T3-BUX-529

Dictionary of Literary Biography

1 *The American Renaissance in New England,* edited by Joel Myerson (1978)

2 *American Novelists Since World War II,* edited by Jeffrey Helterman and Richard Layman (1978)

3 *Antebellum Writers in New York and the South,* edited by Joel Myerson (1979)

4 *American Writers in Paris, 1920–1939,* edited by Karen Lane Rood (1980)

5 *American Poets Since World War II,* 2 parts, edited by Donald J. Greiner (1980)

6 *American Novelists Since World War II, Second Series,* edited by James E. Kibler Jr. (1980)

7 *Twentieth-Century American Dramatists,* 2 parts, edited by John MacNicholas (1981)

8 *Twentieth-Century American Science-Fiction Writers,* 2 parts, edited by David Cowart and Thomas L. Wymer (1981)

9 *American Novelists, 1910–1945,* 3 parts, edited by James J. Martine (1981)

10 *Modern British Dramatists, 1900–1945,* 2 parts, edited by Stanley Weintraub (1982)

11 *American Humorists, 1800–1950,* 2 parts, edited by Stanley Trachtenberg (1982)

12 *American Realists and Naturalists,* edited by Donald Pizer and Earl N. Harbert (1982)

13 *British Dramatists Since World War II,* 2 parts, edited by Stanley Weintraub (1982)

14 *British Novelists Since 1960,* 2 parts, edited by Jay L. Halio (1983)

15 *British Novelists, 1930–1959,* 2 parts, edited by Bernard Oldsey (1983)

16 *The Beats: Literary Bohemians in Postwar America,* 2 parts, edited by Ann Charters (1983)

17 *Twentieth-Century American Historians,* edited by Clyde N. Wilson (1983)

18 *Victorian Novelists After 1885,* edited by Ira B. Nadel and William E. Fredeman (1983)

19 *British Poets, 1880–1914,* edited by Donald E. Stanford (1983)

20 *British Poets, 1914–1945,* edited by Donald E. Stanford (1983)

21 *Victorian Novelists Before 1885,* edited by Ira B. Nadel and William E. Fredeman (1983)

22 *American Writers for Children, 1900–1960,* edited by John Cech (1983)

23 *American Newspaper Journalists, 1873–1900,* edited by Perry J. Ashley (1983)

24 *American Colonial Writers, 1606–1734,* edited by Emory Elliott (1984)

25 *American Newspaper Journalists, 1901–1925,* edited by Perry J. Ashley (1984)

26 *American Screenwriters,* edited by Robert E. Morsberger, Stephen O. Lesser, and Randall Clark (1984)

27 *Poets of Great Britain and Ireland, 1945–1960,* edited by Vincent B. Sherry Jr. (1984)

28 *Twentieth-Century American-Jewish Fiction Writers,* edited by Daniel Walden (1984)

29 *American Newspaper Journalists, 1926–1950,* edited by Perry J. Ashley (1984)

30 *American Historians, 1607–1865,* edited by Clyde N. Wilson (1984)

31 *American Colonial Writers, 1735–1781,* edited by Emory Elliott (1984)

32 *Victorian Poets Before 1850,* edited by William E. Fredeman and Ira B. Nadel (1984)

33 *Afro-American Fiction Writers After 1955,* edited by Thadious M. Davis and Trudier Harris (1984)

34 *British Novelists, 1890–1929: Traditionalists,* edited by Thomas F. Staley (1985)

35 *Victorian Poets After 1850,* edited by William E. Fredeman and Ira B. Nadel (1985)

36 *British Novelists, 1890–1929: Modernists,* edited by Thomas F. Staley (1985)

37 *American Writers of the Early Republic,* edited by Emory Elliott (1985)

38 *Afro-American Writers After 1955: Dramatists and Prose Writers,* edited by Thadious M. Davis and Trudier Harris (1985)

39 *British Novelists, 1660–1800,* 2 parts, edited by Martin C. Battestin (1985)

40 *Poets of Great Britain and Ireland Since 1960,* 2 parts, edited by Vincent B. Sherry Jr. (1985)

41 *Afro-American Poets Since 1955,* edited by Trudier Harris and Thadious M. Davis (1985)

42 *American Writers for Children Before 1900,* edited by Glenn E. Estes (1985)

43 *American Newspaper Journalists, 1690–1872,* edited by Perry J. Ashley (1986)

44 *American Screenwriters, Second Series,* edited by Randall Clark, Robert E. Morsberger, and Stephen O. Lesser (1986)

45 *American Poets, 1880–1945, First Series,* edited by Peter Quartermain (1986)

46 *American Literary Publishing Houses, 1900–1980: Trade and Paperback,* edited by Peter Dzwonkoski (1986)

47 *American Historians, 1866–1912,* edited by Clyde N. Wilson (1986)

48 *American Poets, 1880–1945, Second Series,* edited by Peter Quartermain (1986)

49 *American Literary Publishing Houses, 1638–1899,* 2 parts, edited by Peter Dzwonkoski (1986)

50 *Afro-American Writers Before the Harlem Renaissance,* edited by Trudier Harris (1986)

51 *Afro-American Writers from the Harlem Renaissance to 1940,* edited by Trudier Harris (1987)

52 *American Writers for Children Since 1960: Fiction,* edited by Glenn E. Estes (1986)

53 *Canadian Writers Since 1960, First Series,* edited by W. H. New (1986)

54 *American Poets, 1880–1945, Third Series,* 2 parts, edited by Peter Quartermain (1987)

55 *Victorian Prose Writers Before 1867,* edited by William B. Thesing (1987)

56 *German Fiction Writers, 1914–1945,* edited by James Hardin (1987)

57 *Victorian Prose Writers After 1867,* edited by William B. Thesing (1987)

58 *Jacobean and Caroline Dramatists,* edited by Fredson Bowers (1987)

59 *American Literary Critics and Scholars, 1800–1850,* edited by John W. Rathbun and Monica M. Grecu (1987)

60 *Canadian Writers Since 1960, Second Series,* edited by W. H. New (1987)

61 *American Writers for Children Since 1960: Poets, Illustrators, and Nonfiction Authors,* edited by Glenn E. Estes (1987)

62 *Elizabethan Dramatists,* edited by Fredson Bowers (1987)

63 *Modern American Critics, 1920–1955,* edited by Gregory S. Jay (1988)

64 *American Literary Critics and Scholars, 1850–1880,* edited by John W. Rathbun and Monica M. Grecu (1988)

65 *French Novelists, 1900–1930,* edited by Catharine Savage Brosman (1988)

66 *German Fiction Writers, 1885–1913,* 2 parts, edited by James Hardin (1988)

67 *Modern American Critics Since 1955,* edited by Gregory S. Jay (1988)

68 *Canadian Writers, 1920–1959, First Series,* edited by W. H. New (1988)

69 *Contemporary German Fiction Writers, First Series,* edited by Wolfgang D. Elfe and James Hardin (1988)

70 *British Mystery Writers, 1860–1919,* edited by Bernard Benstock and Thomas F. Staley (1988)

71 *American Literary Critics and Scholars, 1880–1900,* edited by John W. Rathbun and Monica M. Grecu (1988)

72 *French Novelists, 1930–1960,* edited by Catharine Savage Brosman (1988)

73 *American Magazine Journalists, 1741–1850,* edited by Sam G. Riley (1988)

74 *American Short-Story Writers Before 1880,* edited by Bobby Ellen Kimbel, with the assistance of William E. Grant (1988)

75 *Contemporary German Fiction Writers, Second Series,* edited by Wolfgang D. Elfe and James Hardin (1988)

76 *Afro-American Writers, 1940-1955,* edited by Trudier Harris (1988)

77 *British Mystery Writers, 1920-1939,* edited by Bernard Benstock and Thomas F. Staley (1988)

78 *American Short-Story Writers, 1880-1910,* edited by Bobby Ellen Kimbel, with the assistance of William E. Grant (1988)

79 *American Magazine Journalists, 1850-1900,* edited by Sam G. Riley (1988)

80 *Restoration and Eighteenth-Century Dramatists, First Series,* edited by Paula R. Backscheider (1989)

81 *Austrian Fiction Writers, 1875-1913,* edited by James Hardin and Donald G. Daviau (1989)

82 *Chicano Writers, First Series,* edited by Francisco A. Lomelí and Carl R. Shirley (1989)

83 *French Novelists Since 1960,* edited by Catharine Savage Brosman (1989)

84 *Restoration and Eighteenth-Century Dramatists, Second Series,* edited by Paula R. Backscheider (1989)

85 *Austrian Fiction Writers After 1914,* edited by James Hardin and Donald G. Daviau (1989)

86 *American Short-Story Writers, 1910-1945, First Series,* edited by Bobby Ellen Kimbel (1989)

87 *British Mystery and Thriller Writers Since 1940, First Series,* edited by Bernard Benstock and Thomas F. Staley (1989)

88 *Canadian Writers, 1920-1959, Second Series,* edited by W. H. New (1989)

89 *Restoration and Eighteenth-Century Dramatists, Third Series,* edited by Paula R. Backscheider (1989)

90 *German Writers in the Age of Goethe, 1789-1832,* edited by James Hardin and Christoph E. Schweitzer (1989)

91 *American Magazine Journalists, 1900-1960, First Series,* edited by Sam G. Riley (1990)

92 *Canadian Writers, 1890-1920,* edited by W. H. New (1990)

93 *British Romantic Poets, 1789-1832, First Series,* edited by John R. Greenfield (1990)

94 *German Writers in the Age of Goethe: Sturm und Drang to Classicism,* edited by James Hardin and Christoph E. Schweitzer (1990)

95 *Eighteenth-Century British Poets, First Series,* edited by John Sitter (1990)

96 *British Romantic Poets, 1789-1832, Second Series,* edited by John R. Greenfield (1990)

97 *German Writers from the Enlightenment to Sturm und Drang, 1720-1764,* edited by James Hardin and Christoph E. Schweitzer (1990)

98 *Modern British Essayists, First Series,* edited by Robert Beum (1990)

99 *Canadian Writers Before 1890,* edited by W. H. New (1990)

100 *Modern British Essayists, Second Series,* edited by Robert Beum (1990)

101 *British Prose Writers, 1660-1800, First Series,* edited by Donald T. Siebert (1991)

102 *American Short-Story Writers, 1910-1945, Second Series,* edited by Bobby Ellen Kimbel (1991)

103 *American Literary Biographers, First Series,* edited by Steven Serafin (1991)

104 *British Prose Writers, 1660-1800, Second Series,* edited by Donald T. Siebert (1991)

105 *American Poets Since World War II, Second Series,* edited by R. S. Gwynn (1991)

106 *British Literary Publishing Houses, 1820-1880,* edited by Patricia J. Anderson and Jonathan Rose (1991)

107 *British Romantic Prose Writers, 1789-1832, First Series,* edited by John R. Greenfield (1991)

108 *Twentieth-Century Spanish Poets, First Series,* edited by Michael L. Perna (1991)

109 *Eighteenth-Century British Poets, Second Series,* edited by John Sitter (1991)

110 *British Romantic Prose Writers, 1789-1832, Second Series,* edited by John R. Greenfield (1991)

111 *American Literary Biographers, Second Series,* edited by Steven Serafin (1991)

112 *British Literary Publishing Houses, 1881-1965,* edited by Jonathan Rose and Patricia J. Anderson (1991)

113 *Modern Latin-American Fiction Writers, First Series,* edited by William Luis (1992)

114 *Twentieth-Century Italian Poets, First Series,* edited by Giovanna Wedel De Stasio, Glauco Cambon, and Antonio Illiano (1992)

115 *Medieval Philosophers,* edited by Jeremiah Hackett (1992)

116 *British Romantic Novelists, 1789-1832,* edited by Bradford K. Mudge (1992)

117 *Twentieth-Century Caribbean and Black African Writers, First Series,* edited by Bernth Lindfors and Reinhard Sander (1992)

118 *Twentieth-Century German Dramatists, 1889-1918,* edited by Wolfgang D. Elfe and James Hardin (1992)

119 *Nineteenth-Century French Fiction Writers: Romanticism and Realism, 1800-1860,* edited by Catharine Savage Brosman (1992)

120 *American Poets Since World War II, Third Series,* edited by R. S. Gwynn (1992)

121 *Seventeenth-Century British Nondramatic Poets, First Series,* edited by M. Thomas Hester (1992)

122 *Chicano Writers, Second Series,* edited by Francisco A. Lomelí and Carl R. Shirley (1992)

123 *Nineteenth-Century French Fiction Writers: Naturalism and Beyond, 1860-1900,* edited by Catharine Savage Brosman (1992)

124 *Twentieth-Century German Dramatists, 1919-1992,* edited by Wolfgang D. Elfe and James Hardin (1992)

125 *Twentieth-Century Caribbean and Black African Writers, Second Series,* edited by Bernth Lindfors and Reinhard Sander (1993)

126 *Seventeenth-Century British Nondramatic Poets, Second Series,* edited by M. Thomas Hester (1993)

127 *American Newspaper Publishers, 1950-1990,* edited by Perry J. Ashley (1993)

128 *Twentieth-Century Italian Poets, Second Series,* edited by Giovanna Wedel De Stasio, Glauco Cambon, and Antonio Illiano (1993)

129 *Nineteenth-Century German Writers, 1841-1900,* edited by James Hardin and Siegfried Mews (1993)

130 *American Short-Story Writers Since World War II,* edited by Patrick Meanor (1993)

131 *Seventeenth-Century British Nondramatic Poets, Third Series,* edited by M. Thomas Hester (1993)

132 *Sixteenth-Century British Nondramatic Writers, First Series,* edited by David A. Richardson (1993)

133 *Nineteenth-Century German Writers to 1840,* edited by James Hardin and Siegfried Mews (1993)

134 *Twentieth-Century Spanish Poets, Second Series,* edited by Jerry Phillips Winfield (1994)

135 *British Short-Fiction Writers, 1880-1914: The Realist Tradition,* edited by William B. Thesing (1994)

136 *Sixteenth-Century British Nondramatic Writers, Second Series,* edited by David A. Richardson (1994)

137 *American Magazine Journalists, 1900-1960, Second Series,* edited by Sam G. Riley (1994)

138 *German Writers and Works of the High Middle Ages: 1170-1280,* edited by James Hardin and Will Hasty (1994)

139 *British Short-Fiction Writers, 1945-1980,* edited by Dean Baldwin (1994)

140 *American Book-Collectors and Bibliographers, First Series,* edited by Joseph Rosenblum (1994)

141 *British Children's Writers, 1880-1914,* edited by Laura M. Zaidman (1994)

142 *Eighteenth-Century British Literary Biographers,* edited by Steven Serafin (1994)

143 *American Novelists Since World War II, Third Series,* edited by James R. Giles and Wanda H. Giles (1994)

144 *Nineteenth-Century British Literary Biographers,* edited by Steven Serafin (1994)

145 *Modern Latin-American Fiction Writers, Second Series,* edited by William Luis and Ann González (1994)

146 *Old and Middle English Literature,* edited by Jeffrey Helterman and Jerome Mitchell (1994)

147 *South Slavic Writers Before World War II,* edited by Vasa D. Mihailovich (1994)

148 *German Writers and Works of the Early Middle Ages: 800-1170,* edited by Will Hasty and James Hardin (1994)

149 *Late Nineteenth- and Early Twentieth-Century British Literary Biographers,* edited by Steven Serafin (1995)

150 *Early Modern Russian Writers, Late Seventeenth and Eighteenth Centuries,* edited by Marcus C. Levitt (1995)

231 *British Novelists Since 1960, Fourth Series,* edited by Merritt Moseley (2001)

232 *Twentieth-Century Eastern European Writers, Third Series,* edited by Steven Serafin (2001)

233 *British and Irish Dramatists Since World War II, Second Series,* edited by John Bull (2001)

234 *American Short-Story Writers Since World War II, Third Series,* edited by Patrick Meanor and Richard E. Lee (2001)

235 *The American Renaissance in New England, Third Series,* edited by Wesley T. Mott (2001)

236 *British Rhetoricians and Logicians, 1500–1660,* edited by Edward A. Malone (2001)

237 *The Beats: A Documentary Volume,* edited by Matt Theado (2001)

238 *Russian Novelists in the Age of Tolstoy and Dostoevsky,* edited by J. Alexander Ogden and Judith E. Kalb (2001)

239 *American Women Prose Writers: 1820–1870,* edited by Amy E. Hudock and Katharine Rodier (2001)

240 *Late Nineteenth- and Early Twentieth-Century British Women Poets,* edited by William B. Thesing (2001)

241 *American Sportswriters and Writers on Sport,* edited by Richard Orodenker (2001)

242 *Twentieth-Century European Cultural Theorists, First Series,* edited by Paul Hansom (2001)

243 *The American Renaissance in New England, Fourth Series,* edited by Wesley T. Mott (2001)

244 *American Short-Story Writers Since World War II, Fourth Series,* edited by Patrick Meanor and Joseph McNicholas (2001)

245 *British and Irish Dramatists Since World War II, Third Series,* edited by John Bull (2001)

246 *Twentieth-Century American Cultural Theorists,* edited by Paul Hansom (2001)

247 *James Joyce: A Documentary Volume,* edited by A. Nicholas Fargnoli (2001)

248 *Antebellum Writers in the South, Second Series,* edited by Kent Ljungquist (2001)

249 *Twentieth-Century American Dramatists, Third Series,* edited by Christopher Wheatley (2002)

250 *Antebellum Writers in New York, Second Series,* edited by Kent Ljungquist (2002)

251 *Canadian Fantasy and Science-Fiction Writers,* edited by Douglas Ivison (2002)

252 *British Philosophers, 1500–1799,* edited by Philip B. Dematteis and Peter S. Fosl (2002)

253 *Raymond Chandler: A Documentary Volume,* edited by Robert Moss (2002)

254 *The House of Putnam, 1837–1872: A Documentary Volume,* edited by Ezra Greenspan (2002)

255 *British Fantasy and Science-Fiction Writers, 1918–1960,* edited by Darren Harris-Fain (2002)

256 *Twentieth-Century American Western Writers, Third Series,* edited by Richard H. Cracroft (2002)

257 *Twentieth-Century Swedish Writers After World War II,* edited by Ann-Charlotte Gavel Adams (2002)

258 *Modern French Poets,* edited by Jean-François Leroux (2002)

259 *Twentieth-Century Swedish Writers Before World War II,* edited by Ann-Charlotte Gavel Adams (2002)

260 *Australian Writers, 1915–1950,* edited by Selina Samuels (2002)

261 *British Fantasy and Science-Fiction Writers Since 1960,* edited by Darren Harris-Fain (2002)

262 *British Philosophers, 1800–2000,* edited by Peter S. Fosl and Leemon B. McHenry (2002)

263 *William Shakespeare: A Documentary Volume,* edited by Catherine Loomis (2002)

264 *Italian Prose Writers, 1900–1945,* edited by Luca Somigli and Rocco Capozzi (2002)

265 *American Song Lyricists, 1920–1960,* edited by Philip Furia (2002)

266 *Twentieth-Century American Dramatists, Fourth Series,* edited by Christopher J. Wheatley (2002)

267 *Twenty-First-Century British and Irish Novelists,* edited by Michael R. Molino (2002)

268 *Seventeenth-Century French Writers,* edited by Françoise Jaouen (2002)

269 *Nathaniel Hawthorne: A Documentary Volume,* edited by Benjamin Franklin V (2002)

270 *American Philosophers Before 1950,* edited by Philip B. Dematteis and Leemon B. McHenry (2002)

271 *British and Irish Novelists Since 1960,* edited by Merritt Moseley (2002)

Dictionary of Literary Biography Documentary Series

1 *Sherwood Anderson, Willa Cather, John Dos Passos, Theodore Dreiser, F. Scott Fitzgerald, Ernest Hemingway, Sinclair Lewis,* edited by Margaret A. Van Antwerp (1982)

2 *James Gould Cozzens, James T. Farrell, William Faulkner, John O'Hara, John Steinbeck, Thomas Wolfe, Richard Wright,* edited by Margaret A. Van Antwerp (1982)

3 *Saul Bellow, Jack Kerouac, Norman Mailer, Vladimir Nabokov, John Updike, Kurt Vonnegut,* edited by Mary Bruccoli (1983)

4 *Tennessee Williams,* edited by Margaret A. Van Antwerp and Sally Johns (1984)

5 *American Transcendentalists,* edited by Joel Myerson (1988)

6 *Hardboiled Mystery Writers: Raymond Chandler, Dashiell Hammett, Ross Macdonald,* edited by Matthew J. Bruccoli and Richard Layman (1989)

7 *Modern American Poets: James Dickey, Robert Frost, Marianne Moore,* edited by Karen L. Rood (1989)

8 *The Black Aesthetic Movement,* edited by Jeffrey Louis Decker (1991)

9 *American Writers of the Vietnam War: W. D. Ehrhart, Larry Heinemann, Tim O'Brien, Walter McDonald, John M. Del Vecchio,* edited by Ronald Baughman (1991)

10 *The Bloomsbury Group,* edited by Edward L. Bishop (1992)

11 *American Proletarian Culture: The Twenties and The Thirties,* edited by Jon Christian Suggs (1993)

12 *Southern Women Writers: Flannery O'Connor, Katherine Anne Porter, Eudora Welty,* edited by Mary Ann Wimsatt and Karen L. Rood (1994)

13 *The House of Scribner, 1846–1904,* edited by John Delaney (1996)

14 *Four Women Writers for Children, 1868–1918,* edited by Caroline C. Hunt (1996)

15 *American Expatriate Writers: Paris in the Twenties,* edited by Matthew J. Bruccoli and Robert W. Trogdon (1997)

16 *The House of Scribner, 1905–1930,* edited by John Delaney (1997)

17 *The House of Scribner, 1931–1984,* edited by John Delaney (1998)

18 *British Poets of The Great War: Sassoon, Graves, Owen,* edited by Patrick Quinn (1999)

19 *James Dickey,* edited by Judith S. Baughman (1999)

See also DLB 210, 216, 219, 222, 224, 229, 237, 247, 253, 254, 263, 269

Dictionary of Literary Biography Yearbooks

1980 edited by Karen L. Rood, Jean W. Ross, and Richard Ziegfeld (1981)

1981 edited by Karen L. Rood, Jean W. Ross, and Richard Ziegfeld (1982)

1982 edited by Richard Ziegfeld; associate editors: Jean W. Ross and Lynne C. Zeigler (1983)

1983 edited by Mary Bruccoli and Jean W. Ross; associate editor Richard Ziegfeld (1984)

1984 edited by Jean W. Ross (1985)

1985 edited by Jean W. Ross (1986)

1986 edited by J. M. Brook (1987)

1987 edited by J. M. Brook (1988)

1988 edited by J. M. Brook (1989)

1989 edited by J. M. Brook (1990)

1990 edited by James W. Hipp (1991)

1991 edited by James W. Hipp (1992)

1992 edited by James W. Hipp (1993)

1993 edited by James W. Hipp, contributing editor George Garrett (1994)

1994 edited by James W. Hipp, contributing editor George Garrett (1995)

1995 edited by James W. Hipp, contributing editor George Garrett (1996)

1996 edited by Samuel W. Bruce and L. Kay Webster, contributing editor George Garrett (1997)

1997 edited by Matthew J. Bruccoli and George Garrett, with the assistance of L. Kay Webster (1998)

1998 edited by Matthew J. Bruccoli, contributing editor George Garrett, with the assistance of D. W. Thomas (1999)

1999 edited by Matthew J. Bruccoli, contributing editor George Garrett, with the assistance of D. W. Thomas (2000)

2000 edited by Matthew J. Bruccoli, contributing editor George Garrett, with the assistance of George Parker Anderson (2001)

2001 edited by Matthew J. Bruccoli, contributing editor George Garrett, with the assistance of George Parker Anderson (2002)

Concise Series

Concise Dictionary of American Literary Biography, 7 volumes (1988–1999): *The New Consciousness, 1941–1968; Colonization to the American Renaissance, 1640–1865; Realism, Naturalism, and Local Color, 1865–1917; The Twenties, 1917–1929; The Age of Maturity, 1929–1941; Broadening Views, 1968–1988; Supplement: Modern Writers, 1900–1998.*

Concise Dictionary of British Literary Biography, 8 volumes (1991–1992): *Writers of the Middle Ages and Renaissance Before 1660; Writers of the Restoration and Eighteenth Century, 1660–1789; Writers of the Romantic Period, 1789–1832; Victorian Writers, 1832–1890; Late-Victorian and Edwardian Writers, 1890–1914; Modern Writers, 1914–1945; Writers After World War II, 1945–1960; Contemporary Writers, 1960 to Present.*

Concise Dictionary of World Literary Biography, 10 volumes projected (1999–): *Ancient Greek and Roman Writers; German Writers; African, Caribbean, and Latin American Writers; South Slavic and Eastern European Writers.*

Dictionary of Literary Biography® • Volume Two Hundred Seventy-One

British and Irish Novelists Since 1960

Dictionary of Literary Biography® • Volume Two Hundred Seventy-One

British and Irish Novelists Since 1960

Edited by
Merritt Moseley
University of North Carolina at Asheville

A Bruccoli Clark Layman Book

Detroit • New York • San Diego • San Francisco • Cleveland • New Haven, Conn. • Waterville, Maine • London • Munich

Dictionary of Literary Biography
Volume 271: British and Irish Novelists Since 1960

Merritt Moseley

For more information, contact
The Gale Group, Inc.
27500 Drake Rd.
Farmington Hills, MI 48331-3535
Or you can visit our Internet site at
http://www.gale.com

LIBRARY OF CONGRESS CATALOGING-IN-PUBLICATION DATA

British and Irish novelists since 1960 / edited by Merritt Moseley.
p. cm. — (Dictionary of literary biography ; v. 271)
"A Bruccoli Clark Layman book."
Includes bibliographical references and index.
ISBN 0-7876-6015-9
1. English fiction—20th century—Bio-bibliography—Dictionaries.
2. Novelists, English—20th century—Biography—Dictionaries.
3. English fiction—20th century—Dictionaries.
I. Moseley, Merritt, 1949– .
II. Series.

PR881 .B735 2002
823'.91409'003—dc21
2002014238

Printed in the United States of America
10 9 8 7 6 5 4 3 2 1

For Madeline
my love

Contents

Plan of the Series

. . . Almost the most prodigious asset of a country, and perhaps its most precious possession, is its native literary product–when that product is fine and noble and enduring.

Mark Twain*

The advisory board, the editors, and the publisher of the *Dictionary of Literary Biography* are joined in endorsing Mark Twain's declaration. The literature of a nation provides an inexhaustible resource of permanent worth. Our purpose is to make literature and its creators better understood and more accessible to students and the reading public, while satisfying the needs of teachers and researchers.

To meet these requirements, *literary biography* has been construed in terms of the author's achievement. The most important thing about a writer is his writing. Accordingly, the entries in *DLB* are career biographies, tracing the development of the author's canon and the evolution of his reputation.

The purpose of *DLB* is not only to provide reliable information in a usable format but also to place the figures in the larger perspective of literary history and to offer appraisals of their accomplishments by qualified scholars.

The publication plan for *DLB* resulted from two years of preparation. The project was proposed to Bruccoli Clark by Frederick G. Ruffner, president of the Gale Research Company, in November 1975. After specimen entries were prepared and typeset, an advisory board was formed to refine the entry format and develop the series rationale. In meetings held during 1976, the publisher, series editors, and advisory board approved the scheme for a comprehensive biographical dictionary of persons who contributed to literature. Editorial work on the first volume began in January 1977, and it was published in 1978. In order to make *DLB* more than a dictionary and to compile volumes that individually have claim to status as literary history, it was decided to organize volumes by topic, period, or genre. Each of these freestanding volumes provides a biographical-bibliographical guide and overview for a particular area of literature. We are convinced that this organization–as opposed to a single alphabet method–constitutes a valuable innovation in the presentation of reference material. The volume plan necessarily requires many decisions for the placement and treatment of authors. Certain figures will be included in separate volumes, but with different entries emphasizing the aspect of his career appropriate to each volume. Ernest Hemingway, for example, is represented in *American Writers in Paris, 1920–1939* by an entry focusing on his expatriate apprenticeship; he is also in *American Novelists, 1910–1945* with an entry surveying his entire career, as well as in *American Short-Story Writers, 1910–1945, Second Series* with an entry concentrating on his short fiction. Each volume includes a cumulative index of the subject authors and articles.

Since 1981 the series has been further augmented by the *DLB Yearbooks,* which update published entries, add new entries to keep the *DLB* current with contemporary activity, and provide articles on literary history. There have also been nineteen *DLB Documentary Series* volumes, which provide illustrations, facsimiles, and biographical and critical source materials for figures, works, or groups judged to have particular interest for students. In 1999 the *Documentary Series* was incorporated into the *DLB* volume numbering system beginning with *DLB 210: Ernest Hemingway.*

We define literature as the *intellectual commerce of a nation:* not merely as belles lettres but as that ample and complex process by which ideas are generated, shaped, and transmitted. *DLB* entries are not limited to "creative writers" but extend to other figures who in their time and in their way influenced the mind of a people. Thus the series encompasses historians, journalists, publishers, book collectors, and screenwriters. By this means readers of *DLB* may be aided to perceive literature not as cult scripture in the keeping of intellectual high priests but firmly positioned at the center of a nation's life.

DLB includes the major writers appropriate to each volume and those standing in the ranks behind them. Scholarly and critical counsel has been sought in

**From an unpublished section of Mark Twain's autobiography, copyright by the Mark Twain Company*

deciding which minor figures to include and how full their entries should be. Wherever possible, useful references are made to figures who do not warrant separate entries.

Each *DLB* volume has an expert volume editor responsible for planning the volume, selecting the figures for inclusion, and assigning the entries. Volume editors are also responsible for preparing, where appropriate, appendices surveying the major periodicals and literary and intellectual movements for their volumes, as well as lists of further readings. Work on the series as a whole is coordinated at the Bruccoli Clark Layman editorial center in Columbia, South Carolina, where the editorial staff is responsible for accuracy and utility of the published volumes.

One feature that distinguishes *DLB* is the illustration policy–its concern with the iconography of literature. Just as an author is influenced by his surroundings, so is the reader's understanding of the author enhanced by a knowledge of his environment. Therefore *DLB* volumes include not only drawings, paintings, and photographs of authors, often depicting them at various stages in their careers, but also illustrations of their families and places where they lived. Title pages are regularly reproduced in facsimile along with dust jackets for modern authors. The dust jackets are a special feature of *DLB* because they often document better than anything else the way in which an author's work was perceived in its own time. Specimens of the writers' manuscripts and letters are included when feasible.

Samuel Johnson rightly decreed that "The chief glory of every people arises from its authors." The purpose of the *Dictionary of Literary Biography* is to compile literary history in the surest way available to us–by accurate and comprehensive treatment of the lives and work of those who contributed to it.

The *DLB* Advisory Board

Introduction: In Quest of Contemporary Masterpieces

Cyril Connolly was an editor of distinction, a memoirist, a novelist, a cultural commentator, and the friend of some of the major figures of the immediately post–World War I period (Evelyn Waugh, George Orwell, Stephen Spender, W. H. Auden); yet, his lasting image is the one he created most successfully—a miserable failure. He wrote in the final number of his magazine, *Horizon* (December 1949 – January 1950): "It is closing time in the gardens of the West and from now on an artist will be judged only by the resonance of his solitude or the quality of his despair." About himself he claimed, "I have always disliked myself at any given moment; the total of such moments is my life." Also in reference to himself, he declared, "Whom the gods wish to destroy they first call promising." These last two observations appear in his 1938 book, *Enemies of Promise,* an unusual combination of memoir, analysis of style, survey of contemporary writing, and vade mecum for aspiring writers. How to avoid the destruction that the gods visit on the promising, then, is its main topic: how to avoid the enemies of promise (such things as having to earn a living, children, envy).

Put another way, it is a book about how to write a masterpiece, since, as he states in *The Unquiet Grave: A Word Cycle by Palinurus,* 1945), "The more books we read, the clearer it becomes that the true function of a writer is to produce a masterpiece and no other task is of any consequence." But what is a masterpiece? The answer, he suggests in *Enemies of Promise,* is: a book that will last ten years.

> I make it ten years because for ten years I have written about books, and because I can say, and this is the gravest warning, that in a short time the writing of books, especially works of the imagination which last that long, will be an extinct art. Contemporary books do not keep. The quality in them which makes for their success is the first to go; they turn over night.

Connolly's ambition is typically grand and at the same time typically self-effacing—he wants to produce a masterpiece, but he defines a masterpiece by ten years' survival. At least five of his books are in print, *Enemies of Promise* having been republished in 1996, fifty-eight years after its first appearance.

Connolly was one of the most astute commentators on the literary life. He provided a point of entry to an examination of the possibility of masterpieces in today's world of British fiction by investigating which books have "lasted" for ten years. The chosen sample includes:

> I. The winners of 1992 book awards, including the Booker Prize, the Whitbread Prize, the *Guardian* Fiction Award, and others and, in the case of the Booker, all the finalists.
>
> II. Novels named in the annual "Books of the Year" articles published in the quality British newspapers, *The Guardian, The Sunday Times, The Financial Times, The Independent,* and *The Daily Telegraph.*
>
> III. The most recent books published by the writers listed by *Granta* magazine, in 1993, as the twenty "Best of Young British Novelists."

The measure of survival is whether the book is still in print.

I. Award-winning Books for the Year 1992

A. The James Tait Black Award: Rose Tremain, *Sacred Country.*

B. The Booker Prize for Fiction joint winners: Barry Unsworth, *Sacred Hunger,* and Michael Ondaatje, *The English Patient.* (Other short-listed titles: Christopher Hope, *Serenity House;* Patrick McCabe, *The Butcher Boy;* Ian McEwan, *Black Dogs;* Michele Roberts, *Daughters of the House.*)

C. The *Guardian* Fiction Award: Alasdair Gray, *Poor Things.*

D. The Hawthornden Award: Ferdinand Mount, *Of Love and Asthma.*

E. The Whitbread Awards: *Poor Things* (novel of the year); Rachel Cusk, *Saving Agnes* (first novel of the year).

F. The *Sunday Express* Book of the Year: Hilary Mantel, *A Place of Greater Safety.*

G. The W. H. Smith "Thumping Good Read" Award: Robert Goddard, *Into the Blue.*

These are the books that received the most official imprimaturs of 1992. It is true that the standards varied. The *Sunday Express* Book of the Year was deliberately created as an alternative to the Booker and Whitbread awards and was given to a book judged to be "readable"–in other words, not difficult in any modernistic or postmodernistic way; likewise, the "Thumping Good Read" award had populist, rather than artistic, aims in mind.

Of these twelve titles, a majority are still selling well. All the Booker finalists except for *Serenity House* are in print; of these the most popular, judging by Amazon.co.uk sales rankings, is *The English Patient,* which has benefited from a successful motion-picture adaptation and has been reprinted in a movie tie-in version. The novels by Goddard, Mantel, and Tremain are in print. Those which have *failed* to reach the ten-year mark are *Poor Things* (winner of both the Whitbread and the *Guardian* Awards), *Of Love and Asthma,* and *Saving Agnes.* It is possible to get these books by special order. *Serenity House* seems to have vanished without a trace.

Using the Connolly standard, then, two-thirds of the award-winning novels of 1992 are masterpieces. One possible alternative explanation is that the awards themselves, by building sales figures, have kept these novels in print irrespective of their masterliness. The impact of prizes on sales is a hotly debated topic, though, and it seems unlikely to operate at a decade's remove.

II. Books of the Year

These annual articles must be taken with due awareness of their faults. They sometimes provide an arena for logrolling and back-scratching, with many contributors praising their friends, editors, spouses, or lovers, and contributors regularly report choices seemingly designed more to awe than to inform the reader. The book not yet translated from the Czech, the book by a famous author read in manuscript, the annual rereading of Marcel Proust: these are little help to the Christmas book-buyer, ostensibly the reader for whom the articles are provided. One exasperated observer is quoted in *Lord Gnome's Literary Companion* (1994), edited by Francis Wheen, as claiming that such features "mount a finer display of bookworld sottishness than anything else all year." Nevertheless, these articles do provide a venue for influential people to declare which are the best books of the year. An examination of the novels mentioned in the five broadsheet newspapers in 1992 reveals these titles, in addition to those listed above as award winners:

In print
Adam Thorpe, *Ulverton*
Shena Mackay, *Dunedin*
Colm Tóibín, *The Heather Blazing*
Andrew Barrow, *The Tap Dancer*
Jeanette Winterson, *Written on the Body*
Esther Freud, *Hideous Kinky*
Julian Barnes, *The Porcupine*
Christine Brooke-Rose, *Textermination*

Out of print
John Burnside, *Feast Days*
D. J. Taylor, *Real Life*
Vijay Singh, *Whirlpool of Shadows*
Julia O'Faolain, *The Judas Cloth*
Frank Delaney, *The Sins of the Mothers*
Gilbert Adair, *The Death of the Author*

Easily the most often recommended title was *Ulverton,* a first novel providing the history of a fictional English town through the centuries, as told by the voices of a dozen different narrators. Its omission from the various awards was seen by many as an injustice: Penny Perrick, writing in the 29 November 1992 edition of *The Sunday Times* (London), thundered, "May the desert grow up to the doors of all the literary prizes who failed to reward this brilliant first novel." On the other hand, William Startle, in *The Sunday Telegraph* (London) for 20 December 1992, quoted a difficult line of Thorpe's prose and declared, "Such is the perversity of our literary establishment, its wanton enthusiasm for the obscure, that the passage can be found on page 207 of the novel of 1992, Adam Thorpe's *Ulverton.*"

Second most frequently acclaimed was Ondaatje's *The English Patient.* It likewise divided readers; David Sexton, writing in the 27 December 1992 edition of *The Sunday Telegraph* (London), declared that it was "a spurious confection, widely acclaimed by the gullible as 'lyrical,'" and *Private Eye* (27 August 1993) listed his advantages as "foreign, funny name, 'poetic' prose style and so on." On the other hand, in *The Financial Times* (London) for 28 November 1992 both Chloe Chard and Zara Steiner declared flatly that it was "a masterpiece."

The oddest inclusion on the list was Jeanette Winterson's *Written on the Body.* Nobody else mentioned it, but the author herself wrote in the Christmas books pages of *The Sunday Telegraph* (London)–as Andrew Moncur reported in his column in *The Guardian* (26 November 1992)–that "My own *Written on the Body* is this year's most profound and profoundly misunderstood book. A fiction which dismantles the scaffolding of the 19th century novel, replacing time, place, situation, character, even gender, with an intense consciousness. An exaltation of love. An exultation in language. Words unclothed." Was it, then, a masterpiece? The word was not used, though it is possible to infer the author's judgment. And in fact *Written on the Body* has remained steadily in print and currently ranks higher in sales than *Ulverton* though behind *The English Patient.*

How many "masterpieces," then, are on the above list? The first eight books are all in print, the last six out of print. Masterpiece score: 57 percent.

III. The Twenty Best British Novelists

Granta, an influential British literary magazine in the 1980s and 1990s, stirred a sensational discussion by its presentation, in 1983, of what it judged the twenty best British novelists under age forty. This list included many names that almost anybody would have put on such a list: Julian Barnes, Martin Amis, Salman Rushdie, A. N. Wilson, and Pat Barker. Like any such list–consider the fashion for naming the best one hundred books of the twentieth century that flourished around the end of the millennium–it was arbitrary (Why twenty names? Why forty years old or under?), but it came to have an authoritative air, the result both of publicists' use of the honor and of the genuinely high accomplishment of those honored. One of the *Granta* twenty, Ian McEwan, was on the 1992 Booker shortlist; another, Rose Tremain, won the James Tait Black Award with *Sacred Country.*

Emboldened by the 1983 list, or perhaps just feeling a responsibility to maintain its judicial authority, *Granta* published a new list of the twenty "Best of Young British Novelists" in 1993. The names were

Iain Banks
Louis de Bernières
Anne Billson
Tibor Fischer
Esther Freud
Alan Hollinghurst
Kazuo Ishiguro
A. L. Kennedy
Philip Kerr
Hanif Kureishi
Adam Lively
Adam Mars-Jones
Candia McWilliam
Lawrence Norfolk
Ben Okri
Caryl Phillips
Will Self
Nicholas Shakespeare
Helen Simpson
Jeanette Winterson

How well have the authors on this list done in producing literary masterpieces?

There are several odd features about this list. Adam Mars-Jones, who had also appeared on the 1983 list–thus achieving the unique accolade of twice being named one of the twenty best British novelists–had, through 1992, *still* not published a novel. His work up to that time had been short stories. The same is true of Helen Simpson, who as of 2002 has yet to publish a novel (Mars-Jones managed *The Waters of Thirst* in 1993). A. L. Kennedy, in 1993, was the author of one book: *Night Geometry and the Garscadden Trains,* a collection of short stories. The addition of nonnovelists to a list of best novelists may be attributed in part to a desire for diversity, hence the female Kennedy and Simpson, the gay Mars-Jones and the Asian Hanif Kureishi, who was at that time best known as a screenwriter, though his novel *The Buddha of Suburbia* (1990) remains in print.

Other novelists on the list just barely qualified: Will Self's first novel, *Cock and Bull,* appeared in 1992, the same year as Tibor Fischer's debut, *Under the Frog,* and Esther Freud's *Hideous Kinky.* Lawrence Norfolk's *Lemprière's Dictionary* came out in 1991.

What all this inclusiveness suggests is a combination of desperation and ruthless avant-gardism. There must be twenty "best" novelists, and the list will appear even if some of them have written no novels, others only one that is less than a year old. Thus, one might wonder if it makes any sense to scrutinize this list as a guide to possible masterpieces.

Nevertheless, it produces a better showing than might be expected. The novel most recently published before the *Granta* feature is still in print for all these authors:

Iain Banks, *The Crow Road;*
Louis de Bernières, *The Troublesome Offspring of Cardinal Guzman;*
Tibor Fischer, *Under the Frog;*
Esther Freud, *Hideous Kinky;*
Alan Hollinghurst, *The Swimming-Pool Library;*
Kazuo Ishiguro, *The Remains of the Day;*
Philip Kerr, *A Philosophical Investigation;*
Hanif Kureishi, *The Buddha of Suburbia;*
Lawrence Norfolk, *Lemprière's Dictionary;*
Ben Okri, *The Famished Road;*
Caryl Phillips, *Crossing the River* and *Cambridge* (both 1991);
Will Self, *Cock and Bull;*
Nicholas Shakespeare, *The Vision of Elena Silves;*
Jeanette Winterson, *Written on the Body.*

Anne Billson's *Dream Demon* (1989), Adam Lively's *The Snail* (1991), and Candia McWilliam's *A Little Stranger* (1989) are out of print; Simpson wrote no masterpiece novel since she never wrote a novel, and Kennedy and Mars-Jones had in 1992 published only short stories.

Masterpiece score: 14/20, or 70 percent.

These are the novels, and novelists, who were the *critical* favorites of a decade ago. What of the best-sellers? The results are mixed. The two great successes of the British book trade in 1992 were both nonfiction: Andrew Morton's *Diana: Her True Story* and

Madonna's *Sex.* And both are out of print, though Morton has published a revised edition of his book. In the world of fiction, both Ondaatje's *The English Patient* and Unsworth's *Sacred Hunger,* co-winners of the Booker Prize, achieved high sales (and both are still in print). Robert Harris's *Fatherland,* a best-selling novel, is not only still in print but ranks higher in Amazon.co.uk sales than any other book in this list of "masterpieces."

It remains to explore what all this means. These somewhat surprising and, in the end, gratifying findings provoke several reactions.

One is that Connolly was undoubtedly too pessimistic. Writing in 1938, with another world war looming, and constitutionally dubious about the efforts of himself and others, he might have been expected to believe that "in a short time the writing of books, especially works of the imagination which last that long, will be an extinct art." This idea–that novels, or books, or art, or all these are in a parlous state and will soon have passed away from the earth–is a commonplace of cultural commentary. A few years ago a novelist of my acquaintance told me that she expected to see a time, during her life, when reading novels would be about as common as attending the opera. The "death of the novel" has become a cliché, announced again and again. Two years before Connolly uttered his lament, his friend George Orwell was saying that "at this moment the prestige of the novel is extremely low, so low that the words 'I never read novels,' which even a dozen years ago, were generally uttered with a hint of apology, are now always uttered in a tone of pride. . . . the novel is likely, if the best literary brains cannot be induced to return to it, to survive in some perfunctory, despised and hopeless degenerate form, like modern tomb-stones, or the Punch and Judy show."

The causes assigned for the imminent death of the novel are varied. Orwell blames the lack of interest of the "best literary brains" in the genre. To Connolly, the problem seems to be a general cultural decline, accompanied by too much success. Contemporary novels do not keep; "what kills a literary reputation is inflation"; "of all the enemies of literature, success is the most insidious." Others, of course, blame the readers, either because their literacy is too low, their tastes are degraded, or their attention is elsewhere. Another culprit is the rise of competing technology. First the cinema, then television, now video games and the Internet have been given the blame for the death of reading.

A related argument is that reading–or "reading"–will continue, but not of novels. Alternatives include comics; writing on 9 September 1989 in *The Independent* (London), David Lister worried that "We might be dealing with cold-blooded murder–the death of the novel. This is a less than fanciful scenario in Japan, where comics now account for 25 per cent of all published material, and alarm bells may ring in the UK soon." Or perhaps the novel (and other forms of "linear narrative," seen as tyrannizing over the reader) are to be replaced by hypertext. Robert Coover, a distinguished American novelist, published an essay in *The New York Times* (21 June 1992) called "The End of Books," which declared that the novel "as we know it, has come to an end," to be replaced by hyperfiction, which liberates the reader to dictate the structure of his or her reading experience. John Walsh fretted in *The Independent* (London) for 27 August 1996 that the Internet and the electronic book would be the wave of the future; beginning with the acknowledgment that "we are overwhelmed with literary moribundity"–that is, the death of the novel has been announced again and again–Walsh nevertheless believes that "this is different. This could happen. The death of the book, of printed text and of old-style reading is a real possibility, not an academic joke or a post-structuralist conceit."

Or maybe books will continue, but the novel has had its day. From time to time commentators declare that nonfiction has taken on the role of fiction. In 1996 George Steiner told the British Publisher's Association, "We are getting very tired in our novels. . . . Genres rise, genres fall, the epic, the verse epic, the formal verse tragedy. Great moments, then they ebb. Novels will continue to be written for quite a while but, increasingly, the search is on for hybrid forms, what we call rather crassly fact/fiction. . . . What novel can today quite compete with the best of reportage, with the very best of immediate narrative?" And Andrew Marr made news on 27 May 2001 when he insisted in *The Observer* (London) that "non-fiction writing in this country [the United Kingdom] is better–stylistically better, more ambitious, more interesting, more dangerous–than fiction. . . . The tricks of the novel, in rhythm, setting, authorial intervention and characterisation, have been better learned by new generations of historians and biographers than by novelists. As a country, we may be addicted to novels, just as much as the Victorians. But our non-fiction writing is more brilliant."

One final cause for worry about the future of the book, or the novel, in Britain (and we should remember that some ninety thousand books a year are published there, including an estimated twelve thousand novels) is the nature of the publishing and bookselling industries. Novelist Allan Massie, writing in *The Scotsman* (8 August 2000), argues that the author is squeezed. "Nobody owes the author a living. The answer–not unfortunately open to all writers–is to write what the people want to read and buy. In some ways this is more difficult than it was 50 years ago. The market for the serious mainstream novel is smaller than it used to be. . . .

For the writer, the choice is stark. You must either adapt, not necessarily lowering your sights, and work in a popular market . . . or you must find some other way of earning money." This diagnosis will be familiar to anyone who has read Herman Melville's letters to Nathaniel Hawthorne ("What I feel most moved to write, that is banned,–it will not pay. Yet, altogether, write the *other* way I cannot") or, for that matter, Connolly's *Enemies of Promise:* "Every writer should, before embarking, find some way however dishonest of procuring with the minimum of effort, about four hundred a year. Otherwise he must become a popular success or be miserable."

Recent changes in the way the British publish and sell books, some have argued, have exacerbated this perpetual difficulty of the author. One of these changes (equally visible, and worrying, in the United States) is the consolidation of more and more imprints under the ownership of massive publishers, some of which are part of larger, profit-driven, and perhaps Philistine organizations either headquartered abroad (much of British publishing is now owned by the Germans) or answerable to bosses of dubious taste and standards (many imprints have been consolidated under the ownership of Rupert Murdoch, of *News of the World,* Fox Television, and *TV Guide* fame), or both: Murdoch, Australian-born, is now a naturalized American citizen. Between 1980 and 1995 more than fifty long-established family publishing firms, including famous names such as Macmillan, Chatto & Windus, and Hamish Hamilton, lost their independent existence and became part of large media conglomerates. There are now five big publishers (though they publish under many more imprints).

Thus, Stephen Moss declares in *The Guardian* (28 December 1998) that "British publishing increasingly resembles Hollywood. . . . There is a search for an instant return; hence the number of celebrity authors being invited to write novels, often at the expense of good first-time novelists." Michael Sissons, writing in *The Times* (London) for 5 October 1996, agrees: "Publishing is now run, in the main, by salesmen and accountants rather than publishers." And Robin Baird-Smith, the former publisher of Duckworth, a smaller independent firm, writing in *The Independent* (London) on 26 September 1999, was even gloomier. Reflecting on the boom and hype and market churning, he asked: "while all this commercial activity was going on, what was happening to the quality and quantity of books published? In the corporations, the emphasis now had to be on best-sellers. Overheads were so enormous that the demand for return by investors so great, that the only frame of mind was best-sellerdom."

One further structural change affected publishing, in addition to conglomeration: the abandonment in 1995 of the Net Book Agreement, frankly a price-fixing agreement, according to which booksellers were forbidden to sell a book below its cover price. Under pressure from big booksellers such as W. H. Smith and supermarket chains such as ASDA, publishers withdrew from the compact, and the Publishers Association could no longer enforce it. At the time there were suggestions, as Richard Brooks reported in *The Observer* (London) for 1 October 1995, that the collapse of the agreement might "sound the death knell for Britain's literary traditions," because it would "exacerbate a trend towards favouring the big names." Jackie Wullschlager, writing in *The Financial Times* (London) for 23 December 1995, concurred: "Long-term results will be a smaller choice of books and fewer places to buy them . . . the bland, chocolate-box book . . . will now increasingly dominate publishing."

Accurate numbers are hard to come by, and it is not clear if there are fewer books published in the twenty-first century than in 1980 or 1995. Nor is it easy to assess the quality of the ones that are published. Worries that best-sellers and celebrity books would drive out smaller, more ambitious works have not been entirely vindicated, at any rate. Consider the career of Christine Brooke-Rose, author of experimental fiction never likely to reach big sales. Her *Textermination,* published in 1992, was reprinted in paperback in 1997; now, though it ranks 185,044th in the Amazon.co.uk sales figures, it is still in print, ten years after its first appearance. Credit for this fact goes to Carcanet, one of the remaining small publishers.

Another reflection prompted by these investigations is that Connolly was too worried about the perils of success, which he considered the most insidious enemy of literature. Why? "Success is bad for a writer because it cuts him off from his roots, raises his standard of living and so leads to overproduction, lowers his standard of criticism and encourages the germ of its opposite, failure." One's first reaction is to acknowledge that he is talking about a wild sort of success, of the sort that even British authors of literary fiction whom anybody would consider successful–Pat Barker, Martin Amis, John Fowles, Jeanette Winterson–never achieve. Even these writers probably never make enough money to raise them into an entirely different sphere of life, nor are they likely to buy such large homes or become so dependent upon chauffeured limousines that they must publish inferior stuff to keep their incomes going. (One exception might be the case of Amis and his negotiations for a £500,000 advance for *The Information* [1995], for which he was reviled as greedy by some other authors.)

It is true that one successful novel makes the next novel more likely to be published. But that hardly constitutes preventing literature. Nor is it necessarily the case that publishers' hype leads to undeserved sales. Far more likely to prove an enemy of literature is failure.

And what of Connolly's idea of a masterpiece? Surely here he was mistaken. Unless the present day is an unprecedented golden age of British fiction, two-thirds of any selection of current novels, even those named by somebody as books of the year or given a prize, or those written by the "best novelists," are not masterpieces. Good sense suggests that his definition–a masterpiece is a book that lasts ten years–must be rejected.

What has changed since his day? One answer is publishing. Another is bookselling. In the world of publishing, for instance, Connolly wrote before cheap paperback books. Most of the 1992 titles that are still in print are in paperback. The existence of the paperback option presumably permits books to be available when, were only hardback an option, they would have long ago gone out of print.

It is also probable that the larger bookshops, including the virtual bookshops such as Amazon.com and Borders in the United States, Amazon.co.uk and Booksonline.co.uk in Britain, make books less rather than more likely to go out of print. While possibly soulless, and certainly threatening to locally owned, often much more charming small shops, a store such as Barnes and Noble nevertheless stocks many more titles than the average independent and has much more shelf space. On-line booksellers have, in effect, unlimited shelf space. The fierce competition for a place in the bookshop–the losers of which presumably face remaindering–is lessened by large shops with large inventories, no matter what their disadvantages for consumers or authors.

Let us conclude, then, that all those 1992 novels cannot be masterpieces. A masterpiece is something rarer than this. Nevertheless, a book which lasts for ten years is–what?–a good book, say, or a book that enough readers believe is a good book. And the high percentage of the samples used above that are still in print, easily available for readers, at a reasonable price, ten years after their publication is impressive on two counts. One is that competitive pressures, conglomeration of publishers, and the best-seller complex have not yet driven the mid-market books out of print. These books, for the most part, were never best-sellers. Yet they have "lasted." The other is that the book prize judges, the editors of *Granta,* the reviewers and critics and other novelists who construct Books of the Year features have a high success rate themselves. A few of the top novels of 1992 were called masterpieces on their first appearance, and some of the ones that may *be* masterpieces (*Poor Things,* for instance, or *The Death of the Author*) have not survived. But it is not true, as Connolly was writing in 1938, that "contemporary books do not keep." And this fact should be grounds for satisfaction for all those interested in the contemporary British novel.

–*Merritt Moseley*

Acknowledgments

This book was produced by Bruccoli Clark Layman, Inc. Karen L. Rood is senior editor. Charles Brower and Jan Peter F. van Rosevelt were the in-house editors.

Production manager is Philip B. Dematteis.

Administrative support was provided by Ann M. Cheschi and Carol A. Cheschi.

Accountant is Ann-Marie Holland.

In-house prevetting was done by Nicole A. La Rocque.

Copyediting supervisor is Sally R. Evans. The copyediting staff includes Phyllis A. Avant, Caryl Brown, Melissa D. Hinton, Philip I. Jones, Rebecca Mayo, Nancy E. Smith, and Elizabeth Jo Ann Sumner. Freelance copyeditors are Brenda Cabra and Alice Poyner.

Editorial associates are Michael Allen, Michael S. Martin, Catherine M. Polit, Amelia B. Lacey, and William Mathes Straney.

Permissions editor and database manager is Amber L. Coker.

Layout and graphics supervisor is Janet E. Hill. The graphics staff includes Zoe R. Cook and Sydney E. Hammock.

Office manager is Kathy Lawler Merlette.

Photography supervisor is Paul Talbot. Photography editor is Scott Nemzek.

Digital photographic copy work was performed by Joseph M. Bruccoli.

Systems manager is Marie L. Parker.

Typesetting supervisor is Kathleen M. Flanagan. The typesetting staff includes Patricia Marie Flanagan, Mark J. McEwan, and Pamela D. Norton. Freelance typesetters are Wanda Adams and Rebecca Mayo.

Walter W. Ross did library research. He was assisted by Jo Cottingham and the following other librarians at the Thomas Cooper Library of the University of South Carolina: circulation department head Tucker Taylor; reference department head Virginia W. Weathers; reference department staff Brette Barron, Marilee Birchfield, Paul Cammarata, Gary Geer, Michael Macan, Tom Marcil, Rose Marshall, and Sharon Verba; interlibrary loan department head John Brunswick; and interlibrary loan staff Robert Arndt, Hayden Battle, Alex Byrne, Bill Fetty, Marna Hostetler, and Nelson Rivera.

Dictionary of Literary Biography® • Volume Two Hundred Seventy-One

British and Irish Novelists Since 1960

Dictionary of Literary Biography

Brian W. Aldiss

(18 August 1925 –   )

Nicolas Tredell
University of Sussex

See also the Aldiss entries in *DLB 14: British Novelists Since 1960* and *DLB 261: British Fantasy and Science-Fiction Writers Since 1960.*

BOOKS: *The Brightfount Diaries* (London: Faber & Faber, 1955);

Space, Time and Nathaniel (Presciences) (London: Faber & Faber, 1957); revised as *No Time Like Tomorrow* (New York: New American Library, 1959);

Non-Stop (London: Faber & Faber, 1958); abridged and revised as *Starship* (New York: Criterion, 1959);

Equator (London: Brown, Watson, 1958); republished as *Vanguard from Alpha,* together with *The Changeling Worlds* by Kenneth Bulmer (New York: Ace, 1959);

The Canopy of Time (London: Faber & Faber, 1959); revised as *Galaxies Like Grains of Sand* (New York: New American Library, 1960; expanded and revised edition, London: Panther, 1979);

Bow Down to Nul [bound with *The Dark Destroyers* by Manly Wade Wellman] (New York: Ace, 1960); revised as *The Interpreter* (London: Nova, 1961);

The Male Response (New York: Beacon, 1961; London: Dobson, 1963);

The Primal Urge (New York: Ballantine, 1961; London: Sphere, 1967);

Hothouse: A Science-Fiction Novel (London: Faber & Faber, 1962); abridged as *The Long Afternoon of Earth* (New York: New American Library, 1962);

The Airs of Earth: Science Fiction Stories (London: Faber & Faber, 1963); revised as *Starswarm* (New York: New American Library, 1964; London: Panther, 1979);

Brian W. Aldiss (photograph © Studio Edmark)

The Dark Light Years: A Science-Fiction Novel (London: Faber & Faber, 1964; New York: New American Library, 1964);

Greybeard (New York: Harcourt, Brace & World, 1964; revised edition, London: Faber & Faber, 1964);

Earthworks: A Science-Fiction Novel (London: Faber & Faber, 1965; Garden City, N.Y.: Doubleday, 1966);

Cities and Stones: A Traveller's Jugoslavia (London: Faber & Faber, 1966);

The Saliva Tree and Other Strange Growths (London: Faber & Faber, 1966; Boston: Gregg Press, 1981);

An Age (London: Faber & Faber, 1967); republished as *Cryptozoic!* (Garden City, N.Y.: Doubleday, 1968);

Report on Probability A (London: Faber & Faber, 1968; Garden City, N.Y.: Doubleday, 1969);

Barefoot in the Head: A European Fantasia (London: Faber & Faber, 1969; Garden City, N.Y.: Doubleday, 1970);

Intangibles Inc and Other Stories: Five Novellas (London: Faber & Faber, 1969); revised as *Neanderthal Planet* (New York: Avon, 1969);

The Hand-Reared Boy (London: Weidenfeld & Nicolson, 1970; New York: McCall, 1970);

The Shape of Further Things: Speculations on Change (London: Faber & Faber, 1970; Garden City, N.Y.: Doubleday, 1971);

The Moment of Eclipse (London: Faber & Faber, 1970; Garden City, N.Y.: Doubleday, 1972);

A Soldier Erect; or, Further Adventures of the Hand-Reared Boy (London: Weidenfeld & Nicolson, 1971; New York: Coward, McCann & Geoghegan, 1971);

The Book of Brian Aldiss (New York: DAW, 1972); republished as *Comic Inferno* (London: New English Library, 1973);

Billion Year Spree: The History of Science Fiction (London: Weidenfeld & Nicolson, 1973; Garden City, N.Y.: Doubleday, 1973); revised and expanded as *Trillion Year Spree: The History of Science Fiction,* by Aldiss and David Wingrove (London: Gollancz, 1986; New York: Atheneum, 1986; revised edition, London: Stratus, 2001);

Frankenstein Unbound (London: Cape, 1973; New York: Random House, 1974);

The Eighty-Minute Hour: A Space Opera (London: Cape, 1974; Garden City, N.Y.: Doubleday, 1974);

Science Fiction Art (London: New English Library, 1975; New York: Bounty, 1975);

The Malacia Tapestry (London: Cape, 1976; New York: Harper & Row, 1977);

Brothers of the Head (London: Pierrot, 1977; New York: Pierrot/Two Continents, 1977);

Last Orders and Other Stories (London: Cape, 1977; New York: Carroll & Graf, 1989);

Enemies of the System: A Tale of Homo Uniformis (London: Cape, 1978; New York: Harper & Row, 1978);

Science Fiction as Science Fiction (Frome: Bran's Head, 1978);

A Rude Awakening (London: Weidenfeld & Nicolson, 1978; New York: Random House, 1979);

New Arrivals, Old Encounters: Twelve Stories (London: Cape, 1979; New York: Harper & Row, 1979);

This World and Nearer Ones: Essays Exploring the Familiar (London: Weidenfeld & Nicolson, 1979; Kent, Ohio: Kent State University Press, 1981);

Pile: Petals from St. Klaed's Computer (London: Cape, 1979; New York: Holt, Rinehart & Winston, 1979);

Life in the West (London: Weidenfeld & Nicolson, 1980; New York: Carroll & Graf, 1990);

Moreau's Other Island (London: Cape, 1980); republished as *An Island Called Moreau* (New York: Simon & Schuster, 1981); revised and republished as *Moreau's Other Island* (London: Stratus, 2001);

Foreign Bodies: Stories (Singapore: Chopmen, 1981);

Farewell to a Child (Berkhamsted: Priapus Poets, 1982);

Helliconia Spring (London: Cape, 1982; New York: Atheneum, 1982);

Helliconia Summer (London: Cape, 1983; New York: Atheneum, 1983);

Science Fiction Quiz (London: Weidenfeld & Nicolson, 1983);

Seasons in Flight (London: Cape, 1984; New York: Atheneum, 1986);

Helliconia Winter (London: Cape, 1985; New York: Atheneum, 1985);

The Pale Shadow of Science (Seattle: Serconia, 1985);

–And the Lurid Glare of the Comet (Seattle: Serconia, 1986);

The Year before Yesterday: A Novel in Three Acts (New York: Watts, 1987); revised as *Cracken at Critical: A Novel in Three Acts* (Worcester Park: Kerosina, 1987);

Ruins (London: Hutchinson, 1987);

The Magic of the Past (Worcester Park: Kerosina, 1987);

Best SF Stories of Brian W. Aldiss (London: Gollancz, 1988); republished as *Man in His Time: The Best Science Fiction Stories of Brian W. Aldiss* (New York: Atheneum, 1989);

Forgotten Life (London: Gollancz, 1988; New York: Atheneum, 1989);

Science Fiction Blues: The Show That Brian Aldiss Took on the Road, edited by Frank Hatherley (London: Avernus, 1988);

A Romance of the Equator: The Best Fantasy Stories of Brian W. Aldiss (London: Gollancz, 1989; New York: Atheneum, 1990);

Bury My Heart at W. H. Smith's: A Writing Life (London: Hodder & Stoughton, 1990; expanded edition, London: Avernus, 1991);

Bodily Functions (London: Avernus, 1991);

Dracula Unbound (London: Grafton, 1991; New York: HarperCollins, 1991);
Home Life with Cats (London: Grafton, 1992);
Kindred Blood in Kensington Gore: Philip K. Dick in the Afterlife, an Imaginary Conversation (London: Avernus, 1992);
Remembrance Day (London: HarperCollins, 1993; New York: St. Martin's Press, 1993);
A Tupolev Too Far: And Other Stories (London: HarperCollins, 1993; New York: St. Martin's Press, 1994);
Somewhere East of Life: Another European Fantasia (London: Flamingo, 1994; New York: Carroll & Graf, 1994);
The Detached Retina: Aspects of SF and Fantasy (Liverpool: Liverpool University Press, 1995; Syracuse, N.Y.: Syracuse University Press, 1995);
At the Caligula Hotel and Other Poems (London: Sinclair-Stevenson, 1995);
The Secret of This Book: 20-Odd Stories (London: HarperCollins, 1995); republished as *Common Clay: 20 Odd Stories* (New York: St. Martin's Press, 1996);
The Twinkling of an Eye; or, My Life as an Englishman (London: Little, Brown, 1998; New York: St. Martin's Press, 1999);
White Mars; or, The Mind Set Free: A 21st-Century Utopia, by Aldiss and Sir Roger Penrose (London: Little, Brown, 1999; New York: St. Martin's Press, 2000);
When the Feast Is Finished: Reflections on Terminal Illness, by Aldiss and Margaret Aldiss (London: Little, Brown, 1999);
A Plutonian Monologue on His Wife's Death (Folkestone: Frogmere Press, 2000);
Supertoys Last All Summer Long, and Other Stories of Future Time (London: Orbit, 2001; New York: St. Martin's Press, 2001);
The Cretan Teat (Thirsk: Stratus, 2002);
Jocasta (London: Stratus, 2002);
Super-State: A Novel of a Future Europe (London: Orbit, 2002).

Editions and Collections: *Best Science Fiction Stories of Brian W. Aldiss* (London: Faber & Faber, 1965); republished as *Who Can Replace a Man? The Best Science-Fiction Stories of Brian W. Aldiss* (New York: Harcourt, Brace & World, 1966); revised as *Best Science Fiction Stories of Brian W. Aldiss* (London: Faber & Faber, 1971);
A Brian Aldiss Omnibus (London: Sidgwick & Jackson, 1969)–includes *The Interpreter, The Primal Urge,* "The Saliva Tree," "The Impossible Star," "Basis for Negotiation," and "Man in His Time";
Brian Aldiss Omnibus 2 (London: Sidgwick & Jackson, 1971)–includes *Space, Time and Nathaniel; Non-Stop;* and *The Male Response;*
Brothers of the Head; and, Where the Lines Converge (London: Panther, 1979);
The Horatio Stubbs Saga (London: Panther, 1985)–comprises *The Hand-Reared Boy, A Soldier Erect,* and *A Rude Awakening.*

PRODUCED SCRIPT: *Frankenstein Unbound,* BBC Radio, 1974.

OTHER: *Penguin Science Fiction,* edited by Aldiss (Harmondsworth, U.K.: Penguin, 1961);
Best Fantasy Stories, edited by Aldiss (London: Faber & Faber, 1962);
More Penguin Science Fiction: An Anthology, edited by Aldiss (Harmondsworth, U.K.: Penguin, 1963);
Yet More Penguin Science Fiction, edited by Aldiss (Harmondsworth, U.K.: Penguin, 1964);
Introducing Science Fiction: A Science Fiction Anthology, edited by Aldiss (London: Faber & Faber, 1964);
Science Fiction Horizons 1, edited by Aldiss and Harry Harrison (New York: Arno, 1964);
Science Fiction Horizons 2, edited by Aldiss and Harrison (New York: Arno, 1965); both republished as *SF Horizons,* edited by Aldiss and Harrison (New York: Arno, 1975);
Charles L. Harness, *The Paradox Men,* introduction by Aldiss (London: New English Library, 1967);
Nebula Award Stories II, edited by Aldiss and Harrison (Garden City, N.Y.: Doubleday, 1967);
Farewell, Fantastic Venus! A History of the Planet Venus in Fact and Fiction, edited by Aldiss and Harrison (London: Macdonald, 1968); abridged as *All About Venus: A Revelation of the Planet Venus in Fact and Fiction* (New York: Dell, 1968);
Best Science Fiction: 1967, edited by Aldiss and Harrison (New York: Berkley, 1968); republished as *The Year's Best Science Fiction 1* (London: Sphere, 1968);
Best Science Fiction: 1968, edited by Aldiss and Harrison (New York: Putnam, 1969); abridged as *The Year's Best Science Fiction 2* (London: Sphere, 1969);
Best Science Fiction: 1969, edited by Aldiss and Harrison (New York: Putnam, 1970); republished as *The Year's Best Science Fiction 3* (London: Sphere, 1970);
Best Science Fiction: 1970, edited by Aldiss and Harrison (New York: Putnam, 1971); republished as *The Year's Best Science Fiction 4* (London: Sphere, 1971);
Best Science Fiction: 1971, edited by Aldiss and Harrison (New York: Putnam, 1972); republished as *The Year's Best Science Fiction 5* (London: Sphere, 1972);
The Astounding-Analog Reader, 2 volumes, edited by Aldiss and Harrison (Garden City, N.Y.: Doubleday, 1972, 1973); volume 1 republished in 2 volumes as *The Astounding-Analog Reader* (London, 1973);

Best Science Fiction: 1972, edited by Aldiss and Harrison (New York: Putnam, 1973); republished as *The Year's Best Science Fiction 6* (London: Sphere, 1973);

The Penguin Science Fiction Omnibus: An Anthology, edited by Aldiss (Harmondsworth, U.K.: Penguin, 1973);

Space Opera: An Anthology of Way-Back-When Futures, edited by Aldiss (London: Futura, 1974; Garden City, N.Y.: Doubleday, 1975);

Best Science Fiction: 1973, edited by Aldiss and Harrison (New York: Putnam, 1974); abridged as *The Year's Best Science Fiction 7* (London: Sphere, 1974);

Space Odysseys: A New Look at Yesterday's Futures, edited by Aldiss (London: Futura, 1974; Garden City, N.Y.: Doubleday, 1976);

Best Science Fiction: 1974, edited by Aldiss and Harrison (New York: Putnam, 1975); abridged as *The Year's Best Science Fiction 8* (London: Sphere, 1975);

Hell's Cartographers: Some Personal Histories of Science Fiction Writers, edited by Aldiss and Harrison (London: Weidenfeld & Nicolson, 1975; New York: Harper & Row, 1975); includes Aldiss's "Magic and Bare Boards";

Evil Earths, edited by Aldiss (London: Weidenfeld & Nicolson, 1975; New York: Avon, 1979);

Decade: The 1940s, edited by Aldiss and Harrison (London: Macmillan, 1975; New York: St. Martin's Press, 1978);

Best Science Fiction: 1975, edited by Aldiss and Harrison (Indianapolis & New York: Bobbs-Merrill, 1976); republished as *The Year's Best Science Fiction 9* (London: Sphere, 1976);

Galactic Empires, 2 volumes, edited by Aldiss (London: Weidenfeld & Nicolson, 1976; New York: St. Martin's Press, 1977);

Decade: The 1950s, edited by Aldiss and Harrison (London: Macmillan, 1976; New York: St. Martin's Press, 1978);

Decade: The 1960s, edited by Aldiss and Harrison (London: Macmillan, 1977);

Perilous Planets, edited by Aldiss (London: Weidenfeld & Nicolson, 1978; New York: Avon, 1980);

"A Monster for All Seasons," in *Science Fiction Dialogues,* edited by Gary Wolfe (Chicago: Academy Chicago, 1982), pp. 9–23;

The Book of Mini-Sagas I, edited by Aldiss (1985);

The Penguin World Omnibus of Science Fiction, edited by Aldiss and Sam J. Lundwall (Harmondsworth, U.K.: Penguin, 1986);

The Book of Mini-Sagas II, edited by Aldiss (1988);

H. G. Wells, *The Island of Doctor Moreau,* afterword by Aldiss (New York: New American Library, 1988);

"Living in Catastrophe," in *Doris Lessing: Conversations,* edited by Earl G. Ingersoll (Princeton: Ontario Review Press, 1994), pp. 169–172;

Robert Crossley, *Olaf Stapledon: Speaking for the Future,* foreword by Aldiss (Syracuse, N.Y.: Syracuse University Press, 1994);

Wells, *The War of the Worlds,* edited by David Y. Hughes, introduction by Aldiss (New York: Oxford University Press, 1995), pp. xv–xxxvi;

"The Eye-Opener," in *The Best of Interzone,* edited by David Pringle (New York: St. Martin's Press, 1997), pp. 329–341;

Mini Sagas from the Daily Telegraph Competition, edited by Aldiss (London: Sutton, 1997);

Mini Sagas from the Daily Telegraph Competition 2001, edited by Aldiss (London: Enitharmon, 2001).

SELECTED PERIODICAL PUBLICATIONS–UNCOLLECTED: "Remembrance of Lives Past," *Science-Fiction Studies,* 21 (Summer 1994): 129–133;

"Kepler's Error: The Polar Bear Theory of Plurispresence," *Science-Fiction Studies,* 23 (Spring 1996): 1–10;

"The Referee of the War of the Worlds," *New York Review of Science Fiction,* 123 (November 1998): 1, 4–6.

Brian W. Aldiss is a prolific, inventive, and highly skilled writer who escapes easy definition. He is still best known as a science-fiction writer and has garnered all the top awards of the genre. He has also produced a substantial corpus of realistic novels, a major history of science fiction, a rich autobiography, a significant travel book, a small but accomplished body of humorous writing, many essays on literary and cultural topics, and a sheaf of poems. Wide sympathies, a vivid awareness of human vulnerability and resilience, and a concern for the future of humanity and the planet inform all his work; he brings to his writing a rich, eclectic cultural and literary knowledge and a readiness to experiment with language, form, and subject matter. His concern with the craft of writing is shown by his readiness to revise his work when it seems necessary in order to convey his meanings as fully as possible; retitling and rewriting are notable features of his complex bibliography, especially in his earlier career, when he was more vulnerable to magazine editors and publishers who demanded alterations.

Aldiss found early acclaim as a science-fiction writer in the 1950s, and both his short stories and novels in that decade displayed what had already come to be seen by many science-fiction readers as the solid, traditional virtues of the genre: a capacity for compelling storytelling; an ability to convey vividly fear, danger, and violent action; and an imagination that generated futures and alternative worlds that were surprising because of the ways in which they differed from the contemporary world but plausible because of the ways in which they extrapolated from it. Aldiss was not content to rest there, however; he was open to the implications for fiction in general of the *nouveau roman* that emerged in France in the 1950s and of the "New Wave" in science fiction itself that emerged in England in the 1960s; as a novelist and short-story writer, he engaged with both these movements inventively but not uncritically. Since the 1960s he has won increasing respect from critics both for his science fiction and for his more mainstream novels; he has also done much as an editor, historian, and critic of science fiction to raise its profile as a genre worthy of serious critical attention.

Brian Wilson Aldiss was born 18 August 1925, the son of Stanley and Elizabeth May Wilson Aldiss. For the first six years of his life he lived with his family in the flat above the drapers' shop in East Dereham, Norfolk, that his grandfather, H. H. Aldiss, had founded and that prospered throughout the 1920s and 1930s. His childhood was materially comfortable but not altogether happy; in his autobiography, *The Twinkling of an Eye; or, My Life as an Englishman* (1998), he recalls that his mother would threaten that she would not love him if he misbehaved and would compare him unfavorably with an idealized infant sister, born in 1920, who had, according to his mother, lived for six months. Aldiss eventually discovered that she had, in fact, been stillborn. His sense of rejection as a child was compounded in 1931 by the arrival of a younger sister, Betty, in whom his mother found an unalloyed joy that contrasted with her ambivalent attitude toward her son. The theme of the son who fears that his mother may not love him recurs in Aldiss's short stories and novels, for example, "Supertoys Last All Summer Long" (1961), the basis of Steven Spielberg's motion picture *AI* (2001), and *Forgotten Life* (1988). At the age of eight he was sent to St. Peter's Court Preparatory School at Bracton, went on to Framlingham College in Suffolk when he was eleven, and transferred to West Buckland School, Devon, when he reached his fourteenth year. He read widely as a boy; in his contribution to a volume he co-edited with the science-fiction writer Harry Harrison, *Hell's Cartographers: Some Personal Histories of Science Fiction Writers* (1975), he relates that both his fascination with science fiction and his desire to improve its literary quality developed early. He relished the stories in American science-fiction magazines such as *Marvel Science Stories, Amazing Stories,* and *Astounding Science Fiction* but thought them badly written. "By the age of eight, I had begun to appreciate style, the vehicle of fiction, as well as content."

Aldiss with his parents and sister, Betty, 1931
(Collection of Brian Aldiss)

At the age of thirteen Aldiss moved with his family to Gorleston-on-Sea, Norfolk, and he spent his school holidays there. In 1943 he joined the British army, and after training at Britannia Barracks, Norfolk, he entered the Royal Corps of Signals at Catterick Camp, Yorkshire. He was posted abroad in 1944 and served in India, Assam, Burma, Sumatra, and Hong Kong: all of these places provided him with a powerful range of experiences that were to feed both into his science fiction and, more directly, into the second and third novels of his Horatio Stubbs trilogy, *A Soldier Erect; or, Further Adventures of the Hand-Reared Boy* (1971) and *A Rude Awakening* (1978), and into some of his other mainstream fiction, such as *Forgotten Life.* After he was demobilized from the army in 1947, he was entitled to a period of ninety-one days leave and worked on a novel, "Hunter Leaves the Herd," based on an actual event–an infantry sergeant in Sumatra became the first British soldier to desert and join the Republican rebels in exchange for a woman and life in the kampongs (enclosures or villages); the army eventually tracked him down and killed him. "Hunter Leaves the Herd" was never completed or published; although Aldiss had written much short fiction, he found the form of a novel too difficult. Furthermore, the restrictions on profane language in print in England in the late 1940s inhibited his attempt to render his soldiers' dialogue realistically. He amply compensated for this disadvantage when, in more permissive times, he came to write the Horatio Stubbs trilogy.

Aldiss abandoned "Hunter Leaves the Herd" and found a job as an assistant in Sanders' bookshop in Oxford, a post that encouraged both his passion for reading and his desire to write. His first published book, *The Brightfount Diaries* (1955), later drew from his two and a half years of work there. In 1948 Aldiss married Olive Fortescue, who typed out his short stories. He started another novel, "Shouting Down a Cliff," and this time managed to finish it. Although he felt it was unsuccessful, its completion nonetheless pleased and heartened him. Further encouragement came in 1953 when the science-fiction magazine *Nebula* accepted his short story "T," even though it did not actually feature in its pages until 1956. In February 1954 he appeared in print for the first time in the trade journal *The Bookseller,* with a humorous article about the life of an imaginary bookshop, writing under the pseudonym Peter Pica (pica is the name of a small typeface), and in July 1954 his first published science-fiction story, "Criminal Record," came out in the magazine *Science Fantasy.* He was aware, however, that science fiction was still held in low regard. In *The Twinkling of an Eye* he recalls how his boss at Parker's bookshop in Oxford, where he worked after leaving Sanders', saw a copy of *Galaxy Science Fiction* on his desk and remarked: "You don't read that rubbish, do you?" Aldiss replied: "Yes. And I contribute rubbish to it."

Aldiss's ongoing series of articles for *The Bookseller* caught the attention of Charles Monteith, a director of Faber and Faber and a fellow of All Souls College, Oxford. Monteith asked Aldiss to turn the articles into a book, which Faber published as *The Brightfount Diaries.* It is an entertaining, perceptive sequence of sketches, a kind of comic counterpart to the account of Gordon Comstock's period as a bookseller in George Orwell's novel *Keep the Aspidistra Flying* (1936). The book received respectful notices, for example in *The Times Literary Supplement* (*TLS*) and the *Spectator,* though it was also felt to have limited appeal. As Silas Fish put it in the *Spectator* (27 December 1955): "Pleasant enough reading for the bookish who can appreciate its shop-talk, it is too insular to have wider appeal." Nonetheless, *The Brightfount Diaries* had good sales; Aldiss could feel that he had been launched as a writer. That feeling was strengthened when, in December 1955, his short story "Not for an Age" won the short-story prize offered by the *Observer* Sunday newspaper for the best fiction set in A.D. 2500. Among the judges were influential writers and critics such as Angus Wilson and Marghanita Laski. In personal terms, 1955 was a year of both joy and sadness; Aldiss's first son, Clive, was born, but his marriage was in difficulty.

Aldiss took the risk of leaving his bookselling job in 1956 to become a full-time writer. In December of that year his "Tradesman's Exit" shared first place in a competition for a humorous short story held, once again, by the *Observer.* In 1957 he became literary editor of the *Oxford Mail,* and his first collection of short stories, *Space, Time and Nathaniel (Presciences),* was published. It demonstrates his range and inventiveness and is especially notable for "T," the first short story that he ever sold, which the anonymous reviewer of *TLS* (10 May 1957) called "a brilliant new variation on the time paradox." The reviewer's overall judgment was that *Space, Time and Nathaniel* was "an exhilarating debut" but that it was marred by facetiousness and often uncertain execution–charges that have been made against both Aldiss's science fiction and his mainstream fiction subsequently. The review concluded that Aldiss had "a long way to go before he can compete with the experts."

Aldiss improved quickly as a writer, however: his first science-fiction novel, *Non-Stop* (1958), published in revised form as *Starship* (1959) in the United States, demonstrates his capacity to tell a compelling story while raising large issues about the limits of human concepts and perceptions. In *Non-Stop* Roy Complain, a member of a tribe that inhabits a territory called Quarters, leads an expedition into adjacent territories that eventually reveals to him and his companions the truth of their situation; the world in which they live is in fact a huge spaceship, making the enormously long journey back to Earth after a failed expedition to a distant star. The novel vividly dramatizes how human beings may misinterpret reality and traces the trauma and troubling triumph of breaking through to a more accurate understanding of one's condition. Colin Greenland, in *The Entropy Exhibition: Michael Moorcock and the British "New Wave" in Science Fiction* (1983), points out that *Non-Stop* is also an implicit criticism of two linked stories by Robert A. Heinlein, "Universe" and "Common Sense," first published in the American edition of *Astounding* in 1941 and later published as *Orphans of the Sky* (1963). In Heinlein's story, entrapment in a spaceship after a failed expedition promotes heroism; in Aldiss's version in *Non-Stop,* it reveals human weakness. It should be said, nonetheless, that Complain is a kind of hero, although, in a way that is characteristic of Aldiss, he combines resilience with vulnerability. By Aldiss's own account, *Non-Stop* had a better initial reception in the United

Dust jacket for the U.S. edition of Aldiss's 1970 novel, the first of three novels about the sexual adventures of a character named Horatio Stubbs (Richland County Public Library)

States than in Britain, where the reviewer for *TLS* (9 May 1958) found the first two-thirds "excellent, a moving allegory that deserves to be read as literature in its own right" but felt that the last third was contrived. Nonetheless, the novel established Aldiss as a science-fiction writer. In 1958 he won the accolade of the "Most Promising New Author of the Year" at the Sixteenth World Science Fiction Convention.

Aldiss's next novel, *Equator,* appeared in England in 1958 and was republished in the United States in 1959 under the title *Vanguard from Alpha.* The American title highlights the exciting plot of the novel: its protagonist, Tyne Leslie, finds out that the alien Roskians from Alpha Centauri, who have been granted a refuge on Earth in Sumatra, are the advance guard of an invasion force. The English title draws attention both to the physical setting of the novel–Sumatra lies on the equator–and to its metaphorical implications: the equator is the hot center of things, where the action is. Aldiss vividly combines taut scenes of danger and violence, vivid vignettes of Sumatra that draw on his own wartime experience of the tropics, and reflective passages that raise a range of issues. One of these issues is the dubious appeal of action–Tyne has quit his job in diplomatic service for a more exciting life but starts "to wonder about the respect he had held for men of action," "who had seemed to be going round the fastest" but now looked as if they "merely went in circles." Another issue regards free will and determinism–is Tyne in control, a player of the game, or only a pawn in a larger plot? A third issue concerns the possibility of peaceful coexistence between different groups–a possibility of which *Equator* takes a pessimistic view.

Aldiss's second short-story collection, *The Canopy of Time,* was published in the United Kingdom in 1959, the year in which his daughter Caroline was born. The stories range widely in theme, from "O Ishrail!," in which only one person credits an apparently insane man's claim that he is an exiled galactic admiral, to the much-reprinted "Who Can Replace a Man?," in which an attempt by robots to assert their independence when they believe all men have died is quickly quelled when they find a man still living. The anonymous reviewer in *TLS* (18 December 1959) judged that *The Canopy of Time* consolidated the promise of *Space, Time and Nathaniel* but dismissed Aldiss's attempt to link the stories chronologically as "an unnecessary gimmick." For Aldiss himself, however, this arrangement was an important aspect of the collection; he aimed to present the stories as fragments of a hypothetical history of the future that runs from a century or two hence to the end of the galaxy. The collection was published in 1960 under the title

Galaxies Like Grains of Sand, with more-extended linking passages. In his introduction to the 1979 version of *Galaxies like Grains of Sand,* Aldiss's fellow science-fiction writer Norman Spinrad suggests that the 1960 edition is "almost a preview of what will be Aldiss's main concerns and techniques in succeeding years," with its "sophisticated concepts of time expressed through intricate and sometimes convoluted structure," its "unusual shifts of viewpoint within a single story," and its "concern with evolution, devolution, and renewal." Aldiss, however, was dissatisfied with the 1960 edition, and the versions of *Galaxies Like Grains of Sand* that did satisfy him only appeared, with introductions by Spinrad, in the United States in 1977 and in Britain in 1979. These versions gain in coherence, even though they lose two interesting stories from the original *Canopy of Time:* "Three's a Cloud," which turns on a protagonist who has a habit of making small but significant verbal slips (the title of the story is his version of the phrase "three's a crowd"), and "They Shall Inherit," which deals with the temptations and threats of genetic engineering.

In 1960 Aldiss stepped up his campaign to raise the status of science fiction by helping the respected Oxford don, theologian, and science-fiction writer C. S. Lewis to found the Oxford University Speculative Fiction Group. His next science-fiction novel, *Bow Down to Nul,* which appeared in the United States in 1960 and was republished in England under the title of *The Interpreter* in 1961, features a galactic empire ruled by the "nuls," in which one of the colonized planets is "a backward little dump called Earth." The plot is based on the idea that the more widespread the empire, the larger the chances of corruption and exploitation. Aldiss acknowledges that stories about galactic empires had always fascinated him, partly because his wartime military service enabled him to witness directly the disquieting relations between English colonialists and the native inhabitants in India and Indonesia. His remark is a further indication of how thoroughly his science fiction has roots in twentieth-century reality.

Aldiss's role as a promoter of science fiction was enhanced in 1961 when he became editor of the Penguin Science Fiction series and of the first *Penguin Science Fiction* anthology. He went on to edit four further anthologies for Penguin: *More Penguin Science Fiction* (1963), *Yet More Penguin Science Fiction* (1964), *The Penguin Science Fiction Omnibus* (1973), and *The Penguin World Omnibus of Science Fiction* (1986). Two more of his own novels appeared in 1961, *The Male Response* and *The Primal Urge,* both first published in the United States. They took up a topic of key concern to Aldiss: the conflict between sexuality and what he saw as unhealthy repression. Significantly, given Aldiss's view of the repressiveness of British society, *The Male Response* did not come out in the United Kingdom until 1963, and *The Primal Urge* remained unpublished in England until 1967. *The Male Response* is set in an imaginary, stereotypical Africa; when the British edition came out in 1963, D. A. N. Jones, reviewing the novel in the *New Statesman* (4 October 1963), judged it "an amusing fantasy," but the anonymous reviewer in *TLS* (4 October 1963), while acknowledging that Aldiss possessed "some inventive virtuosity," called the Aldiss version of Africa "the superficially realized background for a piece of fiction-journalism."

Aldiss is on surer ground when he satirizes English life in *The Primal Urge,* producing a highly entertaining, sometimes hilarious novel showing the consequences for English society of the invention of "Ers"–"Emotion Registers" or "sex detectors." The Ers are silver discs, worn on the forehead, that change color from silver through shades of pink and red according to the degree of sexual attraction one person feels for another. In portraying a situation in which, as one character puts it, "Inhibitory blocks we've come unjustifiably to regard as keystones in our society are being swept away," *The Primal Urge* anticipates the debates over sexual permissiveness in the England of the later 1960s.

Hothouse (1962), published in the United States in abridged form as *The Long Afternoon of Earth,* began as a series of short stories in the *Magazine of Fantasy and Science Fiction* and received the 1962 Hugo Award for best short fiction. Moreover, its focus on one particular imaginary world helped it to jell into a novel more effectively than the short stories comprising *The Canopy of Time. Hothouse* vividly evokes a world in which a small number of human beings fight for survival against the predatory plant life that is now dominant as a result of increased solar radiation. As in *Equator,* Aldiss once again produces an exciting science-fiction adventure story; but he is also able to give rein more fully than before to his enjoyment of language, to his delight in coining new words, in the names that he creates for his imaginary plants, such as *berrywhisk, dumbler, trappersnapper, crocksock, thinpin, pluggyrug, dripperslip,* and *slashweed. Hothouse* also carries deeper implications. Like *Non-Stop,* it demonstrates a group of human beings coming to recognize the limits of their concepts and perceptions. It also provides powerful images of the instability and fragility of human existence and of the fecundity and ruthlessness of nature. It breaks down the conventional perception in which mammalian, reptilian, and insect life is seen as predatory and plant life is regarded as benign: Aldiss adapts the famous phrase of the nineteenth-century Victorian poet Alfred Tennyson about nature as "red in tooth and claw" to a hothouse world in which plant life is green in tooth and claw.

Dust jacket for Aldiss's 1973 novel, in which a time traveler from the twenty-first century meets Percy Bysshe Shelley, Mary Shelley, Lord Byron, the real-life Victor Frankenstein, and Frankenstein's Monster (Bruccoli Clark Layman Archives)

The Airs of Earth (1963) is a collection of eight short stories that had previously appeared in science-fiction magazines. Characteristically, Aldiss had revised them since their first appearance in print. The stories range widely but touch on typical Aldiss themes: for example, in "A Kind of Artistry" the population of Earth has dwindled to less than two million, and its self-enclosure is strengthened and symbolized by its matrimonial system, in which sons marry their mothers. The story conveys a sense of elegy and entropy, with only an ambiguous intimation at the end of a possible break in the pattern. "How to Be a Soldier" makes ingenious use of a dream sequence in dramatizing the way in which military action in some unspecified future uses a combination of tranquilizers and stimulants ("Fast-plus pills") to turn soldiers into efficient machines who, as they progress up the promotion ladder, repress the possibility of love and tenderness represented by an imaginary woman. "Basis for Negotiation" is a highly dramatic story in which a confrontation between China and the West over the treatment of Chinese nationals in Sumatra escalates into an all-out attack by China on the United States in which, in an anticipation of the "star wars" defense system, Chinese nuclear and "anti-matter" missiles are repulsed by a protective shield; the tale is told from the viewpoint of a gentlemanly British academic appalled by the British government's decision to remain neutral in the conflict. The story both powerfully conveys the danger of nuclear war and implicitly raises challenging questions about the attitudes of the British Campaign for Nuclear Disarmament; by Aldiss's own account, it caused much controversy on its first magazine appearance. "The International Smile" is a comic counterpart to "Basis for Negotiation," in which the discovery of a drug called "polyannamine" makes a potential nuclear war between Russia and the United Kingdom dissolve in laughter. "Shards" combines science fiction with Samuel Beckett, plunging the reader into the bizarre consciousness of what are later revealed to be slices of human brain embedded in fish-like bodies.

In 1964 Aldiss began to develop his interest in the criticism of science fiction, editing and publishing a critical magazine, *SF Horizons,* with his fellow science-fiction writer Harry Harrison. From 1967 to 1976 he and Harrison co-edited *The Year's Best Science Fiction.* Aldiss's next novel, *The Dark Light Years* (1964), focuses on a favorite science-fiction theme, the first encounter between human beings and aliens from other planets. In this case an expedition to find other planets to colo-

Dust jacket for the U.S. edition of Aldiss's 1980 novel, a sequel to H. G. Wells's 1896 novel, The Island of Dr. Moreau *(Richland County Public Library)*

nize captures two six-limbed, omnidextrous "utods" and brings them back to Earth, where they are kept in a zoo; it is possible that the utods may be superior to humanity, but they pursue a practice that humans find it difficult to stomach: wallowing in their own excrement. Their civilization, as Aldiss puts it, is one of "Law and ordure." By creating beings who invert one of the most fundamental human taboos, Aldiss mordantly calls into question preconceptions about the nature of intelligence and civilization. In a review in the *New Statesman* (6 September 1963) Robert Taubman called *The Dark Light Years* "ingenious and sardonic," "a modern morality as much as science fiction and very sharp with its inferences."

The sharp criticism of human prejudice and destructiveness in *The Dark Light Years* continues in *Greybeard* (1964) but it is tempered by an elegiac sadness. *Greybeard* combines science fiction, myth, and fairy tale in a haunting way. Missile testing in space has poisoned the biosphere with hard radiation and rendered humanity sterile. Now the remnant of the human race is growing old: "Of the seven ages of man, little but the last remained." It is rumored that children still dwell in the woods, however, and Algy Timberlane, the "Greybeard" of the title, goes in quest of them through a landscape that is both familiar–it is the Thames Valley around Oxford, where Aldiss has lived for most of his adult life–and strange because of its aging and dwindling human population and the resurgence of animal and vegetable life. Taubman, who had praised *The Dark Light Years* in the *New Statesman,* also praised *Greybeard* in the same journal (2 October 1964), though with reservations; he found it "rich in the imagination of disaster," combining recognizable scenes with others reminiscent of the paintings of the Dutch painters Hieronymus Bosch and Pieter Brueghel, but he also judged it "low on action and less well-organized than the best of Aldiss." Aldiss, in *The Twinkling of an Eye,* has acknowledged that the style of the novel is indebted to Thomas Hardy but suggests that its atmosphere relates more to Richard Jefferies's post-disaster novel *After London* (1885). He has also highlighted an autobiographical subtext in the novel: by this time his marriage had broken up and he was separated from his son and daughter; as he himself puts it, *Greybeard* is "my intensely felt novel mourning the loss of my children."

The "imagination of disaster" identified by Taubman was also strongly evident in Aldiss's short novel *Earthworks* (1965), which portrays a world divided between authoritarian societies and nomads–a world, as the anonymous *TLS* reviewer said, "of nightmare, with the inconsequence of nightmare" and "the inflated language of nightmare." The novelist William Trevor, in *The Listener* (2 May 1968), felt that in *Earthworks* Aldiss "achieves a certain Orwellian chilliness, but spoils the flashes of credibility by introducing a series of ridiculously corny characters." Trevor acknowledged, however, that as a science-fiction writer Aldiss was superior to most. Among the science-fiction fraternity, his status was confirmed when he was guest of honor at the Twenty-third World Science Fiction Convention in London in 1965. That same year was also notable for a development in his personal life: he married Margaret Manson, with whom he had two children–Timothy, born in 1967, and Charlotte, born in 1969.

The journey Aldiss had taken with Manson across Yugoslavia in 1964 resulted in the travel book *Cities and Stones: A Traveller's Jugoslavia* (1966). Yugoslavia is a place to which Aldiss has often returned in his fiction. The title story of his next collection, *The Saliva Tree and Other Strange Growths* (1966), won the Nebula Award for the best novella of 1965. "The Saliva Tree" is a pastiche of H. G. Wells, set in the closing years of the nineteenth century; a young man, Gregory Rolles, witnesses the appearance of a space rather than time machine in the East Anglian countryside; he writes to Wells about it, but by the time Wells arrives in the village the machine and its occupants have departed. Other stories in the collection demonstrate Aldiss's characteristic range, from "Danger: Religion!," which evokes an alternative world in which a Grand Christian Church has gained control of nuclear weapons, to "The Lonely Habit" and "A Pleasure Shared," two well-turned examples of black humor, each told by a serial murderer who unexpectedly encounters another killer. The concluding story in the collection, "The Girl and the Robot with Flowers," is a reflection on the state of science fiction itself, in which, as the narrator, who is also a science-fiction writer, puts it: "Every SF story is getting like every other one."

In the 1960s, in science fiction as in other spheres, the sense that it was time for change grew. One of the science-fiction writers mentioned in "The Girl and the Robot with Flowers" is Michael Moorcock, who was the driving force of the "New Wave" in science fiction that developed in England in the 1960s. In 1964 Moorcock took over as editor of *New Worlds,* a science-fiction magazine that had been founded in 1946, and began to introduce more avant-garde experimental science fiction into its pages. When the original publishers of *New Worlds* decided to close down all their science-fiction magazines in 1966, Aldiss played a key role in obtaining an Arts Council grant that helped *New Worlds* to keep going. Meanwhile his own fiction was developing. In 1967 he published *An Age,* which was retitled *Cryptozoic!* for its American publication in 1968 and for its subsequent British editions. The novel portrays an England moving toward totalitarianism in which most people indulge in mental time traveling. An artist who creates "spatial-kinetic groupages," Edward Bush, is particularly good at this time traveling and is compelled to become a secret policeman who pursues potential subversives in the 1930s and the 1850s before joining in an attempt to overthrow the regime that lands him in a mental home, a psychological wanderer between time zones. *Cryptozoic!* has intriguing moments, but, like future mainstream novels such as *Somewhere East of Life: Another European Fantasia* (1994), it does not hang together.

Aldiss's most cohesive novels in this period were also his most experimental: both first appeared, in earlier versions, in Moorcock's *New Worlds.* The first was *Report on Probability A* (1968), which employs the technique pioneered by the French *nouveau roman* author Alain Robbe-Grillet in a novel such as *La Jalousie* (1957; translated as *Jealousy,* 1959), in which the reader has to infer situations, events, and relationships from precise, austere descriptions of external appearance and behavior. Aldiss complicates this approach with the science-fiction device of multiple dimensions, creating a vertiginous effect as the novel reveals that the watchers on what is assumed to be Earth are under observation by beings in other dimensions who are, in their turn, under surveillance from Earth:

> "There's so much we don't know,"' agreed the Governor. "Meanwhile, all we can do is scrutinize their every movement."
>
> "If we could get our data more directly," Midlakemela said. "If we could only penetrate inside Mr. Mary's house."
>
> "SHE holds the key to the mystery. I feel it in my bones," Domoladossa said. . . .
>
> He was being scrutinized by two Distinguishers on a hillside. They, in turn, were being watched by a group of men in a New York building.
>
> Joe Growleth had been working in the room for five hours and was a little weary. Turning to Congressman Sadlier, he said, "Well, that's how it seems to be. Our robot fly has materialized into a world where it so happens that the first group of inhabitants we come across is studying another world they have discovered–a world in which the inhabitants they watch are studying a report they have obtained from another world."

The novel also raises the question of which of the worlds it evokes can be considered real. A further layer of complexity is added to the novel by its recurrent descriptions of *The Hireling Shepherd* by the nineteenth-century English Pre-Raphaelite artist Holman Hunt, a painting that captures a moment of suspended time with what Aldiss, in an essay in *This World and Nearer Ones: Essays Exploring the Familiar* (1979), calls "intense vision." *Report on Probability A* aroused mixed review responses: the anonymous reviewer in *TLS* (3 October 1968) judged that Aldiss, like Robbe-Grillet and Nathalie Sarraute, was "aiming at literary statics" and that, like them, "he is at once impressive and extraordinarily dull." In contrast, the novelist Wallace Hildick in *The Listener* (2 May 1968) found it "absorbingly interesting," even if "too derivative" of early Beckett, Robbe-Grillet, Jorge Luis Borges, and Franz Kafka. In retrospect, it can be seen as a notable contribution to avant-garde English writing in the 1960s, along with the work of Christine Brooke-Rose and Paul Ableman.

The idea that reality is a fragile and questionable construct is pursued further in Aldiss's *Barefoot in the Head: A European Fantasia* (1969), also first published in

Dust jacket for the U.S. edition of Aldiss's 1985 novel, the final volume of his trilogy about the growth and decline of civilization on an imaginary planet (Richland County Public Library)

New Worlds. In this novel, however, the precise, sober language of *Report on Probability A* gives way to a riot of puns and neologisms, releasing the delight in linguistic inventiveness that was evident, in a more contained way, in the names of Aldiss's fictional flora in *Hothouse.* The disorder of language in *Barefoot in the Head* relates to the world that it evokes–a world devastated by an "Acid Head War" in which the Arab nations have subjected "wesciv" to an "Arablitz" in which planes have dropped PCA (Psycho-Chemical Aerosol) bombs on Europe. The protagonist of the novel is Colin Charteris, a Serbian who has taken his surname from his favorite English writer, Leslie Charteris, the pseudonymous author of the Saint thrillers. Charteris travels to England, where he becomes a guru and Christ figure who leads a crusade of car drivers across Europe. The style that Aldiss employs is exemplified in this vivid passage evoking the growth of the Charteris cult:

> The little fugitive figures were a new tribe, high after the miracle when the Master Charteris had died and risen again in a sparky way after only three minutes after the multi-man speed death up at Aalter. Tribally, they mucked in making legends. Bead groups flowered and ceded, lyrics became old history before the turning night wheeled in drawn. Some of the girls rinsed underclothes and hung them on lines between the kerouacs while others highjinxed the boys or got autoerotic in the dicky seats. A thousand drivniks locusted in the stony patch, mostly British, and the word spread inspired to the spired city.

Barefoot in the Head is a key novel of the fascination and failure of the 1960s counterculture. In *The Listener* (16 October 1969) Stuart Hood called the book "extraordinary" and compared its "dark, sombre, sustained vision" to that of Jean-Luc Godard's movie *Week-end* (1967). Hood found the novel structurally interesting because of its mixture of prose, poems, and pop lyrics and judged the style "dense and powerful," but felt that Aldiss's puns were too often "laboured" and lacking in "associative content." The review in *TLS* (22 January 1970) also had reservations about Aldiss's wordplay: "Is this the punning of Joyce, worth the effort to unravel? Or merely of John Lennon?"

Aldiss's own retrospective attitude to *Barefoot in the Head* has undergone some interesting changes. In "Barefoot: Its First Decade," originally written for a Swedish translation of the novel that was never published and collected in *This World and Nearer Ones,* Aldiss says that he wrote *Barefoot in the Head* to find out whether he preferred "Law and Order–or anarchy and excrement" and "came out on the side of . . . well, against anarchy, let's say." He suggests, however, that "Part of the excitement many people have found in *Barefoot* is because the debate was live to me as I wrote it." He also calls *Barefoot in the Head* "a poetical novel of ideas," the language of which "will have to speak for itself." In *The Twinkling of an Eye,* more than a quarter of a century later, he turns on the novel more harshly, calling it "one of the fake milestones of science fiction" that might "have been better told in plain language." This judgment is too dismissive: *Barefoot in the Head* continues to repay the effort it demands, retains its original excitement, and, with its evocations of displaced people moving across Europe and of global conflict spreading from the Middle East, remains resonant in the world of the early twenty-first century.

Barefoot in the Head marks the extreme of Aldiss's involvement with New Wave science fiction. As he had written back in 1966 to the New Wave anthologist Judith Merril, in a letter quoted in Greenland's *The Entropy Exhibition,* "It's great to be even a splash in a new wave. But even the newest wave gets cast upon the shore." Aldiss's key difference with New Wave writers was that he was in favor of structure while they seemed to reject it: "I'm for structure in fiction because I believe fiction must mirror and/or shape reality and because I believe that the external world has structure: a different sort of structure from fiction's, but fiction is only an analogy of the external world." His conclusion was emphatic: "I feel I am no part of the New Wave; I was here before 'em, and by God I mean to be here after they've gone (still writing bloody science fiction)!"

Aldiss certainly survived the New Wave and went on writing science fiction; but the novel that immediately followed *Barefoot in the Head, The Hand-Reared Boy* (1970)–which he had in fact begun during a break from writing *Barefoot in the Head*–was not science fiction but a first-person account of the sexual development of Horatio Stubbs, a boy growing up in Leicestershire in the 1930s. *The Hand-Reared Boy* can still be seen, however, as related to the 1960s that produced the New Wave because of its sexual frankness, especially in regard to masturbation, the one topic that, in the view of Stubbs and of Aldiss himself, remained taboo, despite the more public airing of sexual matters in the permissive society. Aldiss's determination to break the taboo drives the style of the novel. Compared to the verbal complexities of *Barefoot in the Head,* the prose of *The Hand-Reared Boy* is direct, vigorous, and racy–too direct for the taste of some readers, reviewers, and critics:

> I was introduced to the delights of masturbation early, and had never looked back since then. You might say I was a hand-reared boy. Perhaps I should have been ashamed of all that; I was not. People pretend to be so enlightened about sex nowadays; they talk happily about copulation and such subjects, about adultery and homosexuality and lesbianism and abortions. Never about masturbation, though. And yet masturbation is the commonest form of sex, and tossing off the cheapest and most harmless pleasure.

Despite its preoccupation with autoeroticism, however, *The Hand-Reared Boy* is, in a sense, a traditional moral tale, insofar as Horatio graduates, not to sexual probity, but to an awareness of the reality of the human beings around him; his relationship with an older woman, Virginia Traven, is crucial to his progress in this respect. Its frankness made it hard to get the book into print, however; eleven publishers turned it down, and the twelfth, Hutchinson, initially accepted it and then changed their mind. These difficulties, however, provided valuable prepublication publicity for the novel, and Weidenfeld and Nicolson made an offer to take it on. As preparations for its publication finally got under way, Aldiss became aware that another novel had appeared in the United States that also tackled masturbation with unprecedented frankness: Philip Roth's *Portnoy's Complaint* (1969). While this blunted the pioneering thrust of *The Hand-Reared Boy,* it did not harm its sales and might even have prepared the ground for its popularity. Review response was mixed: the *TLS* reviewer (22 January 1970) liked the "plain language" and felt that the sexual descriptions rang true and were written "too coolly to offer the sly stimulus of pornography." In *The Listener* (22 January 1970) Hood similarly found an anti-aphrodisiac quality in *The Hand-Reared Boy* but judged it a weakness rather than a strength. Hood felt that a potentially interesting topic had been wasted because Aldiss's style was like that of *My Secret Life* (1887) by "Walter"–a work of Victorian pornography that had recently become more widely available in England. "The human beings whose sexual adventures are described are less important than the mechanics of the process." By contrast, Mary Borg, in the *New Statesman* (23 January 1970), pointed out the extent to which the narrative was "elegant, witty and perceptive about a certain kind of middle-class life" and recognized the way in which, at the end of the novel, Stubbs has undergone a "translation" from rutting sexuality to a "consciousness of the complexity of others."

In 1970 Aldiss also produced a collection of fantasy and science-fiction stories, *The Moment of Eclipse.* Two of the stories demonstrate Aldiss's fondness for writing fiction that alludes to previous works of literature or visual art but incorporates them into distinctive new entities–as Hunt's painting *The Hireling Shepherd* was incorporated into *Report on Probability A.* The richly

Wendy, Brian, Charlotte, Margaret, and Timothy Aldiss in Bellagio, Italy, 1989 (Collection of Brian Aldiss)

layered title story, "The Moment of Eclipse," alludes to Hardy's poem "At a Lunar Eclipse" and charts the way in which the narrator's desire to make a movie that will produce the same effect as the poem intertwines with his attraction to a femme fatale who is like a living version of the naked Madonna painted by the Norwegian artist Edvard Munch. As Aldiss explains in his introduction to *A Romance of the Equator: Best Fantasy Stories of Brian W. Aldiss* (1989), "The Day We Embarked for Cythera . . ." alludes to *L'Embarcation pour Cythère* by the seventeenth-century French Rococo painter Antoine Watteau and contrasts an idyllic hillside venue for conversation and festival with a nightmare world of carnivorous cars. "The Day We Embarked for Cythera . . ." is the seed of the novel *The Malacia Tapestry* (1976). Other stories in *The Moment of Eclipse* include a bitingly satirical imaginary interview with Adolf Hitler, "Swastika!"; the highly comic "Working in the Spaceship Yards!"; and the poignant and intriguing "The Village Swindler," set in India and originally written in 1968 when heart transplants were a startling innovation, in which an untouchable offers to sell his heart to the daughter of an Englishman whose father has life-threatening cardiac defects. The collection includes another poignant story that has become better known as the source material for the movie *AI.* "Supertoys Last All Summer Long" is about a boy, David, who fears that he is unloved by his mother–a fear that is justified because, although he does not know it, he, like his teddy bear, is an android. The story is a powerful metaphor for the plight of the child who is afraid that his mother may not love him, as Aldiss himself was. *The Moment of Eclipse* won a British Science Fiction Association Award in 1972, although it is interesting to note that Aldiss later included the title story and several other stories from the collection in *A Romance of the Equator,* a collection of "best fantasy stories," as if suggesting that these stories might be better defined as fantasy than as science fiction.

Aldiss's concern with science and the future emerged in another book of 1970, *The Shape of Further Things: Speculations on Change.* This work of nonfiction is a mixture of both genres and topics. It combines conversation, a journal of daily life in the context of world events, literary history, and speculative essays and covers such topics as science fiction, H. G. Wells, art and the imagination, dreams, and computers. The reviewer for *TLS* (11 September 1970) was dismissive, judging most of it to be "on the level of a bright sixth-form essay." In *The Twinkling of an Eye* Aldiss acknowledges that, by the late 1990s, the speculations about dreams and computers are dated but contends that any new discovery or invention stimulates fresh, if possibly erroneous, thoughts that time will correct. He also points out that *The Shape of Further Things* provoked many letters from readers.

In *A Soldier Erect,* however, Aldiss continues to mine the vein opened up in *The Hand-Reared Boy.* In this sequel, Horatio Stubbs relates his adventures as a soldier in the Royal Mendip Borderers in India and Burma, providing vivid and forthright observations of both foreign parts and private parts that culminate in harrowing scenes of combat, raising the racy romp to a new level of seriousness. These scenes highlight the symbolic significance of sex for Aldiss; it represents life against death. As Horatio puts it at the end of the novel, in his characteristically blunt way: "Probably every man-jack in the Mendips had his hand on his knob that night, giving thanks for survival." A thoughtful review in *TLS* (5 February 1971) argued that *A Soldier Erect* was more memoir than novel but linked it with earlier fictions of soldiering, pointing out Stubbs's likeness to the protagonist of Jaroslav Hašek's *Osudy dobrého vojáka Svejka za svetové války* (1921–1923; translated as *The Good Soldier Schweik,* 1930) and the similarities, sexual frankness aside, between the attitudes of Aldiss's lower ranks and those of Rudyard Kipling's *Soldiers Three* (1888).

While Aldiss was making a new reputation as the author of the Horatio Stubbs novel, his standing as a science-fiction writer was maintained by the short-story collection *The Book of Brian Aldiss* (1972), republished in England as *Comic Inferno* (1973), a title that suggests the blend of humor and intimations of hell in the stories. "Comic Inferno" itself evokes a twenty-second-century world in which robots, from mere mechanical drudges to sophisticated humanoids called "romen," do the work; there is even a R.S.P.C.R., a Royal Society for the Prevention of Cruelty to Robots. One roman, however, writes a book in which he expresses the view that the time has come when the two races, men and romen, must unite–a view that the publisher January Birdlip takes up, though the story ends with the implication, echoing that of "Who Can Replace a Man?," that romen, like robots, will still be subordinate to human beings–the latter being represented, in this case, by publishers out to make a profit. Among other stories worthy of note, "As for Our Fatal Continuity . . ." is an amusing satirical account of the career of a fictional computer artist, while "Send Her Victorious" moves from a dramatic bomb attack on the royal residence of Windsor Castle into an intriguing alternative history with a cast of eminent Victorians, and ends by making reality seem a fragile and dubious construct.

While compiling *The Book of Brian Aldiss,* Aldiss was also completing his massive history of science fiction, *Billion Year Spree* (1973). It is a pioneering work, creating a genealogy for the genre that stretches back beyond the pulp magazines of the 1930s that Aldiss had devoured as a boy to a more established literary classic: Mary Shelley's *Frankenstein* (1818). *Billion Year Spree* has subsequently been revised and enlarged as *Trillion Year Spree* (1986), but it remains a fascinating book in its own right, constantly enlivened by Aldiss's own observations as a major practitioner and a perceptive critic who has read widely both in science fiction and in the traditional canon of English literature. If *Billion Year Spree* seeks to establish the literary lineage of science fiction as well as to acknowledge its sources in popular culture, Aldiss pays further homage to those sources in his compilation *Science Fiction Art* (1975), a large-format book that includes many fascinating reproductions of the covers and illustrations of magazines such as *Amazing Stories* and *Astounding Science Fiction.*

Given the importance that Aldiss attributed to *Frankenstein* in *Billion Year Spree,* and his liking for drawing on earlier literary and artistic works in his own writing, it is perhaps not surprising that he should soon afterward provide his own revision of Shelley's novel in *Frankenstein Unbound* (1973). Twenty-first-century nuclear space wars have damaged the infrastructure of space and a timeslip transports Joe Bodenland, a twenty-first-century Texan and former presidential adviser, to early-nineteenth-century Switzerland, where he meets Mary and Percy Bysshe Shelley, Lord Byron, and Victor Frankenstein and his creation. Bodenland eventually kills the monster with the swivel-gun he has brought from the future, but not before the monster has pointed out that what it represents–scientific and technological progress–cannot be killed (indeed, it is the source of the weapon that Bodenland is using): "though you seek to bury me, yet will you continuously resurrect me! Once I am unbound, I am unbounded." Initially dismissed as self-indulgent, *Frankenstein Unbound* is given more sustained critical attention in Steven Connor's *The English Novel in History, 1950–1995* (1996). While Connor complains about the "awkward lurches of plot," "wearisome passages of banal philosophising," and "spasms of melodrama and sentimentality" in the novel, he identifies a complex and interesting "alternation of respect and rivalry" in its relationship with Shelley's *Frankenstein.*

Whatever its flaws, *Frankenstein Unbound* is a more complex and serious work than *The Eighty-Minute Hour* (1974). Its subtitle, "A Space Opera," was seized on by the reviewer in *TLS* (5 April 1974), who likened it to a galactic production by D'Oyly Carte, producers of the Gilbert and Sullivan operettas. In his autobiography Aldiss has acknowledged it as one of his least successful novels and revealed that it was written spasmodically at a time when he felt, as he had before, that his writing had lost direction. The novel is fragmented by its shifts across Europe and the former Yugoslavia and by slips in time, or "time-turbulences." As always with Aldiss, it has moments of imaginative surprise and of humor, but it is rather a miscellany.

The Eighty-Minute Hour was followed, however, by one of Aldiss's richest and most coherent works: *The Malacia Tapestry.* Malacia is an imaginary city that has tried to put a stop to radical change and scientific and technological development and retains the splendor and squalor of a Renaissance city-state. It is vividly evoked by Perian de Chirolo, an unemployed, impoverished actor who moves between the conservatives and progressives in the city: on the one hand, he kills an ancestral monster and pursues Armida Hoytola, an aristocrat's daughter; on the other, he is asked to play a part in the first magic-lantern melodrama in the city, mounted by Otto Bengtsohn, a progressive who is illicitly developing a "zahnoscope"–a rudimentary form of moving-picture projector. As Eric Korn pointed out in his *TLS* review (23 July 1976), the novel abounds in visual images and in references to means of reproducing visual images, from the fresco to the zoetrope. Korn's enthusiasm for *The Malacia Tapestry* was not shared by Jill Neville in the *Sunday Times* (25 July 1976), who applauded its "delightful verbal inventiveness" but finally felt it was "all fake posturing" and "pure papier-mâché." *The Malacia Tapestry* has continued to win admirers, however, and the element of unreality of which Neville complains could be seen, in a postmodernist critical perspective, as a virtue: Aldiss is exploring here, as elsewhere in his fantasy and science fiction, the nature of reality and the modes and conditions of representation. It is also entertaining.

The novel that followed, *Brothers of the Head* (1977), proved difficult for readers to take at the time of its publication. Illustrated by Ian Pollock, it features two Siamese twins, Barry and Tom, who are joined at the head and possess a rudimentary third head. The novel offers a disturbingly plausible account of their transformation by pop-music promoters into a highly successful rock group, the Bang-Bang–the name alludes to the way in which Barry persecutes Tom and Tom tries to defend himself. Their involvement with a troubled groupie brings them a brief serenity, but then Barry dies. A heart pacemaker is put in to keep Tom alive, but the third head then starts to develop, and Tom can only destroy it by killing himself. The motif of the Siamese twins can be seen as providing a series of uncomfortable images of the divided self, but the exploitation in the novel of difference and disability for metaphorical purposes is questionable. *Last Orders and Other Stories* (1977) has aged better. Its title story, funny and poignant, focuses on three people drinking in a bar as the end of the world draws nigh, while other pieces provide haunting explorations of dreams and reveries, for example, "Year by Year the Evil Gains," which features a figure whom the reader infers to be Josef Stalin's daughter. Aldiss's eminence among science-fiction writers was confirmed in 1976 when the first and only James Blish Memorial Award was conferred upon him.

Aldiss's aversion to communism was taken up in *Enemies of the System: A Tale of Homo Uniformis* (1978). Written in response to a Soviet challenge that a novel showing the complete triumph of communism could never be published in the capitalist West, the work focuses on a group of tourists from a supposedly ideal communist society that combines elements of Aldous Huxley's *Brave New World* (1932) and George Orwell's *Nineteen Eighty-Four* (1949) who are stranded on a visit to Lysenka II, a supposedly primitive planet, and have to react to life in the raw, as represented, for instance, by mothers breast-feeding babies. The novel lacks the intensity of Huxley's and Orwell's dystopias, however, and received a lukewarm response from most critics.

The third Horatio Stubbs novel, *A Rude Awakening,* also produced mixed reactions from reviewers and the book-buying public, perhaps because, in contrast to the two previous novels of the trilogy, its Rabelaisian celebration of sexuality could not counterbalance its bleakness. The action of the novel takes place during Stubbs's last five days in Sumatra, as the British and Indian troops are withdrawing and Sukarno is about to defeat the Dutch colonists. Stubbs's account of his sexual adventures is shot through with pained observations of the human consequences of the fraught politics of the region: for example, one of his lovers, the Chinese girl Tun Su Chi, whom he knows as Margey, is exiled from Shantung province, which has been sacked by the Japanese and is now held by Mao Tse-tung. Displacement, fear, and despair of a kind that sometimes calls to mind Graham Greene mark *A Rude Awakening,* leading Paul Chipchase, a reviewer in the *Sunday Times* (9 April 1978), to suggest that it might be Aldiss's "picture of hell" in which, as the novel puts it, "Life is reduced to a series of packings and unpackings." In *TLS* (19 May 1978) Valentine Cunningham drew attention to what he felt to be a discrepancy between Stubbs's coarse sexual sensibility and his acute awareness of the traumas of postcolonial politics, an observation that is supported by Aldiss's own acknowledgment, in *The Twinkling of an Eye,* that, by the time he came to write the novel, he had "already lost interest in Horatio Stubbs" and felt that he was "too limited a mouthpiece for his fictions."

Aldiss's final short-story collection of the 1970s is *New Arrivals, Old Encounters* (1979). The title story once again takes up the familiar theme of the first contact between humans and aliens; this time the placid aliens are overwhelmed by their awareness of the vast and terrifying tangle of myths and legends that the travelers on the Earth ship bring with them in their psyches. In "Space for Reflection," a five-year-old boy, Gordan Ivan Jeffris, wins a competition for the greatest contribution to a new direction for mankind with an entry that reads: "The universe has a dark corner, the human soul, which is its reflection." His prize is to travel the galaxy and report back to a "superputer"; but the more he discovers, the more difficult he finds it to reach any conclusion other than the reflection with which he won the competition. In 1979 Aldiss also brought out a collection of articles and reviews, *This World and Nearer Ones: Essays Exploring the Familiar,* which is particularly notable for its retrospective reflections on *Barefoot in the Head* and for its ambivalent account of the paintings of G. F. Watts–a name that, in a slightly altered form, figures significantly in *Report on Probability A*.

Aldiss's desire to move, in his mainstream fiction, beyond the limited mouthpiece provided by Horatio Stubbs found its first major outlet in *Life in the West* (1980). In this novel he employs third-person narration, rather than the first person of the Stubbs trilogy, to introduce Thomas C. Squire, a remarkable combination of populist cultural critic, insecure aristocrat, and former secret-service agent. The novel cuts between Squire's experiences at an academic conference on "Intergraphic Criticism" that he is attending and the breakup of his marriage, his many affairs, his childhood experiences, and the deaths of his mother and father. Its geographical range is wide, taking in England, Sicily,

Singapore, and the former Yugoslavia, and it is also much concerned with politics, ideology, and religion. *Life in the West* is a rich and readable novel, but its overall consistency and coherence are open to question, as its first reviewers recognized; for instance, Jacky Gillott, in *The Times* (London) for 6 March 1980, felt that its "many parts" did not "forcefully coalesce to form a wider picture of disintegration," while Eric Korn, in *TLS* (7 March 1980), called it "an uneven novel full of conceits that come off and conceits that do not." The novelist Anthony Burgess, however, included it in his list of the ninety-nine best novels published since 1945.

Aldiss's next novel is *Moreau's Other Island* (1980), republished in the United States as *An Island Called Moreau* (1981). Like *Frankenstein Unbound, Moreau's Other Island* revises and updates a novel by an earlier writer–in this case, *The Island of Doctor Moreau* (1896), by Wells. Calvert Roberts, a U.S. undersecretary of state, arrives on the island as the only survivor of a space capsule that has been sabotaged in a war in 1996. He discovers that the inhabitants of the island are combinations of human and animal surgically engineered by Aldiss's successor to Wells's original Dr. Moreau, the thalidomide victim Mortimer Dart. Roberts's horror is compounded when he discovers that Dart's work is part of the American war effort, particularly with regard to his production of the "SRSR," the "Stand-by Replacement Sub-Race," gnome-like creatures who will be better able to function in the aftermath of an atomic catastrophe. Aldiss echoes Wells's original novel in many respects while developing it in new directions of his own. The philosopher Galen Strawson, in *TLS* (22 August 1980), judged *Moreau's Other Island* "a clear but disquieting success."

After the economy of *Moreau's Other Island,* Aldiss moved on to begin a vast science-fiction epic, the Helliconia Trilogy, in which he creates an elaborate and coherent imaginary world. Helliconia is a planet that moves from intense cold to intense heat in a cycle that lasts for 2,592 Earth years. The first volume, *Helliconia Spring* (1982), shows human beings coming out of caves as the ice of a millenary winter melts: in the prelude Yuli searches for his lost father, becomes a priest, and founds a city. In the rest of the novel a city and civilization develop through the classic stages of epic, pastoral, agriculture, technology, and commerce. In *Helliconia Summer* (1983) civilization develops, but the aboriginal race suffers enslavement, massacre, and diaspora. The third novel, *Helliconia Winter* (1985), is a bitter and powerful tale of conflict, suffering, and exile as the planet grows cold once more.

The story of Helliconia is not a mere impersonal treatise; it is focused through a range of characters for whom Aldiss himself feels affection and with whom readers can identify, such as the summer queen, MyrdemIngagala, and the young Luterin Shokerandt, who leaves his father, the Keeper of the Great Wheel, to seek action and advancement. There are other memorable figures, such as the King of Borlien in *Helliconia Summer,* well described by Nicholas Shakespeare, in his 8 December 1983 review of the novel in *The Times* (London), as "a moody mixture of Hamlet and Henry the Eighth."

Dust jacket for the U.S. edition of Aldiss's 1988 novel, in which an Oxford don learns of his dead brother's life through the deceased man's papers (Richland County Public Library)

The Helliconia Trilogy had also been punctuated by a short-story collection, *Seasons in Flight* (1984). One story in the collection, "The Girl Who Sang," is set on Helliconia, and most of the other stories have folktale elements, even when, like "The Gods in Flight" and "The Plain, the Endless Plain," they deal with nuclear war. "Incident in a Far Country," for example, is a pastiche folktale in which a prince frees his slaves but ends by becoming a slave himself. *Seasons in Flight* is not, however, one of Aldiss's stronger collections. The year after the final volume of the Helliconia Trilogy appeared, *Trillion Year Spree,* the revised and updated version of *Billion Year Spree,* was published. Its co-author was David Wingrove. Although other histories of science fiction had appeared by this time, *Trillion Year Spree* was recognized as a major contribution to the field. By this time Aldiss himself was attracting increasing critical attention. Greenland's *The Entropy Exhibition,* based on an Oxford Ph.D. thesis for which Aldiss had been the external examiner, included an important chapter on Aldiss's work in the context of New Wave science fiction.

With the achievement of the Helliconia Trilogy behind him, the question arose of what Aldiss would do next. A novella, *Ruins* (1987), adumbrates themes of wandering, remembering, regret, and redemption that are developed much more substantially in his next mainstream novel, *Forgotten Life.* This novel focuses on two brothers, Clement and Joseph Winter, whose lives have diverged widely but who, in a strange way, come together after Joseph's death when Clement inherits his older brother's papers. Clement is an Oxford don and practicing therapist married to Sheila, a best-selling author of fantasy novels; his life is ordered and comfortable, though marked by traces of sadness–his marriage has suffered the death of a child and his wife's recent infidelity. Joseph's life, relived through the documents he leaves behind him, was an unsettled one, moving from an apparently loveless childhood to service with the Forgotten Army in Burma to drifting in Sumatra. As with *A Rude Awakening,* reviewers, such as John Melmoth in *TLS* (30 September 1988), noted a sense of bleakness, provoking Aldiss himself to point out, in a letter to *TLS* (21 October 1988), the redemptive notes in the lives of both brothers that sound at the end of the novel. Melmoth also echoed the charge of incoherence that Gillot had made against *Life in the West,* calling *Forgotten Life* "deeply felt but insufficiently organized." In *The Times* (9 October 1988), however, Linda Taylor offered what is likely to be a more enduring verdict: despite some longueurs, *Forgotten Life* is "a cleverly worked, humane and philosophical fiction."

Aldiss concluded the 1980s with *A Romance of the Equator* and launched into the 1990s with a well-received memoir of his writing life, *Bury My Heart at W. H. Smith's* (1990). His first novel of the new decade was both a sequel to one of his own earlier novels, *Frankenstein Unbound,* and another revision and updating of a classic–this time, of Bram Stoker's *Dracula* (1897). In *Dracula Unbound* (1991), Joe Bodenland travels back to 1896, meets Stoker, and persuades him to try to destroy Dracula and his fellow vampires, who, if they survive, will mutate in the far future into a race that will enslave human beings. The novel has an ingenious plot that effectively employs time-travel paradoxes and popular versions of fractal and chaos theory. In his *Times* review (30 May 1991) Tom Hutchinson called *Dracula Unbound* "an astonishing transmutation," but Connor, in *The English Novel in History,* took a less favorable view; contrasting it with *Frankenstein Unbound,* he acknowledged the greater narrative skill of the later novel but found it less interesting than the earlier work, mainly because Aldiss does not attempt to revise the action of *Dracula* as he attempts to revise the action of *Frankenstein.*

Connor's judgment suggests a more general point about Aldiss's work: that his more technically accomplished writing is not necessarily his most interesting. This assessment has implications for his mainstream fiction as well as his science fiction and fantasy. His next mainstream novel, *Remembrance Day* (1993), in fact echoes some of the concerns with time in *Dracula Unbound,* raising the question of to what extent the past may determine the future. It asks whether four people killed in an Irish Republican Army bomb blast at a hotel in Great Yarmouth on 6 July 1991 were predestined to die because of their "histories of prior catastrophe, or else close psychic linkage with catastrophe." Though its focus is Norfolk, it moves widely across Europe and evokes a variety of characters whose lives have been radically altered by the events of the 1980s, such as Ray Tebutt, who has gone bankrupt; Dominic Mayor, who has made a fortune; and Peter Petrik, a dissident Czech moviemaker. Aldiss was disappointed by what he felt to be the limited review coverage given to *Remembrance Day* in England, but he commended reviewers in the United States who spotted the link between his latest novel and an American novel that he had once much admired–*The Bridge of San Luis Rey* (1927), by Thornton Wilder.

The tendency of Aldiss's mainstream novels to roam widely was continued in *Somewhere East of Life: Another European Fantasia.* Its protagonist, Roy Burnell, travels the world listing vulnerable and valued examples of architecture; he has also lost a decade of his own memories. His travels take him to the lands of the former Soviet Empire, especially to Turkmenistan and its capital, Ashkhabad, a remote and largely forgotten region that Aldiss imagined in his novel before visiting it in reality. *Somewhere East of Life* is an enormous and fascinating novel–open, like *Forgotten Life* and *Remembrance Day,* to charges of incoherence but exploratory in a way that seems appropriate to the complex and fast-changing world of the late twentieth and early twenty-first century.

In 1998 Aldiss brought out his substantial autobiography, *The Twinkling of an Eye,* which is both fascinating reading in its own right and a major source of insights into his fiction. That same year, his second

Aldiss and Kingsley Amis at the Groucho Club in London, 1990 (Collection of Brian Aldiss)

wife, Margaret, died; his moving memoir of her illness and death, *When the Feast Is Finished: Reflections on Terminal Illness,* appeared in 1999. As well as looking back on the past, Aldiss also looked, characteristically, to the future: *White Mars; or, The Mind Set Free: A 21st-Century Utopia* (1999), written in collaboration with the distinguished physicist Sir Roger Penrose, aims to imagine what a utopian community on Mars would be like.

Aldiss has also produced three other short-story collections: *A Tupolev Too Far* (1993), notable for "Better Morphosis," in which a cockroach awakes to find that it has been transformed into a "huge pale human thing"–Franz Kafka; *The Secret of This Book: 20-Odd Stories* (1995), which range from the comic spoof of Shakespearean scholarship, "If Hamlet's Uncle Had Been a Nicer Guy," to the evocative "Moon Enigmas"; and *Supertoys Last All Summer Long, and Other Stories of Future Time* (2001), brought out to coincide with the release of Spielberg's movie *AI.* To the title story Aldiss added two further stories about the protagonist, David, and the collection includes a range of other material. It is interesting to see how, in a story first published in 1995, "Dark Society," Aldiss finds an extended metaphor for the Internet in the kind of imagery that recalls the proliferating plant growths of early fiction such as *Non-Stop* and *Hothouse:*

> An undersized military computer operator in Aldershot tapped an unimportant juridical decision into the Internet, addressing it to a distant army outpost in a hostile country. Like the mycelia of fungus, progressing unseen underground in a mass of branching filaments as if imbued with consciousness, so the web of the Internet system spread unseen across the globe, utilising even insignificant Army ops in its blind quest for additional sustenance–and in so doing awakening ancient chthonian forces to a resentment of the new technology which, in its blind semi-autonomous drive for domination, threatened the forces' nutrient substrata deep in the planetary expanses of human awareness.

Such a passage demonstrates Aldiss's stylistic fluency, his capacity to move with the times, and the persistence of deep-rooted and developing thematic and symbolic concerns. He continues to demonstrate his ability to write in a variety of genres with his humorous novel *The Cretan Teat* (2002); *Jocasta* (2002), his rewriting of the Oedipus legend from the point of view of Oedipus's mother; and a novel that combines elements of his science fiction and his mainstream fiction, *Super-State: A Novel of a Future Europe* (2002).

Brian W. Aldiss's writing career is an extraordinary one, in its productivity, its range, and its inventiveness. His fiction searches past, future, and present, the vastness of space and the minutiae of the mind, the palaces of art and the gutters of reality. He is a strong supporter of the importance of structure and narrative, but he is also inclined to wandering, digression, and speculation in ways that often prove fruitful. His standing as a science-fiction writer who has maintained and developed the traditional virtues of the genre but also taken it into new and sometimes experimental areas is secure; his reputation as a mainstream novelist is more uncertain, but his mainstream fiction is richly interesting. The faults noted by reviewers, such as thin characterization, tedious passages, plot contrivances, and incoherence are certainly sometimes present; but they are perhaps inevitable in so prodigious a writer, and they are more than outweighed by his exploratory energy and by his many moments of assured achievement.

Interviews:

Darrell Schweitzer, "Brian W. Aldiss Interview," in his *SF Voices* (Baltimore: T-K Graphics, 1976);

David Britton and Charles Partington, "The Brian W. Aldiss Interview," in *The Savoy Book,* edited by Britton and Michael Butterworth (Manchester: Savoy, 1978);

Paul Walker, "Brian W. Aldiss: Interview," in his *Speaking of Science Fiction: The Paul Walker Interviews* (Oradell, N.J.: Luna, 1978);

Charles Platt, "Brian W. Aldiss," in his *Who Writes Science Fiction?* (Manchester: Savoy, 1980), pp. 297–309;

Rosemary Herbert, "A Chat with Brian Aldiss," *Publishers Weekly,* 236 (10 November 1989): 24;

Stan Nicholls, "Brian W. Aldiss Buries His Heart on Far Andromeda," in his *Wordsmiths of Wonder: Fifty Interviews with Writers of the Fantastic* (London: Orbit, 1993);

Charles N. Brown, "A Moderate Pursuit of Happiness," *Locus,* 35 (September 1995);

Francis Gilbert, "Life of Brian," *Times* (London), Metro section, 28 November 1998;

"Brian Aldiss: Young Turk to Grand Master," *Locus,* 45 (August 2000): 6–7, 63–64.

Bibliographies:

Margaret Manson, *Item Forty-Three: Brian W. Aldiss, a Bibliography, 1954–1962* (Wisbech: Fantast [Medway], 1963)–includes annotations by Brian W. Aldiss;

Margaret Aldiss, *Item Eighty-Three: Brian W. Aldiss, a Bibliography, 1954–1972* (Oxford: SF Horizons, 1972);

Margaret Aldiss, *The Work of Brian W. Aldiss: An Annotated Bibliography and Guide,* edited by Boden Clarke (San Bernardino, Cal.: Borgo Press, 1992).

References:

Michael R. Collings, *Brian Aldiss* (Mercer Island, Wash.: Starmont, 1986);

Steven Connor, *The English Novel in History, 1950–1995* (London & New York: Routledge, 1996), pp. 167–178;

Colin Greenland, *The Entropy Exhibition: Michael Moorcock and the British "New Wave" in Science Fiction* (London & Boston: Routledge & Kegan Paul, 1983), pp. 69–91;

Greenland, "The Times Themselves Talk Nonsense: Language in *Barefoot in the Head,*" *Foundation: The Review of Science Fiction* (September 1979): 32–41;

Brian Griffin and David Wingrove, *Apertures: A Study of the Writings of Brian W. Aldiss* (Westport, Conn.: Greenwood Press, 1984);

Tom Henighan, *Brian W. Aldiss,* Twayne's English Authors Series, no. 555 (New York: Twayne, 1999);

Fredric Jameson, "Generic Discontinuities in SF: Brian Aldiss' *Starship,*" *Science Fiction Studies,* 1 (Fall 1973): 57–68;

Richard Mathews, *Aldiss Unbound: The Science Fiction of Brian W. Aldiss* (San Bernardino, Cal.: Borgo Press, 1977).

Papers:

The Bodleian Library at Oxford University, the Kenneth Spenser Research Library at the University of Kansas (Lawrence, Kansas), and the Rare Books and Special Collections Library at the University of Sydney (Sydney, Australia) have collections of Brian W. Aldiss's papers. The Huntington Library in San Marino, California, has more than one hundred of his letters to his publishers, and the Brian Aldiss Collection at the Dallas Public Library includes letters and papers as well as a variety of other materials.

Paul Bailey

(16 February 1937 –   )

Lorena Russell
University of North Carolina at Chapel Hill

See also the Bailey entry in *DLB 14: British Novelists Since 1960.*

BOOKS: *At the Jerusalem* (London: Cape, 1967; New York: Atheneum, 1967);
Trespasses (London: Cape, 1970; New York: Harper & Row, 1970);
A Distant Likeness (London: Cape, 1973);
Peter Smart's Confessions (London: Cape, 1977);
Old Soldiers (London: Cape, 1980);
An English Madam: The Life and Work of Cynthia Payne (London: Cape, 1982);
Gabriel's Lament (London: Cape, 1986; New York: Viking, 1987);
An Immaculate Mistake: Scenes from Childhood and Beyond (London: Bloomsbury, 1990; revised, 1991; New York: Dutton, 1992);
Sugar Cane (London: Bloomsbury, 1993);
Kitty and Virgil (London: Fourth Estate, 1998; Woodstock, N.Y.: Overlook, 2000);
Three Queer Lives: An Alternative Biography of Fred Barnes, Naomi Jacob and Arthur Marshall (London: Hamish Hamilton, 2001);
Uncle Rudolph (London: Fourth Estate, 2002; New York: St. Martin's Press, 2003).

PLAY PRODUCTIONS: *A Worthy Guest,* Newcastle-upon-Tyne, 1973; London, 1974;
Alice, Newcastle-upon-Tyne, 1975;
Crime and Punishment, adapted from the novel by Fyodor Dostoevsky, Manchester, 1978.

PRODUCED SCRIPT: *We Think the World of You,* television, by Bailey and Trastam Powell, 1980.

OTHER: *The Oxford Book of London,* edited, with an introduction, by Bailey (Oxford & New York: Oxford University Press, 1995);
First Love, edited, with an introduction, by Bailey (London: Dent, 1997);

Paul Bailey (photograph © Jerry Bauer; from the dust jacket for the U.S. edition of Kitty and Virgil, *1998)*

The Stately Homo: A Celebration of the Life of Quentin Crisp, edited, with an introduction, by Bailey (London & New York: Bantam, 2000).

In his book *Three Queer Lives: An Alternative Biography of Fred Barnes, Naomi Jacob and Arthur Marshall* (2001), Paul Bailey details the stories of stage performer Barnes, novelist Jacob, and television personality Marshall, describing how they negotiated in their respectively hostile worlds of early- and mid-twentieth-century England. These "alternate biographies" represent a repeated drive in Bailey's work: to explore the nuances of lives at odds with their surroundings. Whether describing differences of class, nationality, or sexuality, his fiction brings out the details of those points of contact between individuals and society, mapping moments of discomfort and alienation as well as those surprising moments of balance and accommodation. While many of his characters succumb to a suicidal despair, his writing inevitably attends sympathetically to individual lives, creating memorable portraits of both the flamboyant and the everyday.

Paul Harry Bailey was born into a working-class family in Battersea, London, on 16 February 1937. His father, Arthur Oswald Bailey, worked as a street sweeper and died when Bailey was eleven years old. His mother, Helen Maud (née Burgess) Bailey, worked as a household servant and died in the mid 1980s. His brother, David Arthur, was born in 1929, and his sister, Joan, was born in 1931. Bailey's love of theater began early in an all-boys' grammar school, Sir Walter St. John's, and he earned a scholarship at the Central School of Speech and Drama in London. His career as an actor did not pan out, however, and he worked briefly as a store clerk in Harrods before beginning a career as a novelist. In the early 1970s Bailey was a fellow at the University of Newcastle-upon-Tyne and the University of Durham. In 1976 he traveled to North Dakota State University as a visiting professor, where he taught a course on homosexuality in literature and encountered some homophobic hostility while participating on a conference panel in Fargo titled "Forum on Homosexuality." Bailey recalls his apprehension while waiting alone in his hotel room, listening to hostile radio callers asking questions like "When did we last hang one of those freaks?" According to an interview with Amanda Smith for *Publishers Weekly* (26 June 1987), Bailey's companion of twenty-two years, David Joseph Healy, died in the mid 1980s, just days before he completed his 1986 novel, *Gabriel's Lament.*

Bailey's 1990 autobiography, *An Immaculate Mistake: Scenes from Childhood and Beyond,* offers a humorous account of his coming-of-age as an artist, intellectual, and gay man and his struggles to find his place in a family and world that rewards "the natural" and "the normal." Bailey's account remains thoroughly sympathetic and consistently funny, detailing his parents' often perplexed responses to the son they dubbed "The Professor" because of his seemingly eccentric literary, musical, and theatrical tastes. In one scene Bailey's barely literate father brings him home a gift of a tattered copy of Charles Dickens's *Nicholas Nickleby* (1838–1839) and stumbles over the opening lines as he reads the tale aloud to his son. As an adult Bailey recalls the moment and understands his father's hesitation when rereading Dickens: "it was the word 'sequestered' in the novel's opening sentence. . . . 'Sequestered' was totally foreign to him. He'd never had cause to say 'sequestered.' The sight of it on the page had upset him, briefly; had made him keenly aware of his ignorance. The cough and the gulp were his camouflage for that hated 'sequestered.'" Bailey's sympathy for his father's embarrassment typifies his broad understanding of personalities. It also puts his working-class background in direct relationship to his work as an artist and intellectual. In an interview with Smith, Bailey recalls Dickens's lasting influence on him as a writer, recounting that he reads three or four of Dickens's novels every year. Rather than posit his background in opposition to his present position, his biography shows that he is best understood as a product of such an environment.

Bailey's mother emerges, through an unforgettable portrait, as a woman prone to amusing witticisms and equally amusing, albeit banal, clichés, such as her enigmatic and often-repeated formula: "There's *apples* and then there's *apples.*" She would substitute matching terms, everything from *apples* to *boys* to *women,* using the phrase "to differentiate between the respectable and the dissolute, the worthy and the unworthy, the good and the bad." Bailey's sexuality raised two questions that have dominated his life: "Why can't you be more natural?," which was superseded by "When are you going to get married and settle down?" When his mother berates him for carrying a bouquet of flowers in the street, a move that offered proof of his "suspected pansiness," Bailey muses: "It wasn't natural for a boy to be seen bearing flowers; it wasn't natural for a grown man to cry. How many spirits have been broken under the accumulating weight of such absurdly simple truths?" In detailing resistance to such "simple truths," Bailey's autobiography and fiction offer alternate paths, ways of making peace with the ghosts of one's family and beyond. In another scene Bailey recalls waking to hear a male lover praying, begging forgiveness for the gay sex he had just enjoyed. His lover's shame oddly empowers Bailey, whose sympathy frames his lover's confession into an alternate dynamic: "the gift of his abjectness, which helped to release me from mine." Bailey's fiction repeats this dynamic, using a comedic and sympathetic eye to position readers in relationship to characters marked by despair and abjection.

Bailey began writing novels following a lackluster career as a playwright, and his first manuscript was readily accepted by publisher Jonathan Cape in 1967. *At the Jerusalem* won the Somerset Maugham Award and the Arts Council of Great Britain Award for best first novel. Bailey also won the Authors' Club Award in 1970 and the E. M. Forster Award in 1974. Two of his other novels, *Peter Smart's Confessions* (1977) and *Gabriel's*

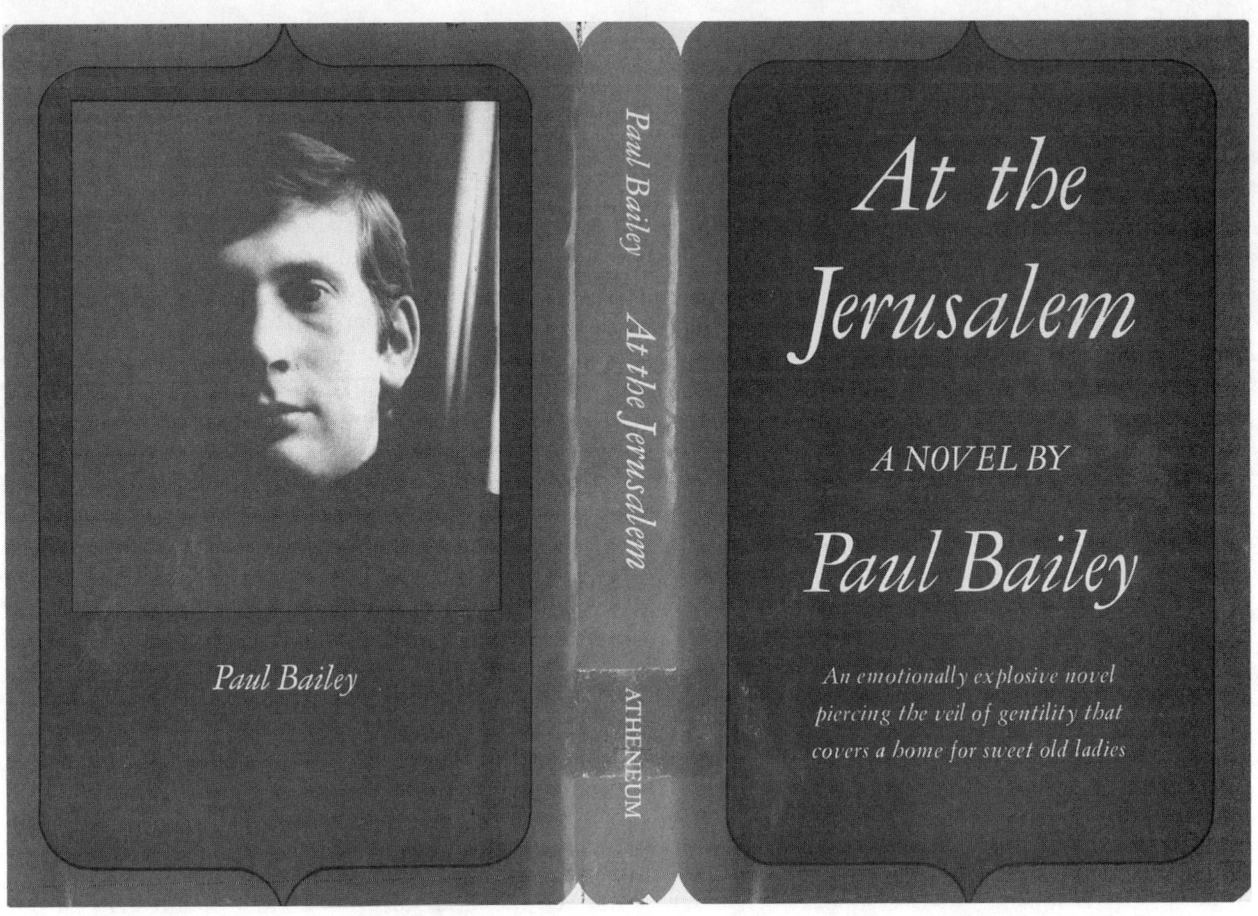

Dust jacket for the U.S. edition of Bailey's first novel, about an elderly woman's attempts to adapt to life in a retirement home (Richland County Public Library)

Lament, were short-listed for the Booker Prize. He has written one biography about a geriatric prostitution ring, *An English Madam: The Life and Work of Cynthia Payne* (1982), and edited a collection of essays on the British expatriate Quentin Crisp, published in 2000. Besides editing a novel for Virago Press and *The Oxford Book of London* (1995), Bailey is a frequent reviewer for *TLS: The Times Literary Supplement* and *The Listener.*

Bailey's first novel, *At the Jerusalem,* tells the story of an alienated and depressed woman, Mrs. Faith Gadny, whose stepson has placed her in a retirement home. The novel traces her struggle to adapt to her new surroundings at "The Jerusalem" while coming to grips with a life recalled as a series of losses. Gadney's inability to join the social group at the Jerusalem follows from her melancholic relationship to her past and the painful deaths of her husband and her daughter. The novel ends with her leaving the nursing home for a mental hospital. The story is sad, but Bailey manages in the end to offer a sympathetic portrait of one woman's misanthropic failures, placing her depressive and seemingly antisocial behaviors in the context of her history of personal loss.

His second novel, *Trespasses* (1970), offers another sympathetic account of a failed life. Ralph Hicks's fragmented and confessional story represents an effort to move toward health following the devastating loss of his wife to suicide. Hicks has lived his life badly, showing little compassion or love to those closest to him. In addition to his wife's suicide, his injured mother practically disowned him. When he accesses his blocked emotions, they manifest in a flood of uncontrollable tears, and he is summarily institutionalized. The novel represents his attempt to write his way toward health through a series of brief vignettes, each associated with a term that links specific characters and events. The story pieces together these fragments, a childhood spent spurning his mother, mourning his father, suffering an unhappy and noncommittal career as a teacher, and an unfulfilling, loveless marriage to a woman he holds in contempt.

As with his first novel, Bailey places the character's failings within a social context, here relating Hicks's coldness to his father's indifference and his struggles with gender socialization. As a young child Hicks is stuck in a tree, and his ensuing rescue marks him as inadequate, a weakness tolerable in a woman, but something that for Hicks points to his failure to "be a man." Bailey subtly links this moment of gender dysfunction to Hicks's more general alienation, as though his failure to succeed in masculinity scars his ability to connect meaningfully with others. In his autobiography Bailey tells of a similar moment in his own childhood, when his cousins taunted him for getting stuck in a tree, and he was shamed for crying: "Crying was what little girls did, because it was in their nature." Despite Hicks's failures as a son and as a husband, Bailey's novel demands that readers relate his shortcomings to the social context out of which he emerged and understand his failures as arising from societal pressures.

While *Trespasses* was critically acclaimed, his third novel, *A Distant Likeness* (1973), was less enthusiastically reviewed, a shortcoming attributed by the reviewer for *TLS* (29 June 1973) to a style of "tiny, cryptic paragraphs collected in short batches separated by blank pages." Once again, the protagonist is in the process of reckoning with an estranged and failed life, this time writing from prison. Police inspector Frank White, who once realized brief fame for arresting a mass murderer, has been undone by his latest arrest, of James Belsey. White, who has recently been left by his own wife, has arrested Belsey for murdering his wife and son but cannot get the man to talk. Much of the story recounts White's conversations with Belsey's daughter and father, as he struggles to put together a portrait of the recalcitrant prisoner. In the end White concludes to the prisoner: "Compared to them, you're a model of sanity." When he slips Belsey a knife in hopes that he will commit suicide, Belsey instead uses it to kill a guard, and White is summarily arrested as his accomplice. The title references the likeness between the two, White's processes of ambivalent identification with and repulsion from the murderer, and the recognition of his own capacity for violence. In *Contemporary Authors* Peter Lewis points to another reading of the title, quoting Simone Weil's notebooks–"Privation is a distant likeness of death"–and further compares the novel to T. S. Eliot's *The Waste Land* (1922) and Dostoevsky's *Crime and Punishment* (1866), calling the novel "a distillation of a super-refined Dostoevskian essence."

Confession is a key element of Bailey's next novel, which he referred to in the interview with Smith as "a comic novel about a man trying to commit suicide." The narrator of *Peter Smart's Confessions* begins his memoir following an unsuccessful suicide attempt. Like so many of Bailey's novels, this dark story of alienation manages to maintain a verbal lightness, tracing the life of an alcoholic with an abusive mother and resentful, chronically lying wife. As an actor Smart has had an erratic career. Despite one well-reviewed play, he is mostly ignored. He has a failed marriage, and his life is marked by a series of suicide attempts. As a young boy he stands patiently waiting at the edge of a slate roof where one of his classmates had been injured but is rescued and brought in out of the rain by his father. His mother recalls that he attempted suicide as a toddler, letting go of her hand and lying in the middle of the road. The mother considers the act a moment of willful spite and punishes young Peter when she gets him home. In another scene he plans to jump from a bridge but is taken home instead by a fellow suicidal woman, whom he ends up marrying out of pity. Susan proves a totally inadequate mother, and Smart responds to her indifference and rage by abandoning her and his son. The bungled suicide that starts the story fails because Smart had taken his dog's tranquilizers by mistake. Such incidents make the story seem generally unlikely. The novel ends with an afterword offered by one of Smart's friends, who relays that Smart ultimately died of cancer, after abandoning acting and becoming a social worker. The novel gains much of its charm from its cast of colorful and unexpected characters, but despite its strengths, *Peter Smart's Confessions* fails to achieve the unified effect of other Bailey novels.

Bailey's next novel, *Old Soldiers* (1980), tells of a chance meeting between two veterans of World War I in St. Paul's Cathedral. Victor Harker is recently widowed and has returned to London after many years following the death of his wife, Stella. At the cathedral he runs into Captain Harold Standish, a Colonel Blimp type, who invites him to an impromptu lunch. As they talk, it occurs to Harker that Standish is soundly eccentric. Standish actually assumes a trio of personalities, of which "Captain Hal" is but one. At times he passes for an indigent named Tommy, who is a favorite at a local Salvation Army. Another change of clothes and false teeth produces the poet Julian Borrow, who lives in an attic papered with rejection letters and holds forth in Hyde Park. The novel follows the adventures of the three personalities and Harker's pilgrimage through the lost East End of his youth. Harker finds the landscape much changed by the Blitz and is haunted by memories of his family and of war, most frequently the disturbing vision of his friend George, whose face and head were blown apart in the trenches only steps from Harker. When Harker invites Standish out for a payback lunch, the weakened and enfeebled Captain Hal barely makes it through the meal, and he collapses following a respite of "frenzy" with a prostitute. Standish is hospitalized, and Harker, whose name and number were in the captain's pocket, arrives at his bedside. There he hears Standish's story, after discovering that they shared a history in France during the war. Standish reveals his real name (Private Eric Talbot) and confesses to having deserted the army in France. Revitalized by a transfusion, he escapes from the hospital and makes a run for the river, where he commits suicide. Meanwhile, Harker dies on his return trip to Newcastle. The novel rehearses one of Bailey's central themes: the respite of a chance friendship balanced against the losses of social alienation and despair. The story also offers a London landscape in transition. Both Harker and Standish resent the growing diversity of a postimperial Britain: "Now the wheel of Empire had been spun arsy-versy: the turban seemed to be as common a sight here as the cloth cap he himself had worn as a youth. . . . Not many years before, he thought, that Indian might have salaamed before me. . . . All that pandering palaver belonged to history now." It seems only fitting that the two "old soldiers" would die in the end: history haunted them painfully, their families were gone, and the transformative miracle of Private Talbot's masquerade was beyond sustaining.

Gabriel's Lament is a coming-of-age story that showcases Bailey's talent for character study. Gabriel Harvey's mother deserts him at an early age, leaving him in the care of his father, Oswald Harvey. Once again, Bailey manages to craft a memorable, oddly sympathetic monster. Oswald Harvey has a gift for language; he is so good with words that his meanness is somehow mitigated by his cleverness. He is violent, bigoted, and cruel, a teller of tales, and a compulsive liar, but his portrait is so powerful, at least from the viewpoint of his sensitive son, that he dominates the novel as he does his son's life. He spins out a fantastic history, raising his son on private myths, like his story of the "Isle of Dogs," where all of the canines from Britain's early years are kept, fed daily by a ship that throws offal over its sides. Like so many of Bailey's novels, the story of *Gabriel's Lament* presents a careful study of class difference. Inheritances arrive from unexpected sources, and the Harvey family moves from abject poverty to wealth. At first Gabriel's mother supports the family by working an unknown job, spoken of only as "my secret place." Then his father comes into money and moves the family to a house described as a veritable mansion, dubbed "Blenheim."

Gabriel is an outsider. As "the only Gabriel" in his school he is always a bit alienated from his peers, and he is further set apart by virtue of his poetic nature and intelligence. His mother is his salvation in his early years, but she disappears when he is a young boy, and he is raised by his abusive father, who drinks heavily and berates his son, calling him "Piss-a-bed" on account of his incontinence. Gabriel finds some relief at the house of his aunt, a Swedenborgian who is alienated from her brother but nevertheless asks Gabriel to remain respectful to his father. Gabriel keeps this death-

Dust jacket for the U.S. edition of Bailey's 1986 novel, about a boy and his abusive father (Richland County Public Library)

bed promise and, despite leaving home at seventeen, remains dutiful by making appearances at holidays and bearing his father's drunken abuse.

While Gabriel leaves home to eke out an independent existence in a boardinghouse, his father becomes obsessed with keeping up class appearances at "Blenheim," however ridiculous and embarrassing his efforts. Gabriel moves into an apartment building, where he keeps company with a countess from Russia and a man from India, two characters who provide some relief from the dominating figure of Oswald Harvey. Gabriel remains hopelessly devoted to his absent "mummy," and in a nod to Bailey's first novel, lands a job working at a retirement home, "The Jerusalem." He befriends a defrocked solicitor and writes a book on itinerant preachers, characters not unlike his father, who captures his son at every opportunity to berate him with what he calls his "Blenheim Lectures." One of the main themes of these lectures is his father's frustration at his son's lack of what he considers a proper male sexuality. He encourages his son to

Dust jacket for the U.S. edition of Bailey's 1998 novel, about a love affair between a British woman and a Romanian poet (Richland County Public Library)

engage in what he calls "Rogering," demanding that he "sow his wild oats." Gabriel has little interest in such manly (or other) pleasures, however, and instead is evicted from his apartment when he is found wearing one of his mother's dresses. As Bailey told Smith in *Publishers Weekly,* Gabriel's lack of libido is a central part of his character, fitting with "the kind of numb state he was in" because of his mother's abandonment and father's abuse.

Whatever charm Oswald Harvey's language affords is offset by his fierce nationalism and racism and his smug sense of British superiority. Like *Old Soldiers, Gabriel's Lament* paints a portrait of a Great Britain in transition, and the novel is rich with descriptive scenes of London neighborhoods. The father rants against the rising populations of South Asians and blacks. When he hears that a family named "Campbell" is moving next door to his beloved Blenheim, he imagines a Scottish family ("the only decent Celts") and is outraged to find the family is black. His racism and class sensibility link with his nostalgia for Victorian Britain and the Age of Empire, and he is characterized by Lewis as "one of Bailey's most brilliant creations and a comic character of Dickensian stature." Interestingly, *Gabriel's Lament,* despite its detailing of suffering and abuse, does not conclude with the suicidal despair that marks other Bailey protagonists. Instead, while in Minnesota at the age of forty, Gabriel discovers the family secret of his mother's disappearance: her suicide. For Jill Johnston, writing in *The New York Times Book Review* (18 October 1987), Gabriel's survival was somewhat unbelievable given the extent of his oppression. Overall, however, the novel was well received, much applauded for its Dickensian breadth and characterizations.

Sugar Cane (1993) opens with the memorable lines: "I work with human genitals. For twenty years, I have examined numerous penises and vaginas. I am a venerologist, and I practice at St Lucy's, in London." The woman who speaks these lines, Esther Potacki, guides readers through a story that manages to link with other Bailey novels, most notably *Gabriel's Lament.* Gabriel returns as Esther's lover (she "brings him out" sexually as he learns to symbolically shed his mother by doffing women's dresses), and together they are privy to a kind of confession. A friend of one of Esther's deceased patients has befriended her. Stephen, known to his dead friend, Antonio, as "Sugar Cane," follows the doctor and charms her with a series of gifts. His attention and their unlikely friendship are part of the injured doctor's return to health. As Judy Cooke described in a *New Statesman & Society* review (28 May 1993), Esther is "pulled back into life by his extraordinary vividness, slyness, occasional trust, frequent evasions." Eventually, Stephen's evasiveness gives way to a recorded narrative, which tells how his life as a prostitute had been preceded by his membership in a sex circle led by a pedophiliac priest known as "the Bishop." Along with other boys, Stephen partook in a variety of sex acts, all part of the (since exposed) Bishop's ritualistic pleasure chapel and confessional.

In her review of *Sugar Cane* Cooke noted that the book is as much about a "transitory, crucial friendship" as it is about sex acts. Bailey's seventh novel, *Kitty and Virgil* (1998), builds on this idea of a passing, yet intense, relationship, combining the idea with Bailey's familiar exploration of suicidal despair. *Kitty and Virgil* tells the story of two lovers, a British woman who indexes biographies and an exiled Romanian poet. They have an affair, taking a good deal of comfort in each other's presence, but in the end it seems their relationship is not enough to sustain Virgil against his past. The story interweaves the lives of Kitty and Virgil, contrasting social history and family backgrounds, finding paths of sympathy between the privileged life of a Londoner and that of a Romanian who has spent years of his life suffering under Nicolae Ceauşescu's oppressive regime. As is typical in Bailey novels, the story is peopled with memorable characters. Kitty's father, Felix, an aging model with a history of wives, has settled for life with a witty butler, Derek, a campy and cutting type. Kitty's twin sister, Daisy, is cruel, petty, and self-centered and struggles to recover from her divorce.

Virgil remains a character marked by distance and frugality. He moves frequently to avoid attachment to people and places. He has few possessions and happily works as a street cleaner. He is repeatedly described as frail and skinny and avoids meat and fowl in his diet. Yet, he and Kitty come to a natural intimacy quickly, forging a life of domesticity over grilled fish. Virgil is portrayed as congenial yet troubled, marked by his poet's wisdom and his sympathetic insight. He demonstrates a capacity for seeing things optimistically, even smiling upon the unbearable Daisy. He is subject to illness, having suffered from tuberculosis as a child and a bad case of flu as an adult. These two episodes are parallel, as his mother's stories interplay with his landlady's and narrative becomes part of the convalescent process. Yet, Virgil's frailty contrasts with his strength. He escaped from Romania by swimming across the Danube and walking across Yugoslavia.

The novel explores the limits of language and of narrative: what remains unspeakable, and the stories that need to be told. It is about overcoming differences through love but also overcoming differences through stories. Virgil tells and retells stories and tales from his youth, folktales that he has learned from his mother. As a student he is drawn to the part of his namesake's *Aeneid* that alludes to unspoken warriors. The novel repeats this emphasis on stories that need to be told, as well as what must not be spoken. Virgil never speaks his father's name, or that of Ceauşescu. His father is a horrific character, one who burdens his son with the story of how he enthusiastically participated in the rounding up and murder of Jews during World War II. For Kitty, Virgil's tales are powerful: "He is giving me the stories that brightened his childhood." The darker stories of Virgil's past are told through a series of letters and poems that he leaves Kitty to read following his suicide in a Paris apartment. In the end Kitty takes up with one of Virgil's compatriot friends. Daisy has recovered from losing her husband to a younger woman, but the one who does not recover is Virgil, for whom suicide seemed the only proper atonement for his father's sins.

Bailey's characters are often distinguished by their relationship with language. The use of language brings his characters (such as the memorable father from *Gabriel's Lament* or the portrait of his mother from his autobiography) to life. Another recurring type of character is the camp queen, the often wickedly eloquent gay man whose verbal wit delights. Characters such as Bernard from *Trespasses* exemplify this type, who has a real-life model in Quentin Crisp, the subject of *The Stately Homo: A Celebration of the Life of Quentin Crisp* (2000), which Bailey edited.

Dramatic phrasing is one of the ways that Paul Bailey manages a high level of energy in his portraits, and his ability with dialogue means that his characters are crafted through economical details. Bailey's fiction repeatedly offers up the revealing phrase that can tell much about a person. It is in part through his verbal inventiveness that Bailey crafts points of sympathy. As he comments in a 1991 interview in *Contemporary Novelists:* "I'm both delighted and appalled by the mysteriousness of my fellow creatures. I enjoy 'being' other people when I write, and the novels I admire most respect the uniqueness of other human beings. I like to think I show my characters respect and that I don't sit in judgment on them. This is what, in my small way, I'm striving for–to capture, in a shaped and controlled form, something of the mystery of life." Bailey's respect for others, his ability to place even the most horrific of characters within the frame of social context, remains perhaps his greatest gift. He invites readers to sympathize with social outcasts, to delay blame and consider the social pressures that make people who they are. His fiction and nonfiction alike celebrate the queer and the camp, the comic ability to persevere through the abjection of social estrangement and alienation.

Interview:

Amanda Smith, "Paul Bailey," *Publishers Weekly,* 231 (26 June 1987): 55–57.

John Banville

(8 December 1945 –   )

Graeme Harper
University of Wales, Bangor

See also the Banville entry in *DLB 14: British Novelists Since 1960.*

BOOKS: *Long Lankin* (London: Secker & Warburg, 1970; revised edition, Dublin: Gallery, 1984);
Nightspawn (London: Secker & Warburg, 1971; New York: Norton, 1971);
Birchwood (London: Secker & Warburg, 1973; New York: Norton, 1973);
Doctor Copernicus (London: Secker & Warburg, 1976; New York: Norton, 1976);
Kepler (London: Secker & Warburg, 1981; Boston: Godine, 1983);
The Newton Letter: An Interlude (London: Secker & Warburg, 1982; Boston: Godine, 1987);
Mefisto (London: Secker & Warburg, 1986; Boston: Godine, 1989);
The Book of Evidence (London: Secker & Warburg, 1989; New York: Scribners, 1989);
Ghosts (London: Secker & Warburg, 1993; New York: Knopf, 1993);
The Broken Jug: After Heinrich von Kleist (Loughcrew, Oldcastle, Ireland: Gallery, 1994);
Athena (London: Secker & Warburg, 1995; New York: Knopf, 1995);
The Ark, illustrated by Conor Fallon (Loughcrew, Oldcastle, Ireland: Gallery Press for The Ark, 1996);
The Untouchable (London: Picador, 1997; New York: Knopf, 1997);
God's Gift: A Version of Amphitryon by Heinrich von Kleist (Loughcrew, Oldcastle, Ireland: Gallery, 2000);
Eclipse (London: Bridgewater, 2000; New York: Knopf, 2001);
Shroud (London: Picador, 2002).

PRODUCED SCRIPTS: *Reflections,* television, adapted from Banville's novel *The Newton Letter,* Channel 4, April 1984;
Seachange, television, RTÉ Dublin, 1994;
The Last September, motion picture, adapted from the novel by Elizabeth Bowen, Trimark, 1999.

John Banville (photograph by Jerry Bauer; from the dust jacket for the U.S. edition of The Untouchable, *1997)*

OTHER: "Introduction: George Steiner's Fiction," in *The Deeps of the Sea and Other Fiction,* by George Steiner (London: Faber & Faber, 1996), pp. vii–xi.

SELECTED PERIODICAL PUBLICATIONS–UNCOLLECTED:

FICTION

"The Party," *Kilkenny Magazine* (Spring–Summer 1966): 75–82;

"Mr Mallin's Request," *Transatlantic Review,* 37–38 (1970–1971): 29–34;

"Nativity," *Transatlantic Review,* 37–38 (1970–1971): 35–39;

"Rondo," *Transatlantic Review,* 60 (1977): 180–183.

NONFICTION

"Vladimir Nabokov," *Hibernia,* 5 August 1977, p. 23;

"Masterly Manic," *Sunday Tribune,* 20 September 1983, p. 5;

"A Calm Gaze into the Abyss," *Irish Times,* 20 April 1987, p. 12;

"A Perfectionist in Art and a Legend in Life," *Irish Times,* 14 August 1993, p. 2;

"The Last Days of Nietzsche," review of *Nietzsche in Turin: An Intimate Biography* by Lesley Chamberlain, *New York Review of Books,* 45 (13 August 1998): 22–26;

"Nietzsche's Complaint," *New York Review of Books,* 45 (5 November 1998);

"The Decade the World Didn't End–or Did It?" *Irish Times,* 8 November 1999;

"Pushed from the Centre of Creation," *Irish Times,* 31 December 1999.

It would be unfair to label John Banville a "writer's writer," because it would suggest he is not a writer easily accessible to the majority of readers. Yet, there is no doubt that Banville's work has attracted much critical opinion emphasizing the author's writerly credentials: his keenness of style, his interest in storytelling, and his commitment to novelistic technique. Such critical assessments often refer to his aesthetics, authority, and clarity as much as to his thematic interests in identity and the unstable nature of truth and knowledge. He is regarded, in that respect, as a highly conscious literary artist, valued for his serious investigation of form. He is also an entertaining writer, and he is an Irish writer.

Banville was born in Wexford and educated locally at the Christian Brothers primary school and St. Peter's College, the main diocesan secondary school. He currently lives in Dublin with his wife, Janet Dunham, whom he married in 1969, and his two sons, Colm and Douglas. Although a relatively private man, Banville has occupied some public roles, as literary editor of *The Irish Times* (Dublin) from 1988 to 1999 and as a member of the Irish Arts Council from 1984 to 1988. He has worked in journalism since 1969. When asked in a 17 September 2000 interview in *The Observer* (London) if he always wanted to be a novelist, he replied, "Well I wanted to be an artist of some kind." Indeed, Banville began to write around the age of eleven or twelve and simultaneously tried his hand at painting. His work often reflects his ongoing interest in art, as well as his interest in science; the stealing of paintings in *The Book of Evidence* (1989) and in *Athena* (1995), for example; or even, in *Eclipse* (2000), in the figure of haunted stage actor of international repute Alexander Cleave. Banville has received various awards for his writing–fewer, however, than the general critical enthusiasm for his work might suggest. *Doctor Copernicus* (1976) was awarded the James Tait Memorial Prize, *Kepler* (1981) *The Guardian* Fiction Prize, and *The Book of Evidence* the Guinness Peat Aviation Award and a short-listing for the Booker Prize.

That this author of around a dozen or so excellent works of fiction has not gleaned more of the glitz and financial celebration of the literary prize circuit is perhaps understandable. Despite his obvious interest in literary style, Banville is not a literary "pyrotechnician" or a writer tied closely to short-term literary trends or triumphs of the singularly contemporary. Having a deep interest in aspects of history and historiography and in the function of fiction as a tool for the investigation of those aspects, his work often investigates the nature of the imagination itself. This commitment to such an investigation often alludes to emotions of delusion or regret. In this respect Banville's work provokes a readerly self-consciousness that can be both enjoyable and unsettling, reminding some readers perhaps a little too well of the power of fiction to shift preconceptions.

Long Lankin (1970), Banville's first book, is a sequence of nine short stories and a novella, "The Possessed." The structural similarity of this book to James Joyce's *Dubliners* (1914) has been widely noted. The title of the book comes from an old Scots-English ballad, "Long Lankin" or "Lamkin." This ballad relates the story of a murder involving a mason's revenge on his former master. The stories are held together as a sequence largely by the recurrent involvement of an interloper in disturbing or unsettling a pattern of life or the run of a relationship, a recurrence that is linked to the plot of the "Long Lankin" ballad. The stories range from investigations of childhood memories, such as in "The Visit" or "Summer Voices," and of love and its rituals, as in "Lovers," to dark encounters with suffering or sacrifice, as in "Nightwind" and ultimately in "The Possessed."

In "The Possessed" the central character, Ben White, frees himself from the influence of his sister Flora, though there is more here than a cry for freedom, and the notion of atonement for sins past hangs heavy. Banville, in fact, questions that nature of freedom itself, not least through showing the results of Ben's journey to be in some senses not an end to angst but a beginning. Indeed, "The Possessed" appears to be a rekindling of the angst, and some of the characters who appear earlier in the short stories, such as Jacob and Norman Collins in "Persona," Julie and Helen in "Sanctuary," and Morris and Liza in "Nightwind," resurface here. Ben White himself appeared previously in "Island."

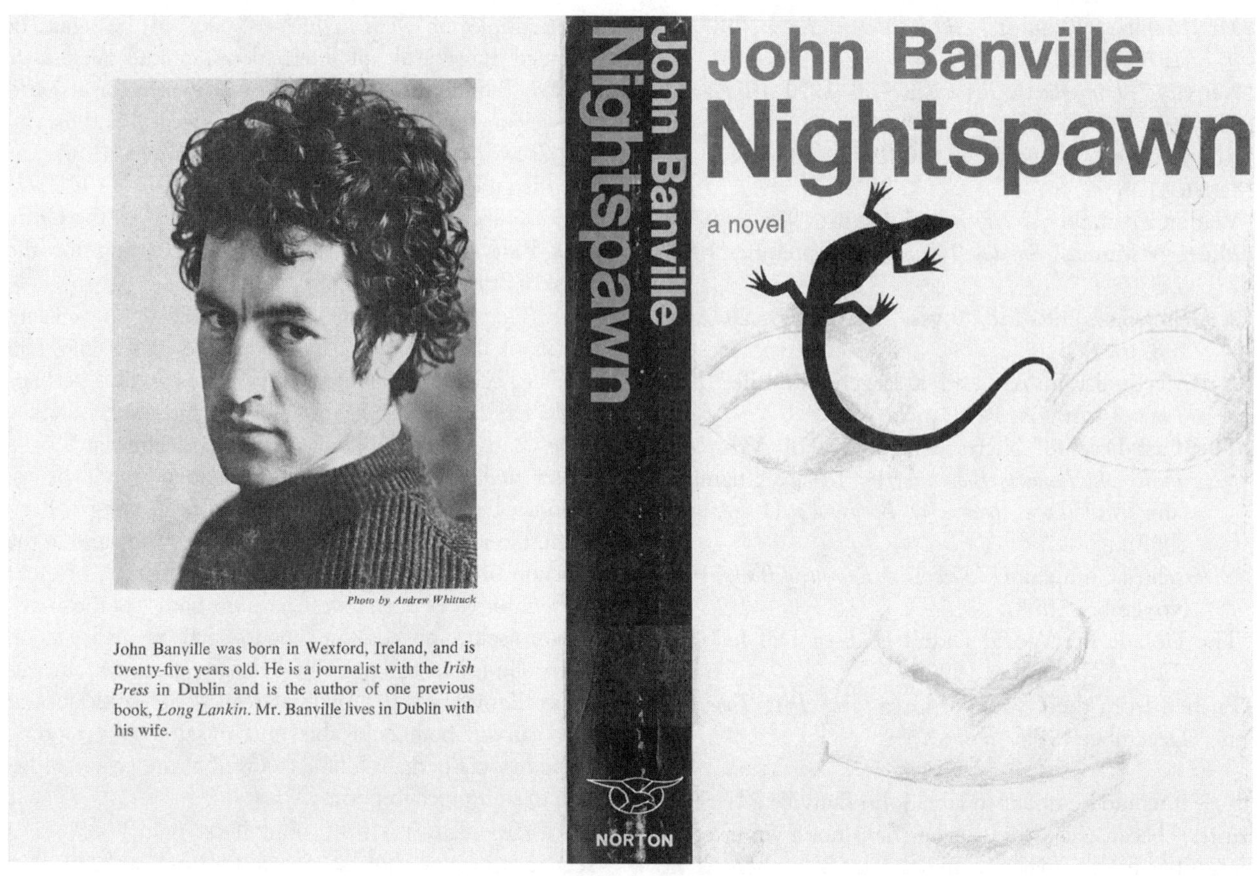

Dust jacket for the U.S. edition of Banville's first novel, in which a young writer encounters strange people and political intrigue in Greece (Richland County Public Library)

Interestingly, in a reprint of *Long Lankin* fourteen years after its original publication, Banville did not reprint "The Possessed," and the removal of the novella from the collection perhaps gives the book a better symmetry. However, whatever can be said about *Long Lankin,* it is important to stress that the work is that of a young writer. Some of the stories date back to when Banville was seventeen years old. Problems critics have found with the book range from Banville's overdependence on the overt use of symbolism and imagery to an awkwardness in the author's attempts to introduce an Irish complexion to thematic concerns that seem better considered universal. Notable Banville scholar Rüdiger Imhof, writing in the *Dictionary of Irish Literature* (1997), suggests certain flaws might be "as a result of Banville's thinking he was being more sophisticated than when he was not." Nevertheless, critical response in *The New Statesman* (30 January 1970) noted that the book was "a ray of hope for the future of fiction"; the reviewer in *TLS: The Times Literary Supplement* (5 September 1970) commented that while *Long Lankin* does entail some "uncharacteristic self-indulgence," the book is "more often truthful and perceptive; and for a writer in his early twenties, is an impressive first appearance."

Nightspawn, Banville's second book, was published soon afterward, in 1971. *Nightspawn* is ostensibly a psychological thriller, but it is also a metafiction in which a "writer" investigates the conventions of fiction. The story of *Nightspawn* is set in modern Greece and revolves around political espionage. It is told by Ben White, the central character of "The Possessed." Ben, a tormented writer, becomes embroiled with a series of surreal characters, not so far removed from the characters readers experienced in the nighttime journeys of "The Possessed." In fact, despite the shift in setting to Greece, *Nightspawn* displays many of the intellectual and artistic preoccupations found in *Long Lankin*–as it does, according to majority critical response, many of the faults of the earlier work.

In a 1981 interview with Imhof, Banville revealed that in *Nightspawn* he wished to "challenge the reader to go on suspending his disbelief in my fiction in the face of an emphatic admission on my part that what I was presenting was fiction and nothing more–and everything more." This playfulness in the realm of the ontological is as much an expression of a young writer's desire to find his way as it is a provocation to the reader to deconstruct the novel itself. If the novel fails, it fails only because the author has yet to find a method of melding his deep concern with the aesthetics of fiction with his knowledge that there is a demand from readers for established and, perhaps, overly worn narrative conventions. He therefore combines a nod toward the historical origins of that demand with a sometimes labored dance around it. For example, Banville seeks out a mythology not only in the Greek setting of the novel but also in the relationship of one character to the next: their representatives within a grid of symbolic mythology. Yet, that grid is often undermined by self-mockery, and the seriousness of myth is deflated, paradoxically, by the author's own seriousness about the flaws in the conventions of fiction. Despite these faults, *Nightspawn* has mostly been considered an accurate foregrounding of Banville's ongoing concerns, and it cannot dismissed for that reason.

A *Saturday Review* writer accurately described *Nightspawn* as a book "full of tricks, a literary sleight of hand, which often seemed to be little more than ends in themselves. Still, for readers who enjoy firework displays, here is a dandy exhibition." The *New Statesman* reviewer praised the author's "scintillating" style but went on to say that the language of the novel was something more to be listened to than read. Banville has not shied away from problems identified with this novel and has made plain, in his interview with Imhof, that he believes the novel has "terrible faults." He also notes, however, that he is "very fond of that book, because I think it is, in a way, the most honest thing I have done."

This statement begs the question regarding in what sense *Nightspawn* is Banville's most honest work. Banville, as literary artist, so naturally situates himself between a use of style and a preoccupation with form that critics have often allowed their own critical traditions to circumvent the writer's aesthetic responses. This fallacious approach is especially apparent in discussions of *Birchwood* (1973), a book that won the Allied Irish Banks Prize and a Macaulay Fellowship from the Irish Arts Council.

The narrator of *Birchwood,* Gabriel Godkin, is attempting to write the story of his childhood. In this novel readers find decay, incest, dementia, and rejection, a baroque brew in which the reinvention and reworking of the past is as much the purpose of the narrator as its revelation. "I am always surprised," writes the narrator, "at the difference between the way things are and the way, before I find them, I expect them to be." This "discovery" is actually intuitive leaping, a creative evaluation, a blurring of the boundaries between revealed and concealed narrative to produce a circular version of truth: seeking out the truth produces in the end the revelation that one is a person who is seeking out the truth. A key element in this process is Gabriel's belief that his cousin Michael is, in fact, his own twin brother, incestuously conceived. This belief is part of Gabriel's pursuit of the much wider question of personal and social meaning. Yet, his story is not a bildungsroman in the traditional sense and certainly no realist social commentary. The narrator is not setting forth in order to reach a point of maturity. Rather, the journey, not the destination, is the crucial fuel for the engine of the narrative. A sense of geographical or physical encapsulation is achieved by locating much of the novel in a crumbling Irish "Big House," a family home.

In part 1 of *Birchwood,* "The Book of the Dead," Gabriel describes the dissolution of the Godkin family. In part 2, "Air and Angels," he joins Prosperos Magic Circus, a newer but even more baroque family than the one the reader has so far encountered. Finally, in part 3, Gabriel returns home to Birchwood and, in the process, confronts the specific instance of Michael's parentage and the wider instance of his own background. This section, titled "Mercury" in a reflection of its relationship to the idea of the messenger moving between gods and mortals, human and divine, ultimately leads the narrator not to the form or truth he was seeking but to the conclusion that all that survives in the end is "imitations" and "fragments."

Writing on *Birchwood,* Martin Amis suggested in *The New Statesman* that "Mr Banville has plenty of talent and style but will get nowhere with this kind of hero, the opinionated sensualist forever spellbound by the difference between himself and everyone else." In Gabriel's writerly search for meaning, however, Banville no doubt presented the first mature evidence of those themes touched upon in *Long Lankin* and in *Nightspawn.* Words here are seen to create a kind of reality, but even when describing painful events they cannot ultimately unearth truth or meaning, only a simulacrum. Significance, then, is illusory; but there is a resonance of wonder at the spectacle of public and personal history that cannot be "transfixed" by the writer, either by Gabriel or, indeed, by Banville himself.

Copernicus of Banville's *Doctor Copernicus* is also a writer, fascinated by words. "Tree. That was its name. And also: the linden. They were nice words." Language and truth are again key themes in the novel. *Doctor Copernicus* is much more overtly an historical novel than anything Banville had written previous to it, albeit with Banville's now well-established proviso that historical truth might not be ascertainable; in fact, it could be a type of parodic reconstruction. Fictional forms, Banville seems to suggest here, are likewise open to such parodic unsettling.

Banville's story of Copernicus's life is broken into four parts: the opening part dealing with his childhood; the second concerning Copernicus's difficult relationship with his brother, Andreas; the third told by his student Rheticus and telling of how Copernicus came to "reveal the secret music of the universe"; and the fourth recounting Copernicus's decline. As in *Birchwood* life is portrayed as characterized by relative chaos and squa-

Dust jacket for Banville's 1981 novel, which fictionalizes Johannes Kepler's years as imperial mathematician of the Holy Roman Empire (Bruccoli Clark Layman Archives)

lor, borne not insignificantly along with the gradual discovery that no language can really match the strength of the central character's scientific vision. Similarly, Copernicus and Andreas, as with Gabriel and Michael in *Birchwood,* carry symbolic weight. Copernicus is the intellectual seeker of something beyond and unearthly, and Andreas is the skeptical, earthbound materialist. If the Copernican revolution can be seen as a further separation between divine and human worlds, then it also contributed to the void formed between them. Thus, in *Doctor Copernicus* Banville gives readers a central character who is aware of the nothingness around which things revolve. He is the artist and writer as much as the astronomer, whose psychology reflects the ultimate emptiness of the "supreme fiction," to borrow Wallace Stevens's term, with which he is dealing. *Doctor Copernicus, Kepler,* and *The Newton Letter: An Interlude* (1982), says George Steiner, writing about *The Untouchable* (1997) in the 4 May 1997 edition of *The Observer* (London), locate Banville as a writer of Irish rather than English fiction, "examples of a genre relatively rare, and indeed suspect, in recent English fiction . . . fables of intellect."

Banville prefaces *Doctor Copernicus* by noting two books on which he has mainly drawn: Thomas Kuhn's *The Copernican Revolution* (1957) and Arthur Koestler's *The Sleepwalkers: A History of Man's Changing Vision of the Universe* (1959). He follows Koestler's account closely, as he does in other works of the tetralogy, which also includes *Kepler, The Newton Letter: An Interlude,* and *Mefisto* (1986) and in which the nature of informed modernity is critiqued. Readers are, that is, no longer innocent of the distance between what humanity would purport to know about the universe and how far from understanding life, and the reason for it, that knowledge still leaves us.

Kepler certainly picks up from where *Doctor Copernicus* leaves off; however, the protagonists of these books are very different personalities. Speaking relatively, Copernicus's genius is suggested, Johannes Kepler's is more declarative; Copernicus is solitary, Kepler gregarious; Copernicus hardly compassionate, Kepler sometimes painfully so. Kepler's greatest discovery, his "secret of creation," is that distances between the five planets known at his time correspond to the ratios of the five Platonic solids. The structure of the novel reflects this "astronomical" reasoning and the subject's prolific career.

Kepler is divided into five parts representing Kepler's main publications: *Mysterium Cosmographicum, Astronomia Nova, Dioptrice, Harmonice Mundi,* and *Somnium.* The number of chapters in each part corresponds to the number of faces of the Platonic solids. The symmetry of the book, however, its harmony, is paradoxical in that Kepler's discovery was quite false. Banville's point about the often fictional nature of fact and the paradoxical nature of fate is in this way made graphic. The concentration of the novel is on Kepler's successful years: from his period of studying with the imperial mathematician Tycho Brahe to his appointment to the same position under Holy Roman Emperor Rudolph II and, finally, to an overview of his writings, in which his last work is decisively a fantasy about a boy and his mother traveling to the moon. Kepler is both scientist and artist, dreamer and pragmatist. Unlike Banville's story of Copernicus, which seems to fall toward despair at the recognition of the void between the desire for knowledge and the limited nature of it, his story of Kepler is one substantially of celebration, supported by the ironic sympathy of the principal narrator of the book. Both Copernicus and Kepler question in the end whether their lives have been a success; both wonder at the limitations of their enterprise and the enigmatic nature of discovery. *Kepler,* however, suggests this questioning is part of the reason for being.

The Newton Letter, the third book in the tetralogy, is a novella. Personalized, subjective, harking back to *Birchwood* in its form, *The Newton Letter* comprises a letter of farewell to "Clio," the muse of history, by an historian who has abandoned plans for a book on Sir Isaac Newton. Newton stands as the material embodiment of absolutism. The book is "an interlude" in that it is situated between the two historical novels of the tetralogy and the contemporary novel, *Mefisto.* It owes something to Johann Wolfgang von Goethe's *Die Wahlverwandtschaften* (1809; translated as "Elective Affinities," 1854) in the choice of character names (for example, Edward, Ottilie, Charlotte) and in its dealings with the nature of and conflicts between the natural and the social order.

The narrator of *The Newton Letter,* after seven years of writing a biography of Newton, no longer believes in his interpretation. This interpretative angst holds a mirror to Newton's own breakdown. The idea of a mechanistic universe ultimately crumbles under questions concerning the impossibility of totalizing narratives. As in *Kepler,* symmetry is shown to be questionable, and as in *Doctor Copernicus,* knowledge is no guarantee of enlightenment. Though the narrator had only to "gather up a few loose ends, and write the conclusion" in order to finish the Newton biography, the conclusive, rationalist nature of those final acts prevents them being possible. The journey is one thing, an innocent and worthy enterprise; to complete it is made impossible by the limitations of language and the uncertain nature of the world.

The final volume in the tetralogy, *Mefisto,* is in the form of an autobiography of a mathematical child prodigy, Gabriel Swan. The name gives away that the novel is a return to the Ireland of the parodic *Birchwood,* not least in the echo of the theme of the twin. "I don't know," writes the narrator, "when it was that I first heard of the existence, if that's the word, of my dead brother. From the start I knew I was the survivor of some small catastrophe, the shockwaves were still reverberating faintly inside me." The book also has links to the preoccupations of Banville's other scientist-artists, with the narrator seeking out a way of showing reality, a representation that works. Both "blessed" and "damned" with the gift of measurement, Swan finally realizes he can only exorcize the demons of his endeavor by writing about it, even though that will not provide him the tools to tie up conclusions and to make sense of things. In the end he decides "In future, I will leave things, I will try to leave things, to chance." Uncertainty rules. Peter Parker, writing in *The Reader's Companion to Twentieth Century Writers* (1995), has noted that Banville attributes the bleakness to the deaths of his parents in the late 1970s and early 1980s.

Awarded the Guinness Peat Aviation Award and short-listed for the Booker Prize, Banville's next novel, *The Book of Evidence,* is the tale of a brutal murder and the theft of a painting, and the first in a triptych that includes *Ghosts* (1993) and *Athena.* Freddie Montgomery, obsessed with a small Dutch masterpiece in the home of a wealthy family friend, is surprised in the act of stealing it by a chambermaid. He takes the chambermaid hostage and gets away in his car, but when she panics, he batters her to death with a hammer. The story, told by Freddie as "evidence" while in custody, is not meant to be a defense; rather, it is a way of coming to terms with the idea of self. Like Banville's other protagonists, Freddie is looking to restore himself. This restoration has a double edge in that Freddie's imaginative thrust is itself painterly, both unreal in its devising of roles and sometimes overcome with the aesthetic qualities of things. Freddie, who once "took up science in order to make the uncertainty more bearable," is now engaged in considering perception, guided, in both a material and an aesthetic sense, by art.

Banville is not suggesting in *The Book of Evidence* simply that the protagonist here has been undone both by science and by art. However, the book does recount a crime that is said, however mockingly, to be brought about by a "failure of the imagination." In fact, Freddie's trust in the imagination goes so far that when his fanciful

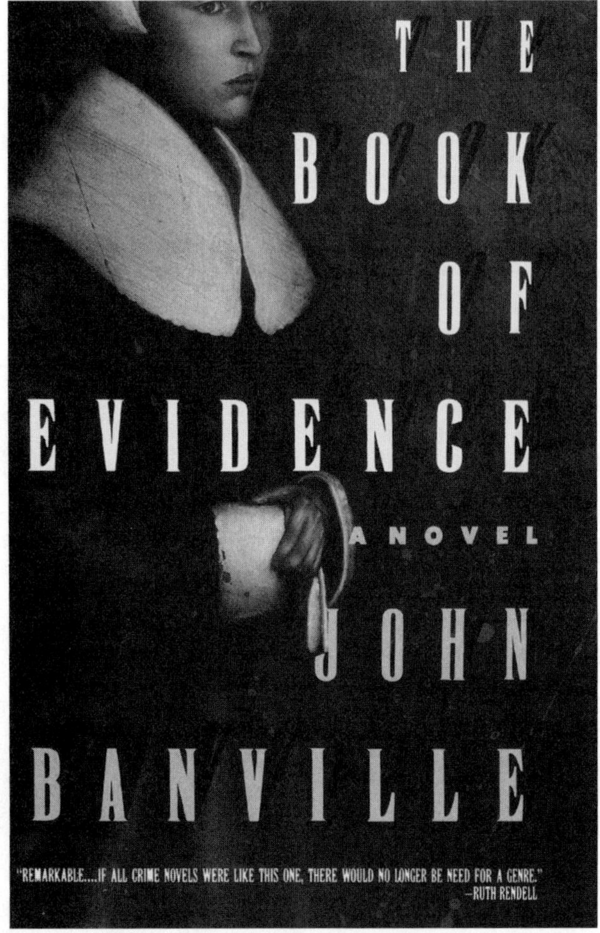

Dust jacket for the U.S. edition of Banville's 1989 novel, in which the narrator attempts to justify his theft of a painting and his murder of a woman (Richland County Public Library)

interpretations are proven inaccurate he is genuinely surprised. His past is, even for him, a "fiction" and, in a nod to Humbert Humbert of Vladimir Nabokov's *Lolita* (1955) he can make amends only through the telling of his story, through making art of his crime and restoring his victim within it.

The Book of Evidence is a convincing evocation of Banville's belief in the power of the imagination to provide consolation for the lack of meaning and symmetry in the world. That this evocation should be made through the voice of a murderer, once a scientist and now an art lover–indeed, a "performer" in both fields–is as much the evidence of Banville's view on the nature of knowledge here as is the plot itself.

Banville's eighth novel, *Ghosts,* begins with the words "Here they are again. There are seven of them. Or better say, half a dozen or so, that gives more leeway." *Ghosts* is apparently narrated by Freddie Montgomery of *The Book of Evidence.* As narrator he is unnamed, but there are clues to his identity. Having served his time in prison, he now moves to a barely populated island to live with the enigmatic Professor Silas Kreutznaer, an authority on the fictitious artist Jean Vaublin, whose work is similar to that of eighteenth-century painter Jean Antoine Watteau, and the laconic Licht. A party of castaways then arrives. The book is divided into four parts, starting in media res with the arrival of the castaways and returning to Freddie's own arrival in the second section. The short third section describes Vaublin's painting *Le monde d'or;* while the fourth, a coda, returns to the present and the imminent departure of the castaways.

There are intertextual games at play in the novel; most obviously, Banville's reference to *Le monde d'or* initiates a link to the visual art of Watteau but also–in his aesthetic positioning, the themes of art and nature, fakes, concealment and escape–to Jean-Jacques Rousseau, Friedrich Nietzsche, Oscar Wilde, William Butler Yeats, and Denis Diderot. The book is filled with references to artists and thinkers, composers, painters–the "ghosts" in the art and knowledge on display in the novel. Ludwig Wittgenstein is mentioned as "poor Ludwig on the snow mountain"; Wilde is referred to in a passage describing "ragged figures" with their "fingernails destroyed, like poor Oscar's, from picking oakum." The narrator alludes to Charles Dickens's *Great Expectations* (1861): "I skulked about for a while in the clayey dampness of the vegetable garden, feeling like poor Magwitch on the run." These references and other similar ones are not meant to alienate the less widely read, nor are they merely a form of intellectual conceit; their purpose is to invoke the richness and range of human thought while acknowledging the disorder of life and the difficulty of finding authentic fact of greater worth than engaging fiction.

In *Athena* Banville has Freddie Montgomery change his name to Morrow "by deed poll," thus narrating both as himself and as a manufactured, or masked, persona. He changes his name this way, at least in part, for "its faintly hopeful hint of futurity, and, of course, the Wellsian echo." As in *The Book of Evidence,* the plot of *Athena* is formed in the Dublin underworld. Montgomery, now Morrow and back in Ireland, gets involved with the shady Morden after agreeing to authenticate eight paintings, the theft of which has been masterminded by the Da, a fancy-dressing character based on Martin "The General" Cahill. Cahill was involved in what was at the time the second largest art robbery in history, taking place in Ireland in 1986. Art and authenticity resurface in *Athena;* so, specifically, does the relationship between writing and the actuality of the world. Morrow writes his account of the affair at the request of a woman, A, with whom he has had a relationship.

Because *Athena* is aimed at A, Morrow's specific, singular audience, the narrator offers metafictional references, is happy to fill his prose with rhetorical questions often linked to the nature of story or self, and comments on the characters and events around him as if they are not merely of his own invention, but also of a larger-than-life kind. "A grotesque among grotesque things," he calls himself. In what is familiar territory to readers of Banville's other works, Morrow is not only creating art but is also called upon to authenticate it. He does so; however, all but one of the paintings he authenticates are copies. Not only that, he eventually realizes that he has been part of a grand game played out between criminals and the police, and the whole artifice of both the events and the writing of his story therefore crumbles away.

In writing to A, Morrow also explores the dimensions of the relationship with her. This relationship borders on the sadomasochistic, their sexual fantasies acted out in the same room in which the paintings are stored. Violent, and engaged in some kind of voyeuristic performance far greater even than Morrow's own, A turns out to be part of the wider game–as does, interestingly, his Aunt Corky, whose death allows him to discover that her origins (said to be Dutch, but not) are a fiction. Her self-invention is reason enough for Morrow's admiration.

Morrow has been both right and wrong. The only genuine painting among the "stolen" collection is the *Birth of Athena* by Jean Vaublin; his aunt is not who he thought she was; and his relationship with A is enmeshed in the questions of authenticity associated with the stolen paintings. There are, in the world of Banville's fiction, no absolutes, either of truth or of artifice, and the making of art melds with the making of the world.

This notion of deception is also explored in *The Untouchable* (1997). George Steiner, writing his review of *The Untouchable* noted that, on the east side of the Atlantic, Banville is "the most intelligent and stylish novelist at work in English today . . . a fastidious master, finely out of tune with the vulgarities of the moment," and that his work "does not require the hype of literary agents and their spurious auctions." *The Untouchable* is based on the life and times of Anthony Blunt, spy and art historian (of the works of Nicolas Poussin, notably for *The Untouchable*), a topic also well covered by Steiner in his article "Reflections: The Cleric of Treason" in *The New Yorker* (8 December 1980).

The novel is driven by political espionage and sexual intrigue. The history here is largely the history of the Cambridge spies (the group that included Blunt, Guy Burgess, Donald Maclean, Kim Philby, and John Cairncross); Banville fictionalizes Blunt as Victor Maskell, though the facts of Blunt's life are not all closely followed. Maskell, for example, is married with children, and Blunt's homosexuality is presented far more as the product of illicitness. Likewise, Banville makes Blunt an Irishman masked as English rather than English proper. This

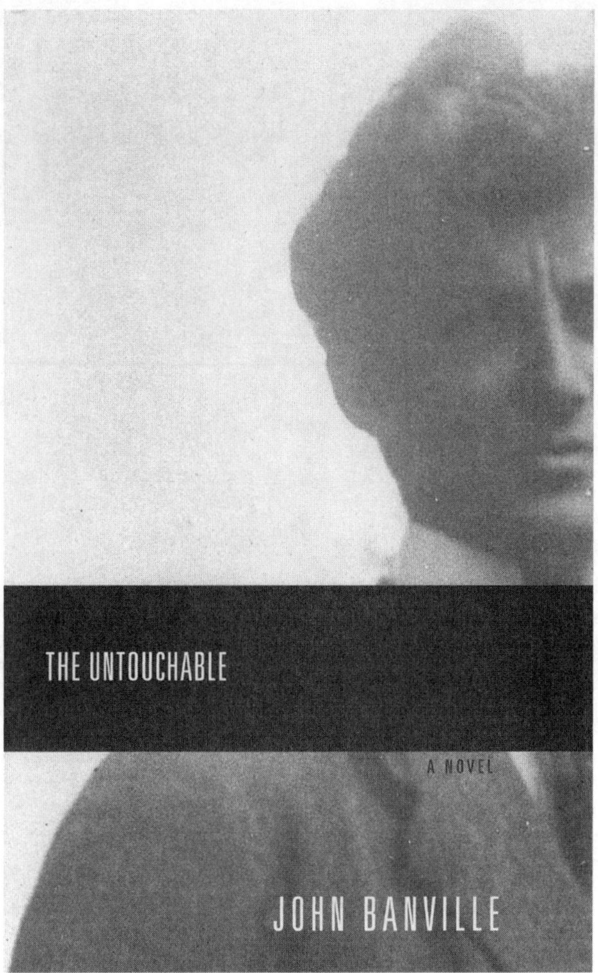

Dust jacket for the U.S. edition of Banville's 1997 novel, a fictionalized account of the life of British traitor Anthony Blunt (Richland County Public Library)

moving of character into the sphere of "Irishness" recalls Banville's much earlier efforts, as far back as *Long Lankin,* to encourage universal themes to reveal their Irish complexions. The change of status means that Maskell can also be used to explore Banville's ongoing interest in the nature of life as a performance. Intriguingly, however, in the 2000 interview in *The Observer* (London) Banville described how he read "the English novelists" when growing up and that *The Untouchable* is a "big acknowledgement to people like Waugh and P. G. Wodehouse."

Central to Maskell's vision of himself, told now as he sets out to write his version of the past, is the painting *Death of Seneca* by Poussin. Though the painting is fictional, its invention refers to Poussin's reading of the work of the ancient Stoic philosophers, which Blunt notes in his own two-volume work about Poussin. Thus, fact and fiction entwine, and the factual story, which is well supplied with intrigue, deception, and treason, does not prevent Banville from further intermingling fact and

Dust jacket for the U.S. edition of Banville's 2000 novel, in which a famous actor retreats to his mother's home to recover from a nervous breakdown (Richland County Public Library)

fiction to explore his own interests in authenticity, performed not necessarily as a linear act of living but as the decidedly writerly act of creating a living character.

Maskell has been acting as a means to an end and now has reached the point at which that acting is exposed. Alexander Cleave, the narrator of *Eclipse,* is an actor who has withdrawn to his mother's old house, having suffered a breakdown during the opening-night performance of a play. Both characters, therefore, are in the throes of self-examination; both have been prevented from these self-examinations previously by the strength and necessity of their fictional existence.

Cleave is successful, but his reputation is now in tatters. His mother's home is meant to be a retreat; however, housing the phantoms of his first loves, of his parents, of his marriage, and of the start of his career, it is hardly that. In fact, the life that he has retreated to find is singularly taken away by that retreat, becoming a ghost itself. Cleave is unsure who he really is. Banville is not suggesting that a man who has lived his life fictionalizing, or performing fictional life, finds it hard to differentiate real life from fiction. Rather, he suggests that all humanity lives in this state in a world that is a melding of elements of both.

Christopher Tayler, writing in *TLS* (29 September 2000), noted that *Eclipse* is "less plot driven than *The Untouchable* or *The Book of Evidence,* but less rarefied than *Ghosts.*" Certainly, when Cleave declares "What do they see in me? What is there in me to be seen? Maybe it is only the surface that they see," there is a strong sense in which this questioning is directed not only at Cleave's audiences but at the reader's perceptions also. Readers are reminded that they are Cleave's audience too, beyond the audiences of his acting. *Eclipse,* after all, is a novel about consciousness, the reader's as much as the protagonist's, an investigation of the ideas of self and of self-creation and a meditation on the role of this consciousness in bridging the gap between past and future.

John Banville's fiction, in short, is that of a skilled stylist with serious interests. It is not fiction without play or fun, however, fiction that ignores entertaining the reader. If there are criticisms leveled at Banville, they most often refer to the primacy of style over narrative substance. Such criticisms are in the minority, however, and Banville's work is most often celebrated for its use of language and its atmospheric use of voice. He has also written some scripts and a considerable amount of literary journalism.

Interviews:

Rüdiger Imhof, "My Readers, That Small Band, Deserve a Rest," *Irish University Review,* 11 (Spring 1981): 5–12;

Ciaran Carty, "Out of Chaos Comes Order," *Sunday Tribune* (Dublin), 14 September 1986, p. 18;

Imhof, "Q. and A. with John Banville," *Irish Literary Supplement* (Spring 1987): 13;

Fintan O'Toole, "Stepping into the Limelight–and the Chaos," *Irish Times,* Weekend section, 21 October 1989, p. 5;

Joe Jackson, "Hitler, Stalin, Bob Dylan, Roddy Doyle . . . and Me," *Hot Press,* 18 (1994): 14–16;

Hedwig Schall, "An Interview with John Banville," *European English Messenger,* 6 (1997): 13–19;

Jane Brown, "John Banville: The Books Interview," *Observer* (London), 17 September 2000, p. 15.

References:

Ingo Berensmeyer, *John Banville: Fictions of Order: Authority, Authorship, Authenticity* (Heidelberg: Universitätsverlad C. Winter Heidelberg, 2000);

Rüdiger Imhof, *John Banville: A Critical Introduction* (Dublin: Wolfhound, 1997);

Joseph McMinn, *The Supreme Fictions of John Banville* (Manchester: Manchester University Press, 1999).

Pat Barker

(8 May 1943 -)

Merritt Moseley
University of North Carolina at Asheville

BOOKS: *Union Street* (London: Virago, 1982; New York: Putnam, 1983);

Blow Your House Down (London: Virago, 1984; New York: Putnam, 1984);

The Century's Daughter (London: Virago, 1986; New York: Putnam, 1986); republished as *Liza's England* (London: Virago, 1996; New York: Picador USA, 2001);

The Man Who Wasn't There (London: Virago, 1988; New York: Ballantine, 1990);

Regeneration (London & New York: Viking, 1991; New York: Dutton, 1991);

The Eye in the Door (London & New York: Viking, 1993; New York: Dutton, 1994);

The Ghost Road (London: Viking, 1995; New York: Dutton, 1995);

Another World (London: Viking, 1998; New York: Farrar, Straus & Giroux, 1999);

Border Crossing (London: Viking, 2001; New York: Farrar, Straus & Giroux, 2001).

Editions: *The Regeneration Trilogy* (London: Viking, 1996; New York: Penguin, 1998)–includes *Regeneration, The Eye in the Door,* and *The Ghost Road;*

Union Street & Blow Your House Down (New York: Picador USA/Farrar, Straus & Giroux, 1999).

Pat Barker is a nearly pure novelist: she writes no short stories, no poetry, but, beginning with her first novel, *Union Street* (1982), immediately declared herself as a major novelist. In the following year she appeared on Granta's list of the "Twenty Best British Novelists," alongside more widely recognized names such as those of Martin Amis, Salman Rushdie, and Julian Barnes. Slightly older than they, she was always aiming to be a writer but found her voice only when, after some false starts, she found her subject matter, which, at least at first, was the lives of working-class people, particularly women, living in northeastern England. Later she staked out another territory: World War I, about which she has written three powerful novels known as the Regeneration Trilogy. The third of these, *The Ghost Road,* won the Booker Prize for fiction in 1995.

Pat Barker (photograph by Paddy Cook; from the dust jacket for the U.S. edition of Another World, *1999)*

Her novels about working-class women often include fatherless children; sometimes the father is dead, sometimes unidentified. The novelist herself was born on 8 May 1943 in Thornaby-on-Tees, England, to a mother whom she declines to identify. Her father was absent; identified as a Royal Air Force (RAF) officer in at least one interview, he was said to have been killed in the war, but Barker later came to believe "they didn't marry and he just buggered off." She learned even later that her mother did not know who her father was. When Pat was seven years old, her mother, Moira, did marry; but Pat was raised by her grandmother and grandfather. Her grandfather was a veteran of World War I, and she was fascinated by his bayonet wound–he used to permit her to insert her finger into it–and both the bayonet wound and the war itself have come to loom large in her fiction. Her grandmother worked in a fish and chip shop; her grandfather was a laborer, whom she remembers seeing wash himself at the kitchen sink. Her grandmother's first husband had been a spiritualist minister, and some of his books, in addition to an encyclopedia, made up the reading matter of her childhood home.

Pat Barker was educated at grammar school (that is, a state-funded selective secondary school), in a girls-only institution that was "so strict that no girl was allowed to talk to a boy even if he was her brother" and then went to London, where she earned a B.Sc. from the London School of Economics and Political Science in 1965. She worked as a teacher, teaching history, politics, and English to "vocational classes of civil servants, horticulturists, police cadets" from 1965 to 1970. In 1978 she married David Barker, now a retired professor of zoology; they have two children, John and Annabel. Her early (unpublished) writing, which has been described as "a series of middle-class novels of manners," took a different and productive turn when she took a creative-writing short course led by novelist Angela Carter. Carter encouraged her to write about her own background. She began to write about "the background she knew: among poor women on deadly assembly lines who raise their children with grit and humour." Though Barker has said that she was liberated by deciding that she was never going to be published, Carter showed her work to Carmen Callil, the publisher of Virago, which published her early novels. The first, *Union Street,* was accepted with an advance of £750 and published in 1982. She has published steadily since that breakthrough. Asked in 2001 what the purpose of fiction is, she said, "to enable people to think clearly and feel deeply about the same subject simultaneously," and her exploration of the struggles of working-class life, war, and the twentieth-century crisis of masculinity answer well to that definition. She lives in Durham, a university and cathedral city near her native Teesside.

Union Street tells the story of seven women. Their lives are linked by a variety of devices: one is propinquity, in that they inhabit the same decayed neighborhood of a declining industrial city. The older ones remember when things were better; now their landscape is one of abandoned houses, scheduled for demolition but until then inhabited by derelicts or used for squalid assignations. In addition to living near each other and (in some cases, at least) knowing each other, these women are united by the bleakness of their lives. Those who work seem limited to the cake factory. The men in their lives are jobless and unreliable and tend to be alcoholic and abusive. In this first novel Barker stakes out a distinctive territory for herself: the lives of workingwomen. There is little about these lives to admire or envy: chaotic, endlessly disappointed, limited, they seem bound to an endless cycle of modest hope followed by major disappointment; too few resources; bad housing, bad employment, bad education. The only things that the women can always count on are conception and birth and, of course, death.

What the author does not do is sentimentalize the women–or demonize the men. At the beginning of *Union Street,* Kelly Brown rises to discover a new man sharing her mother's bed as "Uncle Arthur"; later, after she has been sexually molested during long nighttime rambles, she tells her mother, "Mam, it happened three weeks ago. You've been out every night since then," and the narrator comments, "Kelly looked at her mother. If she longed for love she did not know it. She felt only a renewed and more savage pride in her ability to survive alone." Mrs. Brown is not extraordinary in this milieu: perhaps she is doing her best, but her best is not very good. Likewise, the men, who regularly let the women down, seem almost equally victims of a society that has turned its back on them. They are the miserable products of a postindustrial world. Questioned by one interviewer (who had pointed out that in her first two books, "most of the men are real rotters, and the better ones are usually deficient in some way") as to whether she would be including more good men in her future novels, Barker replied:

> I think more good men; I don't promise more *strong* men. And I don't think I'm making a judgment about the two sexes, in the abstract, as it were. I think I'm writing about a scene in which the heavy industry which employed mainly men, and on which so many men from the working classes relied for their sense of identity, is what's going. And the essence of the social changes in the book is the collapse of that kind of industry and therefore, in a sense, the collapse of the men's identity. The women seem to be far more resilient in the face of this particular type of social change because they have their two roles in the home and outside it. The men seem to me to be very vulnerable to it. I think this is why, perhaps, in the books the men seem weaker than the women.

The women in *Union Street* are linked, finally, by the eldest of them, Alice, who occupies the final section; she is being urged to move out of her home but wants to die there, with dignity. She lives mostly in memory (including, somehow, memories that seem to have leached over from the minds of the other women): for instance,

> Me Dad was the only one made anything of me. . . . But me Mam. I judged her too harshly. Now I look back I see things more her way. She was a hard woman but she had enough to make her hard. Eighteen kids. And we never went without shoes and there was always enough to eat. It might only be broth but there was plenty of it. She was a strong woman. She lived to be eighty and do you know when she died there wasn't a grey hair in her head.

The materials of this novel are energized by the near indomitability of the women; by the honesty of the writing; and by a vigorous kind of humor, the best example of which may come in a neighbor's response to Kelly Brown's rape:

> Mr Broadbent, sparse hair standing up with excitement, spit flying, strode up and down the bedroom floor telling Mrs Broadbent at great length and in some detail how he would punish sexual offenders. Finally, in a burst of civic zeal, he mounted that heap of white and defeated flesh and gave it such a pounding as it had not enjoyed, or endured, for many a long year.

A group of women also dominates *Blow Your House Down* (1984). There is less diversity in them, though, not only because none is very old or very young, but also because they are all prostitutes. They ply their trade in an area much like the one around Union Street; in this case, the alternative employment is not a cake factory but a chicken-processing plant, in which several of the women have spent part of their desperate working lives. They discover that prostitution is better-paid work and that it is much more family-friendly, making child-care options easier.

The occasion for the novel is a period in which a murderer is preying on prostitutes; the career of Peter Sutcliffe, the "Yorkshire Ripper," who murdered prostitutes and other women he identified as prostitutes in the area around his home in Bradford between 1975 and 1981, obviously helps to form the background for the book. Like *Union Street, Blow Your House Down* focuses in turn on different women, each of whom has her own reason for becoming a prostitute and her own way of following the life. Barker makes clear that their lives are the reverse of glamorous: they need someone to watch their children, they want love, they want security. As the violent attacks on prostitutes increase, they are naturally frightened but torn between fear and need for money. Different protective strategies suggest themselves; for

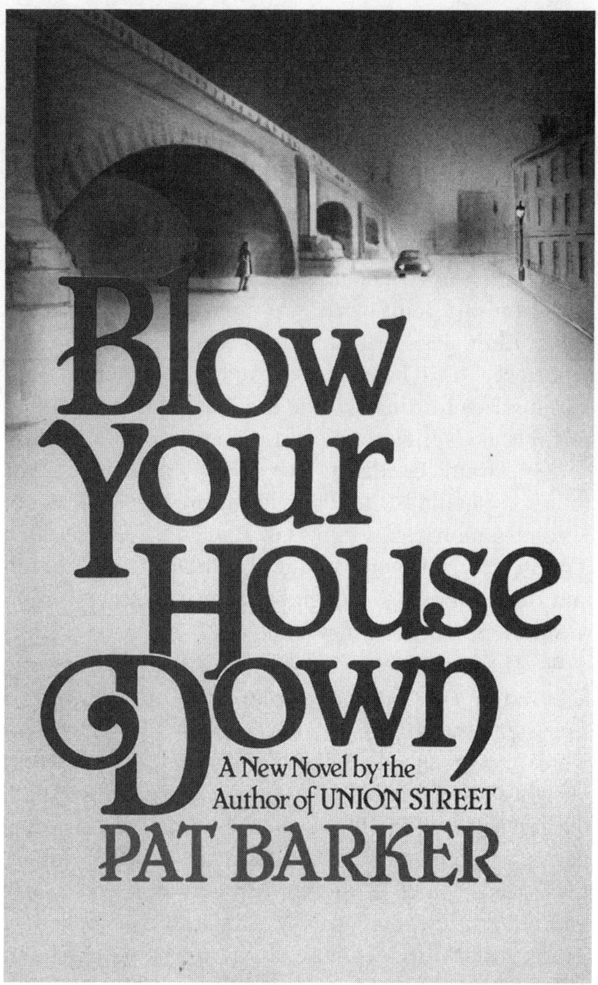

Dust jacket for the U.S. edition of Barker's 1984 novel, about a group of prostitutes menaced by a serial killer (Richland County Public Library)

instance, some of the women work in teams so that when one of them gets into a car with a customer, the other ostentatiously takes down the license-plate number. One suggests that they only go with their regulars, only to be reminded that the murderer probably is somebody's regular. Maureen, one of the more vocal women, shares her own knowledge of the Yorkshire Ripper:

> "I was in Bradford, you know." She watched it sink in. "Oh there was a lot moved out, but there was a lot more stayed. And they were always on: 'Oh he's given it up.' 'He's gone away.' 'He's topped himself.' Like bloody hell. And there were all sorts of ideas flying round. 'Always get out of the car.' 'Never get out of the car.' 'Take the numbers.' 'Work in pairs.' 'Don't bend down.' 'Don't turn your back.' 'Don't suck them off.' Load of rubbish. I never did any of it. I did start carrying a knife and then I thought well, you dozy cow, you're just handing him the weapon. So after that I didn't bother."

The novel occupies itself with both the background–the texture of the lives of women in a shattered, postindustrial landscape, mistrustful of authority (they believe the police are using them as bait to catch the murderer)–and the foreground, the more sensational developments related to the crime. Early on, one of the women, Jean, comments on her partner (and lover) Carol, who seems to have moved to London. Carol turns up dead, however. Later, after a chapter seen from the point of view of the ripper as he kills the aging Kath, Jean believes he has picked her up (he reportedly uses lavender-flavored breath mints) and kills him. Unfortunately, she has killed the wrong man; this mistake seems to explain the epigraph Barker has chosen, from Friedrich Nietzsche: "Whoever fights monsters should see to it that in the process he does not become a monster." Grim as it is, the novel ends with a glimpse of a surviving victim and her loving husband, and then a moving, though somewhat puzzling, vision of starlings swarming above the city.

The hard lives of working-class women are again featured in *The Century's Daughter* (1986; republished as *Liza's England,* 1996), though instead of a chorus of women, the novel centers on one, Liza (Garrett) Wright, born in 1900. The novel is set in 1984–1985, the last year of her life. Liza lives alone, except for a parrot she rescued from a pub being closed; a friend, Mrs. Jubb, comes in to help her out, as she is nearly bedridden. The other major character is Stephen, a young social worker, whose task is to try to get Liza out of her house (she has lived there since 1922) and into an old-person's home, so that her house can be demolished along with the rest of the terrace, presumably to be replaced by soulless high-rise flats like those where Stephen works with vicious youths. On the first page Stephen thinks "he couldn't imagine ever coming to this. To be the sole remaining inhabitant of a street scheduled for demolition. Isolated, helpless, threatened with eviction if you didn't agree to conform and get out." Stephen has an education and a white-collar job, a male lover, agreeable colleagues; and yet in a way he is worse off than Liza. Despite the desperation of her life, she has a vitality that he lacks.

Liza, one of fifteen children born to her mother, loses her favorite brother in the first world war, her son in the second; her marriage, to a man disabled in and mentally weakened by the Great War, is hardly a success, as Frank spends much of his time in spiritualist services and forbids her to work outside the home (though permitting her to wash disgusting butchers' aprons at home for money) before losing his job and his spirits, leaving home, and dying in the workhouse. Her daughter, Eileen, becomes pregnant by a soldier and gives birth to a daughter, Kath, whom Liza rears in the place of her feckless mother. For several years during the worst period of deprivation, Liza spends much of her day collecting coal and dragging it home across the city. The present-day world around her (Stephen's world) is less materially deprived but more morally and psychologically bankrupt; and eventually some of Stephen's youthful clients break into Liza's home and kill her, in a pointless attempt to steal money she does not possess.

As a condition-of-England novel, particularly focused on the blight of the Conservative government of Margaret Thatcher, *The Century's Daughter* may seem too mechanical an assemblage of misfortunes; and indeed, Frances Hill, comparing it to its two predecessors, writes in a 16 June 1990 review for *The Times* (London) that "sentimentality has crept in." In a 3 March 1996 review for the *Sunday Telegraph* Nicholas Bagnall, more caustically, suggests that "Pat Barker lays it on so thick that you'd think she was trying to parody the genre. The char trudges home and you bet her boot-sole will flap. It does. The woman flees from the bombed house: her nightdress will be torn (yes) and will reveal a swinging breast (yes, yes), probably wrinkled (right again)." A more sympathetic reading would note that Liza's spunk and vigor disarm sentimentality; and Barker's evocative prose carries the novel: giving birth to Eileen,

> Liza was absorbed in her long labour and yet not divided from the life of the street that went on all round her. The tramping of feet of men who had work to go to, the squatting on haunches of men who had none, the skitter of a stone over the pavement as children played hopscotch, the hanging-out of washing, the billowing of sheets, the snap and crackle of shirts blowing on the line, women with open-pored, harassed faces chasing a little bacon round and round the frying-pan, always asking, *Will it be enough?,* a cat slinking down the alley, dogs barking, smells of meat and cabbage, the crackle of flames in a grate as fires were lit for the men coming home, then dusk falling, lights going on one by one, windows glowing the colour of their curtains, red and blue and green: all these things and many more revolved around the periphery of her vision, and she felt as her labour went on that she was giving birth to them all.

The Man Who Wasn't There (1988) rounds off the first phase of Barker's career and prepares for her turn toward World War I, though of course Liza's experience with a brother killed and a husband shattered in that war had already begun the move. The novel is a slighter tale than the three novels that have preceded it, with the drabness of the main character's life relieved by a lively and even lighthearted version of his compensating fantasy life. Colin, a twelve-year-old schoolboy, lives with his mother, Viv, another of Barker's rather hard and neglectful mothers, a waitress who lives for her pleasures with her friend Pauline and sex with her employer, the squalid Reg Boyce. In the first scene of the novel Colin has been kept in at school because his mother will not sign his report, though her suggestion is that "If they took the stick to you a bit more often, 'stead of all this keeping you in, they might get somewhere." Colin is fatherless; when he insists on learning about his father, Viv tells him about a shot-down RAF pilot, an affecting story that, unfortunately, he recognizes from a movie.

His alternative life is constructed on the model of movies about life in Resistance France, with his mother and her mate appearing as Paulette and Vivienne, waitresses serving German soldiers, and Colin reassigned a more heroic role as well. Barker interleaves Colin's mental script with his mundane life throughout the novel.

The pattern of consoling fantasy is doubled by Colin's experiences with a spiritualist medium, Mrs. Stroud, who (like Liza Wright's husband) has begun sincerely, lost her gift, but continues to pretend. She acknowledges herself a fraud but insists that her fakery solaces her customers. More oddly, she recognizes that Colin, too, has a gift: "You've got to take care of it, Colin. Don't let it slip away, don't do what I did. You can use it to make yourself look good, you can use it to get even with people, but I'm warning you, if you do, you'll lose it." Whether the reader is supposed to think of Colin as a psychic is unclear, but he is gifted–more intelligent than the people he comes from, though his continued association with the boys from his old school is one source of his problems at the grammar school–and, as his running drama of heroic resistance makes clear, something of an artist.

In a 1993 profile Candice Rodd commented on the apparent break in Pat Barker's career between *The Man Who Wasn't There* and *Regeneration* (1991): "You could almost be forgiven for thinking there are two Pat Barkers–the one writes gritty contemporary feminist novels set in working-class areas of northern England, and the author of profoundly thoughtful fiction about the devastating psychological damage sustained by soldiers fighting in the First World War." Barker has suggested that the historical novel may be a good way to deal with contemporary experience. In conversation with Rodd she also explained the change in direction in another way: "I was fed up with being patronised. You should be able to write about working-class lives and be taken with full seriousness as a creative writer, but you're judged on the authenticity of your sociology. I was always being asked to display my credentials." She cites the interviewer who began by asking what her father did for a living. "He meant: Was 'e down t'mines? And if, as I did, you write about women, sooner or later some critic says: But ah, can she do men?–as though that were some kind of Everest. I took a very conscious decision to change what I wrote about."

Dust jacket for the U.S. edition of Barker's 1991 novel, a fictionalized treatment of World War I poets Siegfried Sassoon and Wilfred Owen (Joseph M. Bruccoli Great War Collection, Thomas Cooper Library, University of South Carolina)

The break is not so sharp as this comment suggests: there are many continuities. One is a concern for northern working-class people; another is an interest in working women (several of the World War I books focus on women working in munitions factories); and the way parents (or lack of parents) shape young lives, as well as war damage, are central to several of the earlier novels.

One immediately apparent difference in *Regeneration* and its sequels, *The Eye in the Door* (1993) and *The Ghost Road* (1995), is the inclusion of real people. Another is the inclusion of real, historical events. In the first category the most important are Siegfried Sassoon, one of the best-known English poets of the Great War; his friends Rupert Owen and Robert Graves; and the physician W. H. R. Rivers, who treated Sassoon and Owen at Craiglockhart Hospital in Scotland. In the second category are the important battles of the war and Sassoon's declaration against the war and its reception in Parliament. Barker's contribution is in the minor

Dust jacket for the first edition of Barker's 1993 novel, the second volume of her Regeneration Trilogy, set in London during the last year of World War I (Joseph M. Bruccoli Great War Collection, Thomas Cooper Library, University of South Carolina)

characters–nurses, other physicians, other patients–who enrich the texture of the novel and in the creation of another wounded officer, Billy Prior, whose importance increases through the trilogy.

The two central characters in *Regeneration* are both involved in paradox and irony. Sassoon, a genuine war hero, has come back to England wounded; but, partly under the influence of Bertrand Russell, Ottoline Morrell, and Robert Ross, he has issued a statement calling for the end of the war and declaring "I am not protesting against the conduct of the war, but against the political errors and insincerities for which the fighting men are being sacrificed." Sassoon is no pacifist, however; he simply believes the British war aims, already unclear, cannot justify the level of slaughter. He reserves his greatest hatred for civilians. The connivance of Graves permits him to be hospitalized rather than court-martialed, and as the novel progresses he continues to feel an obligation to return to France and stand with his men. Likewise, Rivers, who is shown as a humane doctor with enlightened ideas about how to treat war neurosis (especially as contrasted with Dr. Yealland, whose treatment plan includes almost unbelievable brutality, for instance by applying lighted cigarettes to the tongue of a speechless sufferer), is nevertheless an army doctor; and despite his pity for his patients, a successful case is one in which the patient is "cured" enough to return to the front and likely death (Sassoon survived the war; Owen did not).

Barker is effective when portraying the horrors of war. One of the patients at Craiglockhart cannot eat; the incident which precipitated his neurosis was his being blown up and landing with his face in the rotten corpse of a German soldier, which exploded into his mouth. Prior, after a direct hit on some of his men that left him collecting scraps for burial, has found an eye below the duckboards in his trench; sometime later he developed a hysterical inability to speak.

Regeneration, thus, has many sources of interest: What war was like for those fighting it; what a thoughtful, imaginative psychologist makes of his patients. Sex: Sassoon is homosexual; Prior, a bisexual, begins an affair with Sarah Lumb, a munitions worker with the characteristic yellow skin that came with that work. Sarah's mum, Ada, has persuaded her that love between men and women cannot exist, and the narrator tells readers that in Ada's world, "men loved women as the fox loves the hare. And women loved men as the tapeworm loves the gut." Poetry: Sassoon, a confident writer, helps Owen find his artistic voice, in part by persuading him toward (and modeling for him) a tougher, more straightforward kind of war poem. Class: Prior is an anomalous man. He is an officer, but unlike most others, he is from the working class. Rivers thinks of the faces of officers and

> that perpetually harried expression of theirs. Rivers had only ever seen that look in one other place: in the public wards of hospitals, on the faces of women who were bringing up large families on very low incomes, women who, in their early thirties, could easily be taken for fifty or more. It was the look of people who are totally responsible for lives they have no power to save.

Not everything is successful in *Regeneration.* Working in a genre so well established as the Great War novel, Barker occasionally falls into the derivative, as when Prior thinks, "Language ran out on you, in the end, the names were left to say it all. Mons, Loos, Ypres, the Somme. Arras"–which is more or less Frederick Henry's speech from Ernest Hemingway's *A Farewell to Arms* (1929). Nevertheless it is a major accomplishment, properly recognized when *The New York Times* named it one of the four best novels of 1992.

The author was not planning a series when she took up the war theme; presumably, if she had been, she might have started earlier than July 1917 to give herself more scope (the war ended in November 1918). Nevertheless, the first book concludes in November 1917, as Rivers discharges Sassoon to return to France. By the end of the next installment, *The Eye in the Door,* Sassoon has already been wounded again (accidentally shot by his own men while returning from a raid) and is back in a London hospital with a head wound. Prior is also in London, now doing quasi-civilian work for the Ministry of Munitions: he is a sort of spy, a job in which his distaste for pacifists and munitions strikers is a help. As before, however, he is a divided man, because a woman who helped to bring him up, Beattie Roper, is in jail for antiwar activities–convicted of trying to murder Prime Minister David Lloyd George with a poisoned dart–and another old friend, Sean MacDowell, is a leading draft resister who is arrested during the novel and accuses Prior, possibly correctly, of being his betrayer.

The title of the novel seems to evoke the eye in the trench–the traumatic event that brought Prior to Craiglockhart–but refers primarily to the peepholes in the doors of British prison cells (for instance, the one holding Beattie Roper) and the eye drawn around them to remind prisoners that they are always under scrutiny.

Prior is now engaged to Sarah Lumb but sees little of her. Instead, the other side of his sexual nature, the homosexual, involves him with an upper-class married man, Charles Manning, also in the ministry. Manning is friendly with Winston Churchill and other important men in government and society. Prior is also linked, somewhat hesitantly, with Robert Ross (Oscar Wilde's old patron) because both men were involved in the production of a performance of Wilde's *Salomé* (1896). The opposition to this performance brings in the most fantastic part of the novel, which is apparently nonetheless historically accurate: the campaign by a member of Parliament, Pemberton Billings, against "the cult of the clitoris"–unnatural women with diseased and overgrown clitorises who can only be satisfied by bull elephants. Somehow *Salomé* (with its reminder of Wilde's own sexual disgrace) becomes entangled in Billings's insane activities. The female organizer sues Billings for libel but loses. Ross, readers of *Regeneration* will remember, was one of the sponsors of Sassoon's antiwar statement in July 1917.

Once again Prior is uneasily poised between worlds; Manning thinks of him and the status accorded to working-class officers as "temporary gentlemen": "Prior was saved from that not because he didn't imitate–he did–but because he wasn't anxious. Once or twice one might almost have thought one detected a glint of amusement. A hint of parody, even. All the same, the basic truth was the man was neither fish nor fowl nor good red herring. *Socially.* Sexually too, of course, though this was a less comfortable reflection." Prior even has a split personality; as he tells Rivers (now treating him on an outpatient basis): "I was born two years ago. In a shell-hole in France. I have no father." His dissociation produces fugue states in which he acts without later memory, an uncomfortable condition in which he may, for all he knows, have betrayed MacDowell.

The Regeneration Trilogy concludes with *The Ghost Road;* it was awarded the 1995 Booker Prize, an award that probably constitutes a recognition of the whole series. This novel brings the characters up to the end of the war or the end of their lives, whichever comes first: Owen dies within weeks of the end of the war, in the presence of Prior. This novel is a more stripped-down construction than its predecessors: though some of the same characters return, it has a narrowly dual focus on Rivers and Prior and a stronger thematic unity. It is about death. The sections on Rivers often consist of flashbacks to his time as an anthropologist in Melanesia, where he studied the burial practices of South Seas islanders, particularly those who had become disturbed by the end of their headhunting traditions.

Alternating with these passages are scenes of life at the front–the only ones, aside from scattered recollections, in this series. Prior, despite his asthma, has returned to France. For the second half of the novel his experiences are reported in journal entries, one of which bitterly comments on the officers' writing:

> It's like this every evening. And not just letters either. Diaries. Poems. At least two would-be poets in this hut alone. Why? You have to ask yourself. I think it's a way of claiming immunity. First-person narrators can't die, so as long as we keep telling the story of our own lives we're safe. Ha bloody fucking Ha.

Suffice it to say that Prior is not the first-person narrator at the end of the novel. Before that time, though, he has provided unforgettable accounts of death and destruction, including hours spent in a shell hole with a fellow officer whose skull has been largely shot away, leaving him alive, and this brief glimpse of Owen:

> I saw him in the attack, caped and masked in blood, seize a machine-gun and turn it on its previous owners at point-blank range. Like killing fish in a bucket. And I wonder if he sees those faces, grey, open-mouthed faces, life draining out of them before the bullets hit, as I see the faces of the men I killed in the counter-attack. I won't ask. He wouldn't answer if I did. I wouldn't dare

> ask. For the first time it occurs to me that Rivers's job also requires courage.

Perhaps because of the vivid fighting and its obvious waste, *The Ghost Road* seems the most obviously antiwar of Barker's three war novels. At one point Prior thinks back to his first conversation with Sarah: "Loos, she said. I remember standing by the bar and thinking that words didn't mean anything any more. Patriotism honour courage vomit vomit vomit. Only the names meant anything. Mons, Loos, the Somme, Arras, Verdun, Ypres." He has taken over the role of Sassoon, too, as when he adds to an argument about the war among less-experienced officers:

> What do I think? I think what you're saying is basically a conspiracy theory, and like all conspiracy theories it's optimistic. What you're saying is, OK the war isn't being fought for the reasons we're told, but it *is* being fought for a reason. It's not benefiting the people it's supposed to be benefiting, but it *is* benefiting somebody. And I don't believe that, you see. I think things are actually much worse than you think because there isn't any kind of rational justification left. It's become a self-perpetuating system. Nobody benefits. Nobody's in control. Nobody knows how to stop.

With *The Ghost Road* Barker unmistakably moved into a central position in the top rank of contemporary British writers. Eileen Battersby, a perceptive commentator, wrote in the *Irish Times:*

> Two years ago, the English novelist Pat Barker seemed destined to win the Booker Prize with her magnificent novel about men at war, *The Eye in the Door*.
>
> Not only did she not win, she was not even shortlisted.
>
> Considering that the novel, with its powerful characterisation and clear, muscular prose, was so superior to all other British novels published that or any year, its outrageous exclusion could be explained only by suggesting that Barker's honest vision of a frightened England battling with paranoia and resorting to scapegoating the vulnerable, pacifists and homosexuals was dangerously unpatriotic for a conservative, unselfcritical establishment fattened on tales of wartime heroism. But then *Regeneration,* her fifth book and the first of her war novels, should have won in 1991. It was not shortlisted either. Now Barker completes her first World War trilogy with *The Ghost Road.* It is superb; probably the best novel of the year. Again, Barker should win the Booker, but it doesn't really matter. These three novels are among the best British fiction this century.

Another World (1998) turns from World War I to the present, while keeping the war as a central theme. Like her first four novels, it is set in the industrial or postindustrial northeast; like them, it addresses familial stresses and the difficulties of children and adolescents. At the same time, like the Regeneration Trilogy, it is concerned with the cost of war. What is different is that it is set among middle-class people. Nick, the narrator, is a teacher, living with a blended family in a large if rundown house. None of Pat Barker's novels is autobiographical in any deep sense, though all use parts of her experience and knowledge. The World War I veteran of *Another World,* Geordie, has a bayonet wound based on her grandfather's and, like her grandfather, he attributes to his wound the pain that really comes from the cancer that is killing him.

The multigenerational story links Nick; his grandfather Geordie; and the next generation–his daughter, Miranda, and his stepson, Gareth (like so many of Barker's young people, he has always been fatherless). Among the linkages are the irruption of the past into the present and the threat of violence, including violence against loved ones.

The symbolic presentation of the first of these themes occurs when, scraping wallpaper to redecorate a room in their large house, the family discover a painting of another family, crudely defaced by drawn-on genitals, and they seem to see themselves in the picture. Research shows that the people pictured were the Fanshawes, factory owners who had built the house; their children had been suspected of murdering their baby brother; then the older son died on the Somme in 1916. The modern parallel is that Gareth, a troubled and immature boy who spends most of his time playing with a computer, when he is not maliciously cleaning the toilet with his stepfather's toothbrush, is also violent. Early on he kicks a small child and is then subjected to a humiliating attack by some working-class girls; later he throws stones from a cliff and injures his baby brother. His potential for harm is recognized, and by the end of the novel he has been sent off to York, where he can play with computers in his new school.

The violent atmosphere that encompasses the Fanshawes and Nick's contemporary family is generalized as well. Gareth is beaten, Nick is threatened (they live on the edge of a rough neighborhood); while waiting for Miranda at the railroad station, Nick worries; then, the narrator explains, "This is all rubbish, he knows that. But then, like everybody else, he lives in the shadow of monstrosities. Peter Sutcliffe's bearded face, the number plate of a house in Cromwell Street, three figures smudged on a video surveillance screen, an older boy taking a toddler by the hand while his companion strides ahead, eager for the atrocity to come." The references to the Yorkshire Ripper, to the Wests (serial murderers of young women in Gloucester), and to the child murderers of Liverpool establish a somber milieu, which helps to prepare for Gareth's nonlethal but nonetheless horrible assault.

Finally there is Geordie, a 101-year-old veteran of the Great War. One almost suspects Barker of some self-mockery regarding Prior when Helen, one of Nick's colleagues, "tried to get Geordie to frame his war experience in terms of late-twentieth-century preoccupations. Gender. Definitions of masculinity. Homoeroticism. Homo-*what?* asked Geordie." After a half century of refusing to talk about the war, Geordie had permitted Helen to interview him. Once he is dead, Nick reads the transcripts and discovers why Geordie thought he was in hell; having enlisted under the influence of his adored older brother, he saw him, with his guts shot out, suffering in a shell hole and, in terrible compassion, knifed him to death.

The parallels and thematic linkages of this novel are strong enough but not too strong (though some reviewers criticized it for being too schematic); at the end of the novel, Nick reflects on this question:

> Six weeks since they'd uncovered the picture. Six weeks since Miranda stepped back and said, in that soft murmur that had raised the hairs on the nape of his neck, "It's us." Not true, he thinks, even as the covered-up figures rise once again to the surface of his mind. He doesn't regret not telling the family about the Fanshawe murder, because even now he doesn't see how the knowledge would have helped them. It's easy to let oneself be dazzled by false analogies–the past never threatens anything as simple, or as avoidable, as repetition.

The touch of evil suggested by Barker's line, "like everybody else, he lives in the shadow of monstrosities," and her recognition of childhood evil as central to that monstrousness appear again in *Border Crossing* (2001). The germ of what she calls this "bloodthirsty little book" was, she told one interviewer, something she read in a biography of Catherine Cookson, a bestselling novelist from the northeast. As a small child, Cookson was apparently seen by a man on a passing tram in the act of drowning a little boy. "If he had not leaped off the tram and stopped her," Barker asks, "would we have Catherine Cookson, world-famous popular novelist, or Catherine Cookson, the equal of Mary Bell in infamy, the child murderer? What makes the difference is the adult taking responsibility for the child."

Mary Bell, aged eleven when she killed two boys, lies in the background of *Border Crossing,* and so do Jon Venables and Robert Thompson, eleven when they were convicted of murdering toddler James Bulger. Without doubt, knowledge of their real-life crimes helps to create the atmosphere. The anecdote about Catherine Cookson is more troubling, however; it suggests not that a rare, but monstrous, child commits murder, but that many more might do so under the right conditions. The main adult character in *Border*

Dust jacket for the U.S. edition of Barker's 1995 novel, the final volume in her Regeneration Trilogy (Joseph M. Bruccoli Great War Collection, Thomas Cooper Library, University of South Carolina)

Crossing, an adolescent psychologist, realizes that as a youth he could have done violence to a younger boy, had conditions been different.

At the heart of the novel may be the question of evil. Danny Miller, a child murderer, now grown up, asks Tom Seymour, the psychologist, if he believes in evil. The answer is not an easy one.

The plot is set in motion when Tom, out for a walk with his estranged wife, sees a young man throw himself into the canal, apparently in a suicide attempt. He drags him out, dries him off, and discovers that he is Danny. The two are connected; Tom had testified at Danny's trial (for murdering an old woman, not another child), and his testimony seems to have turned the trial. The rest of the novel choreographs a pas de deux between the two men, in which Tom becomes less sure about his original diagnosis, wonders about his own attraction to or projection on Danny, and, simultaneously, works through the disintegration of his marriage, which is strained apparently in part because it is childless. This fact becomes part of the complex relationship with Danny.

Alongside the taut psychological thriller that grows from Danny and Tom's relationship there is a comic sequence about Danny's experience in a provincial creative-writing school. Writing, perhaps, is what he should do: he has charm, plausibility, and a wonderfully developed ability to manipulate. His writing teacher crosses the usual boundary between teacher and pupil. There are many border crossings in this aptly named novel: Julie Wheelwright identified one as "Barker's essential concept of the title's border crossing: the line between two personalities that becomes blurred to the point where the therapist loses professional judgement." Madeleine Kingsley wrote that "in a child's mind . . . victim and bully, the allocation of comfort and punishment, are easily confused." And, as Barker has said, she is powerfully focused on "what is truth and what is fiction," and that border, and its permeability, are central to this novel, as to her others.

When Robert McCrum asked Pat Barker in 2001 if she was in the middle of her writing career, she responded that she did not know, but she had two novels in mind. She told Elizabeth Grice that her next book will deal with child evacuees of World War II, "uniting," as Grice commented, "two of her ineluctable themes: the impact of war on society and the individual and disruption in the lives of children. 'The disruption is a continuing force in the life of a family, which is what I felt about both wars in my own family. I am also interested in the clash of the classes that evacuation brought about.'" This direction seems a promising one, likely to bring further exploration of subject matters–the lives of working-class people, "border crossing," evil, and extremity–that Barker has made her own and incorporated into one of the most powerful bodies of work of any living British novelist.

Interviews:

Jean W. Ross, "CA Interview," *Contemporary Authors,* 122 (Detroit: Gale, 1988): 40–43;

Donna Perry, "Going Home Again," *Literary Review,* 34 (Winter 1991): 235–244;

Candice Rodd, "A Stomach for War," *Independent,* 12 September 1993, p. 28;

James Marcus, "The Politics of Hysteria," *Newsday,* 22 May 1994, p. 34;

Anthony Quinn, "What Sassoon Could Never Resolve," *Daily Telegraph,* Arts section, 2 September 1995, p. 4;

Valerie Grove, "'I know in my bones that book prizes are just three lemons in a row,'" *Times* (London), Features section, 29 September 1995;

Helena de Bertodano, "Booker Prize Blows Her Cover," *Sunday Telegraph,* 12 November 1995, p. 3;

Jane Shilling, "Shaking Off the Ghosts of War," *Daily Telegraph,* 24 October 1998, p. 5;

Alida Becker, "Old War Wounds," *New York Times,* 16 May 1999, VII: 6;

E. Jane Dickson, "Transfixed by the Bloody Battlefield," *Times* (London), Features section, 11 November 2000;

Julie Wheelwright, "Young Lives between the Lines," *Independent,* Features section, 31 March 2001, p. 9;

Elizabeth Grice, "Between Violence and Salvation," *Daily Telegraph,* 31 March 2001, p. 7;

Robert McCrum, "The Books Interview: Pat Barker," *Observer,* Review section, 1 April 2001, p. 17;

Madeleine Kingsley, "A Bridge over Murky Waters," *Financial Times,* Books section, 7 April 2001, p. 4;

Elizabeth Taylor, "Pat Barker Looks at Her Writing and Life," *Knight-Tribune News Service,* 18 July 2001, p. K2704.

References:

Brooke Allen, "Blurring the Borders," *New Criterion,* 19 (May 2001): 62–66;

Nicholas Bagnall, "Paperbacks," *Sunday Telegraph,* 3 March 1996, p. 14;

Andrew Green, "Twentieth-Century War Writing," *English Review,* 10 (November 1999): 40;

Greg Harris, "Compulsory Masculinity, Britain, and the Great War: The Literary-Historical Work of Pat Barker," *Critique,* 39 (Summer 1998): 290–305;

Frances Hill, "Withered by a Cold Northerly," *Times* (London), 16 June 1990;

John Kirk, "Recovered Perspectives: Gender, Class, and Memory in Pat Barker's Writing," *Contemporary Literature,* 40 (Winter 1999): 603–626;

Ankhi Mukherjee, "Stammering to Story: Neurosis and Narration in Pat Barker's *Regeneration,*" *Critique,* 43 (Fall 2001): 49–62;

Katherine G. Nickerson and Steven Shea, "W. H. R. Rivers: Portrait of a Great Physician in Pat Barker's Regeneration Trilogy," *Lancet,* 350 (19 July 1997): 205–210;

Michael Thorpe, "The Walking Wounded," *World and I,* 14 (October 1999): 258–267;

Anne Whitehead, "Open to Suggestion: Hypnosis and History in Pat Barker's 'Regeneration,'" *Modern Fiction Studies,* 44 (Fall 1998): 674–695.

Terence Blacker

(5 February 1948 –   )

Merritt Moseley
University of North Carolina at Asheville

BOOKS: *Neil's Book of the Dead,* by Blacker and Nigel Planer (London: Pavilion, 1984; New York: Harmony Books, 1985);
If I Could Work (London: Walker, 1987; New York: Lippincott, 1988);
Ms Wiz Spells Trouble (London: Piccadilly, 1988; New York: Barron's, 1990);
In Stitches with Ms Wiz (London: Piccadilly, 1989);
Fixx (London: Bloomsbury, 1989);
Henry and the Frights (London: Piccadilly, 1989);
You're Nicked Ms Wiz (London: Piccadilly, 1989); republished as *You're Under Arrest, Ms Wiz* (New York: Barron's, 1990);
The Surprising Adventures of Baron Munchausen (London: Hodder & Stoughton, 1989);
Houdini the Disappearing Hamster (London: Andersen, 1990); republished as *Herbie Hamster, Where Are You?* (New York: Random House, 1990);
In Control, Ms Wiz? (London: Piccadilly, 1990; New York: Barron's, 1990);
Ms Wiz Goes Live (London: Piccadilly, 1990);
Ms Wiz–Banned! (London: Piccadilly, 1990);
Homebird (London: Piccadilly, 1991; New York: Bradbury, 1993);
Time Flies for Ms Wiz (London: Piccadilly, 1992);
The Fame Hotel (London: Bloomsbury, 1992);
Power-Crazy Ms Wiz (London: Piccadilly, 1992);
The Great Denture Adventure (London: Pan Macmillan, 1992);
Nasty Neighbours / Nice Neighbours (London: Pan Macmillan, 1992);
Ms Wiz Loves Dracula (London: Piccadilly, 1993);
Let's Get Divorced! Growing Apart Together with TV's Own Jonathan and Libby Hughes, by Blacker and Planer (London: Ebury, 1994);
Shooting Star (London: Pan Macmillan, 1994);
Pride and Penalties (London: Pan Macmillan, 1994);
Revenance (London: Bloomsbury, 1996);
Ms Wiz, Supermodel (London: Macmillan, 1997);
Dream Team (London: Macmillan, 1997);
On the Wing (London: Macmillan, 1997);

Terence Blacker (photograph by Sheila Rock; from the dust jacket for Kill Your Darlings, *2000)*

The Meaning of Cantona: Meditations on Life, Art and Perfectly Weighted Balls, by Blacker and William Donaldson (Edinburgh: Mainstream, 1997);
Ms Wiz Smells a Rat (London: Macmillan, 1998);
The Transfer (London: Macmillan, 1998);
Ms Wiz and the Sister of Doom (London: Macmillan, 1999);
Ms Wiz Goes to Hollywood (London: Macmillan, 2000);
Kill Your Darlings (London: Weidenfeld & Nicolson, 2000; New York: St. Martin's Press, 2001);
Ms Wiz, Millionaire (London: Macmillan, 2001);
The Angel Factory (London: Macmillan, 2001; New York: Simon & Schuster, 2002).

OTHER: Richard Cohen, ed., *Happy Families: An Old Game with New Faces,* with text by Blacker and others (London: Mandarin, 1992).

SELECTED PERIODICAL PUBLICATIONS–UNPUBLISHED: "Feed Them Books, Not Cod Liver Oil," *Times* (London), 4 October 1997;

"Ghost-Writing: It's the New Rock 'n' Roll," *Independent,* 16 April 2001, p. 3;

"My Stalker Hell," *Independent,* 17 April 2001, p. 3;

"Why Is Everyone Writing A Novel These Days?," *Independent,* 27 June 2001, p. 4.

Terence Blacker's 2000 novel *Kill Your Darlings* tells the story of a failed writer whose pretense of superiority to the literary world alternates with a pathetic attempt to find a place in it. Filled with insights on the art of the ghostwriter, the place of children's books in English letters, and the role Martin Amis plays in the minds of his contemporaries, it handsomely displays the author's talent as a novelist as well as (sometimes mordantly) the fruits of his years of experience as an editor, ghostwriter, journalist, children's author, and novelist. An accomplished impersonator and parodist, Blacker is one of the most versatile writers of his generation.

Born on 5 February 1948 into an army family, the son of Felicity Mary Buxton and career officer General Sir Cecil Blacker who retired from the service as adjutant general, Terence was educated at boarding schools from the age of seven. In "My Stalker Hell" (2001) he says that his childhood was "woefully short of psychologically harmful incidents. What on earth can my parents have been thinking of? Did it not occur to them that, by enveloping me in a so-called 'normal' family, they were depriving me of material and sympathy in future life?" His secondary school, Wellington College, was followed by Trinity College, Cambridge, where he read English. He took his B.A. in 1969. He lived in Paris from 1970 to 1971, working in bookshops, and entered the publishing business in 1974, rising from an entry-level sales position to editorial director of Arrow Publishing. In that role he was an editor, a "fixer" of manuscripts, and sometimes a ghostwriter. He edited *Bachelor Boys: The Young Ones Book* (1984), a spin-off from a popular television show, and later two novels for celebrity jockey John Francome, *Stone Cold* (1990) and *Stud Poker* (1991). In "Ghost-Writing: It's the New Rock 'n' Roll" (2001) Blacker comments on the more unacknowledged part of his editorial work: "for someone hoping to write novels, ghosting was a useful apprenticeship. Unlike other freelance money-earners–notably journalism and teaching creative writing, both of which are harmful–the act of sustained impersonation, of editing and shaping taped conversation into a readable narrative, of suppressing your own voice and personality, was a useful skill for the would-be fiction writer." In "Why Is Everyone Writing A Novel These Days?" (2001) he refers to "publishing's dirty little secret–that you don't actually have to write to be a published writer" because of a "vast army of backroom enablers and facilitators."

At the same time Blacker was writing a column for *Publishing News* under the name Jonty Lejeune, "every author's nightmare editor: a spiv, a snob, randy, on the make," as Maurice Johnson called him. After some years of getting up early to write his own fiction before reporting to work as an editor, he resigned in 1983 to become a freelance writer and editor and spent the 1980s writing children's books–beginning with *If I Could Work* (1987) and *Ms Wiz Spells Trouble* (1988)–consulting, and collaborating on various projects. *Neil's Book of the Dead* (1984), written in collaboration with Nigel Planer, was the first book to appear with his name on it.

His first novel for adults was *Fixx* (1989). Since that time he has continued to write juvenile literature, including many more installments of the Ms Wiz series and four books in the Hotshots series, about a girls' soccer team, as well as the adult novels *The Fame Hotel* (1992), *Revenance* (1996), and *Kill Your Darlings.* He writes an opinion column for *The Independent* and a regular column in *The Author.* From 1991 to 2000 he contributed a weekly column to the *Sunday Times,* a "review of reviews" under the name Harvey Porlock, "scourge of reviewers." He was married on 18 October 1975 to the former Caroline Soper–they are now divorced–and they had two children, Xan, born on 10 March 1977, and Alice, born on 10 May 1979.

His first, most popular, and longest-running series of books for children (fourteen titles so far) focuses on Ms Wiz. A "paranormal operative," or witch, Ms Wiz works benign magic, sometimes with the assistance of children. Deftly plotted, usually around a plan that does not work out, the Ms Wiz books also offer something for adults as well as the target readers (primary-school children). For instance, in *Ms Wiz Smells a Rat* (1998), her husband's objection to Ms Wiz's talking rat, Herbert–"There are three of us in this marriage"–is an echo of Princess Diana's complaint about her husband and his mistress. Likewise, Herbert's poems, written for his beloved Arabella, include lines such as "Ours is the secret, special love / That dare not squeak its name."

Blacker's other series is the Hotshots books, four titles–*Pride and Penalties* (1994), *Shooting Star* (1994), *On the Wing* (1997), and *Dream Team* (1997)–about a girls' football (soccer) team, written for twelve- to fourteen-year-old readers. The Hotshots series grew out of the author's experience coaching his own daughter's football team. Maureen Owens, in *The Times* (London) for 22 February 1997, praised "Blacker's gift for incisive comment interspersed with some shortish footballing descriptions" and said that "the feminist message is skilfully used to examine a range of sexist attitudes from the sharply analytical and frequently funny viewpoint of girls just reaching their teens."

His most notable other books for young people are *Homebird* (1991), the story of a middle-class suburban Londoner who runs away and becomes involved with criminals; *Nasty Neighbours / Nice Neighbours* (1992), about children separated by family enmity; *The Great Denture Adventure* (1992), which shows what follows Grandmother's sneezing out her false teeth; *The Transfer* (1998), about an eleven-year-old football fan who creates a new striker, by "cybertelekinesis," to save his team's fortunes; and *The Angel Factory* (2001), a supernatural thriller about the replacement of human beings (including the narrator's family) by angels. For *The Surprising Adventures of Baron Munchausen* (1989) he rewrote the original stories by R. E. Raspe, first published in England in the eighteenth century.

Children's literature occupies an ambiguous position in English literary life. Gregory Keays, narrator of *Kill Your Darlings,* puts the extreme position: some authors are driven by necessity, he explains, to "remove their brains, don the writing equivalent of nappies and write kiddie-fiction." Those authors, he maintains, "good-hearted and amiable as they may well be, invariably suffer from the writing equivalent of maternal brain-fag." Blacker himself, in "Feed Them Books, Not Cod Liver Oil" (1997), complains that "in spite of the ritual wails of anguish about standards of literacy that issue from politicians and opinion mongers, information about what books parents should buy or avoid is, thanks to the uniquely British snobbery of the reviewing establishment toward children's literature, difficult to find." In addition there are the moral objections, including some to Blacker's *Homebird,* from what he calls "the great army of sanitisers."

He has published three nonnarrative works of parody or satire, all in collaboration. *Neil's Book of the Dead* also grew out of the television series *The Young Ones,* in which Planer played Neil, a hippie; alluding to the Tibetan Book of the Dead, it amusingly satirizes many features of the hippie lifestyle, including tai chi, eating lentils, the Beatles, and Eastern mysticism, poorly understood. There are examples of Neil's poems, for instance:

At Otling Fayre
I did my hair
So I could be like you.
I didn't know
That henna's made
From mud and camel's poo.

Dust jacket for Blacker's 1989 novel, about the rising fortunes of a man who succeeds through prostitution, theft, blackmail, and murder (Richland County Public Library)

Planer and Blacker collaborated again on *Let's Get Divorced! Growing Apart Together with TV's Own Jonathan and Libby Hughes* (1994). It pokes fun at celebrity self-revelation and at New Age–style self-actualization advice and psychobabble, including such notions as Positive Divorcehood, Emotional Algebra, and the need to find one's place on the boy-man-warrior-boy continuum.

The Meaning of Cantona: Meditations on Life, Art and Perfectly Weighted Balls (1997) was written with William Donaldson. The subject, Eric Cantona, was a French soccer star who had come to England to play for Leeds, then Manchester United, and won great celebrity, in part because he was thought to be something of an intellectual. The book consists of a series of *pensées,* not by Cantona but by his followers, the *cantonistes.* It includes some mock philosophizing on football and national differences, and, though it subjects many of the features of English football (its announcers, the nicknaming practices of the players, the clichés) to satire, the book feels like an act of devotion to the game as well.

One of the numbered *pensées* gives the flavor of this book:

> We are what we play. The Frenchman seduces the ball. The Italian renders it a minor work of art. The German organises it. And the Englishman? He kicks it very hard and then spits on the ground in disappointment. Only the Englishman truly cares.

Another may shed some light on the views of Blacker and his co-author (Donaldson is a comic writer):

> In England humour knows its place. It belongs with the professional jester–men with silly haircuts and shiny suits on television; middle-aged drolls having a sideways look at life in newspaper columns and on the radio.

Despite its deliberately fragmented, nonnarrative structure and the elusiveness of its subject, *The Meaning of Cantona* accumulates depth and insight into the fictive footballer until it almost amounts to a novel.

As for Blacker's real novels, written for adults, *Fixx* bears a close relationship to his column in *Publishing News* and his objectionable persona, Jonty. Like him, Jonathan Peter Fixx (also nicknamed Jonty, sometimes) is despicable and unscrupulous, a user, social climber, and even murderer. His is a rogue's progress through the world, such that his survival and even success are a comment not only on amoral man but on the society in which he operates.

This spiv's progress through fashionable Britain takes Fixx from an ordinary childhood in Biggleswade, the son of a shattered World War II hero and a Quaker mother; through prep school, where he runs a prostitution ring, successfully shifts the blame onto another boy, and burns down a hut (killing a college employee) to hide the evidence; into the property market (he stakes himself by stealing and selling his father's Victoria Cross) and the underworld; to the pop music business, his success in which is based on stealing a song, whose real author later kills himself. He blackmails his way into an aristocratic family marriage, then wanders into espionage, working for both sides. Along the way he is responsible for the deaths of several more persons, some in his family, and perhaps commits incest.

This sordid tale is transmitted in a jaunty style, which is the key to the impact of the novel. Sometimes its urbanity reveals Fixx's heartlessness, as in this typical passage about his parents:

> With parts of his already limited cerebrum scattered over a Normandy hillside, Father frankly lacked the wherewithal to be the blinkered authoritarian old bigot he would otherwise have become and Mother, required by any standard of decency to be a nurse rather than a wife, had no alternative but to rein in her wayward and bloody-minded intellect (although it found an underhand, clandestine outlet, as I was later to discover).

Sometimes, in dropping the names of minor celebrities, he seems to be spreading Blacker's indictment of a whole society. Speaking of his public school, he writes: "True, Melton has had its minor celebrities. Archer, the scribbler. Heseltine, the politician. Rice, the songsmith. Colin, the pinko sewer rat. Hunt, the racing driver." Colin is a classmate who becomes his nemesis; the rest of those named are real inhabitants of late-twentieth-century Britain.

Other passages simply characterize Fixx, especially in his pretentious ignorance:

> *Belle dame sans merci.* How aptly that phrase, plucked at random from my extensive knowledge of the *lingua franca,* describes the woman who took the fragile dreams of Jonathan Peter Fixx, held them for an instant in her small, almost childlike hands before letting them fall, grinding them to dust with a turn of a sharp, stiletto heel. Yes, she was, quite literally, "the beautiful lady without thank yous."

Again, his claim that he had earned a great reputation as a shooter with his father-in-law's country house set by "bringing down nine birds (including, to Harcourt's surprise, a heron and a brace of barn owls)" makes a comic, and yet sinister, impression at variance with his self-presentation.

Fixx is in the form of a self-justifying account ("to inspire you with my story, to convince you of my innocence") dictated to his sometime lover and possible daughter, Catherine; it ends with Fixx on his feet again. In its episodic structure, its depiction of a society amoral enough for a villain such as Fixx to triumph, and its dark, ironic moral assessments, *Fixx* is reminiscent of the classic picaresque fiction *Lazarillo de Tormes* (1554) and a powerful first novel. Critical notices were generally positive, with reviewers competing for the right term for Fixx–"the Biggleswade bounder," "a monster of rare and staggering obnoxiousness," the hero of "the scumbag's tale," "a wide-boy from Biggleswade, a yuppie before his time, a talentless go-getter and self-promoter of a type that has prospered more than somewhat in the past 10 years." Robert Nye, writing in *The Guardian* (17 February 1989), summed up, "What Blacker has done is to take a monster and make him almost human by being true to every stray movement of what passes for thought in his mind, with a result that is at once sordid and sublime, and overwhelmingly comic as it zooms back and forth from stars to gutter. You could warm your hands on the crackle of the prose, too, especially in the first two thirds of it."

By the time his second novel, *The Fame Hotel,* came out, Blacker was writing his Harvey Porlock column and was somewhat wary of revenge from reviewers he had scourged. In fact the novel was well enough received; Noel Malcolm, in the *Sunday Telegraph* (6 September 1992), praised its "compelling satire" and the author's ear for dialogue–"The inanities of modern English conversational style are honed and sharpened until they hurt"–though he thought the novel unbalanced, its detective story and its satire in conflict. Andro Linkalter, in the *Sunday Times* (27 September 1992), gave it the backhanded acknowledgment that "there is enough wit here to confirm Blacker's promise as a comic novelist, although it must also be said that for much of its length *The Fame Hotel* betrays the uneven pace and self-consciousness of a second effort."

As its title suggests, the novel is at least in part a satire on the culture of celebrity; it includes a policeman whose main interest is in getting his cases reconstructed on a television show (to disastrous effect), a media clergyman, members of the royal family (offstage), and a compromising tape recording of at least one royal. At the heart of the novel is the dead Oliver Sincton, a ghostwriter, found in a hotel bedroom, stabbed through the neck, handcuffed to the bed, and with a doughnut around his penis. This situation gives rise to two parallel investigations.

In the more conventional one, a policeman named Detective Inspector Potter pursues the solution to the crime; in the other, an old friend of Sincton's, Robin Nicholl, who has been named his literary executor, pursues the information left on computer disks belonging to Sincton. Nicholl is an ineffectual man working in children's novelties who is financially dependent on his wife, Laura Nicholl, a successful novelist. One of the secrets Nicholl uncovers is that his wife was actually dependent on Sincton to ghostwrite her novels. Blacker's explanation of his function clearly reflects on his own history in the profession:

> When projects hit a problem (an overextended biographer, a blocked novelist, a word-blind celebrity), Ollie, the good ghost, would somehow materialise at the right moment. With his help, the biographer miraculously found time to fulfill contracts signed in greed and haste, the novelist recovered her flow, the celebrity discovered articulacy.

This busy thriller-satire includes a kiss-and-tell tabloid figure, Suzi Ashbourn, and a ruthless security service

Cover for the paperback edition of Blacker's 1996 novel, in which the main character is a murderous ghost (Bruccoli Clark Layman Archives)

willing to kill in defense of the good name of the establishment, including the royal family. *The Fame Hotel* is not Blacker's best book, but it is funny as well as dark; its exploration of the ways of authors, ghostwriters, agents, and others involved in manipulating the media and its depiction of a man financially, and then sexually, eclipsed by his wife all give a foretaste of the more powerful use of the same elements in *Kill Your Darlings.*

In a 1997 interview Blacker confided that though he does not believe in God, he believes in ghosts, and his novel *Revenance* has a ghost as its main character. Into Burthorpe, an East Anglian village near Diss, comes a mysterious young woman named Margaret, and shortly afterward, people begin to die mysteriously. Two teenagers having sex in a parked car are felled by a tree that drops onto the vehicle. A secretary is killed at her desk. Two men who try to drive off some "travelers" are themselves killed. It is clear to the reader that Margaret is doing the killing; the mystery is about why she does it and who she is.

She has placed her hopes on the undertaker, Matthew Turville, who she thought might "correct" her, as he corrected the dead bodies under his care; and when Turville, worried about business, said "we need more deaths," Margaret began killing people. This motive explains why some of them seem to "deserve" killing and others do not. As for who Margaret is, she is revealed to be the mistress of sixteenth-century poet and clergyman John Skelton, who was the vicar of Diss. Mistreated by him, she returns (in other words, she is a revenant) to "be rescued from eternity by love."

Along with this ghostly thriller, as readers should expect from Blacker, there is ample satire, in this case on modern village life. Burthorpe is filled with unholy loves: most of the villagers are having affairs; the village shopkeeper is a pervert who spends his time watching dirty videos while dressed in a girl's school uniform; and one woman (Turville's mistress) begins having vivid fantasies about sex with celebrities and is eventually sent off to a private clinic after "her attempted rape of a young milkman from Palgrave while suffering under the illusion that the youth was the film star Kevin Costner with whom she had spent the previous night." The aristocratic landowner is unable to maintain his family estate and ends up turning it into a conference center after, having seen the ghostly Meg, he converts to Christianity.

The only faintly intellectual or literary personage is Miles Larwood, a thanatologist and minor academic writing a book on ghosts, quotations from which help the reader understand the events of the novel. He is the one person in on Margaret's secret. Blacker's description of Larwood is a good example of his characterization:

> Beneath the sandy locks of hair that descended stringily on to the collar of his shirt, he had the stooped shoulders and papery complexion of a man who had spent too much of his life in libraries, whose attention to academic detail had been achieved at considerable cost in terms of general physical comeliness. There had been those, some ten or twenty years ago, who had found in his gaunt, distracted features a sort of ascetic charm, but as his nature (solitary and ruminative) found expression in his face, as the muscle tone slackened around his cheeks and chin, as his own concern for matters of personal appearance, particularly in the nasal area, grew ever more haphazard, it had seemed that Miles's reputation and conversation–neither of which were exceptional–now counted as his strongest personal attributes.

Aside from its mystery elements and the effective satire on modern village life, *Revenance* is concerned with love, real love as opposed to its substitutes and displacements. The spokesperson for this value is Margaret, who explains,

> Why do we return? Why do we come back to meddle in your lives? Perhaps because there is something unresolved, some unanswered question which will not let us rest until we find, even if it takes centuries, the time that will furnish the answer, the person who, in an act of love and revenge, will release us and give us peace.

As her love was devalued by Skelton, she is doomed to be disappointed again by her chosen modern lover.

"Against the odds," wrote Carl Macdougall in the 20 January 1996 *Herald* (Glasgow), "*Revenance* turns out to be a novel about the redeeming power of love, even if it comes from unexpected quarters and in unexpected forms." Macdougall went on to call it "the sort of bleak condition-of-England book in which Blacker specialises. There is less broad comedy than in the earlier novels. Blacker's vision has become . . . well, blacker." John Melmoth, in the 14 April 1996 *Sunday Times* (London), read the novel as evidence of the author's "decidedly dim view of things. *Revenance* is his third novel and his third novel without a single amiable inhabitant. . . . Bad behavior is his fictional territory; naughtiness is fundamental to his view of human nature." Tom Adair, in *Scotland on Sunday* (21 January 1996), welcomed the novel as "a map of our relation to the natural and the supernatural worlds, and of their relationship with each other. Not since *First Light* by Peter Ackroyd (back in 1989) has a comic novel sustained its novelty so acutely, while linking past and present, the terrestrial and the ethereal, the lyrical and the metaphysical aspects of life in quintessential England."

In 1983, *Granta,* the English literary magazine, published its first list of the twenty best young British novelists; it included such promising names as Amis, Pat Barker, Julian Barnes, Graham Swift, Rose Tremain, and, at least according to *Kill Your Darlings,* Gregory Keays, then famous as author of *Forever Young.* Since then most of the others on the list have gone on to greater fame. Keays, the narrator of Blacker's most recent novel, has disappeared. Once profiled in Sunday supplements (shown with his attractive wife, Marigold, in their lovely home), invited to write and read, and expected to publish another book, he now sits in his study trying to write his new novel, "Insignificance," while keeping himself just barely in the literary world with such work as interviewing celebrity novelists for *Professional Writer* and compiling *The Book of Literary Lists.* (Selections from this work, such as "Top Five Peculiar Erotic Habits of the Great Writers," appear throughout *Kill Your Darlings.*) The phrase "kill your darlings," attributed to William Faulkner, speaks of the writer's

Dust jackets for the first U.K. edition and U.S. edition of Blacker's 2000 novel, about the frustrations of a once-promising British novelist (Bruccoli Clark Layman Archives and Richland County Public Library)

ruthless willingness to edit out even his favorite material from his own work. In this novel it also takes on a darker meaning.

Keays is a brilliant creation. He is pathetic: he has seen his wife become successful and rich as a fashionable feng shui designer, and now Marigold, contemptuous of her dependent husband's literary and human failures, is openly unfaithful to him; his son, Doug, is disappointing, mysterious, incommunicative, and possibly crack-addicted; the literary world has forgotten he exists. He is also sinister, possessed of a conviction that the artistic life authorizes anything, from neglect of his family to complicity in dreadful crimes.

His involvement with two writers fuels the complex plot. One of these is Peter Gibson, a student in his creative-writing class who, surprisingly, is an austere, dedicated, and brilliant writer; Keays has an affair with him, and after he breaks it off and Gibson kills himself, he steals the young man's manuscript, which he decides to publish as his own work, titled *terpsichore*. There is much self-delusion about using Peter's work as research material, about his own role in a "deft and complex *pas de deux* with the shade of Peter Gibson, transcribing, reshaping, ordering, editing, often creating several paragraphs of new material," but his daily trips to dispose of the shredded manuscript in remote recycling bins reveals the truth.

The other writer is almost the opposite of Gibson; a famous criminal called Brian (Pussy) McWilliam, he puts his name on books but hardly even pretends to have any hand in writing them. Keays meets him on assignment for *Professional Writer* and becomes entangled in his life–he ghostwrites McWilliam's book *Lolitaville,* a frank account of his sex life with underaged girls that has to be ironized and renamed *Nymph, in Thy Orisons* to reassure the publisher. In return McWilliam provides his own kind of services to Keays.

Most of the interest of *Kill Your Darlings* arises from the picture of Keays and the broader picture of the literary world in which he struggles to hold a place. Keays has written parts of several novels since his early success, and the recital of them is a shorthand history of literary fashions over two decades: "Tell Me the Truth about Love, about Love" (his "zeitgeisty" book of short stories imitating Raymond Carver), "Mind the Gap" (his "London novel"), "Adultery in Hampstead," "Giving It Large" (his "comedy of contemporary male lifestyle"), even his imitation of Irvine Welsh's Edinburgh lowlife fiction, "Gang Hoot Yer Heeb, Auchtermuchty."

One reason that Keays can never complete a project is that he finds himself forestalled by his more successful contemporary, Amis, and his anxiety and envy of Amis provide a strong characterizing note. He worries about whether Amis knows who he is; he refers to him as "the small man"; he even compares physical equipment with him in an accidental encounter in the men's room at a literary festival. When he sees Marigold reading Amis's *Night Train* (1997), he challenges her, producing her response:

> "You hate him because he's done all the things that you should have done, written the books that you should have written."
>
> I allowed a few minutes for the full idiocy of this charge to become clear to her. When I spoke again, it was in cool and measured tones. "As it happens, I had a lot of time for him up to the time of his Eighties novel. No one could regret the catastrophic decline in his talent over the last few years more than I do."
>
> "Poor Gregory. He's sent you round the twist."
>
> "In fact, as a fellow author, I feel profound sympathy for the man. When *terpsichore* appears, he'll be finished. Cultural journalist? Of course. Humorist? Maybe. Serious novelist? Sorry, Mart, you're not even close."

Amis is an enormous figure in English letters, and the representation of Keays's Amis envy assumed unreasonable proportions in some of the reactions to *Kill Your Darlings.* Before its publication, Maurice Chittenden wrote in the *Sunday Times* (23 April 2000) that Amis would be "wickedly portrayed as a philanderer, a bad father and a dinner party bore in a rival author's new work" and claimed that Amis's lawyers would consider libel actions. Chittenden quoted Blacker as saying, "I have never met Amis. . . . I am a tremendous admirer of Amis." Some reviewers seemed to read the novel as a literary roman à clef, others (more accurately) as a "study in self-delusion," a "racy, witty commentary on the media and literary scene," and a "marvellous satire on the arbitrariness of literary celebrity." D. J. Taylor, writing in the *Sunday Times* (16 January 2000), concluded that "However grim in some of its conclusions–and at the very least this ought to be required reading for any bright-eyed teenager who fancies a career as a novelist–much of the action is frankly, and uncomfortably, hilarious: a kind of horrorshow entertainment in which anyone professionally connected to the world of books will scarcely know where to look." David Robson–looking beyond the nervous references to "Mart" and the deft satire on the world of publishing–wrote in the *Sunday Telegraph* (16 July 2000) that "Character after character, from Keays's glacial wife to his young literary protégé, turning neurosis into art, is rendered in a richly three-dimensional humanity, which allows us to laugh at their shortcomings without sneering at them. Best of all is the bitter, complex hero: a man on the cusp of total cynicism, but still capable of personal tenderness and professional idealism."

Melmoth's claim that "bad behavior" is Blacker's "fictional territory" and "naughtiness is fundamental to his view of human nature" is fully borne out by *Kill Your Darlings,* his most fully achieved book. Melmoth's claim, though, that the author has a "decidedly dim view of things" is less sure. A decidedly dim view of bad writers, of rotten husbands, of phony artists, of murderers, thieves, sexual predators–surely one is right to disapprove. Blacker also offers, however, even in Keays, a sometimes touching humanness to go along with the inhuman ambition and self-deception. Moreover, he is a novelist whose truest bent is toward the satirical and the darkly comic.

Perhaps Terence Blacker's gentler feelings are reserved for his children's fiction; and indeed, his more straightforward acts of admiration and political gesture appear in his regular column in *The Independent,* where he addresses questions of authorship, popular culture, war, and peace. In his literary fiction he faces squarely the shortcomings of contemporary men and women and converts his findings into art that is intelligent and deeply satisfying.

Interviews:

Maurice Johnson, "Tricks of the Trade," *Sunday Times* (London), Features section, 6 September 1992;

John Morrish, "The Ghosts of Boyhood Belief: Me and My God. Terence Blacker Talks to John Morrish," *Sunday Telegraph,* Features section, 11 May 1997, p. 4;

Jeremy Boyd Maunsell, "How I Write," *Times* (London), Metro section, 9 September 2000, p. 19.

Melvyn Bragg

(6 October 1939 –)

Gillian Fenwick
University of Toronto

BOOKS: *For Want of a Nail* (London: Secker & Warburg, 1965; New York: Knopf, 1965);
The Second Inheritance (London: Secker & Warburg, 1966; New York: Knopf, 1967);
Without a City Wall (London: Secker & Warburg, 1968; New York: Knopf, 1969);
The Hired Man (London: Secker & Warburg, 1969; New York: Knopf, 1970);
A Place in England (London: Secker & Warburg, 1970; New York: Knopf, 1971);
The Nerve (London: Secker & Warburg, 1971; New York: Knopf, 1972);
Josh Lawton (London: Secker & Warburg, 1972; New York: Knopf, 1972);
The Silken Net (London: Secker & Warburg, 1974; New York: Knopf, 1974);
Speak for England: An Essay on England, 1900–1975 (London: Secker & Warburg, 1976); republished as *Speak for England: An Oral History of England, 1900–1975* (New York: Knopf, 1977);
A Christmas Child (London: Secker & Warburg, 1976);
Autumn Manoeuvres (London: Secker & Warburg, 1978; New York: Knopf, 1978);
Kingdom Come (London: Secker & Warburg, 1980);
Land of the Lakes (London: Secker & Warburg, 1983; New York: Norton, 1984);
Love and Glory (London: Secker & Warburg, 1983);
Laurence Olivier (London: Hutchinson, 1984; New York: St. Martin's Press, 1985);
Abuses of Literacy? Michael Holroyd and Melvyn Bragg Debate the Motion That "Television Is the Enemy of Literature," by Bragg and Michael Holroyd (London: Folio Society, 1985);
The Hired Man: A Musical, by Bragg and Howard Goodall (London & New York: S. French, 1986);
The Maid of Buttermere (London: Hodder & Stoughton, 1987; New York: Putnam, 1987);
Rich: The Life of Richard Burton (London: Hodder & Stoughton, 1988); republished as *Richard Burton: A Life* (Boston: Little, Brown, 1989);

Melvyn Bragg (photograph © London Weekend Television; from the dust jacket for The Sword and the Miracle, *1996)*

A Time to Dance (London: Hodder & Stoughton, 1990; Boston: Little, Brown, 1990);
A Time to Dance: The Screenplay (London: Sceptre, 1992);
Crystal Rooms (London: Hodder & Stoughton, 1992);
The Seventh Seal (London: BFI Publishing, 1993);
Credo (London: Sceptre, 1996); republished as *The Sword and the Miracle* (New York: Random House, 1996);
On Giants' Shoulders: Great Scientists and Their Discoveries from Archimedes to DNA, by Bragg and Ruth Gardiner (London: Hodder & Stoughton, 1998; New York: John Wiley, 1999);

The Soldier's Return (London: Sceptre, 1999; New York: Arcade, 2002);

Two Thousand Years, The First Millennium: The Birth of Christ to the Crusades, by Bragg and Peter Partner (London: Granada Media, 1999);

Two Thousand Years: From Medieval Christendom to Global Christianity, by Bragg and Partner (London: Granada Media, 1999);

The Routes of English, 3 volumes, by Bragg and Simon Elmes (London: BBC, 2000–2001);

A Son of War (London: Sceptre, 2001).

Edition: *The Cumbrian Trilogy* (London: Hodder & Stoughton, 1984)–comprises *The Hired Man, A Place in England,* and *Kingdom Come.*

PLAY PRODUCTIONS: *Mardi Gras,* by Bragg, Alan Blaikley, and Ken Howard, London, Prince of Wales Theatre, 18 March 1976;

The Hired Man, by Bragg and Howard Goodall, Southampton, Nuffield Theatre, 2 February 1984; London, Astoria Theatre, 31 October 1984;

King Lear in New York, Chichester, Chichester Festival Theatre, 1992.

PRODUCED SCRIPTS: *The Debussy Film,* television, by Bragg and Ken Russell, 1963;

Always on Sunday, television, by Bragg and Russell, 29 June 1965;

Isadora, motion picture, by Bragg, Clive Exton, and Margaret Drabble, Hakim / Paris Film / Universal, 1968; released in the United States as *The Loves of Isadora,* 1968;

Play Dirty, motion picture, by Bragg and Lotte Colin, Lowndes / United Artists, 1968;

Charity Begins at Home, television, 1970;

The Music Lovers, motion picture, Russfilms / United Artists, 1970;

Zinotchka, television, 1972;

Jesus Christ Superstar, motion picture, by Bragg and Norman Jewison, Universal, 1973;

Maria Callas: An Operatic Biography, television, 1973;

The Literary Island, television, 1976;

Orion, television, by Bragg, Ken Howard, and Alan Blaikley, 1977;

Clouds of Glory: The Rime of the Ancient Mariner, television, by Bragg and Russell, 1978;

Clouds of Glory: William and Dorothy, television, by Bragg and Russell, 9 July 1978;

Laurence Olivier: A Life, television, 1982;

The Planets, television, 1983;

Land of the Lakes, television, 1983;

Vaughan Williams, television, 1986;

Richard Burton: In from the Cold, television, 1988;

The Modern World: Ten Great Writers, television series, 1988;

The Maid of Buttermere, motion picture, 1989;

The Tall Guy, radio, 1989;

Marathon: The Flames of Peace, motion picture, 1992;

A Time to Dance, television series, 1992;

Classic Widows, television, 1995.

OTHER: *My Favourite Stories of Lakeland,* edited by Bragg (Guildford: Lutterworth, 1981);

Cumbria in Verse, edited by Bragg (London: Secker & Warburg, 1984);

George Bernard Shaw, *The Fabian Society: Its Early History,* preface by Bragg (London: Fabian Society, 1984);

D. H. Lawrence, *Aaron's Rod,* Cambridge Edition of the Works of D. H. Lawrence, introduction by Bragg (London: Grafton, 1989);

Salman Rushdie, *The Wizard of Oz,* edited by Bragg and Richard Maltby (London: BFI Publishing, 1992);

Poems for Alan Hancox, edited by Bragg (Lower Marston: Whittington, 1993);

Thomas Hardy, *An Imaginative Woman and Other Stories,* edited by Bragg (London: Phoenix, 1998);

"Television and the Arts," in *Vision: Fifty Years of British Creativity,* introduction and commentaries by Michael Raeburn (London & New York: Thames & Hudson, 1999).

Melvyn Bragg has published seventeen novels since 1965, an achievement that would satisfy many writers. He has also published twelve nonfiction books, seven screenplays, and two stage plays. He has edited and contributed to other books and written literally hundreds of magazine and newspaper articles. He has written for the *Daily Mail* and the *Evening Standard* and is a regular writer and reviewer for *The Guardian* and *The Observer.*

These accomplishments would suggest that Bragg has had a full career as a modern man of letters, but in fact they represent only a small fraction of his professional life. Prolific writer though he is, Bragg is best known for his work in broadcasting, chiefly in British television, but also in radio. For forty years he has worked in the forefront of British arts broadcasting as a presenter, producer, editor, and writer. He is the preeminent figure in arts broadcasting in Britain. He has brought the arts into the living rooms of the masses with pioneering, award-winning programs on theater, opera, motion pictures, music, the visual arts, and literature. He is a formidable critic and analyst. Further, he has also promoted and made a significant contribution to the popularization of science and the social sciences with important broadcast programs and books on language, the history of science, globalization, democracy, religious history, the history of ideas, and intellectual history. He is president of the National Campaign for the Arts and chancellor of the University of Leeds. He is known as a strong supporter of the Labour Party and was created a life peer in 1998, Lord Bragg of Wigton. He lives in north London at Hampstead and in Cumbria.

Melvyn Bragg was born on 6 October 1939 in the north of England at Wigton, Cumbria, then called Cumberland. Wigton is small–in Bragg's words, a "tight little town"–a market town in a working-class community of farming and engineering industries. His father, John Bragg, was, from time to time, a coal miner, a farm laborer, and factory worker. He went off to the war in the Royal Air Force and returned to work in factory jobs and as a bookie before becoming the tenant landlord of a local pub. His mother, Mary Ethel Bragg, worked in biscuit and clothing factories. Bragg has described an uneventful, warm, and secure childhood, even though the family was poor and times were difficult. He was always reading, never without a book under his arm. He says that the greatest gift his parents gave him was that they left him alone.

Bragg's possibilities might have been limited had not the 1944 Education Act opened up opportunities for children such as he. At eleven he won a scholarship to the local grammar school, the Nelson Thomlinson School, where he did well, not least in mathematics and biology, although, as he remembers, his imagination looked no further than teaching and the civil service as possible careers. Supported by his parents and an enlightened history teacher, he won a scholarship to Wadham College, Oxford, to read modern history in 1958. He graduated with a very good honours B.A. He wrote for the Oxford University magazine *Cherwell,* acted in the Oxford University Dramatic Society, and made a movie with the director Gavin Millar. He has said that, not least, Oxford gave him time to think about himself.

Bragg met Marie-Elisabeth "Lise" Roche when they were both students at Oxford in the late 1950s. Her origins were French. They married in 1961 and had a daughter, Marie-Elsa. Roche was also a writer, and she published a novel, *A Summer's Reckoning* (1968; published in the United States as *The Fool's Heart* in 1969).

Bragg began a career with the British Broadcasting Corporation (BBC) in 1961 as a general trainee in television. Within two years he was a producer for the prestigious arts program *Monitor.* He directed movies, including a portrait of orchestra conductor Sir John Barbirolli. His name first came to broad public notice in 1963 when he wrote *The Debussy Film,* directed by Ken Russell. In 1964 he was appointed editor of *New Release,* the first arts program on the BBC2 television channel.

Dust jacket for the U.S. edition of Bragg's 1968 novel, in which a successful writer leaves London for a remote Cumberland village (Richland County Public Library)

He has been involved in broadcasting in Britain ever since, for the BBC and for Independent Television (ITV), first as a producer, writer, and editor, and later as a presenter. From 1974 until 1978 he was the presenter and producer of the BBC's *Second House, Read All about It,* and an interviewer on *Tonight.* Critical analyses of the arts like his *Second House* and book programs such as *Read All about It* brought a new and popular informality to the stuffy world of British culture in the 1970s. He moved to Independent Television in 1978, first as editor and presenter of *The South Bank Show,* the longest-running arts program on British television, and then as controller of arts for London Weekend Television in 1990. He is a household name, his nasal northern accent affectionately mimicked by stand-up comedians.

His broadcasting career has matured to include his interests in the sciences and social sciences. His radio broadcasting illustrates this development well. From 1988 to 1998 he wrote and presented a weekly Monday morning BBC radio program, *Start the Week,* a general discussion program with a panel chiefly of celebrities in the arts. After a couple of years he decided to change the casting and introduced academics. The audience liked the change, and so he began to concentrate on inviting scientists. He followed this program with a series on the history of science, *On Giants' Shoulders,* and another, *In Our Time,* on which prominent academics discuss cultural and scientific movements and ideas that have changed the world. He has written and presented four radio series on language; *The Routes of English,* chronicling a thousand years of spoken English; and two ITV series on the history of Christianity, specially produced to mark the millennium. He has chaired television forums on globalization and democracy, evolution and human society.

In addition to being a well-known broadcaster, however, Bragg has created a parallel career as a writer. While his fiction writings have won him a few literary awards, his reputation as a novelist has been overshadowed by his broadcasting career. Yet, the sheer volume of his output clearly indicates that writing is an activity that occupies a good proportion of his time. Because he is seen as a television celebrity, his novels are often viewed and reviewed somewhat cynically. There is never a sense, however, that Bragg is cashing in on his celebrity status when it comes to his novels. He clearly thinks of himself as a writer, and, when he is writing novels, his broadcasting life is put aside. There are only a few cases where the celebrity persona enters his fictional plots, and they are perhaps the least successful novels. Significantly, he divides his time between Cumbria and London, because in a sense the tensions between north and south are fundamental to an understanding of Bragg. His best novels are set in the north; his fame emanates from London. Division and tension are not necessarily negative, however, and in Bragg's case it appears that they coexist happily and even productively.

It is difficult not to look back to Bragg's roots in considering his writing. Wigton remains a constant presence in his novels. He has brought his family roots to the fore in his most autobiographical novels to date, *The Soldier's Return* (1999) and *A Son of War* (2001). The community and his contradictory sense of both belonging and of trying to hold it at arm's length for analysis remain strong themes in his novels. The sense of place and landscape stay strong. Bragg himself is a constant reminder of those geographical roots. Despite an Oxford education and forty years in London no one hearing his voice would ever doubt his origins. Beyond place, Bragg's temporal roots are also significant. He was born within five weeks of the outbreak of World War II. His early years were marked by the absence of his father at the war. He grew up during a time of major social change in Britain: the birth of the welfare state, new educational opportunities, and the development of new technology. His career began during the cultural revolution of the 1960s.

He says he manages to balance his writing with his other work by compartmentalizing his life and by not having any hobbies. Because he was already experimenting with fiction when he started his professional career with the BBC, he found ways to fit it in and to continue to write, although at that time he had few hopes of publishing. He was getting up at five in the morning in order to write and then writing on weekends.

Critical accounts of Bragg's life and work tend to say that his reputation as a novelist was established early, in the mid 1960s, by his string of Cumbrian novels. Such an assessment sounds positive and implies security, when in fact this early success has limited Bragg's reputation and perhaps even his writing. He has remained conservative and compromising with both form and content in his fiction. Only in his last two autobiographical novels, intimate portraits of his father, as he admits, has he found his true writing voice. They have brought him more praise as a writer than any of his previous novels, winning prizes and critical acclaim. They have suddenly boosted his literary reputation and, perhaps for the first time in nearly forty years, led to hopes and expectations of Bragg as a serious novelist.

His first published novel, *For Want of a Nail* (1965), was written while Bragg was training at the BBC. It was not the first novel he had written, though the half-dozen efforts he had already made were not, to his own mind, good enough for publication. He was aware that the novel was largely a middle-class genre and that working-class characters were generally relegated to caricature and stereotype. He determined to write about them from a new perspective, from the inside, and with greater honesty and realism. Critical accounts have too simplistically tried to place Bragg's early novels in a postwar-liberal, lower middle class tradition of provincial realism of which Kingsley Amis's fiction is perhaps the best example. Bragg belongs to a different, younger, northern, working-class world, deeply rooted in place and local character. His Cumbrian books are not urban novels, and yet neither are they rural, for despite the fact that Bragg has written and broadcasted on the Lake District, Wigton is outside its pastoral idyll and Romanticism. They are also, to a great extent, timeless novels, with the specifics of dates, wars, and contemporary life glossed over.

For Want of a Nail opens in the wild, John Peel hunting country of Cumberland. Tom Graham is growing up there in a poor family, painfully shy, often confused, wildly imaginative, and yet afraid of change. He is well educated, both formally at the local schools and in the ways of the local world, its histories and peculiar-

Dust jacket for Bragg's 1972 novel, about an orphaned boy in Cumbria (Bruccoli Clark Layman Archives)

ities, by his increasingly eccentric grandfather. The characters, not least Tom, draw on Bragg's own family and childhood–the beautiful mother working hard to keep the family respectable, the father working as a bookie's runner while trying to hold down his factory job, the clever boy who can do complicated arithmetic in his head and can rattle off all the players on the local football team. He is a loner, partly from fear of bullying, partly from choice, partly from neglect. He wonders whether he will be a priest or a boxer. Safe in the ritual of the Anglican Church, he nonetheless needs to be aggressive to make his way in the world. Tom feels misunderstood and betrayed by lies, his own and others', and as he grows into adolescence he turns increasingly within himself. He is selfish and brooding, by turns violent and ashamed, proud in his solitude and yet reluctant to admit that he is totally alone. Oxford offers him the possibility of independence, but the uncovering of the past finally releases him. The plot is predictable: there is a family mystery Tom cannot unravel; he is bright and going places in the world; sooner or later his world will change. The characters are perhaps too black-and-white, the dialogue self-conscious in its effort to be rough and local, and the interjected descriptions of the landscape perhaps a little forced. Yet, altogether the novel is successful, and the narrative is compelling in its simplicity and openness.

The critics liked *For Want of a Nail,* although they inevitably compared it to a high standard of works by Thomas Hardy and D. H. Lawrence. Nevertheless, like Hardy, Bragg characterizes landscape and nature. Tom feels that "the whole earth seemed to be trembling with muted battles of passion," and from childhood he is in awe of The Saddle, the brooding mountain behind the town, "the thought of that fell could bring back the smell of the sweet, heavy fields which flowed from its feet like a train . . . its flint jaws could turn his mind to a flash of white and sear his thoughts with trepidation."

Then, like Lawrence, Bragg writes about a particular local setting that influences characters and events. Further, although Bragg was virtually unknown at this time, the bildungsroman nature of the novel suggested that it might well be autobiographical and, particularly because of the tense, complex relationship between the mother and son, suggested comparisons with Lawrence's *Sons and Lovers* (1913). The novel was perceived to be the work of someone who knew and loved his characters and landscapes well enough to write simply and directly about them. Reviewers predicted a bright future for Bragg, pointing to his originality, thoughtfulness, and imagination and praising his keen eye for people and places.

The Second Inheritance (1966) confirmed Bragg as an important new writer in Britain. The central conflicts of the novel are concerned with connections and divisions, tensions and intimacies. The divisions are social and economic; the connections, personal and geographical. Set on the border between Cumbria and Scotland along Hadrian's Wall, itself a marker of division, it concerns two families, the Langleys and the Fosters. The Langleys have been solid local landowners for generations. Arthur Langley leaves the army to run the family estate when his father dies. His good intentions go astray, however, and he becomes increasingly reclusive, neglecting his responsibilities. A friendship develops between Langley and John Foster, the shy, clever son of an ambitious local tenant farmer. They complement and admire each other. Langley's sister, however, jealous at losing her former close relationship with her brother, decides to form her own connection with Foster. The triangle is strange and intense, but Bragg describes their relationship with sensitivity.

The critics praised not only the novel, describing it as poetic and a masterpiece of atmosphere and character, but also Bragg's promise and potential as a novelist. He was described as a formidable writer with a highly charged imagination. He seemed to have found the perfect landscape, literally and imaginatively, for his writing.

So confident was Bragg that he had arrived as a writer that he left the BBC in 1967 in order to concentrate on freelance broadcasting and writing novels and screenplays. Screenplays paid well and financed his novel writing. Over the next seven years he published six novels despite competition for his time from his growing celebrity in broadcasting and, not least, the suicide of Lise Roche in 1971. His early potential was not then fulfilled. In the novels that followed he wrote about Cumbria and London, the two worlds in which he moves.

Like Bragg himself at the time, Richard Godwin, the protagonist of *Without a City Wall* (1968), is a freelance writer. As Bragg did in 1967, he moves from London to a remote Cumberland village. He is escaping from what he sees as the poisonous waste of his life in London despite his outwardly successful career. He is searching for himself, but in the process he finds Janice, an independent, intelligent woman anxious to escape in the opposite direction. Despite their conflicting purposes they become passionately involved and marry. Richard comes to realize that isolation alone does not guarantee distancing, while Janice feels that to dream alone is everything. Their crises are at once both intensely modern and yet timeless.

The book was praised as the best third novel since *Sons and Lovers* and won the Llewelyn Rhys Memorial Prize in 1969, and yet the critics were not unanimously kind. They noted that while Bragg was defiantly challenging and rejecting the smart, self-conscious world of the new literary novel in favor of a solid, traditional, pastoral narrative, rich in description and dialogue, he occasionally spilled over into self-conscious awkwardness. The plot is stagy at times–a contrived miscarriage, a fractured spine, and characters who arrive from London to provide black-and-white contrasts with Richard's new life.

Bragg's next two novels, *The Hired Man* (1969) and *A Place in England* (1970), together with *Kingdom Come* (1980), published a decade later, make up *The Cumbrian Trilogy,* first published under that title in 1984. The novels trace the lives of the men and women of the Tallentire family from rural Cumberland at the end of the nineteenth century to 1980s London. It is family history, inspired by Thomas Mann's *Buddenbrooks* (1901), and once more suggesting autobiography.

At the start of *The Hired Man* eighteen-year-old John Tallentire sets out at two in the morning to present himself at a hiring fair for agricultural laborers. This experience is a humiliating one for a proud man, and it haunts him and makes him restless and determined to be free. He and his brothers live a life that is hard and pinched and occasionally passionate and violent–the huntsmen drink drops of the fox's blood in their beer, for example, and a fight with spades comes close to murder. John becomes a miner and a union man and moves into the town until the war offers him an escape route, only to be literally trapped underground in a pit accident later while his wife dies at home. The novel ends with him once more at a hiring fair. Nothing, and yet everything, has changed. Attitudes to class, to labor, and to authority have all moved on.

Critics again drew parallels with Hardy, noting how, like Hardy, Bragg shows how over time landscape and inhabitants have grown together. His plain, quiet style was notable only for its difference from the contemporary norm. Bragg was compelled to write immaculately, with clarity and precision, painting even his minor characters meticulously in order to make them convincing and con-

Dust jacket for the U.S. edition of Bragg's 1974 novel, in which the main character is based on his late first wife, Lise Roche (Richland County Public Library)

centrating on emotional depths in the place of sensational plotting or innovative technique. As one reviewer noted, his prose had to be perfect. *The Hired Man* won the 1970 Silver Pen Award of the English Centre of the world association of writers, International PEN.

The second part of the trilogy, *A Place in England,* moves the story forward a generation to John's son, Joseph. He is determined never to be bound as his father was. When the novel begins, he is eighteen years old and working as a footman in an aristocratic house. He is dismissed, however, and so forced to return home. As he later says, the dismissal is the best thing that ever happened to him because it made him free from what was then literally "service." He faces unemployment during the Depression and is in and out of a series of jobs until he joins the air force in World War II, again literally "the services." He comes back in peacetime to the same old situation and might have continued to suffer the degradation of never being his own man except that an opening occurs for him to run a down-at-the-heels pub. This opportunity to be independent is one that he has always wanted and that was denied his father. Joseph has come a long way, much further than his father, but he is still trapped in an inarticulate world, unable to express his feelings, without the words to explain his desires. Like his father's, his marriage suffers.

It takes another generation, Joseph's son Douglas's, for education to be widely available to their class. Douglas is at least in part a fictional self-portrait of Bragg. About to go up to Oxford, he plans a novel that will span three generations of a family like his own, although he worries that it is embarrassing to write about people who might recognize themselves. A clearly realized series of scenes building to a complex whole makes the novel work. By Bragg's subtle, painstaking, understated method, there are not sharp climaxes but rather a series of small turns that bring about the conclusion. The autobiographical elements are clear, and Bragg does not come as close to writing about his own immediate family again until *The Soldier's Return* and *A Son of War.* He has acknowledged that those novels are about his father, but *A Place in England* is undoubtedly their forerunner.

Bragg published four more novels between 1970 and 1978 before he completed the Tallentire trilogy with *Kingdom Come.* The protagonist, Douglas Tallentire, has achieved what his father and grandfather were searching for. His education can make him independent, but, as he too discovers, freedom is not easily achieved, and success and happiness are equally elusive. The difference between Douglas and the earlier generations is that he has the language to articulate his doubts and uncertainties. He moves in a world beyond Cumbria, to London and New York, and faces conflict not just from outside but also personal dilemmas within himself.

At the start of the novel Douglas is literally taking an overview of Cumbria from an airplane, but his move to London and his jet-setting celebrity life also make it possible for him to see his roots objectively. He decides to write a memoir "that could be his lifeline back to writing the stuff he could respect himself for." He provides a neat summary of the entire trilogy: "My grandfather was given a spade, a pick or a gun–labourer, miner, soldier–low wages, bare living; large families encouraged, little education, expectation ground down. My father got a little more, but too late in his life . . . and so he drifts in the straits of possibilities he never had the opportunity to learn to navigate." Meanwhile, of himself he says, "I think I've got choices. I can find ways to be more free and more fulfilled. Some of these are illusory. Some already appear to be no more than alternative methods of self-destruction. But what I have the chance to do is to try to weigh up the balance of a number of things and come to my own conclusions about them."

The ending of the novel brings the trilogy full circle: Douglas's son, John, is getting up and going out before dawn. This John Tallentire is free, however, and life for him is "just about perfect," even if he is fishing in an artificial London pond.

By 1972 Bragg was again working for the BBC. He stayed with them until 1978, when he moved to Independent Television to run *The South Bank Show* for London Weekend Television. The early 1970s were difficult years for him. Bragg's next three novels deal with aspects of Lise Roche's life and breakdown and also with his own sense of emptiness and loss of direction after her death. This loss, perhaps, made him return to the BBC and the sense of belonging and familiarity it represented in his life.

The Nerve (1971) began as a short story but became a novel. It is different from Bragg's other books and more experimental, although it deals with his familiar themes of the north and the south, dislocation, and moving between the two different environments. The protagonist, Ted, is a Cumbrian teacher who has left the north to work in London, teaching and book reviewing. With his eyes streaming with tears because of a nerve infection, he is a figure representing the grieving Bragg. He finds that as a northerner living in the south, there are stereotypical expectations of the person he should be, while back in the north he is perceived as now belonging to the soft, southern, arty, intellectual world. Neither view allows him to be himself. He is trapped by prejudice and yet surrounded by characters who fit the stereotypes that deny him his real identity. *The Nerve* describes Ted's breakdown, but it is its form that makes it experimental. Bragg looks at how the content of a book, its meaning, can shape its form. It is a self-conscious novel at many levels and not altogether successful.

Bragg put the conclusion of the Cumbrian trilogy on hold and published a different novel set in Cumbria, *Josh Lawton* (1972). By now it was clear that Cumbria was his territory. In sharp contrast to the discursiveness and chaos of *The Nerve, Josh Lawton* is tight, simple, and controlled. It is the moving story of an orphan who is variously manipulated and used by those around him for their own ends. Josh's beauty and innocence make him particularly vulnerable. In the mix of loves, friendships, and conflicts of a small community, tragedy seems inevitable. His story is all the more poignant when set against the beauty of the town and the natural landscape and the inarticulateness of the local people, once more a factor in Bragg's fiction. Bragg's narration matches their simplicity and is carefully pitched and controlled in order to elicit reader sympathy. Paul Theroux, writing in *The Times* (London), described the novel as having the lilt and inevitability of an old ballad. With *The Hired Man* it is one of his most successful early novels.

The Silken Net (1974) is a fictional portrait of Roche. Rosemary Lewis is, like her, part French. Her parents are both dead, and she grows up in Cumberland. She remains torn between her life in the north of England and a life in the south or in France. She is also torn between two men, a cultured southerner and a rough northerner. It is a rambling novel, not well focused, and it was criticized for its excessive length. It is far from Bragg's best work but was perhaps a novel he felt compelled to write after his wife's death.

For the first time since 1965 Bragg went four years without producing a new novel. Undoubtedly, this circumstance was owing in part to his being busy producing and presenting television series and specials, screenplays, a stage play, and his important nonfiction book *Speak for England* (1976), an oral history of England since 1900. The book is a series of interviews with locals in Wigton. The people describe their lives, the changes three-quarters of a century have brought, and the experience of what it means to be English. The subject was close to Bragg's heart and one to which he might well have been too close to execute objectively. It was criticized at the time for its form rather than its content, Bragg seeming at times unsure whether he was writing social history or fiction. The same could have been said of his novels to date, however, and it may well be that he published no fiction at this time because the other book filled the role of a novel in his writing life.

Dust jacket for the U.S. edition of Bragg's 1987 historical novel, based on the marriage of Mary Robinson, the "Beauty of Buttermere," and her fraudulent suitor (Richland County Public Library)

When he did return to fiction, with *Autumn Manoeuvres* (1978), it was without his former success. It is a dry novel about politics and an election, said to be based on British prime minister James Callaghan's uncertainty about whether to go to the country at this time. In the novel Jimmie Johnston is a member of Parliament in the Labour Party fighting to keep his Cumbrian seat. Meanwhile, he is facing a domestic crisis as his wife fights her own private campaign for her independence. The situation is complicated by the presence at home of their son and his family. The time span, three weeks, gives a tight unity to the otherwise hectic events of political and domestic intrigue, sex, and violence. In reality it was a phantom election that did not happen, but Bragg takes it up, although to little or no critical acclaim in this novel.

Love and Glory (1983) begins in Manhattan, then moves quickly to London and afterward to Bath, Cumbria, Newcastle, New York, and back on the Roman road to Cumbria, following the route of Willie Armstrong, a television writer. From time to time the narrative moves into the first person, in the form of Willie's notebooks and letters. He is trapped between a loveless marriage and a wild, obsessive affair, with other relationships in which people depend on him, although he is vulnerable and needs help himself. It is a novel that hinges on the analysis of relationships. Bragg's scrutiny of the closeness of a couple on a long car journey, for example, is fine and detailed. He analyzes the scene without actually presenting it. Armstrong's mother is calmly dying of cancer as the novel closes. It ends in the first person, movingly.

Apart from completing the Cumbrian trilogy with *Kingdom Come* in 1980, Bragg had written little fiction of note since the early 1970s until he published *The Maid of Buttermere* (1987). This publication was a turning point in his career as a novelist and is dedicated to Cate Haste, whom he had married in 1973 and with whom he has two children. *The Maid of Buttermere* is an historical novel based on the life of Mary Robinson, the "Beauty of Buttermere," and concerns her involvement with an imposter and bigamist at the start of the nineteenth century. The story had attracted a good deal of contemporary attention: William and Dorothy Wordsworth, Charles and Mary Lamb, Samuel Taylor Coleridge, and Thomas De

Quincey all took an interest and drew public awareness to it beyond the local area. Bragg is often erroneously associated with the Lake District, but *The Maid of Buttermere* is the only one of his novels actually set there. While the novel is a romantic tragedy, a story of truth and lies, innocence and guilt, it is also social history, carefully researched by Bragg. It is a long novel, but this time warranting the expansiveness.

In the novel the self-styled Colonel Alexander Augustus Hope, aristocratic M.P. and soldier, arrives in the Lake District on a mission to marry money. He draws his inspiration as an imposter from a London theater performance he saw years before. He is torn within, however, and cannot fully assume his new character because he likes his old self and wants to be the man who "threatened to break through the ranks of plot." Mary has also been forced to play a role. She is widely famous for her beauty, grace, delicacy, and intelligence. Her father is reluctant for her to marry since her fame attracts wealthy tourists to his pub, while Mary hates "the curio she had become." Disgusted by rich young heiresses and by the crudity of loose servant girls, Hope is drawn to the cleansing beauty of nature and to its human expression, Mary, in a new state of innocence himself. He discovers he no longer needs to act: "if you act as you deeply want to act and if that, sublimely, coincides with what you aim for, then nothing is simpler, nothing is more dynamic, nothing is happier." Meanwhile, he is bound to his contract with his business partner in crime, the corrupt Newton, who holds a terrible power over him. He marries Mary: "This was the best of his life," but she soon realizes he has lied to her. Meanwhile, he is a celebrity, even on trial and at his execution. Coleridge drifts through the novel, writing accounts of Mary and the marriage in the London press.

The novel reads in part like social history, the documentary and the invented blending imperceptibly in newspaper articles, letters, court reports, and people. Mary remains slightly remote as a character, although Bragg convinces the reader of her suffering in the passage in which she discovers the letters that reveal the deceit: "She howled aloud, uncaring, heard all over the tiny village, uncontrolled, a sound which came from a pain all but unendurable. People thought that an animal–a fox perhaps–had caught its leg in the steel jaws of one of the traps in Burtness Wood." There is no sustained psychological analysis of how she feels, however. When she is unhappy, she goes out into the natural world to be alone. Hope's character, on the other hand, is far more fully realized through his thoughts and letters and in the narration. As before, in his best writing Bragg characterizes the natural world. In *The Maid of Buttermere* the brooding Lancaster Sands and fast running tides, "the surge and suck of the ocean," maintain a constant, threatening presence.

The Maid of Buttermere fulfilled the promise Bragg's writing had been suggesting for more than twenty years. For the first time he excelled simultaneously in all the fields he knew best–the local landscape, social history, romantic narrative, moral and psychological issues, and detailed characterization. He did not follow this success with novels of a similarly high caliber, however. The three novels he published over the next nine years, *A Time to Dance* (1990), *Crystal Rooms* (1992), and *Credo* (1996), were all new departures. The success of *The Maid of Buttermere* had perhaps given him the confidence to go off the familiar path.

Bragg wrote the screenplay for the 1989 motion-picture adaptation of *The Maid of Buttermere.* Meanwhile, in the late 1980s and 1990s he was more active than ever in radio and television arts and science broadcasting, writing books to accompany series such as *On Giants' Shoulders: Great Scientists and Their Discoveries from Archimedes to DNA* (1998), *Two Thousand Years, The First Millennium* (1999), and *The Routes of English* (2000–2001). Following his biography *Laurence Olivier* (1984), he published the successful *Rich: The Life of Richard Burton* (1988; published in the United States as *Richard Burton: A Life,* 1989). These books moved his writing career in yet another direction.

A Time to Dance is set in Cumbria, but unlike some of the earlier and later novels, it is not truly local or regional. The book, however, is provincial, in that provincial attitudes and morals shape the action and the characters. An unnamed middle-aged retired banker with an older, invalid wife has fallen in love with Bernadette, a teenage girl. Not only thirty-six years divide them, however. He is a pillar of local respectability who lives in a detached Victorian house, writes articles for local newspapers and magazines, and attends meetings of the Rotary Club; she is working-class and from a disreputable local family–"the rough end of town, Roman Catholic, touch of Irish, gambling, loudness, weekend fighting, petty thieving, gaol and dole and drink." When the novel begins, their affair has inevitably already finished, and he writes the letters to her that make up the book. The reader quickly gets inside the mind of the banker, infatuated and obsessed, and, too easily as Bragg no doubt intends, skeptically judges and condemns him for making a fool of himself for sex. He maintains that he was in love with the girl, however, and his conviction is the key to the success of the novel. From a claustrophobic sense of being trapped by the letter writer's consciousness and obsession, the reader begins to be persuaded that he was and still is in love with her, that the whole experience of that love was more important to him than sex, and that his view of the world has changed. The letters are not sent. They are private, "more a document than a letter," as he says, written for himself, explaining himself to himself, a confession and a catharsis.

Bragg has described *A Time to Dance* as a novel of sexual obsession, and at that romantic, headily sensual level it succeeds. He convinces the reader that as a couple their oddness is purely external, and they enjoy idyllic months together until, reading William Hazlitt, the banker discovers distrust. Suspicion destroys his peace, and so he destroys their love with his unfounded jealousy. As critics pointed out, however, if the novel does not fully succeed, it is at the technical level. Working within the limiting epistolary format, Bragg then interrupts the banker's text with a letter from Bernadette, who powerfully, and with a clear sense of self-respect, analyzes her own feelings, drawing parallels from her reading in James Joyce and Lawrence. Angela, the wife, later writes her story in a letter as well, for the first time revealing the depth of her love and offering the banker his freedom. Their letters fill in the blanks of the past, but they strike the banker as awkward in their unexpectedness and frankness. Perhaps also, from the reader's point of view, they do not quite work as a device because the voice, the tone, the style, and the emotion are too homogenous. The voice is always that of an articulate narrator, consciously writing the parts of a story the reader needs to know. Bragg wrote the television adaptation of the novel, broadcast in 1990.

Crystal Rooms is, for Bragg, another experimental novel. Nonetheless, he returns to familiar themes of north versus south, the innocent northern boy in the corrupt capital, the upper classes, privilege, and celebrity versus poverty and defenselessness. Harry, an orphaned boy from a poor northwestern town, is taken to London by Jake, his Aunt Fiona's boyfriend, mainly to get him out of her way. In the shady world of Leicester Square, Jake abandons Harry. The scenes switch between Harry and the rich and famous. There is more than a hint of Charles Dickens's *Oliver Twist* (1838) to the marginal world Harry finds himself in. He falls into the clutches of a pedophilic pimp but enjoys a fairy-tale rescue by a client, Nicholas, a member of Parliament, and moves into his circle of influential friends, including the rich Jen. Harry's fate is not the narrator's immediate concern, however, and he is put on hold as the novel jumps around in time and between different groups of characters in London and Belfast, in and out of steamy bedroom scenes, to lunches and appointments, and to a soccer match, filling in the blanks of the past and the present. Harry's future is bartered by his aunt, but her blackmailing attempts fail, and he is abandoned a second time, this time in the north. In desperation he runs away to Jen in London with his sister, and the fairy tale that is Harry's story ends well.

Dust jacket for the U.S. edition of Bragg's 1990 novel, about a retired banker's affair with a teenage girl (Richland County Public Library)

Crystal Rooms is a multilayered novel, full of slick dialogue and current media jargon with all the associated superficiality, but it is also a novel about the importance of instincts. Harry does not understand what is happening with the pimp. He is puzzled and alarmed but "he was well taught in the intimations of terror and he knew he was in danger," while at the end Jen realizes that she must "scrape off as many layers as she could from the coatings which had hidden and for a time suffocated her. If she was to live a life unencumbered by the magical realism of her great wealth then an understanding of Fiona was important." The narrative suggests that even Fiona's money-grabbing instinct is right in its way. As a novel about the current state of England, it was well received, although it was not a direction Bragg has since followed.

He next published a novel unlike any of his others. *Credo,* published as *The Sword and the Miracle* (1996) in the United States, is set in the Britain of the so-called Dark

Ages. The book is a mixture of ascertainable historical facts and mythical figures, real events and invention. A huge novel, *Credo* is 750 pages long with a multilayered narrative of overlapping stories and characters. In his afterword Bragg describes its origins in schoolboy cycling trips to Bassenthwaite in the Lake District and an isolated seventh-century church there, St. Bega's. At Oxford he studied the period and later read more and began to write about it, haunted by what he describes as the undeniable spirit of the place with its conflicting sense of mystery and accessibility. At one level *Credo* is a novel of adventure, romance, and war, but at another it questions modern ideas of religious faith and love. An Irish princess, Bega, has been given a relic of the True Cross. She therefore struggles to overcome her emotions and sacrifices her hopes of earthly love to become a priestess and to spread the Word of God. It is a story of saints, warriors, and villains, terror and miracles, set against the wildly beautiful and unforgiving northern landscape.

Credo is romantic and escapist, rich, powerful, and totally absorbing, if eventually a little unconvincing. Bega does not quite work as a character. She is indecisive and a little insipid. So, too, is Padric, her would-be lover. He spends his time becoming a warrior and planning to fight evil without actually acting until well on in the novel. Bragg proves, however, that the Dark Ages were culturally rich and not so dark.

The novel succeeds as an escapist epic, sustaining interest with tremendous battles, bloody violence, and passionate conflict. The characters are wooden, however, and the landscape of mountains, lakes, and coasts, which should be wild and memorable, is not a major factor. Bragg can evoke the northern landscape beautifully, but he does not do so in *Credo.*

The Soldier's Return and *A Son of War* are the first two parts of an autobiographical trilogy. They are Bragg's best novels to date. They suggest that for the first time he has fully achieved what he set out to do as a novelist and that he has found his natural voice. They have won him literary awards and a listing for the Booker Prize. *The Soldier's Return* won the W. H. Smith Literary Award in 2000. *A Son of War* was on the Booker long list in 2001, and although it was not eventually short-listed, the consideration represented a significant move up in literary ranking for Bragg.

Bragg has said that his father's death in the mid 1990s changed the way he thought about him and about his own childhood, family, and upbringing. His aim was to take a real, emotional part of his life, turn it into fiction, and thus liberate it. The novel as a form could do what real life over a period of fifty years had failed to do. He wanted to show that ordinary lives are, as he has said, full of nightmares, cliffs, and chasms that can match any more flagrant and spectacular events even if the people involved endure the hardships and stresses in the quiet, understated way of Britain, where nature and culture demand restraint. Bragg has said that he found himself pulled into a novel that revolved around his father.

The Soldier's Return is about a man coming back from the war in Burma in 1946, as Bragg's father did. The story is about the struggle to rebuild lives damaged by war almost as severely as if the father had been killed. Sam is restless and discontented and finds it difficult to return to the old routine of his civilian life. He is not prepared for the recurring nightmare of the sights and actions of war that he cannot discuss. Ellen, his wife, has come to enjoy her independence in her years alone. She wants a better life, especially for their child. Joe, the son, has grown up with only the idea of a father, an icon, and resents Sam's intrusion, not least into his relationship with his mother. The triangular relationship among father, son, and mother is a difficult one, with tension and jealousy as well as love. There are also wider fundamental issues about family life, the breakdown of family relations, the nature of fatherhood and masculinity, and the shape of seemingly ordinary lives.

At the end of the novel Sam jumps from the train taking him away from his family to a new life alone in Australia. He renounces his freedom. It is a dramatic climax to the novel but not a final resolution.

A Son of War takes the family story from 1946 to 1954. It continues the theme of displacement. At the start Sam is still trying to decide if he has made the right decision in not immigrating to Australia. The family is still not settled as they try to repair the emotional damage of the war. Now that he is to be present, Sam takes a more positive role in Joe's future. So while Ellen wants him to learn singing and dancing, Sam buys him boxing gloves and teaches him to defend himself against the tough local gangs. Life is far from easy for Sam and Ellen. Their marriage is shaky not only because of the tension over Joe but also because Sam acts for them both, refusing to move to the house she wants, changing his job, and buying a rundown pub without consulting her. Joe listens to their quarrels, divided in his loyalties. In the end Ellen does what a working-class wife was expected to do, fulfills her duty and patiently endures the hard life Sam has chosen for them both. *A Son of War* is an understated novel, at least at the emotional level, because Bragg's characters are simple, often uneducated, and inarticulate. There are intense emotions, but the characters do not always have the language to describe them–Sam because of trauma, Ellen because of natural reserve and lack of education, Joe because of his youth. Even so, Bragg goes deep into Joe's developing consciousness, and especially into the secret fears children build into living nightmares.

The novel is dense with the feel of life in postwar Britain, the narrowness of horizons, and the tightness of the small community, positive and negative in extremes. *A Son of War* is a story of slow recovery, growing up, secrets revealed, and small domestic dramas. At the end Joe, facing crucial choices about his future, is persuaded by Sam to stay on at school, thus confirming that the saga will continue.

Bragg says he has found a medium that suits him, writing more truly than ever before, deliberately drawing on his own experience with the facts of his life as a starting point, as he stated in a live forum held by BBC News on 18 June 2001. The result is novels that, as he says, matter more to him than any of his other novels. In a BBC website interview he describes the authenticity of his own voice in his fiction as a hard thing to achieve because "A lot of writers write well but they write rather like other writers. The thing you should try to do is to find the voice that you have–however good it is or isn't, it doesn't really matter, as long as it is like nobody else's voice. I think I have finally got there–with this very plain English, very straightforward–and telling the extraordinary story of ordinary lives." He admits that he is surprised that he did not face up to the situation in his writing earlier. Part of his problem might have been that the situation was not dramatic. As he has said, his father survived the war; Wigton was not blitzed; and lives continued even if the former way of life was dead. Much more difficult to relate than absolute loss was the concept of change in society and particularly at the level of the ordinary family and on the mind of the ordinary man.

Bragg's conflicts are many. He was born into the working class in Wigton, Oxford-educated as an historian, matured in London as a broadcaster and arts journalist, and became a media celebrity with a Lakeland poet's sensibility and a determination to be recognized as a novelist. The issues have all bombarded his fiction from time to time: north and south, landscape, education, articulateness, the meaning of community, and the sense of family. There has been no firm, safe territory for him as a novelist, and he may well remain a victim of his celebrity. He admits to feeling an outsider as far as British fiction is concerned since the late 1960s. Criticized for being conservative and traditionalist, he decided to keep going in his own direction, although he also admits to having made a conscious decision in his forties not to make writing fiction his main work. He has said, "The condition in my life since I was 21 has been making a living and writing fiction." Clearly, however, in his mind the two activities are separate.

The authenticity of *The Soldier's Return* and *A Son of War* suggests that Melvyn Bragg is now writing for himself the novels he always should have written. Bragg manages to connect with an audience, with the common reader as well as with the literary critic. In many ways it is a positive thing that his new stature as a novelist has taken so long to achieve. Had it happened in the 1970s or 1980s, critics would have claimed it was merely the spin-off effect of his celebrity. That did not happen, and it might be said that, in fact, his celebrity has counted against him when it comes to his fiction. His route has been unusual in that he has stayed true to his belief in the power of a tale well told, traditional and provincial though that may be labeled. He does not adopt the role of the successful literary figure, feted and admired from afar. As a novelist he stays true to himself, and in writing about himself he has found success.

Dust jacket for the U.S. edition of Bragg's 1996 novel, about the seventh-century prioress St. Bega (Richland County Public Library)

Interview:

Simon Hattenstone, "True Confessions," *Guardian,* 15 April 1999.

References:

Michele Field, "Melvyn Bragg," *Publishers Weekly* (3 February 1989);

Roger Pybus, "The Fiction of Melvyn Bragg," *Stand* (Summer 1970): 68–74.

Brigid Brophy

(12 June 1929 – 7 August 1995)

Merritt Moseley
University of North Carolina at Asheville

and

S. J. Newman

BOOKS: *The Crown Princess and Other Stories* (London: Collins, 1953; New York: Viking, 1953);

Hackenfeller's Ape (London: Hart-Davis, 1953; New York: Random House, 1954);

The King of a Rainy Country (London: Secker & Warburg, 1956; New York: Knopf, 1957);

Black Ship to Hell (London: Secker & Warburg, 1962; New York: Harcourt, Brace & World, 1962);

Flesh (London: Secker & Warburg, 1962; Cleveland: World, 1963);

The Finishing Touch (London: Secker & Warburg, 1963); republished with *The Snow Ball* as *The Snow Ball. The Finishing Touch: Two Novels* (Cleveland: World, 1964);

The Snow Ball (London: Secker & Warburg, 1964); republished with *The Finishing Touch* as *The Snow Ball. The Finishing Touch: Two Novels* (Cleveland: World, 1964);

Mozart the Dramatist: A New View of Mozart, His Operas and His Age (London: Faber & Faber, 1964; New York: Harcourt, Brace & World, 1964); revised as *Mozart the Dramatist: The Value of His Operas, to Him, to His Age, and to Us* (London: Libris, 1988; New York: Da Capo, 1988);

Don't Never Forget: Collected Views and Reviews (London: Cape, 1966; New York: Holt, Rinehart & Winston, 1967);

Fifty Works of English and American Literature We Could Do Without, by Brophy, Michael Levey, and Charles Osborne (London: Rapp & Carroll, 1967; New York: Stein & Day, 1968);

Religious Education in State Schools (London: Fabian Society, 1967);

Black and White: A Portrait of Aubrey Beardsley (London: Cape, 1968; New York: Stein & Day, 1969);

Brigid Brophy (photograph by Jerry Bauer; from the dust jacket for the U.S. edition of In Transit: An Heroi-Cyclic Novel, *1970)*

The Burglar (London: Cape, 1968; New York: Holt, Rinehart & Winston, 1968);

In Transit: An Heroi-Cyclic Novel (London: Macdonald, 1969; New York: Putnam, 1970);

The Longford Threat to Freedom (London: National Secular Society, 1972);

Prancing Novelist: A Defence of Fiction in the Form of a Critical Biography in Praise of Ronald Firbank (London: Macmillan, 1973; New York: Barnes & Noble, 1973);

The Adventures of God in His Search for the Black Girl (London: Macmillan, 1973; Boston: Little, Brown, 1974);

Beardsley and His World (London: Thames & Hudson, 1976; New York: Harmony, 1976);

Pussy Owl (London: BBC, 1976);

Palace without Chairs (London: Hamilton, 1978; New York: Atheneum, 1978);

A Guide to Public Lending Right (Aldershot: Gower, 1983);

The Prince and the Wild Geese (London: Hamilton, 1983; New York: St. Martin's Press, 1983);

Baroque-'n'-Roll, and Other Essays (London: Hamilton, 1987);

Reads (London: Cardinal, 1989).

PLAY PRODUCTION: *The Burglar,* London, Vaudeville Theatre, 25 February 1967.

PRODUCED SCRIPT: *The Waste-Disposal Unit,* radio, BBC, April 1964.

OTHER: Elizabeth Smart, *By Grand Central Station I Sat Down and Wept,* introduction by Brophy (London: Grafton, 1966; New York: Popular Library, 1966);

"The Young Mozart," in *Opera 66,* edited by Charles Osborne (London: Ross, 1966), pp. 209–230;

Jane Austen, *Pride and Prejudice,* introduction by Brophy (London: Pan, 1967);

The Waste-Disposal Unit, in *Best Short Plays of the World Theatre 1958–1967,* edited by Stanley Richards (New York: Crown, 1968), pp. 37–51;

Maurice Hill and Michael Lloyd-Jones, *Sex Education: The Erroneous Zone,* foreword by Brophy (London: National Secular Society, 1970);

Lionel Salter, trans., *W. A. Mozart: Die Zauberflote/Die Entfuhrung aus dem Serail,* introduction by Brophy (London: Cassell, 1971; New York: Universe, 1971);

"The Way of No Flesh," in *The Genius of Shaw: A Symposium,* edited by Michael Holroyd (London: Hodder & Stoughton, 1979; New York: Holt, Rinehart & Winston, 1979), pp. 94–111;

"The Darwinist's Dilemma," in *Animals' Rights: A Symposium,* edited by David Paterson and Richard D. Ryder (Fontwell: Centaur, 1979).

Brigid Brophy, who died in 1995 after a long struggle against multiple sclerosis, lived one of the most interesting, emblematic careers among writers of her generation. She was an enfant terrible of the 1960s, a fearless and sometimes reckless controversialist, a tireless champion of a broader sphere of human and animal rights, and a campaigner for the dignity and prosperity of the writer's profession. Though she was a public figure for many years, a sort of byword of outrageousness for some observers–and there is no doubt that, her own denials notwithstanding, she did in part court publicity–she was entirely serious about art. *Ars longa, vita brevis;* but for Brophy, a classicist, the life outlasted her literary acclaim. After early and extravagant fame, she has lapsed into later undeserved obscurity. By the time of her death Brophy's work was mostly out of print; after years of campaigning for Public Lending Right (an arrangement permitting authors to be paid royalties on the circulation of their books by public libraries), she was no longer in a position to benefit, her books no longer circulating much.

Those who remember her from the 1960s, when she "leapt upon the literary scene" (in 1953, with the publication of her first novel), testify to her unforgettable impact. *Nova* called her "the tigress, that crafty slasher"; allegedly, the *Sunday Express* threatened to burn her as a witch. Others called her "the arch-priestess of the permissive society, one of the rare and precious human beings who have done something positive, and a saint." Her own self-descriptions are much less extreme, though she insisted that "I am really most interested in intensity. I cannot stand anything that is lukewarm." In 1987 she called herself "an old fashioned Shavian socialist, untinged and untainted by Thatcherism." Her longtime friend Giles Gordon summed her up in his obituary:

> Atheist, vegetarian, socialist, novelist and short-story writer; humanist; biographer; playwright (*The Burglar* had a brief West End run in 1967); Freudian promoter of animal rights; children's author (the adventures of Pussy Owl, only progeny of Edward Lear's pair); tennis fanatic (not least Navratilova) and, on television, football fancier; most loyal of friends; reverer of Jane Austen; lover of Italy; Mozart adorer (her radical *Mozart the Dramatist: a new view of Mozart, his operas and his age,* 1964, was reissued in a new edition in 1989); aficionado of the English National Opera (but not of the Royal Opera House); disliker of "Shakespeare in performance"; smoker of cigarettes in a chic holder and painter of her fingernails purple; mother, grandmother, wife; feminist; lover of men and women; Brigid Brophy was above all an intellectual, which British (though she was Irish) authors aren't supposed to be. We mistrust logical, rational thought in our writers, finding it

Dust jacket for the U.S. edition of Brophy's 1962 novel, about the marriage of a young Jewish couple in north London (Richland County Public Library)

easier to live with instinct, intuition. Brophy was ever the Aristotelian logician.

Brigid Antonia Brophy was born on 12 June 1929. The daughter of a novelist and a teacher–John Brophy and his wife, Charis Weare Brophy–she grew up in London but visited Ireland, her father's home, often and thought of herself (though inconsistently) as an Irishwoman. She was a precocious reader and, she maintained, a hereditary writer. She began by writing poetic dramas, read Oscar Wilde, George Bernard Shaw, and Ronald Firbank (all lifelong devotions) as a small child, and, reportedly, read James Joyce's *Finnegans Wake* (1939) at the age of nine. She learned English and Latin from her mother and the beginnings of her tools as a writer from her father. She remained devoted to both parents but said, ten years after her father's death, that she was closer to him because they had more in common.

When she was eleven years old, she was scheduled to be evacuated from Britain, to escape the German bombing campaign, but at the last minute decided not to go. She was educated at a succession of schools, including St. Paul's Girls' School, and in 1947 matriculated at St. Hugh's College, Oxford, to which she had received a Jubilee Scholarship. She spent four terms at Oxford and was then expelled; different accounts of her life give different explanations of her offense, though she said it was sexual. Suggestions are that her discovery of her bisexuality might have been involved, or some impropriety in chapel; at any rate, she admitted to having been drunk for six straight weeks before her dismissal.

After Oxford, she worked as a shorthand typist in London, writing short stories in her spare time (though the first version of one of these stories was written during a Latin class while she was still at school). Her first collection of stories, *The Crown Princess and Other Stories,* appeared in 1953; it received some admiring reviews. Later that year she published her first novel, the genesis of which she has described:

> In my twenty-fifth year, I sat down to write a narrative poem and rose a fortnight later (a fortnight of which I have no memory) having written instead a brief novel called *Hackenfeller's Ape,* which is probably the best I shall ever write and which already displays at its most intense the violently romantic feeling in a precisely classical form to which most of my fiction aspires.

Hackenfeller's Ape received the Cheltenham Literary Festival first prize for a first novel in 1954. That year Brophy married Michael Levey, who was both the director of the National Gallery (until he took early retirement to care for her after her illness) and the author of many books, including one that he coauthored with Brophy, as well as works on art. Their marriage was closely scrutinized, at least in part because of her provocative pronouncements on the institution–"I think it's highly unnatural to be married," or "my husband is a wife"–as well as her revelations of her bisexuality. By all accounts it was a happy union. They had one daughter, Katharine. Until 1979, when she was diagnosed with multiple sclerosis, Brophy remained a public figure; she broadcast regularly on television and radio, wrote copiously for periodicals, and appeared at literary festivals. Most of her novels appeared in the 1960s; her campaigns on behalf of writers occupied more of her time in the 1970s. She published four books after the onset of illness.

In *Review of Contemporary Fiction* (Fall 1995), Steven Moore attributes the unjust neglect of her work to her being "cursed for being too far ahead of her time; in her 1953 novel *Hackenfeller's Ape* she was writing about animal rights long before the cause became popular, and in 1969 she published the definitive novel about gender confusion (*In Transit*) long before there was a critical context for the topic." Critics are unable to place her as modernist, realist, or postmodernist, though *In Transit: An Heroi-Cyclic Novel,* at least, possesses features "today associated with modernism/postmodernism: tones that run from deadpan black humor to specious seriousness to mock learnedness, typographical unconventionalities, metafictional asides, fractured plots and subplots and juxtaposed set pieces, diagrams and puzzles, puns and portmanteau words, genre parodies and conflations, intertextuality and Barthesian bliss, camp and kitsch."

Brophy's status as a postmodernist is called into question, however, by her interest in Aristotelian logic and her declaration to Leslie Dock in *Contemporary Literature* (Spring 1976) that "I try never to baffle readers deliberately, because that is simply pretentiousness." And claims that she is a high modernist are belied by her impatience with Virginia Woolf, about whom Brophy, in *Don't Never Forget: Collected Views and Reviews* (1966), writes, "For evocation, subtlety of mood, atmosphere–all the qualities the Lupians praise–the sensitive Mrs Woolf can be shamed by an old toughy like [French detective writer Georges] Simenon, who has the literary good sense to approach the intangible through the concrete." The capacity to surprise, perhaps even herself, characterized her writing from the beginning, particularly if her account of how she wrote *Hackenfeller's Ape* is correct.

The novel is about an absentminded professor of zoology who, observing the mating ritual of a rare species of ape at the London Zoo, learns that the male is scheduled for use in a rocket experiment and decides to rescue him. With the help of a modern Moll Flanders he sets the ape free, but liberation causes more problems than imprisonment did. In an interview in *The Beast,* Brophy says she wrote the novel while living near the London Zoo. Deeply affected by pity and terror for what she saw there, she says, "I was trying to establish a parallel between shutting people up in prisons and shutting animals up in zoos." It is partly a study of the animal life of the mind, partly a satire on man–a mixture of intellectual fable, science fiction, and fantastic poem. Unlike Aldous Huxley or William Golding, Brophy does not solidly bond the properties of fable, fiction, and poetry. This flaw weakens the novel, but it also allows an endearing gentleness to play through the more stringent implications of the story, and it leaves space for Brophy's first attempt at a type she draws expertly: the delicate, ineffectual male.

Her second novel, *The King of a Rainy Country* (1956), is Brophy's most naturalistic book, an elegant picaresque tale about a Bohemian girl and her lover. Like one of its own characters, it seems to shrink from the inside of things. There are moments when the prose wriggles with sudden life, however, giving promise of hidden energy. The birth of Brophy's daughter, Kate, in 1957 seems to have released this energy. "The responsibility of becoming this person's mother obliged me to pause and define my own convictions, accounting to myself for how I could be both an artist and a rationalist, and both a Freudian and a Shavian evolutionist. The result was a colossal work of nonfiction, *Black Ship to Hell.*" Published in 1962, this book–compared by Anthony Quinton in the *Daily Telegraph* (London) to Norman O. Brown's *Life against Death* (1959)–is an ambitious exploration of the dynamics of hate. Often maddeningly mechanical in its application of Freudian theory to life, it is still an intellectual tour de force. It was fiercely attacked by reviewers, but Peter Porter summed it up accurately in *The Listener:* "Miss Brophy has found a new way of being creative. She disguises her book as a critical work; it seems to me a loving fiction of opinion. Her respectable progenitors are the great entertainers and explainers Shaw and Auden. They fight for her soul with Colin Wilson."

Black Ship to Hell won Brophy the *London Magazine* Prize for prose in 1962. It also seems to have stimulated her creatively. Between 1962 and 1964 her three most accomplished novels were published. *Flesh* (1962), dedicated to Iris Murdoch, is a cunning fable about sexual awakening. The story is straightforward and concerns the meeting, the marriage, and the marital complications of two young north London Jews. Brophy describes it as "an almost distressingly cold-blooded little story which reads better in the French translation than in English, and which was the first of my novels to have a numerical as distinct from a highbrow success." A *Sunday Times* (London) reviewer called it "not erotic but curious, exploratory, examining the feel of things, the shape of relationships. This detachedly clinical approach is perhaps characteristic of an age which has no moral knowledge, only scientific knowledge. And this, too, may explain why there has been a recent expansion of the comedy of manners." The book is clinical but also poetic, with moments of animal tenderness such as the description of "deep, moist green" chestnut leaves, which, "losing the pleated look of the flesh on a baby's hands, opened to their fullest like the palms of hundreds of adult, caressing hands."

The Finishing Touch (1963), described by its author as a "lesbian fantasy," is a modestly evil comedy about a girls' finishing school on the French Riviera. It has been called "the most concentrated single example of Firbank's influence, really a posthumous monument to him." Again the events are simple. An English princess arrives at the school and innocently precipitates blackmail, scandal, and a startling denoue-

Dust jacket for Brophy's 1963 novel, a "lesbian fantasy" about a girls' finishing school on the French Riviera (Richland County Public Library)

ment. The novel was highly praised. A reviewer in the *Times Literary Supplement* wrote: "Firbank is almost too obviously both the inspiration and the victim of Miss Brophy's waspish and witty tale." A *Daily Herald* reviewer called it "an outrageously indelicate joke made in beautifully mannered prose."

The Finishing Touch is her most decadent book–in *Don't Never Forget* she calls decadence "a rearguard revolutionary movement"–and, as the title suggests, an important contribution to the poetics of masturbation. Awareness of the relationship between literature and pornography led her to crusade publicly for the latter. In 1972 she published, in response to *The Longford Report on Pornography,* a pamphlet, *The Longford Threat to Freedom,* which attacked this "committee of theocrats, paranoiacs, simpletons and puritans" and proclaimed, "Masturbation is one of the few human activities that absolutely cannot do any harm to anyone."

The third and most celebrated of these novels is *The Snow Ball* (1964), a black comedy of manners. The plot is one of intrigue and seduction, the setting is a New Year's fancy dress ball, and the principal characters–dressed as Donna Anna and Don Giovanni–evoke Wolfgang Mozart and Leo Tolstoy. Structurally, according to its author, the novel "attempts to transcribe in literature the erotic perspectives and the chilling effects of a baroque tomb." Such complexity may not be immediately apparent in the narrative, which leads through a series of festive encounters and witty conversations to a bedroom scene recommended by Olivia Manning as "a truer impress of The Act than the much-discussed passage in The Group." Something of Brophy's intention can be glimpsed from the way the main story–the courtship and seduction of Donna Anna by Don Giovanni–is teasingly reflected and refracted by other events at the ball, from the rapid shifts of mood and setting, from the luxurious interiors and freezing exteriors, and from the somber conclusion.

Both in style and subject matter *The Snow Ball* is a study in artifice. The characters, to quote the heroine, are–or aspire to be–"very beautiful, highly-coloured, fantastic reptiles." The best moments have a frigid brilliance. There was a lot of uneasy praise from the critics, and even those who disliked the book conceded its effectiveness. It was described by John Horder in *The Guardian* as Brophy's "breakthrough novel." Murdoch praised it unreservedly in *The Sunday Times* (London), and it was dramatized on BBC television in April 1964.

The Snow Ball is dedicated to Charles Osborne, an Australian who immigrated to England in the 1950s and from 1958 to 1966 served as assistant editor of *London Magazine*. His favorable response to *Black Ship to Hell* led, in Brophy's words, "to my being invited to contribute to the *London Magazine* and by that route I entered journalism, becoming a critic and a propagandist of libertarianism (including liberty for animals) in the papers (most regularly the *Sunday Times* and the *New Statesman*)." She also began to broadcast on television and radio. Her first adult broadcast, in July 1963, was "The Novel as a Takeover Bid"; this talk and subsequent ones were later collected and published in *Don't Never Forget.* After her first television appearance, on "Writer's World" in May 1964, she became a regular television guest throughout the 1960s and 1970s, appearing on *Not So Much a Programme More a Way of Life* in 1964 and 1965, *Late Night Line-Up* in 1965 and 1966, *Enquiry* and *Horizon* in 1965 and 1970, and *The Book Programme* in 1974 and 1976. She joined the Labour Party and became one of the academy of writers who supported Harold Wilson in the 1964 election. She testified as one of the principal witnesses for the defense at the Fanny Hill trial in 1964. In the same year she subjected Kingsley Amis to what a *Daily Mail* (London) reporter called "the most violent public attack on any author I have read since Dr Leavis carved up C. P. Snow." She wrote, for instance, that "Many people's response to the reminder that Lucky Jim is coming to his tenth birthday will be that that's just about how old they thought he was all along."

Her writing at this time became at best trenchantly witty, at worst harsh and arrogant. "The trouble with Miss Brophy," complained Pete Wilsher after a radio talk attacking Huxley in 1964, "is that her haymakers are so wholesale. The undoubted vigour of her invective begins to boomerang on her." Something of this defect mars her radio play *The Waste-Disposal Unit,* broadcast by the BBC in April 1964. The play, she said, "is written in American as a foreign language, the poetic expression of my lethal fascination with that alien tongue which is licking the brains out of my native civilisation." When her stage play, *The Burglar* (a Shavian farce about conflicting moralities), which had enjoyed a successful preliminary run in the provinces, came to the Vaudeville Theatre in 1967, the critics killed it. When it was published in 1968, Brophy prefaced it with a long *apologia pro vita sua,* attributing the failure of the play to the reviewers' hostility to her persona and opinions and suggesting (possibly with some disingenuousness) that "the mantle of pugnacity has been trying to settle on my shoulders for some years now, during most of which I have been too busy with other concerns to give more than a shrug here and there towards twitching it off."

Apart from broadcasts, plays, and the exhibition, Brophy's chief writing during the 1960s was criticism. In *Palace without Chairs* (1978) there is a novelist who has abstained from writing novels, "developing a technique for dealing with his imagination when it preferred the nuclei of fictions: a few he compressed into short stories, but most, even more clearly, he distorted into sometimes rather brilliant critical perceptions about other writers' work. 'All critical insight,' he began one of his critical essays, 'is autobiography by the critic.'" The critical books after *Black Ship to Hell* can be read as simultaneous attempts by the writer's rational self to expose the secrets of her imagination and by her imagination to elude rational exposure.

The first of these critical works was *Mozart the Dramatist: A New View of Mozart, His Operas and His Age* (1964). Brophy says it was "detested by music critics but, happily for me, liked by composers." Her own insistent dedication to music and musicality finds expression in her declaration to Dock that "Everything else I have written (and I think this would probably be true, even if I write an article of 2000 words) is structured on the concerto, in three movements, with a one, two, one-A structure within each movement." One of the reasons *Mozart the Dramatist* creates problems for the reader is that the title implies a study of Mozart's dramatic technique (along the lines of Joseph Kerman's *Opera as Drama,* 1952), whereas in fact the book is a penetrating study of the psychology of an artist in an age of rational enlightenment. Another reason is its abrupt manner. Nevertheless, *Mozart the Dramatist* abounds in fertile suggestions.

In 1966 Brophy published a collection of selected journalism called *Don't Never Forget* (the title is taken from an inscription in English by Mozart: "Don't never forget your true and faithfull friend"). "People (even those who do not mean to be rude)," she wrote in the preface, "often ask me whether my journalism interferes with my serious writing. As a matter of fact, my journalism is serious writing." *Don't Never Forget* bears out this claim. Its subjects include the rights of animals, marriage, opera, detective stories, writers from John Cleland to Patricia Highsmith, and a radio talk on the Profumo affair (commissioned and withheld by the BBC), "The Nation in the Iron Mask." Ian Hamilton attacked the collection for its "mincing aggressiveness and grey slabs of polemical rightmindedness." There is some truth in what he says, but only if the book is read as the sum of its parts. The parts are memorable, emphatic, intense, and brief. She says that wit "is always some form of analysis" and goes on to provide proof, sometimes epigrammatically, sometimes aphoristically. On monogamy: "At present, monogamy is the corset into which we try to fit every married couple–a process which has on so many occasions split the seams that we have had to modify the corset." On the novel: "Soon after the last war an extraordinary fashion broke out among literary public figures for pronouncing that the novel was dead. What the pronouncers probably could have said with truth was that they were dead to novels."

Aggressiveness is more damagingly apparent in the work in which she collaborated with Levey and Osborne. *Fifty Works of English and American Literature We Could Do Without* (1967) is a debunking survey of fifty English and American classics–for instance, *Beowulf,* Edmund Spenser's *The Faerie Queene* (1590–1613), William Shakespeare's *Hamlet* (circa 1600–1601), Charlotte Brontë's *Jane Eyre* (1847), Mark Twain's *The Adventures of Huckleberry Finn* (1884), and other standards. The rationale is that continuing to praise overrated "classics" prevents children from reading good books. There are vivid judgments–Emily Brontë's *Wuthering Heights* (1847) "will wash as a psychological-historical curio or as high old rumbustious nonsense, but not as a great novel"–and links with Brophy's major works (Alexander Pope is praised because he opposed cruelty to animals). Osborne claimed the book was written over a weekend.

Dust jacket for Brophy's experimental 1969 novel, in which a narrator of indeterminate gender never leaves an airport (Richland County Public Library)

In *Black and White: A Portrait of Aubrey Beardsley* (1968) Brophy turned her attention to the psychology of graphic art. *Black and White* is not quite a pioneering study (there was a Beardsley exhibition in London in 1966), and, like much of Brophy's criticism, it is more an attempt to explain the artist to herself and herself to the artist than an exploration of the wider implications of his success. William Empson hinted as much in his otherwise favorable review in *The Listener:* "This is what needs explaining: why did the quality of his line suddenly get under people's skins, a thing which hasn't happened since to any major artist?" The book again demonstrates her gift for condensed precision, however. Its real value is suggested by the fact that W. H. Smith banned it from their display shelves–not because of the text but because of the pictures.

During the middle and late 1960s Brophy's engagement with public opinion and events was at its peak. In October 1965 the *Sunday Times* (London) published her influential essay "The Rights of Animals." This case against vivisection led her into an increasingly active campaign for animal liberties. She spoke in Trafalgar Square in 1967 against factory farming, describing herself later, in an interview in the *Daily Mirror* (London), as "white with terror standing on that bloody plinth in the pouring rain." Her campaign continued throughout the 1970s and 1980s. She contributed a paper called "The Darwinist's Dilemma" (arguing that Darwinism encourages society to regard animals as failed humans) to the Animal Rights Symposium at Cambridge in August 1977, and she was closely associated with the British Union for the Abolition of Vivisection. In 1966 she lectured with missionary zeal to the Fabian Society against religious education in state schools. The lecture was published as a Fabian Tract in 1967, arousing intense hostility and widespread discussion.

In 1969 Brophy published the novel that is certainly her masterpiece. *In Transit* is a wildly experimental, richly comic, philosophically dense, culturally rich work. As the narrative voice is fully aware, *In Transit* invites multiple understandings and misunderstandings, and critical evaluation of it is likewise variable. One critic placed it in her career by saying that in "the late 1960s Brophy's slight lyric grace was nearly destroyed by her tough unreasonableness," characterizing the result as "her most self-exacerbated book," which "expresses the plight of an imaginative writer who has tried too hard to rationalize her irrationality . . . less a novel than a cross between a neurotic essay in criticism and a farcical nightmare." After forty years of experimentation it is harder to state with confidence what is not a novel–even a neurotic essay in criticism or a farcical nightmare may qualify in the aftermath of Julian Barnes's *Flaubert's Parrot* (1984) or John Barth's *Giles Goat-Boy* (1966). Along with her contemporaries Christine Brooke-Rose and B. S. Johnson, Brophy embarked on a brilliant effort to "break up the conventions of the novelistic tradition." The widespread acceptance of postmodernism, metafiction, magical realism, and other alternatives to the realistic text makes clearer Brophy's own early contribution to a new kind of novel. Moore aptly declares that *In Transit* "should be a locus classicus for today's gender critics and advocates of experimental fiction."

Structurally, it is a departure from the form that, Brophy told Dock in *Contemporary Literature* (Spring 1976), underlays the rest of her work–the three-part concerto form: "*In Transit* is an attempt to write in four movements, and with a more complicated development of each theme within each movement." The titles of the four sections are musical, echoing Johannes Brahms's Fourth Symphony–"Section One: Linguistic Leprosy (Allegro non troppo)"; "Sexshuntwo: The Case of the Missing (Re)Member (Andante)"; "Section Three: De Rebus (Scherzo and Fugue)"; "Section Four: Let It All Come Breakdown (Allegro Energico e Passionato)," with a "Codetta (Più Allegro)." The pun in "Sexshuntwo" is a tiny foretaste of the furious wordplay that follows.

Insofar as plot explains the novel, it is about an air traveler named Evelyn Hilary O'Rooley, nicknamed Pat, who decides not to board his airplane as expected but to stay in the transit lounge. O'Rooley is thus in transit between present and past, between destinations, and, it becomes clear, between genders. At a certain point the first-person narrator realizes that he/she no longer knows what his/her gender is. The name is androgynous; the narrator examines her passport, finding it has been blotched with coffee at the point where the sex should be specified, feels his crotch, rubs her face, goes to the restroom, and tries other strategies for discovering the truth. It begins to seem that there is no truth; that the narrator is Patrick or Patricia depending on how the others treat him/her. The second and third sections are narrated in the third person, and the character's name varies from Patrick to Patricia depending on the reactions of others. Brophy's suggestion seems to be, not that human beings are bisexual, but that gender is a socially (or linguistically) constructed category, rather than a given.

The use of an airport as setting is key in the analysis of postmodernity that Brophy is making:

> Perhaps our whole century is in transit–a century whose suctions and pressures seek to dislodge you, its inhabitant, from it; a wind-tunnel of a century, on whose sides we sit insecure, scarcely able to snatch breath for the vacuum-force gale sucking us toward the sci-fi-futuristensce and the gritty, soiled brickdusty, industrial-city-Zephyr sand-blasting us back to the Glasweg-Edwardign rose-red soot-gothi-stone tenements which our own architecture can't/hasn't-time-to think up a replacement for.

Many of Brophy's most persistent concerns appear as themes here: the baroque; opera (there is a lot of an opera called "Al Alitalia"); surrealism; sex, including masturbation, homosexuality, and lesbianism (Pat blunders into a lesbian underworld in the secret corridors of the airport); and freedom, including the freedom of pornography. Much of this last concern is focused on a novel read by the narrator, called *L'HISTOIRE DE LA LANGUE D'OC.* Among the blurbs on the cover of this novel is "'straightforward commercial pornography: and what's wrong with that?'–*Brigid Brophy.*" This is not the only time that Brophy herself appears as a character in the novel.

The use of this "book" is instructive in many ways. First, it is a parody (in a book full of parodies, including a lengthy one of Raymond Burr stories), in this case of the well-known work of sadomasochistic pornography, Pauline Réage's *L'histoire d'O* (1954; translated as *The Story of O,* 1962). The fungibility of language (also always in transit) is demonstrated by the translation of Brophy's version: "The Story of Oc's Tongue." Actually, "la langue d'oc" is a linguistic reference (to the southern part of France, where *oc* was the word for *yes*), and a geographic one (part of southern France is still called Languedoc). But this punning confusion gives rise to an elaborate story of Oc. Oc also becomes "Och"–a Gaelic interjection–and O'C, which takes its place among the other mock-Irish names with which Brophy endows her narrative: O'dysseus, O'pera, and many others.

The richness of Brophy's punning links her to Joyce, a major presence in the background of the book; it also looks forward to Salman Rushdie. Sentences stand out like gems, often multilingual or smutty: the androgynous narrator quotes T. S. Eliot on his/her classical forerunner: "Eyetieresias have fore-sofferto tutto." Three passing Irishmen are overheard saying "It's a very daycent class of fellatio you meet travelling Aer

Dust jacket for Brophy's 1978 novel, about the royal family of a fictional middle European country (Richland County Public Library)

Cunnilingus." The playfulness, as well as the exploration of the real and the fictional, applies even to God:

> In the mytho-kingdom of heaven, Almighty God reefed in his William-Blake nightdress into something more like a blouse (and yet God is not smocked) and faced reality. "Very well," he said reasonably and uncomplainingly, "it turns out to be they who have imagined me, and I who am the fictitious character. But they still have not imagined anyone whom I can imaginarily adore."

Brophy also uses the postmodern practice (though it dates back to Miguel de Cervantes and Laurence Sterne) called "baring the device": usually in one of the narrator's direct addresses to the reader, called successively "Interlude," "Interludibrium," "Interlugubre," "Interlewd," and "Interloo." In the first, for instance, Pat/Brophy explains,

> I've muttered you, my dear Reader, several asides on the subject of the technique of fiction, including some about alienation effects–one of which I am indeed practising on you now, though this (at last openly) Open-Letter to you also serves the representational purpose of signifying by ideogram, while sparing you the sensual experience of, the hiatus I had to live through while I waited for my anyway underweight snack to be delivered to me. . . . I have invited you to inspect and (I hope) concur in the machinery of my narration.

The narrator explains, for instance, that first-person narration helps avoid the necessity for gendered pronouns, *he* or *she,* required for the use of the third person (later, when Pat is too tired to speak, the narration changes briefly into the second person).

There are other elements of *In Transit* that an unsympathetic reader might dismiss as trickery: parallel columns dividing text and commentary, or Italian and English, or two possible permutations of the plot, or male and female; diagrams; a *criticus apparatus* attributed to "Scholiast"; typographical puns. It is wildly funny, and funnily wild, and a brilliant, unfairly neglected contribution to the liberated fiction of the second half of the twentieth century.

Self-exasperation shows again in *Prancing Novelist: A Defence of Fiction in the Form of a Critical Biography in Praise of Ronald Firbank* (1973), which is as long and unruly as its title suggests. "Here is Brigid Brophy," wrote Philippa Pullar in the *Sunday Times* (London), "whose strength and beauty lies in her lyric brevity, writing a fat and heavy volume about someone whose own strength and beauty also lies in lyric brevity." P. N. Furbank in *The Listener* called it "a rum go, a vast ramping book at once so bad and so good one doesn't know whether to cheer or to weep." *Prancing Novelist* is her most quixotic book: a work of creative dissatisfaction and anticriticism, raging in the dark about the most inexplicable artistic property, invention: "the magical faculty which conjures something into thereness where nothing existed before." It is quixotic but also antiquixotic: in a brilliant chapter, "Cervantes and the Label on the Sauce Bottle," Brophy invokes Don Quixote and St. Teresa as opposites who meet in creative madness, the one from an excess of the literary, the other from an excess of the literal. Indeed, her evocation of the character of St. Teresa comes closest to explaining the quality of this sometimes unreadable and occasionally unforgettable book: "Saint Teresa's personality is in strange suspension. It did express itself in art, yet it was, in its capacity as artist's personality, frustrated, because it would not admit its self-expression to be art."

The Adventures of God in His Search for the Black Girl (1973) represents a recovery from solipsism: a series of fables–including a poignant reworking of "The Crown Princess," called "The Singularly Ugly Princess"–and a philosophical novella. A. S. Byatt, reviewing it in *The Times* (London), objected to "a humour based on an apparently colossal optimism." As Brophy wrote in her preface to *The Burglar,* however, "I would hardly have survived the assassination" of *Black Ship to Hell* "had I not transformed myself from masochist and coward into the tough stoic, obstinate egoist or rash Irish lunatic I have been ever since."

Her last sustained works of fiction were *Pussy Owl*–a charming tale of a boastful hybrid "noted for wisdom, intelligence, agility in flight, linguistic ability and for jumping on anyone who gives me cheek," broadcast on BBC television in March 1976 and published in the same year–and *Palace without Chairs,* a psychological fable set in a wintry mid-European Arcadia where everything has gone wrong. It is the most frigid and sterile of all her books. The prose has lost its spring, so that each sentence hits the same flat, dull note. There is, however, a new vigor in naming. Characters called Frumgeour and Skimplepex suggest that her fiction might take a new direction, away from Shavian enlightenment toward the rococo-gothic of Firbank and Mervyn Peake.

Palace without Chairs, dedicated to Michael Foot, is prefaced by a note to readers pointing out that British writers are not paid for the borrowing of their books from public libraries and asking readers to support a Public Lending Right. Despite other activities–serving as vice president of the National Anti-Vivisection Society from 1974 and as vice chairman of the British Copyright Council from 1976–Brophy's chief public activity in the 1970s was the establishing, with Maureen Duffy, of the Writers' Action Group, with the aim of negotiating a Public Lending Right. Though the concept initially aroused intense controversy, in 1979 Foot steered the Public Lending Right Bill through Parliament.

That same year Brophy's life took a catastrophic turn for the worse, as she discovered that she had to live with multiple sclerosis. As she became more and more debilitated, she relied increasingly on her husband, Levey, and her friends–particularly Shena Mackay, whom she had assisted with her fiction and whom she called, in her essay "A Case-Historical Fragment of Autobiography" from *Baroque-'n'-Roll, and Other Essays* (1987), "the finest architect of literary baroque, funny and tragic, and the most Firbankian master of surrealism now extant in the English language." Her illness limited her writing. In 1984 she wrote to Karl Miller, the editor of *The Listener,* asking for some work but also asking for patience: "I am a permanent and more or less total cripple, at least in relation to walking. . . . doing anything is desperately slow and laborious and takes immense planning in advance." In 1989, asked about her reaction to the disappearance of her books from the bookshelves, she replied, "It is impossible not to hope" that readers would rediscover her work. "It is a matter whether people will retain the ability to read."

She was not utterly silenced. She published a book on the cause to which she had devoted much of her time in the 1970s: *A Guide to Public Lending Right* (1983). PLR had been enacted, finally, in 1982, after a ten-year campaign by the Writers' Action Group. Brophy's interest seems to have derived in part from the origins of the idea of compensating writers for the circulation of their books through libraries: it came from her father, John Brophy, who devised the concept of paying authors a penny each time a book was borrowed, called "the Brophy penny." Her book is a lucid account of the campaign and a good overview of postwar British publishing.

That same year *The Prince and the Wild Geese* was published. This short book includes a narrative about a young Irishwoman named Julia Taaffe, visiting in Rome in 1832, and one of her suitors, Grigorii Grigorievich Gagarin. The germ of the book is a collection of drawings and watercolors, executed by the talented Gagarin, dedicated to his courtship of Julia and saved by her heirs. Brophy uses what is known of the two principals (not much), what is known of Rome and Europe in 1832 (a great deal), and her novelistic imagination to flesh out the love story. "Romanticism itself," she declares, "was at springtime." The love story is placed against a background of the English Reform Bill, revolution in France, the youth of Felix Mendelssohn and Hector Berlioz, Aleksandr Pushkin, and other historical events and personages from around the world. If the foreground couple seems attentuated, it is because Brophy has little to go on beyond some charming pictures, and the result is slightly desperate: "As Julia's lovers, sighing for love, crowded about the piano, Prince Grégoire Gagarin may well have conceived a hatred for the wild songs [of] Thomas Moore. . . . he must have feared that she was turning also from the exile of the wild geese." Brophy's interest in the experience of Irishness, European culture, classical music, and the complexities of love triumph over her paucity of materials.

A nonfiction collection, *Baroque-'n'-Roll, and Other Essays,* appeared in 1987. Though not as powerful as *Don't Never Forget,* it includes many interesting essays, including "A Case-Historical Fragment of Autobiography," which describes the onset of her illness, a stumble while she was crossing a street with novelist Elizabeth Jane Howard. The rest of the collection revisits many of her favorites: Mozart, Sigmund Freud, George Bernard Shaw, the baroque, tennis. Animal rights are firmly defended in a criticism of the Labour Party for its support of fishing, a policy rejected by "people who recognise that the love of liberty and fairness is claptrap unless you apply it to animals of every species and not just to animals of the human species in whom it is easy to see ourselves reflected."

Reads, published by Cardinal in 1989, is almost entirely reprinted material from *Don't Never Forget,* with the exception of some reviews of books about cats and actress Ellen Terry, an introduction to a 1987 reprint of Brophy's *The Finishing Touch,* an essay on the Mauritshuis museum, and a 1988 essay on Wilde. One comment stands out as a good summary of her own work in fiction and nonfiction: "The true artistic impulse is, largely, cruel–or at least relentless."

At about that time it became impossible for her to continue living at home. Her husband moved her to a nursing home in Louth, Lincolnshire, where he and his daughter and her family also moved to be near her, until her death, on 7 August 1995.

Brigid Brophy's case is instructive and sad. She wrote a dozen novels and distinguished works of nonfiction. At one time she was one of the two or three best-known women in Britain. Only four of her books have remained in print: her Mozart biography, the pamphlet *The Longford Threat to Freedom,* and two novels reprinted by the Gay Men's Press. Yet, she is an important writer, a major postwar novelist, the author of one of the most inventive and spirited experimental novels of a spirited and inventive decade, and a model of artistic and intellectual independence and power.

Interviews:

Leslie Dock, "An Interview with Brigid Brophy," *Contemporary Literature,* 17 (Spring 1976): 151–170;

Susan Crosland, "Look: A Woman of Substance," *Times* (London), 15 February 1987;

Stanley Reynolds, "Wednesday Women: The Still Prancing Novelist / Interview with Brigid Brophy," *Guardian,* 14 June 1989.

Bibliography:

Steven Moore, "Brigid Brophy: An Introduction and Checklist," *Review of Contemporary Fiction,* 15 (Fall 1995): 7–11.

References:

Mark Axelrod, "Mozart, Moonshots, and Monkey Business in Brigid Brophy's *Hackenfeller's Ape,*" *Review of Contemporary Fiction,* 15 (Fall 1995): 18–22;

Corinne E. Blackmer, "*The Finishing Touch* and the Tradition of Homoerotic Girls' School Fictions," *Review of Contemporary Fiction,* 15 (Fall 1995): 32–39;

Bernard Hoepffner, "Translating *In Transit:* Writing–By Proxy," *Review of Contemporary Fiction,* 15 (Fall 1995): 54–61;

Chris Hopkins, "The Neglect of Brigid Brophy," *Review of Contemporary Fiction,* 15 (Fall 1995): 12–17;

Brooke Horvath, "Brigid Brophy's It's-All-Right-I'm-Only-Dying Comedy of Modern Manners: Notes on *In Transit,*" *Review of Contemporary Fiction,* 15 (Fall 1995): 46–53;

Patricia Lee, "Communication Breakdown and the 'Twin Genius' of Brophy's *In Transit,*" *Review of Contemporary Fiction,* 15 (Fall 1995): 62–67;

Annegret Maack, "Concordia Discors: Brigid Brophy's *In Transit,*" *Review of Contemporary Fiction,* 15 (Fall 1995): 40–45;

Peter Parker, "'Aggressive, witty & unrelenting': Brigid Brophy and Ronald Firbank," *Review of Contemporary Fiction,* 15 (Fall 1995): 68–78;

Patricia Juliana Smith, "Desperately Seeking Susan[na]: Closeted Quests and Mozartean Gender Bending in Brigid Brophy's *The King of a Rainy Country,*" *Review of Contemporary Fiction,* 15 (Fall 1995): 23–31.

Papers:

The Lilly Library at Indiana University in Bloomington holds a collection of Brigid Brophy's manuscripts.

George Mackay Brown

(17 October 1921 - 13 April 1996)

Rob Spence

Edge Hill College of Higher Education, Ormskirk, England

BOOKS: *Let's See the Orkney Islands,* story by Brown, photographs by William S. Thomson (Fort William, Scotland: W. S. Thomson, 1951);

The Storm and Other Poems (Kirkwall, Scotland: Orkney, 1954);

Loaves and Fishes (London: Hogarth, 1959);

The Year of the Whale (London: Chatto & Windus, 1965);

A Calendar of Love and Other Stories (London: Hogarth, 1967; New York: Harcourt, Brace & World, 1968);

Twelve Poems (Belfast: Festival Publications, Queen's University, 1968);

A Time to Keep and Other Stories (London: Hogarth, 1969; New York: Harcourt, Brace & World, 1970);

An Orkney Tapestry (London: Gollancz, 1969);

A Spell for Green Corn (London: Hogarth, 1970);

Lifeboat and Other Poems (Bow: Richard Gilbertson, 1971);

Fishermen with Ploughs: A Poem Cycle (London: Hogarth, 1971);

Poems New and Selected (London: Hogarth, 1971; New York: Harcourt Brace Jovanovich, 1973); enlarged as *Selected Poems* (London: Hogarth, 1977);

Greenvoe (London: Hogarth, 1972; New York: Harcourt Brace Jovanovich, 1972);

Magnus (London: Hogarth, 1973);

Hawkfall and Other Stories (London: Hogarth, 1974);

The Two Fiddlers: Tales from Orkney (London: Chatto & Windus, 1974);

Letters from Hamnavoe (Edinburgh: Gordon Wright, 1975);

Edwin Muir: A Brief Memoir (West Linton, Scotland: Castlelaw, 1975);

The Sun's Net (London: Hogarth, 1976);

Winterfold (London: Chatto & Windus, 1976);

Pictures in the Cave (London: Chatto & Windus, 1977);

Witch and Other Stories (London: Longman, 1977);

George Mackay Brown (photograph by Gunnie Moberg; from the dust jacket for Beside the Ocean of Time, *1994)*

Under Brinkie's Brae (Edinburgh: Gordon Wright, 1979);

Six Lives of Fankle the Cat (London: Chatto & Windus, 1980);

Portrait of Orkney, text by Brown, photographs by Werner Forman (London: Hogarth, 1981); enlarged, with illustrations by Erlend Brown and

photographs by Gunnie Moberg (London: Murray, 1988);
Andrina and Other Stories (London: Chatto & Windus/Hogarth, 1983);
Voyages (London: Chatto & Windus/Hogarth, 1983);
Christmas Poems (Oxford: Perpetua, 1984);
Time in a Red Coat (London: Chatto & Windus/Hogarth, 1984; New York: Vanguard, 1984);
Three Plays (London: Chatto & Windus/Hogarth, 1984);
Christmas Stories (Oxford: Perpetua, 1985);
The Scottish Bestiary, text by Brown, illustrations by John Bellany, Steven Campbell, Peter Howson, Jack Knox, Bruce McLean, June Redfern, and Adrian Wiszniewski (Edinburgh: Paragon, 1986);
Keepers of the House (London: Old Stile, 1986);
A Celebration for Magnus, by Brown and others (Nairn, Scotland: Balnain, 1987);
The Golden Bird: Two Orkney Stories (London: Murray, 1987);
Stone: Poems (Verona, Italy: Kulgin D. Duval & Colin H. Hamilton, 1987);
Two Poems for Kenna (Child Okeford: Words Press, 1988);
Songs for St. Magnus Day: The Seven Jars of Sorrow and Comfort (Oxford: Perpetua, 1988);
The Masked Fisherman and Other Stories (London: Murray, 1989);
Tryst on Egilsay: Hakon and Magnus: Seven Poems (Wetherby: Celtic Cross, 1989);
The Wreck of the Archangel: Poems (London: Murray, 1989);
Letters to Gypsy, text by Brown, illustrations by Simon Fraser (Nairn, Scotland: Balnain, 1990);
Selected Poems, 1954–1983 (London: Murray, 1991);
The Sea-King's Daughter; and, Eureka! (Nairn, Scotland: Balnain, 1991);
In the Margins of the Shakespeare (Monmouth: Old Stile, 1991);
Brodgar Poems (Oxford: Perpetua, 1992);
Foresterhill (Schondorf am Ammersee, Germany: Babel for George Mackay Brown, 1992);
The Lost Village: Poems (Wetherby: Celtic Cross, 1992);
Vinland (London: Murray, 1992);
Rockpools and Daffodils: An Orcadian Diary, 1979–1991 (Edinburgh: Gordon Wright, 1992);
Beside the Ocean of Time (London: Murray, 1994; Calgary: Bayeux, 1994);
The Sea and the Tower (Calgary: Bayeux, 1994);
Orfeo: A Masque (Lastingham: Celtic Cross, 1995);
Winter Tales (London: Murray, 1995);
Selected Poems, 1954–1992 (London: Murray, 1996; Iowa City: University of Iowa Press, 1996);
Following a Lark: Poems (London: Murray, 1996);
For the Islands I Sing: An Autobiography (London: Murray, 1997);
The Island of the Women and Other Stories (London: Murray, 1998);
Northern Lights: A Poet's Sources, edited by Archie Bevan and Brian Murray (London: Murray, 1999);
The Rose Tree (Lastingham: Celtic Cross, 2001);
Travellers: Poems, edited, with an introduction, by Bevan and Murray (London: Murray, 2001).

PLAY PRODUCTIONS: *Witch,* Edinburgh, 1969;
A Spell for Green Corn, Edinburgh, 1970.

OTHER: "Pilgrim," *Lines Review,* 26 (Summer 1968): 5–8;
"The Broken Heraldry," in *Memoirs of a Modern Scotland,* edited by Karl Miller (London: Faber & Faber, 1970), pp. 136–150;
"The Mercenary," *Scotia Review,* 7 (August 1974): 20–23;
"Writer's Shop," *Chapman,* 4 (Summer 1976): 23–24;
"Two Horses, Rose and Terror," in *New Tales of Unease,* edited by John Burke (London: Pan, 1976), pp. 30–40;
"Dark Angels," lyrics by Brown, music by Peter Maxwell Davies (London: Boosey & Hawkes, 1977);
"Night Crossing," *Scottish Review,* 10 (May 1978): 9–11;
"Orpheus with His Lute," *New Edinburgh Review,* no. 44 (November 1978): 18–20;
"An Autobiographical Essay," in *As I Remember: Ten Scottish Authors Recall How Writing Began for Them,* edited by Maurice Lindsay (London: Hale, 1979), pp. 9–21;
"Fiddlers at the Wedding," lyrics by Brown, music by Davies (London & New York: Boosey & Hawkes, 1980);
"Jenny Barraclough," *New Edinburgh Review,* no. 50 (May 1980): 9–11;
"My Scotland: 2: Orkney and Scotland," *Scottish Review,* 36 (November 1984): 15–17;
"Into the Labyrinth," lyrics by Brown, music by Davies (London: Chester Music, 1986);
"Pearl," in *Scottish Short Stories 1986,* edited, with an introduction, by Deidre Chapman (London: Collins, 1986), pp. 27–31;
Edwin Muir: Selected Prose, edited, with an introduction and a memoir, by Brown (London: Murray, 1987);
"House of Winter," lyrics by Brown, music by Davies (London: Chester Music / New York: Edition W. Hansen/Chester Music, 1987);
"The Voyage of the Flood-Tide," in *A Writer's Ceilidh for Neil Gunn,* edited by Aonghas MacNeacail (Nairn, Scotland: Balnain, 1991).

To say that Orkney was important to George Mackay Brown's art is to understate massively. For Brown, Orkney was the source of his art. Its presence is all-pervasive in his poetry and in his prose works. Its history and myth provide Brown with the bulk of the material he used in his fifty years as a professional writer. Brown was born and lived all his life in Stromness, a small town on Mainland, the largest of the Orkney Islands, situated off the northern coast of Scotland. Indeed, save for a few years as a student at Newbattle Abbey and Edinburgh University, Brown scarcely left Orkney. His identification with these islands is complete, and any appreciation of his work must take account of the central position occupied by the lore, language, history, and myth of the islands.

Uniquely in the British Isles, Orkney was Norwegian territory until 1470, when it became part of Scotland. The Norwegian influence is still discernible in place and personal names, in the dialect words used by the inhabitants, and in the store of myth and legend, most noticeably collected in the *Orkneyinga Saga,* a sequence of tales written around 1200. Orkney also has extensive prehistoric remains, mostly of the Neolithic era. These rich resources form the foundation of all of Brown's work.

Brown was born on 17 October 1921 into a poor family: his father, John Brown, was a postman, and his mother, Mhairi Mackay Brown, worked in the local hotel. Brown attended the local school, Stromness Academy, where he discovered his talent for writing in the weekly "compositions" set by his English teacher. Brown writes engagingly in his autobiography, *For the Islands I Sing* (1997), of his voracious reading as a child, moving from the ripping yarns in comics he read as a young boy to his discovery as an adolescent of Romantic poetry. His school education ended when he contracted tuberculosis and was sent to a sanatorium. He never fully recovered his health, but the enforced leisure enabled him to read and develop his literary taste. The illness also meant he could not serve in the forces in World War II; moreover, he was virtually unemployable. These circumstances enabled him to become, perforce, a writer, and in the early 1940s he began to publish news stories, reviews, and eventually a regular column in Orkney's weekly newspaper. These newspaper pieces became a permanent feature of his working life: his final column for the *Orcadian* appeared a week before his death on 13 April 1996.

Brown's life was also colored by a fondness for drink, which bordered on alcoholism. He spent ten years in what he called "a desert of time" doing little other than drinking and writing occasional pieces for the newspaper, together with some early poems. Then, in 1951, he was invited to become a mature student at

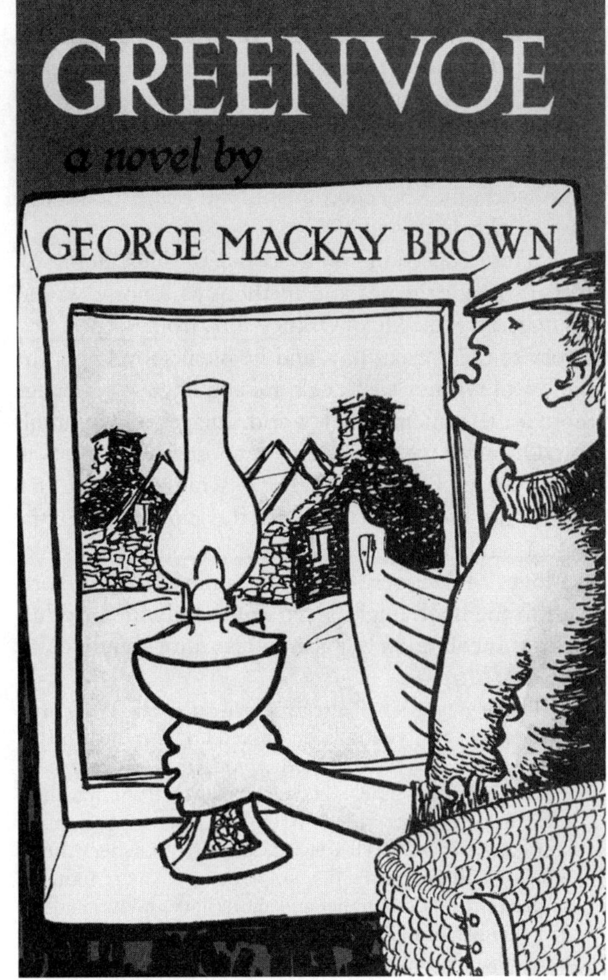

Dust jacket for Brown's 1972 novel, in which a community in the Orkney Islands is taken over by a military-industrial project called Black Star (Richland County Public Library)

an adult education college in Dalkeith, near Edinburgh. This establishment, designed to provide a foundation for degree study, was run by the Orkney poet Edwin Muir. Brown, who admired Muir's work, agreed to attend, and completed his studies there in 1952, before going to Edinburgh University two years later. At this time Brown read Muir's *The Story and the Fable* (1940), which interweaves the quotidian life of the Orkney Islanders with the matter of myth and legend. Muir's book set the pattern for Brown's own work as a poet, story writer, and novelist.

It was Muir who first encouraged Brown to publish, and he was the prime mover behind the publication of Brown's first major collection of verse, *Loaves and Fishes*, published in 1959. By this time Brown was becoming an established poet whose themes–the rituals and rhythms of the seasons in the lives of the farmers and fishermen of Orkney–marked him as a voice distant from the metropolitan concerns of his contemporaries. In stylistic terms, too, Brown owed more to traditional notions of versification than to the then-fashionable pop and free verse of the 1960s. Another volume of poems, *The Year of the Whale* (1965), appeared before the publication of Brown's first literary prose work, the collection of short stories *A Calendar of Love and Other Stories* in 1967.

This collection is a compact illustration of Brown's major themes and methods as a prose writer. His material is the life of Orkney folk, from deepest pre-history to the present day, and he often shows how the shadow of Orkney's rich cultural and linguistic heritage informs the contemporary world. Images and symbols from Orkney's past are often juxtaposed with events in contemporary Orkney. The stories range in their setting across the centuries, from the dark ages to the present, and offer a series of impressions of the lives and loves of a closely knit community. Brown's foreword to the book might serve as not only an introduction to this collection but also to his entire oeuvre:

> Orkney is a small green world in itself. Walk a mile or two and you will see, mixed up with the modern houses of concrete and wood, the "old farm-houses sunk in time"; hall and manse from which laird and minister ruled in the eighteenth century; smuggler's cave, witch's hovel; stone piers, where the whalers and Hudson's Bay ships tied up; the remains of pre-reformation chapel and monastery; homesteads of Vikings like Langskaill where Sweyn Asleifson wintered, the last and greatest of them all; the monoliths of pre-history; immense stone-age burial chambers where the Norse Jerusalem-farers broke in and covered the wall with runes.
>
> Dominating all the islands is the rose-red Cathedral of Saint Magnus the Martyr in Kirkwall, called "the wonder and glory of all the north."
>
> This Magnus was a twelfth-century Earl of Orkney, in a time of terrible civil war. One April morning he heard Mass on the small island of Egilsay; then he walked out gaily among the ritual axes and swords. Next winter the poor of the islands broke their bread in peace.
>
> Round that still centre all these stories move.

Here, Brown in effect lays bare his whole worldview. The small green world of Orkney suffices as his canvas, and he returns relentlessly in all his work to that still center.

The title story in *A Calendar of Love* demonstrates Brown's engagement with the cycle of the seasons, both in nature and in human relationships. The story takes place over a calendar year, during which the central character, Jean Scarth, loses her father and becomes involved with two local men, the womanizing, hard-drinking crofter Thorfinn and the solitary fisherman Peter. She conceives a child, who is born as the snow-drifts of December mark the end of another year, a new life to replace the one that has been lost, just as nature's cycle turns. Brown describes events in starkly unadorned prose. His characters speak in a direct, almost child-like manner, without artifice, seemingly aware of the inevitability of their lives. Jean recognizes this inevitability as the first snow of winter falls and she nears the time of her child's delivery: "And then suddenly, everything was in its place. The tinkers would move forever through the hills. Men would plough their fields. Men would bait their lines. Comedy had its place in the dance too–the drinking, the quarreling, the expulsion, the return in the morning. And forever the world would be full of youth and beauty, birth and death, labour and suffering." Other stories in this collection share the same melancholy tone and sense of the ceaseless renewal made possible by the natural cycle.

Brown's next prose publication was also a collection of short stories, *A Time to Keep and Other Stories,* published in 1969. The collection may be seen as a companion volume to *A Calendar of Love* in that it focuses on the same themes, with a similar cast of characters drawn from Orkney past and present. Their world appears almost a timeless one, though Brown does not shy away from presenting the intrusions of the modern world: in "The Wireless Set," for example, Brown explores the impact of new technology on the lives of a couple whose loss of a son in the war is linked in their minds with the radio he brought to the house before he left. In "Celia," the eponymous antiheroine turns to drink partly as a way of shutting out the horrendous reality of a contemporary world where apartheid is still in place and a vicious war is developing in Vietnam. The religious connotations of the title of the collection reflect Brown's own spirituality: he became a Roman Catholic in 1961, having long held an interest in that faith, and his later work is imbued with his belief.

Between *A Time to Keep* and his next major prose work Brown continued to write and publish poetry, and his poetry formed the basis of his reputation until the publication of *Greenvoe* in 1972. This novel, Brown's first, represents one of his lasting achievements. It is an account of a week in the life of an Orkney community on the fictional island of Hellya as it faces up to its impending demise at the hands of a mysterious military-industrial concern called Black Star. The place is, as Brown describes it in his autobiography, "a kind of tawdry gossipy Eden," and the intrusion of new technology triggers its fall from grace.

The novel is written mostly in a realistic third-person narrative, although one chapter takes the form of a letter written by Johnny Singh, an itinerant peddler on his annual visit to the island. Singh's story is interwoven

George Mackay Brown

GREENVOE

A Novel

One

Slowly the night shadow passed from the island and the Sound. In the village of Greenvoe lights burned in the windows of three fishermen's cottages above the pier

A small dark knotted man came out of one of the doors. He picked up a half-dozen lobster creels from the white wall and carried them across to the pier and down a few stone steps. A motor-boat called the *Ellen* was tied up there. Bert Kerston stowed his creels on board. He untied the *Ellen* and pushed off. He swung the starting handle. The *Ellen* kicked and coughed into life. ~~Her~~ bow ~~tore~~ the quiet water apart.

From the second open door came a mild chant. Samuel Whaness the fisherman was reading Scripture with his wife Rachel. 'He maketh the deep to

Opening page from the manuscript for Brown's 1972 novel (George Mackay Brown Archive, University of Edinburgh)

with an historical narrative compiled by one of the characters, the Skarf, a former fisherman now a Marxist visionary. A third strand in the novel is provided by the rituals of the secret society known as the Ancient Mystery of the Horsemen. These rituals are presented, in a device used by Brown in some of his short stories, in dialogue form with stage directions at the end of each chapter.

The plot of the novel, which is slight, concerns the often-fraught relationships between the islanders. Their way of life is portrayed in five chapters, each charting a day in their doomed collective existence. The characters are reminiscent of those that inhabit the short stories: a mixed bag of the feckless, the earnest, and the drunk. The sensual and fertile Alice has had seven children by seven different men. Her excess is balanced by the sexual frustration of the schoolteacher, Margaret, who is pursued by the captain of the ferryboat, Ivan Westray. Timmy Folster, a simpleton, consumes the industrial spirit sold to him as fuel for his stove. Mrs. McKee, the mother of the Presbyterian minister, is tortured by guilt, manifested in her dreams, in which she finds herself on trial for the indiscretions of her youth. Her son is alcoholic, and she blames herself for that, too.

Into the unchanging lives of these people comes the classic outsider figure, a stranger who takes up residence in the local hotel. None of the islanders can imagine why he is there, and it takes another outsider, Singh, to reveal his function as an ominous agent of change in the form of industrial progress. He is, writes Singh, "Western Man arrived at a foreseen inevitable end." Singh also sees him as ruling the world "with a card index file," and indeed the final chapter of the novel reveals that Black Star does have files on all of the inhabitants of Greenvoe.

The six chapters of the novel are mirrored in the six stations of the ritual initiation ceremony performed by the Lord of the Harvest and the Master Horsemen. Each short ceremony represents a point in the natural cycle of growth and decay. The five stations for the first five chapters–the Plough, the Seed, the Green Corn, the Yellow Corn, and the Dead–are enacted at the end of each day. The final chapter depicts the rapid disintegration of the community as the men from the Black Star project take over Greenvoe and the rest of the island. At first the workers turn the place into a kind of boomtown, but then the inhabitants, persuaded by money from the authorities, are forced to leave, their houses are bulldozed, and the island is turned over entirely to the Black Star project. In a coda that restores the previous rhythms of the narrative, the Lord of the Harvest and the Master Horsemen return ten years after the takeover, and more than eight years since the abandonment of the island by Black Star, to complete their ritual in the midsummer sun. The wheel has come full circle, and the very earth of the island demands that the natural cycle be taken up again. So the novel ends in a ceremony of resurrection, as nature reclaims what has been taken from her.

The novel remains one of Brown's most significant achievements. Its lyrical tone, the dextrous tapestry of its various interwoven narratives, and its darkly symbolic prose style mark it out as a distinctively individual novel, unlike any by Brown's contemporaries. Although it clearly stands against the march of technology at the expense of tradition, it is unsentimental but resolute in its faith in the interdependence of mankind and nature.

Brown's second novel, *Magnus* (1973), takes for its subject the central figure in Orkney legend, St. Magnus the Martyr. The novel is not a straightforward historical narrative, however. Brown's starting point is the account in the *Orkneyinga Saga* of the martyrdom of Magnus, killed by his cousin Hakon after seven years of warfare between them over the sovereignty of the Orkney Islands. The story tells of how Magnus arrives lightly protected at a peace conference on the island of Egilsay, only to be confronted by the much superior forces of Hakon. Magnus, realizing that he has been duped, pleads for banishment or imprisonment, but the nobles of Orkney demand a resolution of the conflict through his death. Magnus meets his end at the hands of Hakon's cook, Lilolf, who smashes his skull with an axe, after receiving Magnus's forgiveness for the act.

The death of Magnus is seen as a martyrdom, and soon he becomes the subject of a cult among the common people, who seek cures for their ailments at the place of his execution. Hakon, against expectations, becomes a much respected earl of Orkney, and the new cathedral is dedicated to the now canonized Magnus. This story surfaces in many of Brown's works, and he acknowledged its significance for him in his autobiography: "These historical events form the backdrop to much of the narrative and verse that I have written. Without the violent beauty of those happenings eight and a half centuries ago, my writing would have been quite different. I was almost going to say, it would not have existed; but of course the talent that will not let one rest would have had to latch on to other themes. There are, fortunately for me, many legendary and historical sources in Orkney from later centuries that any native-born writer can seize on with delight–but still the great story of Magnus and Hakon is the cornerstone."

Onto this story Brown grafts the biblical concept of the "Seamless Garment" of Christianity, woven from the garment worn by Christ at the Crucifixion. The garment can be rewoven by a saint, and the central con-

Dust jacket for the Canadian edition of Brown's 1994 novel, which mixes the history and legends of the Orkney Islands with a young Scotsman's experiences in the 1930s and 1940s (Richland County Public Library)

ceit of Brown's novel is that Magnus is engaged throughout his life on a preordained quest for the garment. Indeed, Brown suggests that there are three garments: the first is that of ordinary existence, the fabric of society; the second garment is the heraldic coat of state to which both Hakon and Magnus lay claim; and the third garment is the coat of sanctity that Magnus must wear for his marriage feast. This immaculate garment will lend a Christ-like status to the wearer, but in order to achieve his aim, Magnus is put to a series of tests, or temptations, all of which he succeeds in resisting, so that he is prepared for the sacrifice on Egilsay.

Brown's account of Magnus's death in chapter 7 of the novel is an ambitious attempt to universalize the event and to link it explicitly with Christ's Crucifixion. After an introduction in which the language of the *Orkneyinga Saga* is rendered in a style reminiscent of the Authorized Version of the Bible, there follows an account of the journey to Egilsay, in which it becomes clear that Magnus is aware of what awaits him and that he goes willingly to his fate. The narrative voice then changes abruptly, replacing Brown's impersonal narrator with a journalistic account of the peace negotiations. The context is now a twentieth-century one, as the report refers to "the dramatic developments in the peace confrontation." Brown's deliberate defamiliarization of the narrative serves to underline his contention that Magnus's martyrdom is as relevant in the twentieth century as it was in the twelfth. This idea is further pointed up when, in a dramatic shift, Lilolf the executioner is presented in first-person narrative as the man charged by a Nazi camp commandant with the execution of Dietrich Bonhoeffer. The chapter also includes a section dealing with the kind of ritual sacrifice that might have occurred in the stone circles of Orkney during Neolithic times. Brown's purpose in these discursive passages is not easy to identify. Certainly, though, this central chapter of the novel establishes the archetypal nature of the sacrifice motif in history and religion.

The action of *Magnus* is largely confined to the events surrounding the central character's death, and the novel is meditative in tone. It is the most avowedly religious of Brown's novels, with the death of the protagonist seen as one of many reenactments of the central event in the story of Christ. Brown concludes his meditation on the nature of the sacrament with this thought: "That was the one only central sacrifice of history. *I am the bread of life*. All previous rituals had been a foreshadowing of this; all subsequent rituals a reenactment. The fires at the centre of the earth, the sun above, all divine essences and ecstacies, come to this silence at last–a circle of bread and a cup of wine on an altar."

Brown's next publication was another collection of short stories, *Hawkfall and Other Stories,* published in 1974, a year that began with his award of the Order of the British Empire for his services to literature. The stories in *Hawkfall and Other Stories* are largely concerned with death: those in *The Sun's Net,* published in 1976, celebrate life, with several stories featuring birth as a central element. Another volume of short stories, *Andrina and Other Stories,* appeared in 1983.

Brown's novel-writing career was resumed in 1984 with the publication of *Time in a Red Coat.* This novel is unique in Brown's canon in not being set mainly in Orkney, although the central character does eventually land on Ottervoe, "an island in the North Atlantic." The protagonist of this narrative is a girl who, in a fairy-tale episode, is given gifts by a White Guardian and a Black Guardian to help her in her journey through life. The White Guardian's gift is a flute carved with the figures of a sun, a horse, and a bird. From the Black Guardian she receives a bag of coins. The main body of the text describes the journeys made by the girl through geographical and temporal space, ranging over the centuries and encountering violence in the shape of wars and battles.

The omens at the birth of the girl are not good. She is born in ancient China, at a time when the people are celebrating a masque of peace, but as she arrives in the world, the barbarians breach the Great Wall. The first chapter describes the preparation for and performance of the masque, which is enacted by puppets. The puppets perform a masque of love and marriage and then one of death. The masque of birth is interrupted by the invasion of the Mongol army, and instead a real birth–the girl's–takes place, followed by a real death, that of her mother.

Armed only with her gifts, the child embarks on her journey through time and space, seemingly condemned to roam the world forever. She does not age and is impervious to the danger she encounters at every turn. The bag of silver and gold coins–described by the Black Guardian as the "earth's whole heart's desire"–is used to pay her way through the centuries.

Clearly, there is little attempt at realistic narrative in this novel. Rather, Brown loads his tale with symbols, repeatedly returning to the dove of peace and the dragon of war. The various conflicts and battles encountered by the girl are described in realistic terms, but the novel operates at a more rarefied level. The narrative frequently takes on a somewhat portentous tone, never more so than when dealing with the effects of the barbarism that is present at the opening of the novel. In a chapter headed "The Longest Journey," for example, a dying soldier–originally from Orkney–replays significant moments of his life as his soul dallies over which road to take, that of Life or Death. In a moment of spiritual enlightenment the soldier realizes a vital truth, described by Brown in words that recall his previous novel, *Magnus:*

> These events, painful enough at the time of their enacting, came now upon our traveller in all their starkness and pity: especially this, that what we do for others' good on earth may end in bitterness and terrible heart-wounds; and yet what we see as "an end" is not the true end; no, all is gathered into a web beyond our computing or comprehension; and while we must seek always to do good, yet that good and every earthly striving to make things well are (because of ignorance and the vain illusions of the self) but rags of the perdurable seamless garment: Truth itself.

The soldier is saved from the Inn of Death by the voice of the girl, who convinces his enemies to dress his wounds and look after him. It provides her with an image of home, too, and in the final chapter an old woman, who is apparently the girl, is now resident on Ottervoe and tells the story of a girl who wandered through the centuries bringing the dove of peace in place of the dragon of war. She says, "it's a lie, like all stories," but her granddaughter, who represents renewal and hope, seems to accept the tale as true. The redemption that ends all Brown's novels consists here in the girl's (and the soldier's) release from time, so that they can live out their lives as mortals.

Time in a Red Coat uses the techniques and language of fairy tale to make a powerful antiwar statement that never reads like polemic because of the poetic richness of the imagery Brown employs. As in all of Brown's works, the potential for renewal and redemption is always present, even at the darkest moments of history.

Brown continued to write poetry and short stories as a counterpoint to his novel writing, producing two major collections of short stories (*The Golden Bird: Two Orkney Stories,* 1987, and *The Masked Fisherman and Other Stories,* 1989) and some important poetry (in particular the 1989 collection *The Wreck of the Archangel*) between *Time in a Red Coat* and his next novel, *Vinland,* published in 1992. This work returns to the familiar historical heritage of Orkney and may be seen to be in some ways a prequel to *Magnus.* The events fictionalized in *Vinland* relate to the period when Orkney, still pagan, was ruled by the grandfather of Magnus, Thorfinn. The central character is not, however, a member of the ruling class but a fictional creation, Ranald Sigmundson, whose career as a sailor and soldier involved him in some of the key events of the time. The result is

Dust jacket for Brown's 1998 book, in which the title story concerns the Scottish legend of the selkie, *or seal-man (Richland County Public Library)*

an entertaining dramatized history, with the stages in Ranald's personal development from pagan boy to converted Christian old man played out against a backdrop of bloody and violent events. The bildungsroman elements are balanced by the historical chronicle of the advent of Christianity on the Orkney Islands, and it is that aspect that the novel emphasizes at its conclusion. In the main narrative, though, Brown takes the reader on an exhilarating journey through Viking history.

The boy Ranald, son to Sigmund Firemouth, a sailor of Hamnavoe (the old name for Brown's hometown of Stromness), is born to the sea and voyages to Iceland with his father in the opening pages of the novel. His adventures begin in earnest when he stows away on Leif Eriksson's voyage across the Atlantic Ocean. As a result of his journey to these newfound lands, he is summoned to the Norwegian court to give an account of his travels. As he reaches manhood Ranald becomes ever more involved in the politics of Orkney and finds himself fighting alongside Earl Sigurd in Ireland.

Ranald, like the girl in *Time in a Red Coat,* longs for peace, and as he grows older he withdraws from public life to farm and to study. Eventually he lives a hermit-like existence as he prepares for his final voyage. The bold soldier-sailor has turned into a Christian philosopher by this stage, one who advocates peace in the words of the Song of Solomon, and in so doing envisions the advent of Magnus: "I am thinking now, rather of a saint who will confront these men of blood and compel them to beat their swords into plough-shares. He will walk through the island in a coat of light, when he comes at last, this saint. People will come to him gladly with their sick minds and bodies. He will set the seal of peace on our cruel history."

The tale of Ranald is told in Brown's characteristic deliberate prose by an omniscient narrator whose approach mirrors the language of myth and fairy tale. *Vinland* begins with a typically simple opening pair of sentences, reminiscent of a children's tale: "There was a boy who lived in a hamlet in Orkney called Hamnavoe. The boy's name was Ranald." Unusually, though, the third-person narrator is constant throughout the novel. Unlike the multiple perspectives of *Greenvoe* or the alienating switches of viewpoint in *Magnus,* this novel maintains a traditional approach, in keeping with its historical theme. Brown is particularly successful at integrating the story of Ranald Sigmundson into the historical record of the earls of Orkney. Philippa

Toomey's review in *The Times* (London) of 19 December 1992 was typical of many in its praise: "Simply written, it casts the spell of a saga, meditating on the mystery of the purpose of a man's life and death." It is Brown's distinctive emphasis on the emotional odyssey of his protagonist as much as the physical journeys he undertakes that sets this novel apart from other historical tales of the Dark Ages.

Brown's final novel, published in 1994 just two years before his death, is the one that garnered more critical praise than any of his other novels. *Beside the Ocean of Time* was short-listed for the prestigious Booker Prize in the year of its publication and was extremely well received by critics. Perhaps even more so than in his previous novels, this work engages with the matter of Orkney myth and legend.

The central figure in the novel is a boy, Thorfinn, who, like Brown himself, is a dreamer. His imagination provides the escape route from the dullness of his life as a schoolboy on the remote island of Norday. The schoolroom of the 1930s gives way in his mind to a succession of more-exotic scenes, as he imagines himself into a twelfth-century Viking voyage to Russia and Byzantium with Earl Rognvald, then at the battle of Bannockburn, then as a Celtic troubadour. In the narrative, twentieth-century reality is juxtaposed with the legends and chronicles of the past. Thorfinn's imagination places people he knows in historical settings, so that Mr. MacTavish the publican is transformed in Thorfinn's mind into a boastful knight at Bannockburn, his Scottish Nationalist beliefs translated into an allegiance to Robert the Bruce.

The coming war casts its shadow on the island, and in a passage reminiscent of the arrival of Black Star in *Greenvoe,* the farms and settlements of Norday are destroyed to make way for the machinery of war; Thorfinn enlists and is eventually captured and imprisoned in a German camp, where he fills his time by writing the stories readers have encountered earlier in the novel. A kindly camp commandant (significantly, he is a southern German Catholic) encourages him, to the point of giving him a typewriter and helping him to dispatch his typescript to a London publisher. After the war he lives in Edinburgh, a "hack historian" churning out romantic potboilers. Then he discovers his true theme and writes a novel that sounds exactly like *Greenvoe:* "He tried something different–the impact on a primitive simple society, close to the elements, of a massive modern technology. He had experienced it at first hand, in his native island, when that pastoral place had been almost overnight changed into a fortress in the months before the Second World War." The novel, like *Greenvoe,* is successful and enables him to return to the now-deserted island with the girl he met years before. The cycle of nature's renewal begins again as they vow to cultivate the land and await the arrival of their son, "who will be the poet." Thus life on the island will begin to take on some of the features of its prewar existence, as Thorfinn and Sophie walk "beside the ocean of the end and the beginning."

Beside the Ocean of Time distills Brown's art in poetically charged prose that manages to, in Thorfinn's words, "dredge something rich and strange out of the mythical past of the islands." Thorfinn, like Brown, perhaps, knows that "It is a seam of rich ore." Also like Brown, Thorfinn writes about what he knows and invests his work with the ancient wisdom that is part of his inheritance.

Following the publication of *Beside the Ocean of Time,* Brown wrote two collections of short stories, the second of which was published posthumously. The first, *Winter Tales,* was published in 1995 and gathers material published, often in obscure journals, over the previous twenty years. The thread that links nearly all the tales in this collection is the familiar one of the encounter between the old Orcadian ways and the forces of the external world. The stories are set variously in the Dark and Middle Ages, the eighteenth century, and the twentieth century; Brown's introduction suggests that they are mainly "calendar tales, that yield their best treasure in midwinter when the barns are full."

Possibly the most surprising and untypical piece is "Lieutenant Bligh and Two Midshipmen," which deals with the relationship between Bligh of the HMS *Bounty* and his midshipman, George Stewart, an Orkney man. The tale focuses on Bligh's first meeting with Stewart, while his ship was anchored at Hamnavoe. From this historical incident Brown fashions a narrative of some pathos, which is influenced by the note he prefaces to the story. In it he reports that Stewart joined Bligh's expedition on the *Bounty* and that he drowned on the way back to face trial after the mutiny. Another eighteenth-century story, "The Laird's Son," has as its first-person protagonist a son forced to abandon the newfound delights of Edinburgh to look after his ailing father's estate in Shetland. There his spirits are unexpectedly raised by the grave respect with which he is greeted and by his observations of the rituals by which the Scottish townsfolk live their lives. The austere simplicity of their way of life contrasts in his mind with the emptiness of the Edinburgh social whirl he has left behind. His short stay includes a celebration of Christmas in a cow byre reminiscent of Thomas Hardy's poem "The Oxen" (1915). Thus, the sophisticate who takes Henry Mackenzie's *The Man of Feeling* (1771) to comfort him on his journey learns true simplicity.

Other pieces in this collection cover more familiar ground. "A Crusader's Christmas" features Rognvald on his way to Jerusalem; "The Architect" concerns a master mason's year on a pagan Orkney Island, culminating in the Christian affirmation of the midnight mass; "A Boy's Calendar" chronicles a year in which a boy absorbs the history of Orkney. In themselves the tales are often slight, but their value lies in the beauty of Brown's natural descriptions. Ultimately, the collection celebrates the tenacity of the Orcadian worldview in an ever changing environment.

Brown's posthumously published collection of stories, *The Island of the Women and Other Stories* (1998), remains true to his lifelong concerns. The title story employs one of the islands' legends, that of the seal-man, or selkie. Brown, as he had done so often, combines evocative historical detail, in this case from the early period of Viking domination, with the oral tradition of the folktale to create a hybrid form–lyrical prose with the cadences of ancient storytelling. That Brown took his role as a storyteller and as a keeper of a tradition seriously is evident in his work. In "Poet and Prince: A Fable" he attempts a fictive account of the role of the writer in society. The story begins in an unnamed European state, where a competition for the post of official laureate is being held, and concludes on a remote Orkney Island, where, as Paul Binding in *TLS: The Times Literary Supplement* (14 August 1998) puts it, "patron and patronized are exiled in lonely symbiotic existence, mutually giving, mutually destructive." Brown's total identification with Orkney and its traditions perhaps lifts him above the status of the officially approved writer-worker; certainly, it is not too fanciful to see him as one of the last bards.

Brown's prowess as a poet led to many collaborations with the composer Peter Maxwell Davies, often involving Brown's words set to his music, though occasionally taking more spectacular forms, as in *A Celebration for Magnus,* a "son-et-lumière" production written to mark the 850th anniversary of St. Magnus Cathedral in 1987. He was also active as a dramatist, largely focusing on Orkney and religious themes in such pieces as *A Spell for Green Corn* (1970) and *The Voyage of St Brandon* (published in *Three Plays,* 1984). To a degree, then, his career as a novelist is secondary to his career in other fields of literary endeavor. The posthumously published *Northern Lights: A Poet's Sources* (1999) provides ample evidence as to the variety of his skills. In this volume many uncollected pieces of prose and poetry are interwoven with his reflections on Orkney life from his weekly newspaper column. A passage written in 1993 shows Brown reflecting on his art and its relationship with his environment: "The ethos and outlook of the islanders has changed greatly since I was a child. People are more prosperous, but the community spirit has everywhere slackened, and the language becomes increasingly impoverished. But sea and islands and hills are still there, and I am thankful that I saw those everlasting things with a child's eye, and the vivid people who lived among them, and their ancient benign rituals."

Perhaps it is true to say that George Mackay Brown was a more accomplished poet than he was a novelist. Even so, the poet's eye informs his prose at every turn, rewarding his readers with a deeply evocative sense of place and history. The critic Tom Scott, writing in *Chapman* (Spring 1990), was accurate when he suggested that "His is essentially a narrative-poetic gift: and poetic means his language sings, intones, even in prose."

Bibliographies:

Osamu Yamada, Hilda D. Spear, and David S. Robb, *The Contribution to Literature of Orcadian Writer George Mackay Brown: An Introduction and a Bibliography,* Studies in British Literature, no. 16 (Lewiston, N.Y. & Lampeter: Edwin Mellen Press, 1991);

Yamada, "A Supplement to the Bibliography of George Mackay Brown," *Dokkyo University Studies in English,* 49 (August 1998).

References:

Alan Bold, *George Mackay Brown* (Edinburgh: Oliver & Boyd, 1978; New York: Barnes & Noble, 1978);

Ian Campbell, "Beside Brown's Ocean of Time," in *Studies in Scottish Fiction: 1945 to the Present,* edited by Susanne Hagemann (Frankfurt am Main & New York: Peter Lang, 1996), pp. 263–274;

Berthold Schoene-Harwood, *The Making of Orcadia: Narrative Identity in the Prose Work of George Mackay Brown* (Frankfurt am Main & New York: Peter Lang, 1995);

Schoene-Harwood, "Narrative Fragmentation and Mythical Closure in the Shorter Historical Fiction of George Mackay Brown," *Scottish Literary Journal,* 22 (November 1995): 41–59;

Tom Scott, "Orkney as Pairt o an Eternal Mood," *Chapman,* 60 (Spring 1990): 32–40;

Hilda D. Spear, ed., *George Mackay Brown–A Survey of His Work and a Full Bibliography,* Studies in British Literature, no. 48 (Lewiston, N.Y. & Lampeter: Edwin Mellen Press, 2000).

Papers:

The George Mackay Brown Archive of manuscript material is housed at the University of Edinburgh.

Louis de Bernières

(8 December 1954 –   )

Nicholas Birns
New School University

BOOKS: *The War of Don Emmanuel's Nether Parts* (London: Secker & Warburg, 1990; New York: Morrow, 1992);
Señor Vivo and the Coca Lord (London: Secker & Warburg, 1991; New York: Morrow, 1992);
The Troublesome Offspring of Cardinal Guzman (London: Secker & Warburg, 1992; New York: Morrow, 1994);
Labels, illustrated by Christopher Wormald (London: One Horse Press, 1993);
Captain Corelli's Mandolin (London: Secker & Warburg, 1994); republished as *Corelli's Mandolin* (New York: Pantheon, 1994);
A Day Out for Mehmet Erbil, illustrated by Eileen Hogan (London: Belmont Press, 1999);
Red Dog, illustrated by Alan Baker (London: Secker & Warburg, 2001; New York: Pantheon, 2001);
Sunday Morning at the Centre of The World: A Play for Voices (London: Vintage, 2001);
Gunter Weber's Confession (London: Tartarus, 2001).

PLAY PRODUCTION: *Sunday Morning at the Centre of the World,* Swansea, Wales, Dylan Thomas Centre, 1999.

PRODUCED SCRIPTS: *A Mad British Pervert Has a Sexual Fantasy About the 10th Street Bridge in Calgary,* radio, Canadian Broadcasting Corporation, 1996;
Sunday Morning at the Centre of the World, radio, BBC Radio 4, March 1999.

OTHER: Joachim Machado de Assis, *Philosopher or Dog?* translated by Clotilde Wilson, introduction by de Bernières (London: Bloomsbury, 1997);
The Book of Job: Authorised King James Version, Pocket Canon Series, introduction by de Bernières (Edinburgh: Canongate, 1998; New York: Grove, 1999);
"The Death of Miss Agatha Feakes," in *Shorts: New Writing from Granta Books* (London: Granta, 1998);

Louis de Bernières (photograph by Rupert Conant; from the dust jacket for the U.S. edition of Señor Vivo and the Coca Lord, *1992)*

"Feathers in our Knickers," in *Does the Sun Rise Over Dagenham? and Other Stories: New Writing from London,* foreword by Mark Lawson (London: Fourth Estate, 1998);
Hartley Coleridge, *Bricks Without Mortar: A Selection of Poems from Hartley Coleridge,* edited by Lisa Gee, introduction by de Bernières (London: Picador, 2000);

Steve Clark, *Captain Corelli's Mandolin: The Illustrated Film Companion,* introduction by de Bernières (London: Headline, 2001).

SELECTED PERIODICAL PUBLICATIONS–UNCOLLECTED: "The Brass Bar," *Granta,* 43 (Spring 1993): 23–31;

"Our Lady of Beauty," *Paris Review* (Fall 1998): 67–79;

"A Conditional Being," *Sunday Telegraph* (London), 14 February 1999;

"The Turks are so wonderful with children," *Guardian,* 1 January 2000.

Louis de Bernières helped broaden the canvas of British fiction in the 1990s, gaining a considerable popular appeal with his use of Latin American and continental European settings, his willingness to allow history and politics to be constituents of the novelistic canvas, and his ability to create recognizable yet individual characters. Without being deliberately experimental, he breaks out of novelistic forms as they have been traditionally conceived. At times de Bernières's work deals with themes–such as the brutality of war and political oppression–that might be soft-pedaled by more genteel or formalistic writers. Yet, part of his appeal is a strong comic sensibility. De Bernières is unafraid to laugh, or to encourage the reader to laugh, at situations with respect to which the only permissible literary attitude might be deemed one of dead seriousness. Although his books are ambitious in scope, their sense of fun and their use of satire to portray cultural intricacies make them accessible to a broad audience.

De Bernières is best known for *Captain Corelli's Mandolin* (1994; published in the United States as *Corelli's Mandolin*), an historical novel set on the Greek island of Cephallonia during World War II, which was adapted into a motion picture directed by John Madden that was released in 2001, starring Nicolas Cage, Penélope Cruz, and Christian Bale. De Bernières's earlier Latin American trilogy has been overshadowed by the success of his fourth novel, but it represented an important step in integrating the themes and techniques of the Latin American novel into a British fictional tradition often criticized for being parochial and formally nonexperimental.

Louis de Bernière-Smart was born in London on 8 December 1954 to Reginald Piers Alexander de Bernière-Smart and Jean Ashton de Bernière-Smart. His father was an army officer who spent time overseas in the Middle East. De Bernières grew up in Hambledon, Surrey, and as a teenager attended Bradfield College (the equivalent of an American high school). In 1969 de Bernières spent four months at Sandhurst, the British military academy, but found it was not suitable for him. After leaving Sandhurst, de Bernières spent approximately a year in Colombia, where he served as a private tutor and worked on a livestock farm. This period provided the inspiration for the setting of his first three novels. He then matriculated as a baccalaureate student and graduated with a degree in philosophy from the University of Manchester in 1977. He obtained a certificate of education at Leicester Polytechnic in 1981 and a master of arts degree from the University of London in 1985. He worked variously as a mechanic, bookseller, motorcycle courier, landscape gardener, and (for the majority of the time) as a teacher. In 1982 a motorcycling accident temporarily immobilized de Bernières, and he took up writing as a way to cope with his sudden enforced leisure.

In the late 1980s de Bernières began publishing short fiction in prominent British literary magazines such as *Granta* (an excellent credential for an aspiring British novelist during this period). These stories established the characteristic tone of de Bernières's narratives, in which the writer seemed to have read and assimilated much previous fiction, all the while striving for a notable idiosyncrasy of style. The Surrealist label is, in broad measure, applicable to de Bernières's early work; however, the discerning reader can see much in it that the Surrealist label does not quite cover, including a matter-of-fact tone that balances the unlikeliness of incident often to be found in the plots of the stories.

De Bernières's first novel, *The War of Don Emmanuel's Nether Parts,* was published in Britain by Secker and Warburg in 1990; the U.S. edition was published by William Morrow two years later. For this novel, de Bernières was honored with a regional award of the Commonwealth Writers Prize in 1991. *The War of Don Emmanuel's Nether Parts* is the first book of de Bernières's Latin American trilogy, a group of novels that decisively put the author on the literary map. The book is set in an imaginary South American country, mostly reminiscent of Colombia but also having echoes of Venezuela and, especially in the Portuguese diction in the represented patois of the characters, of Brazil. *The War of Don Emmanuel's Nether Parts* has no British characters, though the title character, Don Emmanuel, is descended from Welsh forebears. Even though most readers would assume that de Bernières's Latin American trilogy draws on his personal experiences in the region, there is no character in any of the books that could serve as a straightforward surrogate for the author. In this way de Bernières' work is similar in its South American setting to that of the Pakistani-American novelist Zulfikar Ghose in his Brazilian trilogy, though de Bernières' style is more narratively oriented and exhibited with more flair.

Dust jacket for the U.S. edition of de Bernières's 1990 novel, the first book of a trilogy set in an imaginary Latin American country (Richland County Public Library)

The War of Don Emmanuel's Nether Parts has an episodic structure. The book is divided into forty-three chapters, which, with a length (in the British edition) of 376 pages, averages just less than 9 pages per chapter. Each chapter has a title that signals the narrative content to be found therein. For example, chapter 12 is titled "Federico Is Taught To Be A Guerrilla and General Fuerte Is Captured." This device, reminiscent of many eighteenth- and nineteenth-century novels, both foregrounds and subverts the general emphasis on plot in the novel. The chapter titles signal the reader that plot is important; yet, by revealing the action to be found in the chapters, the titles do away with any sort of short-term narrative suspense. The reader's attention is thus partially deflected from what is happening in the chapter to how the author is presenting what happens.

The Latin American setting of the book and its nostalgic yet buoyant embrace of traditional narrative were the features of *The War of Don Emmanuel's Nether Parts* most discussed by reviewers on both sides of the Atlantic. The reviewers, however, did not know quite what to make of de Bernières's writing. Thus, aspects of the book that de Bernières might well have intended as narrative strategies were interpreted as flaws. Susan Lowell, for example, reviewing the novel for *The New York Times* (1 March 1992), said that "The characters tend to be types: clever peasants, wise whores, haughty dames transformed by love, knights-errant. And in fact this book, although labeled a novel, is really a romance."

Many reviewers of this volume and subsequent books in the trilogy compared de Bernières to Gabriel García Márquez, the Colombian novelist who won the 1982 Nobel Prize in literature. They noted that de Bernières shared the Colombian writer's interest in using the magic realist mode to represent social upheaval. Reviewers also mentioned that de Bernières's outlook was generally more optimistic than that of García Márquez. Part of this difference is no doubt attributable to de Bernières's more playful sensibility, but some of it can be seen to stem from being an outsider, in which context the more celebratory aspects–rather than a fundamental bitterness toward the social situation of Latin America, as with García Márquez–might be seen as part of the author's demonstration of his attachment to the setting. Another difference is generational; de Bernières is twenty-six years younger than García Márquez. Although de Bernières's Latin American trilogy was published in the 1990s, the Latin America it describes is largely an abstracted and fictionalized version of the region as it was in the 1970s and 1980s.

The action of *The War of Don Emmanuel's Nether Parts* begins when Doña Constanza, a wealthy local landowner, decides to divert the Mula River in order to save her swimming pool from drought. This action threatens local farmers, who are dependent on the river for their economic livelihood. The effect of Doña Constanza's action that ignites resistance, however, is the threat the diversion poses to the bathing habits of Don Emmanuel, a cultivated gentleman of partially Welsh descent who likes to bathe his "nether parts" in the river and is both bewildered and outraged by the diversion. Don Emmanuel is but one of an array of individuals and groups dissatisfied with prevailing conditions. Remedios is a young female political activist who decides she must join the rebel guerrillas' military struggle because of the excessive fragmentation of the civilian political parties on the Left. General Fuerte is an unusually reflective military officer who decides that he cannot countenance his service's prevailing methods of repression and torture, as represented by the sadistic Captain (later Colonel) Rodrigo Figueras, the principal villain of the book. Federico is an idealistic and imaginative young man who ends up joining the guerrillas less out of political resentment than out of an abstract sense of wanting to perform good deeds and see that justice is done.

The book, as befits its episodic structure, has no one main character. Instead, the action weaves between the several principal characters, picking up one thread of narrative, then going to other threads for a few chapters, and eventually returning to any given thread within a range of no more than five chapters. Although the principal characters meet one another at various times, there is never a single point at which all the threads converge. General Fuerte's character experiences the most development in the book. At the beginning of the novel he is a skeptical but loyal general who is a part of the military establishment. He is captured by the guerrillas and tried for crimes against humanity; his willingness to die in punishment not for his own personal misdeeds but for those of the military establishment he has served impresses the guerrillas, and they spare his life. Doña Costanza similarly is kidnapped and begins to change her perspective on life, particularly after she begins a love affair with a guerrilla named Gonzago. Her repentance, though, is not as complete as the general's, and her transformation occurs more out of passion than out of a full intellectual reconsideration.

The turning point of the action is a rain of cats that occurs in chapter 27, "Of Cures, Cats, and Laughter," which is one of a few chapters that take the form of a first-person letter written by a French emigré named Antoine to his mother, a passage from which serves as a good example of de Bernières's descriptive style:

> If that were not strange enough, we were afflicted immediately afterward in that area with the most extraordinary plague, though I hasten to add it is a benign one. You may have noticed (how could you help it?) that there are muddy paw marks on the paper and that my handwriting is unusually erratic. This is because there has been a large black cat trying to sit on the paper as I write and also taking swipes at my pen as it moves. "What is so strange about that?" I hear you say. "My son loves cats." What is so strange, Maman, is that we are absolutely inundated with a flood of cats of biblical proportions. I cannot describe to you the sheer quantity of these animals that have appeared out of nowhere! They are sitting on fence posts, on gates. They are draped voluptuously across roofs and branches; they are in the Jeep, in my house, in the stable, in the fields. I cannot sit out at night, as is my wont, because three or four cats instantly leap on my lap and onto my shoulders, and they also occupy Françoise's hammock on the porch. I have to turn them out of my sink before I can wash my hands and also out of the shower last thing at night.

The rain of cats represents a kind of absurd excess that in the context of the harsh setting of the novel acts as an act of deliverance. The analogies to the biblical flood are played up in a mock-epic way, with the rebel community eventually being characterized as "postdiluvian." The rain of cats acts as a kind of signal that fortune is on the side of the rebels, and, indeed, they escape from Colonel Figueras, who is later blown up by a land mine. General Fuerte dies, too (or dies naturally after a Lazarus-like resurrection), as a kind of final expiation; the reverence accorded his memory heralds a potentially more moderate tone to the existing government. The novel ends with the rebels founding (on old Inca ruins) the utopian community of Cochadebajo de Los Gatos, the name derived from the *gatos* (cats) who become a kind of emblem of the freewheeling exuberance of the new community. De Bernières's affection for cats is well known; his 1996 interview with Helena de Bertodano for *The Daily Telegraph* (London) mentioned his Burmese cat, Toby. This community verges on earthly paradise; yet, it is an escape from society, and in the settled parts of the country injustice and corruption remain notwithstanding General Fuerte's sacrifice.

Despite its rollicking tone, *The War of Don Emmanuel's Nether Parts* is mainly preoccupied with politics. Elements of the narrative seem reminiscent of journalistic accounts of Latin America by English-speaking writers in the 1980s. The episode in which the army invades the vacant British possession of the Isle of Pigs resembles the Falkland Islands War between Britain and Argentina in 1982. The cameo portraits in chapter 33 of the economics minister, Dr. Jorge Badajoz, whose neoliberal policies dismantle the manufacturing base of the country in a futile attempt to generate short-term prosperity by increasing foreign exports, and of the mayor of the capital city, Raoul Buenanoce, who builds a lavish Inca theme park as a tourist attraction (an unsuccessful one, it turns out) even as the Indian peoples it represents are being oppressed by the state structure, are only moderate exaggerations of actions undertaken by the neoliberal governments of the region in the late 1980s–such as those of Rául Alfons'n (Argentina), José Sarney (Brazil), and Jaime Lusinchi (Venezuela). De Bernières's ultimate vantage point is nonetheless much more abstract. He is asking questions having do to with political philosophy: What is a just society? Is armed resistance against an unjust order legitimate? What are persons of conscience to do when they realize that, for all their personal virtue, they are but cogs in an immoral system? The distance provided by the foreign setting enables de Bernières to use it as a laboratory for working out these ethical and political dilemmas.

Dust jacket for the U.S. edition of de Bernières's 1991 novel, the second book in his Latin American trilogy, about a philosophy student who successfully campaigns against a narcotics kingpin (Richland County Public Library)

The middle novel in the Latin America trilogy, *Señor Vivo and the Coca Lord,* was published in Britain by Secker and Warburg in 1991 and in the United States by William Morrow the following year. Like its predecessor, it was awarded a regional Commonwealth Writers Prize, the honor being bestowed in 1992. The book assumes the reader knows the plot of the previous novel, though certain names and events are mentioned only in an inconspicuous way. Dionisio Vivo is a young man studying philosophy at the University of Ipasueña, located in the city of the same name. Vivo is outraged by the hegemony of the cocaine trade over his country and writes a series of letters to the newspaper in protest. He falls in love with Anica Moreno, an Amazon-like woman from the regions near the Amazon. Vivo is the son of a high-ranking general and as such has a reasonably privileged place in the society. Dionisio Vivo's best friend, the policeman Ramon, supplies the practicality that the sometimes dreamy Vivo lacks and protects his friend from excessive harassment by the authorities. Vivo's great antagonist is El Jerarca, the coca lord of the title, whose avarice and sense of his own entrenched power recoil against both Vivo's activism against the drug trade and the general spirit of enlightenment and idealism that Vivo represents.

Señor Vivo and the Coca Lord has an episodic structure and narrative chapter titles that are similar to de Bernières's first book. At 279 pages, it is shorter, and the general impression the book gives is of a more tightly knit unit. Rather than a panoply of characters, as in the first book, de Bernières's second novel centers on one primary protagonist, Vivo, and a restricted circle of associates and antagonists. This tighter focus enables the author to achieve greater depth of character and concentrate more on elaborating upon the themes of the book than on relating a series of incidents. This depth is greatest in a particularly searing scene in which Anica is tortured and raped by El Jerarca's henchmen. *Señor Vivo and the Coca Lord* also has a more dramatic and suspenseful finale, in which Ramon gives his life to defend Vivo, and the latter triumphs over El Jerarca, ending the coca lord's reign of terror. Vivo then establishes himself beyond the reach of power in Cochadebajo de los Gatos, though unlike the refugees of the first book, whose rebellion has been forgotten, his accomplishments still resonate in the metropolitan center of Ipasueño. As if to make sure not to give the book an overly upbeat ending, de Bernières relates a final anecdote: the nation receives aid from abroad to destroy drug crops and plant legitimate crops such as coffee. By a kind of bureaucratic perversity, though, the grant only applies when a legitimate crop replaces a drug crop, not when coffee or such is planted afresh. Thus, there is an (unintended) incentive to plant drug crops, then receive money for uprooting the plants. This closing note of irony acts as a restraint upon the often exhilarating developments in the main sequence, in which Vivo continually finds his aspirations falling short of the realities his society is prepared to accept.

Vivo does not accept the constraints of the society in which he has matured. He looks for a world elsewhere, a world in which the principles of the philosophers he has read can be realized. Vivo's reading of philosophy is an important element of the book. The philosophers that Vivo reads are of the European tradition, similar to those de Bernières might have read as a philosophy student at the University of Manchester in the mid 1970s. De Bernières portrays Latin America as what the Brazilian social theorist José Guilherme Merquior called "el otro ocidente" (another West)–a part of the West far more disadvantaged and unstable than Europe and North America, but still an heir to the same traditions of classical, Christian, and Enlightenment thought. The Latin America of the trilogy is a place that, though possessing a troubled and damaged societal history, is still a part of Western civilization. Vivo himself is a kind of emissary for the renewed embrace of Western civilization and values. His efforts to introduce the idea of rational reflection in a world of brutality, and of personal loyalty in a context of pure exploitation, make him both admired and feared by different sectors of the society.

Vivo's father, the general, bears significant resemblances to General Fuerte in the first book. Although de Bernières does not always represent the military this positively, all his novels include military figures and settings, a motif perhaps attributable to his father's military experience or to his own short tenure at Sandhurst. The high status possessed by Vivo's father gives him special advantages. It protects him from retribution for some of his actions; yet, it also gives him leverage to effect social change in a way that others might not. An intriguing minor character is President Veracruz, the head of state of the imaginary country. He is ineffectual and unresponsive to his people. Yet, his eccentricity as an aloof, neurotic, withdrawn politician is benign compared to El Jerarca and some of the military, and if he were the only problem with the setting depicted in the book, the tone of the novel would be far less dark.

Señor Vivo and the Coca Lord received reviews similar to those that *The War of Don Emmanuel's Nether Parts* had received. Interestingly, John Lennard, writing for *TLS: The Times Literary Supplement* (21 June 1991), called the book "science fiction" and de Bernières has been included in reference books on science fiction, such as *Magill's Guide to Science Fiction and Fantasy Literature* (1996), edited by T. A. Shippey. This classification comes despite the generally realistic and present-day or near-present settings of his books. De Bernières's use of unlikely plot incidents might account for his being termed a science-fiction writer, though it is more likely the utopian dimension of de Bernières's work that has led critics to place it in a science-fictional context.

The Troublesome Offspring of Cardinal Guzman (1992) is the last and most ambitious volume in the Latin American trilogy. At 387 pages and divided into two parts, the novel is a final capstone on the imaginary world the author has created. Each book of the Latin American trilogy emphasizes a different dimension of experience: in *The War of Don Emmanuel's Nether Parts* the focus is on politics; *Señor Vivo and the Coca Lord,* with its philosophically minded protagonist, is the most intellectually oriented of the three books; and in *The Troublesome Offspring of Cardinal Guzman* religion receives the spotlight. This focus is not just because of the title character, Cardinal Dominic Trujillo Guzman; the cardinal's brother, Salvador, attempting to mock his brother, pretends to be a priest and intones obscene passages from the first-century B.C. Latin poet Catullus that the uneducated locals believe to be church Latin; and another character is Father García, the local parish priest who is urbane and compassionate yet becomes insane. In addition, a principal motif of the novel is "The New Albigensian Crusade." This crusade is prompted when Cardinal Guzman develops a monster in his belly, which prompts him to kill his own son, who is then transformed into a hummingbird. Guzman makes statements that the military uses to justify the suppression of the rebels as an act undertaken in God's name. The original Albigensians were heretics in thirteenth-century southern France who were suppressed by the Roman Catholic Church, and by likening his contemporary dissenters and mavericks to the Albigensians, de Bernières gives them a heretical aura. Conversely, he gives them an historical pedigree, also signaled in the conceit of the resurrection of a sixteenth-century Spanish conquistador, Conde Xavier Pompaya de Estremadura, who is freed from a frozen glacier and joins the rebels.

The organization of the novel differs slightly from that of its predecessors. Some chapter titles are narrative, but sometimes the chapters are given the title of a general theme or the name of the character who relates a first-person narrative within them; the titles are often repeated within the fifty-six chapters, creating a recurring pattern. One reappearing narrator is the Mexican musicologist, an outsider who becomes wealthy as a result of popularizing what he thinks is a traditional folk tune but is in fact a piece of music composed by Dionisio Vivo. Since Mexico, though a Latin American nation, is not in South America, his first-person narration provides a somewhat detached perspective on the action. Several characters from the previous books, such as Remedios, Doña Constanza, and Señor Vivo, also reappear in subordinate roles.

De Bernières's depiction of religion in the novel, specifically the presence of Cardinal Guzman and other priests in the context of Latin American social revolution, is influenced by the ecclesiastical movement known as "liberation theology" that flourished in Latin America from the late 1960s to the early 1990s. Liberation theology, while upholding many traditional Christian doctrines, stressed the establishment of "base communities" (small groups of Christians gathering to study Scripture and work for social justice) centered in the historically oppressed classes and emphasized a "preferential option for the poor"–an alignment of the Church with the interests of the poor rather than the wealthy–that often took the form of protesting actively against social injustice, particularly under authoritarian military dictatorships. Thus, the attitudes toward reli-

De Bernières, with the tool featured in "The Brass Bar," his 1993 essay about his stint as an automobile mechanic (photograph by Barry Lewis)

gion in the book fall outside traditional Left-Right antagonisms in that the Left is usually perceived as anticlerical, especially in Hispanophone countries. The title is inherently paradoxical, since Roman Catholic priests are supposed to remain celibate and thus not have offspring. De Bernières's portrait of Cardinal Guzman's erotic self-realization is not merely lascivious, however, though reviewers such as James Polk, writing in *The New York Times Book Review* (8 May 1994), saw the author as championing "good times and fornication" (quoting from the end of the third chapter of the novel). Cardinal Guzman is depicted as a human being who happens to be a priest and is afflicted with relatively normal human failings. In a sense, his love for women enables him to share more in the daily life and fate of his flock. De Bernières's frequent references to the Bible are sometimes jocular in spirit, but this jocularity is set against a background of deep understanding of the biblical material. His interest in the Bible can be seen in his writing an insightful introduction to an edition of the Old Testament Book of Job in 1998. In addition, the epigraph to *Señor Vivo and the Coca Lord* is from the biblical Song of Solomon.

As befits the tragicomic tone of the book, the ending is muted and ironic. The rebels beat back their opponents, not through their own efforts but through the miraculous manifestation of a devastating mudslide that overwhelms the military forces. President Veracruz is impeached and humiliated; however, clearly his successor, former foreign secretary Lopez Garcilaso Vallejo, while less corrupt, will not be a truly enlightened or effective leader. But the community of Cochadebajo de los Gatos have instilled in themselves a spirit of resilience and autonomy and will no longer be intimidated by overbearing tyrants.

After publishing *The Troublesome Offspring of Cardinal Guzman,* de Bernières decided to end the Latin American series, though he had originally conceived it as five books. De Bernières's fourth novel, *Captain Corelli's Mandolin,* was published in both Britain and the United States in 1994. The novel was titled *Corelli's Mandolin* in the United States, which was in fact its original, working title, according to the contributor's note accompanying de Bernières's autobiographical piece in *Granta,* 43 (Spring 1993). In *Captain Corelli's Mandolin* de Bernières revisits a well-known era in history (World War II) but does so by using a peripheral venue (the Greek island of Cephallonia in the Adriatic). Cephallonia is, or was before de Bernières's novel made it a popular tourist destination, a little-known island, overshadowed by Corfu and Ithaca. In *Captain Corelli's Mandolin* the leading citizen of Cephallonia is Doctor Iannis, a wise, skeptical man of science, whose puttering intellectuality (he is writing a history of the island) stands in gentle contrast to the naiveté of his daughter, Pelagia, and the other locals. Cephallonia, though parochial, seems to bask in blissful harmony. This equilibrium is shattered once the Italians invade the island.

Fascist Italy, though nominally a full partner with Nazi Germany in the Axis alliance, was definitely a junior ally. Under Benito Mussolini, Italy had already taken over Albania in 1939. To prove it could keep up with Germany in the latter's parade of military conquests in Europe, Italy served Greece with a trumped-up ultimatum and invaded in October 1940. Cephallonia was one of the first parts of Greece to be taken. De Bernières does not just show the private reverberation of this event in the lives of his main characters, Doctor Iannis and Pelagia; he also goes into the mind of Ion Metaxas, the Greek dictator, who, though often criticized by historians of the period, is portrayed in the book as more or less a man of honor. The tone of de Bernières's narrative is lyrical and romantic but laced with a dry, often mordant humor. The book relates a large-scale historical sequence yet also focuses on the private lives of a few Cephallonian individuals. The particular emphasis is on the love life of Pelagia, who at the beginning of the book is engaged to Mandras, a strapping young fisherman from the island, but in the course of the book falls in love with Captain Francisco Corelli, head of the Italian forces, who soon develops a personal rapport with Pelagia that wins out over the inevitable initial suspicion. The ambiguous stance of the Italian occupiers of Cephallonia serves de Bernières as a metaphor for the ambiguity of the Italian position in World War II. Fascist Italy was allied to Nazi Germany but was not as thoroughly totalitarian, and the Italian occupiers end up feeling as much or more in common with the Greeks as with their German allies. De Bernières assiduously evokes Cephallonia as a physical and social setting, even though, as he mentioned in a 1999 interview with the British Broadcasting Company, he had spent only a short time in Cephallonia before writing the novel. Greek words, such as *kalimera* for "good morning" and *agapetos* for "beloved," are occasionally inserted to lend an air of authenticity, and the houses and customs of the islanders are rendered with vivid specificity. De Bernières takes full advantage of thousands of years of recorded history of the island, skillfully interspersing Christian and pagan, classical and Byzantine, ancient and modern referents:

> Ever since the time when the Goddess Io had been instrumental in the killing of Memnon by Achilles and had precipitated the accidental shooting of Procris by her own unsuspecting husband, the island had been a prodigy of wonders. This itself was no wonder, for the island possessed a saint unique to itself, and it was as if his numinous power was too great and too effulgent to be contained within himself.
>
> St Gerasimos, withered and blackened, sealed inside his domed and gilded sarcophagus by the reredos of his own monastery, dead for five centuries, rose up at night. Decked in scarlet and golden robes, precious stones and ancient medals, he rattled and creaked his way discreetly among his flock of sinners and the sick, visiting them in their homes, sometimes even going abroad to his native Corinthia, there to visit the bones of his fathers and wander amongst the hills and groves of his youth.

Captain Corelli's Mandolin repeats the pattern of *The Troublesome Offspring of Cardinal Guzman* with chapter titles that are either the names of characters (who give alternated interior monologues) or bare descriptions of the action. The viewpoint of Carlo Piero Guercio, "L'Omosessuale" (the homosexual), a fellow Italian soldier who is surreptitiously in love with Corelli, is presented through first-person narration and, in the third person, that of the German officer Günter Weber, described with only slight facetiousness as "the good Nazi."

Captain Corelli's Mandolin was not an instant best-seller, though it won the regional 1995 Commonwealth Writers Prize. Yet, the book became extraordinarily successful, remaining what publishers and booksellers call a "steady seller" five or six years after its release. A steady seller is a book with undramatic initial sales but a persistent popularity that eventually surpasses books that begin spectacularly and then peter out. By 1999 *Captain Corelli's Mandolin* had sold more than 900,000 copies worldwide; by 2001 sales had exceeded two million copies. The novel became particularly popular among adult reading groups, usually informal gatherings of from five to twenty people, normally in a private home or in a bookstore. Indeed, *Captain Corelli's Mandolin* can be seen as being a sociological as much as a literary phenomenon, for its success as much as that of any other book registered the rise of the reading group in Britain in the 1990s. The popularity of the novel among reading groups more than made up for its lack of presence on traditional best-seller lists. It became a cultural token even among those who had not read it, and made its way into popular culture, as evidenced not only by the 2001 motion-picture adaptation but also by the book being pictured prominently in the 1999 movie *Notting Hill* starring Hugh Grant and Julia Roberts, in a scene in which the character played by Grant is reading the novel. De Bernières's book generated a new sort of novelistic tourism. People began to visit Cephallonia and even to retire there, just because it was the setting for *Captain Corelli's Mandolin.*

Why did the novel achieve this sort of popularity while de Bernières's earlier novels had not? One possibility might be the setting of Cephallonia, not in itself but as a small, isolated community suddenly subject to war and occupation. The emergence of heroism and valor out of previously ordinary circumstances is reminiscent of such stories as the Italian writer Giovanni Guareschi's *Mondo piccolo Don Camillo* (1948; translated as *The Little World of Don Camillo,* 1950). As in the Italian novel, in de Bernières's book a heroic parish priest helps to alleviate the pain his flock is suffering, though in this case it is the unidealized Greek Orthodox Father Arsenios. The central love story of the novel between Corelli and Pelagia has a lyricism lacking in de Bernières's earlier books. The popularity of *Captain Corelli's Mandolin* might reflect the traditional appeal of World War II as a setting for historical fiction, with the new wrinkle of the Greek front, a theater traditionally undertreated in blockbuster novels about the war, contributing added luster. Tom Holland, writing in the *New Statesman* (4 December 1998), hypothesized that the popularity of the book might have had to do with "the British being sentimental about Greece" in a kind of romantically nostalgic way.

One of the major differences between the Latin American trilogy and *Captain Corelli's Mandolin* is the perceived political partisanship of the latter. In *Captain*

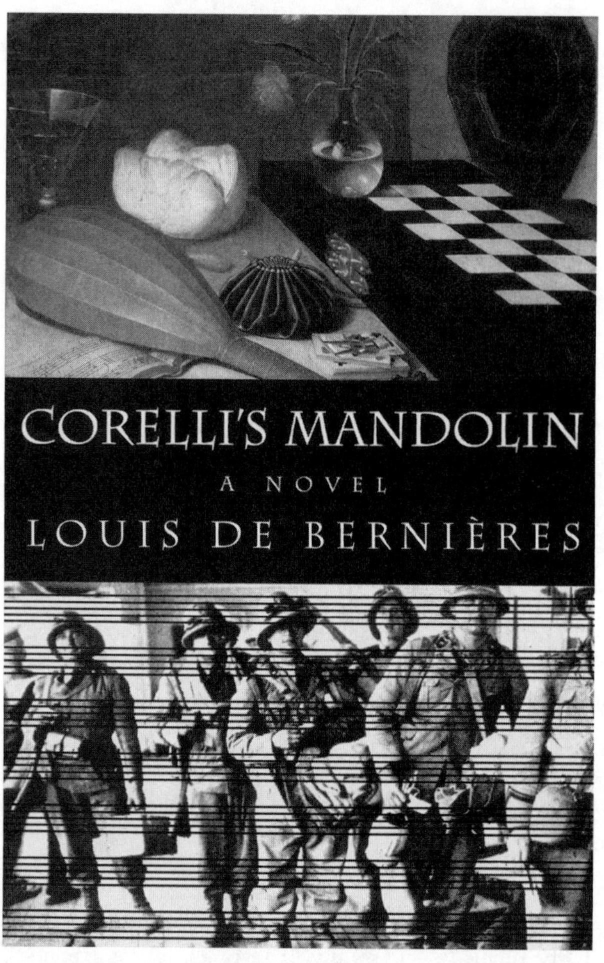

Dust jacket for the U.S. edition of de Bernières's 1994 novel, the basis for a 2001 movie (Richland County Public Library)

Corelli's Mandolin de Bernières is fiercely critical of the Greek Communists. One of the ways in which de Bernières develops the unlikely romance between Corelli, the outside occupier, and the local girl, Pelagia, is by having Pelagia's Greek suitor, Mandras, value his ideological adherence to the Greek Communists more than his love for her. The romance between Pelagia and Mandras is strained in direct proportion to Mandras's involvement with the Communist partisans. This negative portrayal of the Communist resistance led to denunciations of the book by the Greek Left as well as by the British Communist Party newspaper, *The Morning Star,* which, according to Seamus Milne in *The Guardian* (30 July 1999), accused de Bernières of being ideologically anticommunist. In the Latin American trilogy, however, de Bernières, while not lauding Communists as such, is sympathetic to the guerrillas' revolutionary aims, and he is critical of the manner in which the military authorities tend to castigate their opponents as invariably being Communist. *Captain Corelli's Mandolin* is much more politically explicit than are de Bernières's earlier novels. At the end of the book de Bernières appends an author's note once again criticizing the Greek Communist partisans and commending the British government of Prime Minister Clement Attlee for intervening against them in the 1940s. He also compares the situation in 1940s Greece to the bloodshed in the 1990s attendant on the breakup of Yugoslavia, and he calls for a more interventionist posture there on the part of the British authorities. This attention to the politics of the time when the book was written is different from the Latin American trilogy, which, though published between 1990 and 1992, registers the end of the Cold War only tacitly.

The setting in the Latin American trilogy is imaginary, though based on reality. De Bernières's approach in *Captain Corelli's Mandolin,* however, is almost documentary, especially in the chapters dealing with Metaxas and the actions of the Italian army, as well as the material about the history of Cephallonia. There is much straight historical exposition, not just to set up the plot or premise of the book but as an integral component of the narrative. What is notable here is that de Bernières had spent a significantly longer amount of time in Latin America than he had in Cephallonia. The more empirically rendered milieu was based on the area less thoroughly experienced in actuality. Although Iannis, Pelagia, Mandras, and Corelli are not "round" characters in the novelist E. M. Forster's sense of the term, they are perhaps less stereotypical than the landowners and rebels of the Latin American trilogy. The novel also features some more comic characters, such as the young, insouciant maiden Lemoni and the pine marten Psipsina, who have particularly endeared themselves to readers. Psipsina the pine marten is one of the most memorable portraits of a pet in late-twentieth-century fiction. Its pointless death has been noted by many readers as being one of the most gripping moments in the novel. The mandolin played by Captain Corelli, which gives the novel its title, expresses the persistence of hope and spirit in terrible circumstances and symbolizes the triumph of the healing strains of music over the fearsome bombs and guns of warfare. De Bernières enjoys restoring and repairing mandolins and other musical instruments as a hobby, and the mandolin motif in the novel gains from an understanding of the material and technical aspects of playing this instrument as much as the more allegorical significance of the idea of music as a redemptive force.

An issue debated among readers is whether the last hundred pages, which extend beyond the 1940–1945 setting of most of the book, are truly needed. Characteristic of these complaints is the comment by W. S. di Piero in *The New York Times Book Review* (13 November 1994) that in the last hundred pages "the novel loses its momentum." In these closing chapters the action flashes forward almost to the time of the writing of the novel, though the narration is not entirely proleptic. Dr. Iannis is long dead, though the descendants of Psipsina still flourish. Pelagia's daughter, Antonia, marries an older businessman and produces a son named Iannis after his great-grandfather. In 1993 (symbolically, perhaps, after the end of the Cold War) an aged Corelli returns to Cephallonia and meets the young Iannis near the ruins of the house where the old doctor had once lived. Corelli, ashamed of the misdeeds of the Italians in the war, has become a Greek citizen. He has fulfilled his musical aspirations and written three concertos, the first, perhaps significantly, performed in 1954, the year of de Bernières's birth. Corelli and Pelagia discuss old times and renew their relationship amid an awareness of the passage of time and the hopeful emergence of the youngest generation. Although the last few chapters are really just an extended epilogue, they do make explicit the significance to the present day of the otherwise historical events recounted in the novel.

De Bernières was a Markin-Flanagan Distinguished Visiting Writer at the University of Calgary, Alberta, in 1996; while there, he read his *A Mad British Pervert Has a Sexual Fantasy About the 10th Street Bridge in Calgary,* which was broadcast on radio by the Canadian Broadcasting Corporation. In 1997 One Horse Press published a second edition of de Bernières's 1993 book, *Labels,* a short, comic piece about a man obsessed with collecting cat-food labels, which originally appeared in a limited edition of two thousand numbered and signed copies. With his savings and the money from *Captain Corelli's Mandolin,* de Bernières purchased an eighteenth-century rectory in Norfolk, near the home of his friend Elizabeth Jane Howard, the writer.

In 2001 de Bernières had three books published: *Red Dog* and *Sunday Morning at the Centre of the World: A Play for Voices* in October of that year and *Gunter Weber's Confession* in December. The latter work, published in a limited edition of 350 copies, covers familiar territory, comprising a sort of sequel to *Captain Corelli's Mandolin,* an additional chapter in which the "good" German officer Weber returns to Pelagia's and Dr. Iannis's house after the Italian soldiers are massacred.

In contrast, *Red Dog* is a curious departure for de Bernières. Set in the desert mining region of Western Australia, it is a collection of interrelated tales about the exploits of the flatulent, nomadic Red Cloud kelpie (an Australian breed of collie) of the title. De Bernières told Wyndham in their interview for *The Age* (Melbourne) that he got the idea for the book during a visit to Australia when near the town of Dampier he noticed a bronze statue "of a dog that used to hitch rides and go wherever he wanted to." Intrigued, de Bernières later returned to interview people who remembered the dog, a local legend in the 1970s, using their stories and earlier published accounts as the basis for his short narrative. He told Wyndham, "I had always had it in mind to write a children's book but I'd never had a decent story before." Critical reaction was mixed. Sandra Howard in a 13 October 2001 review in *The Spectator* (London) praised the "youthfully doggy style" of the book and said that in it de Bernières "brilliantly evokes the red heat of Australian summers." In *Booklist* (15 September 2001) Benjamin Segedin called the book "delightful" and noted that de Bernières "is rapidly establishing himself as a master storyteller." In contrast, an unsigned notice in *Kirkus Reviews* (1 August 2001) described the stories of Red Dog as "only mildly interesting," complained that the book "has some charm, but it's awfully slack, its paragraphs swollen by pointless filler," and sourly concluded, "The thousands of readers who loved *Corelli's Mandolin* have waited impatiently for its author's next novel, so one understands why this innocuous little non-book was published. But

Dust jacket for the U.S. edition of de Bernières's 2001 book, a fictionalized account of the life of an Australian dog (Richland County Public Library)

why was it written?" Paul Bravmann, in a brief review in *The New York Times* (7 October 2001), concluded that "Unlike de Bernières's previous work, 'Red Dog' is terribly thin, suitable only for uncritical Australophiles and dog lovers, or as bedtime stories en route to an unruffled sleep." Such negative comments, however, may be at least partially motivated by what de Bernières called "the tall-poppy syndrome" in his interview with Wyndham, the desire of critics to "cut down" popular writers.

Sunday Morning at the Centre of the World marks another departure for de Bernières. Modeled after Dylan Thomas's *Under Milk Wood,* which was originally a radio play in 1954 before being staged in 1956, de Bernières's "play for voices" was also first broadcast on radio before its stage debut, at the Dylan Thomas Centre in Swansea, Wales, in 1999. De Bernières's play features a narrator who describes various residents of Earlsfield, the South London neighborhood where the author lived for a decade, and the residents themselves, who, as Howard puts it in the same article in which she reviewed *Red Dog,* "are allowed to colour in and plump out their own characters with fruity dialogue." She described the play as "beautifully readable, tender and poetic."

De Bernières was at one point reported to be working on a novel about the medieval Albigensians, a natural topic given the motif of The New Albigensian Crusade in *The Troublesome Offspring of Cardinal Guzman.* But this project evidently yielded to a novel about a community of Christians and Moslems living in southwest Turkey in the early twentieth century, a narrative encompassing World War I and the Gallipoli campaign, the breakup of the Ottoman Empire, and the subsequent destruction of the mixed community in the "ethnic cleansing" of the 1920s. De Bernières had already explored this setting in a short piece, *A Day Out for Mehmet Erbil* (1999), published in a limited edition of fewer than three hundred copies. He told Susan Wyndham in a 20 October 2001 interview for *The Age* (Melbourne) that his new long novel, provisionally titled "Birds Without Wings" and two-thirds written, was "about people who always managed to live together peacefully being torn apart, and about the ambiguity of human nature–people who can be horrible and violent one minute and show great hospitality and generosity the next."

Louis de Bernières is one of those rare writers who has successfully managed to bridge the divide between so-called literary fiction and popular fiction, having written both critically acclaimed novels and a worldwide bestseller. By extending the boundaries of the novel to include explicitly historical and political material, and by leavening postmodern narrative techniques with the gusto of his storytelling, de Bernières has become one of the most distinctive writers working in Britain at the beginning of the twenty-first century.

Interviews:

Nicci Gerrard, "A Soldier and His Musical Instruments," *Observer* (London), 3 April 1994;

Helena de Bertodano, "The Real Captain Corelli," *Daily Telegraph* (London), 14 September 1996;

Susan Wyndham, "From the Red Heart," *Age* (Melbourne), 20 October 2001.

References:

Nicholas Farrell, "False note on Il Duce," *Spectator* (London), 27 March 1999, pp. 20–21;

Andy Harris, *Captain Corelli's Island: Cephallonia,* photographs by Terry Harris (London: Pavilion, 1999);

Tom Holland, "Best-seller," *New Statesman* (4 December 1998): 64;

Emily A. McDermott, "Every Man's an Odysseus: An Analysis of the 'Nostos' Theme in 'Corelli's Mandolin,'" *Classical and Modern Literature: A Quarterly,* 20 (Winter 2000): 21–37;

Seamus Milne, "Novel damned by Captain Corelli's model," *Guardian,* Weekend section, 29 July 2000, p. 10;

Richard Sheppard, "Savagery, Salvage, Salves and Salvation: The Historico-Theological Debate of *Captain Corelli's Mandolin,*" *Journal of European Studies,* 32 (March 2002): 51–61;

Sascha Talmor, "An Englishman in Latin America: *The War of Don Emmanuel's Nether Parts* by Louis de Bernières," *History of European Ideas,* 17 (January 1993).

Anita Desai

(24 June 1937 -)

Dan Friedman
Yale University

Anita Desai (photograph by Jerry Bauer; from the dust jacket for the U.S. edition of Baumgartner's Bombay, *1989)*

BOOKS: *Cry, the Peacock* (London: Peter Owen, 1963);
Voices in the City: A Novel (London: Peter Owen, 1965);
Bye-Bye, Blackbird (Delhi: Hind Pocket Books, 1968);
The Peacock Garden, illustrated by Jeroo Roy (Delhi: India Book House, 1974; London: Heinemann, 1979);
Where Shall We Go This Summer? (Delhi: Vikas, 1975);
Cat on a Houseboat (Delhi: Orient Longmans, 1976);
Fire on the Mountain (Bombay: Allied Publishers, 1977, London: Heinemann, 1977; New York: Harper & Row, 1977);
Games at Twilight, and Other Stories (London: Heinemann, 1978; New York: Harper & Row, 1980);
Clear Light of Day (London: Heinemann, 1980; New York: Harper & Row, 1980);
The Village by the Sea: An Indian Family Story (London: Heinemann, 1982);
In Custody (London: Heinemann, 1984; New York: Harper & Row, 1985);
Baumgartner's Bombay (London: Heinemann, 1988; New York: Knopf, 1989);
Journey to Ithaca (London: Heinemann, 1995; New York: Knopf, 1995);
Scholar and Gypsy (London: Phoenix, 1996);
Fasting, Feasting (London: Chatto & Windus, 1999; New York: Mariner, 2000);
Diamond Dust: Stories (Boston: Houghton Mifflin, 2000); republished as *Diamond Dust and Other Stories* (London: Chatto & Windus, 2000).

PRODUCED SCRIPT: *In Custody,* motion picture, adapted by Desai and Shahrukh Husain from Desai's novel of that title, Merchant-Ivory Productions, 1993; also released as *Hifazaat.*

OTHER: Rabindranath Tagore, *The Home and the World,* translated by Surendranath Tagore, introduction by Desai (Harmondsworth, U.K.: Penguin / New York: Viking Penguin, 1985);
Mitch Epstein, *In Pursuit of India,* introduction by Desai (New York: Aperture, 1987);
Attia Hosain, *Sunlight on a Broken Column,* introduction by Desai (London: Virago, 1988);
Anne Brontë, *Agnes Grey,* Virago Modern Classics, no. 359, introduction by Desai (London: Virago, 1990);
Lady Mary Wortley Montague, *Turkish Embassy Letters,* edited by Malcolm Jack, introduction by Desai (Athens: University of Georgia Press, 1993; London: Pickering, 1993);
Ismat Chughtai, *The Quilt & Other Stories,* translated by Tahira Naqvi and Syeda S. Hameed, preface by Desai (Riverdale-on-Hudson, N.Y.: Sheep Meadow, 1994);

Salman Rushdie, *Midnight's Children,* introduction by Desai (London: David Campbell, 1995; New York: Knopf, 1995);

Vanessa Baird, ed., *Eye to Eye, Women: Their Words and Worlds. Life in Africa, Asia, Latin America and the Caribbean As Seen in Photographs and in Fiction by the Region's Top Women Writers,* introduction by Desai (Oxford: New Internationalist, 1996; London & New York: Serpent's Tail, 1997).

One of the most accomplished fiction writers of English today, Anita Desai has established herself through the consistency of her formidable body of work. From acclaimed children's fiction–*The Village by the Sea: An Indian Family Story* (1982) won the *Guardian* Prize for Children's Fiction in 1983–to collections of poignant short stories, and from several scholarly introductions to a screenplay for an award-winning movie, Desai's writing has been consistently of the highest quality. Her lucid and penetrating novels for adults constitute the central pillar of her achievement and are becoming increasingly widely read. Desai's novels deal with the intimate psychological worlds of individuals whose identities, thoughts, and emotions are affected by their different and often clashing affiliations to, among others, familial, geographical, linguistic, professional, class, ethnic, and national groups. Desai herself has been affiliated with different groups–as an Indian woman writing in English she has been categorized as an Indian or a feminist writer. Although she self-consciously shares many concerns with other Indian and women writers, those categories do scant justice to the careful consideration of the pressures of selfhood found in her novels.

The notion of place, and the movement toward or away from a specific place, is important in providing both a physical and spiritual context for her characters. Whether they are in the city or the countryside (a territorial opposition she often uses), the concrete particulars of a particular location, often a surprisingly diverse neighborhood in India, matter to Desai. Almost invariably, her characters travel physically as well as mentally and emotionally, either running away from home or on a quest for something. During these travels Desai uncovers some of the psychological "truth that is nine-tenths of the iceberg that lies submerged" by representing the inner and hidden life of her characters. Although she is not a political writer, the actions and psychic turmoil of the characters reflect the larger political turmoil in their worlds. Without turning the characters into mere ciphers, she is, as Anthony Thwaite pointed out in a review of *In Custody* (1984) in *The New Republic* (18 March 1985), "such a consummate artist that she suggests, beyond the confines of the plot and the machinations of her characters, the immensities that lie beyond them–the immensities of India."

Anita Mazumdar was born 24 June 1937 in Mussoorie, a hill station just north of Delhi, to a German mother, Toni Nime Mazumdar, and an Indian father, D. N. Mazumdar, an engineer. One of three children (she had a sister and a brother), she was barely ten years old at Independence and the subsequent partition of the subcontinent into India and Pakistan. That event, as is the subject of national and personal independence, is a recurrent theme of her writing. Although the Mazumdar family spoke German and Hindi at home, Desai's short stories in English span the pre- and post-Independence eras, starting when she was seven (publishing her first story at the age of nine) and continuing to the present in anthologies and periodicals, including *Thought, Envoy, Writers Workshop, Quest, Indian Literature,* and *Harper's Bazaar.* She received her early education at Queen Mary's Higher Secondary School in New Delhi, and then at Miranda House, Delhi University, where she received a B.A. with honors in English literature in 1957. In December of the following year she married Ashvin Desai, a businessman, and together they have raised four children: Rahul, Tani, Arjun, and Kiran (who is now a novelist in her own right).

Besides selling well, her novels have won considerable recognition from her peers. Since winning the Winifred Holtby Prize from the Royal Society of Literature in 1978 for *Fire on the Mountain* (1977), Desai has received several awards for her writing. Although she has not yet won the Booker Prize (the foremost literary award in Britain), three different judging committees have short-listed Desai's novels over a twenty-year period–*Clear Light of Day* (1980), *In Custody,* and *Fasting, Feasting* (1999). Recognition for her talent and achievement spans three continents: in India she was appointed a member of the Advisory Board for English of the National Academy of Letters in Delhi; in Great Britain she is a Fellow of the Royal Society of Literature; and in the United States she is a member of the American Academy of Arts and Letters. Academia has also recognized her work, and since the 1980s she has held a variety of impressive fellowships and teaching positions in England and the United States. These have included positions at Smith College (1987–1988), at Mount Holyoke College (1988–1993), and, since 1993, at the Massachusetts Institute of Technology (MIT). In England both Girton and Clare Hall Colleges at the University of Cambridge have honored her with fellowships: at Girton, she was a Helen Cam Visiting Fellow in 1986–1987 and an honorary fellow in 1988; at Clare Hall, she was an Ashby Fellow in 1989 and an honorary fellow in 1991.

Desai wrote short stories during the early years of her marriage when her children were young, and she only published her first novel, *Cry, the Peacock,* in 1963. In *Cry, the Peacock* Desai portrays a marriage in which each partner has a radically different way of understanding the other and the world that surrounds them. The novel foreshadows several themes that recur in her work–the problems of independence, of communication, the influence of the West, and the tensions of religious and domestic interaction. It also displays the first use of the tripartite structure that she has used on several occasions. Four of her first five novels are explicitly tripartite–*Voices in the City* (1965) being the exception–and many of the later ones also consist of three sections, even though the sections may be interwoven or only notable through their absence. The three-part structure allows the establishment of a character in a place in the first part–in the case of *Cry, the Peacock,* Maya in her garden. Then, in the second part comes a chronological, geographical or perspectival dislocation–for Maya this dislocation is her marriage to Gautama that forces her to move into his house and to deal with his philosophy. Finally, in the third part there is often an unsatisfactory resolution or ambiguous closure that shows how the dislocation of the second part provides no escape from the limitations of the first part: what is hard-won through the novel is not freedom, but experience. In *Cry, the Peacock* the experience is particularly painful as Maya comes to realize what her marriage and the way she ended it mean to her.

The story deals with the summer leading up to Maya's murder of her husband, Gautama. Their names allude to the Hindu principle of illusory reality and the Buddha, respectively. Gautama, who was a student of Maya's father, is significantly older than she, and when she marries him and moves to the city, she does so almost, but not quite, as a result of a pact between the two men. Maya and Gautama espouse what he calls the attitudes of attachment and detachment, respectively. He cites the *Bhagavad Gita* in his plea to her to become less attached to every little thing, but to no avail. Framed by the two brief sections at either end of the book–the death of Maya's dog, Toto, in part 1, and Maya's terrible final scream in part 3–the philosophical opposition of the married couple structures the book. Their opposition prevents the couple from communicating with one another, and, not for the last time in Desai's work, the failure of communication between characters leads to a calamitous and violent ending.

The novel is set in India just before Independence, and there are allusions to the anti-British protests, though Maya is blissfully ignorant of them. The influence of colonial rule is shown as pervasive but not necessarily any more evil than the differing influences of

Dust jacket for the U.S. edition of Desai's 1977 novel, about interfamily conflict that culminates in a rape-murder and an act of arson (Richland County Public Library)

Islam, Buddhism, and Hinduism. Her anglophile father reads her English fairy tales as a child, and she names her doll Rose and her dog Toto (after Dorothy's dog in the 1939 movie *The Wizard of Oz*). As the marriage and the contemporaneous Independence movement (for which it is a partial allegory) lead to violence, the reader is shown on a personal level how close independence is to obsession and isolation. Characters in a carefully studied psychological book, Maya and Gautama also represent codes struggling for a hold on the future of India. The mutual incomprehension and abrupt ending of the marriage reflect the violent disengagement of the relationships between the Raj and the local population and among the Buddhist, Moslem, and Hindu communities around the time of Indian independence. Despite the gloomy ending, the novel is not overly judgmental; the challenge of independence is presented with all its ambiguities and ambivalences, but the scream that closes the book reminds the reader of the weight of decisions and the price of belated understanding.

Published two years later, *Voices in the City* is the first of her Indian family novels. Although it deals with an entire family and not just a marriage, it shares two of Desai's early themes with *Cry, the Peacock:* first, missing family members, and second, the movement between the city and the country. In *Cry, the Peacock,* Maya's father spoils her after his wife dies, and his son runs away in rebellion. He himself eventually leaves for Europe just before the climax of the novel and the struggle for independence, leaving Maya with no one to turn to as her communications with Gautama disintegrate. In *Voices in the City* the family about whom the story is told is also missing a key parent–in this case the father, about whom the reader learns nothing–as well as the eldest son, Arun, who leaves for Europe to go to boarding school at the start of the novel. Set in Calcutta, this novel covers the adventures of a family whose children come to the city as they reach adulthood. The reader experiences the arrival in the city of the family and the gradual disenchantment of each of the three remaining children: Nirode, Monisha, and Amla. Then, in the final section, their mother arrives in Calcutta from the almost mythical country home in Kalimpong.

In *Voices in the City* Monisha is unable to compromise with a world that values her only according to her ability to bear children. None of the siblings find anything but despair in their interactions with the surrounding "box-wallahs"–the dull greedy salesmen who run Calcutta–but, unlike her brother and sister who turn to writing and drawing respectively, Monisha finds no solace in her writing. She becomes isolated and silent, and she eventually commits suicide by self-immolation. This action prompts her brother Nirode to compare her to Kali, who is the goddess of Bengal, of knowledge and ignorance, of life and death. For Desai, whose father was Bengali and has often expressed deep admiration for Rabindranath Tagore–the Bengali poet who became the national poet of India–this reference to the patron goddess of Bengal has a deep resonance. The two surviving siblings belong to a group of characters in Desai's work who are unwilling or unable to relinquish an ideal that exists beyond the chaos and crush of the everyday world and use religion, philosophy, or art to attain the ideal. *Cry, the Peacock* uses religion and philosophy, *In Custody* uses poetry, and *Journey to Ithaca* (1995) uses religion; references to Tagore are found in all of the early works.

In *Bye-bye, Blackbird* (1968), her first novelistic foray into a country beyond India, Desai takes the reader to a bigoted England into which the first waves of commonwealth immigration are just settling. The influx of "coloured" immigrants or "blackbirds" (hence the title) is viewed with general suspicion by the white population. Even the Millers, who emigrated from Germany as the Muhlsteins before the war, are scornful of their Indian lodger, Adit Sen. Adit and Sarah, the central couple in the book, are an interracial couple who were married in England. Right at the beginning Adit and his friend Dev are openly called "Wogs" while on the bus. This derogatory term, which originally referred to people from northern Africa, is now used indiscriminately to refer disparagingly to all dark-skinned foreigners. Even when they are insulting immigrants, the locals do not distinguish between Punjabis, Sikhs, Bengalis, Arabs, or Africans. Even Sarah's friend Bella, who introduced Sarah and Adit, recounts a story her uncle had told her about being in India and seeing widows performing suttee, throwing themselves onto the burning funeral pyres of their husbands. She does not even flinch when the anachronism of her story is pointed out (the practice was abolished in British India in 1829 and had died out in the Indian states by the middle of the nineteenth century). By undermining the polarity of black and white, as well as the supposed unity of each color, Desai is exploding the misconceived opposition of color and history.

The book begins with Dev's arrival in England with some money from his father to attend the London School of Economics (LSE), but he does little or nothing about registering or enrolling in classes. Eventually, Adit becomes sick of England, just as Dev becomes enamored of it, and they trade places (Dev takes Adit's house and job). On a pivotal trip to visit Sarah's parents, Dev, more moody than ever, falls in love with the domestic tameness of the English country, the land. On the same trip Adit finally feels the snobbish racist rejection by Sarah's mother of both him and Sarah and realizes that neither she nor Sarah's father has any interest in him or even in Sarah. Sarah, white and born in England, has a resiliently stoic temperament and is recognized by the old Sikh grandmother who lives downstairs as someone who will be more at home with the forthright challenges of India than with her mother's reserved country prejudice. Although she is pregnant when Adit says he has to go back to India, Sarah is excited to go with him, and their new child is a symbol of hope for the journey. "Will the baby be black or white?" is the foolish question asked by one of the teachers at the school where Sarah works–it will be neither but rather a hopeful synthesis.

Food is the main symbol of mutual acculturation in the novel. Throughout the book, and throughout Desai's work, the tug of war over cultural practice is felt most strongly in the kitchen. There is a comical opening scene in *Bye-bye, Blackbird* that introduces the theme, in which Dev, while trying to make breakfast in the Sens' suburban kitchen, is confused by cat hairs in the tea cosy, claustrophobically closed windows, and the strange mixture of English and Indian artifacts on the sideboard. He ends up making little and breaking much. The kitchen provides, on the one hand, the quiet calm and afternoon tea of England, and on the other, the chaotic activity and spicy fried *pakoras* (chickpea flour fritters) of home. Like the hot tea that everyone drinks, the cultural practices that surround tea-drinking have been produced, developed, and consumed by a mixture of the Raj, England, India, Anglo-Indians, and Indians in England.

Narrower in scope, less nuanced in its characterization, and more rigidly structured, *Where Shall We Go This Summer?* (1975) reads like an earlier work than *Bye-bye, Blackbird.* As in *Cry, the Peacock,* the novel centers on a desperate wife in a marriage in which husband and wife are out of kilter with one another. The main character, Sita, like the characters in *Voices in the City,* is torn between the life of the city and an impossible nostalgia for the country. Instead of the infertility that Monisha suffers, Sita's fecundity brings her to the point of despair and forces her back to the country in her one act of truth, or perhaps of betrayal. In an act of nostalgia and insanity she goes to the countryside to "not have the baby," hoping that her reconnection with an idyllic past will somehow inspire a status quo in her womb that will end neither in birth nor abortion. The destinies of Sita and her unborn baby are formally linked to the fate of the independent Indian polity through the division of the book into three parts. These are divided by year and season between the "present" and the immediate aftermath of Independence–into "Monsoon 1967," "Winter 1947," and "Monsoon 1967."

Unlike the Sens' unborn child in *Bye-bye, Blackbird,* which heralds a new future, however uncertain, Sita's unborn child is tied to the past. For this, her fifth pregnancy, Sita flees to the island of her childhood home that was given to her father by a wealthy follower. Sita's father was a spiritual leader of the independence movement–a "second Gandhi." Unlike the first one, he was ill educated and depended more on charisma and a strange brand of political, social, and moral rhetoric to excite his supporters. In 1947, with the advent of Independence, he retired to the country with his family and *chelas* (disciples), to his island home. Here he chose to settle and put into practice some social experiments. These experiments seem to be getting further and further away from any rational, civilized ideas of governance. He ends up grating pearls, rubies, and gold into medicine that he gives to the villagers, understanding that their faith is more important to them than any medicine he could provide. Sita is searching for the type of faith that her father provided, but there is nowhere left to find it and no one with whom to share it.

Dust jacket for the U.S. edition of Desai's 1980 novel, the first of her books to be short-listed for the Booker Prize (Richland County Public Library)

Published in 1977, *Fire on the Mountain* is also about an attempt at escape and its eventual futility. Nanda Kaul has survived longer as a mother and a matriarch than has Sita and feels that she has earned her solitude in the Simla hills at Kasauli. When her great-granddaughter Raka arrives, she is worried that she will lose her tranquillity. The peace is indeed shattered in the closing pages by two events, neither of which occur in the way that Nanda Kaul had feared. There is no escaping the multiple conflicts that dog the societies Desai portrays. *Fire on the Mountain* shows the clash of generations between Raka and Nanda Kaul, of classes between the hill station and the village below, of business between the farms and the factory, and of values between the educational programs sponsored by the central government and the traditions of the local villagers. The action comes to a head, as it so often does in Desai's novels, with violent gender conflict. The arranged child marriage by which Preet Singh is trying to ally his family with a rich man in the next village is overshadowed by his rape and murder of frail Ila Das, who has been arguing against it.

It is unclear whether Raka's act of arson that follows the rape-murder and lends the novel its title mirrors her great-grandmother's attempted escape from society, is a dramatic response to Preet Singh's horrific attack on Ila Das, or is an attempt to burn away the equally ineffective poles of disengagement and engagement that Nanda Kaul and Ila Das symbolize, respectively. The three-part structure ("Nanda Kaul at Carignano," "Raka comes to Carignano," "Ila Das leaves Carignano") illustrates the changing context as Nanda Kaul stays ensconced in the same place. Established at her retirement home in the first part, she is disturbed by Raka in the second part, and any possibility of her rationalizing the new status quo is destroyed in the third part. Perhaps the fire on the mountain is the only way that the new generation can clear all the prejudice away, but perhaps it is merely wanton destruction; Desai leaves the reader on the brink of despair but not without hope.

The most successful of her family novels, *Clear Light of Day* was the work that first drew the attention of critics and the Booker Prize judges when it was published in 1980. In a highly favorable review on the front page of *The New York Times Book Review* (23 November 1980) Anne Tyler said that Desai "constructs her plots with infinite care, relying less upon physical events than upon a mosaic of details thoughtfully selected and arranged" and that *Clear Light of Day* does "what only the best novels can do: It totally submerges us." The details that concern her in this case are the minutiae of family life as the four children of the family grow up in old Delhi. The neighborhood is sedate and dusty, as opposed to New Delhi, which the children imagine as fast, modern, and glamorous. During the Independence period both of their parents and their aunt die, and Arun (the older brother) runs away with Hyder Ali, their wealthy Muslim neighbor and landlord, whom he admires tremendously and in whose library he has grown up. Despite the suddenness of these traumas, it is the small misunderstandings over the decades that have allowed the links between the family members to decay and that provide Desai with material that she handles exquisitely.

The contemporary action begins when Tara comes home to India for the summer and, despite her husband's coolness to the idea, decides to stay with her elder sister, Bim, and her younger, mute, idiot brother, Baba, at the family home. Tara has been traveling the world with her diplomat husband but fails to understand the hypocrisy of his explanations of the state of India. Despite her intellectual shortcomings she perseveres in her attempts to understand Bim and Baba's situation in order to reconnect them with herself, Arun, and the new generation of the family embodied by her two bright daughters who arrive at the end of the novel. Gradually, and in an order that is thematic rather than chronological, the reader is shown the strands of the past that have brought the family members to where they are emotionally and geographically. Along with the characters, Desai questions their previous investment of meaning in each of the events and memories of their childhood and, story by story, some never told, but only referred to, some repeated by various characters, the reader pieces together a narrative of the family.

The tension between Urdu and Hindi (and the pressure upon Islam in India) that led Raja to accompany Hyder Ali into exile in *Clear Light of Day* is revisited more poignantly four years later with *In Custody*. The novel also dramatizes the tension between worldly and spiritual concerns through the confrontation between the greatest living Urdu poet and a young professor of Hindi who idolizes him. Despite his profound love for Urdu poetry and his monograph on the famous poet Nur, Deven Sharma has had to make a compromise and has chosen to teach Hindi in Mirpore in order to support his wife and child. Deven meanders through a succession of events, failing to assert himself in any way, and sees his dream of interviewing Nur turn into a nightmare and then a complicated burden. Beset by spurious friends and self-interested colleagues on one hand, and a family with concrete needs and an idol with feet of clay on the other, Deven, over the course of little more than a summer, passes through a series of trials without either succeeding or failing. By the end of the novel the burden of the various types of debts he has incurred are inseparable from the custody of the soul and spirit of Urdu poetry with which he feels Nur has entrusted him. Desai collaborated with Shahrukh Husain on the screenplay for the 1993 motion-picture adaptation of the novel; directed by Ismail Merchant and released in Urdu with English subtitles, the movie version won the National Film Award of India for Best Film in 1993.

Baumgartner's Bombay (1988) is structured around presenting a scene and then telling the stories that lead back to the scene and explain it. It begins with Lotte, a German expatriate friend of the eponymous Hugo Baumgartner, wailing while reading the wartime postcards from her dead friend's mother, which came only until 1941, stopping, the reader presumes, because she was killed by the Nazis. Gradually the reader learns the story that led up to Hugo's horrible, meaningless murder, the events of the day preceding his slaying being interspersed with the events of his life and its occasional intersections with Lotte. The irony of the novel lies in the agency of Hugo's murder. Even after fifty years in India and a lifetime of passive disavowal of his Jewish roots, he is still caught up in the backwash of a European culture that had expelled him and murdered his people, one to which he no longer belongs (having literally and symbolically traded in his German passport for an Indian one). His murder is carried out by Kurt, a drug-crazed parody of the Nietzschean superman, a supremely selfish blonde German traveler whom Hugo happens to have taken home after finding him slumped with no money in Farroukh's restaurant, where Hugo is a regular. Farroukh assumes that Hugo and Kurt share a kinship since they are both German. Hugo, though he knows better, feels an eager but scared compulsion to look after one last stray.

Hugo's living companions are a scruffy collection of former street cats that he rescues, keeps, and feeds but, unlike these animals, who love him and share his space, Kurt shows no gratitude and kills Hugo for the silver cups that his racehorse had won. Ironically, the horse never actually belonged to Hugo. He and his business partner, Chimanlal, used to slip off to the racetrack, and, thanks to Hugo's intuitive betting suggestions and Chimanlal's money, they won enough to buy the horse. The trips to the racetrack, inextricably associated with an early memory of his father not wanting to take Hugo as a child with him to the races, came to end with the death of his business associate. When Chimanlal's son took over the business, there was no paperwork to show that Hugo had an interest in the animal. Chimanlal's son breaks with his father's generation in both attitude and action. Kurt, while totally different from Baumgartner's generation of Germans, continues the work of the wartime Germans, if in an entirely different manner. The superfluity of Baumgartner's murder is breathtaking and shakes any assumptions that the reader may still have about the nature of India and what can be found there.

Dust jacket for the U.S. edition of Desai's 1988 novel, about a German Jew who escapes the Holocaust by immigrating to India, where he is eventually murdered by a psychopathic German hippie (Richland County Public Library)

Although given a generic classification of "Religious fiction" by the Library of Congress, Desai's 1995 book, *Journey to Ithaca,* is less about organized religion and more about the broader possibility of emotional and spiritual self-realization. The novel follows three adventurers caught up in "a kind of love triangle set against the madness of extreme spiritual searching"–as Richard Bernstein put it in a review in *The New York Times* (30 August 1995). They journey from Europe to India in search of some nameless spiritual feeling that they cannot find in France, Germany, or Italy. The two main protagonists are, like Hugo Baumgartner, upper-middle-class Europeans in India but, unlike him, Sophie and Matteo, both children of bankers, have freely chosen to run away together to India. The final section of the novel throws their diverging journeys toward self-realization into new relief by relating the story of how Laila, known fondly to her ashram as "the Mother," had also come from abroad. The description in the novel of the foreign provenance of a revered Indian mystic undoes more of the essentialist assumptions about Indian society that were undermined in *Baumgartner's Bombay,* while at the same time examining the ongoing fascination Europeans have for India as the destination of a spiritual pilgrimage.

Despite its relative neglect by awards committees, *Journey to Ithaca,* a book that Desai dedicated to her four children, is noteworthy for the technically complex and adventurous way that it ties together several of her enduring concerns. Although this novel is the story of a marriage, Desai's description of Sophie and Matteo's adventures is unlike her other family or marital dramas as she interweaves three geographically and chronologically disparate stories. Despite this formal mixture, and their avowed quest for the "Truth," as Paul Gray pointed out in *Time* (21 August 1995) all "three princi-

Paperback cover for the 2000 U.S. edition of Desai's 1999 novel, about a spinster living with her parents in Delhi and her brother attending school in Massachusetts (Richland County Public Library)

pals seem so monomaniacal about their journeys that they remain, in the end, inaccessible." The final section of the book is Sophie's attempt to communicate with her husband by joining what she knows to what Matteo believes, marking the most persistent attempt by a wife to build a bridge to communicate with her husband in Desai's work. Sophi tries to communicate by writing a biography of "the Mother" whom Matteo so idolizes. Her search is interwoven with a biography of Laila that may be Sophie's final book, or may just be the story as Desai is telling it. As Sophie's research and the Mother's biography follow one another from Alexandria to Cairo, to Paris, and then to India, there is a mounting hope that the biography can display meaning in the similarity between Laila's pilgrimmage and that of Sophie and Matteo. This similarity can help Sophie and Matteo, or their children, understand how they belong to one another and in the world.

Published in 1999, *Fasting, Feasting* tells the story of a Delhi family: the parents, referred to as the indivisible unit, MamaPapa, their son, Arun, and two daughters, Uma and Aruna. The girls are neglected as soon as Arun is born. MamaPapa dedicate the family to helping him improve the family name by going to study abroad, but when he is finally accepted by a college in Boston, his sister Uma sees that he is unmoved, and "the years of scholarly toil had worn down any distinguishing features Arun's face might once have had." Of the whole family it is Uma, the slow and clumsy eldest child, who elicits the reader's sympathy. As the novel opens, she is a spinster living almost like a servant in her parents' house. Flashbacks throughout the first part of the novel describe how this situation came about. The family is tricked twice out of her dowry as they try to marry her off even though she has no such wish. Both times she is sent home by her husband's family and arrives home where, notwithstanding her innocence, she is accociated with disgrace. Despite her blamelessness, she is considered to be shamed and is hidden away at home. Although belittled by everyone in the family apart from her Aunt Mira Masi, she is the only character who seems to transcend her physical situation for fragments of time, reaching a selfless ecstasy during a "fit" in an ashram and while nearly drowning during a religious trip out into the Ganges.

As one might expect from the title, *Fasting, Feasting* is a "novel not of plot but of comparison," as Sylvia Brownrigg observed in a review in the on-line journal *Salon* (17 February 2000). The longer first section deals with Uma's life in India and the second with Arun's life in Massachusetts. In part 2 of *Fasting, Feasting* the destination of the "missing" son is described for the first time in one of Desai's novels. Unlike the travels of Maya's rebellious brother in *Cry, the Peacock,* Arun in *Voices in the City,* or Raja in *Clear Light of Day,* Arun's trip to the United States is presented in the novel. Uma has seen how Arun has been ground down by MamaPapa's ambitions for him and now, on the other side of the world, Arun sees Uma's frustrations mirrored in the frustrations of his hosts' bulimic daughter. The comparisons that Desai draws are not between the states of surfeit and scarcity but between the states of mind that lead to the actions of fasting and feasting. The respective freedoms and wealth of sons and daughters in India and the United States are shown to fluctuate between these extremes without finding a happy medium.

In Anita Desai's fiction neither nostalgia nor the yearning for the exotic offer anything but illusions to be shattered. She deals with both the past and the geographically remote as daily claims on characters' feelings that must be treated with equal and lucid attention but no favoritism. *Clear Light of Day* marked the culmination of her first period of writing. Since then, Desai has written novels that, without leaving her main interests behind, have pushed the borders of her careful style and the scope of her intense scrutiny. Each time she publishes a new novel, it becomes more likely that it will be the one for which her stylistic control and broadened scope are recognized by a Booker Prize.

Interviews:

Corinne Demas Bliss, "Against the Current: A Conversation with Anita Desai," *Massachusetts Review,* 29, no. 3 (1988): 521–537;

Florence Libert, "An Interview with Anita Desai," *World Literature Written in English,* 30, no. 1 (1990): 47–55;

Magda Costa, "Interview with Magda Costa, Barcelona, 30 Jan 2001," <http://www.umiacs.umd.edu/users/sawweb/sawnet/books/desai_interview. html> [1 January 2002].

References:

Fawzia Afzal-Khan, *Cultural Imperialism and the Indo-English Novel: Genre and Ideology in R. K. Narayan, Anita Desai, Kamala Markandaya, and Salman Rushdie* (University Park: Pennsylvania State University Press, 1993);

Shyam M. Asnani, "Anita Desai's Fiction: A New Dimension," *Indian Literature,* 24, no. 2 (1981): 44–53;

Suman Bala and D. K. Pabby, eds., *The Fiction of Anita Desai,* 2 volumes (New Delhi: Khosla, 2002);

Usha Bande, *The Novels of Anita Desai: A Study in Character and Conflict* (New Delhi: Prestige Books, 1988);

Meena Bellioppa, *Anita Desai: A Study of Her Fiction* (Calcutta: Writers Workshop, 1971);

Pippa Brush, "German, Jew, Foreigner: The Immigrant Experience in Anita Desai's *Baumgartner's Bombay,*" *Critical Survey,* 8, no. 3 (1996): 277–285;

O. P. Budholia, *Anita Desai, Vision and Technique in Her Novels* (Delhi: B. R. Publishing, 2001);

Mohini Chakranarayan, *Style Studies in Anita Desai* (New Delhi: Atlantic Publishers, 2000);

Radha Chakravarty, "Figuring the Maternal: 'Freedom' and 'Responsibility' in Anita Desai's Novels," *ARIEL: A Review of International English Literature,* 29, no. 2 (1998): 75–92;

Chandra Chatterjee, *Surviving Colonialism: A Study of R. K. Narayan, Anita Desai, V. S. Naipaul* (Antwerp, Belgium: Universiteit Antwerpen / New Delhi: Radha, 2000);

K. Chellappan, "Being and Becoming in Anita Desai's *Where Shall We Go This Summer?*" in *Subjects Worthy Fame: Essays on Commonwealth Literature: In Honour of H. H. Anniah Gowda,* edited by A. L. Mcleod (New Delhi: Sterling, 1989, pp. 10–16;

Bidulata Choudhury, *Women and Society in the Novels of Anita Desai,* Creative New Literatures Series, no. 6 (New Delhi: Creative Books, 1995);

Richard Cronin, "The Quiet and the Loud: Anita Desai's India," in his *Imagining India* (Basingstoke, U.K.: Macmillan, 1989), pp. 45–58;

R. K. Dhawan, ed., *The Fiction of Anita Desai,* Series in English Language and Literature, no. 10 (New Delhi: Bahri, 1989);

Kunj Bala Goel, *Language and Theme in Anita Desai's Fiction* (Jaipur, India: Classic, 1989);

N. R. Gopal, *A Critical Study of the Novels of Anita Desai* (New Delhi: Atlantic Publishers, 1995);

Graham Huggan, "Philomela's Retold Story: Silence, Music, and the Post-colonial Text," *Journal of Commonwealth Literature,* 25, no. 1 (1990): 12–23;

Jasbir Jain, "Anita Desai," in *Indian English Novelists: An Anthology of Critical Essays,* edited by Madhusudan Prasad (New Delhi: Sterling, 1982), pp. 23–50;

Jain, "The Use of Fantasy in the Novels of Anita Desai," in *Explorations on Modern Indo-English Fiction,* edited by Dhawan (New Delhi: Bahri, 1982), pp. 227–237;

Shashi Khanna, *Human Relationships in Anita Desai's Novels* (New Delhi: Sarup, 1995);

Inder Nath Kher, "Madness as Discourse in Anita Desai's *Cry, The Peacock,*" *Commonwealth Novel in English,* 5, no. 2 (1992): 16–23;

Shantha Krishnaswamy, "Anita Desai: The Sexist Nature of Sanity," in her *The Woman in Indian Fiction in English, 1950–80* (New Delhi: Ashish, 1984), pp. 236–280;

Judie Newman, "History and Letters: Anita Desai's *Baumgartner's Bombay,*" *World Literature Written in English,* 30, no. 1 (1990): 37–46;

Michael Parker and Roger Starkey, eds., *Postcolonial Literatures: Achebe, Ngugi, Desai, Walcott* (New York: St. Martin's Press, 1995);

Virender Parmar, *Women in the Novels of Anita Desai: The Archetypes and Patterns of Quest* (Jalandhar, India: ABS Publications, 2000);

Usha Pathania, *Human Bonds and Bondages: The Fiction of Anita Desai and Kamala Markandaya* (New Delhi: Kanishka, 1992);

K. J. Phillips, "Ambiguous Tragic Flaw in Anita Desai's *Fire on the Mountain,*" *International Fiction Review,* 17, no. 1 (1990): 3–8;

Madhusudan Prasad, *Anita Desai: The Novelist* (Allahabad, India: New Horizon, 1981);

Bommatapalli Ramachandra Rao, *The Novels of Mrs. Anita Desai: A Study* (New Delhi: Kalyani, 1977);

Ramachandra Rao, "Themes and Variations in the Novels and Short Stories of Anita Desai," *Journal of Literature and Aesthetics,* 2, nos. 2 and 3 (1982): 74–79;

Sangeeta Ray, "Gender and the Discourse of Nationalism in Anita Desai's *Clear Light of Day,*" *Genders,* 20 (Fall 1994): 96–119;

Dieter Riemenschneider, "History and the Individual in Anita Desai's *Clear Light of Day* and Salman Rushdie's *Midnight's Children,*" in *The New Indian Novel in English: A Study of the 1980s,* edited by Viney Kirpal (New Delhi: Allied Publishers, 1990), pp. 187–199;

Minoli Salgado, "When Seeing Is Not Believing: Epiphany in Anita Desai's 'Games at Twilight,'" *Journal of Modern Literature,* 20, no. 1 (1996): 103–108;

Kajali Sharma, *Symbolism in Anita Desai's Novels* (New Delhi: Abhinav, 1991);

R. S. Sharma, *Anita Desai,* Indian Writers Series, volume 18 (New Delhi: Arnold-Heinemann, 1981);

Sharad Shrivastava, *The New Woman in Indian English Fiction: A Study of Kamala Markandaya, Anita Desai, Namita Gokhale & Shobha De,* Creative New Literature Series, no. 14 (New Delhi: Creative Books, 1996);

Tony Simoes da Silva, "Whose Bombay is it, anyway?: Anita Desai's *Baumgartner's Bombay,*" *ARIEL: A Review of International English Literature,* 28, no. 3 (1997): 63–77;

Brijraj Singh, "The Fiction of Anita Desai," *Humanities Review* (New Delhi), 3, no. 2 (1981): 40–43;

Sunaina Singh, *The Novels of Margaret Atwood and Anita Desai: A Comparative Study in Feminist Perspectives* (New Delhi: Creative Books, 1994);

Indira Sivanna, *Anita Desai as an Artist: A Study in Image and Symbol* (New Delhi: Creative Books, 1994);

Katharine Capshaw Smith, "Narrating History: The Reality of the Internment Camps in Anita Desai's *Baumgartner's Bombay,*" *ARIEL: A Review of International English Literature,* 28, no. 2 (1997): 141–157;

Mrinalini Solanki, *Anita Desai's Fiction: Patterns of Survival Strategies* (New Delhi: Kanishka, 1992);

Ramesh K. Srivastava, ed., *Perspectives on Anita Desai,* Indo-English Writers Series, no. 6 (Ghaziabad, India: Vimal, 1984);

A. V. Suresh Kumar, *Six Indian Novelists: Mulk Raj Anand, Raja Rao, R. K. Narayan, Balachandran Rajan, Kamala Markandaya, Anita Desai,* Creative New Literatures Series, no. 9 (New Delhi: Creative Books, 1996);

J. P. Tripathi, *The Mind and Art of Anita Desai* (Bareilly, India: Prakash Book Depot, 1986);

Ranu Uniyal, *The Fiction of Margaret Drabble and Anita Desai: Women & Landscape,* Creative New Literatures Series, no. 40 (New Delhi: Creative Books, 2000).

Jenny Diski

(8 July 1947 -)

Ann Hancock
University of the West of England, Bristol

BOOKS: *Nothing Natural* (London: Methuen, 1986; New York: Simon & Schuster, 1987);
Rainforest (London: Methuen, 1987);
Like Mother (London: Bloomsbury, 1988; New York: New American Library, 1988);
Then Again (London: Bloomsbury, 1990);
Happily Ever After (London: Hamilton, 1991; London & New York: Penguin, 1992);
Monkey's Uncle (London: Weidenfeld & Nicolson, 1994);
The Vanishing Princess (London: Weidenfeld & Nicolson, 1995);
The Dream Mistress (London: Weidenfeld & Nicolson, 1996; Hopewell, N.J.: Ecco, 1999);
Skating to Antarctica (London: Granta, 1997); republished as *Skating to Antarctica: A Journey to the End of the World* (Hopewell, N.J.: Ecco, 1998);
Don't (London: Granta, 1998);
Only Human (London: Virago, 2000; New York: Picador USA, 2001);
Stranger on a Train (London: Virago, 2002).

PRODUCED SCRIPT: "Murder in Mind," television, *Screen One,* BBC1, 2 October 1994.

SELECTED PERIODICAL PUBLICATIONS–UNCOLLECTED: "Conflict and Joy," *Guardian,* 24 December 1993, pp. G2, G4;
"And Not a Shop in Sight," *Observer,* Review section, 19 July 1998, p. 2;
"Falling in Love at 53," *Observer,* Review section, 27 August 2000, p. 4.

Jenny Diski (photograph by Jerry Bauer; from the U.S. edition of Only Human, *2001)*

Jenny Diski made a fairly late start to her writing career; she was nearly in her forties by the time she published her first novel. During the 1990s she established a reputation as an intelligent novelist and essayist who accepted the challenges of uncomfortable subject matter and adopted an original approach to it. The rigorous exploration of contemporary thinking has been the dominant force in her writing, though she has also shown awareness of the experiments with narrative notable in much modern fiction.

Diski was born Jennifer Simmonds in London on 8 July 1947, the only child of a second marriage for both parents. Her father, James Simmonds, formerly Zimmerman, was a first-generation East End Jew, as was her mother, born Rachel Rayner. The family lived for Simmonds's first eleven years at Paramount Court, a block of flats in Tottenham Court Road in central London. As a black marketeer, Simmonds's father provided relative wealth in her early years, which was manifested in clothes, skating and ballet lessons, and the trappings of social advancement. The marriage was not, however, happy or successful, and Simmonds's father left when she was six years old, plummeting her mother into a breakdown. Simmonds was placed in foster care until her mother was discharged from the hospital and her father returned. Diski's many accounts of her childhood, in fiction and interviews, focus on the extreme instability of her mother and the vicious antagonism between her parents. Diski described her mother as "mad," and certainly she did not provide adequate maternal care. In an interview with Andy Beckett in 1996, she said: "There are very few positive things I can remember about my mother. . . . Sometimes I sit down and try . . . but on the whole it is her grotesqueries that I remember." As Simmonds neared the end of her time at primary school, at eleven, her father left permanently.

Her mother, unwilling either to work or to accept payments from the Department of Health and Social Security, was virtually destitute after bailiffs, required to leave only a bed and chair, claimed most of the family's belongings. While Simmonds and her mother were awaiting eviction, social workers visited and arranged for Simmonds to go to a progressive Quaker boarding school in Letchworth, Hertfordshire. She stayed only a few terms and returned to her mother, who had found work as a housekeeper, though she soon lost the position. At the age of thirteen Simmonds found her father again with a new partner, Pam, and lived briefly with them. It was not, however, a solution for Simmonds, who developed negative feelings about families, as she stated rather provocatively to Frederic Tuten in 1999: "I find families vile and dangerous, and I don't find love that relates to family life very plausible." Living with her father failed, and Simmonds returned to the boarding school until her behavior prompted staff to ask her to leave just before she turned fifteen.

Back with her mother, now in Brighton, Simmonds responded to the immense turmoil and insecurity of her life by taking an overdose, which was followed by a period of several months in a psychiatric hospital in Hove. The doctor who was treating her would not give permission for her to return to either of her dysfunctional parents, and she could not go back to the boarding school. It was her good fortune that the writer Doris Lessing, whose son had been in Simmonds's class at the boarding school, offered her a home, where she remained for four years. Lessing found her a school and encouraged her to write, though Simmonds discarded all the stories from that time. Shortly before she was due to take her A levels, her father died from a heart attack. Two days after his death, on a date that seems to be imprinted on Diski's consciousness, 22 April 1966, she saw her mother for the last time.

Without taking her exams, she left Lessing's home to live alone in a bed-sitter, again experiencing problems so severe as to necessitate three years in psychiatric hospitals, including the Maudsley in London. As Diski told Tuten, she "went into a spin from 20 to about 23." Toward the end of what she refers to as the "bin period" she became heavily involved in the excesses of 1960s London; she "did a lot of sex, drugs and rock and roll–mostly drugs, not much rock and roll." Another major overdose during this period brought her close to death.

After many years in which Simmonds had become accustomed to institutionalization and constant interrogation by therapists of all kinds, she made a considered decision to reject madness, when she was confronted with the prospect of being sent back again to the first hospital that had treated her, and to find work. She completed a teachers' training course and taught for five years, participating in a project to start a school in Camden for children who had been excluded from regular school. During this time she married; she and her husband, Roger, invented the name Diski. Her only child, Chloe, was born in 1977. The marriage was short-lived, but her former husband remained a friend. Later, she started a B.S. course in anthropology but left after two years, before obtaining a degree.

In her thirties Diski finally began to write for publication. She has frequently suggested that writing was the only career that would ensure the solitariness that is so important to her and that it was the only work she ever really wanted to do. Recollections of "plans to be the world's greatest writer" at the age of eight appeared in a piece on the horrors of family Christmases in *The Guardian* in 1993. Suzie Mackenzie, writing in *The Guardian* (9 October 1991), suggested that "her books read like episodes from an autobiography," and it is clear that her harrowing relationship with her mother, brought to a halt when Diski was still a teenager, haunts her writing. Madness, confusion about identity, desertion of children, powerlessness, and emotional withdrawal are all strong themes in her work. Diski herself, while acknowledging autobiographical material in her fiction, does not see her writing as therapy. "I don't write to make myself better," she told Michael Dibdin in 1991.

Her first novel, *Nothing Natural,* a bold investigation into the difficult subject of sadomasochism, was published in 1986, when she was thirty-nine. Diski said in an interview with Angela Neustatter for *The Guardian* that "I was intrigued because sado-masochism is so utterly unacceptable." The protagonist, Rachel, a single mother who earns a living teaching children excluded from school, relishes her self-sufficiency and is cynical about "coupledom." She feels that she is in control of her life but finds herself relinquishing that power when she becomes involved with Joshua, who coldly draws her into an occasional relationship that functions only through ritualized violent sex. She recognizes and analyzes the inadequacies she believes are responsible for Joshua's sadistic behavior but nevertheless finds herself a willing victim. As she becomes more and more dependent on his visits, she experiences unease about his control over her: "she wanted, needed, his control over her body but not over her life." While she responds to the vulnerability Joshua brings out in her, she is fearful of the power game that she seems inevitably to lose.

After the suicide of Pete, a troubled adolescent in state care whom she has been teaching, Rachel descends into severe depression. Partly through the desire to be alone and partly through guilt toward those who are looking after her, particularly Isobel, her adoptive mother, she has herself admitted to a hospital but flees when it appears that the doctors are prepared to hold her against her will for treatment.

The main narrative is framed by chapters relating to Rachel's return from Cornwall, where she sought refuge from the hospital doctors with a friend. The opening chapter describes Rachel's suspicions about Joshua's possible involvement in a rape that had been reported in her newspaper. From the start the reader has this suspicion in mind about Joshua, as well as Rachel's assertion that "Joshua was a catastrophe that had happened to her; a growing tumour she had most uneasily learned to live with." In the final chapter the narrator returns to the newspaper article as Rachel agonizes over Joshua and her relationship with him. Her apparent complicity with him is acted out as she writes him a letter describing a fantasy of rape in her home, but almost without volition she reports to the police that a man has been watching her house at night, giving a description of Joshua. What starts out as a "gift" for Joshua turns into a bid for power as the police catch him in an apparent act of rape. It seems that the diminishing of Joshua, who looks "smaller and rather pathetic" in front of the police, frees Rachel, but perhaps only to her self-imposed isolation and to the status of victim.

Diski thought that many readers misunderstood the ending of the novel, in not recognizing that Rachel "cops out completely," as she told Tuten. Certainly it provoked controversy on account of content that many found shocking and some repellent and ensured that Diski was noticed as a new novelist. The novel was successful in terms of sales and was reviewed more extensively than might be anticipated for a first novel.

A second novel, *Rainforest,* followed a year later. It opens with a first-person account in the present tense of Mo's current job as a cleaner in private houses. Her job fulfills her desire for order, for restoring things to the way they should be. She is, however, haunted by memories of a trip to a rain forest that has left her unable to return to her previous life as an academic and in need of weekly sessions with a doctor. Life is held at a distance, in fear of chaos causing mental collapse.

Subsequent chapters reveal how Mo reached this point in her life. Told in the third person, they describe her work as a lecturer in the life sciences department of a university and the field trip she undertook to study the ecosystem of the rain forest in Borneo. Her practical, sensible, and organized approach to her university work is contrasted with that of her colleague, Liam, who risks his secure family life and his career to pursue a young student, Grace, with whom he is infatuated. Mo's longing for control and emotional distance is also challenged by a younger man, Joe, who is appointed by the university to cover for her absence on the field trip. His views on man's alienated relationship to nature are in direct contradiction to her belief that people live "as part of a balanced natural system." Though she is attracted to him, his casual and impulsive attitude toward sexual relationships threatens her.

In the rain forest Mo carries out her neat and precise measurements of the contents of the forest floor, searching for a "coherent pattern," avoiding the intimacy that is on offer from a colleague at the base camp, and feeling an increasing anger and anxiety. An unexpected visit from Joe, during which she gives in to her desire for him, and his equally unexpected departure disorientate her and precipitate her into chaos. "Joe and the forest. They were the same. Both dangerous, beguiling the unwary into forgetting to be watchful. Each hid cruel and sudden surprises." She suffers a terrifying breakdown from which she only partially recovers, reducing her life to minimal human contact and a single room that is an "almost empty space that requires nothing" of her. She achieves some contentment but only at the expense of engagement with the world.

A less likable character than the protagonist of *Nothing Natural,* Mo follows a trajectory similar to Rachel's, ending up in a fragile state and fighting to keep madness at bay through controlled isolation. Both characters live life on the margins, a place where Diski's heroines are often to be found. Frances, the main character of *Like Mother* (1988), makes a determined choice to be an outsider, despite the attempts of others to steer her toward conventional feminine roles. Two narratives run side by side: the story of the upbringing of Frances in postwar Britain and a

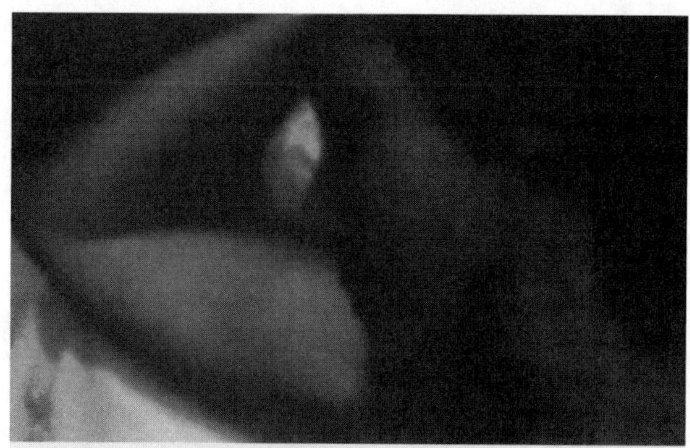

Dust jacket for the U.S. edition of Diski's 1996 novel, about a middle-aged woman in an unsatisfying relationship and a bag lady, who may be the woman's mother (Richland County Public Library)

metafictional narrative provided by Nony (short for nonentity), Frances's baby, a child born with limited brain function. This second narrative offers a commentary on Frances's story and on storytelling in general. It is in the form of a dialogue, the "listener" invented for that purpose perhaps representing the role of the questioning reader, responding with commonsense bewilderment to the oddities of the tale.

There are clear autobiographical elements in the story of Frances, the only child of Ivy and Gerald, a Jewish couple who thrive in the black-market world immediately after World War II but never realize their expectations of an affluent life. Her mother brings Frances up to be a "good girl," always nicely dressed, but when Frances finds badness within, she recognizes where her energy lies. As her parents' marriage disintegrates–her mother a drunk, her father merely pathetic–Frances retreats into a secret wickedness, her "private place." She comes to define badness as passivity, a kind of refusal. "Refusal was the real point. Refusal to tell, refusal to allow anyone to know what she knew." With Sandra, her beautiful friend who, unlike Frances, lives to please, and more so with Stuart, a boy who fell in love with her when she was twelve, Frances experiments with wickedness, seeking unconsciousness with stolen ether, stealing from shops, and never being caught. Her goal is oblivion and caring about nothing, a refusal to relate to the world. The objective seems to have been achieved when she makes dancing her career, something defined as "solitary, difficult and essentially pointless." When that too fails her, she agrees, as "another refusal," to marry Stuart, who believes that one day she will love him and behave in a normal way; but she does not change, and he leaves when she refuses to abort their seriously defective child.

Nony gives Frances pleasure as the "ultimate refuser," an anhydranencephalic who cannot respond in any way. At the end of the story Frances is dying of cervical cancer, and Nony's life expectancy is also short; Frances merely sees the longed-for oblivion at hand. The neat conclusiveness of the ending is, however, undercut by the reader/listener in the second narrative, who finds Frances's illness implausible. The "truth" of the story is constantly put in question as the nature of stories, with beginning, middle, and end, is exposed and juxtaposed with the "little empty circles" of Frances's own short-story writing. The contrivance of fiction is emphasized in the novel; this absence of realism makes Frances's almost incredible detachment from those around her more acceptable and allows the reader to dwell on the themes of the novel.

Diski's interest in storytelling and in issues of personal identity is again in evidence with *Then Again* (1990). The central narrative, in which the protagonist, Esther, struggles with the problems of her troubled fourteen-year-old daughter, Katya, is juxtaposed with the story of another Esther, a young victim of the Inquisition, which comes to the contemporary Esther not quite in her dreams but in a border time between sleeping and waking. The concurrent stories are paralleled as both Katya and the earlier Esther (later called Elizabeth) ask challenging questions and are in various ways punished by the demands of the prevailing ideologies.

Katya believes she has found grace and stops eating in acknowledgment of her discovery of God. Medical authorities deem her psychotic, though competing explanations are offered for her condition. The doctors diagnose hormonal imbalance, a chemical cause. Esther's friend Ben, a psychotherapist, however, finds family conflict the source of the problem.

Katya's attempts to explain herself meet resistance, particularly from an impatient priest who scorns her experiences and convinces her of her wickedness. In a desperate state Katya runs away and is raped by a man who finds her wandering the streets. Only Sam, a young man squatting in a derelict house, is prepared to help her, tending her even when she cuts herself and lapses into a catatonic state. Ben is clearly not to be trusted. Having taken advantage of Esther's vulnerable state by becoming her lover after Katya left, he later deceives Esther about Katya's treatment when she is brought into the hospital by the police. He had promised a drug-free therapy but in fact admits her to a psychiatric hospital. "They want to stop her asking questions," says Sam.

The earlier Esther who permeates modern Esther's consciousness is a young Jewish girl, adopted by a Christian family and renamed Elizabeth when all of her family and community are murdered. Her sense of her own difference from those around her, both in looks and intelligence, strikes a chord in Esther, who was herself adopted and is increasingly uncertain of her own identity. The clear parallel, however, is with Katya. Elizabeth begins to doubt the beliefs she has been brought up with. She appeals for help to Father Anselm, another outsider embittered by his incarceration with "peasants." He encourages her in heresy but only as entrapment. Having taken her to a hut in the woods, purportedly to meet like-minded people, he dupes the innocent girl into having sex with him before having her arrested. Finally, she is put to death as a sorceress and heretic.

Through the experiences of Elizabeth and Katya, Esther is forced to question her own apparently liberal attitudes as the two stories in the novel expose inadequacies of modern thinking and medical practices. Katya is brutally treated, just as Elizabeth was, too easily labeled insane for daring to be different. Ben, the contemporary priest of mental health, is little different from the sinister, treacherous Father Anselm. A network of connections provides a complex investigation of madness, religious faith, morality, and rationality. Esther incorporates what she has learned, taking on Elizabeth's story as her own, achieving a degree of peace in her knowledge but also an awareness of the limits of her understanding. The novel closes with the question that preoccupied Katya and Elizabeth–"what for?"

With four novels published in quick succession, Diski became established as a writer capable of presenting difficult ideas in an accessible fictional form. Her tendency to put under scrutiny widely accepted contemporary beliefs, including many feminist ideas about the representation of women (though she is an avowed feminist), assured her of a reaction from readers. Some have found her too concerned with ideas and her novels overly schematic, and Diski admitted to Beckett in an interview in 1996 that ideas are always her motivation. "The books start out with ideas. . . . The novel comes afterwards. . . . It's always a bit of a nuisance when I have to move people around and make them do things."

There is a lighter tone than usual in Diski's fifth novel, *Happily Ever After* (1991), though her characteristic darkness is also lurking. It revives a character from *Rainforest,* Liam, revealing the consequences of his desertion of wife and children. Living as a virtual alcoholic in a dilapidated house, he is still obsessed with Grace, who has married him but does not return his worship of her body. He is, though, loved by Daphne, the sitting tenant, a "dried-up, 68-year-old ex-lady novelist" inhabiting the top floor of the house. By chance the house is where Daphne spent part of her childhood with a "dark, deserted, demented" mother. These hopeless cases are joined by Sylvie, an aimless "eternal visitor" who stays with anyone who will look after her. Her six-year-old daughter, Divya, has been in the care of social services almost since birth. After she moves, reluctantly, into Liam's house as a tenant, she experiences terror at being required to take responsibility for herself and sinks into self-pity. Daphne dreams of escape with Liam, while he dreams of monkhood. For none of the characters is the house a home.

The "quiet despair" experienced by most of the occupants is shared by Jock, the social worker responsible for Divya. Visiting Sylvie and Divya in their squalor, Jock convinces himself that the child should stay with her depressed and incompetent mother, acknowledging that there is no answer to the problems of such a deprived child. When Liam realizes that Grace is lost to him, he attempts to drink himself to death but is prevented by the determination of Daphne to gain his attention and affection. In a bizarre scene she climbs into Liam's bed, after tying him down as he sleeps, and attempts to rape him. Weakened by a hangover or genuinely transformed, Liam falls in love. Daphne takes charge of her life and his by persuading her former publishers to give her an advance on a new novel, *Happily Ever After,* and to buy her a motor home. As the odd couple prepare to leave, Divya turns increasingly to Daphne, but she is unable to help her, despite the empathy she feels for the child's condition. Instead she works on her book, which is a version of Diski's novel, desiring "only to write a novel about a love that ends in happiness."

After traveling through Europe together, Daphne and Liam rebuild a ruined house in Spain and plan to settle down. In London, Jock has found a horrifying way to deal with his anxiety about Divya. Close to breakdown himself, he takes Divya out as a treat, gives her sleeping pills, and lowers her into a river to drown. It seems to him the only thing to offer a child doomed to a life of pain and sadness. Daphne too tries to make things right; "wasn't she living the outcome of her decision to be happy?" Yet, she still feels the urge to roam and has to move on.

The final chapter gives ironic concessions to closure. The narrative returns to the house, now empty and awaiting sale. Sylvie, rendered a legitimate victim by Divya's death, returns to her previous life in other people's households. Liam has finished his house but is unaware of the underground spring that will bring about its collapse. Daphne is traveling alone, "chatting with the Lord," as she has throughout the novel. In a final burst of self-referentiality, she describes the ending of her novel: "Everyone is going to live happily ever after. I don't have to say what all the happily ever afters will be, do I?" A strange crying still haunts the house where two unhappy children–Daphne and Divya–spent time, but no one hears it. Reviewers appreciated the sharp irony of the writing in this "comedy" that, as the reviewer in the 14 November 1992 edition of *The Times* (London) wrote, "stretches the definition of black humour to breaking point."

In 1994 Diski wrote a script, "Murder in Mind," for the occasional BBC1 crime series *Screen One,* shown on 2 October, starring Charlotte Rampling as a therapist who counsels patients to kill themselves and Trevor Eve as the detective who fails to stop her, succumbing himself to suicide. Andrew Billen in *The Observer* (25 September 1994) described it as a "crisp satire on New Age cures for age old miseries" in an interview with Rampling just before the program was broadcast. Another novel, *Monkey's Uncle,* was published in the same year. Charlotte Fitzroy's "descent into madness" opens this complicated, sometimes surreal novel. As is inevitable with Diski, who has considerable first-hand experience of interpretations of mental illness, a variety of reasons are offered for Charlotte's problems: childhood trauma (her father's desertion); the recent death of her daughter in a road accident; hormonal imbalance; the collapse of Communism; a hereditary defect. Experimenting again with multiple narratives to explore madness, Diski tells three entwined stories. Two Charlottes exist: the one "up-top," the depressed self, negotiating the miseries of mental illness; and Charlotte-the-Escapee, the mad self, who exists in an alternative dream reality, populated by an articulate orangutan and those key influences on twentieth-century thought, Sigmund Freud, Karl Marx, and Charles Darwin. In addition, there are selected episodes from the unhappy life of Robert FitzRoy, captain of the *Beagle*–the ship on which Darwin served as naturalist–whose biography Charlotte has been reading. His doomed exploits and eventual suicide encourage her to identify with him as a putative ancestor.

Charlotte's treatment in the hospital illustrates the grim realities of depressive illness. "It felt like that top layer of skin had been removed, and suddenly the depression was exposed to the air." As a character she is rather nebulous, remote from her children, whom she seems unable to love just as her mother failed to love her, and let down by the political movements she devoted her energies to. Marx and Freud "*just weren't good enough*"; Darwin as "full of holes as your socks probably are." She tells her past to Matthew, her therapist, with whom, predictably, she falls in love. His implicit rejection of her and a visit from her son's girlfriend on her return from the hospital precipitate an overdose. Despite her obvious despair, she makes a remarkable recovery, which suggests to the doctors that at least a part of her wanted to live.

Other parts of the novel move self-consciously into an imagined world, reminiscent of Lewis Carroll's *Alice's Adventures in Wonderland* (1865), and indeed, as if to make the point absolutely clear, every chapter is prefixed with an extract from that novel. Charlotte's companion is Jenny, a vocal orangutan that Charlotte had seen at the zoo. They drink tea and have discussions about evolution, and now and then meet up with the three elderly gentlemen who promised so much for the twentieth century. All Karl, Sigmund, and Charles are really interested in, however, is acquiring more food and, in a series of Mad Hatter's tea parties, indulging in vague, puerile bickering about their differing points of view. Diski ridicules these icons of popular thought, but there is little real analysis of their ideas.

There were some reservations expressed about the literary quality of *Monkey's Uncle.* While it was praised for its bold originality, serious intent, and precise, subtle writing, some reviewers were irritated by its flaws: too much material that seems without purpose; an unwieldy form; and, as Jenny Turner for *The Guardian* (15 March 1994) suggested, a sacrifice of the demands of narrative to "structures which exist only in intellectual space." It was, however, generally perceived as thought-provoking and interesting; Rachel Cusk, writing in the 7 March 1994 edition of *The Times* (London), called it "a spirited look at the contemporary liberal psyche."

Diski's collection of short stories *The Vanishing Princess* (1995) was greeted with enthusiasm, though the by-now common criticism that her fictions are too schematic or formulaic was in evidence. Her skill in writing about sexual desire and sexual acts was applauded, as were her intelligence and wry humor. The stories are about women and their obsessions, dark and strange but relieved by witty narration. The collection begins and ends with a fairy tale, taking the familiar motif of the princess in captivity in a tower, but unlike some other contemporary women writers, notably Angela Carter, who have reworked traditional tales to give their heroines a more active and interesting destiny, Diski leaves her princesses perpetually waiting for their stories to begin. Oblivious of the world or even of their own identities, they do nothing. One just disappears; the other, readers assume, sits it out until her death.

Many of the remaining stories take women, often in conventional roles of wife or mother, who deny expectations. In "Housewife" an ordinary married woman engages in an adventurous sexual liaison that is not discovered and does not impact on her marriage. In "Wide Blue Yonder" a young woman on holiday in the Caribbean with her husband and young son realizes that she has sacrificed her right to pleasure and choice in her ordered and dull life. She achieves euphoria, not the anticipated terror, when her mat floats out to sea. "This was, she thought, the most complete pleasure she had ever experienced." The protagonist of "Bath Time" charts her life in terms of unsatisfactory baths, from the Dettol scrubs imposed by her mother to the compromises of marriage and motherhood. After waiting many years, she achieves her dream bathroom in which she can spend a long-anticipated uninterrupted day. The stories deal often with painful experience, with unhappiness and anxiety, but Diski adopts a cool, astringent tone for emotion, reserving intensity for passages of sexual exploration.

The Dream Mistress (1996) makes many demands upon the reader with its potentially confusing narrative structure. Diski described it in a 1999 interview with Tuten as "about storytelling, about writing really, where stories come from and where they go to in their improbable way." Chapter 1 sets up a conventional narrative; forty-six-year-old Mimi has an argument with her boyfriend in a cinema, leaves by a back way, and finds a tramp unconscious in an alley. The old woman, named Bella by paramedics, is taken to the hospital, where layer upon layer of stinking rags have to be removed before she can be attended to. This story is, however, quickly rendered strange when, in an abrupt change of point of view in the second chapter, Bella, who does not know who she is, starts to describe in surrealist fashion her body stripped of all flesh, its internal workings in evidence; it is as if the nurses' unwrapping extends right to the bone. This alarmingly visceral account is a striking metaphor for the key question in the novel: "who knew where one properly addressed the centre of oneself?"

Dust jacket for the U.S. edition of Diski's 2000 novel, a modern version of the biblical story of Abraham and Sarah (Richland County Public Library)

Once the opening episode has established the focus of the novel, little happens in the present-time narrative. Mimi returns from the cinema, and Jack comes home much later, having obviously been with another woman. After sex with Mimi, followed by a row, Jack leaves. For the remainder of the novel Mimi is lying in bed remembering and dreaming, though it is not always clear which is which. Mimi's memories of her mother, Leah, and of the development of her relationship with Jack are the most straightforward, usually appearing in numbered chapters. Chapters with no number but a heading–"Bella" and "Mask"–tell stories of a woman who has been facially disfigured in an accident and is taken care of by a man who abandons wife and children to do so. One might see this character as an alternative Mimi. Another woman in these chapters seems to be a redeemed version of Leah who spends time as a novice nun and later performs an unwitting miracle before she becomes the bag lady whom Mimi finds. There is also one numberless, nameless chapter, preceded by a blank page, which provides some links for those readers alert enough to find them.

Mimi has for a time been falling asleep, at odd times in inappropriate places, perhaps as a means of escape, but she does not dream. The merging fragments of stories are, however, the products of Mimi's consciousness, her explorations of herself and her relationships. They are justified by the novel's epigraph from Freud: "those dreams best fulfil their function about which one knows nothing after waking." Mimi is rather like Mo in *Rainforest,* damaged and distant, having built a "wall of serenity" around herself. Jack, like Joe in the earlier novel, breaks down the protective wall, with profound consequences for the fragile protagonist.

"Painful," "profoundly disturbing," and "unsettling" were adjectives applied to this novel. The incoherence of the narrative was exasperating to some reviewers and justifiable to others; Alex Clark in *The Sunday Times* (19 October 1997) said, "Diski writes extraordinarily well of the fictions we weave in order to survive . . . and in this novel she makes a virtue out of incoherence and disintegration." In November 1997 Diski read an excerpt from *The Dream Mistress* with a corneal operation from a 1960s television medical documentary projected behind her during a symposium titled "Violence and the Arts" for the London Film Festival. The performance was described as a "charmingly casual but thought-provoking meditation on the body" by Chris Drake in *The Independent* (28 November 1997).

Skating to Antarctica (1997) is probably Diski's best-known and most appreciated book, described by Michèle Roberts in *The Times* (29 May 1997) as "her best and most moving book to date." In this mix of travel book and memoir, a poignant, yet unsentimental, voice exposes Diski's vulnerability with honesty and no self-pity as she revisits her acutely painful past. The longing for oblivion, for a blankness in which memory is erased, has been evident in many of Diski's fictional characters, represented as a desire for whiteness, for emptiness. A visit to Antarctica gives expression to those feelings, a "hopeful voyage into whiteness." As she travels forward as a tourist on her literal journey into the ice, Diski also returns to the ice-skating of her childhood and to a mother with whom she was always on thin ice. The memories are in part generated by her reluctant assent to her eighteen-year-old daughter's curiosity about her grandmother, which leads Diski back to the Tottenham Court Road flat and discussions with neighbors who still remember the family. Detective work on Chloe's part reveals something of the life of Diski's mother after they parted company when Diski was Chloe's age. The distressing details of Diski's youth with two suicidal and abusive parents are juxtaposed with witty accounts of her fellow travelers on the voyage to Antarctica. For many readers the recurrence in Diski's fiction of unloved children, absent fathers, deranged mothers, and distant, fearful women was fully explained by this book. As Christina Patterson wrote in *The Observer* (1 June 1997), "If there was ever any doubt that Diski's masterful portrayal of isolation, depression and despair was rooted in personal experience, it is firmly dispelled by this, her first work of non-fiction." *Skating to Antarctica* was much lauded for its candor and originality. It was awarded the Mind Book of the Year award in 1998 for the book that had made the most significant contribution to public awareness of mental health problems; the award was a result of an accident by her publishers, according to Diski, who, until recently, has not allowed her work to be submitted for prizes.

Diski's next publication, *Don't* (1998), was also a work of nonfiction, an absorbing collection of short essays, most of them having originally appeared in the *London Review of Books,* to which she has been a regular contributor. It consists primarily of book reviews and essays based on personal experience. Diski brings her independent, witty, and clear-sighted view to the iconic and the merely famous: Madonna, Robert Maxwell, Howard Hughes, Princess Diana, Marlon Brando, Greta Garbo. Throughout her writing career Diski has been a prolific reviewer of books, films, television, and radio. In addition to her work for the *London Review of Books,* she has written book reviews and a weekly radio column for the *Mail on Sunday,* written regularly for *The Observer,* and even did a supermarket column, "Off Your Trolley," for *The Sunday Times* in 1993. She has also contributed reviews and articles on many subjects to *Sight and Sound* and *The American Scholar.* Gerald Jacobs of *The Independent on Sunday* (9 August 1998) suggested that, with *Skating to Antarctica* and *Don't,* "having made her mark as a novelist, Diski is now in the front rank of non-fiction."

Diski returned to fiction with *Only Human,* subtitled *A Comedy,* in 2000. It is a retelling of part of Genesis (chapters 11 to 22), a modern version of the story of Abraham and Sarah, or, as they were before God's pronouncement, Abram and Sarai. After the lucid confessional of *Skating to Antarctica, Only Human* seems less overtly autobiographical than many of Diski's novels. Sarai is, at the beginning of the novel, wounded by family like Diski's other female characters. Her position in Terah's household is secure–he is her father–but her mother was a slave girl, and only her longing for a female child persuades Terah's wife, Emtelai, to accept Sarai. Her sex too displaces her; as a girl she is invisible, excluded from the ritual recitation of the generations, when Terah names her brothers, but "the final name . . . was never spoken." Sarai is, however, a strong, resilient woman who, unlike Diski's previous heroines, is much loved and herself capable of intense feeling. The novel is in part the love story of a devoted brother and sister who are ordered by their father into marriage to ensure offspring and, with initial difficulty, transform their relationship into the intimacy of husband and wife. Only in this novel does Diski attempt an exploration of enduring, faithful love, but it is significantly placed in an ancient, mythical context, distanced from contemporary life.

Much of the narrative follows Abram and Sarai in their wanderings through the desert. First, the whole family has to leave their home and business in disgrace after Haran, Sarai's younger brother, kills himself. Later, when Abram finally realizes what Sarai has known for many years, that she will never conceive, he experiences an angst that isolates him from Sarai and leaves him open to a call from God to set out as his chosen one to a new land. With Sarai "no longer the central passion of his life," Abram surrenders himself to God's will. Diski gives priority to Sarai in her story of a deeply patriarchal world, rendering the destruction of Sodom and Gomorrah in a brief paragraph and making little of God's command that Abraham sacrifice Isaac, the child of Abraham and Sarah's old age who surprises them with his arrival long after the couple has pronounced: "Now there can be no more surprises." The novel's framing device of Sarah as an aged woman on her deathbed, with an audience of eager seekers after truth, casts her as a source of wisdom, though, as Diski's regular readers might anticipate, she denies them any comfort. For Sarah, "it was all endings. Always. Endings, starting and ending, but no conclusion."

The originality of the novel is evident not only in Diski's revision (but at the same time faithful retelling) of the biblical story but also in her choice of God as a first-person narrator, interrupting the third-person narrative of Abram and Sarai with philosophical reflections on mankind and, with a novelistic self-consciousness, on the processes of creation. All too human, God becomes exasperated with his beings, who seem to act of their own accord, escaping his authorial control. Humor and irony are generated by God's willfulness and neurosis as he embarks on a contest with Sarai for possession of Abram and at the same time tries to wrest the story from her: "The story's mine, not hers, never was hers. The interruption is the narrative, the interruptor is the narrator. As if her story could be the story. . . . I am the Word and the maker of time." The divine is rendered comical and inconsistent, laughed at occasionally even by Abram, but God learns from his creations the range of human emotions–fear, jealousy, self-doubt, anxiety, "the anguish of desire." Diski undercuts the grandeur of biblical language and thought with anachronism–God's utterances become informal as he is "getting the hang of time" or jokily working "the old three times three trick," which "always works a treat" in gaining the full attention of his creatures–and commonsense straight talking, as in this exchange between Abram and Sarai:

> It seemed a long way to come for nothing very special.
>
> "This land. Canaan. This is where my seed will develop into a nation."
>
> She stopped herself from snapping that so far his seed had failed to develop into a single baby, and she could not see how it was going to make the leap directly into nationhood now. Abram never was strong on irony and he looked even less likely to appreciate it at the moment.

Reviewers thought that Diski met well the challenges of this novel. Maggie Gee in *The Sunday Times* (29 October 2000) commented that *Only Human* is "held together by a wit and control that Diski's last novel, *The Dream Mistress,* seemed to lack."

The unexpected appearance of love in Diski's fiction was echoed in her life at the time of the publication of *Only Human.* Between August and November 2000 *The Observer* printed a series of pieces in which Diski charts the progress of her relationship with a new lover, whom she refers to only as the Poet. Diski has testified many times in print to her desire to live alone and the difficulties she experiences with relationships. She has always expressed a cynical distrust of romantic love. The articles in *The Observer* describe her surprise and anxiety at her own actions in not only planning to share her life with a man, but also leaving London, where she had lived all of her life, for Cambridge, to buy the house across the road from the Poet. The contradictions were not lost on her, as she reports in *The Observer* on 27 August 2000: "I am . . . buying a house in the provinces–all, my dears, in wild pursuit of my heart's desire. In the first place I don't do wild; and in the second, I don't have a heart." After an "extremely busy" early life, the "whole aim for the second half of my life was for nothing whatever to happen." In 2002 Diski ventured again into travel writing, following up the successful *Skating to Antartica* with *Stranger on a Train,* which, like the earlier book, combines memoir with an account of a journey, this time around North America by Amtrak. Though envisaged by Diski as a book "about nothing happening," she is unable to avoid contact during the journey with a few fellow travelers who are drawn together in camaraderie by their smoking habit. Adam Mars-Jones in *The Observer* (18 August 2002) described the book as "often fiercely funny" and found interest in the "entertaining encounters" in smoking cars which Diski describes. Rachel Aspden in the *The Guardian* (17 August 2002) was less convinced: "Flashes of insight along the way provide sparse compensation for her own summary of the journey: 'Blankness outside as well as in the empty centre.'"

Contradiction is the mark of Jenny Diski's fiction. She can adopt a tone that is bleak, clinical, and cold, or compassionate and witty. At times her novels are in danger of too much abstraction; at others she writes with concrete precision about observable realities. In her concentration on the problematic lives of women she finds common ground with many contemporary feminist writers, but feminist assertions are exposed to the same critical scrutiny as are other beliefs that underpin the value systems of society.

Interviews:

Angela Neustatter, "Terror in the Human Jungle," *Guardian,* 10 June 1987, p. 26;

Michael Dibdin, "One Damn Thing after Another," *Independent on Sunday,* Review section, 22 September 1991, p. 30;

Suzie Mackenzie, "True Stories," *Guardian,* 9 October 1991, p. 21;

Andy Beckett, "Mother of Invention," *Independent on Sunday,* 5 May 1996, pp. 32–33;

Frederic Tuten, "Jenny Diski," *Bomb,* 66 (Winter 1999): 42–47.

References:

Gerd Bayer, "'A Sterile Promontory': Jane Rogers's and Jenny Diski's Views of the Future," *Arachne: An Interdisciplinary Journal of the Humanities,* 6 (1999): 79–92;

Silvia Caporale Bizzini, "Language and Power in Jenny Diski's *Rainforest,*" in *Theme Parks, Rainforests and Sprouting Wastelands: European Essays on Theory and Performance in Contemporary British Fiction,* edited by Richard Todd and Luisa Flora (Amsterdam & Atlanta: Rodopi, 2000), pp. 29–39;

Janina Nordius, "Molds of Telling: Metafictional Sliding in Jenny Diski's *Like Mother,*" *English Studies,* 72 (1991): 442–453;

Victoria Rosner, "Gender Degree Zero: Memoirs of Frozen Time in Antarctica," *a/b: Autobiography Studies,* 14 (1999): 5–22.

J. G. Farrell

(23 January 1935 – 12 August 1979)

Michael C. Prusse
Zürcher Hochschule Winterthur & Universität Zürich

See also the Farrell entry in *DLB 14: British Novelists Since 1960.*

BOOKS: *A Man from Elsewhere* (London: Hutchinson, 1963);
The Lung (London: Hutchinson, 1965);
A Girl in the Head (London: Cape, 1967; New York: Harper & Row, 1967);
Troubles (London: Cape, 1970; New York: Knopf, 1971);
The Siege of Krishnapur (London: Weidenfeld & Nicolson, 1973; New York: Harcourt Brace Jovanovich, 1974);
The Singapore Grip (London: Weidenfeld & Nicolson, 1978; New York: Knopf, 1979);
The Hill Station: An Unfinished Novel; with Two Appreciations and a Personal Memoir, and an Indian Diary, edited by John Spurling (London: Weidenfeld & Nicolson, 1981).

OTHER: "J. G. Farrell Comments," in *Contemporary Novelists,* volume 2, edited by James Vinson (London: St. James / New York: St. Martin's Press, 1972), pp. 399–400;
"J. G. Farrell," in *Bookmarks,* edited by Frederic Raphael (London: Quartet, 1975), pp. 49–52.

SELECTED PERIODICAL PUBLICATIONS–UNCOLLECTED: "Views," *Listener,* 30 August 1973, pp. 272–273;
"The Pussycat Who Fell in Love with a Suitcase," *Atlantis,* 6 (Winter 1973–1974): 6–10.

J. G. Farrell (from the dust jacket for the U.S. edition of The Singapore Grip, *1979)*

The writing career of J. G. Farrell was cut short by his unexpected death by drowning when he was fishing on some rocks close to his new home in Kilcrohane, County Cork, Ireland. The obituaries and memoirs published by friends and critics recognized the loss of a major literary figure. Farrell, whom his biographer, Lavinia Greacen, labeled "that most elusive of twentieth century novelists," has remained popular with the reading public, as is demonstrated by the many reprints of his Empire trilogy–according to Ronald Binns in *J. G. Farrell* (1986) "probably the most ambitious literary project conceived and executed by any British novelist in the 1970s." In academic circles Farrell did not make a major impact until the mid 1990s. His work has mostly been read as political; depending on the critic, he has been credited with reactionary conservative, radical Marxist, or liberal humanist views. These wildly opposite interpretations, as well as the fact that the novelist frequently derided idealism in his narratives, support the conclusion that the Irish poet Derek Mahon had already reached at an early stage: Farrell is, in fact, a

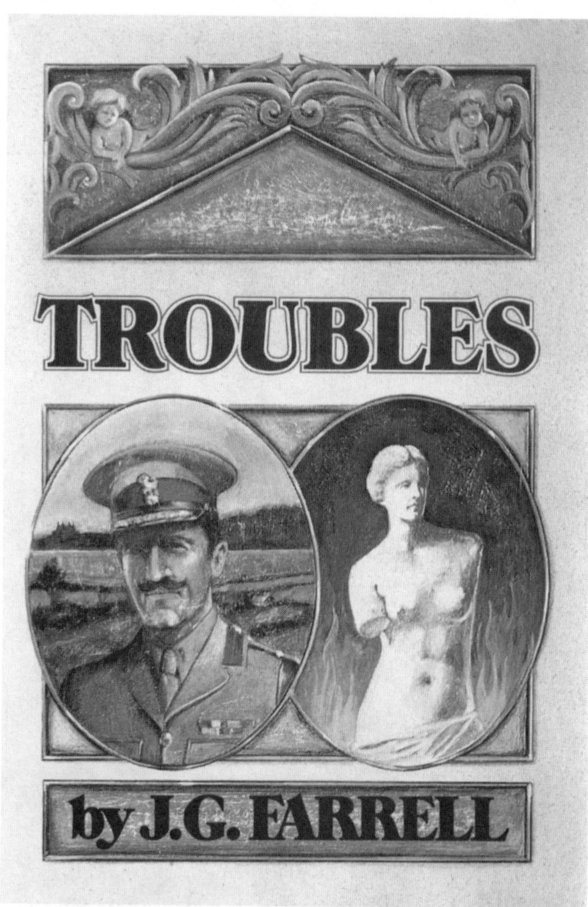

Dust jacket for the U.S. edition of Farrell's 1970 novel, in which a decayed Irish coastal hotel becomes a metaphorical setting for the Irish political "troubles" (Richland County Public Library)

philosophical writer, who is preoccupied with analyzing the human condition as such rather than with propagating a particular ideology. Recent criticism has, in the words of Peter Morey, agreed upon "an interpretation of the novels of J. G. Farrell and Paul Scott as examples of post-colonial fiction, since both partake of oppositional and interrogative narrative practices which recognize and work to dismantle the staple elements of imperial narrative."

Born to Anglo-Irish parents in Liverpool on 23 January 1935, James Gordon Farrell grew up as the second of three brothers in a family that, apart from the ties with Britain and Ireland, was also shaped by the colonial experience: William Farrell, the author's father, had worked as an accountant in Bengal for some time, where he had also married Prudence Josephine Russell, a former receptionist and secretary to a doctor, in 1929. The Farrells moved to Ireland after World War II, but Jim was sent to Rossall, a public school in Lancashire, England. This early experience of existing in two worlds–the Irish boy in a British boarding school and the British boy on holiday in Ireland–sharpened Farrell's vision and prepared the ground for his portraits of Britons who do not just feel, but actually are, completely out of place in the colonies. After leaving Rossall, Farrell taught in Dublin and spent some time working on the Distant Early Warning (DEW) in the Canadian Arctic. His studies at Oxford were interrupted when he contracted polio–an illness that left him partially crippled and had a profound influence on his fiction, in which disease is an ever-present threat and metaphor.

In 1960 Farrell left Oxford with a third class honours degree in French and Spanish and went to live in France, where he taught at a lycée and began to write fiction. After a false start–his first three novels combine contemporary settings with avant-garde writing, which the novelist later dismissed as "casting around"–Farrell, who wanted "to write universal as opposed to regional novels," realized, as he told George Brock in *The Observer Magazine* (24 September 1978), "that the really interesting thing that's happened during my lifetime has been the decline of the British Empire." In his Empire trilogy, which he began on a Harkness Fellowship in the United States and then largely composed in a tiny flat in Knightsbridge, London, the novelist proceeded to unmask the negative effects of British imperialism not only on the colonized but in particular on the colonizers themselves. This quality, combined with the ability to spin a good yarn, brought him to the attention of a large public and won him major literary prizes. Farrell was in the middle of writing a seventh novel when he drowned. His influence lingers: book reviews still cite him as an eminent model, and he even resurfaces in fiction; in Alison Lurie's novel *Foreign Affairs* (1984), the protagonist, Vinnie Miner, reads a Farrell novel on her flight from New York to London and, more significantly, the writer Stephen Cox in Margaret Drabble's *The Gates of Ivory* (1991) is clearly modeled on Farrell himself.

The first step in Farrell's writing career was an attempt to exorcize the nightmarish experience of contracting polio in an autobiographical novel, "Lung," which remains unpublished. His first book, *A Man from Elsewhere* (1963), was deliberately set apart from his personal past, set outside the British Isles and tightly controlled in structure, tone, and argument. The narrative relates how Sayer, a journalist for a communist paper, tries to uncover dark secrets in the life of Regan, a dying novelist who is about to be awarded an important Catholic literary prize. The plot is patently patterned on the famous quarrel between the two best-known representatives of French existentialism, Jean-Paul Sartre and Albert Camus. Sayer, representing Sartre, and Regan, representing Camus, argue about the same contentious existentialist issues: the position that murder can be vindicated as an expedient in overthrowing tyranny (Sartre) versus the stance that there are no ends that justify unjust means (Camus). Sayer's task is complicated by an affair he has with Regan's daughter, Gretchen, and his mission eventually turns out to be a complete failure. Reviewing the book for *The New Statesman* (20 September 1963), Bernard Bergonzi pounced on the weaknesses of the novel: "Many first novels are excessively autobiographical, but *A Man from Elsewhere* suffers from the opposite fault of being a cerebral construct, dreamed up out of literature and the contemporary French cinema." Simon Raven also criticized the structure of the narrative in *The Observer* (15 September 1963), but was, on the whole, more generous: "Mr. Farrell's style is spare, his plotting lucid and well timed; his expositions of moral or political problems are pungent if occasionally didactic."

Farrell's second publication, *The Lung* (1965), is closer to the author's autobiography because he describes in authentic detail the oppressiveness of being encased in an iron lung after an attack of polio. However, the novelist again chose to distance the narrative from his own experiences by resorting to comedy: the solitary hero, Martin Sands, is another existentialist loner and appears to be modeled on Malcolm Lowry's Consul in *Under the Volcano* (1947) rather than on Farrell himself. Characterized by an insatiable thirst for alcohol and sex, Sands is indifferent toward the world and even toward his illness. His stay in hospital is marked by a series of escapades, among them the seduction of his stepdaughter, Marigold, and eventually he is discharged by the doctors into an uncertain future. *The Lung* received favorable reviews: the anonymous critic in *The Observer* (31 October 1965) stated that "Mr. Farrell gives the pleasantly solid impression of really having something to write about," and on 11 November 1965 the reviewer of *The Times Literary Supplement* (*TLS*) added that "Mr. Farrell's is an effective, potent brew, compounded of desperation and a certain wild hilarity."

A Girl in the Head (1967), Farrell's third novel, was the result of a prolonged creative struggle, but the book was certainly the author's most ambitious effort so far. The protagonist, the impoverished Polish count Boris Slattery (an alias for the Irish impostor Mick Slattery), experiences disenchanting moments in the drab seaside resort of Maidenhair Bay. He lives in the constricting household of the Dongeon family–V. S. Naipaul's *A House for Mr. Biswas* (1961) may well have served as a model–and his marriage to Flower Dongeon is at a dead end. Boris enjoys the company of Dr. Cohen, a dying alcoholic, and he has sex with an underage teenager, June Furlough. His fantasies revolve around the

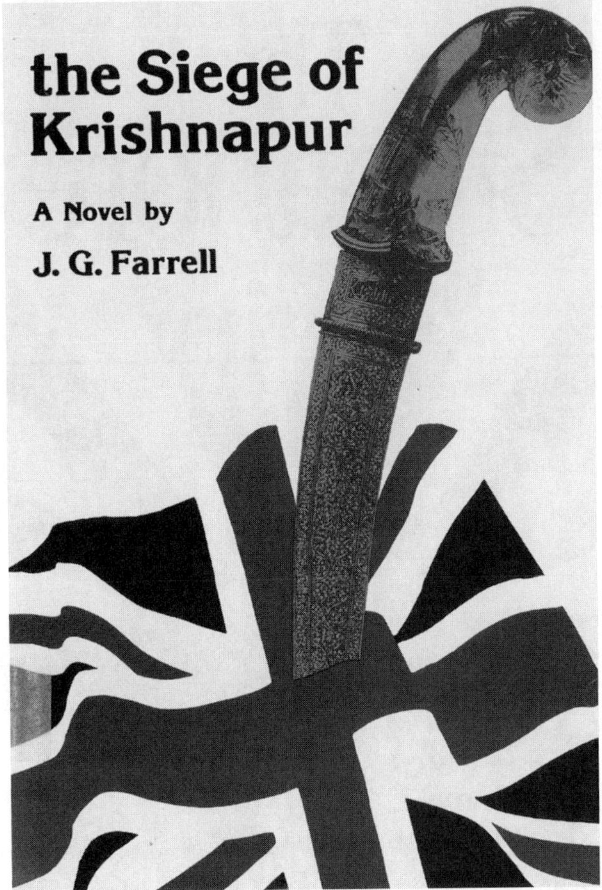

Dust jacket for the U.S. edition of Farrell's Booker Prize–winning 1973 novel, set during the 1857 Indian mutiny against British colonial rule (Richland County Public Library)

arrival of Ines, a Swedish summer guest and the "girl in the head" of the title. Like Sands in *The Lung,* Boris is modeled on Lowry's Consul; however, Boris also has obvious parallels with Humbert Humbert in Vladimir Nabokov's *Lolita* (1955). Ian Hamilton, writing for *The Listener* (13 July 1967), disliked the novel, suggesting that Farrell had at best achieved an "adroit pastiche" of Samuel Beckett's deadbeats. Martin Levin, by contrast, in *The New York Times Book Review* (23 March 1969) praised the author's "flair for giving the ridiculous an inspired originality," while the anonymous critic in *TLS* (20 July 1967) prophetically announced that the novel's "verbal assurance and resourcefulness show that Mr. Farrell is not content to coast along merely imitating his previous work. Such a deliberate extension of range is perhaps a hopeful sign for a talent which, after three novels, still has not found the mode in which to fulfil its attractive promise."

In his first three novels Farrell was concerned with the plight of individuals who have to face an apparently meaningless life. The novelist found a new

Dust jacket for the U.S. edition of Farrell's 1978 novel, which portrays the British economic exploitation of Singapore just prior to World War II (Richland County Public Library)

mode of expression when he realized that his message would gain in relevance if his fiction were set in the past. On Block Island, off the Rhode Island coast, Farrell discovered the remains of an old, burned-down hotel, which inspired him to create the Hotel Majestic, the setting of *Troubles* (1970). His family background was a further reason why he directed his attention toward the violent common history of Britain and Ireland. *Troubles* relates the story of the fierce struggle for Irish independence. Registering events through the uncomprehending eyes of Major Brendan Archer, the melancholy hero of the novel, the narrative exposes the hardened stances of Irish and British nationalists and highlights the vain pretensions of the British Empire. Archer, shell-shocked in the trenches of World War I, comes to stay in the Majestic, a decaying grand hotel on the Wexford coast, because he wants to clarify his position with regard to Angela, his mysterious fiancée, who soon fades away with leukemia. His inertia prevents Archer from leaving, and against his will he is drawn into the political hostilities but fails to understand either faction: neither his host, Edward Spencer, a bigot Protestant landowner, nor Sarah Devlin, an Irish Catholic girl he falls in love with, can provide him with convincing reasons for the destructive spiral of violence that besets the island. His belief that there is "no need to abandon one's reason simply because one is in Ireland" is quickly checked by Sarah, who informs him that "in Ireland you must choose your tribe. Reason has nothing to do with it."

Eventually, history catches up with the lodgers at the Majestic when the hotel burns down. The building is a powerful symbolic structure since the process of decaying alludes in multiple metaphors to what was going on in Ireland and the rest of the empire at the time. By making use of the crumbling Majestic, Farrell linked his book intertextually to the Irish tradition of the Big House novel, a fact that was noted by several critics. The novelist Elizabeth Bowen, author of the Big House novel *The Last September* (1929), praised *Troubles* in the journal *Europa* (1970) for generating excitement and for reflecting yesterday "in today's consciousness." After reading *Troubles,* Vivian Mercier labeled Farrell "a born story-teller" (*The Nation,* 8 November 1971), and the Irish novelist William Trevor, writing in *The Guardian* (8 October 1970), called the novel a "clever book" and "a *tour de force* of considerable quality." Farrell was awarded the Geoffrey Faber Memorial Prize for *Troubles,* and the prize money allowed him to travel to India to do research for his next novel.

The Siege of Krishnapur (1973) at last brought Farrell's work to the attention of a larger audience since it won the 1973 Booker Prize. Taking up material that had been used and abused in fiction frequently enough before–the Indian Mutiny of 1857–Farrell created a magnificent blend of adventure, Victorian ideas, and criticism of the empire. When Mr. Hopkins, a high-ranking civil servant in Krishnapur, notices signs of unrest among the native populace, he decides to have the residency fortified. The other Britons ignore his warnings, however, and are absorbed by picnics, balls, horse races, and pig-sticking–activities that they find infinitely more captivating than any concerns the Indians might have. Farrell highlights their irresponsible behavior by having one party play blindman's buff when the country is already seething. The decadence of the colonizers also shows in a scene in which a horse is given champagne, and servants are called demeaning nicknames such as "ant" or "monkey."

The outbreak of the mutiny duly surprises the British, and the shocked survivors withdraw to the residency, where they not only fight for their lives but also engage in violent quarrels about religion, the origins of cholera, and other issues of the Victorian age. Hopkins, a supporter of the Great Exhibition of 1851, has brought a collection of relics of this event to his residency: these include ingenious inventions and pieces of art that glorify progress. During the monsoon season the earthen walls are diminished by the downpours, and the desperate defenders throw these emblems of their civilization on top of the walls in order to keep the earth from being washed away. Farrell reduces these artifacts of the Victorian age from their representative status to mere means of defense and thus illuminates how British notions of superiority collapse in the course of the siege. Ultimately, the depleted garrison is rescued by a British relief force.

Hopkins's main opponent is Fleury, a would-be poet who renounces his ambitions and evolves into a robust Victorian adventurer. His metamorphosis helps him not only survive but also succeed in matters of the heart. Hopkins, by contrast, loses faith in civilization and comes to the conclusion that the "British could leave and half India wouldn't notice us leaving just as they didn't notice us arriving. All our reforms might be reforms on the moon for all it has to do with them."

Newsweek (21 October 1974) reviewer Walter Clemons recommended the novel enthusiastically as "a work of wit, lively historical reconstruction and imaginative intensity." John Spurling in *The New Statesman* (21 September 1973) called it "a masterpiece," and Julian Symons hailed Farrell in *The Sunday Times* (2 September 1973) as "one of the half-dozen British writers under forty whose work should be read by anybody inclined to think that no interesting novels are being written today."

Hopkins alludes to the main concern of Farrell's next novel, *The Singapore Grip* (1978), when he reflects toward the end of *The Siege of Krishnapur* "that a people, a nation does not create itself according to its own best ideas, but is shaped by other forces, of which it has little knowledge." In *The Singapore Grip* Farrell attempts to expose those other forces, laying the blame at the door of the capitalist economic system.

Despite the threat of a Japanese invasion, the members of high society in Singapore celebrate their economic prowess at garden parties while incompetent officers of the army, navy, and air force quarrel about preeminence. The shortsighted economic exploitation of the Far Eastern colonies, which lies at the root of the success of the colony, now renders any common line of defense against the Japanese impossible, as the various inhabitants of Singapore–Britons, Indians, Malayans, Chinese–have no common interest. Farrell analyzes the colonial economy in detail, using a fictitious company, Blackett and Webb, as his model: in compelling chapters he describes how Burmese rice-growing communities were destroyed solely because it proved profitable to Western entrepreneurs and how native producers of rubber were systematically swindled by the colonial authorities.

Dust jacket for Farrell's posthumously published 1981 novel, about a British doctor and his family in the Indian city of Simla during the 1870s (Richland County Public Library)

The huge amount of factual information is not included in the text in dull blocks but is cleverly woven into the narrative: among the unusual venues for conversations about these matters are a brothel, a Chinese dying house (where elderly people are sent to die), a tennis court, and various burning buildings. In the course of these discussions Farrell ridicules the notion that Britain's ruthless exploitation of her colonies can be balanced by the benefits of civilization such as schools, hospitals, and courts.

The most significant figure in the novel is the archcapitalist Walter Blackett, who has no scruples about trying to turn any situation to his advantage. The fact that Walter is shown to be all too human at the same time makes the character all the more credible. His antagonist, Matthew Webb, the idealistic heir to 50 percent of the company, finds it difficult to perceive events in a realistic fashion–a handicap that is symbolically stressed in his myopia and the constant trouble he has with his glasses. Farrell also offers short glimpses into the lives of the native population and even into the experiences of Japanese soldiers while they are fighting in the jungle or in the rubber plantations.

Farrell's assault on capitalist economy has often been interpreted as Marxist; this interpretation is questionable, however, since Farrell also exposes the delusions of political idealism with the figure of Webb. The novelist's political leanings remain open to debate, but, as his speech on receiving the Booker Prize demonstrates, he clearly saw himself taking the side of the weak and persecuted. While later critics have perceived Farrell's amalgamation of fact and fable as successful "deconstructing and rewriting" of history, as Michael C. Prusse wrote in *"Tomorrow Is Another Day": The Fictions of James Gordon Farrell* (1997), many contemporary reviewers felt that the novel suffered from an overload of factual information. Lucy Hughes-Hallet, writing in *Vogue* (1 September 1978), considered the narrative "weighted with indigestible chunks of information," while Isabel Quigly in *The Financial Times* (21 September 1978) felt that the protagonists have to squeeze through a too tightly wrought net of facts. On the other hand, some critics were delighted with *The Singapore Grip:* John Mellors in *The Listener* (28 September 1978) thought of it as "an exciting adventure story" that he found "utterly absorbing," and fellow novelist Timothy Mo wrote in *The New Statesman* (15 September 1978) that the book was "this brilliantly idiosyncratic and funny writer's most successful yet."

Two years after Farrell's death on 12 August 1979, John Spurling published his last manuscript under the title *The Hill Station* (1981). The fragment shows the writer attempting to extend his art; moving away from groups of besieged Britons, he focuses on a survivor from Krishnapur, Dr. McNab, who travels to the mountain resort of Simla in the company of his wife and her niece. Although the hero is a doctor, life in Farrell's Simla before Rudyard Kipling used it as the setting for some of his stories is fraught with dangers, because disease is as omnipresent as in all of Farrell's fiction. The plot involves religious controversy, an outbreak of rabies, and unrequited love and unrolls in a stable society that is not threatened by a menace as dramatically existential as a siege. The narrative tantalizingly creates another look at Britons outside their home ground but with a touch of Jane Austen, an author whom Farrell greatly admired. Most critics were pleased with the decision to publish Farrell's novel fragment. Penelope Lively, writing in *Encounter* (August 1981), thought "it was going to be a fine novel," and in *The Observer* (26 April 1981) Derek Mahon identified the debts that it owes to Thomas Mann's *Der Zauberberg* (1924; translated as *The Magic Mountain,* 1927). Paul Theroux, writing in *The Sunday Times* (26 April 1981), ascertained that "there is enough of it to cast a spell," while in the *British Medical Journal* (18 April 1981) David Simpson argued that *The Hill Station* was further proof of "Farrell's most distinctive talent–his reworking of history as fiction."

J. G. Farrell has become a seminal author in academic circles because he has been identified as a forerunner of postcolonial literature and thus as a relatively early British "rewriter" of the imperial past who is conscious of the fact that, as E. L. Doctorow said in his essay "False Documents" (1977), "there is no history except as it is composed." Farrell perceived his function as re-creating the past through the insignificant events that are left alone by historians, as he notes in "J. G. Farrell Comments" in James Vinson's *Contemporary Novelists* (1972): "catching colds, falling in love, or falling off bicycles. It is this real life which is the novelist's concern (though needless to say, realism is not the only way to represent it)." These individual experiences allowed Farrell to subvert the official version of history and to explain the present state of affairs to his readers because "about the past they are more susceptible to clarity of vision." It is difficult to say where his career would have led, but Mahon probably comes close to the truth when he sums up Farrell's ambitions: "He measured himself, I suspect, against the giants of modern literature; and given the time, he might have joined them."

Interviews:

Stephanie Nettell, "James Farrell," *Books & Bookmen* (October 1963): 27;

Malcolm Dean, "An Insight Job," *Guardian,* 1 September 1973, p. 11;

Derek Mahon, "Spotlight," *Vogue* (June 1974): 138;

Caroline Moorehead, "Writing in the Dark, and Not a Detail Missed," *Times* (London), 9 September 1978, p. 12;

Dean, "Grip of Empire," *Guardian,* 13 September 1978, p. 10;

George Brock, "Epitaph for the Empire," *Observer Magazine,* 24 September 1978, pp. 73–75.

Bibliographies:

Ralph J. Crane, "J. G. Farrell: An Annotated Bibliography," *Eire,* 28 (1993): 132–148;

Crane, "J. G. Farrell: A Bibliography of Primary and Secondary Sources," in *J. G. Farrell: The Critical*

Grip, edited by Crane (Dublin & Portland, Ore.: Four Courts Press, 1999), pp. 196–210.

Biography:

Lavinia Greacen, *J. G. Farrell: The Making of a Writer* (London: Bloomsbury, 1999).

References:

Bernard Bergonzi, "Fictions of History," in *The Contemporary English Novel,* edited by Malcolm Bradbury and David Palmer (London: Arnold, 1979), pp. 42–65;

Ronald Binns, *J. G. Farrell* (London & New York: Methuen, 1986);

Laurence Bristow-Smith, "Tomorrow Is Another Day," *Critical Quarterly,* 25 (Summer 1983): 42–52;

Ralph J. Crane and Jennifer Livett, *Troubled Pleasures: The Fiction of J. G. Farrell* (Dublin & Portland, Ore.: Four Courts Press, 1997);

Crane, ed., *J. G. Farrell: The Critical Grip* (Dublin & Portland, Ore.: Four Courts Press, 1999);

Margaret Drabble, "Things Fall Apart," in *The Hill Station: An Unfinished Novel; with Two Appreciations and a Personal Memoir, and an Indian Diary,* edited by John Spurling (London: Fontana, 1982), pp. 178–191;

David Farrar, *Brodie's Notes on J. G. Farrell's The Siege of Krishnapur* (London: Pan, 1981);

Chris Ferns, "'First as Tragedy, Then as Farce': J. G. Farrell's Retelling of History," *Dalhousie Review,* 67 (1987): 275–285;

Benny Green, "J. G. Farrell," *Spectator,* 25 August 1979, p. 20;

Lars Hartveit, "The 'Solitary Passage Over the Switched Points of History' and the Experience of Dislocation in J. G. Farrell's *The Singapore Grip,*" *English Studies,* 70 (1989): 566–580;

Fiona MacPhail, "Major and Majestic," in *The Big House in Ireland: Reality and Representation,* edited by Jacqueline Genet (Dingle, Ireland & Savage, Md.: Brandon, 1991), pp. 243–252;

Neil McEwan, "J. G. Farrell: Empire trilogy," in his *Perspective in British Historical Fiction Today* (London: Macmillan, 1987), pp. 124–158;

John McLeod, "Exhibiting Empire in J. G. Farrell's *The Siege of Krishnapur,*" *Journal of Commonwealth Literature,* 29 (1994): 117–132;

Peter Morey, "The Burden of Representation: Counter-Discourse through Cultural Texts in J. G. Farrell's *The Siege of Krishnapur,*" in his *Fictions of India: Narrative and Power* (Edinburgh: Edinburgh University Press, 2000), pp. 109–133;

Charles Palliser, "J. G. Farrell and the Wisdom of Comedy," *Literary Review,* 1 (15–18 October 1979): 14;

Michael C. Prusse, *"Tomorrow Is Another Day": The Fictions of James Gordon Farrell* (Tübingen & Basel: Francke, 1997);

John Riddy, *J. G. Farrell, The Siege of Krishnapur: Notes* (Harlow: Longman, 1985);

Margaret Scanlan, "Elizabeth Bowen's *The Last September* and J. G. Farrell's *Troubles,*" in her *Traces of Another Time: History and Politics in Postwar British Fiction* (Princeton, N.J.: Princeton University Press, 1990), pp. 40–62;

Frances B. Singh, "Progress and History in J. G. Farrell's *The Siege of Krishnapur,*" *Chandrabhaga,* 2 (1979): 23–39;

Michael Thorpe, "Making History: Fiction, History and the Indian 'Mutiny,'" *World Literature Written in English,* 26 (Spring 1986): 179–187.

Papers:

The *Papers of James Gordon Farrell (1935–1979): Manuscripts of his Novels, of Unfinished Novels, Plays etc., with some Notebooks and Presscuttings* are held under this title at the Manuscript Library of Trinity College, Dublin, under the reference number TCD MSS 9128–60.

Eva Figes

(15 April 1932 -   )

Juliette Wells
Yale University

See also the Figes entry in *DLB 14: British Novelists Since 1960.*

BOOKS: *Equinox* (London: Secker & Warburg, 1966);

Winter Journey (London: Faber & Faber, 1967; New York: Hill & Wang, 1968);

The Musicians of Bremen, retold by Figes, illustrated by Horst Lemke (London: Blackie, 1967);

The Banger, illustrated by Joanna Stubbs (London: Deutsch, 1968; New York: Lion Press, 1968);

Konek Landing (London: Faber & Faber, 1969);

Patriarchal Attitudes: Women in Society (London: Faber & Faber, 1970; New York: Stein & Day, 1970; republished, with a new introduction by Figes, Basingstoke: Macmillan, 1986; New York: Persea, 1987);

Scribble Sam, illustrated by Stubbs (London: Deutsch, 1971; New York: McKay, 1971);

B (London: Faber & Faber, 1972);

Days (London: Faber & Faber, 1974);

Tragedy and Social Evolution (London: Calder, 1976; New York: Persea, 1990);

Nelly's Version (London: Secker & Warburg, 1977; New York: Pantheon, 1988);

Little Eden: A Child at War (London: Faber & Faber, 1978; New York: Persea, 1987);

Waking (London: Hamilton, 1981; New York: Pantheon, 1981);

Sex and Subterfuge: Women Novelists to 1850 (London: Macmillan, 1982); republished as *Sex and Subterfuge: Women Writers to 1850* (New York: Persea, 1988; London: Pandora, 1990);

Light (London: Hamilton, 1983; New York: Pantheon, 1983);

The Seven Ages (London: Hamilton, 1986; New York: Pantheon, 1986);

Ghosts (London: Hamilton, 1988; New York: Pantheon, 1988);

The Tree of Knowledge (London: Sinclair-Stevenson, 1990; New York: Pantheon, 1990);

The Tenancy (London: Sinclair-Stevenson, 1993);

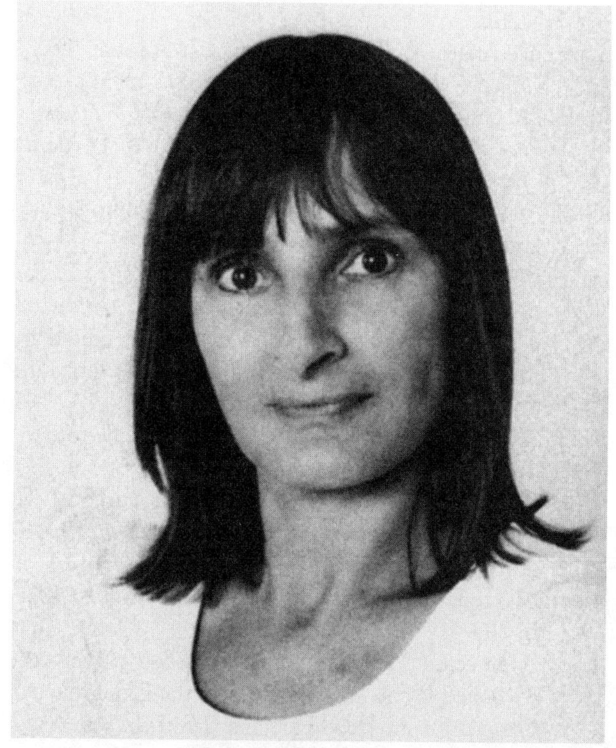

Eva Figes (photograph by Jerry Bauer; from the dust jacket for the U.S. edition of The Tree of Knowledge, *1990)*

The Knot (London: Sinclair-Stevenson, 1996).

Edition and Collection: *Nelly's Version; Light; Waking* (New York: Quality Paperback Book Club, 1994);

Nelly's Version, introduction by Susan Faludi (Chicago: Dalkey Archive Press, 2002).

PRODUCED SCRIPTS: *Time Regained,* radio, BBC Radio 4, 22 May 1980;

Days, radio, BBC Radio 2, 27 February 1981;

Dialogue Between Friends, radio, BBC Radio 3, 30 July 1981;

Punch-Flame and Pigeon-Breast, radio, BBC Radio 3, 25 July 1983;

The True Tale of Margery Kempe, radio, BBC Radio 3, 5 April 1985.

OTHER: *Classic Choice,* edited by Figes (London & Glasgow: Blackie, 1965);

Modern Choice, edited by Figes, 2 volumes (London: Blackie, 1965, 1966);

"The White Road to Blackmail," in *Woman on Woman,* edited by Margaret Laing (London: Sidgwick & Jackson, 1971), pp. 113–130;

"Bedsitter" and "Obbligato," in *Signature Anthology* (London: Calder & Boyars, 1975), pp. 33–47;

"On Stage," in *Beyond the Words: Eleven Writers in Search of a New Fiction,* edited by Giles Gordon (London: Hutchinson, 1975), pp. 113–128;

Women Their World, edited by Figes, Abigail Mozley, and Dinah Livingstone (Gisburn: Platform Poets, 1980);

"On the Edge," in *London Tales,* edited by Julian Evans (London: Hamilton, 1983), pp. 51–59;

Maria Edgeworth, *Belinda,* introduction by Figes (London & Boston: Pandora, 1986);

Edgeworth, *Patronage,* introduction by Figes (London & New York: Pandora, 1986);

Women's Letters in Wartime: 1450–1945, edited, with an introduction, by Figes (London: Pandora, 1993; London & San Francisco: Pandora, 1994).

TRANSLATIONS: Martin Walser, *The Gadarene Club* (London: Longmans, 1960); republished as *Marriage in Philippsburg,* adapted by James Laughlin (Norfolk, Conn.: New Directions, 1961);

Elisabeth Borchers, *The Old Car,* illustrated by Werner Maurer (London: Blackie, 1967; Indianapolis: Bobbs-Merrill, 1971);

Bernhard Grzimek, *He and I and the Elephants* (London: Deutsch/Thames & Hudson, 1967; New York: Hill & Wang, 1967);

George Sand, *Little Fadette* (London & Glasgow: Blackie, 1967);

Renate Rasp, *A Family Failure: A Novel* (London: Calder & Boyars, 1970; New York: Orion, 1970);

Manfred von Conta, *The Deathbringer: A Novel* (London: Calder & Boyars, 1971).

SELECTED PERIODICAL PUBLICATIONS–UNCOLLECTED:

"The State of Fiction: A Symposium," *New Review,* 5 (Summer 1978): 14–15;

"The Long Passage to Little England," *Observer* (London), 11 June 1978, p. 29;

"About Men About Women," *Observer* (London), 13 February 1994, p. 25;

"Confronting the Ghosts of Berlin's Past," *Times* (London), 5 June 1997, p. 21.

Best known in England for her germinal feminist study *Patriarchal Attitudes: Women in Society* (1970), Eva Figes is the author of several novels that explore new methods of representing human experience. Although she considers herself a European rather than an English writer, her concern with reshaping the form and content of the conventional realist novel aligns her with the generation of British experimental novelists of the 1960s and 1970s. Figes's personal history as a child refugee from the Holocaust informs her recurrent interest both in the meaning of language and in figures who are haunted, marginalized, and unsure of their identities. She places particular emphasis on the quotidian experience and inner life of women, both contemporary and historical, and frequently plays with the boundaries between fact and fiction, poetry and prose.

Eva Unger was born in Berlin on 15 April 1932, the elder child and only daughter of Emil Eduard Unger, a textile-industry representative, and Irma Cohen Unger, both of whom were well-off and thoroughly assimilated German Jews. Her early childhood was sheltered and indulgent, with parents and servants cooperating to protect her and her younger brother from the realities of Adolf Hitler's rise to power. She experienced her father's internment in the Dachau concentration camp, which began with an arrest on *Kristallnacht* (Crystal Night)–as the November 1938 pogroms were ironically called–as merely an unexplained absence. In a 1978 essay in *The Observer* (London), Figes writes that her father "would probably not have come out of Dachau if the Gestapo had not been corrupt as well as brutal"; however, he was released only after he had contracted scarlet fever in the prison camp. His illness prevented the family from fleeing to Bangkok as they had planned, but he eventually secured an English visa for the family through his professional connections as a representative for British textile firms. The four Ungers departed for England in 1939, shortly before Eva's seventh birthday.

Figes's 1978 memoir, *Little Eden: A Child at War,* depicts her difficult adjustment to English life, concentrating on the year 1941, when, as a nine-year-old, she was evacuated from London to Cirencester. Her father served in the British army in a special unit for foreign refugees, while her mother worked as a seamstress to support the family. Her family's sudden loss of wealth resulted in a profound lifestyle change and descent in class, while her physical differences from her English schoolmates exacerbated the barriers of language and nationality. Unger, who already knew how to write German script, was especially pained by having to abandon the German language and to relearn how to read and write. Unger maintained contact with her first language by studying it in school and reading books on her family's shelves, although her parents forbade her to speak German, especially in public. As she recalls in *Little Eden,* "one must never be heard speaking one's own language, which had become that of the enemy. It was all right to outdo the other children on the playground by yelling *Donner und Blitzen, Achtung* or *Heil Hitler,* the odd phrases picked up from the radio and particularly, since the war, radio comedians, but no more. The language of childhood had become the tongue of lunatics and maniacs, and a sort of mental curtain came down, dividing this from intimate exchange, lyric and song, which had to stay secret and hidden."

If asked, Unger's parents gave their nationality during the war years as "stateless." Unger became aware of her identity as a Jew when one of her patriotic schoolmates, who commonly taunted her for being German, called her in addition by that name. Her parents' efforts to protect her had worked all too well: she had never heard the word before and did not know what it meant. Her mother enlightened her by sending her to the local cinema to watch the newsreels of atrocities at Bergen-Belsen. "At last," states Figes in *Little Eden,* "I knew what it meant to be a Jew, that shameful secret which had been hinted at but kept from me for so many years." Unger also gradually became aware of her mother's anguish at not knowing for certain the fate of her own parents, who had been left behind in Berlin. Figes notes in a 1994 essay in *The Observer* (London) that Irma's distress affected her as well: "my mother took out her suffering on me, the nearest available object." Figes herself experienced nightmares well into adulthood that she ascribes to survivor's guilt. As she explains in her 1978 essay in *The Observer* (London), "All Jewish survivors of the holocaust have to cope with a sense of guilt, however irrational that sounds. It was clearly absurd for me, at six, to feel guilty about having left relatives behind, so my rational mind dismissed the idea and my guilt found expression in my dreams."

A bright spot in Unger's childhood and young adulthood was her love of reading and creative writing. One year during the war, she asked for a pocket torch (flashlight) for Christmas, not for walking in the blackout (as her mother imagined) but so that she could read secretly under the bedclothes. A red-covered copy of William Shakespeare's play *As You Like It* (1599–1600), which Unger obtained and devoured while at Cirencester, had a particularly powerful effect: as she recalls in *Little Eden,* "I was fascinated by words half understood but pregnant with more meaning than anything I had read before." As a young adult, she read her way through the public library, preferring the works of Charles Dickens above all others. At the same time, she wrote essays for class that her teachers admired as well as stories and poems in her private notebooks, dreaming of growing up to be a writer. In an essay included in the 1971 anthology *Woman on Woman,* Figes draws an explicit connection between the development of these interests and her growing sense of herself as an outsider in English culture: "I became aware of myself, and my isolation, at the same time as I became aware of reading and books and my wish to write."

While Unger attended a coeducational state school, Kingsbury Grammar, her parents sent her brother, who was less academically inclined than she, to a public school (in Britain, a school independent of the state educational system, traditionally preparing students for admission to a university). The distinction irked her, especially as she began to consider college. Her parents hinted that she should find a job or get married. She persuaded them by winning the only state scholarship from her school to Queen Mary College of the University of London, where she studied English literature, receiving a B.A. with honors in 1953.

The following year she married John George Figes (pronounced Fie-jess), a personnel manager who held a degree in history. She was motivated in part by a strong desire to leave home, as she recalled in a 1993 interview with Jan Moir for *The Guardian* (London): "I had a row with my parents and met my husband the next day." They had two children, a boy (Orlando Guy) and a girl (Catherine Jane), before divorcing in 1963. In her *Woman on Woman* essay Figes discusses her divorce in practical and legal terms, as a case study of the challenges women face in collecting support payments. She also remarks in retrospect that she was hesitant about combining writing with marriage, judging that "the demands of such a relationship would inevitably conflict with the inner demands of the creative process." During her children's early years Figes worked as an editor for a variety of publishing houses, first freelance and then full-time after the divorce. She was with Longmans, Green and Company from 1955 to 1957, Weidenfeld and Nicolson, Ltd. from 1962 to 1963, and Blackie and Son, Ltd., from 1964 to 1967. She particularly enjoyed editing children's books at Blackie and Son, Ltd., a job that, as she told Michele Field in 1987, was "cosy and undemanding–and it gave me time to write." Between 1960 and 1971 she also wrote three children's books, edited two literary anthologies, and completed several translations, mostly of contemporary German literature.

Except for brief periods of working as a writer-in-residence at universities and traveling to literary events, Figes has continued to reside in London. A disciplined writer, she sets herself the daily task of writing at least eight hundred words. She told Michelene Wandor in 1983 that her ideas for novels choose her rather than the other way around, with an image, incident, or anecdote often serving as a starting point.

Figes's first novel, *Equinox,* is one of her most autobiographical: published in 1966, it explores issues familiar to her from her then-recent divorce. In the course of a year, a woman named Liz, who is turning thirty, confronts increasingly debilitating feelings of despair, which both contribute to and result from her disintegrating marriage. Capturing both Liz's troubling thoughts and the aridity of her external life, Figes alternates between third-person narration and interior monologues that are reminiscent of the work of such modernist writers as Virginia Woolf. Figes's eye for minute but telling details, which is one of the hallmarks of her fiction, is already evident in *Equinox,* as is her ability to confront and convey characters' bleak emotional states. As is true with many of Figes's works, critics' responses divided between appreciation of these qualities and irritation at her lack of linear storytelling and traditional character development: Kenneth Allsop praised the novel in a 28 January 1966 review for *The Spectator* (London) for the "unblinking accuracy" of Figes's portrait of Liz, while B. A. Young, in *Punch* (23 February 1966), faulted Figes for writing "so affectedly it's hard to follow the story."

Winter Journey (1967), which received the *Guardian* Fiction Award for that year, reached a wider audience and received greater critical acclaim than *Equinox.* Like the earlier novel, *Winter Journey* is spare in both size and tone. Structured around a single day, it follows the mundane activities of an elderly man, Janus, who is close to death. Making efforts to "keep moving" in spite of physical pain, he tends to drift into impressionistic, wide-ranging memories of earlier episodes in his life. Critics praised in particular Figes's effective conveyance of Janus's moment-to-moment sensations and thoughts: Robert Nye, in *The Guardian Weekly* (13 April 1967), commended her ability to go "beyond gesture to fix the most fugitive moments of existence in a pattern true to themselves." Others, however, continued to object to Figes's unconventional narrative techniques; for example, writing in *Library Journal* (1 March 1968), Charles D. Pipes characterized the reader of *Winter Journey* as "stumbling over the pebbles of poetic prose scattered along a somewhat arid plot."

With the success of *Winter Journey,* Figes left her work in publishing to write full-time. She began *Konek Landing* (1969) after her first trip back to Germany as an adult. Dedicated to Figes's maternal grandparents, the novel takes as its theme the survivor's guilt that had long dogged her personally. In her 1978 *Observer* (London) article Figes calls *Konek Landing* "an epic story of a survivor of the holocaust who cannot come to terms with the present or resolve the problem of killer and victim." In an essay in the *New Review* (Summer 1978) Figes claims Franz Kafka as a significant influence on her work, and his effect is particularly visible in the setting of this novel, a nameless and oppressive central European country, as well as in the nightmarish experiences of its protagonist, the orphaned Jew Stephan Konek. Although Figes considers *Konek Landing* to be one of her most important novels, her narrative experimentalism, which is more extreme in this work than in *Equinox* or *Winter Journey,* alienated many of her critics such as Jonathan Raban, who judged the novel, in the *New Statesman* (5 September 1969), to be "monotonous and often incomprehensible."

The 1970 publication of *Patriarchal Attitudes,* Figes's next book and her first work of nonfiction, was a sensation in England, inundating her with mail and requests for public appearances. A polemic, the work concerns the oppression of women, as understood in both historical and ideological terms. Praised for its coolly reasoned arguments, persuasive use of evidence, and trenchant analysis, *Patriarchal Attitudes* was, as Figes states in her introduction to the 1986 edition, "the right book at the right moment," coming just before Germaine Greer's *The Female Eunuch* and Kate Millett's *Sexual Politics,* both published that same year. Although Figes long resisted being labeled as a feminist, a category she found restrictive, *Patriarchal Attitudes* established her as one in the British public mind. In the 1990s a plethora of journalists sought her views on feminism then and now, as well as on the enduring popularity of *Patriarchal Attitudes,* which has frequently been reprinted. With typical acerbity, Figes told Moir that the book "stands the test of time well. . . . In fact, I think it stands up better than the rest. All the other authors have recanted in one way or another."

Figes's next novel, *B* (1972), addresses the sources of creativity and the relation between reality and fiction through a complicated, self-reflexive story. A novelist named Paul Beard writes about a novelist named B., whose life appears to be distinct from Beard's own but who turns out to resemble Beard quite closely. In *B,* Figes creates the effect of metafictionality by deploying narrative tricks and cultivating riddles and uncertainty; on the whole, critics judged these efforts to be overly ambitious and ineffective.

Following her reception of a C. Day Lewis Fellowship in 1973, Figes published *Days* (1974), in which she tracks the thoughts and observations of a single charac-

Paperback cover of the 1988 U.S. edition of Figes's 1977 novel, about an amnesiac who seeks clues to her identity (Richland County Public Library)

ter, a nameless female hospital patient. From her bed, the woman reflects on her surroundings and reminisces about her previous life. Reviewers criticized Figes's decision to reproduce rather than reenvision the deadening experience of hospital routine: writing in the *New Statesman* (18 January 1974), Timothy Mo declared that if "Figes wished to convey the texture of hospital monotony as rebarbatively as possible she has succeeded, but surely the point is to transform the experience imaginatively." Figes's attempts to allegorize her narrator's situation as emblematic of women's lives in general also drew criticism, as from Valentine Cunningham, who asserted in *The Listener* (24 January 1974) that "*Days* bids over-ambitiously to embrace the plight of all women, and its sympathies become rapidly too diffuse." Figes later adapted *Days* into a radio play, a genre in which she produced several other works, all in the early 1980s.

In an essay published in *Beyond the Words: Eleven Writers in Search of a New Fiction* (1975) Figes comments on the development of her art through her first five novels, explains her motivation for recasting the traditional novel, and presents her view of the function of fiction writers. Having once aimed "to create a kind of poetry in novel form," she now considers herself principally concerned with "finding some way of expressing the peculiarities, awfulness and seemingly ungraspable qualities of life itself." This effort, she explains, requires "constant literary innovation since familiar fictional modes deal with aspects of living that have long been grasped and have nothing unfamiliar or unexpressed about them." She emphasizes that the "new connections" and "new networks" she creates in her novels, while distinct from the conventional form of a nineteenth-century novel, "nevertheless do create a narrative of a kind and do impose a sort of order on chaos. I am using a different grid, which I first have to construct by a painful process of trial and error." To her, the duty of the novelist is not to entertain or reassure but to "shock into awareness, startle, engage the attention."

Ambiguity, which interests Figes in various ways throughout her work, is at the heart of *Nelly's Version* (1977), whose main character has no memory of her past. The woman, who signs herself into a hotel as Nelly Dean–the name of the housekeeper in Emily Brontë's *Wuthering Heights* (1847)–records her impressions of the places that she visits and the people whom she meets, some of whom claim to know her. An unresolved thriller of undiscoverable identity, the novel raises questions about the reliability of perception. British reviewers were divided. Some appreciated the complicated effects Figes achieves through her character's disorientation: Peter Lewis, in *Stand* (1977–1978), compared the novel to the plays of Harold Pinter, noting that "harmless conversational remarks suddenly take on a sinister implication, and Eva Figes obtains some Pinterish comedy out of verbal ambiguity." Others, however, objected to what they saw as Figes's excessive emphasis on the constraints of women's lives and conventional identities: in a 30 July 1977 review in *The Spectator* (London) Peter Ackroyd contended that Figes had harnessed "'modern' literature in order to make a limited and political point." American reviewers, who read *Nelly's Version* over a decade later, generally appreciated the enigmatic quality of the novel, praising Figes's ability to imbue ordinary encounters and conversations with uncertainty and unusual significance; for example, Alida Becker wrote in the *St. Petersburg Times* (30 October 1988) that "it is in the apparently pedestrian details that the terrors, inequities and sometimes the triumphs of life reveal themselves most eloquently," and she described the novel as "a puzzle of astounding and perhaps insoluble intricacy."

Figes's work was partially supported in the years from 1977 to 1979 by a fellowship from the Arts Council of England. In the middle of this period she published two essays that put forth a stronger and more political version of her artistic credo than does her 1975 *Beyond the Words* piece, the first a contribution to a forum in *The New Review* (Summer 1978) about the state of English fiction, and the second an 11 June 1978 piece in *The Observer* (London) to mark the publication of her wartime memoir, *Little Eden*. In both, Figes emphasizes her identity as a European writer and her conviction that contemporary fiction must reinvent itself in order to address the realities of the twentieth century. Responding to British critics' lack of sympathy for experimental novels in general and hers in particular, she theorizes in the *Observer* essay that English readers are satisfied with–and, indeed, prefer–the comforts of conventional storytelling because their world was left largely untouched by such horrors as the Holocaust: "The English still write in the style of Arnold Bennett because they still inhabit his world. England was never invaded, never touched by cataclysm." In the *New Review* piece, she likens her motivation for artistic creation to the painful movement of a piece of shrapnel lodged in a war veteran's flesh: "I am European by birth, even though I write in English. My starting-point is inevitably Kafka. The English social realist tradition cannot contain the realities of my own lifetime, horrors which one might have called surreal if they had not actually happened. For me the old forms are hopelessly inadequate, and can only say things that are no longer worth saying." Of critics' mixed assessment of her own work, she states in the same essay that she no longer expects "to be regarded as anything more than an oddity, out on a limb." She is particularly contemptuous of the American literary market, asserting that "America provides rich commercial pickings, and everyone knows that Americans like bad books." Figes could not know, of course, that in the next decade her works would achieve considerable popularity among American readers, especially women.

In *Waking* (1981) Figes chooses a particularly constrained "grid" through which to convey the experience of her unnamed narrator or narrators: seven episodes of wakefulness at different stages of life. In each brief chapter a woman reflects on her body and its changes, her often unsatisfying relationships, and her desires. As with *Days* and *Nelly's Version,* Figes's decision not to name her characters invites them to be considered not only as individuals but also as archetypes. Although reviewers praised *Waking* for its wealth of detail and lyricism, in which it resembles Figes's earliest novels, many critics objected to the pervasive solipsism resulting from Figes's tight focus on the thoughts of each sleepless narrator. A. Alvarez, for instance, characterized the novel in *The New York Review of Books* (13 May 1982) as "written in poetic prose: no plot to speak of, all mood and sensibility" and criticized the monologues as being limited to "a kind of rhapsody of the self."

In the nine years between *Days* and *Light* (1983), Figes published two books of literary criticism, the well-regarded *Tragedy and Social Evolution* (1976) and *Sex and Subterfuge: Women Novelists to 1850* (1982). The first discusses tragic drama in the context of specific historical and social conditions, while the second addresses women writers' contribution to the development of the English novel. Figes enjoyed alternating between works of fiction and nonfiction, as she told Wandor in 1983: "I find that non-fiction writing is a great release because it's so easy for me; once you've done your homework and got your facts right, it's like putting a knife through butter." She declared that she views her past roles as novelist and critic as being distinctly separate, indicating too that she plans to reserve her future energy for fiction alone: "I think that in the non-fiction I was fulfilling a role more as a citizen, and in the novels as an artist. I now feel that I want to function as an artist, and it's time for other people to change the world if they're ever going to." Asked what influence her nonfiction works have had on her novel writing, Figes stated that they have affected the way she writes about women, with *Patriarchal Attitudes* in particular causing her to turn her attention from male characters to female ones. Figes's attention in *Sex and Subterfuge* to the kinds of novels women have historically chosen to write can also be viewed in relation to her own approach to the form: in her introduction to the book, for instance, she builds on a statement of Woolf's, asserting that "the best of women's fiction tends to be short and compressed."

With *Light,* Figes applies her lyrical prose to an historical figure for the first time, depicting a single day in the life of the painter Claude Monet and his household at Giverny in the summer of 1900. From before dawn to night, Figes attends to the nuances and variations of light, which preoccupy Monet, as well as to the perceptions and emotional states of the family members, servants, and guests whose lives intersect with his. Critics on both sides of the Atlantic hailed the novel as Figes's best yet, singling out for praise her rendering of Monet's artistic vision and process of creation. Writing in *The New York Times Book Review* (16 October 1983), Joyce Carol Oates commended Figes's rendering of "Impressionism in words," calling the novel a "prose poem" that demonstrates the still-vital possibilities of experimental fiction. Figes's novels have often been likened to those of Woolf, owing to the two authors' common use of the stream-of-consciousness technique and attention to women's quotidian experience, and the comparison has not usually been favorable to Figes. Oates, however, judged *Light* to be a worthy descendant of Woolf's great modernist novels: "The parallel with *To the Lighthouse* [1927] and *The Waves* [1931] is instructive rather than distracting, for Miss Figes has applied Woolf's idiosyncratic vision to a subject as ambitious as Woolf's; that *Light* is self-consciously derivative in technique does not detract from the beauty of its images and prose." The third of Figes's novels to be published in the United States, *Light* brought Figes to the attention of American readers, who enthusiastically received her as a "new" author.

Several reviewers of *Waking*–such as Carol Rumens in *TLS: The Times Literary Supplement* (23 January 1981)–concluded from its seven-part structure that Figes had produced a woman's version of Shakespeare's seven ages of man in *As You Like It*. *The Seven Ages* (1986) takes a different approach, depicting stages in women's history through the voices of seven generations of women, all of whom are related to the central character of the novel, a retired midwife living in contemporary England. Influenced by Günter Grass's novel *Der Butt* (1977; translated as *The Flounder,* 1978), which treats cooking throughout human history, Figes focuses on women's experiences of medicine and woman healers through the ages. The ambitious two-thousand-year sweep of the novel is anchored by Figes's trademark eye for detail as well as by an uncharacteristic use of the conventional tools of the novelist: speaking to Caroline Rand Herron in 1987, Figes herself called the book "a novel in every sense, because it has loads of narrative and character." While critics praised Figes's weaving of vivid historical fact into the novel, they viewed her effort to convey a feminist message as less successful. Angeline Goreau's review in *The New York Times Book Review* (22 February 1987) was typical: "In deliberately turning her attention from the history of 'events' and kingdoms to the history of ordinary lives, Ms. Figes has appropriated for fiction the trend that has informed the best historical writing in the last two decades. The marriage is largely successful, but her enthusiasm may have carried her too far. She sometimes writes as though the events of history were no more than an elaborate fiction created by the powers-that-be (men) for their own invidious purposes."

In her 1987 interview with Field, Figes reflected anew, and less combatively, on the shape of her literary career and her philosophy of writing: "I certainly felt when I was beginning, in the 1960s, that I was in some sort of vanguard, but . . . one gets more conventional the more one writes. When one starts, one starts with *precepts*–and then gradually adapts them to what one really wants to do. I no longer think there are any hard and fast rules, except that you must do something different each time and it's got to be exciting. And the first person you've got to excite is yourself–or you wouldn't do it." She also stated that she feels less isolated among English novelists than she did in her early days: "on the whole there are now a lot of English writers who are doing interesting things."

Figes's next novel, *Ghosts* (1988), was published in the same year that she received a Society of Authors traveling fellowship. Like *Days* and *Waking, Ghosts* focuses entirely on the perceptions and memories of an unnamed female narrator. Figes crafts her prose into short bursts, ranging in length from a single sentence to a brief paragraph, that create the effect of poetic stanzas. The narrator meditates on change and loss, both personal and external; she attends to the minute signs of the succeeding seasons even as she reflects on day-to-day encounters and recollections. Reviewers praised the novel for its vividness and particularity, which achieve more than mere verisimilitude: in the *Los Angeles Times Book Review* (22 January 1989) Kirsten Grimstad observed that "the only force opposing the suction of time and change seems to reside in the created work itself, in the carefully measured prose and in poetic images that capture and evoke the passing moment, the individual, the feeling."

Figes returned to the historical novel form in *The Tree of Knowledge,* published in 1990, the same year in which she was elected a fellow of Queen Mary College, her alma mater. The novel is a dramatic monologue in the voice of the aged, impoverished Deborah Milton Clarke, a daughter of the famous seventeenth-century English poet John Milton. Prompted by curious visitors to recall her childhood and her relationship with her father, Deborah unfurls a bitter tale of oppression and woe, in which she blames societal mores in general and her father in particular for her lack of opportunities. As in *The Seven Ages,* Figes draws on historical sources–here, Milton's biography and writings–in order to enrich and ground her fictional narrative, which encompasses several generations of the Milton family. Critics of *The Tree of Knowledge* were, characteristically, divided: Andrew Sinclair, writing in the 20 September 1990 issue of *The Times* (London), found Deborah's monologue to be persuasive and powerful, a "tour de langue" (feat of language), while others, such as Sybil Steinberg in *Publishers Weekly* (22 February 1991), judged it monotonous or ideologically heavy-handed. *The Tree of Knowledge,* as were *Light* and *The Seven Ages,* was published in the United States as a mass-market paperback and reached a relatively wide, appreciative readership.

The Tenancy (1993) represents a departure for Figes: a straightforward third-person narrative full of named characters and obviously portentous events, it is not overtly experimental either in content or form. Edith, its protagonist, settles her mother in a nursing home and moves into a rented city flat, anticipating the freedom of living alone. Her indulgence of herself and her complicated memories is interrupted, however, by an escalating series of disturbing occurrences in the building, which authorities do nothing to stop. As in *Nelly's Version,* Figes relies on subdued prose to set a sinister, suspenseful tone, a tactic that many reviewers judged unsuccessful. An unattributed review in the 14 May 1994 issue of *The Times* (London) characterized the book as "a short and succinct urban nightmare," while in the 22 May 1994 issue of that same newspaper, Pam Barrett judged that "even the plethora of unpleasant incidents fails to convey the necessary atmosphere of menace." *The Tenancy* was Figes's first novel in more than a decade not to be published in the United States.

Figes's novel *The Knot* (1996) treats five stages in the life of protagonist Anna Hart, from infancy to motherhood, with particular focus on her developing use of language and her conception of the power of words. As a child, Anna chats to herself and puzzles over the relationship between words and things; as a teenager, she experiments with her identity by changing the way she describes herself and notices the discrepancy between what adults say and how they act; as an articulate young woman, she confronts the difficulty of making herself understood; with her own baby, she revisits the nonsense words and questions familiar to her from her own childhood. Critics generally acclaimed Figes's representations of Anna's experience of language as compelling and universal: "the author repeatedly takes your breath away by the accuracy with which she reminds you of a childhood or adolescent sensation you had forgotten," wrote John Berger in the 17 March 1996 issue of *The Observer* (London). Some reviewers, however, faulted the novel for failing sufficiently to transform the commonplace: Figes's mimicry, asserted D. J. Taylor in *The Guardian* (15 March 1996), lacks "the degree of stylisation, the sense of experience given a defining extra twist, necessary to make it interesting."

In the 1990s Figes's opinions were frequently sought by the British press regarding both the progress of feminism and also the writings of her daughter, Kate, who has published nonfiction works on women's contemporary social status and the experience of motherhood. (Figes's son, Orlando, is an award-winning author of volumes of Russian history.) Because of her associations with Holocaust survivors and Holocaust literature, Figes served as a judge for the 1997 Jewish

Dust jacket for the U.S. edition of Figes's 1990 historical novel, in which the protagonist is the daughter of the seventeenth-century poet John Milton (Richland County Public Library)

Quarterly–Wingate Literary Prizes. The panel of judges conferred the nonfiction prize on *Fragments: Memories of a Wartime Childhood* (1996), Carol Brown Janeway's translation of Binjamin Wilkomirski's *Bruchstücke: aus einer Kindheit 1939–1948* (1995), but the award was subsequently withdrawn when, as was widely reported, Wilkomirski's highly praised memoir was discovered to be a work of fiction. Figes also contributed two personal essays to London newspapers on the subject of her maternal grandparents' fate in the Holocaust. In the first piece, published in the 13 February 1994 issue of *The Observer* (London), she discusses her terrifying sense of obligation, which increased after her own parents' deaths, to discover the exact date and place of their demise. The second article, published in the 5 June 1997 issue of *The Times* (London), concerns a recent journey back to Berlin, where she located her grandparents' names in the memorial book for Berlin deportees: "And there it was in black and white: Emil Cohen, likewise Ella Cohen, deported on April 2, 1942, to Trawniki. Place of death, Trawniki. Verschollen. Missing, lost." Both the sight of the entry and the trip itself, which included visits to landmarks familiar from her childhood, brought Figes a measure of peace.

In one sense, the guiding principle of Eva Figes's career as a novelist has been variety. Several of her novels span lifetimes or even millennia, while others focus tightly on a single day (*Winter Journey, Light*) or year (*Equinox*) in a protagonist's life. Sometimes she restricts herself to a single character's perceptions, as in *Waking* and *Winter Journey,* and sometimes she moves fluidly among narrators. While some of her novels focus on the experiences of nameless Everymen and Everywomen, others represent the effects of historical states and events, whether the Holocaust (*Konek Landing*) or women's experiences through the centuries (*The Seven Ages* and *The Tree of Knowledge*). Still others are informed by elements of Figes's personal history: *Equinox* involves the consequences of a decaying marriage, *Konek Landing* explores survivor's guilt, and *The Knot* treats a woman's experience of learning and using language. Figes's prose ranges from lyrical to deliberately pared down, encompassing both precise, concrete details and near nonsense. Common to all of Figes's novels, however, is an intense interest in ever changing states of consciousness, the passing of time, the relation of memory to present experience, the significance of the commonplace, the universal resonance of individual lives, and the uses of brevity and compression. In a given novel these enduring preoccupations combine with a particular premise and narrative style to produce, as Figes told Field in 1987, "something different each time." Although Figes's critics and readers have judged some combinations to be more successful than others, her unflagging commitment to innovation and experimentation has earned her the respect of a dedicated, if rarely broad, readership.

Interviews:

Michelene Wandor, "Art and Reason," in *On Gender and Writing,* edited by Wandor (London: Pandora, 1983), pp. 152–155;

Michele Field, "Eva Figes," *Publishers Weekly,* 16 January 1987, pp. 56–57;

Caroline Rand Herron, "Artist First, Feminist Second," *New York Times Book Review,* 22 February 1987, p. 7;

Laurel Graeber, "New Beginnings in Middle Age," *New York Times Book Review,* 25 September 1988, p. 9;

Jan Moir, "Public Lives: The Feminist Time Forgot," *Guardian* (London), 27 October 1993, p. 8.

References:

Ellen G. Friedman, "'Utterly other discourse': The Anticanon of Experimental Women Writers from Dorothy Richardson to Christine Brooke Rose," *Modern Fiction Studies,* 34, no. 3 (1988): 353–370;

Andrea Gutenberg, "Thresholds and Boundaries: Limit Plots in Eva Figes, Penelope Lively and Sara Maitland," in *Engendering Realism and Postmodernism: Contemporary Women Writers in Britain,* edited by Beate Neumeier, Postmodern Studies, no. 32 (Amsterdam & New York: Rodopi, 2001), pp. 191–205;

Martha Tuck Rozett, "Constructing a World: How Postmodern Historical Fiction Reimagines the Past," *CLIO,* 25, no. 2 (1996): 145–164;

Anna Maria Stuby, "Eva Figes's Novels," in *Engendering Realism and Postmodernism: Contemporary Women Writers in Britain,* edited by Neumeier, Postmodern Studies, no. 32 (Amsterdam & New York: Rodopi, 2001), pp. 105–116;

Stuby, "'A Piece of Shrapnel Lodges in My Flesh, and When It Moves, I Write'–The Fiction of Eva Figes," *Anglistik & Englischunterricht,* 60 (1997): 113–127;

Aranzazu Usandizaga, "Childhood and Self in Eva Figes's *Little Eden,*" *BELLS: Barcelona English Language and Literature Studies,* 1 (1989): 207–214.

Margaret Forster

(25 May 1938 -)

Merritt Moseley
University of North Carolina at Asheville

See also the Forster entry in *DLB 155: Twentieth-Century British Literary Biographers.*

Margaret Forster (photograph © Tara Heinemann; from the dust jacket for the U.S. edition of Lady's Maid, *1991)*

BOOKS: *Dames' Delight* (London: Cape, 1964);

Georgy Girl (London: Secker & Warburg, 1965; New York: Berkley, 1966);

The Bogeyman (London: Secker & Warburg, 1965; New York: Putnam, 1966);

The Travels of Maudie Tipstaff (London: Secker & Warburg, 1967; New York: Stein & Day, 1967);

The Park (London: Secker & Warburg, 1968);

Miss Owen-Owen Is at Home (London: Secker & Warburg, 1969); also published as *Miss Owen-Owen* (New York: Simon & Schuster, 1969);

Fenella Phizackerley (London: Secker & Warburg, 1970; New York: Simon & Schuster, 1971);

Mr Bone's Retreat (London: Secker & Warburg, 1971; New York: Simon & Schuster, 1971);

The Rash Adventurer: The Rise and Fall of Charles Edward Stuart (London: Secker & Warburg, 1973; New York: Stein & Day, 1974);

The Seduction of Mrs Pendlebury (London: Secker & Warburg, 1974);

William Makepeace Thackeray: Memoirs of a Victorian Gentleman (London: Secker & Warburg, 1978); republished as *Memoirs of a Victorian Gentleman: William Makepeace Thackeray* (New York: Morrow, 1979);

Mother Can You Hear Me? (London: Secker & Warburg, 1979);

The Bride of Lowther Fell: A Romance (London: Secker & Warburg, 1980; New York: Atheneum, 1981);

Marital Rites (London: Secker & Warburg, 1981; New York: Atheneum, 1982);

Significant Sisters: The Grassroots of Active Feminism 1839–1939 (London: Secker & Warburg, 1984; New York: Knopf, 1985);

Private Papers (London: Chatto & Windus, 1986);

Elizabeth Barrett Browning: A Biography (London: Chatto & Windus, 1988; New York: Doubleday, 1989);

Have the Men Had Enough? (London: Chatto & Windus, 1989);

Lady's Maid (London: Chatto & Windus, 1990; New York: Doubleday, 1991);

The Battle for Christabel (London: Chatto & Windus, 1991);

Daphne du Maurier (London: Chatto & Windus, 1993); republished as *Daphne du Maurier: The Secret Life of the Renowned Storyteller* (New York: Doubleday, 1993);

Mothers' Boys (London: Chatto & Windus, 1994);

Hidden Lives–A Family Memoir (London & New York: Viking, 1995);

Shadow Baby (London: Chatto & Windus, 1996);

Rich Desserts & Captain's Thin: A Family & Their Times, 1831–1931 (London: Chatto & Windus, 1997);

Precious Lives (London: Chatto & Windus, 1998; Thorndike, Me.: Thorndike Press, 1999);
The Memory Box (London: Chatto & Windus, 1999);
Good Wives?–Mary, Fannie, Jennie & Me, 1845–2001 (London: Chatto & Windus, 2001).

PRODUCED SCRIPTS: *Georgy Girl,* motion picture, adapted by Forster and Peter Nichols from her novel of that title, Columbia, 1966;
Elizabeth Barrett Browning: Conversations Between Elizabeth Barrett Browning and Her Latest Biographer, Margaret Forster, video, Films for the Humanities and Sciences, 1992.

OTHER: *Drawn from Life: The Journalism of William Makepeace Thackeray,* edited, with an introduction, by Forster (London: Folio Society, 1984);
Selected Poems of Elizabeth Barrett Browning, edited, with an introduction, by Forster (London: Chatto & Windus, 1988); also published as *Elizabeth Barrett Browning: Selected Poems* (Baltimore: Johns Hopkins University Press, 1988).

SELECTED PERIODICAL PUBLICATIONS–UNCOLLECTED: "When to cling on and when to say 'enough,'" *Daily Telegraph* (London), 21 September 1998, p. 12;
"Books: Inspirations," *Independent* (London), 7 November 1998, p. 16.

Margaret Forster, who began publishing fiction in 1964, has had an extraordinary career, producing twenty-nine books, including biography, fictionalized autobiography, one edition of poetry, three books of memoirs, and most significantly, nineteen novels. Her longevity and sustained high level of achievement have been recognized by external awards–but mostly in the field of nonfiction. Several of her biographies have won awards; even her *Rich Desserts & Captain's Thin: A Family & Their Times, 1831–1931* (1997), the history of a family of Carlisle biscuit makers, won a Lex award, given by the *Financial Times* (London) for the best work of business history. Her novels, on the other hand, reap the rewards of publication and good sales but seem critically undervalued. *Have the Men Had Enough?* (1989) was short-listed for the Sunday Express Book of the Year Award in 1989. This prize, which she did not win, was created to celebrate more "readable"–that is, more popular, less artistically ambitious–works than those nominated for the Booker Prize. The impression that she gives in interviews suggests that she is not writing for critical esteem.

In fact, Forster seems in many ways a pure writer. She hates all journeys; she does not like music; she dislikes public appearances, literary events, launch parties, and the other paraphernalia of literary life. In a 1993 interview with Angela Lambert she called herself "a housewife and a loner," and she told Rosanna Greenstreet in a 1992 interview that the greatest love of her life is "reading and my husband," that is, Hunter Davies, also a writer. "Reading" may be modest here, for sustained writing has been the basis for her long and outstanding career. She maintains that she does not plan her writing but writes out of obsession, and her practice is business-like; Angus Calder, a 1997 interviewer, reported, "She writes, according to her husband, ten pages a day in copper-plate handwriting, never rereads what was written the day before and has never taken more than seven weeks to write a novel. She cannot be doing with endless revision: 'It bores me. I like a novel to be alive when it leaves me.'" Forster has frequently spoken (and written) of the demands family and children make on women's lives. In middle age she has become more free and maintains her artistic fertility at a rate of a book nearly every year.

Forster, the daughter of Arthur G. Forster and his wife, Lilian, was born 25 May 1938 in Carlisle, in the northwestern corner of England in what was then Cumberland (now part of Cumbria). Her family was working-class; her father was a manual worker, and her maternal grandmother was a servant and the illegitimate daughter of a servant, though Margaret's mother was more educated and had a white-collar job before marrying Arthur. The middle child, Margaret grew up smart, troublesome, with ambitions beyond her family; she began school early, was admitted to a grammar school (that is, an academically selective state school) and then to Somerville College, Oxford University. She received her B.A. in 1960 and immediately married Hunter Davies, with whom she had lived off and on during their undergraduate years (he was at Durham University). Her marriage, and its longevity, stand out against her declaration in *Good Wives?–Mary, Fannie, Jennie & Me, 1845–2001* (2001) that "I never wanted to be a wife, that feeble creature who obeyed." They moved to London, where she taught at a girls' school from 1961 to 1963. From 1977 to 1980 she reviewed books for *The Evening Standard* (London). For most of her married life, her work has been writing, accommodating the rearing of their three children: Caitlin, born on 6 March 1964; Jake, born on 24 May 1966; and Flora, born on 31 October 1972. She and Davies continue to live in north London and in the Lake District.

Four years after receiving her degree Forster published her first novel. She had written, as she called it in a personal interview in 2002, a long "Dickensian-type novel based on my experiences as an au pair girl in Bordeaux," which was rejected but with encouragement.

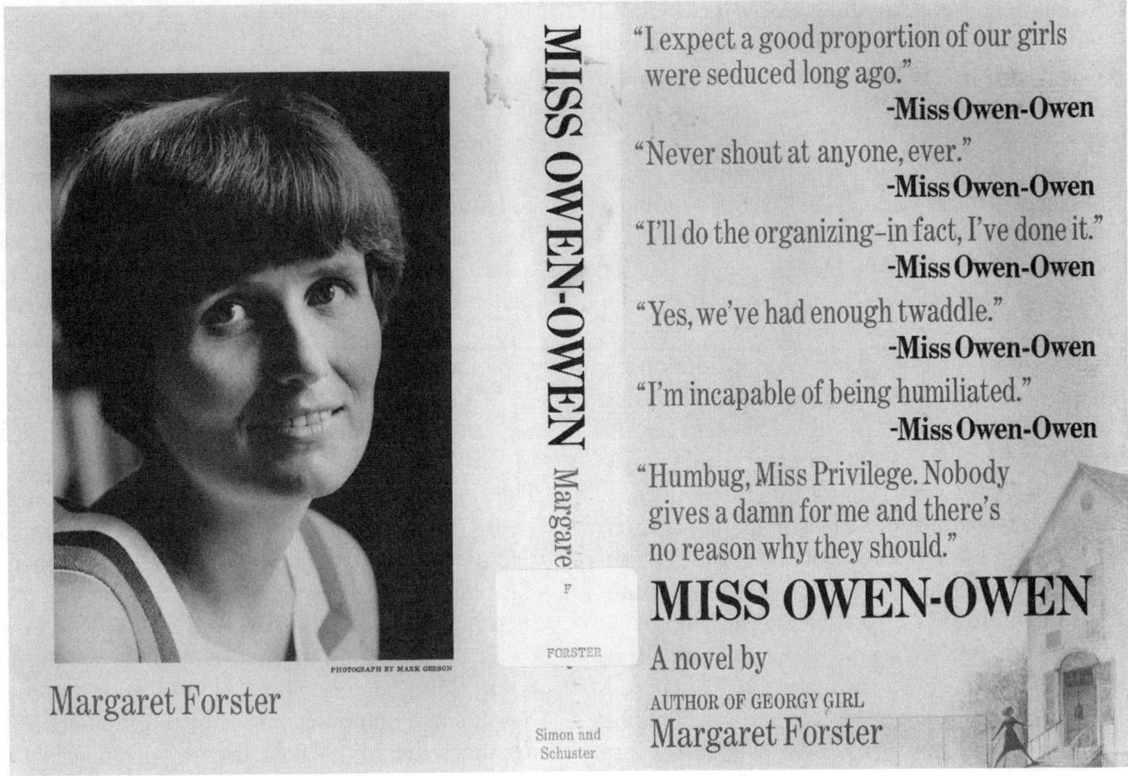

Dust jacket for the U.S. edition of Forster's 1969 novel Miss Owen-Owen Is at Home, *about the newly appointed headmistress at a girls' grammar school (Richland County Public Library)*

She then wrote *Dames' Delight* (1964) in imitation of J. D. Salinger's *Catcher in the Rye* (1951). She has expressed regret for it, in part because she was sued for libel and, as a result, had to remove good parts of the novel and hand over her advance to a lawyer. As is the case for some other novelists her first published book is her most autobiographical. *Dames' Delight,* a lighthearted academic novel, is about Oxford. A northern girl from a working-class background, Morag Graham goes down to Oxford; the novel covers her first two terms. She worries about love, has boyfriends, but remains a virgin; she basically has two friends, of whom one (Amanda) has affairs, the other (Rachael) is a rich girl enjoying an affectation of weirdness. Morag breaks rules and gets into trouble because one of her boyfriends embarrasses the college in print; she is afraid she is going to be sent down for going to London without permission, and for other violations, but instead is congratulated because she has done well on her preliminary exams, though she never does any work to speak of. Fairly early she gets permission to live outside the college by pretending to be too stressed by dormitory life, and thereafter she has a place to invite boys and give parties.

Like other academic novels this book includes coming-of-age lessons; as a friend tells her, "The trouble with you, Morag, is that you don't understand the nature of sex. It's like eating and going for walks and drinking–it's a need. It's wrong not to satisfy it. But love's quite different, dear, and you mustn't mix it up with sex." She gets by on her intelligence; accounts of her academic work are mostly comic. For instance,

> The question Miss Graveney had set was: "Consider the effects of the Roman occupation on the early English settlements." It meant precisely nothing. I began to panic, then I remembered hearing someone say once that education didn't mean knowing things, it meant knowing how to find out things. I felt rather pleased. All I had to do, proceeding from first essentials, was to find out when the Roman occupation began and ended, and then where the early English settlements were. If they were in the same place as the Romans the connection would be obvious. There was nothing to worry about.

The novel ends on a low-key note, with a gesture of disillusionment. Called from a party to be told by her tutor that she has performed with distinction on her exams, Morag tells her, "Anything I ever had before I came, Oxford has taken away. Like enthusiasm. Once I knew William Rufus was an absolute bastard, now I'd be scared to say so even if I was sure," and returns to her party.

University life for Forster was followed by life in a London flat. Her next novel, *Georgy Girl* (1965), is about that sort of life. One of her most celebrated books, it was made into a 1966 motion picture starring Lynn Redgrave, James Mason, and Alan Bates, for which Forster and Peter Nichols wrote the screenplay. This novel features a clear-sighted look at London life among young people in the "swinging sixties"; likewise, it is an acute study of masochistic relations between the sexes and the classes. Georgy (Georgina) is the daughter of Ted and Doris, who are servants to a rich man. Both Doris and Georgy find Ted's self-abasing admiration of the rich James disgusting; but Georgy is in a similar doormat relationship to her flatmate, Meredith. Meredith is a monster of egotism and selfishness; a musician, she borrows money from Georgy and from her lover Jos, who is also a musician but has taken a menial job. Meredith is pregnant; she and Jos, thinking the child may be his, marry listlessly, though she has aborted two of his previously. While she is in the hospital, Jos and Georgy become lovers, and when Meredith decides to get rid of the baby, Georgy takes it on. As the novel ends she is going to marry James Leamington, her parents' wealthy employer.

Georgy's motivation is subtly developed. One of her strongest convictions is of her own ugliness. She is big and homely; Meredith frequently comments on her ugliness, and her father once said, when Georgy turned up oddly dressed for a party, "'I wish to God I had a daughter who looked like a daughter and not a navvy' . . . Doris reckoned that was the beginning of Georgy's real obstinacy." In compensation for her homeliness, she has gone in for eccentric dress and being quirky and sharp-spoken. But the novel explores her generous need to love and be loved, which leads her to mother the baby Sara, even at the cost of her relationship with Jos. Georgy has a friend, Peg, who is more homely and obviously resents Georgy's partial success in escaping her loveless life. As Jos thinks, "She looked the picture of misery and all the old pity, which was once the only emotion he'd felt for her, came back. She was such a stupid, silly bitch. Once she'd been Meredith's catspaw, making herself ill with jealousy and the conviction that she was ugly and useless and doomed to a dreary life, and now she was Sara's. It was as though she had a talent for martyrdom."

Forster has reportedly distanced herself from her novels of the 1960s, but this distancing is unfortunate, as their standard is high and they do not suffer unduly from comparison with her more recent works. *The Bogeyman* (1965), the result of rewriting her first rejected novel, is an especially strong book. A study of a dysfunctional family headed by a bitter and violent teacher, it is uncompromising on how families tear at each other. Jack, the father, and Edith, the mother (a full-time homemaker), have two teenagers, Natalie and Justin, and a baby, Sebastian; with the exception of Sebastian, the rest hate each other. The mildest figure is Dutch au pair girl Christina Podva, who makes an effort but cannot stand the atmosphere and the family's exploitation of her.

Jack, when Edith complains that her life is nothing but cooking and cleaning, replies, "My life is working my guts out at a job I hate for three people I hate. Full stop. If you want to know why I go on, then I don't know. Because I'm scared to kill myself, I suppose, or because I've got some twisted sense of responsibility." The etiology of his misery in his teaching job, at which he is not very good, is clear. And his impact on the family is profound. Both children run away during the book; Edith, after some shoplifting, goes into a mental hospital and comes back blissful and indifferent following shock therapy; Natalie tries to poison her father but is prevented by Justin, who nevertheless beats his father up before leaving.

The atmosphere in the household is typified by the children's reactions to the decision to recruit an au pair: Justin and Natalie "told them it was the most stupid idea that had ever entered their thick heads. As Natalie said, either Justin or her father would end up in bed with the wench and there would be another bastard of a baby in the family."

The Bogeyman depicts a spectacularly unhappy family; but there are few novelists whose characters regularly speak so harshly to family members as Forster's. Plain, even rough, speaking may be a trait of her own family. Valerie Grove visited her for a 1991 interview for *The Sunday Times* (London) and recorded her discourse with her husband–"Oh shut up, Hunter," "Do stop simpering, Hunter," "Oh leave us alone, Hunter, for heaven's sake"–and judged that the "incessant putdowns" were a sign of their closeness.

The Travels of Maudie Tipstaff (1967) begins in territory often visited in Forster's novels: "the buildings" in Glasgow, where poor people, like Maudie, live in a room and a kitchen and sleep on a "bed in the wall." Maudie is a crotchety old Scotswoman, bigoted and narrow-minded; after her husband leaves her, she decides to do some traveling and spend four months with each of her three grown children, two daughters and a son. Her comic travels take her from Glasgow to London (by bus); thence to a rural setting in northwestern England; and then by plane to Malta. Her three children provide an array of possible adult outcomes, though none of them is satisfying to their mother. Jean, the oldest daughter, is well married, living in a prosperous London suburb. Maudie reflects that "Until Edward came along, Jean had been a good and loving daughter, knowing where her duty lay and doing it accordingly. She had brought her pay packet home and given seven-tenths to her mother and one-tenth to the church and kept a fifth for herself, which was as it should be." The life Jean now lives seems sterile to Maudie; there is no housekeeping to do, no shops nearby, and no neighbors to drop in. Second daughter Sally is a marked contrast: whorish and slatternly, she lives on a farm and is married to a farm laborer. She neglects her husband, children, and home. Her friend Grace, theoretically a cleaning woman, is in fact her partner in drunken dancing outings and casual affairs. Here at least Maudie has something to do, caring for the children and cleaning the house.

Robert, single but with a girlfriend, Eleanor, lives in Malta; he is idle and sybaritic and offends Maudie by naked swimming and self-sufficiency. Maudie, reflecting on her travels, "curled herself up on the bed and sniffed to herself and experimented with wishing she had never had any children at all." She seems to learn that everybody is on his own; when she is at home she is lonely, but with her children she feels isolated. She finally makes a confidante of Eleanor and tells her that she does not believe in love, married for children and a family and regretted it every day of her life, and resents Robert and Eleanor for being in love.

The stresses and dubious rewards of marriage and motherhood are also at issue in the next novel, *The Park* (1968). Unlike most of Forster's novels, which are quite traditional in structure, this one is organized more architecturally than chronologically. Six women regularly come to a park in London, and though they see each other often, they are distant. Their lives are bound together by three devices. One is an old man who sees them regularly and names them Moany Face, the Gypsy, the Girl, Chatterbox, Blue Hat, and Nell. Each chapter gives a series of glimpses into each life; one chapter, for instance, ends with all but Nell having sex. Like the old man, the personified park unites these six lives: "The park closed, exhausted. It thought all the women coy and sickly with their daydreams. All they did, as they walked up and down and round and round, was daydream, wanting this and that, anything but what they had got." Finally, they are drawn together by being present at a catastrophe: "Nell's" (her real name is Faith) son falls into a pond and drowns. For a while they interact. The last chapter once again gives a look at each woman's life; change comes to all of them, mostly improvement, and all but one will never visit the park again.

There is the usual unsentimental Forster take on the ambivalence toward husbands and the difficulties of motherhood (typically none of the women has a paid job). Liza thinks of her children: "If only they would go to bed like that every night and sleep all night, she would love them completely. It was only in the night she hated them."

The next novel marks a major change in being about an unmarried, childless woman, another failed teacher (like Jake in *The Bogeyman*), though with the difference that she is full of self-confidence and pride in her educational theories and practices. *Miss Owen-Owen Is at Home* (1969) provides the story of a newly appointed headmistress at the Seacrill County High School, a selective school for girls. Miss Owen-Owen faces many difficulties: among them are the newly elected Labour government, determined to end selective grammar schools, and her brother Nigel, imprisoned in Dartmoor Prison for rape and murder. Her determination to believe that the girl Nigel raped was responsible for her own fate is connected with her own odd sexual notions. She insists, for instance, on introducing sex seminars, in which the married teachers will be required to answer questions from the girls: "That was the greatest duty of the modern girls' school, and Miss Owen-Owen was determined not to shirk just because she had never suffered it herself. She had never known what it was like to battle against sexual desires. She had never had any." To one girl who is pretty and whom she has seen kissing a boy, she volunteers the observation, "Quite a lot of people think you're either a whore or a cock-teaser."

Her determination to change everything–the amount of Latin studied, the way girls prepare for exams–combines with her Gestapo mentality and her readiness to spy, dismiss, and interfere to make her brutally unpopular. She has only two supporters, one of them an incompetent teacher in the school whom she treats hatefully, though she knows she should not. Miss Owen-Owen is something of a tragic figure: aware of her errors, she is nonetheless unwilling, or even unable, to apologize or change her mind about anything. She knows she is unpopular, "blundering on and making enemies and yet could not cry stop." Having made a fool of herself at a public meeting, she must now resign and leave town. "It had all been a romantic notion. Funny, nobody would ever have put her down as a romantic. But that was what it had been. She had seen herself not exactly as a knight in shining armour, but as a kind of figure of light rescuing people from darkness–the darkness not of ignorance, but of complacency."

Dust jacket for the U.S. edition of Forster's 1970 novel, in which a spoiled young woman pursues a series of unsuccessful marriages (Richland County Public Library)

Fenella Phizackerley (1970) is one of Forster's most acid novels. It is the picaresque story of a girl whose only distinction is that she is beautiful. Spoiled by her father, who has given her a ridiculous name as part of his making her believe she is exceptional, she has no interior life of which to speak, no sympathy for others, no friends, no unselfish thoughts, no interest in anything outside herself, and she is proud of herself. Leaving school at fifteen, she meets and marries a thirty-four-year-old academic because he has an Aston Martin. They live in Hampstead, where she moves from laziness to adultery and is sent packing back to her parents. She tries to open a shop but does not know enough and soon marries a young, pimply aristocrat and lives with him and his parents in a big country house; after he dies, apparently of venereal disease, she goes abroad and contracts a "marriage" with an already married American adventurer. As the novel closes she is back with her father, an auctioneer, working as a secretary, not unhappily.

A pure study of a character, *Fenella Phizackerley* includes several attempts to sum up the protagonist. During her first courtship, the narrator explains, "There was a good deal to know about Laurence, but Fenella never got to know it. There was a lot less to know about Fenella, and Laurence soon knew it all." Her graduate-student lover tells her, "You're labeled 'bed only'–and don't have any ideas you're Helen of Troy or somebody. You're not even all that beautiful, so hang onto your husband, Mrs. Winstanley. You may need him." Finally, the narrator concludes (and the tone is that of a moralist finishing a fable): "So lived Fenella Phizackerley, her flights of fancy quite dead. She discovered that she was, except for her beauty, a very ordinary person, suited to very ordinary pursuits. She longed for nothing except easily attainable things like a new coat or longer holidays. Her contacts with other people were few, but she did not worry about it. She had recognized that she was misanthropic by nature and did not let that worry her."

Mr Bone's Retreat (1971) is another of Forster's wonderful studies of isolated characters, in this case William Bone, an elderly eccentric, living in a fine eighteenth-century house in London. On Christmas Eve he ends up admitting a couple of young hippies, Alex and Sophie, who are homeless, not really married, and expecting a child: "he managed to look at the voices, a furtive look, but sufficient. A young man and a very young girl. Both were wet. The young man had his arm round the girl. His gaze now flickering lower, William saw the bulge of the girl's stomach and shivered. He had a horror of pregnant women." He lets them have a flat, despite his disapproval of them and despite Alex's obnoxious behavior, which includes unquestioning exploitation of William and neglect of Sophie (Sophie is less selfish, knows they are using William, but makes excuses for Alex despite his mistreatment of her).

William's life is lived out in relation to Agnes Joliffe, an old friend who lives in his basement; his architect friend, Pullen; Agnes's daughter; and the new lodgers, Alex and Sophie. Unknown to the rest of them, he is dying of cancer and has made preparations for suicide if the pain becomes too great.

William Bone is a complex man. As Agnes reflects, "The man was such a dear, dear man, but such an irritant, such a fool. She supposed he aroused women's maternal instincts, and certainly she had always wanted to protect and comfort him. When young, of course, William had also aroused other, less philanthropic instincts, not only in her but in many others, but she did not think he knew about that." (His retreat from women, or from shared life, is the retreat of the title.) His friend Pullen maintains a friendship based on raillery: "The sport lay in the vicious teasing Pullen gave William. He teased him, nastily, about everything. He teased about sex, pretending William was a well-known poof, or about Mrs. Joliffe, pretending she was his mistress. He teased him about his running, pretending he ran in the park only to rape young girls and not to keep fit." The unnamed omniscient narrator explains that "William was a man whose whole being precluded intimacy."

Despite his eccentricities, his remoteness, his fear of intimacy, Bone is actually an admirable man. A veteran of both world wars, he protects Sophie and Agnes, provides for Sophie's child (named for him), and punches the repellent Alex.

After eight novels in seven years the author diversified her work. Between 1971 and 1990 she published twelve books. Of these, three were biographies–*The Rash Adventurer: The Rise and Fall of Charles Edward Stuart* (1973), *William Makepeace Thackeray: Memoirs of a Victorian Gentleman* (1978), and *Elizabeth Barrett Browning: A Biography* (1988); two were edited anthologies, *Drawn from Life: The Journalism of William Makepeace Thackeray* (1984) and *Selected Poems of Elizabeth Barrett Browning* (1988); and one was a history, *Significant Sisters: The Grassroots of Active Feminism 1839–1939* (1984). Of these works the most significant are the last one and the books about Browning, which bore fictional fruit as well. During the same period Forster also published six novels.

The Seduction of Mrs Pendlebury appeared in 1974. It is a fascinating study of an aging couple, immiserated by the passage of time and the mentally unbalanced bitterness of the wife. Stanley and Rose Pendlebury are retired (he from a government clerkship, she from domestic service) to a bungalow in a part of London that has begun gentrifying; they know hardly any of the neighbors, who are mostly younger and middle-class, while they are working-class. Stanley is patient and stolid; Rose is volatile, paranoid, and cruel. They talk of visiting their son in Australia but never go; it appears that he has gone to the ends of the earth to get away from Rose.

When a new family moves in next door–Tony and Alice Oram and their daughter, Amy–Rose unexpectedly takes a liking to them, plays with the girl, and visits Alice. Having no close relationships with others, she becomes overdependent on this one; at one point she goes to call on Alice and, when nobody answers, decides "She'd been treated like dirt, made to look small." Actually, Alice is at the hospital having a miscarriage. On another occasion Rose has a spell of dementia in which she thinks Tony is coming to their house and scratching the furniture.

The novel provides views of many characters' consciousness, as well as some authoritative commentary by the narrator, for instance: "Rawlinson Road, for all Rose Pendlebury's criticism, had become a friendly place. People knew each other, talked to each other, even helped each other. . . . Rose Pendlebury knew nothing of it. She saw them coming and going, heard the voices voicing in a way that set her teeth on edge, and retreated into the core of her house." But she, with her exaggerated and proud privacy that seems almost agoraphobic, cannot see her averagely friendly, normal neighborhood:

> Standing on the doorstep while Stanley fumbled about for his key such a longing overcame her to get in the house and never leave it that she whimpered with impatience. Every time she closed her eyes with exhaustion she saw hundreds and hundreds of people as they had walked past her, trapping her, in Oxford Street. None of them cared. They were all busy, all rushing, all trampling her down. The only sanity was inside her own front door minding her own business, or out in the garden playing with that child.
>
> "O for heaven's sake hurry up!" she shouted and banged her fists in Stanley's back.

The pathetic feature of Rose Pendlebury is that, like Miss Owen-Owen, she is to some extent aware of her own self-lacerating behavior. As she and Stanley leave the bungalow, she reflects sadly on her treatment of Alice: "All her life, she would live with the loss of the only person ever to like her better than she liked herself, the only person willing and able to make her see her fellow humans as friendly and giving. The girl, Alice, had been a blessing, but she was not a saint. It was only natural that she never wanted to see her again." Even this statement is untrue, since Alice is on her way over to show her her new baby, but Rose has again put the most negative construction on events.

Following a biography of Thackeray in the guise of a first-person memoir (what Forster describes in the opening pages as "a nightcap sort of book which the reader could dip into at his leisure and smile and sleep for a little while then wake up and read a little more and so on, suiting himself as he wants"), Forster produced *Mother Can You Hear Me?* (1979). This novel was part of a trend that, though not radically divergent from her earlier work, became perceptible in Forster's work from the late 1970s on. To call any of her books "problem novels" makes them seem schematic and preachy, and they are not. And the earlier books dealt with "problems," of course: the problem of a man driven by hatred of his work to hate his life and his family was at the heart of *The Bogeyman,* for instance. Nevertheless, particular social problems, often those that mostly affect women (care of aged parents, the choice of single parenthood, the responsibility for criminal offspring), imaginatively rendered, are crucial in most of her novels after the late 1970s. Joan Smith wrote about *Mother Can You Hear Me?* in a review of *The Battle for Christabel* (1991) in *The Guardian* (2 May 1991) that the novel "is one of the most painfully honest I have ever read. It raised agonizing questions about female identity, asking whether the role of mother leaves anything over for the individual woman, and whether daughters can ever shake off the past." The mother-daughter relationship is often at the heart of these works (as it had also been in such earlier books as *The Travels of Maudie Tipstaff* and *Mr Bone's Retreat*).

In *Mother Can You Hear Me?* Angela Bradbury, a married mother of four living in London, is repeatedly tugged, physically and emotionally, into the struggles of her parents. The elder Bradburys live in Cornwall, and Mrs. Bradbury has been in failing health for a decade or more. Her husband cares for her, with love that is inseparable from pugnacity. At the beginning of the novel Mrs. Bradbury's health has taken a turn for the worse, and a period begins during which Angela (sometimes with her sister, Valerie) visits; worries about what is to be done with her; takes her on failed holidays and houses her in London, until she finally dies there. This story line is the main plot of the book; the secondary one is about the relationship between Angela and her own daughter, Sadie, who is a difficult fifteen-year-old. Reminiscences of Sadie's childhood, printed in italics, alternate with the story of Angela and her parents.

In one sense the novel is about the problem of aged parents and to what extent one should lament the death of an old, ill, and miserable human being. This part of the book is made (as Smith commented) "painfully honest" in part by making Mother not lovable. In one excruciating family outing she contradicts her husband, and the narrator relates that "Mother's showing off had failed in its object, which was to publicly humiliate him and goad him into making a fool of himself." She whines and plays on her daughters' guilt. And yet she is a pitiful character, not only because she is ill. She has married only to have children, has been disappointed in her children, and at this point is a misery.

In another sense the book is about mothers and daughters. Angela and Valerie, the daughters, are the ones expected to care for Mother, not their two brothers; Angela is the one denounced by her aunt for failing her mother. Particularly because of having tried to raise her own daughter differently and produced such a spoiled and often hateful child, she ponders the relationship frequently.

> It was a trap. She ought to have known–she had known–having a mother, being a mother, they were both pledges to eternity, promises to be something impossible. She had tried so hard to break the chain but it was too tough and strong. She did not know which was worse–the agonizing pain of failing to be the daughter Mother needed and wanted and had a right to expect or the misery of failing to be the mother her daughter needed and had an equal right to expect.

Mother Can You Hear Me? brilliantly provides the texture of a tense family, in a way reminiscent, sometimes, of *The Bogeyman:*

> "When I was young," Angela repeated, but ladled out soup at the same time so that everyone began eating and ignored her, "I thought I would always want everyone to tell me the truth, but now I'm not so sure. The trouble is–"
>
> "Mum," Sadie said, "wrap up."
>
> "Why? Why should I?"
>
> "Because we don't want to hear you rambling on–do it if you like but we won't listen."
>
> "Why not?"
>
> "It's boring."

The death of her mother liberates Angela. Oddly, it seems to improve Sadie, as well, as she appears at the funeral, testifies to her love for Grandma, and even helps out a little. At the end of the novel they have their only civil conversation, even showing signs of affection

Dust jacket for the U.S. edition of Forster's 1971 novel, about an elderly eccentric who opens his home to a hippie couple on Christmas Eve (Richland County Public Library)

on Sadie's part, and the last words show that Angela is "without resentment," which is unusual for her.

Perhaps in reaction against a painfully honest exploration of contemporary social problems, the next novel is more sensational and more romantic, as the subtitle promises. *The Bride of Lowther Fell: A Romance* (1980) includes enough surprising and unusual plot elements for three or four of Forster's more conventional books. There is mysterious or disputed parentage; a madwoman raving about her impending marriage to "the Earl"; various attacks on the narrator including a slain rabbit and a sheep's head left at her house and a home invasion in which she is blindfolded, tied to a pole, and groped; and an oppressive atmosphere in which everybody knows everybody else's business and everybody seems related.

The narrator, Alexandra Grove, is a young single woman living in London. She has a long-term lover, Edward, from whom she is estranged. As she explains,

> At thirty years old, then, I had achieved most of the things I wanted, even if in the most tragic way. And I was happy. For ten years I had enjoyed my position in life and pitied others who were obliged to settle for less, who hungered after what I had, or who had made decisions which later had turned out to be wrong. Invariably, these mistakes hinged on marriage and maternity. . . . Children complicated what might still have been a simple issue.

Children (as Forster is always keen to note) do complicate simple issues. In this case, Alexandra's twin sister and her husband die in a plane crash, leaving their thirteen-year-old son, Casper, in her care. She takes this event as the occasion for a major change in her life, moving to Cumberland (in the English Lake District, though the attractions that draw tourists are not much in evidence). The novel concerns her efforts to come to terms with her neighbors, including the creepy Crosthwaites, who live on one side, and the mad, Miss Havisham-like Miss Cowdie, on the other; with various local men who are erotically drawn to her; and with her own fears and secrets. The novel ends in a sensational shoot out and revelation of suppressed truths.

Forster explains the origin of her next novel: "I'd been judging the Booker, and so many novels that year were brittle farces, so I thought I'd like to try" her own farce. *Marital Rites* (1981) is a short novel, a study of what appears to be (and in some ways really is) an ideal marriage and the effect on that marriage of the husband's infidelity. Anna and Robert Osgood have been married twenty years. Robert is a publisher; Anna, like most of the wives in Forster's fiction, does not have a paid job but stays at home and cares for her children (the most important of them, Sarah, being a sardonic, sexually active eighteen-year-old). Anna has recently expressed herself–in a group of four neighbor women who function chorally during this novel–strongly about the supine way in which one of her friends behaved when her husband betrayed her. Immediately, her certainty and forcefulness are put to the test. Robert writes a letter confessing that he has been having an affair with a young woman, Claire, who works in another publishing firm; he loves her, but still loves Anna, dreads destroying his marriage, but is unwilling to give up Claire. He seems to behave out of a scrupulous desire to be honest; both Claire and, when he unwisely confides in her, his daughter, Sarah, suggest that the thing to do would be keep the affair secret.

A minor farce ensues when Anna decides to pretend that she has not received the letter and enlists the aid of Robert's secretary to pretend it was not sent. Later the secretary, Betty, reveals that it was in fact sent. Anna and Claire speak; Anna and Betty speak; Robert and Betty speak. But Robert and Anna cannot speak of it. Her decision to pretend nothing has happened eventually "works." On a weekend away, as Sarah insists they "sort things out," nothing is ever said. Her passivity contrasts strikingly with her earlier advice about somebody else: "She could have gone straight round and hit him and brought him to his senses. . . . She should never have left his side, morning, noon or night. She should have gone to his office, followed him to lunch, just generally have made his life hell."

Marital Rites is a subtle, if perhaps minor, study of fidelity, honesty and dishonesty in marriage, love, and the role of children and friends in a troubled marriage. As the novel ends the narrator reveals that "the marriage of Anna and Robert Osgood endured and was good. They were still a legend, except to themselves. . . . They kept their secret and prospered by it and were never found out." The tone of the final sentence sheds a curious light on this summary: "The rites of marriage continued and were preserved and that was all that mattered, wasn't it?"

Forster makes canny use of her research. Just as her later work on Browning resulted in a biography, an edition of her poems, and a novel, so her Thackeray work resulted in both the 1978 fictionalized memoir and the 1984 anthology, *Drawn from Life*. Her next book was one of her most significant nonfiction works, one that sheds considerable light on her own life and on the lives of women in her novels. Published in 1984, *Significant Sisters* provides biographies and analyses of eight important women, including Elizabeth Blackwell, the first American woman to practice medicine, Elizabeth Cady Stanton, Florence Nightingale, and birth-control advocate Margaret Sanger. Although hardly a scholarly biography of any of these women, the book gives useful introductions to them and provides a shapely narrative.

More interesting are the reflections on feminism and on Forster's life. For instance, she writes,

> Feminism is full of riddles. One of the most intriguing is why it has not attracted an enormous rank-and-file following among women themselves, why it is still as necessary as it was in the nineteenth century to ask a woman if she is a feminist. The plain truth is that not only do large numbers of women feel apathetic but many more actively hate feminism. This is because right from the invention of the word it has been both misrepresented and misunderstood. . . . Feminism, both for men and women, is the most attractive and peaceful of doctrines.

And, though she pays high tribute to these pioneers for establishing the conditions that enabled her life as wife, mother, housekeeper, and writer, she muses, "I have been a feeble feminist. I have gradually come round to understanding that there is still a trap. It isn't marriage itself; it isn't motherhood alone; it is some subtle force which is not yet either fully understood or controlled. There is something in women which prevents them striking out as men do." Such a comment sheds considerable light on her books. One of the key insights here, though, is the extent to which feminist insistence that women have the right to control childbearing has changed women's lives forever. In her novels and her memoirs, Forster insists that involuntary conception marks the greatest difference between women of the past and their sisters in the second half of the twentieth century, including herself.

Private Papers (1986) is another study of family dynamics, focusing, again, on the mother-daughter relationship. It is also something of an experiment in form, using the interplay between two documents (one called "Private Papers") to give two much different first-person accounts of family life. The two narrators are Penelope Butler and her eldest daughter, Rosemary. Penelope, born in 1915, is writing an account of her life in 1984. Rosemary, a painter, has discovered it while looking for family photographs and reads her mother's story, interrupting it from time to time with her own comments, outcries, corrections, and emendations. It seems at first that the reader is to understand Rosemary's contributions as her thoughts, particularly as they have a highly informal tone: "Who *is* she talking to, writing for? Is this a diary or a letter?" but it becomes clear that Rosemary, too, is writing, leaving her own testimony. At the end she writes,

> I'll leave her precious papers where I found them, but I'll leave my own too–it's only right that my perspectives should count for as much as hers. Her papers are no longer private. I have made them my property, I have walked all over her memories, opinions and judgements, I have been a trespasser without mercy. And I have absolutely no regrets. In the unlikely event of Mother discovering and objecting to what I have done, I shall defend myself with pride. I shall say, "Mother, I am *your* daughter." Then we'd see what the fuck she makes of that.

Penelope is an orphan; raised without any family at all she marries Oliver, a man who has only a mother and no other close relatives. Starved for family, Penelope places what Rosemary at least considers an inordinate and even grotesque emphasis on family (especially after her husband is killed on D-Day). She has two daughters, then adopts another, and finally has a third.

The adopted daughter, Jess, accidentally electrocutes herself; the oldest, Rosemary, becomes a bohemian, lives with unsuitable men, has more than one abortion (one of which Penelope knows about), and, at a fairly advanced age, decides to have a baby without being married. In this novel, where almost everything goes wrong, she loses the baby. Celia, the second daughter, abandons a promising academic career and becomes first a gardener, then a social worker; she also makes poor choices in men, living first with an abusive and controlling policeman, then with an older Irish former convict and tramp. And the youngest daughter, Emily, marries but then divorces. The only one of the daughters to become a mother, she loses her son when he is killed in the Falklands War. So the family that began with the sole Penelope moves into the third generation with only Vanessa, Emily's daughter.

It is a melancholy narrative of a family in which "family" has been both an unfair ideal and an impossible goal. The primary interest of *Private Papers* is the question of causation. The daughters seem both to claim that they are happy with the way their lives have turned out (except for Emily) and to blame their mother. She expresses bewilderment about how it has all happened. The other source of fascination is in the juxtaposition of the two voices–Penelope's and Rosemary's–in the private papers: Penelope stately, dignified, sentimental, and (necessarily) self-justifying; Rosemary vigorous, sarcastic, profane, and, at least overtly, unapologetic and proud.

While researching her biography of Browning, Forster became aware that a good anthology of her poems was not in print; the result was her 1988 edition of *Selected Poems of Elizabeth Barrett Browning.* The same year her biography of the poet appeared. The stimulus for this latter book, aside from the gap of some thirty years since the previous full biography, was the discovery of about a thousand new letters by the poet. As Alison Hennegan, reviewing the book for *The Guardian* (24 June 1988), summarized, "Margaret Forster's aims are three-fold: to distinguish myth from reality; to suggest explanations for the bewildering array of contradictions which Elizabeth managed, usually, to hold in perilous equilibrium; and, most important of all, to draw readers back to the poetry itself." Browning is the kind of subject to appeal to Forster; she wrestled with the problem of balancing love, marriage, parenthood, and creative work; her relationship with her mother was an important shaping experience in her life; she was a proto-feminist, having read Mary Wollstonecraft and forsworn marriage by the age of twelve. Her progressive principles were sometimes shamed by insensitive practice, particularly in her treatment of Wilson, her maid, whose story Forster tells in *Lady's Maid* (1990).

Published in 1989, *Have the Men Had Enough?* is one of Forster's most well-received and most powerful books. This novel is another study of family versus fulfillment, focusing on an old woman, "Grandma McKay," who, after a long life in "the Buildings" in Glasgow, has been moved to London by her son Charlie. She denies that she should have had pleasure in her life–because she had bairns. The acute problem facing the family (Charlie and his wife and two children; his brother, Stuart; his unmarried sister, Bridget) is what to do about Grandma, now that she is incapable of caring for herself. She has Alzheimer's disease, which becomes steadily worse through the book until she dies. The title of the book comes from one of Grandma's catch phrases: she worries constantly about "the men's tea." She is an odd mixture–she favors men, especially if they are tall and strong, but actually dislikes them, thinking they cause trouble. She relies on her two adult sons but has always loved her daughter more. The secondary meaning of "have the men had enough?" has to do with the unjust distribution of care. Bridget has essentially sacrificed her life for her mother; now caring for Grandma McKay falls more and more on Charlie's wife, Jenny, and teenage daughter, Hannah. The men feel less guilt and are reconciled to the idea of institutionalizing their mother.

The moral questions raised by the book are exacerbated by the fact that Grandma is genuinely difficult in her dementia, even disgusting. Early in the book she is eating with her hands at a family dinner:

> then she takes her bottom teeth out (the top set are already out, lost sometime between breakfast and lunch

Dust jacket for the U.S. edition of Forster's 1980 novel, in which a single woman moves to the English Lake District to take care of her orphaned nephew and encounters an atmosphere of Gothic mystery (Richland County Public Library)

and likely to turn up any place from the peg basket to the biscuit tin). She uses them as a scoop, grating them through the shallows of the gravy to fish out a potato, and Adrian laughs and Dad smiles and Mum moves her face not a muscle and Paula closes her eyes and Bridget snatches the teeth, rushes to the sink, sluices the teeth, rams them back into Grandma's mouth.

In his review for *The Guardian* (10 March 1989) Jonathan Coe observed that by the end of the novel "we realise . . . that only when the men have had enough (because it is still the men who organise, earn and legislate) will anything ever be done to prevent these situations from arising." He summed up, "If there was a prize for the writer of the most socially useful novel of the year, Margaret Forster would be a clear favourite; and since there are already prizes for the best and most entertaining, I sincerely hope she wins one." Interestingly, Coe thought of the problem this novel dramatizes as the "army of unpaid nurses and social workers who make it half their life's work to look after aged parents." In his 17 March 1989 review for *The Independent* (London) Auberon Waugh, on the other hand, diagnosed it as unbridled longevity: "Forster's brilliant and desperately relevant new novel invites us to contemplate the alternative to 'premature death': death in the new government-sponsored state of full maturity."

In *Lady's Maid* Forster takes the servant, Elizabeth Wilson, who provided invaluable assistance to Elizabeth Barrett and Robert Browning, from the subordinate (though still important) position she occupied in the 1989 biography and gives her her own voice and her own story. Told in alternating third-person narration and letters written by Wilson to her mother and others, it recounts how she came from Newcastle to London and began to care for the poet. She helps and encourages Barrett to try harder and be less victimized by her unnamed medical condition; she assists the courtship by Browning; and she continues with them when they leave England for Italy, where she marries an Italian. There is considerable edge to the novel, including discussions of marriage as slavery, and a sharp awareness of Barrett's jealousy of Wilson, who is not supposed to have a "follower"–as men were called if they showed an interest in servants. In her review of Forster's 1988 biography of the poet, Hennegan sharply noted the poet's "sickeningly unfeeling treatment of Wilson, the maid to whose discretion and loyalty the Brownings owed their courtship and marriage, but whose right to remain with her child and husband they denied. In her poems Elizabeth espoused the rights of working women, attacked the man-made fiction of legitimacy, defended the sacred rights of maternity: at home, Wilson was a Servant Problem." Like *Have the Men Had Enough?, Lady's Maid* examines the inequality of obligation, in this case on the basis of class rather than gender. Wilson must leave her own child behind for the Brownings' convenience; when she gets a holiday they grant her the privilege of taking along Pen, their own son. Privilege, and insidious but covert and usually unexamined assumptions, rule the relationship between the lady and her maid.

Since 1991 Forster has continued her impressive output with four novels, two books of family memoir and another that combines biography with personal memoir, a full-scale biography of Daphne du Maurier, and the history of a biscuit manufacturer in Carlisle. While the novels again explore complicated social and moral questions (adoption of mixed-race children, illegitimacy, and always mother-daughter relations), the nonfiction books show a marked turn to Carlisle (the city of her birth).

Published in 1991, *The Battle for Christabel* centers on a child. Christabel (named for famous English feminist Christabel Pankhurst) is the offspring of Rowena, a feckless woman who, determined to have a child and preferring a black father, used an unnamed and now untraceable West Indian to engender her daughter. Now Rowena is dead and the question is: what will happen to Christabel? The father never knew he had a child and is in Barbados. Rowena has left no instructions. Her wealthy Scottish mother is too old to take on a child; her sister, a widowed flautist with a busy traveling schedule and a grown daughter of her own, is always on tour. The narrator of the novel, Isobel, who was Rowena's best friend, takes an interest. Unfortunately, when she decides to try to arrange adoption, she invites the Department of Social Services in, and, with that step, she and Rowena's family have lost control, if they ever had it. Christabel is first placed "in care" and then fostered with a couple whom none of Rowena's friends or family like. That their dislike is class-based complicates matters: Christabel's foster parents speak ungrammatically and prefer store-bought cakes to home baking. When Isobel marries and tries to adopt Christabel herself, she comes up against the power of the DSS and its preference for a mixed-race family.

There is much anger against the social services, social workers, bureaucrats, and so on; there is also some awareness by Isobel (who is not a relative and has no family claim on Christabel) that her difficulties, though not her "fault," may result from her personality: "It is still not feminine to be strong, still not an attribute admired in women unless it is concealed or unless it is glossed over with a conventional appearance and the use of what is called charm. I have no charm." In her 2 June 1991 review for *The Independent* (London) Maureen Feely commented: "Isobel comes away happy to have discovered what it's like to have an urge for a child; I came away understanding that a society doesn't reveal its obsession with class and race until people start to argue about who controls that child. This disturbing and highly readable book far surpasses its modest intentions." And Joan Smith was equally positive in her review for *The Guardian*: "*The Battle For Christabel* is something rare, a novel of ideas expressed not through ideology but through character and feeling; in that territory of dread and reconciliation which is the family, Forster reigns supreme."

Following publication of *Daphne du Maurier* (1993), which was generally well received for more than just its somewhat sensational revelation of du Maurier's bisexuality, Forster turned to another timely social novel. Even more than transracial adoption, the popular mind had been occupied–horrified, really–by the murder in Liverpool of a three-year-old, James Bulger, by two ten-year-old boys, who lured him away from a shopping center, battered him to death, and left him on railroad tracks to be dismembered. *Mothers' Boys* (1994) is not exactly about that event, instead being written out of another traumatic event closer to the author, but it is about boys and violence.

The novel studies two families affected by a shocking act of violence. Sixteen-year-old Leo, in the company of a hardened criminal and on LSD, has randomly attacked Joe, another boy, kicked and knifed him, and smeared him with excrement. Leo is arrested but will say nothing about his crime, convicted, and sent to a youthful-offender facility. Before his sentence is up he escapes, and with the complicity of his great-grandfather gets away to London. Joe, the victim, is traumatized by his experience, mostly by the memory of his shame rather than his physical wounds, but is apparently recovering as the novel ends.

The focus is on the families of these boys and particularly their mothers. Leo is actually an orphan, his English mother and African father having been murdered before his eyes; he lives with his grandmother, Sheila Armstrong, and her ineffectual husband, Alan Armstrong. She and her husband are working-class. The other family, Sam and Harriet Kennedy, is upper-middle-class. The two women have some things in common, such as worrying about their boys, husbands who are somewhat shut out, and even a shallow relationship that begins when Sheila writes a letter of apology to Harriet.

The most interesting part of this novel is the psychology of the victim, Joe, and even more of his mother. She handles him with kid gloves, permits him to treat his parents cruelly, and begins to arouse the resentment of her older son and her husband. The husband indeed denounces her cultivation of unhappiness:

> I should have warned you long ago . . . about how ridiculous you've become, how bitter, and about how much damage you're doing, and how I'm sick of this tragedy queen stuff. I'm sick of it and I couldn't care less whether you come with me to Edinburgh, I don't even know if I want you to come, you'd kill the weekend before it started. I'm going because I want to enjoy myself–yes, that filthy word, enjoy, have some pleasure again, and I'm not ashamed of wanting to do it.

Although he may be seen, in some ways, as an evasive male leaving women to do the emotionally difficult work, it is true that when toward the end of the novel Joe learns to drive, buys a car, and gets a girlfriend, Harriet's worry that it will all end in tears becomes almost indistinguishable from a regret that he is return-

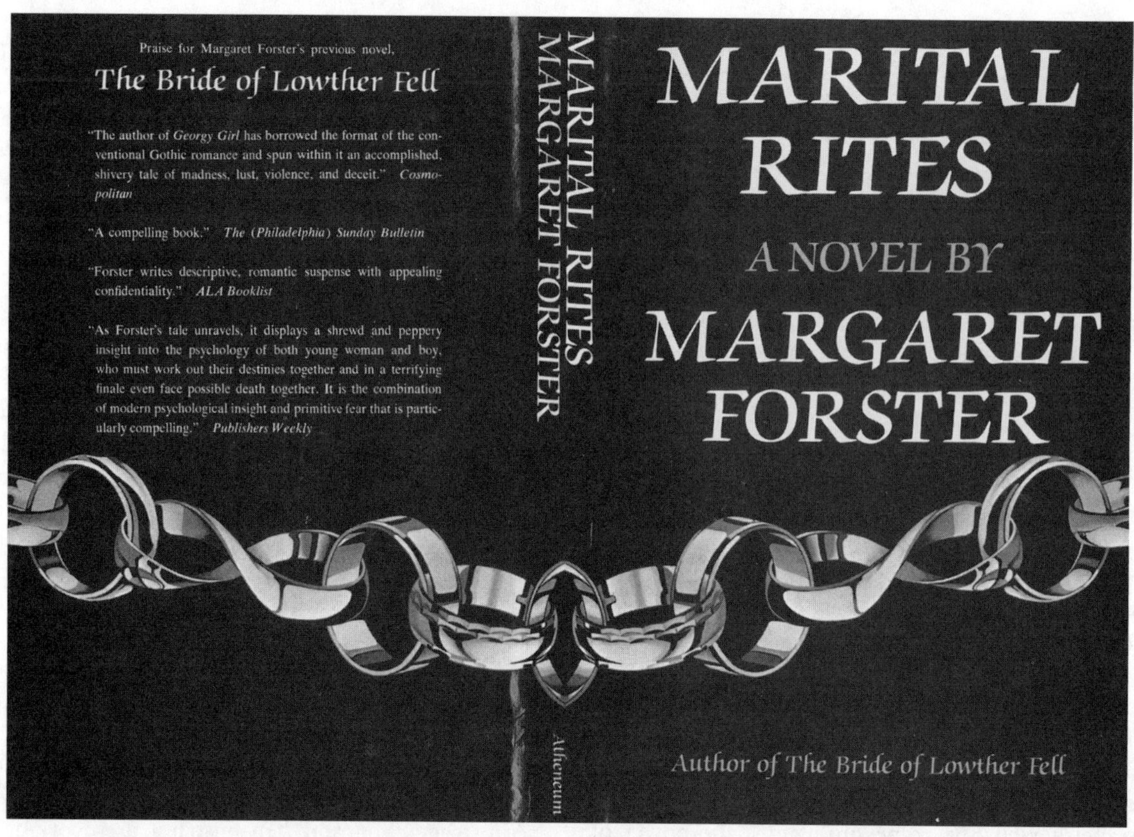

Dust jacket for the U.S. edition of Forster's 1981 novel, about a wife's passive response to her husband's infidelity (Richland County Public Library)

ing to normality. Blame is never particularly placed–or rather it is shared. As Candia McWilliam wrote in her 12 June 1994 review for *The Independent* (London), Forster "aerates the sticky mass of life and its entanglements, processing and working through them with trenchant fairness."

"The sticky mass of life and its entanglements" makes a good summary of what Forster faces in *Hidden Lives–A Family Memoir* (1995), and in the next book, a fictional revisiting of this material, *Shadow Baby* (1996). There are many meanings of "hidden lives." One is the lives of average women before Forster's generation, including that of her own mother. Another is the hidden early life of her grandmother, who refused to discuss any part of her life before she was twenty-three; the most sensational is Forster's grandmother's illegitimate daughter, hidden from family knowledge until she turned up screaming at her mother's funeral.

The book is a study of three generations of women. Grandmother, born Margaret Jordan in 1869, was herself illegitimate and had an illegitimate daughter, successfully hidden away but traced in the present day by her granddaughter. A servant, Margaret Jordan, married a butcher, became a homemaker, and had three daughters. The first daughter, Lilian, received some education but then married "down" to a machinist in a factory. She had three children herself, of whom the middle child was Margaret Forster. The book tells the story of these three lives. It has fascinating things to reveal about grandmother Margaret, the lives of servants in Carlisle, the stigma of illegitimacy, and marriage and motherhood for her; more poignantly, about Forster's own mother, who appears to her as a thwarted self; and, finally, about Forster's life, including her own marriage in comparison with that of her family. About her mother, she reflects: "I tried to work out why a woman as beautiful (to me) and clever and good and kind didn't have what she wanted even if I didn't know what it was she did want. How had this state of affairs come about? I decided it was because she had made one fatal mistake: she'd got married. Simple. She'd got married and then had children, all part of being married and inevitable, I thought, and trapped herself." Her determination to be different helps to explain her studiousness, her university education, her career, and her more equal marriage.

But so do vast changes in women's lives. The nature of domestic work, and to some extent the expectations of men, along with birth control, make for a new world for women, and this motivates Forster's moving conclusion:

> All of us, all three representatives of different generations, always have put family first but in my case, in the case of my generation, it has not been at ruinous cost. I'm not, and haven't been, crippled by the family. I don't pay an enormous emotional price for the having of one. I have been able to be myself within its confines. . . . Let no one say nothing has changed, that women have it as bad as ever. They do not. I am glad, glad not to have been born a working-class girl in 1869 or 1901. Everything, for a woman, is better now, even if it is still not as good as it could be. To forget or deny that is an insult to the women who have gone before, women like my grandmother and mother.

The book also holds some insights into the author's novels, revealing that Georgy was her mother, "trading everything, if necessary, for children," and detailing the connections between the university life in *Dames' Delight* and her college years spent intermittently living with Davies.

Shadow Baby is, in the words of Lucy Hughes-Hallet in her 9 June 1996 review in *The Sunday Times* (London), "about maternal love: children's craving for it, mothers' experience of it and, more prominently and more contentiously, mothers' capacity for not feeling it." It retails two apparently separate stories of illegitimate maternity (though they turn out to be closely connected). One is set in and around Carlisle and is obviously based on the family history unearthed in *Hidden Lives.* A rural orphan, Leah is impregnated by a rich local playboy and gives birth to a daughter, Evie. When Leah marries she insists on abandoning her daughter to a relative, upon whose death Evie ends up in the workhouse, then becomes a servant. Eventually, she accidentally locates her mother but is spurned by her. Her mother has a legitimate daughter who also has an illegitimate daughter after her fiancé is killed in World War I, but she keeps her. Evie turns up at her mother's funeral and introduces herself; later, like Forster's hidden aunt, she dies in an asylum.

This story is intercut with another, set closer to the present time, in which a girl named Hazel, aged eighteen, gets pregnant and is bullied by her mother into having the baby in Norway and giving her up for adoption. Like Evie, she eventually tracks her mother down in London, receiving a cold welcome. When last heard from, she has become pregnant, though she has an abortion and is sterilized, in some macabre way, perhaps, putting an end to the chain of unwanted pregnancies and unloved daughters.

Both featured mothers–Leah Arnesen and Hazel Walmsley–want little to do with their daughters; both are married to husbands who are more sympathetic toward the daughters than are their wives. The shadow of the title is multivalent, pointing toward the effort to keep the illegitimate daughters in the shadows, the shadows they cast over their mothers' lives, and the literal shadow of Evie at her mother's front door, which is never opened to her; there is also this account of Hazel giving birth to the girl who will be Shona: "She heard the gurgling cry, knew the shadow had a voice, but she never felt the body from which it came. She did not weep, not then, she felt too frozen, hypnotised by the enormity of what she had done. A feeling of outright panic mixed with a new fear in her, the fear of one day being called to account, and her mother not being there to manage everything." As Caroline Moore reacted in her 16 June 1996 review in *The Sunday Telegraph* (London), "Maternal feelings cannot be denied with impunity; but nor, years later, can they be created ex nihilo: resentment, guilt, or even embarrassment are more likely to fill the void."

In 1997 Forster returned to the story of Carlisle with *Rich Desserts & Captain's Thin,* a history of Carr's, a biscuit-making firm important in the Carlisle of her youth, begun by Quaker merchants of progressive and humane principles. McWilliam, writing in *The Independent* (London) (12 October 1977) declared that the "story of a business carefully built up, flourishing to the point where it is part of a nation's pride, and then subverted by family schism and fate and lost to outside forces can never be uninteresting."

Forster's next book, *Precious Lives* (1998), is a sort of sequel to *Hidden Lives,* though where the earlier book seemed most interested in childbirth and its consequences, this one is about death. There are two main characters in this book, both dying. Forster's father, the factory machinist familiar from *Hidden Lives,* is ninety-four. A no-nonsense, unreflective, northern working man; incapable of expressing affection; impatient with assistance or helplessness, he lives in his own bungalow and gardens into his nineties. Finally and inevitably, he begins to fail, accepts assistance unwillingly, goes into a home, and dies. Meanwhile, Margaret's sister-in-law Marion is dying of cancer. An interesting woman who had married young, without education, she later began to take courses, qualified as a social worker, and, at about the same time, realized she was a lesbian. She knows for some time that death is inevitable and, as Forster learns with surprise, finds the hardest part of it is the boredom of living while dying.

Memory and its burdens have been important in many of her novels; these, and the problems of mother-daughter relations, figure importantly in *The Memory*

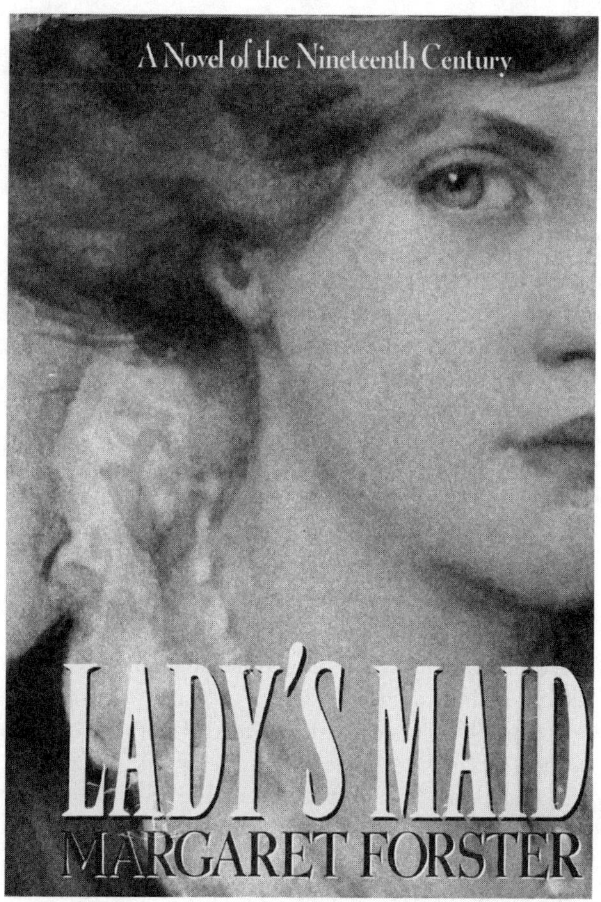

Dust jacket for the U.S. edition of Forster's 1990 historical novel about Elizabeth Barrett Browning's maid (Richland County Public Library)

Box (1999). Catherine Musgrave, the protagonist (and, unusually for Forster, the first-person narrator), is thirty-one, the age at which her mostly forgotten mother died. Her father and her stepmother (whom she has loved, and who has been a good parent to her) have recently died. While clearing out their Oxford home she finds a "memory box" that her mother, knowing she was dying, made for her. It contains mysterious objects–an address book, a shell, gull feathers, a photograph–and she decides to follow where they lead to discover the secrets of her mother's life. They lead her to Cumbria, to the West Indies, and to the discovery, among others, that her mother had had a love affair before marrying her father and had undertaken challenging sailing voyages despite her frail health.

Her discoveries are less sensational than those Forster had made about her own family; but they help her change her life. Catherine is a thirty-something single woman who, by her account, "had made a mess of much of my life. I had done things with which I did not particularly care to acquaint those who did not know." She has a lover, Tony, whom she fends off, and one cousin, Rory, a confused homosexual living in London. What she learns about her mother helps her clarify her own hesitations, or retreat: "I think I came at last to understand the effect my mother's death had had on me. I never consciously thought anything as extreme as 'If I have a baby I will die,' but there may have been something of that fear in my attitude."

Forster's 2001 book is another work of nonfiction, combining women's history with personal reminiscence. *Good Wives?–Mary, Fannie, Jennie & Me, 1845–2001* is much concerned with what it means to be a wife, or a good wife, what sorts of sacrifices wifehood requires, and whether they are ever justified. The other three women of the title are Mary Livingstone (1821–1862), who lived a harrowing life as wife to the explorer and missionary David Livingstone; Fanny Stevenson (1840–1914), wife of Robert Louis Stevenson; and Jennie Lee (1904–1988), married to Aneurin Bevan, an important Labour M.P. and cabinet minister. There is a sort of evolution from unquestioning self-suppression through a dawning feminism to Jennie Lee, who refuses to be a housekeeper, keeps her own name, but still sacrifices part of her own life (she was also a member of Parliament) to her marriage.

Interspersed with these lives is that of the author. She writes in her prologue, "I never wanted to be a wife, that feeble creature who obeyed." Yet, she is a wife, though without ever having promised to obey her husband. Later she writes ruefully, "I know that, unlike Jennie, I have been a bad wife." (To her, a good wife is independent.) "I am a disgrace to my own feminist aspirations. To be obliged to admit, as I am obliged to admit, that I do not know how much money we have is disgraceful."

In the epilogue she asks,

> why do women get married today? Why do they still go through these rituals, however basic they have become, which turn a woman into a wife? I know why Mary Livingstone did, I know why Fanny Stevenson did, I know why Jennie Lee grudgingly did, and I know why I myself did. We all had our very different reasons, but the reasons why women today are still prepared, even eager, to become wives are much harder for me to identify and understand.

Thus, she is still training her scrutiny on the family, on women's lives, and on the problems of making a society, with the kind of intelligence and fierce honesty that characterize her fiction and nonfiction as well.

Reviewing *Hidden Lives* for *The Toronto Sun* (21 June 1996) Heather Mallick provided an overview of Forster's career that catches its most important qualities:

> Forster, a prolific British novelist and social historian, is one of those rare writers who can't seem to get anything wrong. She aims at her target, she knows precisely what she wants to say and she writes, quickly, within a couple of months, the very book she had intended. Forster, who wrote *Georgy Girl,* on which the Lynn Redgrave movie was based, is also the author of *Significant Sisters,* the best feminist history extant, and several wonderful novels about the pains and pleasures of family life. She is a chronicler of our cruel little ways within the family; she can be harsh; she gives no quarter whatsoever.

For whatever reason–her popularity? her productivity?–Forster has been seriously undervalued in critical esteem. She has never won the Booker Prize, the Orange Prize (a feminist award, open only to women authors), or the Whitbread Prize. Academics have shown little interest in her. Her name has never appeared in the *MLA Bibliography.*

And perhaps these omissions would not trouble Margaret Forster. Despite her lack of prizes or scholarly study, her body of work is a major one. She writes brilliantly–though her work never flaunts its brilliance–about the most important matters life contains: birth, death, parenthood, aging, relations between the sexes and among the classes, memory, and the burden of the past on the present.

Interviews:

Valerie Grove, "Virgin Birth," *Sunday Times* (London), Features section, 17 March 1991;

Rosanna Greenstreet, "The Questionnaire: Margaret Forster," *Guardian,* 11 April 1992, p. 39;

Angela Lambert, "From 'Georgy Girl' to the man in Daphne," *Independent* (London), 17 March 1993, p. 23;

Graham Lord, "The Arts: Writer's cramp and wedded bliss," *Daily Telegraph* (London), 7 April 1993, p. 19;

Kate Clanchy, "A favourite aunt with a zest for life," *Scotsman,* 19 August 1997, p. 13;

Max Davidson, "Cracker: The True Story," *Daily Telegraph* (London), 27 September 1997, p. 5;

Greenstreet, "Property: My First Home," *Daily Telegraph* (London), 14 August 1999, p. 8.

Carlo Gébler

(21 August 1954 –   )

Michael J. Hayes
University of Central Lancashire

BOOKS: *The Eleventh Summer* (London: Hamilton, 1985; New York: Dutton, 1985);

August in July (London: Hamilton, 1986);

Work and Play (London: Hamilton, 1987; New York: St. Martin's Press, 1987);

Driving through Cuba: An East-West Journey (London: Hamilton, 1988); republished as *Driving through Cuba: Rare Encounters in the Land of Sugar Cane and Revolution* (New York: Simon & Schuster, 1988);

The T.V. Genie (London: Hamilton Children's, 1989);

Malachy and His Family (London: Hamilton, 1990);

The Glass Curtain: Inside an Ulster Community (London: Hamilton, 1991);

Life of a Drum (London: Hamilton, 1991);

The Witch That Wasn't (London: Hamilton Children's, 1991);

The Cure (London: Hamilton, 1994; New York: Penguin, 1994);

W.9. & Other Lives (Belfast: Lagan, 1996; London & New York: Boyars, 1998);

Frozen Out: A Tale of Betrayal and Survival (London: Mammoth, 1998);

How to Murder a Man (London: Little, Brown, 1998; New York: Boyars, 1999);

The Base (London: Mammoth, 1999);

Father and I (London: Little, Brown, 2000; London & New York: Boyars, 2001);

Dance of Death: A Version of August Strindberg's Dance of Death (Belfast: Lagan, 2000);

Caught on a Train (London: Mammoth, 2001).

Carlo Gébler (photograph by David Barker; from the dust jacket for the U.S. edition of How to Murder a Man, *1999)*

PLAY PRODUCTION: *Dance of Death,* adapted from August Strindberg's *Dödsdansen,* London, Tricycle Theatre, 1998.

PRODUCED SCRIPTS: *Night,* television, London Weekend Television, 1972;

Croagh Patrick, television, Radio Telefis Éireann, 1978;

The Beneficiary, television, based on the short story by Anton Chekhov, Radio Telefis Éireann, 1979;

Over Here, television, Radio Telefis Éireann, 1980;

Rating Notman, motion picture, National Film Finance, 1981;

Country and Irish, television, BBC 4, 1984;

Two Lives: A Portrait of Francis Stuart, television, BBC4, 1985;

George Barker, television, London Weekend Television, 1987;

Plain Tales from Northern Ireland, television, DBA Television, 1993;

David Calvert, television, ARTE, 1994;

Life after Death, television, BBC4, 1994;

The Joint's Not Jumping, television, BBC, 1995;

No Other Purpose, television, BBC, 1995;

Baseball in Irish History, television, BBC4, 1996;

Put to the Test, television, BBC, 1998;

The Suspecting Glance: Conor Cruise-O'Brien, television, Radio Telefis Éireann, 2000;

December Bride (by Sam Hanna Bell), radio, BBC, 2001.

SELECTED PERIODICAL PUBLICATIONS–UNCOLLECTED: Review of *Death and Nightingales,* by Eugene McCabe, *Spark* (Enniskillen, Ireland);

"At the Depot," *Fortnight Review,* 343 (October 1995): 24;

"Archer's Poison Arrows" [review of *Jeffrey Archer: Stranger Than Fiction,* by Michael Crick], *Fortnight,* 344 (November 1995): 34;

"The Taxi Driver's Story," *Fortnight,* 344 (November 1995): 28;

"The Garageman," *Fortnight,* no. 345 (December 1995): 24;

"A child of history" [review of *Unholy Ghosts,* by Ida Daly], *TLS: The Times Literary Supplement,* 1 March 1996, p. 24;

"Kat," *Fortnight,* no. 347 (March 1996): 28–29;

Review of *Camus: The First Man, Fortnight,* no. 347 (March 1996): 34–35.

"I have a narrative that makes some sort of sense of what happened." This sentence, taken from Carlo Gébler's memoir of his fraught relationship with his father, *Father and I* (2000), can be taken as a leitmotiv for his formidable body of novels: a catalogue of titles that has produced, out of the crosscurrents of intense personal feelings, family disorientation, and oppression, a study of the individual in the recent history of Europe and a powerful affirmation of the importance of the novel. Each of Gébler's books has been well reviewed and praised, though he still often receives the sort of critical attention–in terms of placement and length of reviews–accorded to "minor" novelists. Yet, critics have used such epithets as "hypnotic," "intriguing," and "compelling" to describe his novels. More important than these encomia, however, is the developing scope of his work as a whole. His experiments with time, cinematic use of imagery, and narrative voices drawn both from history and from across Europe constitute a major achievement. Above all, he explores the individual both within the domestic circle and as a determinate figure in society as a whole.

Karl Ernest Gébler was born on 21 August 1954 to forty-year-old novelist Adolphus Ernest Gébler and Edna O'Brien, an aspiring writer in her early twenties. Adolphus, known as Ernest, was the son of a Czech clarinetist, Adolph, whose itinerant engagements had landed him in Dublin, where he had married a local girl. The union of Ireland with continental Europe was a potent yet familiar cultural mix in Catholic Ireland. Ernest Gébler's own marriage–following his divorce from Leatrice Gilbert, his American wife–to O'Brien, a girl from the rural, traditionalist west of Ireland, affirmed a similarly idiosyncratic union.

Gébler, who was named after Karl Marx, curiously shared this forename with Ernest's firstborn, a son Leatrice had taken when she returned to the United States, whom Gébler did not meet for some forty years. His name was changed to Carlo during childhood by his mother and grandmother. In 1956 his younger brother, Sasha, was born, and two years later the family immigrated to England. Although Ernest continued writing, it was Edna who felt released into creative freedom and became the more successful of the two. In late 1962 the marriage ended, and for several years the boys lived with their father until, in late 1965, they went to live with their mother.

In September 1968 both were accepted as boarders at Bedales School in Hampshire, a liberal coeducational school that encouraged the arts and achieved good examination results. When in 1972 O'Brien was the subject of a television arts profile, Gébler, on the strength of a movie made for school, was commissioned to make a Super-8 insert for the program. From then on, television and movies not only launched his career but became inextricably part of his consciousness as a writer.

In 1973 Gébler went to York University to study English; his degree course included both the modern novel and Soviet cinema. Completing his studies with an upper second class degree in 1976, he went to the National Film School. While preparing his graduation movie, in Galway in the summer of 1978, he, by his own account, literally "stumbled" on the grave of William Joyce, "Lord Haw Haw." This notorious figure had broadcast to Britain on behalf of the Nazis during World War II, and after the war he was executed as a traitor. The incident led Gébler to other "traitors." A seaman, Stoker Rose, became the subject of the movie he wrote and directed called *Rating Notman* (1981), which was short-listed for the BAFTA (British Academy of Film and Television Awards) Film Award in 1983. Another subject, the Australian-born Irish novelists Francis Stuart, who wrote speeches for Joyce and

Dust jacket for the U.S. edition of Gébler's 1985 novel, about a ten-year-old boy's coming-of-age on his grandparents' farm in Ireland (Richland County Public Library)

also broadcast from Berlin, became both the subject of a movie as well as a friend. These particular narratives afforded Gébler the opportunity to explore the corrosiveness attendant on secrecy, bullying, and inflexibility in personal and social relationships. They prompted scrutiny of the Continental as well as the Irish part of his cultural heritage. During the 1970s and early 1980s Gebler flourished as both a producer and scriptwriter for movies and television. At the same time he also began to establish himself as a writer of reviews, articles, and stories for prestigious publications such as *Critical Quarterly, The Guardian,* the *Los Angeles Times, TLS: The Times Literary Supplement,* and *The Sunday Tribune.* From 1986 to 1987 he was the television critic for the *Times* (London) and from 1999 to 2000 he wrote a regular column for *Jazzwise.* At this time he writes regularly for *Fortnight Magazine,* in Belfast.

Married, Gebler lives with his wife Tyga and their five children in Enniskillen, Northern Ireland. As a well-established author he gives readings worldwide and runs creative-writing workshops; in addition, he has been writer-in-residence one day a week at Maghaberry, a category A prison. His commitment to writing and the arts as well as his outstanding achievements was recognized in 1990, at the early age of thirty-six, by election to Aosd'na (The Irish Academy). In May 1999 he was confirmed as a member of An Chomhairle Eala'on (The Irish Arts Council).

In the early 1980s *The Literary Review* published several of Gébler's short stories. One, about a young boy going to the races with his grandfather, was expanded into his first novel, *The Eleventh Summer,* published in 1985. Dedicated to his mother, it is a deceptively simple narrative of a boy's coming-of-age during a holiday in Ireland. Autobiographically based (both Gébler and his brother, Sasha, spent holidays with O'Brien's parents on their farm in Tuamgraney, County Clare), it culturally resonates with many children of Irish parents living in England who "went home" from urban England to relatives in rural Ireland. Gébler, the storyteller and image-maker, does more than simply reminisce, however, producing a densely textured account of personal and cultural clashes.

The prologue has the narrator, Paul Weismann, waking up as his dreams turn into reveries on the morning of his first planned return in twenty years. In the first chapter ten-year-old Paul goes to stay with his grandparents after his mother's death, which, it is hinted, might have been suicide. The family, in spite of the farm, are in straitened circumstances because of his grandfather's drinking and betting on horses. Because one horse, appositely named Green Fields, had refused to leave the starting line, large sums were lost and the old man went on a weeklong drunk. Chapter 1, the original short story, reprises Green Fields's story when Red River Rose collapses while leading and has to be shot. Paul cannot prevent his grandfather from going into a pub and getting obliterated on brandy. Granny's tears in the night that wake Paul alert readers to the secret territory of adult disappointment.

Three strands run through the novel: the story, Paul's physical perceptions and reactions, and his burgeoning inner life. Most important, it is the story of his beginnings as an artist. It also holds intimations of Ireland's transition from President Eamon de Valera's fantasies of poverty-stricken but happy Catholic peasantry into a modern country, the "Celtic tiger" of the European Common Market.

The story is rich in idiosyncratic characters, including Andy at the cottage; Mr. McKenna, who drives the grandfather; Joseph the farmhand; and Granny, who tries to hold things together and be a mother to Paul. Three characters dominate Paul's narrative, however: his grandfather, whose self-destructive willfulness and alcoholic binges give rise to images of a mythic Celtic twilight; Philomena, Paul's young cousin and the obscure object of his only partially understood desires; and his absent father, whose stern anti-Catholicism counterpoints the abiding rituals of Catholicism and whose arrival to take him home finally marks the passage into adulthood.

The grandfather is not only an important narrative force in the plot but is also the source of a major linking image between the young and adult Paul. He gives Paul £1, which he changes into pennies and puts in a jar. Later, he goes outside after lunch to find that the jar of pennies is gone. At the end of the chapter he looks in vain for faces in the clouds, but all he sees are clouds "moving like old-fashioned sailing ships across the blue, still sea." Metaphor has replaced anthropomorphism. Paul's capacity to see images does not disappear entirely, however. Under the stress of his grandfather coming home drunk after buying drinks for the harvesters, Paul imagines a serpent waiting "to leap out through grandfather's mouth and devour everyone in sight." In its way it does happen: the grandfather falls asleep with a lighted cigarette that burns the house down and kills him. After the funeral, "in the sky above, he noted with something like satisfaction, there was a cloud shaped like a winged snake which appeared to be floating away."

On Philomena's visits there is a mutual, secretive exploration of sexuality. At night Paul imagines undressing her. During his enforced bedrest after being thrown from a haywagon by a bolting horse, Paul is visited by Philomena. In an elaborate reconstruction of how she was once hypnotized, Paul engages in the game and persuades her to get into bed with him and take off her clothes. Lying naked on top of her, Paul shares with Philomena an intimation of the "secret" of what adults do together. The abiding impact of the scene is an innocent, delicate but clandestine, physical exploration mutually undertaken.

Some weeks after the conflagration a letter arrives from his father in England: an accusatory, logical, graceless letter announcing he is coming to take him home to England. Within Paul an inner hardness replaces his more gentle, susceptible self. He never sees Granny again–cards arrive at Christmas, from Granny and Philomena, but that summer has passed into a regretful memory. The epilogue telling of his return shows everything altered. Joseph, still child-like, is now working for the factory as well as farming in a small way and is married with six children. Philomena has gone to England. Granny died some years previously. The one thing that remains is the lost jar of pennies, which he finds. He determines to salvage his memories, as corroded as the pennies, and in the act of writing retrieve something of the lost self. "Paul is a wonderful narrator, completely believable because he is so earnest and smart and serious," wrote reviewer Roberta Smoodin in the *Los Angeles Times Book Review* (22 December 1985); Smoodin praised Gébler as "one of the most sensual fiction writers at work today. Though 'The Eleventh Summer' is only his first novel, his sensibility seems fully matured, rounded, rich."

In his second novel, *August in July* (1986), Gébler continues the theme of writing the past to recover self. The novel covers a year in the life of August Slemic, a Polish exile in late middle age, and writing is explored as a self-consciously psychotherapeutic act. The novel opens with August writing about his youthful desire to write and ends with his psychiatrist's letter affirming that "Any work of this kind helps to draw out the poison."

The narrative is simple and sentimental, covering the period from Christmas 1980 to New Year 1981, with the crucial episodes, his adultery and his wife's accidental death from a fall while he is out, occurring on the eve of Diana Spencer's wedding to Prince Charles in July. The most significant aspect of the novel is its portrayal of displacements: August trapped in his past, by wordplay trapped in July, exiled from his country and from the bright promise of love. Where Paul embraces writing intuitively, August recognizes it as a means of pretending his life is someone else's, thus putting a shape and form to it.

The richness of the novel lies in August's account of his memories, the vivid gallery of characters, and the subtle dialogues on the different aspects of love. Running through the novel are images that have autobiographical significance for Gébler himself and that evolve themes expressed in *The Eleventh Summer*. At the end of that novel Paul feels an inner rigidity forming; August, however, knows he has an emotional hardness he wants to overcome "to lose my casing: I would become a beautiful creature with whirring wings and a body the colour of petrol."

The novel starts on Boxing Day 1980 at August's home, with Eunice, his wife, and their son, Damien, visiting. There is evident irritation between father and son, who cannot be bothered to tune the clock radio he bought August for Christmas. Damien hurries away about his own concerns, and August goes to lie down but starts writing in the notebook Eunice bought for him. The complex and subtle treatment of time, which mirrors August's inner states rather than chronology, is signaled by the next chapter, which cuts to the eve of the royal wedding. It is an ordinary working day overshadowed by what the reader has learned of August's life. He and Eunice sleep in separate bedrooms, but he is courteous and concerned about her, adding poignancy to his proper but real emotional interest in his employee Emma.

The next chapter switches back to December 1980, launching a continuous rhythm between August's self-scrutiny through writing and his family and social life. This structure allows the exploration of a crucial memory of childhood to come halfway through the novel. On Sundays in Warsaw, August went with his mother to visit his Uncle Peter. On one occasion, when August was eleven years old, he wandered into his uncle's bedroom and saw his mother kneeling before Peter, engaged in oral sex. Though he does not fully understand it until later, the formation of the carapace has begun. At eighteen he leaves for England, deliberately without visiting his mother's grave, both culturally and emotionally displaced.

The denouement of the novel starts on the evening before the royal wedding. August goes to a party alone. He takes recently divorced Marjorie home; on the way a cat gets run over. After they spend the night together he goes home in spite of her wanting him to stay. His door is bolted and he cannot get in; neither can he wake his wife, so he goes to a phone box to wake her. August's efforts are in vain, however, as Eunice is dead from a fall. In the final chapter, set on Boxing Day 1981, August learns that Eunice had been having an affair: "The days grew shorter and my soul grew darker."

Reviews of this novel included reservations–"This is a meticulous study, done with great sympathy," wrote Martin Seymour-Smith in the *Financial Times* (22 March 1986). "The problem is that its low-keyedness too often becomes mere banality." There were also more positive evaluations, such as Christopher Wordsworth's in *The Guardian* (24 April 1986): "In his second novel . . . Carlo Gébler develops a sensitive talent and brings off something quite unusual by writing about a glum and boring character in an interesting way, style, organisation, and insight doing the trick."

In his next novel, *Work and Play* (1987), Gébler's protagonist is Fergus Maguire, a young Irishman moving between Ireland and England. Again the novel experiments, this time with a straightforward linear narrative exposition but with a series of mainly short chapters. Fergus is trying to live, to throw off addiction, paranoia, and alienation: as *The Sunday Times* review put it, "a mirror of our times." While it is that, in its sensitivity to the nuances of everyday relationships it is also part of Gébler's continuing inquiry into the implications of the personal within social contexts.

At the beginning of the novel Fergus, a university dropout, is living in the Irish countryside, cleaning himself up from drug addiction. He goes to the family home in Bray with its view over Dublin Bay. His relationship with his mother is easy, if deferential on her part. His father, however, is unkind and dismissive of him.

When Fergus and his father go together to the beach, his father has a heart attack, later dying in hospital. Their relationship and its effects on Fergus continue after his father's death, however. Circumstances are aggravated by the father's will, which disinherits him in favor of his sister. He returns to England and his former circle of friends.

The novel portrays Fergus in his accommodation, at work and at play with friends and acquaintances. Each situation generates a subplot that reveals aspects of Fergus as he struggles to reach some kind of wholeness and authenticity in himself. In the flat below his live an Asian family, the Singhs, who are being terrorized by the National Front. They seem churlishly uncooperative when he goes to the police on their behalf, and the police do nothing anyway. Later that night there is a fire in their flat, and he tries to rescue them but collapses in the smoke. Mrs. Singh and her two sons die. The whole incident reveals the nature of cruelty but also of thoughtlessness and incomprehension arising from lack of readiness to understand.

The only writing Fergus does is to answer the letters sent to International Television, the company he works for, in the course of which he comes by a copy of a book titled *The Torture Papers,* published by the writer, Mr. Wiggins, himself. The paranoid fantasies, described in enumerative physical detail and of which readers are given an example, could be a parody of his father's writing. Wiggins pursues him about having a movie made of the book. The revelation that ensues is that all people think of themselves as the center of life. Fergus reminisces about his father and realizes he must move forward and escape his preoccupations. His friends give him the context in which to realize he is the only one who can make sense of his life. He has to rescue himself through thought for others, lack of self-centeredness, and love.

Through Laura, his girlfriend from school, he meets Jennifer. On an evening out the girls strip in a restaurant, high on drink and drugs. Fergus saves them all from arrest by swallowing a packet of cocaine but gets involved with Curry, a policeman, who tries to turn him into an informer. When he avoids the issue the police later plant drugs in his flat: he discovers them and destroys them before the raid. It transpires that Jennifer had told the police what happened–the restaurant incident was the direct cause of his persecution. By understanding why she implicated him, and by accepting that his sister, Pippa, will not share the inheritance, he frees himself, realizing what the alternative would be: "Each time April came there'd be a little less hope and joy and a little more reproach and regret."

Reviewer Jay Parini, writing in the *Los Angeles Times* (15 May 1988), commented on this conclusion: "The novel ends with an explicit moral, with Fergus understanding that he must exercise his freedom: 'He knew now what the penalties would be if he didn't.' One cringes, slightly, when a novelist makes a 'point' so nakedly. But one accepts it from this writer because one accepts everything else in his wonderfully unassuming realistic novel."

In 1988 Gébler published a book of travel and observations, *Driving through Cuba: An East-West Journey,* and in the next year he published the first of his children's books, *The T.V. Genie.* His next adult fiction, *Malachy and His Family* (1990), marks what might be considered the end of his first phase as a novelist and the beginning of the second. The early novels concentrated on the inner lives of the narrators. In this novel Malachy comes from the United States to meet the British family he has never known, including a younger half brother, also named Malachy, and a half sister, Eva. The situation has autobiographical echoes of Gébler and his American older brother. In an interview with Gébler for the 28 January 1990 edition of *The Times* (London), Paddy Burt called it "a potent package wrapped in innocuous-looking paper."

Dust jacket for the U.S. edition of Gébler's 1987 novel, in which a recovering drug addict attempts to come to terms with his dismissive father's death (Richland County Public Library)

Malachy, like the earlier narrators, writes about his responses to his new family, but the responses are contingent on the new rather than the familiar. Furthermore, readers' perceptions have been shaped by the British Malachy, who uses his half brother's diary for a college project titled "Home." He adds background on their forebears that his half brother was not in a position to know. The O'Neill family brings together two twentieth-century histories, father John Michael's Irish history and mother Teresa's Hungarian background.

The narrative is simple: Malachy meets his new-found family, comes to stay with them, and joins in family events and activities. His feelings for his half sister, Eva, develop into a sexual love, with attendant guilt, and tragedy ensues. Gébler generates complexity out of the histories of his father and stepmother. Moreover, incidental background and vignettes give tone and moral force to the narrative.

When Malachy arrives at the airport his treatment by immigration officials differs markedly from that of a French-speaking couple trying to get to see their son at Keele University. They are black and are refused entry: prejudice and petty tyranny are continually exposed in Gébler's books. On the train station platform Malachy questions a Mr. Shrotton about his trainspotting, the compulsion he has followed from childhood that has yielded eighty-five notebooks of train numbers. His answer, that it is in the genes, launches the major theme of the book; as Eva says, "I think . . . all the bad which happens stays in the blood."

According to the British Malachy's research, John-Michael's maternal grandfather was driven from his ten-acre farm with his family by armed constables acting with indifferent brutality. The humiliation and sense of failure led to drunkenness and bullying. One of the daughters, Margaret, married Walter O'Neill and "When Walter drank Walter was a killer." John-Michael is caught in a double bind: his mother surely cannot love his violent father, but she does not love her children enough to leave him. John-Michael's life became "binges alternating with periods of sobriety, just like his father before him." Malachy's mother Teresa's Hungarian past covers the history of central Europe from the end of World War I. The focus of her background story is her intelligent mother, Maria, through whom readers get a woman's perspective on events. Maria marries an idealistic young printer, Stephen Gara. Her response to life is not unlike John-Michael's: dogged practicality with occasional outbursts of frustrated rage. At the time of the Soviet invasion of what is now Czechoslovakia the disappointed Stephen throws himself under a tram. Teresa had already immigrated to England at the time of the Hungarian uprising in 1956. On Eva's twenty-first birthday the family goes to an airfield for a birthday flight. Eva dances across the tarmac, running into a spinning propeller blade.

In his early novels Gébler writes from the point of view of male protagonists confronting and responding to occasions of personal disillusion by a retreat into a self-protective shell. Eventually they realize that to live they must break out of the shell. In order to rescue themselves they try to objectify their distress by writing or, like Fergus in *Work and Play,* by accepting love. In *Life of a Drum* (1991) the narrator is a woman, Catherine Janovsky née Baring, hanging on to a lower-middle-class existence. Her diffident spirit tumbles through life: as Catherine's prologue puts it, "Life's a series of blows. What is it Rudi used to say? 'What is born a drum is beaten till death.'"

In the prologue Catherine is lying in bed, her lover is downstairs talking to a former lover, and she is musing on how she got into the present relationship. The final chapter takes up this issue again, and after three predictable answers, a fourth reason is offered—not so much an answer as a defining happy memory of her father, who left when she was a young child. They were at a pub on a sunny day, and her father made a daisy chain for her mother, which Catherine eventually took and threw into a wishing well. Her wish was that her father could stay home with her and her sister. When her father learns the true explanation his anger evaporates. "My dad called me to him and lifted me on to his lap. I put my head against his chest and he stroked my hair." Magic and dreams in Gébler's books give way to defining physical moments.

The foreground narrative in the novel is Catherine's "surprisingly happy" arranged marriage to Rudi, a Polish immigrant who wants to stay in Britain and is willing to pay £2000 for a marriage of convenience. Catherine has been working for fourteen years for a firm of importers. Her itinerary from Tehran to Beirut to Nicosia to Riyadh, mostly driven by geopolitical upheavals, ends with her return to England at age thirty-four. She accepts the proposition partly for the money, partly out of passivity; in the end accepting Rudi but refusing his money. Rudi gets a job in airport security, supplementing their income by "liberating" small quantities of goods from the warehouse and selling them. She falls in love with him and he with her. They are about to go on holiday when he dies of a heart attack.

The main part of the novel is her trepidation at coping with the funeral and realizing that Rudi has left what to her are huge debts of about £3000. Above everything is her grief. Finally she tries to start her life again, borrowing money from a former lover, Claus, who runs an art gallery, and to sustain the chance relationship she has struck up with Johnnie. Counterpointing these events are memories of formative experiences with her father: she learned "Never to expect too much. Never get promises from those you love. Take what you get and ask for nothing more." Set against the resigned melancholy, however, is the retrieval of the memory, in the final chapter, of sitting on her father's knee in the pub garden in the sun. Experience that can be so harmful can also be positive. Robert Nye, writing in *The Guardian* (21 February 1991), commented briefly on *Life of a Drum:* "This has a shrewd edge, and a faithfulness in its working out of the conversation between the heroine and her modern London environment, which make it attractive. Gébler knows what he is trying to do, and does it without fuss." In *The Independent* (23 February 1991) Richard Burns called Catherine "a triumph of the plausible" and her story "a triumph of the small scale."

In the year *Life of a Drum* was published, 1991, Gébler's father, whose approbation he had sought in vain, had a bad fall and had to be settled in a nursing home. That same year Gébler also published a nonfiction book, *The Glass Curtain: Inside an Ulster Community,* engaging the problems of that troubled community.

In his next novel, *The Cure* (1994)–following another children's book, *The Witch That Wasn't* (1991)–Gébler returns to the rural Ireland of his first novel. It features the same lyricism, introspection, and portrayal of characters' aspirations, as well as the cruelty and desperation. Critical reaction frequently noted the negative light *The Cure* casts on rural Ireland, although Gébler also evinces a deep understanding of the individual as an actor, for better or worse, in the social group. Furthermore, he answers the question of why so many of his damaged protagonists have sought some kind of salvation through writing their own stories.

The central narrative incident is based on a true crime committed in rural Ireland, near Clonmel, at the end of the nineteenth century. Bridget Cleary, wife of Michael, falls ill and does not readily recover. Believing her to be possessed by fairies, he resorts to herbalism and magic rites, finally burning her to death in their own cottage. Various neighbors and relatives participate in the crime, and Cleary is sentenced to twenty years penal servitude. Novelist Tibor Fischer, writing in the *Financial Times* (12 November 1994), judged that it was "a tribute to Gébler's skill that this climactic immolation seems inevitable."

Gébler, however, places his first acquaintance with the story in an incident from childhood. Jim Christie, somewhat autobiographical, as with Paul Weismann in *The Eleventh Summer,* goes back to Ireland with his father. They visit Mr. Egan, a ninety-five-year-old former member of the Royal Irish Constabulary who was based in Drangan, Tipperary, and witnessed the crime firsthand. He shows father and son his cuttings and notebooks and tells the story over a couple of days. The father borrows the notebooks and never returns them. This story is framed in its turn by a more recent incident: the death and cremation of the narrator's father and his discovery of the notebooks in an old Jacob's Biscuits tin.

The objectivity of the policeman's notes is supplemented by the interpretive views and choices of the narrator, who is influenced by his own childhood. "It's because of what's happened to an author that a book gets written, not the social circumstances. All fiction is autobiography." This summation in the epilogue leads the reader back to the prologue and permeates any subsequent reflection on the story with the presence of the storytellers. Gébler offers fictions that incorporate the mixture of motives and emotions that occur in life, validating them with his own narratorial presence. The main story sketches incidents from the lives of the two main characters, Bridget and Michael. Bridget learned at school, where she was bullied, that resistance can give way to resignation. Michael, whose mother was ill and taken to the hospital without his knowledge, was left without explanation because of his father's silence. When she did return, and he asked where she had been, his father's terse response "up in Kearney's," the local site of a falbed fairy fort, only confirmed his belief in fairy deception, power, and wickedness. Their inclinations are confirmed by adult experience of overt and covert social forces. Social hierarchy and rational order are maintained by Dr. Crean, the local medical practitioner, by the police, and by the Catholicism of Father Ryan. The hidden world, which fails the infertile Bridget, is promoted by Mrs. Whelan, the local wisewoman who uses her fairy power to help the infertile, and by Dennis Ganey, the herb doctor (as his name translates from the Irish). For the superstitious the covert world of malign forces is the more real, with fatal consequences.

The powerful climax is when Michael douses Bridget in paraffin and sets her aflame; the burning of Bridget takes place over an evening and the following day. The point of view moves from participant to participant, all of whom are drawn into Michael's dark pathological vision. The sequence ends with the main participants standing at night around the fairy ring of Kilnagranagh Hill calling in vain for Bridget to come out. The story ends with Bridget being buried in unsanctified ground with only a few onlookers and the police present.

Avoiding anticlimax, the last chapter sums up the aftermath in notes from Egan's notebooks. There is an epilogue, however, in which the narrator recalls his mother's death. Finally, as an adult, he reflects on why he has written down the story: "Another person's suffering and death–that is the principal thread. . . . the weight of a human life is incalculable."

In the 24 November 1994 edition of *The Times* (London), David Park called *The Cure* "a powerful exploration of a primitive and insular society, trapped in a cleft between superstition and science, burdened by poverty and harboring both self-loathing and a repressed sexuality. Gébler beds the novel in the convincing and concrete reality of daily existence and writes in a clear and unassuming style, evoking an indifferent landscape and the lives which looked to it for sustenance." Fischer summed it up as "First rate, but not a book likely to be promoted by the Irish Tourist Board."

A book of short stories, *W.9. & Other Lives* (1996), followed and then a young person's book, *Frozen Out: A*

Dust jacket for the U.S. edition of Gébler's 1998 historical novel, about the members of a secret terrorist society in Northern Ireland (Richland County Public Library)

Tale of Betrayal and Survival (1998), in which a young woman, Phoebe, faces sectarianism in Northern Ireland. *Frozen Out* coincides with Gébler's next novel, *How to Murder a Man* (1998). Another historical novel, it inquires into the effects of experience on the individual, the impact of character on society, and above all the potential of storytelling to help understanding. In a detached, controlled voice Gébler recounts a world pervaded by barbaric cruelties and dialogues frequently informed by cunning, desire for control, and terror.

There is an almost Dickensian array of characters, many with their own mixture of both good and evil. Rody Donohoe, a hired assassin, is a brutal murderer but is caring in his relationship with his lover Geraldine and her three children and finally, by his own lights, dignified in execution. Croker Flanagan, a simple-minded giant, is bullying and, in his naive way, religious. The central characters are Thomas French, the new agent for the Beatonboro' estates, and Issac Marron, an estate tenant, also leader of the Ribbonmen, a secret terrorist society. The story of a pair of lovers, Tim Traynor and Kitty McKenna, intersects with the conflict between French and Marron.

The aim of the Ribbonmen is control of society on their own terms. Among their chief objectives is the preservation of tenants' rights, rights by which a tenant could sell succession to his holding. French is trying to get the estate on its feet again with a proposal that tenants in arrears get these arrears paid off by returning the land to the estate. Any money made from auctioning their goods and cattle they keep, and in addition he pays passage to the United States for themselves and their families, where they can make a new debt-free start.

Kitty is the only daughter of tenant farmers who pay their way. Tim, orphaned in his teens, has an acre of poor land, the earnings from which he supplements by doing odd jobs around the estate. Kitty's parents do not see him as a suitable match, and the two are parted. The loss of their joyful eroticism and natural celebration is more acutely felt since it has existed in the midst of brutality. Tim goes to Marron to join the Ribbonmen and achieve a sense of power to offset his frustration. He is accepted since he works in French's garden and is in an ideal position to observe Fernch's routine, so pointing the way for the assassins.

The novel is a metaphor for any terrorist-dominated society. Being one of the terrorists gives power to the powerless, but in the need for secrecy, it takes away individuality, releasing more primitive responses. When Tim attacks Croker with a spade for letting his goats trample his acre, he is acting out of character. He is sought by the constabulary and also blamed by Marron for drawing attention to himself. The lovers are reunited, but when they try to escape the situation for the United States they are executed by the Ribbonmen. Gillian Fairchild, writing in *The Daily Telegraph* (16 May 1998), observed: "The story indicates that violence in Northern Ireland is passed from generation to generation. Is the author therefore also denying the likelihood of a lasting peace? His unpleasant but powerfully memorable book undoubtedly invites that interpretation."

The reader is told a good deal about French, his relationship with his wife, his diligence in his work, and his compassion. About Marron, Gébler offers nothing other than his pedestrian sense of order, both in habits and relationships. Only through dialogue does he provide a sense of Marron's terrifying perception of others' weaknesses, the source of his power. In the final confrontation between him and French, the human wins out over the fanatic. As French and Micky Laffin, the bailiff, sit like two characters from Samuel Beckett at the end, however, the reader recognizes there is no ending, only the continuous struggle against inhumanity.

In the same year *How to Murder a Man* was published, Gébler adapted August Strindberg's *Dödsdansen* (1901; first translated as *The Dance of Death,* 1912) for the Tricycle Theatre in London by changing the setting to a British army camp in the west of Ireland from 1913 to 1916. His interest in Strindberg has accompanied the added depth his dialogue has acquired, particularly in *The Cure* and *How to Murder a Man.* It may not be irrelevant that Strindberg's preface to *Fröken Julie* (Miss Julie, 1888) laid out a project for development of character that included all kinds of motivations: physical, emotional, and mental as well as chance, a facet that Gébler has added to his sensitivity to dreams, myths, and visual perception.

Gébler's memoir of his relationship with his father, *Father and I,* is honest and uncompromising in its scrutiny of both himself and of his perceptions and feelings toward his father. It is equally honest in its appraisal of his father's behavior, written in full awareness that others do not necessarily share his views.

The strengths of Carlo Gébler's writing are moral seriousness, deft style, and subtle analysis of the interplay of historical forces and individual predispositions. Reviewing *How to Murder a Man* and *W.9. & Other Lives* in *The Observer* (19 April 1998), Sylvia Brownrigg summed up many of the best qualities of his fiction: "Gébler's stories are understated, with a stylish humility. . . . He is not afraid of explicit, rather old-fashioned conclusions. . . . Gébler's characters are often moving in their stumbling attempts at love, their lunges towards marriage. . . . Gébler's adeptness at emotional nuance enriches his quiet tales." Focusing particularly on *How to Murder a Man,* she writes, "Gébler works well with the conventions of historical fiction, and travels with confidence between the different figures in his story." Park, in his review of *The Cure,* observed that he "has demonstrated an imaginative and subtle understanding of the complexities of Irish society. Where others attempt to focus on the big picture and succeed only in the reproduction of cliché, Gébler . . . often arrives at compassionate insight through approaching his subject matter from oblique angles."

Interviews:

Paddy Burt, "Keeping the Black Dog at Bay," *Times* (London), 28 January 1990;

Sally Weale, "Real Lives: In the Name of the Father," *Guardian,* 19 September 2000, Features section, p. 4.

Joanne Harris

(3 July 1964 –)

Merritt Moseley
University of North Carolina at Asheville

BOOKS: *The Evil Seed* (London: Warner, 1992);
Sleep, Pale Sister (London: Arrow, 1994);
Chocolat (London: Doubleday, 1999; New York: Viking, 1999);
Blackberry Wine (London: Doubleday, 2000; New York: Morrow, 2000);
Five Quarters of the Orange (London: Doubleday, 2001; New York: Morrow, 2001);
Coastliners (London: Doubleday, 2002; New York: Morrow, 2002).

SELECTED PERIODICAL PUBLICATION–UNCOLLECTED: "The Two of Me: As an Anglo-French Child in 1960s Yorkshire, Joanne Harris, the bestselling author of *Chocolat,* Had to Cope with Constant Prejudice–and the Nickname Froggy," *Sunday Telegraph,* 24 February 2002, p. 1.

When Joanne Harris followed two obscure early novels with *Chocolat* (1999), she suddenly made herself into one of the most celebrated of contemporary English novelists. That novel became a best-seller and in 2000 was made into a successful motion picture; moreover, it gathered interest and even love among readers–a majority of them women–attracted by the author's combination of sensuous evocativeness, particularly of French life; powerful and perhaps somewhat old-fashioned plotting; and touches of the supernatural. In the three years following the publication of *Chocolat* she has published a novel each year. The first three have been called the "food trilogy," both because their titles mention food and drink and because Harris is concerned with food and describes it artfully. Harriet Lane, in an interview for *BBC News Online* (14 March 2002), referred to her as the inventor of "gastromance." Her 2002 novel, *Coastliners,* is not unconcerned with food but shifts scene–to another part of France–and perceptibly darkens the overall mood, perhaps in a move back toward her early Gothic fiction. Lane aptly sums up her work so far: "quirky, sensuous books set in the French countryside." Her popularity has brought some easy dismissal of her works which, according to literary editor Boyd Tonkin (*The Independent,* 15 April 2001), "straddle the literary and popular ends of the trade."

Joanne Harris (photograph by Adine Sagalyn/Agence Opale; from the dust jacket for the U.S. edition of Five Quarters of the Orange, *2001)*

Joanne Michele Sylvie Short was born on 3 July 1964 in Barnsley, South Yorkshire. Both her parents, Robert and Jeannette Short, were teachers; her English grandparents ran a sweetshop, and she lived above it for the first few years of her life. She was an only child until age ten, and this fact, she told Catherine Deveney in *Scotland on Sunday* (4 March 2001), "made her introverted and quite solitary. 'I didn't necessarily get on very well with other kids because I didn't have the means of communicating with them. I read enormously and lived in a fantasy world for years, virtually all the time. Everything was imagination.'" She was educated at Wakefield Girls' High School and Barnsley Sixth Form College, then read modern and medieval languages at St. Catherine's College, Cambridge. She had met her future husband, Kevin Harris, during her sixth-form year, as a result of some graffiti scrawled on her school desk. They played in a rock band together at college and married in 1991. He is a freelance land researcher; they have one child, daughter Anouchka.

After graduating, Harris had a brief career in accountancy, then took a teacher training course. For ten years she taught modern languages at Leeds Grammar School, while writing fiction. The success of *Chocolat* permitted her to give up her teaching job. She continues to live in Barnsley (to the evident surprise of her frequent interviewers, who seem to expect her to move either to France or to London, which she disdains). Her high visibility–perhaps even more associated with the movie version of *Chocolat* than with any of her books–seems not to have changed her much, as she continues to write steadily. Although she has professed satisfaction with the motion picture of *Chocolat,* despite some changes that she thought either "dumbed it down" or removed potential sources of offensiveness (for instance, making the most obstructive character a village mayor rather than a Catholic priest), she has expressed plans to adapt *Coastliners* for the screen. As Lane reported, she is also working on another novel, which she describes as "a tale of witchcraft, dancing and nuns in seventeenth century France. 'It's a sort of habit ripper,' she says."

The most important biographical fact about Harris is her dual nationality and cultural heritage. Her father met her mother while on an educational exchange in France and brought her, a native of Brittany, back to live in Yorkshire. Harris grew up half-French and half-English. There were disadvantages: she was routinely called "Froggy" as an insulting anti-French nickname, and she felt estranged from her schoolmates and other Barnsleyites. On the other hand, she learned French like a native, so that she had some difficulty understanding how other people could only speak one language (she still speaks French with her daughter); and she spent summers with her mother's family in France. Her long immersion in France and French life (including, alongside frequent visits, her mother's French cookery) has laid the groundwork for her fiction. Though she says that Italian admirers have urged her to set a novel in Italy, she writes about the culture she knows, either firsthand or through family stories.

Julian Barnes, who also writes extensively about France, partly because he came to love it on childhood trips with his parents (also teachers), comments perceptively in his *Something to Declare* (2002): "Knowing a second country means choosing what you want from it, finding antitheses to your normal, English, urban life; discarding the sense of responsibility you feel about your own country, giving yourself a rest from the bilious emotions stirred by your own public representatives." Barnes goes on to specify that (similar to Harris) "My partial France is provincial in topography and contrarian in spirit; a France of the regions rather than the centre, of José Bové rather than sleek-suited Eurocrat, of Cathar martyr rather than papal legate." Harris, too, has been accused of sentimentalizing France, though her inclusion of–for instance–anti-Gypsy violence, anti-Semitism, and wartime collaboration with the Nazi occupiers hardly expresses a determination to idealize the French.

Harris's first two novels are set in England. *The Evil Seed* (1992) is a vampire novel. Its setting is Cambridge, and there are elements of a typical "student novel," though, as Kevin Patrick Mahoney wrote on the website *AuthorTrek,* Cambridge makes for an ideal location: "it is absolutely the right place for her shadowy monsters to remain hidden in plain view, since there are always new faces each year." Readers who know that Harris studied languages at Cambridge will be surprised neither by the setting nor by the range of literary and artistic references that decorate *The Evil Seed,* most of them having to do with the Pre-Raphaelite Brotherhood. Mahoney declared it "Harris' most carnivalesque book. I don't think it's the blood and guts which frightens you, it's just that the prose makes your heart beat with so much adrenaline, so much pace, that your senses are liable to be heightened."

Mahoney, who maintains a comprehensive website on Harris (www.geocities.com/SoHo/Nook/1082/joanne_harris_page.html), calls her next novel, *Sleep, Pale Sister* (1994), "a quite complex work" and a "rare and bloody fiction." Set in the nineteenth century, it carries allusions to C. L. Dodgson (Lewis Carroll), particularly in the suggestions of pedophilia hidden beneath her protagonist Henry Paul Chester's paintings of young girls, and to art critic John Ruskin, whose failed marriage is invoked by the name Euphemia, or Effie, given to Chester's favored model. *Sleep, Pale Sister* is a Gothic romance, complete with dark secrets, laudanum addiction, and the whiff of anti-Catholicism familiar from the English Gothic tradition. Harris told Marla Addison in an interview for the website *CountryBookshop,* "My first books were much closer to category

Dust jacket for the U.S. edition of Harris's 1999 novel, in which a French village is transformed after a free-spirited woman opens a chocolate shop (Richland County Public Library)

fiction than my recent ones. At the time I was aiming for a kind of literary horror/gothic genre, but my publishers had difficulty marketing them. Predictably they ended up in the horror section, largely unread. . . . I'm still fond of my early books, though; I'm glad I wrote them, and in spite of their faults, I'd love to see them in print again."

Exasperated by her husband's attention to a televised soccer match, Harris asked him what women do as obsessively as men watch football; his answer–"eating chocolate"–is credited with giving her the idea for her next novel. Five years divided *Sleep, Pale Sister* from *Chocolat,* and in that time Harris moved from the Gothic genre to something like magic realism. She also found her métier in writing about France. The reaction of readers to *Chocolat* was markedly different, too. It sold slowly at first but then became more popular as a result of word of mouth. One of the publicists for the movie version, as quoted by John Arlidge in *The Observer* (24 September 2000), said, "'People started talking about it and one day you walked on to a train and there were loads of people–mainly women–reading it.' As its popularity grew, one reviewer asked, 'Is this the best book ever written?'" It was likewise recognized by the critical establishment, being nominated for the Whitbread Prize for best novel.

Chocolat is an example of "cloistral fiction"–the kind of novel in which a closed system, usually a small town, is changed by the irruption into it of an outside force (other examples are Mark Twain's *The Mysterious Stranger,* 1916, and Harris's favorite book, Emily Brontë's *Wuthering Heights,* 1847). In this case the closed system is the French village of Lansquenet in the region of Lot-et-Garonne; the outside force is Vianne Rocher, a mysterious woman who arrives, accompanied by her daughter, Anouk, and opens a chocolate shop on the main square. That she arrives on Shrove Tuesday; that she is studiedly indifferent to religion and the whitewashed church across the square; that she is an unmarried mother; that her treats constitute a threat to the parishioners' Lenten deprivations; and that she announces her plans for a grand "Festival du Chocolat," to be celebrated on Easter Sunday, bring her into conflict with the town's embittered and twisted priest, Père Francis Reynaud. The battle lines are drawn: between Roman Catholicism and paganism (Vianne is the daughter of a witch, reads tarot cards, and celebrates magic), between intolerance and life-affirming acceptance.

Michèle Roberts, another half-French novelist who writes in English about France and religion, is an interesting commentator on Harris's work. In *The Independent* (24 February 2001) she argued that the "simplistic Catholic split" of Harris's childhood "lives on, of course, in the form of oppositions between men and women, good and evil, body and spirit. Joanne Harris's novel *Chocolat* depicted a French village reenacting them. Harris reverses the oppositions, so that to the sympathetic reader, the female chocolate-maker is Good and the repressive male priest is Bad. The struggle is between the pagan forces of darkness, or dark chocolate, and heavenly light." The town, and the book, are divided, perhaps too schematically, into good and bad. The good are, generally speaking, the poor in spirit, the downtrodden (abused wives, Gypsies), lonely old men, most women, and joyous misfits. The bad are the priest and the priest-ridden and the anxious bourgeoisie.

The alternating narrators are Vianne and the priest, Reynaud, who is tormented both by his own weaknesses and by a secret sin. His accounts make it clear that he is not just against sin and enjoyment but, in some deep way, against life: gardening in the churchyard, he finds that

> So many scents disturb me. I would like orderly rows of shrubs and flowers, perhaps with a box hedge around the whole. This profusion seems somehow wrong, irreverent, a savage thrusting of life, one plant choking another in a vain attempt at dominance. . . . as I dig and prune and cut, the serried green armies simply fill the spaces at my back, pushing out long green tongues of derision at my efforts.

The colorfully populated cast includes, as one of its most important representatives, Armande, an aging widow who refuses to behave respectably, shocking her daughter Caro, a prissy middle-class wife and one of the most implacable opponents of Vianne's La Celeste Praline. (The clash between an old but still vital person and his or her uptight and materialistic children is a theme Harris returns to several times.) Armande is contemptuous of her daughter but naturally allied to Vianne and Anouk and, later, the Gypsies who visit the village with unfortunate consequences. As readers will expect, Vianne changes Lansquenet, lightening its drab life with her brilliant confections (vividly described by Harris) and their overt sensuousness–for instance, a delicacy called "nipples of Venus." As the novel ends, she is moving along to work her magic elsewhere, thinking, "The wind smells of the sea, of ozone and frying, of the seafront at Juan-les-Pins, of pancakes and coconut oil and charcoal and sweat. So many places waiting for the wind to change. So many needy people."

Reviews of *Chocolat* were mixed: Roberts criticized the writing as "unremarkable, often loose and unfocused," but said that it "rises to poetry when different kinds of sweeties are named and precision is called for." Lucasta Miller, in *The Independent* (21 March 1999), decried the pathos; Ron Charles, writing in the *Christian Science Monitor* (21 January 1999), regretted "Vianne's dalliance with the occult." Nevertheless, he said this "high-calorie fantasy is a strange blend of romance and feminism. Your sweetheart will think you're gallant and politically correct all at the same time," and called it "perfect light fare for a romantic winter night." Others who praised the book sometimes did so in condescending ways, often using gustatory metaphors: "*Chocolat* is made of spun sugar," Janice Harayda wrote in *Newsday;* one of the strongest reviews, by Kit Spring in *The Observer* (11 April 1999), ended: "Vianne is such a life-affirming character, and the book is full of colour, tastes and scents, that as you are lured on by the plot and the wonderful descriptions, your senses are left reeling. This novel is a celebration of pleasure, of love, of tolerance. Read it. But only if you're not on a diet."

Reviewers seemed less keen about *Blackberry Wine* (2000). Perhaps this was an example of the common reaction against an author's follow-up to a widely celebrated novel. There are many reminders of *Chocolat.* The main French setting is again Lansquenet, and some characters return; there are magical occurrences, including a revenant dead man; again food and drink are important, and lovingly described; and the story is of regeneration and renewal. Unlike the renewal of the village and its people in *Chocolat, Blackberry Wine* concerns the renewal of a desiccated man.

Yorkshireman Jay Mackintosh is a writer of one book, called *Three Summers with Jackapple Joe;* now he is blocked, dissatisfied with his girlfriend and his students in a writing class. He suddenly buys an old house in Lansquenet, moves there, and becomes a part of the village. He also begins to cultivate the land. There he is visited by the spirit of Jackapple Joe, a retired miner on whom Jay based his novel. Joe is a wise heart, a natural healer, and a sort of benevolent fairy godfather presiding over Jay's rebirth. As in *Chocolat,* there is a clear and relatively Romantic scale of values: nature, the country, poor people, and traditional ways are good; high culture, London, modern innovations, and efforts to simulate tradition are bad.

The most unusual feature of this novel is its narrative posture. Though Mackintosh is the protagonist, the narrator is a bottle of wine. "Fleurie, 1962," the last bottle remaining in a case of twelve laid down in the year of Jay's birth, listens from the cellar and relates, in a perky style, what happens. The reasons for this choice are not immediately obvious, and, since Fleurie knows what Jay is thinking–is, in effect, an omniscient narrator–the implications of it are fudged. The questionable narratological logic was criticized by some reviewers, along with other improbabilities involving rail connections and French property law. Details of verisimilitude, of course, are irrelevant in a novel that turns on practical magic, whose plot is spurred by a spirit from the dead. Susannah Herbert, writing in the *Daily Telegraph* (26 February 2000), summed up:

> Essentially, this is a novel for those who feel there must be more to modern fiction than "black single mothers and Glaswegian dope addicts and gratuitously using the word 'fark.'" This *cri de coeur* is Jay's, screamed at a classful of earnest young London creative-writing students as he prepares his escape to Lansquenet–but it might just as well have come from Harris, who patently shares her hero's belief that stories without "magic" do not count as stories at all.

Dust jacket for the U.S. edition of Harris's 2000 novel, narrated by a bottle of wine (Richland County Public Library)

Roberts (one of those who detected improbabilities in the stipulations about French life in the novel), wrote in *The Independent* (12 March 2000), "Best read as romance or fairy-tale, the story offers a heart-warming myth of creativity, identity and love that's perhaps a little too sugary if you like your wines full-bodied and dry."

The following year Harris published *Five Quarters of the Orange:* again set in France, again with a title referring to food. This novel is a step in a different direction, however. With a firmer historical positioning (1942, in Occupied France) and set in a different region of France–the village of Les Laveuses, on the Loire, near Angers–it also delves into darker matters. It cannot be accused of being sugary.

Actually, though wartime is central to the novel, it occupies two different time periods, between which the narrative alternates. In the present, the elderly Framboise Dartigen (now widowed and going under the name Francoise Simon) has returned to Les Laveuses, unrecognized by its inhabitants, and bought and restored her old family home. She has two surviving siblings: elder brother Cassis, who inherited the house but has lost his money and sells it to her, and elder sister Reine-Claude, or Reinette, who has been a prostitute in Montmartre and is now institutionalized. Framboise has two adult daughters, Pistache and Noisette. Most troublingly, she has a nephew, Cassis's son Yannick, who along with his wife, Laure Dessange, a food writer, torments her and eventually brings about the exposure of her secret past.

The present-day story includes her establishment of a small creperie, where she becomes successful by serving dishes based on her mother's recipes. She has inherited her mother's journal, which includes both her recipes and a disjointed narrative of events in her life in the 1940s. Framboise's main ally is Paul Hourias, a childhood friend who she believes no longer remembers her. Her nephew and niece discover where she is, pursue her for her recipes, encourage their son to damage her business, make veiled demands for her property, and threaten to reveal her secrets. They are the sort of yuppies, hungry for property development and fashion and impatient of old people and tradition, who constitute the villains in several of Harris's novels. By means of revived memory, a gradual interpretation of her mother's writings, and a growing intimacy with Paul, Framboise reconstructs the events of 1942 that made her family outcasts in Les Laveuses.

The central event was the execution of ten villagers in retaliation for the murder of a German soldier. The connection of the Dartigens with that event was complicated and included the collaboration of all three children with the German occupiers, an equivocal relationship between their mother and the dead soldier, and a complex relationship, generally, between the French and the Nazis. The soldier was Tomas Leibniz; Framboise idolized him, loved him even, while Cassis and Reinette became entangled with him in different ways. They both wanted luxuries–cigarettes, movie magazines–and in return for them they passed on information about their neighbors to Tomas, who is involved in the black market, who has an illegal radio, who is selling parachute silk. In response he uses their knowledge not to punish the guilty but to blackmail them for further luxuries. He is an operator, a charming rogue. He is also the friend of the three Dartigens, particularly of Framboise, whom he assists in her summer-long efforts to catch a legendary pike called Old Mother. His death is an accident resulting directly from her success in catching Old Mother; eventually, Framboise's mother is blamed and, after the Nazis retaliate against the village, the family is driven out. Framboise has never known the full story but discovers it in the "present" narrative, where she also owns up to it, under threat of exposure by her nephew's shrewish wife.

There are many themes running through *Five Quarters of the Orange.* One is the myth of the noble French Resistance, along with the myth of the utterly evil Nazis. Leibniz is the most charming character in the book; the villagers accommodate the Germans quite comfortably. Another is the intolerance of small-town life. Framboise's mother is preserved from some sort of lynching only by a then-incomprehensible and apparently miraculous savior. A third is the discomforts and strains of family life. Framboise is uneasy with her siblings, indifferent to her father (killed by the Germans), and later remote with her own daughters. She exploits her mother's terrible headaches, the onset of which always includes the smell of oranges, by deliberately poisoning her with stolen oranges. The mother's need for opiates to survive her migraines leads her, in turn, into the local café, La Mauvaise Réputation, and into an affair with Leibniz. Perhaps the profoundest theme has to do with the legacy of the past in the present. Framboise begins the novel with her mother's only material bequest to her, the book including her recipes as well as her hints of her private life, and that legacy broadens through the plot.

Some reviewers of *Five Quarters of the Orange,* perhaps misled by the food metaphors, seemed stuck in grooves of predictable reaction. Tom Jaine, for instance, wrote in *The Guardian* (7 April 2001): "The apparent charm of the author–*Chocolat* was a runaway success–seems to lie in her evocation of a French never-never land where things may occasionally turn nasty, but saccharine always flows." By contrast, Caroline Gascoigne, in the *Sunday Times* (8 April 2001), recognized that "Harris is on assured form, expertly unfolding a story that, answering critics of her earlier work, is firmly rooted in the real world." In *The Independent* (16 April 2001), Helen Stevenson summed it up as "a grown-up, unpatronising book, written from a French point of view for, I would say, an English readership; from the inside for the outside, with zest." Amanda Craig used her review in the 31 March 2001 edition of *The Times* (London) as an occasion to take a broader look at Harris's work: "Joanne Harris tends to be looked down on by the literary establishment. Too unpretentious, too accessible and now (following the success of the film *Chocolat*) too rich, she is seen, in the sneering words of one literary editor, to be working her way through a menu with a succession of novels revolving around food. Yet like Framboise, the narrator of *Five Quarters of the Orange,* she deserves to have her virtues recognised." Craig goes on to acknowledge that some highbrow readers might object to the quantity of "redemption, courage and love" but praised the novel as "vastly enjoyable and utterly gripping . . . a dark antithesis to *Chocolat.*"

Perhaps Harris has become tired of reviewers using her food interests as a shortcut to judgment. Her 2002 novel, *Coastliners,* makes no reference to food in its title nor does its cover depict anything edible. Though of course its characters eat and drink, no lavish celebrations of what they consume feature in the narrative. She has moved her setting again: this time to an island called Le Devin, off the coast of Brittany. In a 2002 newspaper article the author provided some insight into the sources of this novel. After an account of her childhood in Yorkshire, sometimes made uncomfortable by her half-French status, she describes summer holidays with her French grandfather. "He had a fisherman's cottage on Noirmoutier, an island off the Vendée coast, and we spent all our summer holidays there together. . . . It was idyllic." Le Devin, the locale for *Coastliners,* is described similarly: "one of the many islets caught like crabs in the shallows off the Vendée coastline. Eclipsed by Noirmoutier on the coastal side. . . ." Harris also explains what happened to that fisherman's cottage after her grandfather's death: "Death–and its promise of inheritance–brings out the ugly in people, and in the absence of a will, the three sisters could not agree how to proceed." One of them bought out the rest, paying an unfairly low price, then demolished the cottage and built a new and lavish villa.

This account provides some insight, perhaps, into Harris's impatience with the predations that grasping younger people threaten over the lives, memories, and property of their elders, present in her novels from *Chocolat* through *Coastliners,* in which two sisters are in fact divided over their father's property. One loves it for what it is–a ramshackle house and a boatyard–while the other's eyes glitter for what it can be turned into.

Madeline Prasteau is the traditional daughter, who, in accordance with island wisdom that claims that "Everything returns," has come back to Le Devin after ten years in Paris. Her parents have divorced; her islander father remained, and she accompanied her outsider mother, who disliked the island life, to Paris, where they lived in poverty while Madeline trained as a painter. Her mother having died, Madeline comes home. Meanwhile, sister Adrienne has married wealth, embraced bourgeois life and its aspirations, and turned against her sister's love for Le Devin as it has always existed.

The island is divided, rather schematically, in the somewhat Manichean way Lansquenet is, though here the division is as much geographical as social. At one end is the village of Les Salants, poor and struggling, Madeline's home; at the other is the more prosperous La Houssinière, overseen by the ambiguous plutocrat Foxy Brismand, whose money threatens Les Salants but has also funded Madeline's education (his son has mar-

Dust jacket for the U.S. edition of Harris's 2001 novel, about the complex relationship between a French family and a German soldier during the Nazi Occupation (Richland County Public Library)

ried her sister). The complex texture of competition between the two villages has been changed by a new threat to Les Salants. Its sand is eroding, its fish have fled, and increasingly its streets and cemetery are flooded. The villagers are fatalistic, but Madeline discovers that a new shore defense, built by Brismand for the beach at La Houssinière, has changed the patterns of the currents and is washing sand from Les Salants to its more favored neighbor. She organizes an effort to construct an inventive floating reef made of tires that changes the currents again; with its fish coming back, new sand on its beach, and, for the first time, tourists visiting, Les Salants is revitalized.

Brismand is, as Madeline and the reader suspect, playing a deep game. The other important characters in Madeline's story (colorful villagers and chatty nuns aside) are two other men. One is her father, GrosJean, who has lost the habit of building boats and almost the ability to speak, spends much of his time at the cemetery where his dead brother lies, and is finally shown to be preoccupied by an unsuspected memory. The other is the mysterious Flynn, or Rouget (nicknamed for his red hair), an Irishman who helps old GrosJean, devises the artificial reef, and generally contributes to the happiness of the people of Les Salants–reminiscent in a way of Vianne's contribution in the village of Lansquenet. Flynn is not what, or who, he at first appears to be; or even who he secondarily appears; and his ambiguous relationship to the island, and to Madeline, who becomes his lover, is one of the springs of the action.

Harris is working imaginatively with the idea of islands. The novel begins with a little disquisition on how islands are different. The difficulties of island life are a running theme–the threat from shifting currents, oil spills, bad weather, invading jellyfish, even the difficulty of getting goods or services (the closest thing to a doctor on the island is a veterinarian) or getting out from under one another's observation. Madeline, in her account of coming back, moves the island idea into metaphor: "I was not planning to stay. However potent the illusion of time suspended, I had another life now. I had changed. I was no longer an island."

Though it is small, Le Devin houses long-running feuds between two fishing families; competitions for the one young, sexy girl in Les Salants; something like a "bright lights, big city" attraction, which brings the young people of Les Salants to La Houssinière for smoking, motorbike gangs, and fugitive sex. There is an island saint, Ste. Marine-de-la-mer, whose image is lost and then found and in whose name apparent miracles take place, and a drowned church whose phantom bell rings to announce disasters.

Helen Stevenson's review of *Coastliners,* in the *Scotsman* (16 March 2002), expressed exasperation over what she deemed the predictability of Harris's landscape, plot, and food interests, "the determined female protagonist," the supernatural, and other elements, but continued:

> What was new to me, what I had not remembered from the previous books, was the occasional passage of writing where the plot and the thudding melodrama and the sentimentality all stood aside, and a description stilled my eye on the page, and made me, for a moment, glad I had read so far. Harris's knowledge of France is completely authentic, and present in the detail. For this book she has studied the sea, the island community, the nautical detail, meticulously, and it shows. It gives the novel interest and weight.

Maggie Gee, writing in the *Sunday Times* (10 March 2002), was also divided but declared that "Joanne Harris . . . manages to make her new 479-page novel about life on a tiny, divided Breton island seem as brief and honeyed as a fairy-tale or film. Everything about her style is aerodynamic: short paragraphs, sentences and chapters, clear, briefly sketched images, quick-fire dialogue, and an easily swallowed, rounded form for every scene."

Psychological depth in her characters is not Joanne Harris's greatest strength, though the almost mute GrosJean Prasteau is a memorable creation; instead she specializes in plot–which, in the balancing of moral forces and the usually more-or-less happy endings, is vulnerable to characterization as melodrama–and even more in evocation of place and sensation. Le Devin is a starker place than some of her earlier settings, and there is nothing here like the chocolate shop and the nipples of Venus, but she has a sure touch in conveying the look, the sound and feel, and especially the taste and smell of places and things. Rachel Simhon, in the *Daily Telegraph* (24 March 2001), insisted that "to dismiss Joanne Harris's novels as sentimental misses the point. She is an old-fashioned writer in the finest sense, believing in a strong narrative, fully rounded characters, a complex plot, even a moral, for goodness sake. Her novels may be whimsical, but like the best fairy stories they cast an irresistible spell."

Interviews:

Marla Addison, "Interview," *CountryBookshop* <http: www.countrybookshop.co.uk/journal/interview/harris. phtml>;

Kevin Patrick Mahoney, "Joanne Harris Interview," *AuthorTrek,* March 2000 <http:www.geocities.com/SoHo/Nook/1082/joanne_harris_interview.html>;

John Arlidge, "Life Is Sweet for Author of Surprise Bestseller," *Observer,* 24 September 2000, p. 7;

Gloria Goodale, "An English Writer Gets a Taste of Hollywood," *Christian Science Monitor,* 15 December 2000, p. 19;

Catherine Deveney, "Sweet Success," *Scotland on Sunday,* 4 March 2001, Spectrum section, p. 20;

Boyd Tonkin, "Joanne Harris: Is there Life after Chocolat?" *Independent,* 15 April 2001, Features section, p. 7;

"The Modest Talent," *Sunday Age* (Melbourne), 27 May 2001, Agenda section, p. 5;

"Chocolat and Chips," *Observer,* 15 July 2001, Review pages, p. 4;

Harriet Lane, "Success on a Plate," *BBC News Online,* 14 March 2002 <http:www.bbc.co.uk/hi/english/audio-video/programmes/breakfast/newsid_1871000/1871151.stm>.

Angela Huth

(29 August 1938 –)

Cecile M. Jagodzinski
Illinois State University

BOOKS: *Nowhere Girl* (London: Collins, 1970); republished as *Somehow I Had to Find a Brass Band* (New York: Coward-McCann, 1970);
Virginia Fly is Drowning (London: Collins, 1972; New York: Coward, McCann & Geoghegan, 1973);
Sun Child (London: Collins, 1975);
South of the Lights (London: Collins, 1977);
Monday Lunch in Fairyland and Other Stories (London: Collins, 1978); revised as *Infidelities: Short Stories* (New York: Potter, 1979);
The Understanding (Ambergate, U.K.: Amber Lane Press, 1982);
Wanting (London: Harvill, 1984; New York: Macmillan, 1984);
The Englishwoman's Wardrobe, photographs by Kenneth Griffiths (London: Century, 1986);
Eugenie in Cloud Cuckoo Land, illustrated by Dianna Dunn (London: Deutsch, 1986);
Such Visitors: Stories (London: Heinemann, 1989);
Invitation to the Married Life (London: Sinclair-Stevenson, 1991; New York: Grove, 1992);
Land Girls (London: Sinclair-Stevenson, 1994; New York: St. Martin's Press, 1994);
The Trouble with Old Lovers: A Play (London & New York: S. French, 1995);
Another Kind of Cinderella and Other Stories (London: Little, Brown, 1996);
Wives of the Fishermen (London: Little, Brown, 1998; New York: St. Martin's Press, 1998);
Easy Silence (London: Little, Brown, 1999; New York: St. Martin's Press, 2001);
Of Love and Slaughter (London: Little, Brown, 2002).
Collection: *Land Girls; Wives of the Fishermen: Angela Huth Omnibus* (London: Abacus, 2001).

PLAY PRODUCTIONS: *The Understanding,* London, Strand Theatre, 11 May 1982; New York, Neighborhood Playhouse, 12 January 1999;
The Trouble with Old Lovers, Basingstoke, Haymarket Theatre, 9 February 1995.

Angela Huth (photograph by Sophie Litchfield; from the dust jacket for the U.S. edition of Land Girls, *1994)*

PRODUCED SCRIPTS: *The Summer House,* television, BBC, 1969;
"Special Co-respondent," television, 24 July 1970;
"The Emperor's New Hat," television, BBC, 1971;
Paul and Michelle, motion picture, by Huth and Vernon Harris, Paramount, 1974;
"Virginia Fly is Drowning," television, BBC, 1975;
"The Englishwoman's Wardrobe," television, BBC, 20 November 1986;
"The Understanding," television, Yorkshire Television, 1987;
"Sun Child," television, Yorkshire Television, 1988;
Past Forgetting, radio, Radio 4, 20 November 2001.

RECORDINGS: *Invitation to the Married Life,* read by Huth, Oxford, ISIS Audio Books IAB960705, 1996;

Nowhere Girl, read by Huth, Oxford, ISIS Audio Books IAB961205, 1996;

Such Visitors, read by Huth, Oxford, ISIS Audio Books IAB970608, 1997;

Sun Child, read by Huth, Oxford, ISIS Audio Books IAB980110, 1998;

Easy Silence, read by Huth, Oxford, ISIS Audio Books IAB000512, 2000;

South of the Lights, read by Huth, ISIS Audio Books IAB970709, 2001.

OTHER: *Island of the Children: An Anthology of New Poems,* compiled by Huth, illustrated by Jane Ray (London: Orchard, 1987);

Casting a Spell and Other Poems: An Anthology of New Poems, compiled by Huth, illustrated by Ray (London: Orchard, 1991).

SELECTED PERIODICAL PUBLICATIONS–UNCOLLECTED: "Why Some of Us Get More and More Irritable As Time Goes By," *Times* (London), 14 April 1976, p. 10;

"A-level Lit Crit," *Times* (London), 30 September 1977, p. 19;

"Spirit of Christmas," *Times* (London), 22 December 1984, p. 9;

"Title Fight," *Daily Telegraph* (London), 24 May 1995, p. 20;

"Q–The Greatest Life-Giver I Ever Met," *Daily Telegraph* (London), 11 June 1999, p. 19.

Angela Huth has worked as a journalist but is best known for her novels about contemporary English life, people's explorations of love and longing, and the simple human desire to be connected to someone–sometimes at great cost to one's self.

Angela Maureen Huth was born in London 29 August 1938, the elder of two daughters of actor, director, and producer Harold Edward Strachan Huth and Bridget Nickols Huth. Educated at private schools in England (Guilsborough Lodge School and Lawnside), she continued her studies at a convent school in Switzerland, then studied art at the Ecole des Beaux-Arts in Paris, the Annigoni School of Art in Florence, and the Byam Shaw Art School in London. Huth commented on this finishing-school sort of education later on in life, in a 26 August 1991 interview with Danny Danziger for *The Independent* (London): "I had a mother whose theory was that the way to be well educated was to speak perfect French like her, and to this end there was quite a lot of suffering in my childhood." The slight bitterness expressed here is nowhere evident when Huth speaks of her father, who died in 1967; she apparently adored him and regretted that he did not live to read her first novel.

After her "coming out" party in 1956, Huth embarked on a career in advertising and journalism. After a brief stint in the art department of J. Walter Thompson Advertising, she became travel editor at *Queen* magazine, then woman's page editor for *The Sunday Express* (London). In 1965 Huth became the first woman reporter on *Man Alive,* a pioneering British Broadcasting Corporation (BBC) television documentary series. From 1969 to 1970 she served as the presenter for *How It Is,* also on the BBC. Aside from her work as a fiction writer, Huth continues her work as a journalist and reviewer for various newspapers and magazines.

Huth met her first husband, Quentin Crewe, in 1959 while both were working at *Queen* magazine. Despite his disabling muscular dystrophy, Crewe was a well-known journalist, travel author, food critic, and bon vivant. Huth and Crewe married in 1961. A son, Caspar, died just four days after his birth; their daughter, Candida Crewe, born in 1964, is now a novelist and freelance journalist. The couple divorced when Candida was five but remained friends until Crewe's death in 1998. Huth's second marriage, to film producer Tony Palmer, lasted less than a week.

On 24 June 1978 Huth married James Howard-Johnston, elder son of Rear Admiral C. D. Howard-Johnston and Lady Alexandra Trevor-Roper. Howard-Johnston is University Lecturer in Byzantine Studies at Oxford and a fellow of Corpus Christi College. His specialty is sixth-century A.D. Byzantine history, but he is also interested in the history of the Near East in the seventh century. He is the author of scholarly essays and the more popular *The Scholar and the Gypsy: Two Journeys to Turkey, Past and Present* (1992), written with Nigel Ryan. Huth and Howard-Johnston have one daughter, Eugenie, born in 1981.

Huth began writing at an early age, composing stories for her sister, Trish. In a 23 May 1984 interview with Bryan Appleyard for *The Times* (London), she said that she was worried that her experiences would pass by unrecorded, so, from the age of five, "she has written feverishly, describing every thought and incident." In an interview with Jerome Boyd Maunsell in *The Times* (London) for 11 March 2000, she called writing "one of the great pleasures in my life," she begins with a title, then decides on a genre: "All I need is the first and last sentence, and then it's my usual adventure into the unknown, trying to get from A to B."

Huth claims her stories and characters are "imagined," but they seem to be full of people who, like

Dust jacket for the U.S. edition of Huth's first novel (1970), about a young woman who is unlucky in love (Richland County Public Library)

Huth, have strong feelings about living in Oxford, the way Englishwomen dress, and the everyday work of preparing and serving meals. Huth is unapologetically old school, and in *The Times* (London) of 14 April 1976 she described herself as "sufferer of incurable punctuality." She has been outspoken in public expressions of her opinions: in a 30 September 1977 letter to *The Times* (London) she called for a return to the good old days when memorization was a required part of a good English education; in a 22 December 1984 letter to *The Times* (London) she protested the absence of traditional Church of England services on Christmas Eve; and in a 24 May 1995 letter to *The Daily Telegraph* (London) she criticized a fellow author for getting titles of nobility wrong. These personal likes and dislikes seep their way into her characters, who tend to exhibit either proper manners and kindness or coarseness and cruelty. Like Jane Austen, to whom Huth is often compared, Huth's themes are civility, manners, and social custom, and her characters display a need for privacy that often runs counter to the modern tendency to discuss, weigh, and pummel the reader's feelings and opinions to death. And, for Huth, as it was with Austen, marriage is a central concern. In Huth's novels and short stories, people nearly always seem to define themselves in terms of their relation to that social institution. For the married, attraction to persons other than one's spouse seems inevitable; at the same time, the comfort and dependability of one's partner usually trump infidelity.

Nowhere Girl (1970), Huth's first published novel, follows the adventures of Clare, a hapless young woman who seems to fall in love with all the wrong men. The book opens at the funeral of Clare's first husband, Richard. There she meets Mrs. Fox, an eccentric but wise widow whose vitality and optimism provide a bracing contrast to Clare and her bad choices. Mrs. Fox still speaks of her husband, Henry, in the present tense and shares with Clare her memories of him, from his first declaration of love to the raucous Salvation Army band she had arranged for his funeral celebration. Mrs. Fox, quoting Austen, says that "one's happiness must in some measure be always at the mercy of chance," but Mrs. Fox seems able to direct her own happiness, while Clare leaves hers completely to chance.

Separated from her second husband, Jonathon, Clare takes up with Joshua, a man who is "bad at sharing things." The first-person narrative recollects Clare's two marriages and two spouses, each begun in hope and innocence and ending in irritation and disappointment. The structure of the novel mirrors Clare's indecision, as her memories tack back and forth between past and present, between current and past loves. She seems to have no identity of her own: her three men call her, not by her Christian name, but Little One, Suki Soo, and Face. A miscarriage (her second) leaves Clare feeling empty, her insides "a scooped-out hole." The physical and emotional pain of the loss of the child is compounded by Joshua's declaration that he is too thoughtless to truly care for her. Her hopes of reconciling with Jonathon are dashed when she learns he has taken up with someone else. The death of the solid and dependable Mrs. Fox leaves Clare completely alone, searching for a brass band to celebrate Mrs. Fox's funeral.

Reviewers of the book seemed undecided about whether Clare deserved her victimhood, and they tended to register either sympathy or repugnance. Critical commentary tended to focus on the character, not on the quality of Huth's writing.

The title character in *Virginia Fly is Drowning* (1972) is "raped, in her mind, on average twice a week." These fantasies are compensation for her virginal life, spent at home with mother and father. Her virginity is sensationalized in a television interview that makes her a minor celebrity. Virginia loses her virginity to her American pen pal, Charlie, in a sordid scene completely at odds with her romantic expectations, and she finally agrees to marry her occasional companion, an elderly professor of music for whom she feels absolutely no passion.

The New York Times Book Review (27 May 1973) critic Caroline Seebohm found fault with the character of Virginia but praised Huth's "neat, lively style." She seemed unable, however, to separate Huth from her powerless, pathetic central character. Seebohm blamed Huth for Virginia's helplessness, and she wanted a completely different sort of book, one in which the author explains the existence of a thirty-one-year-old virgin. The writer of the unsigned 7 September 1972 review in *The Times* (London) found the book "unrelieved by any true command of style," while Virginia C. Jones, in a review for *Best Sellers* (15 June 1973) thought it "trivial and of no interest." But others found the story a sensitive picture of the gap between dreams and reality, and one woman's passive acceptance of society's roles for her–first as object of desire and eventually as dutiful wife and mother.

Told from the third-person point of view, *Sun Child* (1975) opens in sunshine and laughter, with the child Emily observing her obviously still-in-love parents, Fen and Idle. Fen, much younger than her husband, is charming, incompetent about the house, and almost child-like in her gaiety and joie de vivre. She is a fitting partner for Emily but is surprisingly unmatched to her husband, a diplomat frequently away from home on business. Idle is so much the formal gentleman he wears his "London shirts" even when he is home for the weekend.

With Emily, the reader watches the gold fade from the couple's marriage as Fen, almost unwittingly, falls in love with sometime actor and entrepreneur Kevin. Emily is immediately suspicious of Kevin, a friend of her uncle, and watches warily as he and Fen succumb to each other's newness and charm. Clinging to the hope that her parents will not part, Emily wishes for a little brother to restore her parents' closeness to one another.

A visit to Fen's mother at Christmas restores neither Fen and Idle's marriage nor assuages Emily's feelings of panic. All Emily wants, she tells her grandmother, is "a really boring life with Mama and Papa just there all the time." Grandmother (a "mad, evil witch" in Emily's eyes) responds like a grownup, not a loving grandmother:

> Emily, my dying wish will be that you may never have a boring childhood, or a boring life. Pain, yes. We all need a little of that. Incomprehensible happiness, yes. Ups and downs. Excitements and disappointments, but never boredom.

Fen's careless friendship with Kevin, and Idle's growing comfortableness with his secretary, mark the end of the golden relationship. Immersed in their own concerns, Fen and Idle have fallen out of the habit of loving each other, and so they easily pick up the habit of loving someone else. The novel closes as Emily watches her mother, clothed like a "harbinger of autumn," leaving her husband and child to go live with Kevin.

South of the Lights (1977) is a novel of English village life. The beautiful hen-keeper Brenda remains reluctantly engaged to Evans, the local postman, while Evans's retired father, Henry, is exhausted by the smothering attentions and baked goods of his kind wife, Rosie. Only a chance glimpse of a seemingly glamorous woman dressed in a leopard coat begins to revive the older man. His obsession for "The Leopard," as he calls her, is destroyed when he sees her up close in the local pub, with her nylon coat, tired, made-up face, and a lustful companion. Henry becomes overwhelmed with "the emptiness of reality"; as Henry tells his wife, "there are a lot of dead people walking about. You run into them everywhere." Only the aptly named Lark, a self-contained girl with hopes of a singing career, seems fully alive. But she dies, painfully, from an unspecified disease, "silvered by gin" and the final magical triumph of a singing engagement.

Dust jacket for the U.S. edition of Huth's 1984 novel, about an actress being stalked by a director of stage plays (Richland County Public Library)

Reviews of the novel ran the gamut of opinion. In a 30 June 1977 review for *The Times* (London), Philip Howard noted Huth's ability "for getting inside the skins of all sorts and conditions of ordinary people (who are, of course, not ordinary at all)." But Peter Ackroyd, writing in the 2 July 1977 issue of *The Spectator* (London), was critical: "Poor little Lark dies for us as a form of therapy: the most unrealistic character has to be sacrificed in order to convince us of the reality of the others." Julian Barnes, in *New Statesman* (1 July 1977), found it "the most narcoleptic novel I've read in a long time," an opinion he regretted having to express in the face of the "quiet competence of the construction and the decent plainness of the style." In *TLS: The Times Literary Supplement* (19 August 1977) Jane Miller was scathing in her criticism of Huth's treatment of the lower-class characters and what she saw as Huth's pretentious vocabulary. Miller dismissed *South of the Lights* as a "tears and laughter" romantic novel that omitted the laughter.

Huth's short-story collection *Monday Lunch in Fairyland and Other Stories* (1978) was republished the following year in the United States as *Infidelities.* The two books have thirteen stories in common, but *Infidelities* excludes the three stories in the British edition that do not deal with relations between the sexes and adds two new stories. The themes of *Monday Lunch in Fairyland and Other Stories* take their cue from the title story, in which Anna's married lover tells her, "visits to fairyland are nothing to do with anything else. If you plan them right they can go on for ever and ever. Just things to look forward to, and to look back on." Anna's marriage, her lover's marriage, and their own affair all take place in separate, compartmentalized worlds. These sorts of divisions are repeated throughout the collection: silences, deaths, differences of opinion, and, most of all, infidelities of various sorts separate the characters. In "Thinnest Ice," a man believes his wife's frequent absences from home mean she is having an affair. His confidence in her is already destroyed by the time he discovers she has been learning to ice-skate in order to please him. The woman in "Loving Gourmets" is expecting passionate lovemaking on a vacation to France; instead, it is the gourmet food, not she, that is the object of her companion's devotion. In "Mind of Her Own" a wife and mother decides not to go on yet another family vacation. For her, vacations consist of peeling potatoes and taking care of the family in a place less pleasant than home. Her uncharacteristic decision lands her in a mental hospital, where she comfortably settles in. Only visits from her family interrupt the rhythm of her days and her fantasies about Mr. Rochester, the love interest of the eponymous heroine of Charlotte Brontë's novel *Jane Eyre* (1847).

Reviews of both collections were mixed, as were judgments of individual stories: what one reviewer panned, another praised. In her 4 March 1978 review for *The Spectator* (London) Mary Hope thought the collection like "those beautifully made fancy cakes you used to get in countries poor in ingredients . . . amazingly artful and tasting of nothing at all," and in the *TLS* (3 March 1978) Anne Duchêne reproached Huth for "some conventional dead writing." But other critics praised Huth's style and what Robert Kiely, writing in *The New York Times Book Review* (9 December 1979), called her "little illuminations of love and marriage," with their simultaneously comic and poignant insights into human nature.

Throughout the 1970s Huth wrote original television scripts and adaptations of her own novels. Two of her plays have been produced and published: *The Understanding* (1982); and *The Trouble with Old Lovers* (1995). The first drama was not well received, despite the casting of Ralph Richardson in a central role. In a backhanded compliment to Huth, Benedict Nightingale, in the *New Statesman* (21 May 1982), supposed that, like Henry James, another novelist of manners, Huth's talents were not suited to the drama: "Drama was too extrovert a form for his inward and delicate talent." *The Trouble with Old Lovers,* written in the mid 1980s, was not produced until 1995 and never made it to the London stage.

Wanting (1984) tells multiple stories of unrequited love. "The despair of wanting," as one of the main characters puts it, seems to underlie everyone's lives. Some expressions of this desire are suppressed by duty or despair; others are manifested in frightening ways. The heroine of the novel is Viola, an actress who inspires the passion of Harry Antlers, an unpleasant stage director, who, when he is not stalking or terrorizing Viola, is eating, sweating, and cursing "the general brightness of the world." Since her youth, Viola has been beloved by Richard, now married to Sonia, who is confined to an asylum. Such is Richard's sense of duty to his marriage vows that he cannot ever contemplate divorce, or even an affair with Viola. Viola's brother, Gideon, is off in New York, sharing an apartment with Hannah, whose decorating instincts Huth treats in appropriately satirical manner. Alfred, a widower; Edward, a student of moths; and Maisie, Richard's sister, round out the cast of characters; they, like all the others, are similarly infected (or inspired) by desire. Huth signals the rightness or foolishness of all these potential pairings in a variety of ways. Those destined for failure are characterized by the inconsiderateness and cruelty of one of the partners: Harry, for instance, lacks pity for those in love with him; Sonia menaces Richard with threats of suicide; Alfred is haunted by the "pinched, mean, unfriendly" face of his dead wife, Eileen. But for Viola and Richard, and finally Gideon and Maisie, there are moments of pure happiness when consciousness of the joys of the moment can be transformed into memories that will not fade. As Viola says, "Hope can die, but a conviction that something would have been right, had it been given the chance, can exist forever." The novel ends with Maisie and Gideon's wedding, Viola and Richard's parting, and the formation of a mutually beneficial partnership between Harry and Hannah.

Some reviewers regarded the book as a realistic look at the possibilities for fulfilling desire. Nicholas Bagnall and Sally Cousins, in the *Sunday Telegraph* (5 November 2000), called it a "wry black comedy, "and Sara Laschever, in the *New York Times Book Review* (25 August 1985), saw it as "an engaging light read." But Sakvar Altinel in *TLS* (15 June 1984) thought Huth had not quite managed to help the reader feel the pain and pathos of the thwarted lovers; and Harriet Waugh, in a 30 June 1984 review for *The Spectator* (London), found the book unfocused and lacking a real feeling for the characters. Waugh missed the mark, though, when she asked for Harry to be less grotesque and for Viola to let go of her good manners. Huth's point is exactly that: there are people in the world who are bullying and unattractive, and there are those for whom standards and codes of conduct matter.

Invitation to the Married Life

a novel by

Angela Huth

Dust jacket for the U.S. edition of Huth's 1991 novel, about happy and unhappy spouses (Richland County Public Library)

The idea for *The Englishwoman's Wardrobe* (1986) came to Huth at a wedding. Huth always takes care to tell readers of her characters' taste in dress and interior design–indeed, clothes often mark the woman, from the old-fashioned dress of Isabel in "Laughter in the Willows" to the synthetic coat of the middle-aged Leopard, who is the occasion of desire in *South of the Lights.* This coffee-table book provides photographs (by Kenneth Griffiths) and interviews with English women of various occupations and social classes, ranging from Huth's friend Princess Margaret to author Jilly Cooper. Her introduction is sometimes astringent–"any *group* of

Dust jacket for the U.S. edition of Huth's 1994 novel, about three young women who volunteer as farmworkers to replace men serving in World War II (Richland County Public Library)

Englishwomen is hardly cheering to the eye. . . . There are few sights more depressing than a gathering of academics' wives (except, perhaps, a clump of councillors' wives)"–and sometimes sympathetic:

> there are also plenty of signs that the Englishwoman is not wholly dowdy. At least her clothes display a spirited sense of individuality–she will not be dictated to, bossed about, persuaded to wear the latest thing should it not appeal. . . . With a wise sense of priority, she puts her wardrobe into the second division of important things in her life–surely its rightful place.

Maeve Binchy (*Books,* August 1987) was horrified at the very notion of women speaking so freely to Huth about their clothing. But this little diversion from Huth's more serious work in some sense embodies the challenges her female characters face: how to tend to a necessary aspect of life without appearing superficial, how to express personal preference and individuality (in dress, in habits, in lovers) without bankrupting one's husband or causing envy among one's friends.

Between 1986 and 1991, Huth wrote or edited three children's books: *Eugenie in Cloud Cuckoo Land* (1986), *Island of the Children* (1987), and *Casting a Spell and Other Poems* (1991). The first book Huth wrote for her younger daughter, Eugenie; the other two are compilations of poetry that Huth solicited from others, some not known as writers for children. Contributors to the two anthologies include such luminaries as Ted Hughes, Seamus Heaney, Kingsley Amis, and Joan Aiken. These, along with some authors not known for their poetic work, produced two atypical collections of children's verse. While Connie Bensley in *TLS* (4 December 1987) found some of *Island of the Children* unsuitable for bedtime reading, Imogen Woods in *The Independent* (30 November 1991) thought the poems of *Casting a Spell* "easy on the ear, but without the relentless cheeriness of much children's verse."

Such Visitors (1989) comprises two new stories and eleven that had been previously published. Most people are, as the character in the title story says, "such visitors in each other's lives–mere visitors. Even husbands and wives." Huth revisits the same sort of people who appeared in her earlier collections. There is the man in "Sudden Dancer" who learns to dance to please his wife, only to learn that she resents his intrusions into her nights out alone. Anna, the wife and mother in "The Fuschia Auberge," escapes from her family vacation and fantasizes about an affair with the handsome stranger M. Cadeau, who treats her to a glass of champagne. Sybil Steinberg, the reviewer for *Publishers Weekly* (11 May 1990), characterized the stories as "banal tales," but for the most part, critics considered the collection an accomplished depiction of the absurdities of love and the ease with which repeated disappointment can lead to passivity and hopelessness.

Invitation to the Married Life (1991) dissects the lives of four married couples and three single people who are in various stages of love or infatuation. The event that propels the plot is an invitation to a country ball being hosted by the shallow, affection-starved Frances and her husband, Toby, whose chief amusements are computer programming and watching badgers at night. The novel opens with Rachel and Thomas–she, continually depressed, is happy only when she can escape to sleep in her luxuriously appointed bedroom; he, in between adulterous affairs, is ripe for a new liaison. Mary and Bill are happily retired, contented with one another and with their lives; only Mary's neurotic fear of being the first to die disturbs her equilibrium. Their daughter, Ursula, and her husband, Martin, an Oxford don, are the only other happily married couple in the novel. Martin's old bachelor friend, Ralph, is in love with Ursula. And Ralph's mother, Rosie, a charming and talented painter of indeterminate age, is pursued by Thomas, who has fallen "irretrievably, ecstatically" in love with her. Huth's descriptions of her characters' peccadilloes tell us much about love and loneliness. Ralph makes "lists of instructions to himself to provide the necessary discipline of a solitary life" and only occasionally allows himself the luxury of thinking about Ursula. Small habits and attentions, good and bad memories can glue together or tear apart a relationship. For Bill, "The sawing of a tree, and the loving of a wife, could occupy you wholly"; his attentive and silent concern for his wife's privacy sustains their long marriage. For Frances, however, marriage is just a series of "meeting, parting, meeting, parting . . . their way of dealing with the gulf that divides all human souls." Even the contented Ursula realizes that "The sadness in marriage is that you can never quite perceive each other's experiences."

Reviews of *Invitation to the Married Life* were generally positive, with the editors of *The Antioch Review* (Spring 1993) praising Huth for doing "what Jane Austen did in her day: observing the daily life of the middle class with insight and wit." But John Nicholson damned it with faint praise in an 8 August 1991 review in *The Times* (London), declaring: "Not much happens in a Huth novel, though the pages pass without pain." Ellen Pall in *The New York Times Book Review* (24 January 1993) and Duchêne in *TLS* (26 April 1991) both criticized the book for the excessive number of principal characters, with Duchêne suggesting that Huth have "another shot at it: but with fewer people."

Huth's *Land Girls* (1994), set in World War II England, tells the story of three young women who go to the country to perform farm chores in place of the young men off at war. The story begins in the present, as Prue, Ag, and Stella meet for their annual luncheon to reminisce and bring each other up to date on their lives. The remainder of the novel describes the lives of the three during their time on the farm belonging to taciturn Mr. Lawrence and his kind, solid wife, Faith. Prue is the flirt, the lower-middle-class hairdresser who does her face and puts ribbons in her hair even when she drives a tractor. Ag is a classics scholar, pining for a fellow student she barely knows, and Stella is the shy one, in love with navy man Philip, whom she has seen only three times. The action takes place over the course of the farming year, from October through harvest time of the following year. During that time, all three girls have flings with the farmer's son, Joe (exempt from military service because of his asthma), and all three struggle with the arduous physical work and their own romantic and emotional cravings. A subplot revolves around farmworker Ratty and his harridan of a wife, Edith.

The novel received critical praise, despite its romanticized treatment of life in the Women's Land Army. In a 12 March 1994 review for *The Daily Telegraph* (London) Imogen Lycett-Green maintained that Huth's "sharp observation and careful eye for detail" saved the book from sentimentality. Huth's descriptions of the hedging, plowing, and milking cows, and the details of material life in the 1940s, from makeup to food, "build a pleasingly substantial impression of a particular historical moment," claimed Lucy Hughes-Hallett in a 17 March 1994 review in *The Times* (London). It is the fact of this World War II setting that enables Huth to write so refreshingly of a more innocent time, said fellow novelist Anita Brookner in a 12 March 1994 review in *The Spectator* (London). The girls are allowed to be girls, not women, as they might be in a postfeminist age; they also grow into friends, and not competitors, even though all are bedded in turn by the handsome Joe. "This is primarily a novel about work," argued Brookner. Huth's plain style and treatment of themes such as duty, honor, and fidelity suit the "unspoilt, almost prelapsarian character" of the novel. A 1998 motion-picture version of the novel, directed by David Leland, with a screenplay by Leland and Keith Dewhurst, was widely panned for its prettiness and triviality; Huth herself opined in the 17 October 1998 issue of *The Independent* (London) that "The person who wrote the script didn't feel it necessary to read the book. He wrote a nice story about his own childhood on a farm and used my characters' names, that's all."

Another Kind of Cinderella and Other Stories (1996) focuses on people who share a common characteristic: their separateness from others. Even partners in a marriage feel alone, and the single people, such as Isabel in "Laughter in the Willows," have become "used to being a lone figure in a coupled society." The sense of aloneness is intensified by an inability to decide whom they can trust. Isabel wonders if she should marry the charming but slightly demonic Jacques. "Alternative Behaviour" is the journal of a woman whose husband is dying of cancer. The couple's closeness is threatened when their rebellious daughter comes back home to treat her father with alternative therapies. In "Squirrels," old maid Vera Brindle, continually resisting the social workers who want to put her away, spends her life weighing household items and drawing pictures of the squirrels that have taken up residence in the roof. When Vera dies, surrounded by squirrels and bits of caved-in ceiling, the reader is only slightly distraught, happy that she was able to stay in her own home until the end. "Mistral," set in France, depicts Annie, faithful servant of bachelors Gerald and Arthur. One day her

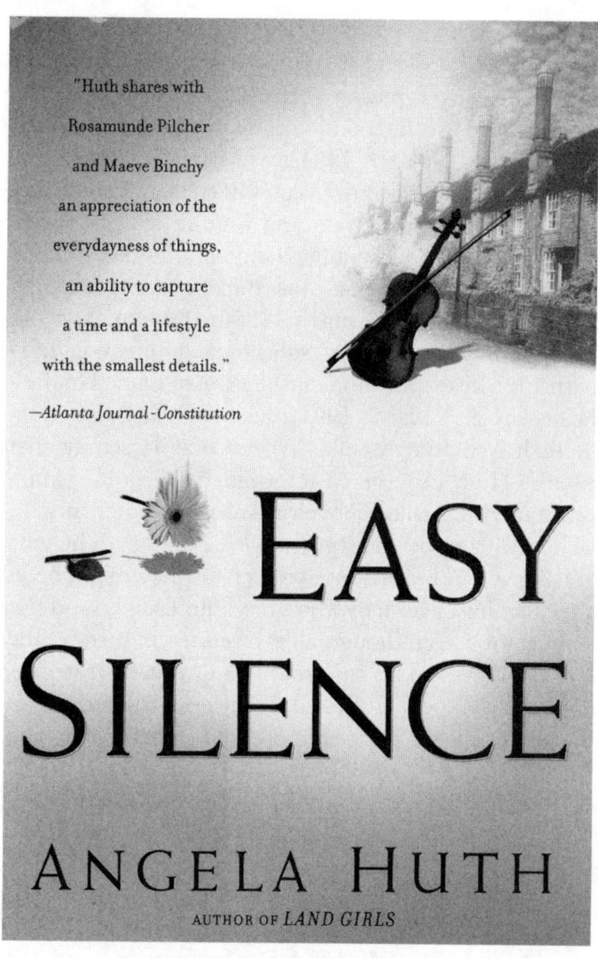

Dust jacket for the U.S. edition of Huth's 1999 novel, in which a musician decides to kill his wife after he becomes infatuated with another woman (Richland County Public Library)

composure disappears, and she lets rain a shower of fruit, flour, and dishes. The brothers, temporarily chastened, fix their own dinner for the first time, while Annie records it all in writing. It is unclear whether Annie lets loose her repressed anger or if she imagines the episode. These stories offer a challenge: Huth is liberal with her sympathies, even toward slightly unpleasant people. In Huth's fictions, as in life, it is hard to take sides: decisions about other human beings are always complicated and uncertain.

Like *Land Girls,* Huth's *Wives of the Fishermen* (1998) chronicles female friendship. Huth told Valerie Grove, in a 15 March 1998 interview for *The Times* (London), that she finds women's friendships "fascinating," since "there is always an element of treachery there." Her visit to a fishing village in Scotland inspired the themes and at least one of the characters in the novel; she found "a sort of sadness in the air and a sense of a desperate community." *Wives of the Fishermen* focuses on Annie, beautiful and selfish, and her plain, dependable, and loyal friend Myrtle.

Their lifelong friendship and Myrtle's happy and contented marriage to Archie (the only boy Annie could never snare) stand in contrast to Annie's childless and empty conjugal life with Ken. While Myrtle does not need roses, "just assurance," Annie's consumerism forces her husband into trading on the black market. Ken's involvement with Archie's death at sea tests the women's friendship, as does Myrtle's eventual ability to attract the attentions (and friendship) of the available single men in town.

The setting, an isolated Scottish coastal town, and the traditional occupation of both women's husbands lend the book the feel of some mythical past. In fact, Kate Grimond, in a 28 March 1998 review for *The Spectator* (London), thought the trappings of fable, fairy tale, and romance carpeted the book: "the large, selfless girl of simple poetic tastes winning the hero over the materially minded, egocentric lass; a clumsy tortoise and a fickle hare." Despite some quibbles about the authenticity of Huth's treatment–including a geographical error, noted by Patricia Nicol in a 15 March 1998 article in *The Sunday Times* (London)–reviewers were pleased with the book, one calling it "a gem of a novel."

Huth's novel *Easy Silence* (1999) seems to draw together the various themes she has touched on in her earlier work: how to maintain fidelity, how to honor a spouse's privacy, how to appreciate the comfortable, easy silences spent with those one loves and not mistake them for boredom. Murder, insanity, and jealousy inhabit the thoughts of Huth's principal characters in this novel. William, violinist in a string quartet, becomes infatuated with the new violist, Bonnie, and so resolves to kill his wife, Grace, his beloved "Ace," as he calls her. Grace, an amateur painter of flowers, at first basks in, but then becomes terrified by, the attentions of young neighbor Lucien, who turns out to be both a psychopath and a matricide. Silences and rests, conversation and music, are clues to character and to relationships in this novel. William and Grace enjoy their companionable silences as well as the set times they have for conversing with one another; similarly, the three male members of the quartet cherish both their silences and their music-making. But when Grace spends time with Lucien, the "mutual recognition" she shares with William disappears, and when William plays a duet with Bonnie, they venture into "dangerous territory."

Critics praised Huth's portrait of middle-class, middle-aged married life, but generally disbelieved the blackly comic aspects of the novel. As Patrick Gale, in his 14 August 1999 review for *The Daily Telegraph* (London), remarked, "her observations on the small rituals that prop up an enduring marriage can . . . be acute, which makes the unbelievability of the central plot point all the more glaring."

Huth's latest novel, *Of Love and Slaughter* (2002), is set in contemporary rural Devon. The central plot revolves around George Elkin, a solicitor who has given up his practice in order to farm his deceased father's land, and Nell and "Prodge" Prodger, a sister and brother who live nearby. Nell loves George, but George marries Lily, an old acquaintance from Oxford. The recent epidemics of foot-and-mouth disease and BSE in Europe serve as a backdrop to the personal stories of these four people. Reviewers were nearly unanimous in their criticism of Huth's attempt at social realism: the heavy-handedness of her attacks on government, with its indifference to the lives of real people, eclipsed the stories about human character. As Peter Parker in the *Times* (London) (28 July 2002) put it: "Unfortunately, this plot feels as if it has been grafted on to an expository essay on the death of British farming." And in *The Sunday Telegraph* (30 June 2002), Max Davidson lamented the fact that, "in her justified anger at the state of British farming," she " has forfeited the artistic detachment necessary in any storyteller."

Richard Cobb, in *TLS* (7 July 1989), called Huth "a devastating miniaturist," while Judy Cooke, in *The Guardian* (23 June 1989), said that "energy seeps away" "whenever a wider range of experience is described." But, according to Appleyard, Huth herself "loathes the idea of any 'big' issues intruding on her work." Her major theme is love–an experience that ranges from the passionate to the humdrum, from the obsessive to the quotidian. Angela Huth's novels show the readers characters falling in love over a satin-lined sleeve or a pair of topaz eyes, but also those who remain contentedly in love because of the everyday courtesies and kindnesses they share in friendships, marriages, and families.

Interviews:

Elisabeth Dunn, "Pouring Out Understanding," *Times* (London), 18 April 1982, p. 37;

Bryan Appleyard, "Raging Calm of a Country Wife," *Times* (London), 23 May 1984, p. 11;

Josephine Fairley, "The Lady's Not for Pressing," *Times* (London), 17 November 1986, p. 15;

Danny Danziger, "The Worst of Times: The Torture Just Dripped into Me," *Independent* (London), 26 August 1991, p. 10;

Valerie Grove, "Making a Ripple," *Times* (London), 11 March 1998, p. 14;

Lynda Lee-Potter, "Three Husbands, One Affair, and My Old Friend Princess Margaret," *Daily Mail* (London), 28 August 1998, pp. 32–33, 35;

Naim Attallah, *Dialogues* (London: Quartet, 2000);

Jerome Boyd Maunsell, "How I Write," *Times* (London), 11 March 2000, Metro section, p. 23;

"We Could Have Danced All Night," *Times* (London), 12 May 2001, Weekend section, p. 2.

References:

Quentin Crewe, *Well, I Forgot the Rest: The Autobiography of an Optimist* (London: Hutchinson, 1991);

Jonathan Sale, "Passed/Failed: Angela Huth," *Independent* (London), 23 April 1998, p. E10;

Kathleen Tynan, "Marital Whoas," *Vanity Fair* (December 1992): 190.

Robin Jenkins

(11 September 1912 -)

Ingibjörg Ágústsdóttir
University of Iceland

See also the Jenkins entry in *DLB 14: British Novelists Since 1960.*

BOOKS: *So Gaily Sings the Lark* (Glasgow: MacLellan, 1950);
Happy for the Child (London: Lehmann, 1953);
The Thistle and the Grail (London: Macdonald, 1954);
The Cone-Gatherers (London: Macdonald, 1955; New York: Taplinger, 1981);
Guests of War (London: Macdonald, 1956);
The Missionaries (London: Macdonald, 1957);
The Changeling (London: Macdonald, 1958);
Love Is a Fervent Fire (London: Macdonald, 1959);
Some Kind of Grace (London: Macdonald, 1960);
Dust on the Paw (London: Macdonald, 1961; New York: Putnam, 1961);
The Tiger of Gold (London: Macdonald, 1962);
A Love of Innocence (London: Cape, 1963);
The Sardana Dancers (London: Cape, 1964);
A Very Scotch Affair (London: Gollancz, 1968);
The Holy Tree (London: Gollancz, 1969);
The Expatriates (London: Gollancz, 1971);
A Toast to the Lord (London: Gollancz, 1972);
A Far Cry from Bowmore and Other Stories (London: Gollancz, 1973);
A Figure of Fun (London: Gollancz, 1974);
A Would-Be Saint (London: Gollancz, 1978; New York: Taplinger, 1980);
Fergus Lamont (Edinburgh: Canongate, 1979; New York: Taplinger, 1979);
The Awakening of George Darroch (Edinburgh: Waterfront/Glasgow Herald, 1985);
Just Duffy (Edinburgh: Canongate, 1988);
Poverty Castle (Nairn, Scotland: Balnain, 1991);
Willie Hogg (Edinburgh: Polygon, 1993);
Leila (Edinburgh: Polygon, 1995);
Lunderston Tales (Edinburgh: Polygon, 1996);
Matthew and Sheila (Edinburgh: Polygon, 1998);
Poor Angus (Edinburgh: Canongate, 2000);
Childish Things (Edinburgh: Canongate, 2001);

Robin Jenkins (Bruccoli Clark Layman Archives)

Lady Magdalen (Edinburgh: Canongate, forthcoming 2003).

Editions: *The Thistle and the Grail,* with introduction by Cairns Craig (Edinburgh: Harris, 1983);

The Cone-Gatherers, with introduction by Iain Crichton Smith (Edinburgh: Harris, 1980; London: Penguin, 1983);

Guests of War, with introduction by Isobel Murray, Scottish Classics Series, no. 10 (Edinburgh: Scottish Academic Press, 1988);

The Changeling, with introduction by Alan Spence (Edinburgh: Canongate, 1989);

Fergus Lamont, with introduction by Bob Tait (Edinburgh: Canongate, 1990);

Just Duffy, with introduction by Margery Palmer McCulloch (Edinburgh: Canongate, 1995).

OTHER: "The Writer on Writing," in *The Cone-Gatherers* (Harlow: Longman, 1991), pp. v–viii;

"Cardwell Bay 1937," in *Fallen Angels: Paintings by Jack Vettriano,* edited by W. Gordon Smith (London: Pavilion, 1994), p. 92.

SELECTED PERIODICAL PUBLICATIONS–UNCOLLECTED:

POETRY

"Homemaker," "Tavira," "Waiting," "Desolation," and "Next Morning," in *Chapman,* 71 (Winter 1992–1993): 72–75.

NONFICTION

"Novelist in Scotland," *Saltire Review,* 5 (1955): 7–10;

"Why I Decided Scotland Must Be Seen Through Fresh and Truthful Eyes," *Glasgow Herald,* 12 October 1982, p. 11.

Robin Jenkins was praised by Eleanor Morton as "one of Scotland's finest contemporary writers" and by Douglas Gifford in *Books in Scotland* (Spring 1996) as "one of the great novelists in English." Yet, Jenkins has never gained international recognition despite the serious critical attention given to many of his novels. Even in Scotland, public and academic recognition of his work has been marginal when compared with his more successful contemporaries. Jenkins is undeniably a Scottish writer, but he has remained an outsider in the Scottish literary scene. He has kept himself at a distance from the literary circles of Scotland and has been reluctant to promote his work in the media and elsewhere. This self-chosen isolation is perhaps one of the reasons Jenkins's work has not been more widely acclaimed. It may also contribute to the fact that it is problematic to place his work within specific literary traditions or movements. Jenkins's own insistence that he does not belong to any literary tradition manifests his strong opposition toward categorization and may have reinforced the idiosyncratic nature of his literary approach. Although critics have tended to classify his writing as following traditionalist or realist models, his work, especially from the 1970s onward, breaks from traditional narrative methods and challenges the realist model. Jenkins regards himself as a realist, while he also holds that the shifts in narrative perspective that are such a prominent feature of his technique reflect his belief that there is, as he told Glenda Norquay, "no absolute truth." These facts may have a bearing on Cairns Craig's assertion in the *Edinburgh Review* (Spring 2001) that Jenkins "uses the techniques of traditional realism precisely to subvert the certainties . . . which realism was designed to support."

In his work Jenkins explores themes and issues such as the influence of Calvinism on Scottish society, the question of urban versus rural values, the vulnerability of children and the fragile nature of innocence, the effects of class division and the injustices of capitalist ideology, the cruelty and futility of war, and humanity's fallen state in a world of hypocrisy and spiritual lassitude. In the case of the novels set abroad, he explores racial prejudice and cultural conflict in the context of the dubious legacy of British imperialism. Jenkins's work portrays human isolation and the difficulties of communication in a disillusioned, mechanized world and highlights the inadequacy of language in representing the reality of individual experience and emotion. Above all, Jenkins's treatment of his recurrent concerns is driven by intense ethical awareness. He wants to examine the moral inconsistencies and hypocrisies of human nature; his fiction forces readers to see themselves as they are and shocks them into recognizing humanity's moral weaknesses. Throughout his work Jenkins toys with the idea of attainable moral perfection, the idea that pure goodness can exist in a world of selfishness and greed. At the same time, his narratives stress the near impossibility of achieving such goodness through showing that humanity is by nature morally fallible and limited. Jenkins has said that he is more interested in characters than plot and prides himself on being an ironist. Although many of his narratives appear to be relatively simple, Jenkins's irony disrupts this apparent simplicity, making it problematic to reach a straightforward interpretation of their underlying meanings. It is a common tendency among Jenkins's readership to overlook his deeply ironic approach, thus failing to appreciate the inherent ambiguity of his work.

John Robin Jenkins was born on 11 September 1912 in Cambuslang, a small mining village in Lanarkshire, Scotland. He hardly knew his father, James Jenkins, who fought in World War I and died of rheumatic fever in 1919, shortly after returning home from the war. Jenkins's mother, Annie Robin Jenkins, was left on her own to support a family of four children by working as a cook and housekeeper.

Jenkins did well at school and was awarded a bursary for his secondary education at Hamilton Academy. In his teens he went to various churches, trying to find a spiritual home, but eventually decided that none of them suited his beliefs and became a professed atheist. Jenkins studied English at the University of Glasgow and finished an M.A. there in 1936. In 1937 he married Mary McIntyre Wylie and taught English in a primary school in Glasgow for four years. The couple eventually had three children: Helen, Ann, and Colin. When World War II broke out, Jenkins had become a committed pacifist and registered as a conscientious objector. He was exempted from military service and worked for the Forestry Commission in Argyll between 1940 and 1946. After the war Jenkins resumed teaching, this time at a secondary school in the deprived East End area of Glasgow. During this period Jenkins first started writing seriously. In 1955 he moved to a post in Dunoon Grammar School. Two years later he left Scotland and over the next decade taught abroad, at Ghazi College in Kabul, Afghanistan, from 1957 to 1959; in the British Institute of Barcelona University from 1959 to 1961; and at Gaya College in Sabah, Malaysia, from 1963 to 1968. Two years after returning to Scotland, he retired from teaching and devoted himself to writing. He has lived in Toward, south of Dunoon, since 1968, although he has also lived and written for periods in Spain, California, and Canada. In 1999 Jenkins received an Order of the British Empire for services to literature.

Jenkins's first novel, *So Gaily Sings the Lark* (1950), is one of several novels that reflect his years in the forestry service, telling the story of David Sutherland, a young miner who travels from Lanarkshire to Argyll to work in forestry. The novel appears at first to echo the preoccupations of the Scottish Literary Renaissance in its implications that a more simple, self-sufficient, and natural way of life is to be found in the countryside and that rural Scotland can offer a sense of unity and continuity that would not be achieved in an urban environment. Through revealing that country life is beset by similar moral and social problems to those of life in the city, however, Jenkins's novel ultimately rejects Scottish Renaissance suggestions of a harmonious fusion of man with nature. Compared with much of Jenkins's other work, *So Gaily Sings the Lark* is an unremarkable novel and has received minimal critical attention, but it introduces many central characteristics of Jenkins's writing, such as his tendency to render ambiguous the conclusions of his novels by suggesting possible alternative resolutions to the plot.

Jenkins's second novel, *Happy for the Child* (1953), received considerable attention and earned him the *Daily Sketch* Book Find Award. It is the first of a line of novels to deal specifically with the effects of poverty and class distinction in urban Scotland and introduces one of Jenkins's favorite concerns: the innocence, vulnerability, and corruptibility of children. John Stirling is a poor boy, the "lad o' pairts" who has the chance to rise above his social circumstance through intelligence and hard work. He feels ashamed of his background and endeavors to keep it hidden from his wealthier schoolmates but is painfully aware of his cowardice and ingratitude to his hardworking mother. The antithesis to Stirling is Gourlay, a dunce at school, rebellious and given to nasty pranks. Gourlay provides Stirling with a negative alternative against which to measure his own position; conversely, Stirling's brilliance at school provides the positive alternative that Gourlay desperately lacks. Initially, narrative presentation of Stirling and Gourlay appears to establish clear-cut binaries of good and evil, but Gourlay's role as symbolizing evil is gradually called into question through the brutal revelation of Gourlay's miserable domestic circumstance. The empty despair of his situation finally renders trivial the worries that cause Stirling's depression and isolation at school. Jenkins's deconstruction of opposites in this novel highlights the impossibility of classifying moral behavior into categories like good and evil, right and wrong. It also reflects Jenkins's approach to difficult moral questions in his work: he seldom draws clear lines between moral opposites and does not present his characters or story lines in black and white but rather in different shades of gray, changing constantly according to the use of narrative irony and ambiguity.

His third novel, *The Thistle and the Grail* (1954), received positive reviews and, two years after its publication, was described by George Blake as "a long, resourceful, eloquent, occasionally coarse, slightly improbable and always challenging tale of life in an industrial townlet in Lanarkshire." Its central theme is football, and its aim is to show football as the new religion of Scotland. It charts the efforts of a junior football club (the Thistle of the title) to win the cup (the Grail) for the first time. The central character is Rutherford, the president of the football club, whose professional success and material comfort are a source of guilt for him, since he feels that by advancing socially he has betrayed his ideals of social justice. Through Rutherford's development, Jenkins raises serious questions regarding the validity of idealism, community values, and the limits of human moral ability. The story of Rutherford's predicament is framed by Jenkins's satirical, often comic, treatment of football. By virtue of its name, the Thistle team and its followers are presented as an ironic symbol of Scotland and the Scottish nation, while football and religion become almost indistinguishable from one another through the vocabulary used: football supporters are "worshippers," football players are "martyrs," and goalposts are "altars." Setting up an analogy between football fanaticism and extreme religion, Jenkins criticizes the self-image of a community or a nation that relies so heavily on "religion" for a sense of identity that it fails to see the sources wherein its real identity can be found.

Jenkins's subsequent novel, *The Cone-Gatherers* (1955), is one of his shorter and smaller-scale works, but it is also among his most widely known novels and is the only one of his books that is regularly taught in Scottish secondary schools. It has a conventional, clear-cut style and poetic quality, and its focus on the struggle between good and evil has clear biblical echoes. The novel has been compared to John Steinbeck's *Of Mice and Men* (1937), and Moira Burgess suggested that Jenkins's novel is "far more ambitious and profound" than Steinbeck's. It is set during World War II, and the action takes place on the Runcie-Campbell estate, where the brothers Neil and Calum, who is a hunchback with angelic beauty of face and moral purity of soul, gather cones. The opposite to the brothers' unobtrusive and decent nature is the evil Duror, the estate gamekeeper, who hates Calum and sees him as the personification of his own "stunted, misshapen, obscene, and hideous" life. Duror's descent into evil culminates in his murder of the innocent Calum, reflecting indirectly on the atrocities being committed by the Nazis outside the isolated setting of the woods. While Duror's moral decline warns of the evil inherent in human nature, Calum functions as a Christ figure whose ultimate death can be read as a symbolical sacrifice to atone for the sins of humanity. The conclusion of the novel, however, with its echoes of the Crucifixion and its implications of atonement and renewal, has failed to convince many readers, in particular the reaction of Lady Runcie-Campbell to finding the murdered Calum, defined by Edwin Morgan as an "implausible catharsis."

Guests of War (1956) is also set during World War II, and it describes the evacuation of hundreds of women and children from Glasgow to the countryside to safeguard them against German bombs. It can on one level be seen as a social comedy, but it also carries serious undercurrents in its commentary on social division and the moral hypocrisies of international warfare. War, as the title indicates, is a central theme, and its importance is emphasized through the repeated use of words and phrases that relate to warfare. Jenkins uses the concept of war on three levels. First, war is a symbol for the clash between the guests and the hosts of the story, the Gowburgh dispossessed and the Langrigg privileged, who are presented as virtually alien to each other despite their common cultural heritage. Second, it is central to the development of the protagonist, Bell McShelvie, a slum housewife who welcomes the war as an opportunity to escape to the country idyll of her childhood and whose feelings of guilt, self-accusation, and sense of moral inadequacy cause her great inner struggle. Third, there is the real war happening in Europe, which Edgar Roy, the young teacher who accompanies the evacuees to Langrigg, is waiting to join. An idealist who does good on behalf of the evacuees, Roy assumes the role of chivalrous hero. He is the "savior" of the Gowburgh women and children, but his future in the air force will cast him in an entirely different role, as he will bring death and misery to countless innocent German civilians. Jenkins's presentation of Roy is therefore highly ironic, and what Gifford, in "God's Colossal Irony: Robin Jenkins and *Guests of War*" (1986), termed Roy's "Galahad energy" is purely superficial.

Jenkins's next novel, *The Missionaries* (1957), has received little critical attention. The missionaries of the title are officials and police who are sent to a small Scottish island to evacuate a group of religious fanatics who claim that the island has spiritual meaning as their home and sanctuary and refuse all offers of accommodation elsewhere. Despite their skepticism, not one member of the mission is unaffected by the atmosphere on the island, and Jenkins's employment of startling symbolic allusions adds to the air of fantasy in the story. Again, religion plays an important role, emphasized by the use of vocabulary and images connected with religion and worship. The novel was described by Alastair R. Thompson as "a study of faith in decline and of faith discovered," and Jenkins, in an interview with Norquay, has commented that it is "a deliberate attempt to create an allegory–a mixture of fantasy and realism."

The Changeling (1958), one of Jenkins's best-known early works, charts the efforts of Charlie Forbes, a well-meaning schoolteacher, to "save" one of his pupils, the poor, sly, but intelligent Tom Curdie, by taking him on holiday with his family; however, his plan has disastrous consequences. While acknowledging the kindness of Forbes's gesture, the narrative perspective also suggests that his actions are partly motivated by selfish reasons, thereby rendering ambiguous the teacher's true motives. Initially suggesting an "ideal" goodness that should positively affect the characters and circumstances of the story, the narrative voice then goes on to deconstruct that apparent idealism. It turns out that Curdie's exterior remoteness conceals a fundamental sensitivity and that any show of kindness is a threat to his self-sufficiency. Thus, it is shown that goodness can be "cruel" in being a threat to

Dust jacket for the U.S. edition of Jenkins's 1978 novel, about a young man whose pursuit of absolute goodness alienates those around him (Richland County Public Library)

the basic need for survival, and despite the best intentions, kindness is liable to fail when challenged by circumstances it does not have the resources to deal with. Forbes's goodness is inadequate when faced with the complexity of Curdie; it is beyond his capacity to understand the boy's suffering, and the frequent juxtaposing of Forbes's perspective and his troublesome family affairs with the much more real anguish of his pupil sets the tone for the tragic outcome. Ultimately, the symbolic meaning of the title is fully revealed, as Tom has become a changeling, trapped between two worlds and belonging to neither. He has become an exile within his own society, unable to penetrate the world of the Forbeses and those who share their code of existence, unable to return to his old environment because of his lost independence. He belongs with the recurrent social outcasts of Jenkins's fiction, such as Gourlay of *Happy for the Child,* whom Jenkins uses to expose the immorality and hypocrisy of class segregation, simultaneously emphasizing the fragmented state of Scottish society through these characters' inability to function within it.

While it has been argued that *The Changeling* ends on a note of melodrama, critics generally agree that this conclusion is necessary to emphasize the folly and futility of Forbes's gesture and to reveal the hopelessness of solving "dilemmas of class and equality by single acts of kindness," as David Craig observed. Conversely, melodrama has been seen to detract from the quality of Jenkins's subsequent novel, *Love Is a Fervent Fire* (1959). Hugh Carstares, an army veteran, is posted to Argyll as the new district officer in the forestry service. At his arrival there, he becomes infatuated with the proud, bitter, and revengeful Constance Kilgour, a decayed aristocrat who has an illegitimate daughter. The narrative is intensely psychological, and there is a feeling of underlying menace within Jenkins's portrayal of Carstares and Constance's complex and troubled relationship. Sexuality carries almost Freudian, archetypal overtones of danger and threat, while also inspiring happiness, optimism, and anticipation. While the novel ends on a positive note, the narrative voice makes it clear that achieving perfection in this relationship will be difficult, yet emphasizes that love, though imperfect, fallible, and often poisoned by selfishness or other human faults, should always be cherished, no matter how limited. The ironies and paradoxes of love are there; readers are asked to accept that love is always subject to one's own fallibility.

Some Kind of Grace (1960) signals an important change in Jenkins's writing; it is the first of a line of the novelist's works that are based on his years abroad. During the next fourteen years, all except three out of Jenkins's eleven published works have a setting outside Scotland. Jenkins's native background and his passion for Scotland are nevertheless evident, since most of the foreign narratives focus on Scots abroad, exploring specifically Scottish reactions to and clashes with the foreign environment, its culture, and its inhabitants. Jenkins's own years abroad fall within a period that was marked by the rapid decline of the British Empire, and this decline is especially felt in his Borneo stories, where the problematic change from colonial dependence to self-government is made explicit. Jenkins's interest in questions of morality, the limits of idealism, and social hypocrisy is even further manifested in his foreign work, especially in the context of his treatment of racial difference and colonial subjugation. Throughout, the foreign fiction questions the moral value of imperial appropriation and exploitation of colonies' resources, which suggests that Jenkins was deeply sympathetic toward natives and colonies subjected to British rule. Overall, the colonial awareness of the foreign work poses serious questions regarding Britain's relationship with its former colonies and Scotland's part in the British Empire.

While the central theme of *Some Kind of Grace* is the mystery and elusiveness of grace, the novel is also a shrewd observation of Afghanistan and its people, exposing the harshness, brutality, and social injustice of Afghan life. The country is shown as controlled by the regime, by strict law and arbitrary justice, and by nepotism and corruption in official ranks. Yet, although Afghanistan was never a colony, British influence is shown to be considerable, and Jenkins's novel implicitly criticizes the British diplomats' show of racial arrogance toward the citizens of a country that has welcomed them as guests.

Similar divisions between the British and their hosts, or between East and West, are apparent in Jenkins's next novel, *Dust on the Paw* (1961), which is among Jenkins's best and most ambitious works. The novel has attracted widespread praise; Bernard Sellin, in "Robin Jenkins: The Making of the Novelist" (1986), describes it as a "large-scale, elaborate examination of the buffer zone between two alien cultures," and other critics have compared it with the works of major British novelists such as E. M. Forster and Graham Greene. Set in Afghanistan during a period of cultural revolution and political reform, *Dust on the Paw* focuses on a large international mix of characters and reaches its climax at "Jeshan" (the annual celebration of Afghan independence) when the *shaddry* (the robes and veil worn by Afghan women) is abolished. The story focuses on two sets of interracial relationships, that of the Afghan Abdul Wahab, a patriotic and idealistic scientist, with his handicapped and determined British fiancée, Laura Johnstone, and that of the British teacher, poet, and idealist Harold Moffat with his beautiful, dignified, and artistic Chinese wife, Lan. The narrative action revolves around a debate initiated by the secretly racist Moffat as to the question of British interference with Wahab's plans to marry Laura; and around Wahab's sudden rise to power in Afghan political circles. The circumstances of Wahab and Moffat are presented as parallel or mirrored situations, and the failure of both men to live up to their ideals shows a discrepancy between moral principle and social behavior that is a prominent theme in Jenkins's work. The treatment of this issue in the novel is made especially poignant in the character of Wahab, who is one of Jenkins's more interesting and complex protagonists. Possessed of an intense self-awareness, Wahab acknowledges the transitory nature of human ideals and recognizes his own corruptibility.

The title of the novel is a quotation from the Persian poet Abu al-Qasim Firdawsi, or "the Homer of Persia," who wrote that the powerful ones of the earth are the lion's paw and that the humble are the dust on it, and is especially significant to Wahab's development. The title indicates how power can be unequally distributed, but while the novel gives clear precedence to the humble it also makes clear that dust and lion need each other and are interrelated concepts. In Wahab, Jenkins brings dust and lion together: living in poverty and degradation one moment and holding a position of power the next, he is in essence both dust and lion. His inner conflict, between the ambition for power on one hand and the desire for humility on the other, is symbolically reflected in the title.

After his subsequent novel, *The Tiger of Gold* (1962)–among Jenkins's least successful novels, it tells the story of a Scottish girl who falls in love with an Indian prince–Jenkins returned temporarily to Scottish settings in *A Love of Innocence* (1963). Although it has become one of Jenkins's lesser-known novels, it attracted positive criticism in *The Times Literary Supplement* (24 May 1963), in which the reviewer commended the plot for being "as simple and as tortuous as a Grand Master's chess game." Set in 1960, the novel tells the story of the adoption of two Glaswegian brothers to a Scottish island. Jealous of his wife's continuous adultery, their father brutally murdered their mother three years previously and is now in a mental asylum for criminals. This central plot provides the basic framework for a complex tale of innocence, moral ambivalence, and redemption. Various subplots, dealing with a broad range of characters, such as frustrated spinsters, barren wives, and religious bigots, add further to the depth and elaborateness of the novel. In particular, the narrative shows a dark, disturbing side of the experience of children, and here the ironic significance of the title becomes evident: the ultimate question posed asks to what extent people will cherish and love the kind of innocence that children represent, when the children in their care are of deprived, dubious, and even criminal parentage.

In his next work, *The Sardana Dancers* (1964), Jenkins turned back to foreign settings, although this novel is not set in an Eastern country subjected to British influence or authority. Set in Spain, it is the story of English twins Jonathan and Madeleine Broxmead, both aspiring artists unsure of their creative talent, who are sustained in their easy and luxurious lifestyle by the annuity left to Jonathan by his aunt. Their comfortable but dull life is transformed by the unexpected arrival of two strangers, one a young woman from Barcelona who is on the run from the police for anti-Franco activities, the other a male, working-class Scot-

Paperback cover for Jenkins's 1993 novel, about a Glaswegian retiree and his wife who relocate to the Arizona desert (Bruccoli Clark Layman Archives)

tish painter of extraordinary genius. Through the juxtaposition of different social and moral perspectives, Jenkins explores many issues and themes, ranging from the relationship between morality and artistic creativity, to confrontations of class, to politics and nationalism. Above all, it is a story of human fallibility, personal growth, and self-discovery, but these central aspects are focused in the story of Jonathan's love for the Catalan Montserrat and in the narrative concern with human unity, symbolized in the title and the sardana, a native Catalan folk dance that Jenkins employs to suggest that human life, for all its diversity, is in effect one universal cycle in which all participate.

A Very Scotch Affair (1968) returns to Scotland, although Spain also plays an important, though secondary, role. The novel has generally been well received, and Norquay, in "Moral Absolutism in the Novels of Robert Louis Stevenson, Robin Jenkins and Muriel Spark: Challenges to Realism" (1985), notes that it is second only to *Fergus Lamont* (1979) in revealing Jenkins's "attitudes to the mind and morality of Scotland." Its protagonist, Mungo Niven, a cynical and disaffected insurance supervisor, leaves his dying wife, family, and home in a Glasgow slum for the chance of an easier and more luxurious life in Spain with his wealthy mistress. Mungo is self-deluded, callous, vainglorious, and selfish, but he also experiences moments of intense self-awareness and self-blame that invite some sympathy from the reader, and the shifting narrative perspective further reveals that Mungo is not the only severely flawed character in the novel. The idea of moral complexity and of a shifting or "split" reality is central to Jenkins's presentation of Mungo, as is indicated by Sellin in "Commitment and Betrayal: Robin Jenkins' *A Very Scotch Affair*" (1996): "Mungo Niven is a problematic character, a round complex character who can be at the same time a lecherous egotist and a man sincerely concerned with the degradation of culture and environment in an increasingly materialistic world." Presented as the most intelligent of the family, Peggy Niven understands her father's need to break free of the slum; her "guilty sympathy" for Mungo originates in her knowledge that "she too was a traitor, ready to escape when the chance came." The underlying suggestion of the novel is that, despite his cruelty toward his wife, Mungo's challenging of his repressive environment is courageous and valuable in a way that most of his family and neighbors are unable to comprehend. His unpleasantness is thus closely related, as Norquay put it in *DLB 14: British Novelists Since 1960* (1983), to a "paradoxical sense of value and worth."

Jenkins turned back to foreign settings in *The Holy Tree* (1969), arguably his most "postcolonial" novel, and certainly one of his finest works. It is set in the former British colony of Kalimantan (Sabah, or Northern Borneo) and centers on political tension and the receding power of Britain in the face of Kalimantan's forthcoming independence. Jenkins's colorful evocation of the ethnic variety of Kalimantan, along with his ironic depiction of the British expatriate community, highlights how racial prejudice and cultural tension have been created by the consistent aggression and exploitation of colonialists, in this case both the Chinese and the British.

The Holy Tree is Jenkins's only Borneo story that has a Borneo aborigine for a protagonist. Michael Eking, a nineteen-year-old Dusun boy, dreams of getting a college education and thus escaping the poverty and ignorance of his kampong, or village. This desperate ambition leads him to betray political rebels, one of them his brother, to the police. Michael is one of Jenkins's more equivocal creations, naive yet deceitful, child-like yet worldly, dedicated yet treacherous. Narrative juxtaposition of different perspectives in the novel emphasizes the moral ambiguity of Michael's character and actions. Moreover, his enthusiasm for becoming "Westernized," which, by implication, includes becoming morally corrupt, adds a satiric slant to Jenkins's treatment of colonization. Through his portrayal of Michael, Jenkins questions whether Western ideology is not guilty of moral decadence among its more positive values of democracy and freedom of speech. The imposition of British values has left an indelible mark on Kalimantan society and character, demonstrated most poignantly in the misguided notions of Michael, who is, in Francis Russell Hart's words, "caught in a postcolonial social web."

The Expatriates (1971) is also set in Kalimantan and underlines once more Jenkins's satirical perspective on British imperialism and his concern with the moral hypocrisy of racial prejudice. The portrayal of sexual relationships between races in the novel has clear symbolic meaning, especially since the relationship presented is initialized by a white man's rape of a native woman and is subsequently based on his emotional, sexual, and financial dominance over her. This symbolic pattern of subjugation and dominance is repeated in "Imelda and the Miserly Scot," one of the short stories in *A Far Cry from Bowmore and Other Stories* (1973), which features stories set in Borneo, Afghanistan, and India.

The main character of *A Toast to the Lord* (1972) is the religiously confident Agnes Tolmie, whom Alan Bold describes as "besotted with religion" and "a product of Scotland's theocratic state of mind." The result of thinking herself one of God's chosen, Agnes's manipulative behavior leads to the death of her parents and the murder of her fiancé. Her almost superhuman strength in the face of horrible death is presented in ambiguous terms, and ultimately, the reader has no way of knowing exactly what impact the tragedy has on her, because no narrative access is given to her thoughts and feelings after it happens. Instead, one has to rely on other characters' perspectives, which differ in their interpretation of events, and the narrative perspective subsequently wavers between total conviction of Agnes's spiritual worth and an absolute rejection of her as either stupid or mad. By suddenly removing narrative access to the protagonist, Jenkins thus makes it practically impossible to make definite judgments about Agnes's behavior in the last chapters of the novel.

This method of removing narrative access to the protagonist at a crucial point in the story reoccurs in *A Figure of Fun* (1974), which is set in Malaysia and centers on the question of whether to meet strange, unwanted, and unsavory moral challenges and defy the prejudice of friends and compatriots or to follow the herd, do what is expected, and accept a life of conventionality and moral mediocrity. Mediocrity wins, but the real value or "truth" of such an outcome is again rendered ambiguous through Jenkins's manipulation of narrative point of view. In *A Would-Be Saint* (1978) Jenkins uses the receding protagonist to even greater effect. It is an unsettling and enigmatic novel, charting the development of "would-be saint" Gavin Hamilton from his childhood until he is in his late thirties and working in forestry in Argyll at the end of World War II. His moral sensibility sets him apart from others from an early age, and by always turning the other cheek–in private life, football, and war–he demonstrates the kind of humility and virtue that he feels are lacking in his society. His moral pilgrimage consists of trying to achieve an absolute goodness, or "saintliness," that could prove inspirational to his fellow beings. Gavin is presented as a Christ figure, and the skepticism and suspicion shown to him by other characters are made analogous with what would be the likely reaction of people should Christ appear in the modern world. At the same time, Jenkins presents Gavin's goodness in highly ambiguous terms. Other characters are unsure about Gavin's motives and feel uncomfortable in his presence, and it is frequently implied that his goodness and charity are not altogether spontaneous but spring from pride and are practiced merely to prove himself morally superior to the rest of fallible humanity. In many ways Gavin is an unpleasant character, his cool, detached moral calculations taking precedence over human love and involvement. His deliberate retreat into isolation coincides with Jenkins's gradual removal of narrative access to his protagonist, with the result that Gavin has ultimately moved altogether beyond the comprehension of other characters and of the reader.

Gavin is one of several characters in Jenkins's fiction whose unconventional, extreme behavior and actions isolate them from their society and render them incomprehensible, even unpleasant, to other characters and the reader. Like Agnes Tolmie before him, and like the protagonists of *The Awakening of George Darroch* (1985) and *Just Duffy* (1988) after him, Gavin inhabits an almost fabulistic or mythic realm of extremes. These characters' moral and/or religious stances reject compromise and challenge the mediocre morality of their society, where charity and self-denial are disregarded in favor of material comfort and respectability and where the majority pay only lip service to the moral and social teachings of Christ. Initially, by creating these characters, whose apparently unblinking faith, charity, virtue, and prodigious awareness of human cruelty and immorality stand in sharp contrast with the "halfway house" ethics of their community, Jenkins forces an understanding of the corrupt morals of politicians, the

Church, and society in general. Yet, as the stories progress, doubt is cast on each protagonist's moral or spiritual value, so that the reader eventually has to question their motives: Are they genuine or false? Are they based on moral and spiritual superiority or do they arise from pride, stubbornness, and attention-seeking? Are they merely manifestations of insanity? As each character is pushed further toward extremes in terms of their behavior and social interaction, the reader can no longer identify or sympathize with their actions. Thus, while Jenkins's portrayal of extremes forces a recognition of the moral and spiritual lassitude of the world, his deeply ironic and ambivalent approach to Agnes, Gavin, Darroch, and Duffy ultimately subverts any former indication of their moral and/or spiritual value. In this respect, all four texts seem to include a deconstructive element; they originally appear to establish a system of superior ethical or religious values (the absolutes of goodness and spirituality) that are then undermined, questioned, and deconstructed through narrative ambiguity and irony.

In her 1993 essay on the "disruptive" element of Jenkins's fiction, Norquay argues that his "recent writing can be seen as both a continuation and a development of his previous work, but in both respects maintaining a disruptive character which is distinctively his own." Norquay's estimate is that the challenges in Jenkins's work, which operate as a force for disruption, "emerge more sharply in the period since 1979" and that since then Jenkins has "both built upon and diverged from his early works." This definition is appropriate in terms of the directions in which Jenkins's later Scottish narratives have progressed. Thus, *Fergus Lamont,* considered one of Jenkins's most important later developments and certainly among his finest novels, continues the ruthless social analysis that characterizes much of his earlier fiction, interrogating Calvinist morality and highlighting the fragmented nature of Scottish society and the great divergence between social classes in Scotland. Simultaneously, *Fergus Lamont* diverges from the earlier fiction in terms of both narrative technique and narrative approach to these concerns. Unlike his earlier narratives, Jenkins's novel here juxtaposes two different time settings within the story line: the story of Fergus's eventful past, which takes up most of the narrative space, and occasional flash-forwards, signaled by passages in italics, which relate the present life of the old and impoverished Fergus as he writes his memoirs. Fergus's memoirs then include several leaps forward in time that hint at future events in his life and the fate of other characters. Thus, Jenkins breaks his usual habit of laying out his narratives in a straightforward time sequence in which no prior knowledge–except for through suggestive symbolism, imagery, and foreshadowing–is given of events to come. On another level, the first-person narrative means that the interpretation of events is entirely dependent upon Fergus's biased vision, and the reader is forced to identify with a character one is otherwise inclined to dislike. Ultimately, the kilted Fergus, whose odyssey from poverty to riches and back into poverty brings him into contact with every level of his society, becomes an ironic parody of the schizophrenic state of Scotland.

While the narrative structure of *Fergus Lamont* indicates a move toward "postmodern" methods in Jenkins's writing, *Poverty Castle* (1991) reveals the author at his most innovative–and self-reflexive–yet. Its narrative form and its function as metafiction constitute a definite break from Jenkins's usual narrative techniques. It is, on the one hand, a story of a dying novelist, Donald, who wants his last novel to be "a celebration of goodness, without any need of irony." On the other hand, it is the novel Donald writes, which focuses on the Sempill family, who use part of their inherited fortune to buy a derelict country house that they name Poverty Castle. Later in the story a working-class girl, Peggy, the university roommate of the eldest Sempill girl, is introduced. The Sempills seem the model of happiness and success, and initially there is an atmosphere of love and benevolence, but the narrative soon reveals cracks in the Edenic image of the Sempills and their world.

The Sempills' happiness derives from their isolation from and ignorance of the outside world, while there are also hints of the father's alcoholism and the mother's mental instability. These problems are never discussed or resolved but only hushed up, as if bringing them into the open would shatter the positive image of the family. The name of their home, Poverty Castle, is moreover oxymoronic by implication and thus highlights the paradox that lies at the heart of the Sempills' supposed happiness. Ultimately, Donald fails in his intention of celebrating goodness through his portrayal of the Sempills, but an alternative, more realistic model of goodness is established in the character of Peggy, whose "limited but genuine goodness," as Horst Prillinger characterizes it, triumphs over the Sempills' artificiality. Through the story of Donald and his novel, Jenkins comments on the nature of fiction making and questions the ability of literature to do justice to the complexities and paradoxes that characterize society and human moral capacity. At the same time, *Poverty Castle* is highly self-reflective; the efforts of Donald the novelist have an obvious relevance to Jenkins himself and may be read, as Norquay does in "Disruptions: The Later Fiction of Robin Jenkins," as an ironic comment on Jenkins's own "inability to settle for the comfortable and comforting."

Paperback cover for Jenkins's 2001 novel, about an elderly widower trying to come to terms with a lifetime of dishonesty about his humble origins

Jenkins's next novel, *Willie Hogg* (1993), is the story of retired hospital porter Hogg and his apparently simple wife, Maggie. They get the sudden news that Maggie's missionary sister is dying of cancer on her Christian mission to the Navajo Indians in the Arizona desert, and after a Glasgow tabloid newspaper gets interested in their story, a publicity fund is set up for them to travel to Arizona. Their journey marks a major change: Maggie, formerly portrayed as a lost and bewildered simpleton, becomes sensible, confident, and determined, while Willie feels nervous and vulnerable. In the days before and after Maggie's sudden death in the desert, Willie is forced to reassess her abilities, his feelings for her, and his own views of humanity and religion. Significantly, Willie and Maggie are transferred from an enclosed, even parochial, urban locale to the desert landscape of Arizona, where they encounter the very different culture of the Navajo Indians. This extreme dislocation of both physical self and inner sensibility forces the changes that take place in both characters.

In *Leila* (1995) Jenkins returns once more to foreign settings, but although the novel has attracted critical attention, critics are not agreed on the level of its quality. It is remarkably similar to *A Figure of Fun,* although the political and historical element is much stronger than in the earlier novel, and Jenkins's exposure of the imperial legacy emerges more clearly and effectively than before. Jenkins's next publication, *Lunderston Tales* (1996), is a collection of short stories united by the setting of Lunderston and focuses on provosts, shopkeepers, ministers, plumbers, hairdressers, rich widows, golfers, and visiting prostitutes from Glasgow. The writing of *Lunderston Tales* represented a personal challenge for Jenkins, as expressed in his foreword to the book: while suggesting that Scotland's failure to vote for home rule in the 1979 referendum made it "a country that, too supine to take itself seriously, does not deserve to be taken seriously by any other country," Jenkins stresses that nevertheless, "paradoxically, its individual people are as interesting as any in America or Russia." The wide scope of issues dealt with in the collection, local as well as universal, manifests the validity of Jenkins's assertion. Jenkins's playful sarcasm spares neither individuals, organizations, nor politicians, but there is more optimism and more affection in Jenkins's irony than in many of his other depictions of Scotland. His portrayal of the Lunderstonians' gossip, parochialism, and self-righteousness is delicately poised between controlled anger, impartiality, compassion, and humor.

Matthew and Sheila (1998) is the story of two children: Matthew, who sets himself apart through his apparently simpleminded goodness and sensitivity, and the beautiful and talented Sheila, who shows her nasty side only to Matthew, claiming to have killed a baby and one of their classmates, and plots the murder of her own father. Jenkins described his intention in a 1999 interview with Ingibjörg Ágústsdóttir as being to portray true goodness in Matthew and pure evil in Sheila, but this set of binary opposites does not survive for long in its original form. By making Matthew become consumed with ideas of Calvinist grace, thinking he is one of "those favourites of God who could do no wrong, or rather who, if they did what in others would be called wrong, were immediately absolved and protected from punishment," Jenkins–given his critical view of Calvinist ideology–undermines the notion of Matthew as good. Other flaws in Matthew's character become apparent, especially his hatred of his new stepmother. The evil mentality of Sheila is never proved either, just hinted at; all along, there is the possibility that her evil is merely an illusion, sustained by Matthew's vivid imagination and Sheila's possibly false boasts of doing evil deeds. As a result the boundaries between the concept of good and evil as portrayed in the two children become increasingly blurred as the story develops, and the reader is eventually left unsure about the qualities of either character.

Jenkins's subsequent novel, *Poor Angus* (2000), tells the story of Angus McAllister, a painter who has returned to Scotland from Basah in the Far East to find inspiration for masterpieces on his native Hebridean island. It is a tragicomedy that focuses on Angus's rejection of his former mistress from Basah and his refusal to help her in the fight over the custody of her daughter. The novel tackles the role of the artist; through Angus's perspective, artistic talent is perceived as a sign of grace, thus justifying the true artist's show of selfishness and cruelty to others. Being an artist sets one aside while necessitating the use of other people to achieve artistic perfection. The novel therefore asks whether artistic merit justifies the means by which art is created. Ultimately, the true value of Angus's art is undermined and questioned via Jenkins's portrayal of his selfish nature. For all his intimations of immortality and artistic greatness, Angus is really, as the ironic title suggests, "poor" in spiritual, emotional, and moral terms.

Jenkins's 2001 publication, *Childish Things,* reiterates how central the issues of morality and self-knowledge are to his literary vision. The protagonist and narrator, seventy-two-year-old, recently widowed Gregor McLeod, wavers between self-interested opportunism and self-flagellation and guilt. One minute he questions his own capacity for genuine despair and grief, the next he fantasizes about being involved with rich widows for the sake of their possessions. It soon emerges that McLeod has lived his life in disguise, trying to escape memories of his underprivileged and unhappy childhood. He has put on appearances and even lied to his family about aspects of his past, but the truth of his origin has tormented him all his life. When his friend, a Californian film star, hires Glaswegian private detectives to uncover his lies, McLeod eventually has to face up to his past and acknowledge the callousness and moral cowardice that characterized his treatment of his mother. The novel encapsulates Jenkins's central thematic concerns; it highlights once more the deep-set divisions that lie at the heart of Scottish society and character, explores the issues of familial loyalty and moral fallibility, and charts McLeod's development from betrayal, selfishness, and conceit toward self-knowledge and, perhaps, ultimate redemption.

Robin Jenkins's next novel is *Lady Magdalen* (2003), an historical novel about the wife of the Marquis of Montrose. As in most of his fiction, Jenkins's choice of subject is a challenging one; little is known about Lady Magdalen, which gives Jenkins plenty of artistic license in her portrayal. It is to be expected, moreover, that the Scottish Covenanting Wars, in which the Marquis of Montrose played a leading role, will be an important theme, perhaps continuing Jenkins's ruthless investigation of the forces that have influenced Scottish religious life, culture, and mentality. Without doubt, what Sellin, in "Commitment and Betrayal," describes as Jenkins's "moral rigidity, the hard uncompromising stare with which he views his characters and the present world," will also be present in this forthcoming novel. Jenkins is never easy on his readers, and they might at times find his deeply ironic perspective and his seemingly arbitrary use of symbolism difficult to fathom. Even so, these idiosyncratic qualities are part of what makes reading Jenkins's work an enriching process of learning about Scotland, the world, and human nature.

Interviews:

Glenda Norquay, "Moral Absolutism in the Novels of Robert Louis Stevenson, Robin Jenkins and Muriel Spark: Challenges to Realism," Ph.D. thesis, University of Edinburgh, 1985, pp. 436–451;

Winifride Logan, "The Symbolism of Good and Evil: Studies in the Novels of Robin Jenkins," dissertation, University of Glasgow, 1991, pp. 42–48;

Eleanor Morton, "Easily led by his creations," *Glasgow Herald,* 12 February 1999, p. 24;

Ingibjörg Ágústsdóttir, "A Truthful Scot," *In Scotland,* 1 (Autumn 1999): 13–22.

References:

George Blake, *Annals of Scotland, 1895–1955: An Essay on the Twentieth-Century Scottish Novel* (London: BBC, 1956);

Alan Bold, "The Reflective Novel: Jenkins and Urquhart," in his *Modern Scottish Literature* (London & New York: Longman, 1983), pp. 205–212;

Moira Burgess, "Robin Jenkins: A Novelist of Scotland," *Library Review,* 22 (1970): 409–412;

Cairns Craig, "Robin Jenkins–A Would-Be Realist?" *Edinburgh Review,* 106 (Spring 2001): 12–22;

David Craig, "A National Literature? Recent Scottish Writing," *Studies in Scottish Literature,* 1 (1963–1964): 151–169;

Douglas Gifford, "God's Colossal Irony: Robin Jenkins and *Guests of War,*" *Cencrastus,* 24 (1986): 13–17;

Gifford, "Spring Fiction: Dreams of Love and Justice," *Books in Scotland,* 57 (Spring 1996): 8–15;

Francis Russell Hart, "Novelists of Survival," in his *The Scottish Novel: A Critical Survey* (London: Murray, 1978), pp. 272–286;

Maurice Lindsay, "The Scottish Renaissance," in his *History of Scottish Literature* (London: Hale, 1977), pp. 375–441;

Edwin Morgan, "The Novels of Robin Jenkins," in his *Essays* (Cheadle Hulme, U.K.: Carcanet, 1974), pp. 242–245;

Glenda Norquay, "Disruptions: The Later Fiction of Robin Jenkins," in *The Scottish Novel Since the Seventies: New Visions, Old Dreams,* edited by Gavin Wallace and Randall Stevenson (Edinburgh: Edinburgh University Press, 1993), pp. 11–24;

Norquay, "Moral Absolutism in the Novels of Robert Louis Stevenson, Robin Jenkins and Muriel Spark: Challenges to Realism," Ph.D. thesis, University of Edinburgh, 1985;

Horst Prillinger, *Family and the Scottish Working-Class Novel, 1984–1994* (Frankfurt am Main & New York: Peter Lang, 2000), pp. 42–47, 79–83, 111–118, 145–156, 185–190;

Bernard Sellin, "Commitment and Betrayal: Robin Jenkins' *A Very Scotch Affair,*" in *Studies in Scottish Fiction, 1945 to the Present,* edited by Susanne Hagemann (Frankfurt am Main & New York: Peter Lang, 1996), pp. 97–108;

Sellin, "Robin Jenkins: The Making of the Novelist," *Cencrastus,* 24 (1986): 7–9;

Alastair R. Thompson, "Faith and Love: An Examination of Some Themes in the Novels of Robin Jenkins," *New Saltire,* 3 (1963): 57–64;

Roderick Watson, *The Literature of Scotland* (Basingstoke: Macmillan, 1984), pp. 453–454;

Jack Webster, "Why This Rare Scottish Talent Hides Potential Classics in a Farmhouse Drawer," *Glasgow Herald,* 25 June 1984, p. 7.

A. L. Kennedy

(22 October 1965 –)

Andrew Biswell
King's College, Aberdeen University

BOOKS: *Night Geometry and the Garscadden Trains: Short Stories* (Edinburgh: Polygon, 1990);
Looking for the Possible Dance (London: Secker & Warburg, 1993);
Now That You're Back (London: Cape, 1994);
So I Am Glad (London: Cape, 1995; New York: Knopf, 2000);
Tea and Biscuits (London: Phoenix, 1996);
Original Bliss (London: Cape, 1997; New York: Knopf, 1999);
The Life and Death of Colonel Blimp (London: British Film Institute, 1997);
Absolutely Nothing (Glasgow: Mariscat Press, 1998);
Everything You Need (London: Cape, 1999; New York: Knopf, 2001);
On Bullfighting (London: Yellow Jersey Press, 1999; New York: Anchor, 2001);
Indelible Acts (London: Cape, 2002; New York: Knopf, forthcoming 2003).

PLAY PRODUCTIONS: *The Audition,* Edinburgh Festival Fringe, 1993;
Delicate, Royal Leamington Spa, Motionhouse Dance Company, March 1996;
True (Requiem for Lucy Palmer), Glasgow, Tramway Theatre, 2000.

PRODUCED SCRIPTS: *Totally Out of It,* television, BBC, 1993;
Just To Say, television, BBC, 1994;
The Year of the Prince, television, BBC, 1994;
There's an End to an Auld Song, television, BBC, 1995;
Ghostdancing, television, BBC, 1995;
Stella Does Tricks, motion picture, adapted by Kennedy from her short story "Friday Payday," Compulsive Films / Sidewalk Productions, 1997;
For the Love of Burns, television, BBC 2, 1999;
Dice, television, by Kennedy and John Burnside, CBC, 5 November 2001.

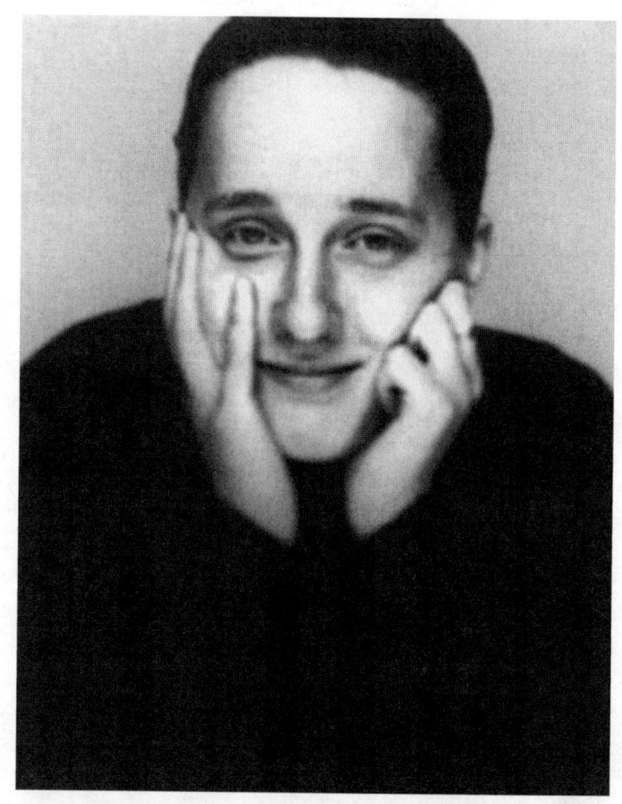

A. L. Kennedy (photograph by David Thompson; from the dust jacket for the U.S. edition of So I Am Glad, *2000)*

OTHER: *The Ghost of Liberace,* edited by Kennedy, Hamish Whyte, and Meg Bateman, New Writing Scotland, no. 11 (Aberdeen: Association for Scottish Literary Studies, 1993);
A Sort of Hot Scotland, edited by Kennedy, James McGonigal, and Bateman, New Writing Scotland, no. 12 (Aberdeen: Association for Scottish Literary Studies, 1994);
Last Things First, edited by Kennedy, McGonigal, and Bateman, New Writing Scotland, no. 13 (Aber-

deen: Association for Scottish Literary Studies, 1995);

"Not Changing the World," in *Peripheral Visions: Images of Nationhood in Contemporary British Fiction* (Cardiff: University of Wales Press, 1995), pp. 100–102;

"True," in *New Writing 4,* edited by A. S. Byatt and Alan Hollinghurst (London: Vintage/British Council, 1995), pp. 27–31;

"Awaiting an Adverse Reaction," in *New Writing 6,* edited by Byatt and Peter Porter (London: Vintage/British Council, 1997), pp. 43–46;

New Writing 9, edited by Kennedy and John Fowles (London: Vintage/British Council, 2000);

Jean Rhys, *Good Morning, Midnight,* introduction by Kennedy (London: Penguin, 2000).

A. L. Kennedy is one of the most consistently energetic and critically acclaimed novelists to have emerged from Scotland in the closing years of the twentieth century. Since the early 1990s she has produced novels, collections of short stories, nonfiction books, stage plays, television scripts, a motion-picture screenplay, and several journalistic pieces. Her critical reputation has steadily broadened as her readership has become international. Initially hailed as a major new voice by the Edinburgh press, she has subsequently been lauded in the columns of newspapers and magazines published in London and New York and elsewhere in North America. Reviewing the U.S. edition (1999) of her short-story collection *Original Bliss* (1997) in *The New York Times* on 14 February 1999, the poet Thomas Lynch declared that "Kennedy is a world-class fiction writer." It might also be said of Kennedy herself, as Lynch said of one of her fictional characters, that she is "neither solely female nor mostly Caledonian."

The hallmarks of her literary style are clearly on display in her earliest published stories and novels. Kennedy specializes in austere, emotionally loaded fiction and naked, at times almost painfully confessional, nonfiction. Rejecting the modernist experimentalism of such writers as James Joyce and Virginia Woolf, she is a writer who is inclined toward realist narratives that are nevertheless deeply charged with meaning and resonance. The short stories typically function as enigmatic fragments, whose context and location may be difficult to work out on a first reading. Depression, loneliness, paranoia, suicide, prostitution, child abuse, infidelity, wife beating, sadism, sexual fetishism, and mental breakdown are consistent themes throughout Kennedy's published fiction and nonfiction. But this apparently bleak worldview is lightened by occasional moments of sublimity and creative or religious fulfillment. Furthermore, the narrative voice often undercuts the intense suffering that Kennedy describes with odd flashes of humor and irony.

In addition to her considerable fictional output, Kennedy is known throughout the British Isles as a regular performer of her work at arts centers and literary festivals, and since 2000 she has worked as an occasional political columnist for *The Guardian* newspaper in London, in which capacity she has made contentious public statements on the conduct of the government of Prime Minister Tony Blair, the dubious ethics of animal cloning, and the U.S. intervention against the Taliban in Afghanistan. Significantly, with her story "Night Geometry and the Garscadden Trains" she is also the youngest writer to be represented in *The Oxford Book of Scottish Short Stories* (1995), edited by the poet-professor Douglas Dunn.

Alison Louise Kennedy was born 22 October 1965 in Dundee, on the east coast of Scotland, to R. Alan Kennedy and Edwardine Mildred Price Kennedy. In many respects Kennedy might be thought, along with her near-contemporaries Don Paterson and W. N. Herbert, for example, to have put Dundee on the literary map. (Most well-known Scottish writers have come from Edinburgh or Glasgow.) Perhaps partly as a result of her success, other Dundonian writers, such as the Scots novelist Matthew Fitt (born in 1968), are now beginning to find a wider audience. One of the crucial aspects of Kennedy's writing is that she appears to be working against the grain of traditional Scottish culture. In *On Bullfighting* (1999) she speaks dismissively about the historical hallucinating that has long characterized Scottish oral poetry and music. With reference to the folk song "Mhairi's Wedding," she writes:

> For those of you lucky enough to have never encountered this piece of pseudo-Celtic pap I will say that its first words are *Step we gaily, on the go, heel for heel and toe for toe,* and that it then deteriorates. It mentions–I can hear it fucking mentioning–herring and oatmeal and peat and several other elements vital to the noble, rural, ceilidhing Gaelic life.

Kennedy acknowledges that in recent decades Scottish literature has been engaged in a rejection of what she terms "romanticised tartan lunacy." Although her cultural formation is almost exclusively Scottish, Kennedy has stated that she has always felt partly "a foreigner" in Scotland. Her mother is of Welsh origin, and she explains in *The Life and Death of Colonel Blimp* (1997) that her parents had returned from Australia shortly before she was born, and that, as a result, "I did not sound like the people I met in my home town, or the children I was educated with in school. I could learn the language–I still have a protective tendency to bor-

Dust jacket for the U.S. edition of Kennedy's 1995 novel, in which a man claims to be the reincarnation of the seventeenth-century French poet and duelist Savinien de Cyrano de Bergerac (Richland County Public Library)

row other people's accents–but it was not the language of my heart and mind."

Kennedy is notoriously reticent about the details of her private life; however, a careful reading of her published works, together with newspaper and radio interviews, reveals a surprising amount of biographical information. Her parents divorced when she was eleven years old, and she continued to live in Dundee with her mother, a schoolteacher. Her father was a professor of psychology, but she has stated in interviews that the dominant male figure throughout her childhood was her maternal grandfather, J. H. Price, to whom her early books are dedicated. She told Stephen McGinty, in a 30 May 1999 interview for *The Sunday Times* (London), "My grandfather was the stable one. He was a big influence on me. The more I think about it, the greater he was. . . . It makes a difference in you if you are a woman. It's your first relationship, the first man you go out with." Speaking of her absent father, she said, "I think if he had stayed around and I had grown up to 18 we might have had some form of relationship, not father-daughter but pals. But that just didn't happen. He comes to readings but there isn't much to say. It is all too late."

Kennedy attended Dundee High School, a private institution in the city, from 1970 until 1983, and she developed her interest in poetry and drama while studying there. She told Gillian Glover in an interview for *The Scotsman* (1 December 1995): "If ever there was an explosion, it happened to me in fourth or fifth year at school. That's when I became a manic reader. Especially poetry. Then I became obsessive, really obsessive about theatre, and read lots of play texts. I just stayed at home and read."

Between 1983 and 1986 Kennedy studied for her B.A. degree in theatre studies and drama at the University of Warwick in Coventry, England. She resided a few miles away from the campus in Royal Leamington Spa. Warwick provides one of the locations for her first novel, *Looking for the Possible Dance* (1993). Jenny Turner, who interviewed Kennedy for *The Guardian* (London) in 1994, placed the origin of her earliest short stories in the dramatic monologues she wrote while studying there. Although none of Kennedy's work was published during her undergraduate years, she regularly composed performance pieces for herself and others.

The intellectual milieu that formed Kennedy at Warwick, founded in 1965 as one of the "new" postwar English universities, was one in which the history of the activism of the 1960s and 1970s still lingered, though the period of intense student political activism was largely over by the time Kennedy arrived. The Departments of Theatre Studies and English (in which Kennedy took some undergraduate courses) both participate in the university's long tradition of feminist and gender-based scholarship. Germaine Greer, who is now a professor of English at Warwick, was a junior lecturer in the English department between 1967 and 1971, and she wrote her groundbreaking feminist manifesto, *The Female Eunuch* (1970), while teaching there. Another literary figure who studied at Warwick in the 1980s was the novelist Jonathan Coe, who graduated in 1986, the same year in which Kennedy completed her B.A. degree. Coe was writing a doctoral thesis on the works of Henry Fielding and Samuel Beckett. He was simultaneously working on his first published novel, *The Accidental Woman* (1987). There is no evidence to suggest that the two writers knew each other at this time. When Coe later reviewed Kennedy's first novel, his enthusiasm was muted.

After graduating, Kennedy worked at various temporary jobs, including brief periods spent selling household brushes and double glazing, and she claimed state unemployment benefits while working on her first book. She has spoken about a period of "significant depression" in her early twenties, but she declines to go into detail about this subject or any other aspect of her personal life. From 1988 to 1989 she was a community arts worker for the Clydebank and District Council, in West Dunbartonshire in west central Scotland, where she organized creative-writing workshops for groups of schoolchildren and single parents; from 1989 to 1991 she was writer-in-residence for Hamilton & East Kilbride Social Work Department, a metropolitan region in South Lanarkshire about twelve miles south of Glasgow; and from 1989 to 1995 she was writer-in-residence for Project Ability, a Glasgow-based art center dedicated to creating opportunities for disabled people to gain access to the visual arts. From 1989 until 1995 she edited a low-budget underground literary magazine, *Outside Lines.*

In 1987 Kennedy moved to Glasgow, where she still lives and works. She occupies a large and architecturally distinguished flat above the Great Western Road in the city center. She lives alone, is unmarried, and she does not drink, smoke, or take drugs. Before sitting down to write, she usually removes her shoes. Although she has disclosed these few biographical facts in interviews, she is otherwise zealous in guarding her privacy. She told McGinty, "There are certain things I need to have in place for my work. I need not to be in pain. If I'm in anything approaching a relationship I also feel quite well. I am like anybody else: I don't like being on my own, but I effectively have been all my life. That is a bit of a pain in the arse, frankly."

Kennedy's first book, a collection of fifteen short stories, *Night Geometry and the Garscadden Trains,* was published in 1990 by Polygon, a small Scottish press based in Edinburgh. The title story is an eloquent cri de coeur, narrated by an anonymous woman who recalls her disastrous marriage to a bed-hopping man named Duncan. The "night geometry" of the title refers to the couple's interlinked positions while sleeping. They find that they breathe in unison at night, but after discovering his infidelities she learns how to breathe independently. A railway accident provides the pivotal moment of the story. The narrator's usual commuter train fails to run, and she returns home unexpectedly to find Duncan in bed with another woman. Her monologue is characterized by sharp and witty asides: "You can imagine the situation. . . . with both of us constantly washing away the feel of his current mistress. We went through a lot of soap." The narrator realizes that she has been cast reluctantly in the part of the wronged wife and that this position is itself a cliché. Finally, however, she arrives at a kind of bitter wisdom, and she remarks that "half of some things is less than nothing at all and . . . contrary to popular belief, people, many people, almost all the people, live their lives in the best way they can with generally good intentions and still leave absolutely nothing behind. . . . This is not enough."

"The Role of Notable Silences in Scottish History" is a haunting, first-person confessional piece about a hack journalist. The unreliable narrator of the story begins by telling the reader that she has difficulty telling the truth. She regards this as a symptom of Scotland's troubled (and at least partly fantasized) history. "There's no point in being Scottish if you can't make up your past as you go along," she says. Her semimystical reflections on the geography of Glasgow recall the works of other contemporary British writers about cities, particularly those of Peter Ackroyd and Iain Sinclair. She describes a chance encounter in a public library with another writer (possibly a maniac), who has filled several unpublished notebooks with his own thoughts on the "strange effects" of the city. After the man is murdered–he is the innocent victim of a random stabbing in a Glasgow pub–she takes possession of his writings. Thinking back on their brief involvement, she remembers an evening they spent together wandering the dark streets of the city, communicating with the ghosts of the past:

> We felt Highland mutineers running and running, solemn English soldiers, patrolling a January bridge and the hard shots of muskets, tapping at the bodies of discontented men. . . . The street full of weavers, lying still. Murderers hang, tramways open, exhibitions are held and mothers give birth to children of great importance. Always there are voices, of all kinds, alone and singing or harsh above the heads of the crowds.

The reader is left in a state of uncertainty as to the precise nature and provenance of these visions. The story has no easy solution beyond offering itself as a piece of "loud music" or a set of spectacles through which to view the historical grievances of the Scottish people.

The Scottish poet Kathleen Jamie, who reviewed the book in *TLS: The Times Literary Supplement* (5 April 1991), welcomed Kennedy's "compassionate" interest in "the silent majority," meaning those ordinary Scottish lives that usually go undocumented. Singling out a few stories for particular praise, Jamie nevertheless ended on a note of reservation: "Though emphatic, the stories eventually have a sameness about them. Together, they seem not to lend each other strength, but rather to sap it. The result is a lack of dynamism, as if the writer were unable yet to divine her source of energy and channel it into strong work." In retrospect, this pronouncement looks like a grudging and needlessly harsh judgment on what was, by any standards, a highly promising first collection. *Night Geometry and the Garscadden Trains* was subsequently awarded the Saltire First Book of the Year Award by *The Scotsman,* the *Mail on Sunday*/John Llewelyn Rhys Prize, and a Scottish Arts Council Book Award, all in 1991.

Kennedy's first novel, *Looking for the Possible Dance,* was published in London by Secker and Warburg in 1993. The heroine, Margaret Hamilton, is a Scottish student who is educated, as Kennedy was, at an English university. Her mother has died young, and much of the novel deals with her close relationship with her father, her sense of loss following his death, and with her intense affair with Colin, a fellow Scot who becomes a satellite-dish salesman. Margaret returns to Scotland to take up a job at a community center, but she falls out with her humorless employer, who then begins to persecute her.

The disrupted chronology and haphazard, episodic structure of the novel seem to be signs of apprentice work, as if the author were not yet fully comfortable working at such expansive length. The first two hundred pages are largely uneventful, but the book builds to an ultraviolent finale, in which Colin is abducted by a sadistic loan shark and subjected to unspeakable tortures while a soundtrack of Mozart plays in the background. This touch may be a distant echo of Anthony Burgess's 1962 novella, *A Clockwork Orange,* in which the central character is subjected to aversion therapy accompanied by the music of Beethoven.

Kennedy's novel also reflects bitterly and ironically on Scottish culture, notably through a "found" text on the *ceilidh* (a Gaelic word, meaning a gathering for the performance of songs and stories), which has been written by Graham, one of the minor characters: "As every languageless, stateless, selfless nation has one last, twisted image of its worst and best, we have the ceilidh. Here we pretend we are Highland, pretend we have mysteries in our work, pretend we have work. . . . We feel angry and sad and Scottish. Perhaps we feel free."

When Coe reviewed the novel in *The Guardian* (23 February 1993), he praised the careful attention Kennedy had paid to Margaret's interior life. "It's refreshing," he wrote, "to find a writer so minutely alert to the nuances of the sort of lives (young, impoverished, disaffected but unbowed) which have not been well served by much contemporary fiction." But he concluded with a list of hesitations, and complained that, above all, the novel "desperately needs an injection of plot." Lucasta Miller wrote in a 27 February 1993 review in *The Times* (London) that the novel "evokes a sense of empty monotony and the impossibility of intimacy. . . . Eschewing experimental fireworks, its theme and style are quietly conventional."

In 1993 Kennedy was included in the "Twenty Best Young British Novelists" list published by *Granta* magazine. Responding to the list in a 3 May 1993 piece in *The Times* (London), the writer Julie Burchill said of Kennedy: "Praise the Lord and pass the orchids, a real writer is among us, with a beautiful first novel."

A second collection of stories, *Now That You're Back,* was published by Jonathan Cape, Ltd., in 1994. Kennedy's editor at Cape is the Aberdeen-born poet Robin Robertson, whose impressive list of Scottish, Welsh, and Irish writers includes Irvine Welsh, Alan Warner, Janice Galloway, Mike McCormack, and Niall Griffiths.

In the story "Christine," Kennedy makes another excursion into the supernatural. The eponymous figure is a woman who has the ability to read the minds of those around her. She is clumsy as a schoolchild, but this is because she is acutely aware of the other children's hostile thoughts about her. Years later, she meets one of her former tormentors and finally confides that she possesses telepathic powers. "It was a shock. It was an invasion," he says. "Someone telling me precisely what I am thinking, beat by beat–that seems to affect my soul." After another interval, the male narrator meets Christine again. She has become a nun, which is apparently a natural consequence of the life of hardship she has been forced to lead up to this point. It appears that she has been sending him dreams during the interval since their last meeting. Kennedy implies that Christine is possibly an angel or a martyr who has been sent to test those whom she meets–but few people in the story demonstrate any capacity for goodness.

"The Mouseboks Family Dictionary" is a comic story with a serious point. It takes the form of a surreal A–Z, in the course of which a coherent narrative about inherited money emerges. Following the death of their old aunt, various members of the Mouseboks family go into her attic, where a vast sum of money is said to be stored. They discover, in a series of locked boxes, a few banknotes, a large collection of mice, and a substantial quantity of mouse droppings. It is clear that the mice have eaten the money and that the deceased aunt has had an elaborate joke at their expense. For reasons that are unclear, the family members then agree that they will all change their first names to "Francis." Several epigrammatic utterances are made, of which the most relevant would seem to be "Betray your children often, and they may learn and grow." This experimental story is almost unique among Kennedy's fiction in deviating from a straightforward realist presentation of events.

"Friday Payday," by contrast, is a solid piece of urban realism. It tackles the issue of child prostitution in London. The central character is a displaced Glaswegian girl of about fourteen who works for a heroin-addicted pimp named Danny. Although she dreams of returning to Scotland, the girl "knew what she was qualified for–hand relief or up the kilt." Readers learn something of her appalling home life before she became a prostitute: "Father called it having a cuddle and said it was her mother's fault. He'd used to do this with her mother but then she'd gone to somewhere else and he still needed someone because he was a normal man." The girl's voice comes across strongly, and her thoughts are spiced with Scots expressions: "bogging," "crabbit," "treating you like a wean." Such deviations from standard English are unusual in Kennedy's writing, and they add a certain plausibility to this story. "Friday Payday" attracted the attention of the motion-picture director Coky Giedroyc, who commissioned Kennedy to write a full-length screenplay. The result was *Stella Does Tricks* (1997), a movie that received few published reviews in Britain but that met with more success in Australia, Germany, and the United States.

Reviewing *Now That You're Back* in *The Financial Times* (London) of 5 February 1994, Shena Mackay wrote, "Too many of the pieces here are arch makeweights without humour or psychological truth." But she added that three or four of the stories, including "Friday Payday," demonstrated a pleasing level of what she termed "delicate realism."

Kennedy's second novel, *So I Am Glad* (1995), is a violent and magical story set in Glasgow. It is reminiscent of the works of Angela Carter (in its magic realism) and Ian McEwan (in its extreme sadism). The book has two distinct plot threads. Jennifer Wilson, a radio newsreader and professional voice-over artist, recollects her sadomasochistic affair with a man named Steven, in which she has assumed the dominant role. The evident relish with which she describes their sexual antics is presumably intended to disturb the reader. She cheerfully observes, "I only told you I was calm. I never even suggested that I was nice." By her own admission, Jennifer is devoid of feeling but not of guilt. Her well-suppressed compassionate side is brought to the fore by the sudden arrival in her shared flat of Martin, an amnesiac who requires her care. Martin gives the novel its true focus. His body is covered in scars and he secretes a glowing liquid when he sweats. He believes himself to be the reincarnation of Savinien de Cyrano de Bergerac, the notorious seventeenth-century French writer, soldier, and duelist. Either Martin is a dangerous fantasist, or he is telling the truth. Jennifer chooses to believe his story, mainly because her life is otherwise surrounded by professional lies and personal deceptions.

Dust jacket for the 1999 U.S. edition of Kennedy's 1997 short-story collection, in which the title novella depicts an unhappily married Glasgow housewife who becomes involved with a self-help guru (Richland County Public Library)

Jennifer's narrative centers on various kinds of pain, both physical and psychological. "Tenderness is dangerous," she says, "softly cataclysmic and never in the places you'd expect." The reader cannot be sure whether this ambiguous statement refers to the genuine warmth she shows to Martin or to her sadistic joy in beating up Steven.

Reviewing *So I Am Glad* in *The New York Times* (27 February 2000), David Sachs spoke of Kennedy's "bold vision and masterly prose." He added: "Nimbly skirting the comic-book nuances (displaced cavalier amok in Glasgow), the novel persuasively portrays a dignified gentleman, a reformed duellist, tightly coiled, prone to 'dangerous enthusiasms.' Reincarnation has humbled him [Martin] but brought hope."

In 1996 Kennedy was appointed one of the judges for the Booker Prize for fiction. The winning novel was *Last Orders* by Graham Swift.

Kennedy's next book is in many respects her strongest, as critics were not slow to recognize. Published in 1997, *Original Bliss* is a collection of ten short stories followed by a 150-page novella, which gives the book its overall title. The novella "Original Bliss" occupies more than half of the book. At the center of the tale is Mrs Helen Brindle, an unhappily married Glasgow housewife, who spends her sleepless nights consuming junk television and self-help books. Having lost her religious faith, she regards herself as "God's widow." A possible source of salvation presents itself in the form of Professor Edward E. Gluck, whose books are among Mrs Brindle's reading matter. Gluck, who is said to be on the shortlist for a Nobel Prize, has developed a pseudophilosophical system known as "The Process." Mrs Brindle sends him a fan letter in the hope that he will be able to make sense of her predicament. She travels to Stuttgart, Germany, to attend a series of lectures he is giving there. The two protagonists meet, but Mrs Brindle is initially overawed by his intelligence, and their conversations are inconclusive. Gluck asks her, "Would you like a religious experience . . . or would you like a definition of a spiritual experience? . . . I certainly can't give you a spiritual experience." Yet, he is intrigued by the force of her personality, and he confesses that his early life and relationships with his parents were deeply unhappy. The positions are quickly reversed as Gluck's confessions become more intimate, and it is evident that he hopes to find some personal sense of wholeness through his (entirely platonic) dealings with Mrs Brindle. He tells her that, in spite of his immense fame, he desires only to be good, and he acknowledges that, although she is by no means an intellectual, she possesses a fundamental goodness that he lacks. Gluck confides that he is an erotomaniac, hopelessly addicted to pornographic magazines and videos. With Mrs Brindle's help, he believes that he will be able to overcome his squalid, masturbatory impulses. She returns to her husband in Glasgow but not before she has given Gluck permission to correspond with her.

Back in Scotland, Mr Brindle–whose first name is never disclosed to the reader–persuades himself that his wife is carrying on an adulterous affair. He discovers Gluck's letters and begins a vengeful campaign of horrifying domestic violence against his wife. These violent episodes are narrated with a remarkable degree of authorial detachment, with the emphasis firmly on anatomical details:

> He had taken her hand and closed it in a drawer. She had made his damage worse when she wrenched her fingers free without understanding where they were. . . . She tried to lift her hands and discovered that one wouldn't lift. It was stuck. A burst of nausea and a white, high sound happened when she pulled on her arm and when she looked at her fingers, the four fingers of her right hand that were already an unfamiliar shape and bleeding and a little hidden by four flaps of sheared-away skin. She could see the light of one of her bones.

At crucial moments such as this one, Kennedy's prose is entirely drained of any emotional content. Judgment (from the reader's point of view) seems imperative, but it is rendered more difficult by Mrs Brindle's less than fully convincing justification of her husband's violent abuse. He is, as she sees it, merely the instrument of a Calvinist God, and she readily submits to his violence as a possible way of regaining her lost faith: "She was at fault and whatever happened, it was meant. God's will." Something is being said here, or at least implied, about her complicity in these acts of almost unbearable cruelty. But what Kennedy's novella conspicuously lacks–and surely this omission is deliberate–is any kind of moralizing commentary from the omniscient, third-person narrator. Although the action is focalized through Mrs Brindle, it is difficult to know her emotional response to the circumstances acting upon her. One might say that "Original Bliss" is an "open work" (to employ Umberto Eco's critical term), which allows for a variety of conflicting responses. This artfully achieved ambiguity is undoubtedly one of the chief strengths of the novella. After an unexpected plot twist, the novella concludes on a note of affirmation, attempting to overlay a religious significance onto the foregoing events. This strategy is a risky one to have adopted, but Kennedy ends the novella with characteristic panache.

The novella "Original Bliss" is the most accomplished, mature, and consistently rewarding piece of fiction that Kennedy has published to date. Catherine Lockerbie wrote in *The Scotsman* of 11 January 1997, "Although of startling intelligence, she is the least aridly cerebral of writers. . . . Original Bliss, however uncomfortable, only adds to the now copious evidence that here is a writer of linguistic brilliance, balm-bearing humanity and blissful originality."

Published in 1997 and commissioned as part of the British Film Institute "BFI Film Classics" series, *The Life and Death of Colonel Blimp* is Kennedy's first nonfiction book. It is a close reading of Michael Powell and Emeric Pressburger's 1943 movie, but the emphasis throughout is on Kennedy's personal response to the motion picture, and the reader is given several autobiographical digressions. The displaced European Jewish screenwriter Pressburger gave her, she says, "the first signs of a free and wonderful desire for the perfect Home which my life, my thought, my action and my love can always grow towards. He gave me an insatiable ache, but one which is to do with living and creating and not with death." She argues that *The Life and Death of Colonel Blimp* "is more poignant and savagely forgiving, more melancholy, troubling and revealing, than almost any other cinematic work I have encountered."

Everything You Need (1999) is Kennedy's boldest novel to date. Set between the years 1990 and 1997, the book describes the troubled relationship between Nathan Staples, a depressive author given to suicide attempts, and his daughter, Mary Lamb, who has been raised by two homosexual Welsh uncles and is unaware of her true paternity. Nathan lives on a remote island, having deliberately cut himself off from the modern world. Mary, who is an incipient writer, is invited to become part of the colony of artists and eccentrics that he has established there. Nathan, who has become stifled by the trashy genre fiction that he writes for a living, hopes to rediscover his own original voice through the selfless and redemptive act of teaching his daughter how to become a writer.

Everything You Need is an undisciplined sprawl of a novel, which lacks the focus and direction of Kennedy's other works. There is much talk in the book about the agonies of artistic creation, and Nathan descends into surly resentment on the subject of publicizing his work. Little justification is given for the contempt he expresses for his readership, and the reader is led to the conclusion that he is driven by a severe and largely incomprehensible misanthropy. His publisher, an amiable drunk named Jack Grace, is treated more sympathetically. Nevertheless, it is disappointing that Kennedy, whose reputation was founded on her close scrutiny of quotidian life, should have felt moved to produce an overloaded book that merely talks about the business of writing rather than showing the reader why writing is supposed to be important. It is a deeply solipsistic performance, and the typographical eccentricities (long passages are written in italics or upper case) do little to inject interest to a chaotic narrative.

There are a few compensations. Nathan's short stories, the texts of which are given in full, are unfailingly interesting, and they remind the reader that Kennedy is capable of writing well when she is not writing about being or becoming a writer. The characterization of Mary is perhaps the strongest feature of the book, and the narrative is sensitive to alterations in her discourse as she grows in years, experience, and confidence.

The reviews of *Everything You Need* were mixed. Toby Mundy claimed in the *New Statesman* (24 May 1999) that the book was defeated by "overkill," and he objected to "the unremitting scatology, the obsessions with pain, desperate sex, wounds and death." Carey Harrison wrote, in the *Chicago Tribune* (9 September 2001), that "the unweeded repetitiveness of *Everything You Need* reads like a cry for help, or at least for an editor not awed by Kennedy's rising fame. Sadly, its self-indulgence drains from this novel everything that is singular and fresh, rendering it . . . distinctly passé." Lorraine Adams responded more generously in *The Washington Post* (8 December 2001): "In this novel Kennedy has traded the intense precision of her earlier work for a more capacious virtuosity. . . . Reading Kennedy, one gets the feeling that our era has produced a writer commensurate with its complexity and lushness, its vulgarity and absurdity." The mixtures and ambiguities of the novel were neatly summarized by Gail Cauldwell in *The Boston Globe* (12 August 2001), who wrote that *Everything You Need* was "a smart, captivating, exhausting novel."

On Bullfighting is an odd blend of documentary and confessional writing, published in 1999 as part of the Yellow Jersey Press series of nonfiction books about sport, which also includes Jonathan Rendall's lugubrious gambling memoir, *Twelve Grand* (1998). Kennedy's book begins with the author standing on a window ledge high above the Great Western Road, suffering from a painful spinal injury and contemplating suicide. Deciding not to jump, she travels instead to Spain to find out about the corrida. Bullfighting, she argues, has much in common with writing. Going on the journey and subsequently shaping it into narrative form are presented as restoring, life-affirming acts: "I wanted to discover if the elements which seemed so much part of the corrida–death, transcendence, immortality, joy, pain, isolation and fear–would come back to me. Because they were part of the process of writing and, good or bad, I miss them."

On Bullfighting is in part a rejection of the unattractive machismo of Ernest Hemingway's *Death in the Afternoon* (1932); however, Kennedy's study is not in any sense a work of feminist appropriation. It is, on the contrary, a serious-minded attempt to see past the bravado and distortions of Hemingway's account of the same territory. Kennedy writes of her affinity with the Spanish playwright and poet Federico García Lorca, who was shot dead by a fascist firing squad in 1936. She draws biographical parallels between herself and Lorca, with whom she claims to share an interest in "contemplating the horrors, the fascinations and the strengths of death." She is appalled by the depth of her own interest in the bloodthirstiness and immense cruelty of bullfighting. When she witnesses a matador being gored on a bull's horns, she continues to photograph the spectacle, aware that she may be taking pictures of a dying man. She continues to believe, as Lorca did before her, that bullfighting possesses a purgative and religious significance. Regardless of the questionable ethics of such a sport, no reader of Kennedy's book will doubt that she succeeds in communicating the thrill of the corrida. A glossary of Spanish bullfighting terminology is helpfully included as an appendix.

Stephanie Merritt wrote, in the 14 November 1999 issue of *The Observer* (London): "This is an unhappy book; a book about dreams sought, and about failure. Kennedy returns again and again to the loneliness of the matador as a means of mitigating her own pain." In his review in *The New York Times* (30 March 2001) Richard Eder stated that Kennedy "possesses the artist's timeless vision. She writes somewhat as Goya paints: with pain, terror and beauty. . . . She makes no claims to healing but she has picked up a metaphor, which for a writer may be the closest thing to it."

Kennedy has become an increasingly prominent and unfailingly mercurial figure on the British literary scene, as a Fellow of the Royal Society of Arts (since 2000), and as a judge of the Guardian First Book Prize (2001) and of the Orange Prize for Fiction (2002). A new collection of twelve short stories, *Indelible Acts,* is scheduled for publication by Jonathan Cape in October 2002.

On 5 August 2001 Kennedy delivered the annual PEN lecture at the Edinburgh Book Festival. The lecture is a strongly worded argument against censorship, in which she addresses the problem of evil and defends the novelist's right to deliver what she calls "unpleasant news." Speaking out on behalf of imprisoned writers abroad, A. L. Kennedy, as published on her personal website, offers an implicit commentary on her own fictional project as a whole: "The knowledge of evil is entirely, desperately necessary and in fiction we meet it intimately, deeply and in perfect personal safety. . . . We are not all monsters under the skin, but we misunderstand ourselves if we believe that evil cannot at least tempt and bewilder us. . . . The defence of fiction and all it in turn defends must be total to be in any way effective."

Interviews:

Jenny Turner, "Portrait: A Person of Substance," *Guardian,* 28 January 1994, Weekend section, p. 16;

Gillian Glover, "Call Me A. L.," *Scotsman,* 1 December 1995, p. 14;

Stephen McGinty, "Death Becomes Her," *Sunday Times* (London), 30 May 1999, Books section, p. 13;

Catherine Lockerbie, "A Writer Apart," *W Magazine,* 18 (Summer 1999): 13–20;

Yvonne Nolan, "A Dream Not Her Own," *Publishers Weekly,* 23 July 2001, pp. 43–46.

References:

A. L. Kennedy Website, 6 May 2002 <http://www.a-l-kennedy.co.uk/>;

Julie Burchill, "Young, British and Unreadable," *Times* (London), 3 May 1993, p. 12;

Dominic Head, *The Cambridge Introduction to Modern British Fiction, 1950–2000* (Cambridge: Cambridge University Press, 2002), pp. 153–154;

Catherine Lockerbie, "Anatomy of an Original Voice," *Scotsman,* 11 January 1997, p. 16.

Angela Lambert

(14 April 1940 -)

Merritt Moseley
University of North Carolina at Asheville

BOOKS: *Unquiet Souls: The Indian Summer of the British Aristocracy, 1880–1918* (London: Macmillan, 1984); republished as *Unquiet Souls: A Social History of the Illustrious, Irreverent, Intimate Group of British Aristocrats Known as "The Souls"* (New York: Harper & Row, 1984);

1939: The Last Season of Peace (London: Weidenfeld & Nicolson, 1989; Santa Barbara, Cal.: Clio Press, 1989);

Love Among the Single Classes (London: Bodley Head, 1989; Harmondsworth, U.K. & New York: Penguin, 1990);

No Talking After Lights (London: Hamilton, 1990; London & New York: Penguin, 1991);

A Rather English Marriage (London: Hamilton / New York: Penguin, 1992);

The Constant Mistress (London: Hamilton / New York: Penguin, 1994);

Kiss and Kin (London & New York: Bantam, 1997);

Golden Lads and Girls (London & New York: Bantam, 1999);

The Property of Rain (London & New York: Bantam, 2001).

SELECTED PERIODICAL PUBLICATIONS–UNCOLLECTED: "Schools that put girls in a class of their own," *Independent* (London), 26 March 1991, Focus section, p. 16;

"Jeanette: Could anyone be as good as she thinks she is?" interview of Jeanette Winterson, *Independent* (London), 23 January 1998, p. 16;

"How to write convincing fiction: Make it up," *Daily Telegraph* (London), 4 May 2002, p. 7.

Angela Lambert (photograph © Nick Dolenz; from the dust jacket for Love Among the Single Classes, *1989)*

Angela Lambert is a journalist, an historian, and a novelist–roughly in that order, though she remains all three. Beginning in 1989, she has published seven novels, which constitute a study of the way lives are shaped by history, by accident, by class, and by love.

Angela Maria Helps was born 14 April 1940, the child of John Donald Helps and Edith Paula Alice Helps. Her father was a civil servant and her mother a homemaker. She declared in 2001, in unpublished correspondence, that she regarded her date of birth as "a piece of extraordinary good luck, since it meant that I was one of the first wave of women to benefit from the Pill, feminism and equal (if still far from perfect) opportunities." As a girl she attended a boarding school, and, she told Maureen Paton in an interview for *The Guardian* (30 December 1998), "the memory of being dumped by her unfeeling parents" remains with her and is part of the subject of *No Talking After Lights* (1990). She felt ignored by her parents–her father an imperious husband of the old school, her mother a deferential wife. Their marriage has both provided material for her fiction and fueled her own feminism. She told Jean W. Ross in a brief interview for *Contemporary Authors* (1993), "Since the age of twelve I always knew I was a writer. I always had greater ease and fluency with words than with anything else."

She attended St. Hilda's College, Oxford, where she read PPE (Politics, Philosophy, and Economics); shortly after graduating with honors from Oxford in 1961, after a time spent as a maid to William Francis Hare and his wife (fifth earl of Listowel and Baroness Listowel), she married Martin John Lambert in December 1962. Her marriage ended in 1967 after her husband abandoned her for another woman, leaving her as a single mother to support her daughter, Carolyn Ruth, then four years old, and son, Jonathan, then eighteen months old. Since that time she has supported herself and her three children, two daughters and a son (a second daughter, Marianne Vizinczey Lambert, was born of a short relationship when Lambert was thirty-one).

Her work was primarily in journalism, aside from a time (1964–1967) spent as a civil servant in the private office of a Labour cabinet minister, Francis "Frank" Aungier Pakenham, seventh Earl of Longford. She was an assistant editor for the magazine *Modern Woman* in 1962; she was the only female reporter on an all-male news desk at Independent Television News from 1972 to 1976, a television reporter for London Weekend Television from 1976 to 1977, and a reporter for Thames Television from 1977 to 1988. In the latter year she joined *The Independent* (London), a newly launched daily newspaper, where she remained until 1995. She has also been a journalist for *The Daily Mail* (London) and currently writes interviews and features for *The Sunday Telegraph* (London) and freelance reviews and opinion pieces for other newspapers and magazines, as well as occasionally broadcasting on the radio. She has expressed some regret, in her interview with Paton, about the cost to her children of her years as a single parent, working in journalism, characterized by "my businesss [*sic*], my poverty–and my infatuations." Since 1986 she has lived with her partner, television director Tony Price, spending some part of each year in the French cottage she bought many years ago; she has seven grandchildren.

She began writing fiction, according to her interview with Paton, after she came down with a nearly fatal disease, portal hypertension, in 1979. She has suffered recurrences since, and explained in the unpublished 2001 correspondence, "You will find that sickness and death play a considerable part in most of my novels . . . and that's why." Her busy journalistic career was varied by book authorship, beginning in 1984 with *Unquiet Souls: The Indian Summer of the British Aristocracy, 1880–1918* which was followed by *1939: The Last Season of Peace* in 1989. She then began writing fiction and subsequently published seven novels, though she said in 2001 that she hoped to return to nonfiction, perhaps with a biography.

Lambert's two social histories share an interest in liminal moments–the period just before World War I and the one just before World War II–and an ambiguous, perhaps not fully reconciled, attitude toward class. She told Ross in their 1993 interview:

> It is difficult for anyone who is not British to comprehend the degree to which snobbery, accent, and the class system dominate this society. As a socialist and something of a republican, I deplore it; as a novelist and an observer of human behaviors, I am fascinated by it. The nuances of class, and the arrogance or subservience it generates, are a major influence upon people's behavior towards one another in this country. Both my two books of social history and my novels (particularly the second and third) explore this English trait.

Her own situation in the class system is, or at least was, solidly middle class: the child of a civil servant, she attended boarding school and Oxford, and she was employed by members of the aristocracy (though, in one case, as a maid). In a 1998 interview of working-class novelist Jeanette Winterson, she caused a quarrel by making the (surely correct) observation that middle-class children, too, can have difficult childhoods.

Published in the United States in 1984 as *Unquiet Souls: A Social History of the Illustrious, Irreverent, Intimate Group of British Aristocrats Known as "The Souls,"* Lambert's first book appeared earlier that same year in the United Kingdom with the more revealing, and certainly less hectic, subtitle *The Indian Summer of the British Aristocracy, 1880–1918.* It is a study of a constellation of families who seemed to turn away from traditional Victorian assumptions and practices late in the nineteenth century; they included the Asquiths, Balfours, Curzons, various lords and ladies, and perhaps most importantly, Tom Nairn noted in his review for *The Guardian* (11 October 1984), "a manufacturing family which in the middle of the last century moved into the upper echelons and acquired both landed property and political power," the Tennants. Lambert is interested in the greater (though far from extreme) social flexibility, the intellectual vitality, and the more interesting lives of this new social constellation. In an early summing up, she contrasts them with the established "Marlborough

Dust jacket for Lambert's first novel, about a divorced librarian and her unhappy relationship with a Polish immigrant (Bruccoli Clark Layman Archives)

House set" revolving around the Prince of Wales. The Souls

> never counted among its innermost ranks more than forty or fifty people, though the same number again might have been considered as "occasional Souls." It was not easy for an outsider to gain full acceptance. The Souls prided themselves above all on their intellect, their aesthetic sensibility, their unique interpretation of the taste and manners of their time. These were the qualities that secured entry to the charmed circle. Their houses, their clothes, but above all their conversation were different from the rest of their class. Only twice during the previous history of the English aristocracy had intelligence been regarded as a desirable, let alone an essential, attribute. The first time was during the reign of Elizabeth I. The second was the heyday of the Holland House set, a century before.

There are some moving pages on the effect on these families of World War I–their sons' disproportionate loss of life because they were officers and physically fit. Lambert does not claim too much for them, and, in general, her attitude strikes a judicious balance between cynicism and adulation.

In 1989 she published *1939, The Last Season of Peace*. The "season" in the title is the social season, the time of debutantes "coming out," and the book focuses on the women who underwent the process in the final season before World War II, from about May to the end of July 1939–that is, almost up to the beginning of the war. The book includes many interviews with surviving debutantes, period photographs, and anecdotes. Lamber wonders,

> Since the Season was expensive, exhausting and a social ordeal for all but the most poised, why did anyone–parents or daughters–submit to it? Setting aside for a moment its real purpose, to introduce eligible young people to one another in a safe and enjoyable setting, what other function might it fulfil? Certainly most of the debutantes, and their escorts claim fifty years later that it was fun. . . . The Season, then, was a forum in which to see and be seen by perhaps two thousand people, of whom several hundred were contemporaries of both sexes . . . a forum which gave a girl a chance to prove herself and make her mark in a few short months, knowing that whatever impressions she created might remain for the rest of her life. . . . a social testing ground.

As in her previous history, Lambert finds these people interesting but is not lost in admiration of them, nor blind to their own limitations, particularly of imagination. As Nicola Shulman noted, in her 16 April 1989 review for *The Times* (London), it was not her intention "to ridicule or despise her subjects for their self-absorption and frivolity"–for instance, their confessions that they were almost unaware of the impending war, their rigidly short list of acceptable conversational topics, their unawareness that their empty dance cards were of little moment while people were dying elsewhere. "On the contrary, she goes to lengths to explain that behavior was wholly justifiable, because of their education, if that is what one can call the kind of intellectual footbinding that girls of this type were subjected to." In the *Los Angeles Times* (17 September 1989) reviewer Benjamin Kilborne called *1939* "a sheer pleasure to read . . . an intelligent, witty and well-constructed study of the London debutante season of 1939, the last of its kind."

In 1989 Lambert also published her first novel, *Love Among the Single Classes.* The central character is a divorced woman of forty-four, Constance Liddell, whose need for love is so strong that, though she is an intelligent and aware woman, it overbalances her judgment and leads her to greater unhappiness than her original loneliness. Divorced from Paul (with whom she remains on friendly terms, however), she has three children, two of them out of the home and one still living with her. She answers a personal ad from a man who says he wants marriage; the man turns out to be Iwo Zaluski, a Polish immigrant. He has been in London for four years, having left his wife and adult daughters in Poland. Despite Iwo's predictability and lack of apparent promise for Constance, she is soon besotted with him. In the face of the warnings of her former husband, her children's dislike for Iwo, and the presence of an old friend, Andrew, who is apparently in love with her, she is set on Iwo.

The novel is structured in three sections: "The Librarian's Obsession" (Constance is a librarian); "The Polish Obsession"–though the Polish Iwo is never obsessed with Constance, he is obsessed with Poland and Polishness; and "Dissolution." The ultimate failure of the relationship is apparent to a reader from an early point, and Constance is aware of Iwo's disappointing lack of promise–as well as his "infidelity" with other women and his unresolved relationship with his own wife.

In *Love Among the Single Classes* Lambert explores two related problems. One is the way in which her protagonist (and perhaps, by extension, other members of the single classes) chooses the wrong love object. The other is the predicament of single people generally, and the author clearly means to generalize this predicament far beyond Constance. The title of the novel claims class status for the unmarried, as does Constance's early explanation that "It's true that I have a susceptible heart–but then, we who are members of the single classes, unmarried and unattached, are always waiting to fall in love." She is part of an awkward generation; she is liberated enough to have sex without marriage, but she still wants–badly–to be married; as she says, "I remain hidebound by the pre-pill morality and my parents' fossilized attitudes."

In his review for *The Guardian* (7 April 1989) Norman Shrapnel commented that "There's a slight scent of good soap about *Love Among the Single Classes,* Angela Lambert's first novel, and it's also the sort of book advanced feminists would once have wanted to burn." Lambert is a proud feminist, and so is Constance Liddell in her way, but she nevertheless shares some fairly conventional observations. Considering her former husband's new girlfriend, she says, "Behind that white-faced, black-haired mask is a woman who wants a husband and babies. It is the undoing of us all." And she explains why she is so determined to be married, in the face of all Iwo's unfitness and uncooperativeness: "Because a man is safe-conduct through this man's world. A lone woman is open to exploitation, ridicule, and attack. She has to be forever on her guard, conciliating, avoiding, anticipating trouble, because being alone means being exposed."

In *No Talking After Lights,* published in 1990, Lambert moved backward to Constance's youth to focus on Constance King's unhappy adjustment to a new school, Raeburn, to which she comes at age eleven. Her parents are going out to Kenya and have to leave her at a boarding school, though they seem to her, and apparently are, excessively indifferent to her sufferings.

There are similarities here with Charlotte Brontë's Jane Eyre, and even with Charles Dickens's David Copperfield (Constance attracts friends, like the young David, because she tells stories well); however, the novel is no collection of stereotypes but rather an original account of a young girl's state of mind and heart. Called Goggles, then Goggsy, because of her glasses, she writes to her parents begging for permission to leave; at one point she tries unsuccessfully to run away; when, at the end, she is given permission to leave she realizes that she no longer wants to do so.

Along the way she is challenged by the rules of confidentiality (a persistent thief invites her confidence) and bemused by the striations of class. Little things, particularly the way the girls decorate their space, tell important stories:

> Anyone coming into the dormitory–Matron, prefects, other girls–could see at a glance if someone's people

> were young, glamorous and rich, and deduce whether they lived in town or in the country, whether family pets were low-status ones like cats, rabbits, guinea-pigs, or high-status ones like a large dog or two, a horse or pony. Sometimes the pictures showed a house in the background. Being rich mattered very much indeed, but boasting about being rich was the worst kind of swanking.

Alongside the story of Constance and the girls in the dormitory there are interesting pictures of the lives of the staff. Two of them are lesbians, living together; the younger loves the older, who in turn loves a girl in the top class. She is (perhaps understandably) embittered and sarcastic and, finally, dangerously cruel: she refuses to permit Constance to seek medical attention for a seriously infected finger. The most sympathetic portrait is of the headmistress, Mrs. Birmingham, who has ridiculous qualities (she is first introduced as "the massive Easter Island presence of the Headmistress, the Hon. Henrietta Birmingham") but is kind, understanding, and long-suffering. She has a dying husband and has lost three brothers in World War I.

The troubles that afflict the girls are not of world-historical importance. One of them is groped by a gardener; there are the petty thefts; there is a polio scare. But Lambert knows that misery is not a function of the gravity of its causes:

> None of the grown-ups took these little melodramas seriously. Childhood, after all, is an innocent, unclouded time. Children are like tumbling puppies or singing birds. Even the most loving and sensitive parents, grannies or teachers assume that adolescent emotions are undeveloped and fleeting. How *could* they be serious, funny little monkeys? It was a tiresome phase and of course they all exaggerated wildly, but thank goodness it didn't last. Adults have forgotten the agony of growing up, when feelings are vast and incomprehensible, primitive and turbulent.

Constance wonders, "why is everyone happy except me? How do they do it? They giggle and chat and muck about. They do things together–pets and gardening and things–and they all sort of belong, all except me. Why is it so hard to be happy?"

In her 26 March 1991 article in *The Independent* (London) Lambert acknowledges the autobiographical impulse behind the novel, but insists that "I hated my school for every minute of seven years." Reviewers responded to the truth of feeling of the novel: Barbara Trapido wrote in a 30 September 1990 review in *The Sunday Times* (London) that "It tells a sensitive, engaging and quietly unfolding story in a surprisingly neglected area of adult fiction"; Candice Rodd, who called it a "lively and atmospheric novel" in her 28 October 1990 review in *The Independent* (London), recommended, "Quick, read on–if necessary with a torch under the blankets after lights."

Dust jacket for the U.S. edition of Lambert's 1989 book, about the London debutante season just prior to the outbreak of World War II (Richland County Public Library)

As she used her school experiences for *No Talking After Lights,* the author acknowledged in her interview with Paton that her parents and the nature of their marriage underlie her next novel, *A Rather English Marriage* (1992). This statement is odd because most of the novel is about the relationship between two widowers. Roy Southgate, a retired milkman, a member of the respectable working class, and Reginald "Reggie" Conyngham-Jervis, a retired company director and former Royal Air Force (RAF) squadron leader (a title he still insists on using), meet in the hospital, by coincidence: their wives both die during the same night. Roy is undone by the loss of his beloved wife; Reggie hardly notices his own wife's death.

But he does begin to notice how helpless he is without her. He lives in a big house in Tunbridge Wells; his wife owned the house and in her will has only left him permission to live in it, leaving the title as well as most of her considerable wealth (of which he was unconscious) to nieces. After her death he has no idea how to prepare himself a meal or where clean shirts come from.

A well-meaning social worker and a vicar suggest that Roy move in with Reggie; the explanation given is that he will provide company for the lonely man. Although assured by the social worker that he will be there as an equal, Roy is almost immediately placed as Reggie's servant. At once he becomes "Southgate" to Reggie; in return Reggie is "Sir," or "Squadron Leader" (Roy was a sergeant in the war). Class tells. The less worthy man almost effortlessly assumes command and exploitation of the much better one, who knows he is being used (Reggie treats Roy as a servant but never pays him anything) but humbly accepts the treatment, for the most part, except when he loses his temper.

Reggie's courtship of a smarter younger woman comes to nothing when he has a stroke and she (who, both of them were fully aware, would only have married him for money) realizes that she cannot nurse an invalid and, even more crucially, discovers that he is not rich. Roy moves back to his own home, which he opens to his daughter-in-law and her two noisy children (left homeless when Roy's son was imprisoned for bigamy), and he eventually remarries, to an old friend of his wife. The strengths of this fine novel are in the characterization of the two main male characters, in the exploration of marriage, and in the subtle analysis of social forces.

Reggie's wife, Mary, has left him a letter to read when the will is opened, in which she tells him, "Marriage is a funny thing, it isn't easy, it hasn't been what we expected, has it? We've had a rather *English* sort of marriage." By the same token, Roy tells him, as he moves out, "It's been like a kind of marriage in a way, hasn't it? You and me living together here these last, what is it, nine months must be, sort of both looking after each other."

Reggie is a fascinating creation, an obtuse man, living in the past (his conversation is an irritating patchwork of RAF slang and boring war stories), with few friends (keeping friends seems to have been his wife's job); his blindness, narcissism, and utter self-absorption are such that of course he has not helped to look after Roy, any more than he has done his wife, Mary. He looks back on his marriage:

> I do not know, he thought, when I last kissed my wife. Was it months before she died, or years? He had not touched her, kissed her, listened to her, worn her gifts, met her eyes . . . and, by ignoring her, had diminished her to a creature who asked nothing of him. . . . Yet . . . isn't that what we all secretly want, Reggie wondered, once the first fine frenzy is over? He had more or less assumed that all husbands were like him, all wives like Mary, all marriages like theirs: a smooth-running service arrangement, give and take–me giving women status and taking home and comfort, organization, *order*.

Observing Roy, he realizes that there is more to marriage than that. Roy's own thoughts about life, though simple, are almost noble: "This, Roy used to think, was why people were born: to bring up children and teach them to be good; to cherish and protect one another; to work hard and honestly; and to retreat at the end of the day into their snug and individual paradise. He was perfectly content; he asked for nothing more."

Lambert explained to Paton that Roy and Reggie are both her father. "Roy is my father in character, and Reggie's marriage is my parents' marriage. For the last 25 of their 45 years together, my father never really observed my mother. She would ring me up to complain that he hadn't spoken to her for 24 hours." Reviewers generally admired this book. In the 7 November 1992 issue of *The Times* (London) Rebecca Fraser found it a "grave and moving dissection of the long-term institution"–that is, marriage; Lucasta Miller wrote in a 14 November 1992 review in *The Financial Times* (London) that it is "observant, wry, and ultimately poignant. Successfully avoiding sentimentality, it offers a credible dramatisation of class tension and generational conflict." In the 29 November 1992 issue of *The Daily Yomiuri* (Tokyo) Tim Sevenoaks chided Lambert for lack of ambition, placing her in a group of writers he called the "Nanny Pack," but, despite some uneasiness, summed up:

> We have a nicely constructed novel of many merits, one of the greatest of which is the unfashionable artistry of Lambert's whole, textured characterization. This is a mysterious and rare gift. When one comes across it in a novel like this, where not very much happens and verbal pyrotechnics are subordinated to orderliness, one is reminded that it alone has the power to make a novel enthralling.

And, in the most positive account of Lambert's fiction to this point, under the title "a severe moralist," Katie Owen related this novel to its two predecessors and declared in the 11 October 1992 books section of *The Sunday Telegraph* (London), "Lambert's fiction is firmly rooted in middle-class realities, and has a soft, traditional flavour and a richness of detail that makes it deceptively comfortable reading despite some brilliant social satire. But within her minutely realised bourgeois world, human acts of cruelty and indifference are observed with pinprick accuracy, and authorial retribution is sure to follow."

Constance Liddell has a small walk-on part in this book. The local librarian, she knows Roy Southgate and by the end of the novel has taken up with a new man, declaring with great delight that he is "*not Polish.*"

Readers of *No Talking After Lights* will remember that King had a sister, Stella, though she is only an offstage presence in that book. Now named Laura, she is the central character in the next novel, *The Constant Mistress* (1994). In a personal communication in 2001 Lambert commented that, "though I regard it as a failure, it qualified both as a book about several generations of an extended family AND a 'feminist' novel, examining–many thought, disapprovingly, though that was never my intention–the fate of women who seek the route of liberation (Laura) against domesticity (her sister Constance)."

It is easy to see why the author might regard the novel as a failure. There is an implausibility in its central situation. Laura King, aged forty-four (the same age as Constance in *Love Among the Single Classes*), a cosmopolitan translator who has never married, has contracted hepatitis C and is dying. She summons thirteen former lovers to a dinner party; twelve come. To them she explains, "I have a year, at most two, left to live. I would like to shake off all care and business by spending that time in your company." They agree and so she embarks on a rotation of spending one month with each of them. She takes them more or less chronologically, from her college lover to lovers from her forties. In each case the visit provokes flashbacks of their initial relationship and particularly of their sexual pleasures. This structure works out less mechanically than one might think, as some of the stays prove unsatisfactory and are aborted. Most of her lovers are high-flyers, and most are rich. Many of them are now married and Laura seems surprisingly obtuse about why the wives do not welcome her with delight.

The novel traces her physical deterioration as a result of disease. In addition to a study of the process of dying, it is something of a study of love. The people who really love Laura are nice men to whom she does not respond sexually, or they are extremely old, or gay.

At the heart of Laura's emotional reaction to her impending death is guilt; she has had an affair with Paul, at that time married to her sister, Constance, conceived a baby, and aborted it at her mother's urging. This guilt is why she believes she does not deserve to live and rejects a transplant that might save her life.

Dust jacket for Lambert's 1990 novel, about an eleven-year-old girl who is sent to an English boarding school when her unloving parents go to Kenya (Bruccoli Clark Layman Archives)

The suggestion that *The Constant Mistress* is a feminist novel deserves some examination. No doubt Laura King has liberated herself from traditional feminine restrictions on sexuality; she takes pride in "her own capacity for sexual pleasure as well as the skill to give it," a quality she learned from her former lover Joe. And yet the slightly repellent way that Laura judges all the other women in the novel (admittedly, they are mostly married to her former lovers, except for her sister, who is divorced from one) is hardly sisterly.

Oddly, the novel seemed nearly ignored by reviewers. The one full-length review, by Phillipa Gregory in the 30 October 1994 issue of *The Sunday Times* (London), is decidedly mixed. She concedes that "As a story of a woman's journey through illness to death, it is humane and understanding. The grim realities of a progressive disease are charted with a pathologist's accuracy. Although it may be fanciful about love and sex and a woman's conscience indeed at times it is so melodramatic as to attain high camp at heart it is an honest book about the decay of a woman's body, and the rise of her spirit." But she also says that Laura "may claim to be a liberated woman but she sounds like a whore"; and she seems impatient with Laura's only moderately polymorphous sexuality:

> Explicit, but not erotic, these affairs with the elderly, the perverse, the virginal and the outright incompetent serve as a contrast to Laura's One Great Sin which to preserve the dramatic tension of the novel I will not reveal; other than to reflect that I have heard worse, and that I think that having your nipples brushed vigorously with a hairbrush, without your consent, is a good deal worse and she tolerates that for years.

Brief notices of the paperback edition judged that "Lambert has created an implausible plot within a compelling narrative which explores terminal illness and the sexual liberation of the last three decades," as Rosalind Powell put it in a 17 December 1995 review in *The Observer* (London), and that "It's a marvellous idea and Angela Lambert realises it, on the whole, with wit and inventiveness, no miracles are requested, and none granted, in what is a compulsively readable novel," as Arminta Wallace noted in the 11 November 1995 issue of *The Irish Times* (Dublin).

At about this time the placement of Lambert in the world of English fiction seems to have changed. The move from a literary novelist and severe moralist with a fine grasp of middle-class detail to the writer of a "compulsively readable novel," a move signaled by the small number of reviews, most of them of the paperback edition, may have resulted from the change in subject matter; if far from what the British call a "bonkbuster," *The Constant Mistress* has a high quotient of unmarried sex, which, if not "casual," is nonetheless not committed. The new placement was certainly accelerated by the move to a new publisher, Transworld Publishers, Ltd., for her next book, which appeared under the Bantam imprint. The result was a situation that Lambert by no means welcomed; that is, her identification as a romance novelist, "putting me," as she lamented in her unpublished 2001 communication, "out of bounds for all serious reviewers."

Her next novel, *Kiss and Kin* (1997), further established her as a "romance novelist"; she received the Parker Romantic Novel of the Year Award from the Romantic Novelists' Association in 1998 for it. Although undoubtedly pleased by the recognition and the prize (£5,000), the author was also clearly a bit uneasy about the criteria, stating not only that "I never thought of myself as a writer of romantic novels," but that she did not read them, either, as Dalya Alberge reported in a 16 April 1998 article in *The Times* (London). The presenter of the award, Jeffrey Archer, showed some of the status anxiety of the romance genre when he declared that Leo Tolstoy's *War and Peace* (1865–1869) is romantic fiction.

It is true that *Kiss and Kin* is far from what is usually considered the subject matter of the romantic novel; the lovers are people in late middle age, and there are no heaving bosoms, as such–which is not to say that the passion between them is not deep, strong, and lasting. There is love at first sight; there are lovers who cannot live without each other.

The novel begins with Harriet Capel, a widow living in Dorset. She thinks back on her marriage without strong emotion, acknowledging that she has never been in love or enjoyed sex. The plot begins when she goes up to London to visit her son and daughter-in-law. There is a long-standing feud between the Capels and the Gaunts, the family of Harriet's daughter-in-law, growing out of careless and insulting remarks made at the wedding, compounded by misunderstanding and stubbornness. Oliver Gaunt (who has come to London alone, leaving his wife in France) approaches the door and sees Harriet through the window: "Oliver felt the blood drain from his face and an answering flush rose in hers. Dry-mouthed, tachycardic, he thought, good grief, I am falling in love!"

The two middle-aged adults begin an affair, undetected by their children (who are nonetheless happy that the bad feeling between the families seems to be melting away). The affair is brief and is terminated by the unexpected, and undesired, arrival of Clarissa, Oliver's wife. Sure that she is losing him, Harriet drives back to Dorset and is killed in a road crash. Oliver, who has informed his wife of the affair and told her he is leaving her, of course stays put when Harriet dies; but after the wedding reception for his other daughter, Philomena, back in France,

> Oliver climbed the stairs to their bedroom. He pulled open his bedside drawer, found an old envelope and wrote on the back of it I AM INCONSOLABLE. He took out and unwrapped the pistol and without pausing for a second held it to his right temple and fired. It was precisely eight months, almost to the minute, since Harriet had died. Sometimes it is the man who loves most.

The novel makes use of the *Romeo and Juliet* (1594–1595) parallel usefully but not too obtrusively. Harriet Capel is almost a Capulet, and almost Juliet-like, she dies in despair (though not intentionally). Unlike William Shakespeare's play, this novel has a solidity of social detail that places the passion into a complex life. The younger generation, their friends and siblings, and Oliver's old friends all contribute to the texture, as do passages such as this one, in which the happiness they are all feeling in a pizza restaurant, just before Clarissa arrives to spoil everything, is compared to the kind of threshold moment Lambert wrote about in her first two books:

> There is a pause when the tide is full, before it turns and flows the other way. In that moment time seems sluggish. It dawdles. The water gathers itself and waits. That pause precedes any momentous change and is recalled with nostalgia, like a lost Golden Age. Such were the final few summers before the Great War; the decades before the French Revolution; the glittering Court of the last Tsar. . . . Such too were the Kennedys' Camelot years. In this dreamlike interval things happen separately, unhurriedly, deliberately, as though frames of film were being examined slowly, one by one, rather than flashing across the screen too quickly for single moments to be isolated. Oliver held Harriet's hand, Hugo, his two feet clamped firmly on either side of the cage underneath his chair, basked in the knowledge that he was the centre of attention, Julian and Philomena talked to each other for the first time since the feud had begun thirteen years ago, Roddy and his wife looked proudly at their three handsome children, and the two little girls sitting next to Ulrike trusted her never to leave them. A dreamlike interval: perfection achieved.

For whatever reason–and one of them may be that this novel genuinely is not Lambert's finest work, but the "romantic" pigeonholing is largely responsible–there were few reviews; these tended to be paragraphs in reviews of more than one book, or even reviews of the 1998 audio book (read by Sian Phillips) or a 17 April 1999 radio play broadcast on BBC Radio 4; and reactions were mixed, including some condescending faint praise. In *The Sunday Times* (London) of 28 February 1999 Karen Robinson (reviewing the audio book) said that "Angela Lambert combines seriously adept storytelling–you really are kept guessing until the final minute–and acute social observation of generations of family life." In her 29 June 1997 review of the novel for *The Sunday Times* (London) Joan Smith detected signs of hasty writing and summed up, "Well-meaning though it is, and passionately engaged with its protagonists, it feels in the end like a novel that does not actually need readers," and in a 14 June 1997 review for *The Daily Telegraph* (London) Gillian Fairchild, amid jocose references to Harriet and Oliver's "jubilant genitalia," semipraised the book for "neat observations on family dynamics" but judged that "with its unsurprising characters and convenient melodramatic ending, this novel is not as sharp as some of her previous ones."

Dust jacket for Lambert's 1992 novel, about a retired milkman and a former Royal Air Force squadron leader who set up housekeeping together after their wives both die on the same night (Bruccoli Clark Layman Archives)

Kiss and Kin was followed by *Golden Lads and Girls* (1999), which shared with its predecessor both a texture of allusions to Shakespeare (in this case, *Cymbeline,* 1609–1610) and an awareness that erotic love does not end with the loss of youth. It also shared an absence of critical attention; the one extended review it received, by David Robson in the 25 April 1999 issue of *The Sunday Telegraph* (London), recognized that "Having won the 1998 Romantic Novelist Award, Angela Lambert is stuck in an inglorious pigeon-hole. But she is a more interesting writer than she might appear. . . . Unusual storylines, light years from the banalities of Mills and Boon"–the most common, almost generic, brand name for British romances, comparable to the American Harlequin Romances–"are her forte."

In some ways this novel recapitulates concerns from Lambert's work up to 1999. The novel appears with a family tree at the beginning, which includes (in unimportant branches) Reggie Conyngham-Jervis of *A Rather English Marriage* and Henrietta Birmingham of *No Talking After Lights*. The main character, Hermione Staunton, is a debutante but of a cohort disrupted by war (she comes out belatedly, in 1922). The setting of the beginning is reminiscent of Lambert's first book of social history; here the unidentified narrator places it for readers: "This was May, 1911, the mythical Indian summer of the British Empire; the climax of the Edwardian era, soon to end with the death of the King, whose giant bulk and giant heart were fighting a losing battle." What happens in this Indian summer is an idyllic love affair between two children, Hermione and her neighbor Sandy Gordon-Lockhart. They are the children of wealth and privilege. Soon, the Gordon-Lockharts move to Scotland, separating the children, it seems, forever; their letters are intercepted by disapproving parents.

What follows is a broad-scope study of a woman's life in twentieth-century England. Hermione never marries; her only experience of sex for most of her life is her rape by a servant on Fireworks Night. She grows up and lives unhappily with her selfish, snobbish mother. After her brother's death in World War I she is made her father's heir, and she manages his business. For a time she attends art school and gets a taste of Bohemian life after the war. In World War II she turns her Devon estate into a hospital and helps treat the wounded. Throughout her adulthood she uses the enormous wealth she has inherited for good works. As an old woman she meets Sandy's grandson, a doctor, then is reunited with Sandy.

The love story is believable and well handled, as is the social history. Lambert is interested in the changes in women's lives, particularly the changes resulting from the Pill and the freedom to manage reproduction. Hermione lives too early for the Pill; in her case menopause fills the same role. The novel is also focused on class, which, as Lambert has insisted, generates "arrogance or subservience," two objects of her scrutiny in *Golden Lads and Girls*. The chief illustration in *Golden Lads and Girls* is the relationship between Hermione's parents. Her father, Jack Staunton, is a self-made millionaire, a Lancashireman; her mother, Phoebe, is the daughter of impoverished Scottish aristocrats, the Campbell-Leiths. They all, including Phoebe, despise Jack Staunton, use him (Phoebe is pregnant by another man when she marries him, and treats Jack with contempt thereafter), and her family regularly borrows money from him. This arrogance is mixed with greed, and, as the narrator reveals,

> No twig or branch of the Campbell-Leiths was unmoved by the fact that Hermione Staunton controlled a huge fortune and each member of the family could think of several good reasons why he, she, or their children should inherit it. Prejudice against money that had originated "in trade" dissolved at the prospect of being willed it, for curiously, those who have not had to work to get rich often feel superior to those who have–when surely it ought to be the other way round?

Lucy Atkins's "at a glance" review in the 23 May 1999 issue of *The Sunday Times* (London) characterized the novel as "straightforward, intermittently frothy and enjoyable, despite old-fashioned values and characters who can be divided into baddies and goodies." In his review for *The Sunday Telegraph* (London), Robson considered it at greater length and found some slackness in the treatment of Hermione's long life; he wrote that "Romantic feelings are explored in characters normally regarded as too young, or too old, to entertain such feelings in their fullest, deepest sense. The result is a touchingly upbeat story, in which an artificial plot is illuminated by moments of rare humanity."

In 2001 Lambert turned to a much different subject. *The Property of Rain* has almost nothing to say about the upper middle class in England or fine social distinctions, or the period just before World War I (its aftereffects are darkly important, though); the narration intercuts a 1980s media investigation with the story of the events under investigation; and in general this novel is an ambitious new start for its author.

There are two focal characters, both impoverished peasants, both born in 1921. Sam Savage grows up in rural poverty in Suffolk, the youngest child of Abel Savage, a drunken, violent farm laborer, destroyed by his experiences in World War I, and his wife, equally a victim, who has retreated from her bleak marriage into religious mania. There are stark contrasts between the harsh life the Savages live and that of their rich landlord, who eats well during the Great Depression while his workers go hungry.

Sam shows some promise in school, recognized by his teacher, Miss Jamieson. He takes up with Edith, a girl who shares his class background and some promise herself. Throughout his school years his nemesis is Jake Roberts, a coarse and sadistic bully; finally, in 1935, Sam joins the army to get away from his father, encouraged by a sympathetic vicar, the Rev. Mr. Persimmons. Unfortunately, the vicar encourages Jake to join up too, as a "mate" for Sam, and together they are sent to India.

Meanwhile, the other main character, Lakshmi, is growing up in India. An Untouchable child living in

Dust jacket for Lambert's 2001 novel, about a soldier who is forced to take part in a brutal gang rape and murder in India and years later kills the rape ringleader in revenge (Bruccoli Clark Layman Archives)

dire poverty, an unwanted fourth daughter, she has too many siblings, some of whom die. The girls get married, unhappily. Her father considers himself fortunate to have found a job as a sweeper for the British army, and he stays away from home, drinks, and goes with whores. Lakshmi is engaged to her much older uncle. When the monsoon comes, and her sister's mud house is washing away, Lakshmi goes, with her younger brother, to the British camp to find her father; unfortunately, they cannot read warning signs, and they climb a fence and approach a barracks. Jake Roberts drags Lakshmi inside and the men rape her one after another, to death. The last rapist is Sam, shamed and bullied by Jake into taking part. The soldiers throw Lakshmi's body into an incinerator, where it does not burn, but after a brief inquiry and cover-up nothing is ever done about the crime. Sam returns to Suffolk and marries Edith, but he is impotent and it is clear that the crime that ended Lakshmi's life has blighted his as well.

Jake is also back in town, now working as a slaughterer (Sam is a mailman), and during a great flood–the historically factual, and carefully researched, floods of 1953, which drowned hundreds in a single night–Sam murders Jake with an oar. He hopes that his demons will have been exorcized. This conclusion in 1953 is intercut with the 1980s visit to Sam of a television documentary team. The interest of the documentary makers casts a retrospective significance over the events of 1935, as the narrator's rhetorical crosscutting between Sam's and Lakshmi's stories (before Sam ever goes to India) has already prepared the reader for a connection between the two characters.

There is nothing melodramatic about this novel; the only improbability is the inescapable haunting of the basically good Sam by his nemesis Jake, which is a bit like the relationship between Orlick and Pip in Dickens's *Great Expectations* (1861). The novel is clear and understanding on the causes of family dysfunction, as in the account of Abel Savage's ruination on the Western Front: "He was not the man he had been, not as father or husband. His head roared with a tinnitus of terror that became even more vivid in his sleep. He dreamed of earth hurled skywards by exploding shells, trees stripped of greenery in midsummer, fields plundered by marching boots, nothing growing, no order of the seasons, no sense, no safety."

Sam, a great reader of Rudyard Kipling, looks forward to India, but it is not as he had expected: "He would have liked to share his wonder and bewilderment with Edith–or Mr Persimmons–or even his teacher, Miss Jamieson–but they were thousands of miles away. He wanted India to be as he had imagined and not as it was. Swarming right up to the cast-iron gates of the cantonment, piling up behind its perimeter wall, out there in the dark, the real India was noisy, smelly, teeming, chaotic and–Sam finally admitted to himself–frightening."

In a 6 May 2001 review in *The Sunday Telegraph* (London) Jessica Mann praised the social criticism and the research, and she concluded that "The novel is as instructive as a sociology textbook, but Angela Lambert writes with passion and precision, bringing genuine emotional power to her evocation of two degraded environments and one tragic incident." Reviewing the book in the 19 May 2001 issue of *The Times* (London), Amanda Craig recognized the ambition of the novel and, while she disapproved of some of its structural devices, wrote that "*The Property of Rain* will be too dark for those who have enjoyed the romantic tinge to Lambert's previous works. It is, however, more interesting for being so, and its flaws do not prevent it from being gripping, passionate and intelligent."

Angela Lambert's strengths lie somewhere between Mann's "sociology textbook" and Craig's "romantic tinge." Every one of her books has something to say about the powerful role that love and passion play in lives–and she is interested in tracing that power across the spectrum of lives, not just those of the young and beautiful. And her social observation, her continuous sharp awareness of the role of class and the nuances of distinction and division, make her an accomplished practitioner of the social realist's art. The "minutely realised bourgeois world"–though there is nothing bourgeois about the world of *The Property of Rain*–the "richness of detail," and the "brilliant social satire" noticed by critic Owen in her 1992 review of *A Rather English Marriage* combine with fertility of invention and an engaged moral awareness to make her a reliably engaging novelist whose books activate readers' hearts as well as minds.

Interviews:

Jean W. Ross, *Contemporary Authors,* volume 138, edited by Donna Olendorf (Detroit, Washington, D.C. & London: Gale, 1993), p. 264;

Maureen Paton, "The Eternal Child," *Guardian,* 30 December 1998, Features section, p. 13;

Neasa MacErlean, "A Way With Words But Not With Thrift: Writer Angela Lambert Admits Her Faults to Neasa MacErlean," *Observer* (London), 5 March 2000, p. 36.

Sara Maitland

(27 February 1950 -)

Ruth P. Feingold
St. Mary's College of Maryland

BOOKS: *Daughter of Jerusalem* (London: Blond & Briggs, 1978); republished as *The Languages of Love* (Garden City, N.Y.: Doubleday, 1981); republished as *Daughter of Jerusalem: A Novel* (New York: Holt, 1995);

Tales I Tell My Mother, by Maitland, Zoë Fairbairns, Valerie Miner, Michèle Roberts, and Michelene Wandor (London: Journeyman Press, 1978; Boston: South End, 1980);

A Map of the New Country: Women and Christianity (London & Boston: Routledge & Kegan Paul, 1983);

Telling Tales: Short Stories (London & West Nyack, N.Y.: Journeyman Press, 1983);

Weddings and Funerals, by Maitland and Aileen La Tourette (London: Brilliance Books, 1984);

Virgin Territory (London: Joseph, 1984; New York: Beaufort Books, 1986);

Vesta Tilley: A Cultural Study (London: Virago, 1986);

More Tales I Tell My Mother, by Maitland, Fairbairns, Miner, Roberts, and Wandor (London: Journeyman Press, 1987);

A Book of Spells: Short Stories (London: Joseph, 1987);

Arky Types, by Maitland and Wandor (London: Methuen, 1987);

Three Times Table (London: Chatto & Windus, 1990; New York: Holt, 1991);

Home Truths (London: Chatto & Windus, 1993); republished as *Ancestral Truths* (New York: Holt, 1994);

Women Fly When Men Aren't Watching: Short Stories (London: Virago, 1993);

A Big-Enough God: Artful Theology (London: Mowbray, 1994); republished as *A Big-Enough God: A Feminist's Search for a Joyful Theology* (New York: Holt, 1995);

Angel and Me: Short Stories for Holy Week (London: Mowbray, 1995); republished as *Angel & Me: Stories* (Harrisburg, Pa.: Morehouse, 1997);

Pandora's Box: A Three-Dimensional Celebration of Greek Mythology, illustrated by Christos Kondeatis (London: Duncan Baird, 1995; Boston & London: Bulfinch Press, 1995);

Sara Maitland (photograph by Nigel Perry; from the dust jacket for Ancestral Truths, *1994)*

The Ancient Egypt Pack: A Three-Dimensional Celebration of Egyptian Mythology, Culture, Art, Life and Afterlife, illustrated by Kondeatis (Boston: Bulfinch Press, 1996; London: Duncan Baird, 1997);

Angel Maker: The Short Stories of Sara Maitland (New York: Holt, 1996);

Virtuous Magic: Women Saints and Their Meanings, by Maitland and Wendy Mulford (London: Mowbray, 1998; New York: Continuum, 1998); republished as *Virtuous Magic: Meanings in Female Sainthood* (London: Mowbray, 1999);

Brittle Joys (London: Virago, 1999);

Gardens of Illusion: Places of Wit and Enchantment, photographs by Peter Matthews (London: Cassell, 2000);

Awesome God: Creation, Commitment and Joy (London: Society for Promoting Christian Knowledge, 2002); republished as *A Joyful Theology: Creation, Commitment, and an Awesome God* (Minneapolis: Augsburg Fortress, 2002).

PRODUCED SCRIPTS: *Morning Story,* radio, BBC Radio 4, 20 March 1989;

Short Stories for Long Nights, television, Channel 4, 19 December 1989;

Morning Story, radio, BBC Radio 4, 25 March 1991;

"Risk," television, *Obsessions,* Channel 4, 1992;

Pleasures of War, motion picture, Finetake Productions, 1999;

"Other Voices," radio, *Afternoon Theatre,* BBC Radio 4, October 2001.

OTHER: *The Happy Unicorns: The Poetry of the Under Twenty-fives,* edited by Sally Purcell and Libby Purves, introduction by John Wain (London: Sidgwick & Jackson, 1971)–includes contributions by Maitland;

"Andromeda," in *Bananas,* edited by Emma Tennant (London & Tiptee: Blond & Briggs, 1977);

Antonia White, *The Hound and the Falcon: The Story of a Reconversion to the Catholic Faith,* introduction by Maitland (London: Virago, 1980);

"Abortion and the Sanctity of Life," in *Catholicism and Conflict,* edited by Terry Drummond, Jubilee Lent Lectures, 1982 (London: Jubilee Group, 1982);

"The Errant Unicorn," in *On Gender and Writing,* edited by Michelene Wandor (London & Boston: Pandora, 1983);

"Two for the Price of One," in *Fathers, Reflections by Daughters,* edited by Ursula Owen (London: Virago, 1983; New York: Pantheon, 1985);

Walking on the Water: Women Talk about Spirituality, edited by Maitland and Jo Garcia (London: Virago, 1983);

"Heart Throb," in *Passion Fruit: Romantic Fiction with a Twist,* edited by Jeanette Winterson (London: Pandora, 1986);

"Let Us Now Praise Famous Women and Our Mothers Who Begat Us," in *Stepping Out: Short Stories on Friendships Between Women,* edited by Anne Oosthuizen (London & New York: Pandora, 1986);

Mary Brunton, *Self-Control: A Novel,* introduction by Maitland (London: Pandora, 1986);

Margaret Laurence, *The Stone Angel,* afterword by Maitland, Virago Modern Classics, no. 251 (London: Virago, 1987);

"Passionate Prayer: Masochistic Images in Women's Experience," in *Sex and God: Some Varieties of Women's Religious Experience,* edited by Linda Hurcombe (London: Routledge & Kegan Paul, 1987);

"Gluttony," in *The Seven Deadly Sins,* edited by Alison Fell (London: Serpent's Tail, 1988);

"Lady with Unicorn," in *The Virago Book of Ghost Stories,* edited by Richard Dalby (London: Virago, 1988);

Very Heaven: Looking Back at the 1960's, edited, with an introduction, by Maitland (London: Virago, 1988);

"Futures in Feminist Fiction," in *From My Guy to Sci-Fi: Genre and Women's Writing in the Postmodern World,* edited by Helen Carr (London: Pandora, 1989), pp. 193–203;

The Rushdie File, edited by Maitland and Lisa Appignanesi (London: ICA/Fourth Estate, 1989; revised edition, Syracuse, N.Y.: Syracuse University Press, 1990);

Louisa May Alcott, *Eight Cousins,* introduction by Maitland, Virago Modern Classics, no. 337 (London: Virago, 1990);

Alcott, *Rose in Bloom,* introduction by Maitland, Virago Modern Classics, no. 338 (London: Virago, 1990);

"Justice," in *The Seven Cardinal Virtues,* edited by Fell (London: Serpent's Tail, 1990);

"Fall from Grace," in *The Penguin Book of Modern Women's Short Stories,* edited by Susan Hill (London: Penguin, 1991);

The Virago Book of Ghost Stories: The Twentieth Century: Volume Two, edited by Dalby, introduction by Maitland (London: Virago, 1991);

"One Dark and Starry Night," in *The Man Who Loved Presents: Seasonal Stories,* edited by Alison Campbell, Caroline Hallett, Jenny Palmer, and Marijke Woolsey (London: Women's Press, 1992);

"For the Menopausal Woman," in *A Certain Age: Reflecting on the Menopause,* edited by Joanna Goldsworthy (London: Virago, 1993; New York: Columbia University Press, 1994);

"An Edwardian Tableau," in *The Oxford Book of Historical Stories,* edited by Michael Cox and Jack Adrian (Oxford & New York: Oxford University Press, 1994);

Alison R. Webster, *Found Wanting: Women, Christianity and Sexuality,* foreword by Maitland (London: Cassell, 1995);

Rachel Lever, ed., *To Her Naked Eye: Short Writing by Women,* introduction by Maitland (London: Pyramid, 1996);

The Martyrdom of Perpetua, introduction and commentary by Maitland (Evesham: Arthur James, 1996);

The Passion of Perpetua and Felicity, introduction by Maitland (Cambridge: James Clark, 1996);

Genesis: The Book of Beginnings: Abridged from the Text of the Revised English Bible, foreword by Maitland, introduction by Lawrence Boadt, The Lion Classic Bible Series (Oxford: Lion, 1997);

"The Loveliness of the Long Distance Runner," in *A Whole Other Ball Game: Women's Literature on Women's Sport,* edited by Joli Sandoz (New York: Noonday, 1997);

"The Secular Saint," in *After Diana: Irreverent Elegies,* edited by Mandy Merck (London: Verso, 1998), pp. 63–74;

"The Burning Times," in *The Mammoth Book of Lesbian Short Stories,* edited by Emma Donoghue (London: Robinson, 1999; New York: Carroll & Graf, 1999).

An eclectic and unorthodox author, Sara Maitland has written fiction, popular and academic theology, journalism, social and literary criticism, screenplays, biography, and the text for illustrated books on subjects as disparate as Greek mythology and gardening. In a prolific career she is best known, however, for her feminist theology and for her novels and short stories, which have won a wide following as well as several awards.

Maitland herself sees more similarities than differences among her various works, writing in a statement posted on the website of the 1999 cultural-exchange program *Island Voices 3* that "they're all about the same things . . . about sex and gender and risk and beauty and stories and language and power and glory." Indeed, many of these themes and elements can be traced throughout her body of work, although they seldom turn up in precisely the combinations one might expect. Particularly unusual is the manner in which Maitland integrates her religious and literary impulses in her fiction, creating finely nuanced and sometimes startling takes on the role of the spiritual in everyday life. Many of Maitland's characters are deeply religious (generally Catholic), but their faith does little to elevate them above the muck and strife of the world. As a character in her novel *Home Truths* (1993) observes about his brothers and sisters, "the members of this family who claim not to believe in God always swear by his name, and those of us that do use sex and lavatories"–and it is precisely this mixture of the sacred and the profane, the complexity of belief and contemporary life, that infuses Maitland's fictions.

All of Maitland's novels, as well as many of her short stories, focus on the lives of women–in particular, on women at moments of crisis. These crises are never simple, nor are they simply resolved; in fact, many never achieve full resolution. Weaving back and forth in time, Maitland carefully reconstructs her protagonists' lives, showing what twists and turns brought them to the point where the reader makes their acquaintance, while at the same time pushing them forward to a climax of self-discovery or decision. To this extent she is a realist author, operating in the same theater as many other contemporary women writers. Pure realism, however, is not her goal: she told Ruth P. Feingold in an unpublished 13 March 2002 interview that she sees "a kind of thinness in a lot of contemporary realism, in its intense specificity. . . . It can't carry larger messages." Her fictional universe, thus, is one in which realism mixes seamlessly with fantasy, creating a mythopoeic mode often compared to that of fellow British writer Angela Carter. Maitland considers herself a "fabulist," by which she means "both someone who writes fables, and someone who inserts the fabulous into the daily." Tracing her literary heritage to the world of fairy tales and fables, she strives for a balancing point between timelessness and contemporaneity, the universal and the particular.

Sara Louise Maitland was born 27 February 1950 in London, to Adam Maitland and Hope (Fraser-Campbell) Maitland, though she grew up primarily in southwestern Scotland. Her father had been a master printer, the managing director of a large printing company, but took early retirement to go home to Scotland and run his ancestral estates–thus becoming an "unskilled agricultural laborer," as he liked to put down on forms. Her mother did the day-to-day work of running the household and raising six children, of whom Sara was the second eldest. Sara describes her childhood home as green and lush, an almost paradisial pastoral landscape, near which most of her family still lives.

Sara Maitland returned to England in 1961: first to boarding school, then to study English literature at St. Anne's College, University of Oxford, which she entered in 1968. Although she had not anticipated making the move permanent, she has, in fact, ended up spending most of her adult life on the southern side of the border. In 1971 she received her B.A., and over the next two years she published her first short story, married an American, Donald Hugh Thomson Lee (on 24 June 1972), and gave birth to her first child, Mildred McNab Lee. Mildred is now an actress living in the United States. A son, Adam Maitland Lee, was born in 1981. Maitland and her husband separated in the 1990s and divorced in 2002.

The years Maitland spent at Oxford were pivotal for developing the political, intellectual, and spiritual ideals that would go on to inform her life and writing. Oxford was a focal point in the emergence of second-

Dust jacket for the U.S. edition of Maitland's 1978 novel, Daughter of Jerusalem, *in which a feminist agonizes over her inability to conceive a child (Richland County Public Library)*

wave feminism and in 1970 was the site of the first national feminist gathering in Britain. Although she says she had not thought much about feminism before the conference, from that time on it became central to the way she looked at the world: in her *A Map of the New Country: Women and Christianity* (1983) she calls it "my first ever conversion experience." This first conversion, moreover, was shortly followed by another: the heady turbulence of the late 1960s, which Maitland calls "profound and exciting and liberating" in her *A Big-Enough God: Artful Theology* (1994), opened her eyes to the possibilities and power of not only feminism and socialism but also of Christianity. Maitland had been raised a Presbyterian but was not overtly religious; by her teen years she had simply stopped thinking much about Christianity one way or another. In college, however, she awoke to religion as a logical extension of the social and political creeds that had emerged to give shape to her life: "made brave by hope and anger," she says in *A Big-Enough God,* "I was tough enough for the enormous God whom I met." It is this "enormous" God–fierce, seductive, transformative–that grounds Maitland's theology and informs her fiction. In 1972 she formally converted to Anglicanism; that same year her husband became an Anglican priest.

Maitland's career as an author began hand in hand with her work as part of a feminist writers' collective–a group she helped found–in response to the intellectual isolation she experienced upon moving to a small village in the southwest of England shortly after her marriage. Centered in London, the collective–made up of Maitland, Zoë Fairbairns, Valerie Miner, Michèle Roberts, and Michelene Wandor–met regularly for three or four years, during which time the members worked on their own projects and on a group short-story collection, *Tales I Tell My Mother.* Published in 1978, this collection was hailed as the first explicitly feminist British publication, and it has gone on to be regularly taught in schools; the group, all of whom have become well-respected authors, published a sequel about a decade later, *More Tales I Tell My Mother* (1987)–and followed this second volume with a twentieth-anniversary set of stories broadcast by the British Broadcasting Corporation (BBC).

In 1978 Maitland also published her first novel, *Daughter of Jerusalem,* which was immediately hailed (along with Roberts's first book, *A Piece of the Night,* published the same week) as one of the first contemporary British feminist novels. The protagonist of *Daughter of Jerusalem,* Liz, is a committed feminist who is as devoted to (and dependent on) her women's group as she is to her husband, Ian. As the novel opens, Liz is doing everything she can to keep from falling to pieces on the street, and even her group cannot help her. She and Ian have been trying to conceive a child for five years; she has been seeing a fertility specialist for almost a year; and she has just been given the bad news: she and Ian are both biologically capable of having children–Liz just cannot seem to ovulate when he is around. Her specialist suggests, none too subtly, that she see a psychiatrist–it is a suppressed rejection of motherhood, he claims, a "confusion about [her] gender rôle," that is causing her difficulties.

Cast into a vortex of guilt, despair, and anger–anger at her doctor, anger at herself, anger at her friends who are having babies or abortions–Liz struggles throughout the novel with the question of whether or not she is to blame for her inability to get pregnant. All the nontraditional choices she has made in her life are placed under scrutiny: did she fall in love with Ian, a gay man four years her junior, because she was not enough of a "Real Woman" to accept a "Real Man"?

Has joining the women's movement–marching, even, in support of abortion rights–somehow made her incapable of carrying a child? Moreover, her guilt about her supposed lack of femininity is matched by her guilt for what she perceives as her inadequate commitment to feminism–for, as she tells her friend Nancy, "I know it's 'wrong,' 'bad feminism,' that stuff, but if I was persuaded that conforming to some doctor's feminine ideal would get me pregnant, I'd conform." Nonetheless, unconvinced–or afraid of what she might find out–Liz puts off visiting the psychiatrist.

Daughter of Jerusalem is written in nine chapters, designated "April" through "December." The nine-month span is, of course, not coincidental, and the metaphor is enhanced through the ending of each chapter: a series of vignettes of biblical women–Mary, Sarah, Delilah–conceiving, trying to conceive, and finally (in December), giving birth. And on Christmas Day, just as Ian pours out his own insecurities and anguish over their childlessness to her, Liz suspects that she may finally be pregnant. It is a tentative moment, one still full of much uncertainty–but also of hope. The biblical parallel of Mary in the stable, also filled with hope and uncertainty about what her new motherhood may have in store for her, concludes the novel. *Daughter of Jerusalem* won Maitland the Somerset Maugham Award in 1979.

After publishing *Daughter of Jerusalem,* Maitland decided to take what she thought would be a quick break from fiction, to explore the lives of contemporary women working in new ways within Christianity. Although first envisioning her book-in-progress as a series of interviews with women that would simply present the state of things as they were, Maitland soon became radicalized. Speaking with women in Britain and America about their experiences, she realized that the issues such a book would explore demanded, also, a serious investigation into what she increasingly saw: as she put it in the introduction to *A Map of the New Country,* the book that resulted, "massive underlying questions about the whole structure of institutional Christianity." Published in 1983, *A Map of the New Country* is both objective and personal, journalism and prophecy. In it, Maitland explores the work that Christian women, and Christian feminists in particular, had done over the prior few decades; she envisions her portrayal of this work as a kind of cartography that can serve to guide other women–including herself–to explore new spiritual territory. All Christianity, she writes, is fundamentally a journey: "out of Egypt and into the painful freedom of the wilderness; out of Babylon and exile back to our true home. . . . Until the comfortable compliance is recognised for what it is–both slavery and disobedience–the journey cannot be at all." The complacency of the institutional church, and the oppression of women it engendered, were both, to her mind, antithetical to the true spirit of Christianity.

Maitland's second novel, *Virgin Territory* (1984), was published a year after *A Map of the New Country* and in many ways can be read as a fictional version of the feminist theology of the earlier volume. The novel delves much more explicitly than *Daughter of Jerusalem* into the relationship of spirituality to everyday life, bringing Christianity to the forefront by focusing on a nun who is having a crisis of faith. Sister Anna, a woman in her late thirties, entered the novitiate within months of graduating from college; she has always been secure in her vocation and is a valuable member of her Latin American missionary community. Her life is irrevocably altered, however, when a fellow nun, Sister Kate, is raped one night; angry, shaken, she becomes suddenly completely unable to cope, convinced that God is furious with her. Considering leaving the order, she is sent instead by her mother superior on a research sabbatical to London, to give her a chance to sort things out.

Sister Anna's academic project, though, only compounds her difficulties: researching the spread of Catholicism to Latin America, she becomes newly aware of the depredations committed in the name of the church–and often with its direct assistance: "With the laughter of the Fathers in her ears, she could not escape the fact that it was . . . with the blessing of the pope, by people who prayed and received the sacraments that the golden lands of hope and promise had been ruined, despoiled, assaulted. Raped." These "fathers" are the voices of male authority, sacred and secular, that Sister Anna increasingly hears–whether in or outside of her head, she does not know. Desperate for safety and security, she is alternately threatened and cajoled by these aural apparitions, who berate her for her insufficient faith and promise that if she submits to their will, she will be protected. The voices clamor for her acquiescence, yet more and more she wonders about the responsibility of the Catholic Church for oppression, including the oppression of women: "The Jesuits in Brazil had penned the native Indians in corrals and treated them like slaves to 'protect them' . . . Like women, like women now. . . . penned in kitchen or convent–to protect whom from what? Were the rules of enclosure, applying to women religious only, to keep the nuns in or the evil out? Whose evil?"

As Sister Anna struggles with her religious and psychological crisis, she simultaneously becomes embroiled in two relationships outside of the church that likewise test her sense of self and mission. The first is with Caro, a badly brain-damaged three-year-

Dust jacket for the U.S. edition of Maitland's 1984 novel, about a nun in Latin America who suffers a crisis of faith after one of her fellow nuns is raped (Richland County Public Library)

old girl, whose physical therapy Anna volunteers to help with at the suggestion of her confessor. The second is with Karen, a lesbian she meets in the British Library, a "freelance socialist feminist intellectual" with whom Anna strikes up an unlikely, and challenging, friendship. Each of these two introduces Anna to a frightening aspect of herself she has never before addressed: Caro to "the bad little girl . . . monster and freak" who resists being molded into a form acceptable to others; and Karen to her own previously unacknowledged sexuality.

Events are brought to a climax when Anna learns of the death of her dearest friend, Sister Kate, shot after leaving their order to join a guerilla group to fight imperialism in Latin America. Guilty over leaving Kate behind to deal with her anger alone in the aftermath of the rape, over never having told Kate how much she loved her, Anna begins to make love to Karen–then backs off in a frenzy of guilt, rupturing the friendship, and leaving herself alone once more to find her way.

Still tormented by her internal voices–those of the "Fathers," and those that she ascribes to Caro–Anna realizes that she can and must reject both the structured, but limiting, safety of the convent and the utter chaos of simple rebellion. In the end she finds that her path lies not in abandoning her religion but rather in breaking away from its patriarchal structures: "she had to go and seek the country of the Mothers." Anna writes requesting dispensation from her mother superior, her father, and Karen. Then, melding feminist spirituality with liberation theology, she heads back to Latin America on her own, "to learn to be a grown-up woman."

After *Virgin Territory,* Maitland spent the next several years dividing her time between literary and cultural criticism, short stories, and group projects. In the first category, she published a 1986 study of late-Victorian British music-hall star Vesta Tilley, who was best known as a male impersonator. She also edited a book about the 1960s, *Very Heaven: Looking Back at the 1960's* (1988), and collaborated with Lisa Appignanesi on *The Rushdie File* (1989), a collection of articles, interviews, and other documents related to the fatwa placed on author Salman Rushdie after the publication of his novel *The Satanic Verses* (1988). Over the same five-year span (1984–1989), she collaborated on three works of fiction: a volume of short stories, *Weddings and Funerals* (1984), written with Aileen La Tourette; the second volume of stories from her writers' collective, *More Tales I Tell My Mother;* and a novel, *Arky Types* (1987), co-authored with writing collective member Wandor.

Weddings and Funerals, the first of these publications, is a book of ten stories divided into five sections: comprising stories of weddings, sin, madness, birth, and funerals. Each section consists of one story by Maitland and one by La Tourette; alternating who wrote first, the authors composed their work in response to one another. More consistently and overtly fantastical than her novels, Maitland's stories in this book–as well as in her aptly named first solo collection, *A Book of Spells* (1987)–are hauntingly evocative of fairy tales, albeit of vaguely disquieting ones absent from most children's bookshelves. Witches, herbalists, saints, and dwarves populate the pages, each giving their own eerie twist to reality. *Arky Types,* in contrast, is an absurdist contemporary take on the epistolary novel. Written as a series of letters between not just the two authors but also a huge cast of characters–some real, some fictional, some mythical–the novel is in many ways, Maitland has said, a satire of the British women's movement.

In 1990 Maitland's third solo novel, *Three Times Table,* appeared to much acclaim. Maitland's personal favorite among her novels, *Three Times Table* is an intricately crafted portrait of three women–a mother, daughter, and granddaughter–each of whom is facing a momentous decision about her future. Set over the course of one twenty-four-hour period, largely in the house the three share, the novel examines each character in turn in a series of gradually expanding chapters that eventually explore, in flashback, all the major turning points of the women's individual and joint lives.

Rachel, seventy-four, is a paleontologist, the respected senior curator of dinosaurs at the Museum of Natural History in South Kensington. A lifelong believer in Darwinian gradualism, she has slowly and secretly, in recent years, come to accept the tenets of catastrophe theory: the idea that evolution has occurred in sudden bursts, spurred by such events as meteor strikes. To openly embrace catastrophe theory, however, means to reject her entire life's work, represented by the skeletal reconstruction that first brought her to prominence. She has written a paper clearly explaining her new beliefs, calling for the dismantling of her exhibit; the paper is typed and ready for publication, ready to be presented to the board of the museum–but she still has not decided what to do: "tomorrow I'm going to have to destroy it, order it to be taken down. . . . it's even worse than that. I don't know if I can, if I have the courage. I may cheat, lie, deceive; it's my dinosaur, my father's dinosaur, my life work. . . . I wish I was dead." Limited in her professional achievement by her husband, as well as by the mores of her times, Rachel has only this one successful bit of fieldwork to cling to; without it, she is not sure where she will be.

Rachel's daughter Phoebe, thirty-seven, is a former mathematical prodigy who is now a professional gardener. Her drama emerges much more slowly than Rachel's but is, if anything, even more severe. Traumatized in college by the death of her beloved father and by her initial reaction to the event–anger, at being called away from her studies–Phoebe impulsively forswears her first love, mathematics. In so doing, however, she discovers that she has also somehow wrought a permanent and fundamental change in her psyche: "because she could not do her work she found she could not do anything else either: she was suddenly cut off from all delight and pleasure and engagement and feeling. She simply could not." Phoebe has spent her life since drifting, unable to make a passionate commitment to anything or to anyone. Now, though, she has discovered a sinister new love: a tumor in her breast. "Strange and vital, so entirely her own and so secret," the carcinoma suggests to her the mysterious power of growth–and despite the knowledge that what she is doing is "insane and dangerous," she refuses to go to a doctor, to let the tumor be destroyed. The same night during which Rachel ponders the fate of her paper, Phoebe struggles with the question of whether or not she will keep the appointment she has made with a surgeon the next day.

Maggie, fifteen, faces the strangest dilemma of the three. A seemingly normal high-school student, she is in fact the possessor of a secret even more powerful than her mother's: her closest friend and constant companion is a dragon, Fenna. Conjured in early childhood out of a compound of myth and her grandmother's science, Maggie's dragon, despite his origins, is anything but imaginary–and is absolutely vital to her being:

> Fenna is the one purely joyful thing in Maggie's life. . . .
>
> Fenna is flame and fire, and moves on the wings of the night that are dragon-wings, to dance with taloned claws and mock at hopes of safety.
>
> Fenna is the dark force of the imagination as well as its golden dancing;
>
> Fenna is chaos as well as order, and brings, on fiery dragon breath, the full danger of the chasm.
>
> Fenna and Maggie belong to each other.
>
> For Maggie, this is the primal sentence. Not the first words spoken, but from before the surfacing of memory she has known this. It is her first self-conscious sentence. It is the sentence around which she has shaped her identity.

Fenna has taught her to fly, quite literally, and has safeguarded her for ten years–but Fenna himself is now a danger to Maggie. Increasingly isolated from her peers, unable to menstruate, Maggie is trapped by Fenna in the world of childhood. To grow up, she must reject him–yet she may not survive his anger at her betrayal.

Maitland remarked in a 2002 interview that "what the book is about is the absolute importance of the imaginary, and its dangers. It's about finding balances: Maggie's gone too far: she's trapped outside the real, and it's dangerous for her." In contrast, "Rachel has to make room for the imaginary." By the close of the novel, each has done precisely that: Maggie, in renouncing Fenna, sends him to her grandmother, who welcomes him with an explosion of joy, feeling "as though she'd given science and herself new hope of heaven." *Three Times Table* is the only one of Maitland's novels to have no explicit Christian references; yet, it can be read as having an explicitly Christian theme: that of renunciation. Each of the three main characters must make the conscious decision to give up something central to her understanding of her identity, in order to have the possibility to move on, to grow into the next stage of her life. No promises are

Dust jacket for the 1994 U.S. edition of Maitland's 1993 novel, Home Truths, *in which a woman tries to remember a disastrous vacation in Zimbabwe during a tense family holiday in the Scottish Highlands (Richland County Public Library)*

made about the superiority of that gained over that relinquished; there is only an understanding that growth, however painful, is a requisite part of life.

In 1993 Maitland, increasingly unhappy with the political and spiritual implications of belonging to a national church, converted to Roman Catholicism. Her next major works of fiction and theology can, like *A Map of the New Country* and *Virgin Territory,* be read in part as a double-barreled exploration of similar spiritual concepts–concepts that are themselves an outgrowth of ideas from the earlier books. Published in 1994, *A Big-Enough God* arose out of a series of Lenten lectures Maitland was invited to give to Anglican clergy of London. In it, she offers her suggestions for a path of spiritual journeying, by reporting on her own search for a workable personal theology, as the subtitle of the 1995 U.S. edition, *A Feminist's Search for a Joyful Theology,* makes clear. When it comes to theology, Maitland writes, "I am . . . in the literal sense of the word, an amateur–a lover. As a lover, I cannot help but desire that theology should be more playful, more open, more giving, should respond to me more sexily than is its habit." Her theology, however, must do more than seduce her: it must be a theology that affirms difference and diversity as desirable, that has transformative political and social potential, that is both mystical and ethical. Maitland's God must be an ultimately unknowable one, in any rational or logical sense; moreover, her God must be, finally, "Big-Enough–a God who is in the final count larger, cleverer, more infinite than her creation or my theology can describe her." Maitland's God is one who presides over a "dense, disorderly, chaotic and joyful universe," one in which there is "evolution, and indeterminacy, and generosity, and chance. There is risk and beauty and joy." Neither consolatory nor avenging, the God that Maitland envisions is one who challenges humans to risk everything, if only for the beauty of it.

This challenging God is, at first view, distinctly absent from the pages of Maitland's 1993 novel, *Home Truths* (published in the United States as *Ancestral Truths,* 1994). *Home Truths* centers on the story of Clare Kerslake, a society photographer in her thirties who, on vacation with her lover, David, in Zimbabwe, comes to grief while hiking up Mount Nyangani. On their ascent, Clare and David violate every possible one of the fifteen safety rules posted for their protection at the foot of the mountain; caught in a sudden fog, they then lose their way. When Clare is carried down off the mountain three days later, battered and bleeding, she has lost her camera; her right hand, smashed past the point of saving; her lover–and also any recollection of what has happened on the mountainside. Three explanations are offered for David's disappearance: he may have fallen into a crevasse; he may have been kidnapped by bandits or freedom fighters; he may have been punished for his disrespectful attitude by the ancestral spirits of the mountain. Or there is a fourth possibility, which Clare suggests in her delirium: she may have killed him.

The primary action of *Home Truths* takes place six months after Clare's accident, when she is summoned by her mother to join the family for their annual two-week retreat at Skillen, her ancestral shooting lodge in the Scottish Highlands. Simultaneously grateful for her family's love and resentful of their interference, Clare finds herself swiftly caught up in a changeable household dynamic compounded of old alliances and loyalties, equally old resentments, and the multiple pressures of all the seven siblings' extremely divergent lives. Quite apart from any specifics of plot, *Home Truths* excels in its portrayal of these adult children's interactions with one another and with their loving, devout, micromanaging parents.

The unspoken agenda for the holiday, which everyone including Clare recognizes, is to get her to remember what happened to her–and to David–and to talk. Always insecure, however, Clare is now even touchier because of her amputation and the expensive myoelectric prosthesis her mother has procured for her, but which she has yet to learn to control. Her family knows there is a "careful balance [to] preserve between teasing and intruding," but they do not always succeed. It is but small consolation to Clare that she is not the only one occupying the hot seat: her brother Ben, their mother's favorite, has just been publicly disgraced. An Anglican priest, he has appeared photographed in the Sunday tabloids in leather and nipple ring, under the headline "Vicar in Gay Drag Orgy." He, too, owes the family an explanation.

As Clare begins the slow process of sorting through her memory, she looks back not only to her last days with David but also to events and emotions from years before. The reader soon learns that Clare and David's relationship was an unpleasant one, David being an arrogant and manipulative man who did all he could to dominate her. Yet, Clare remained with him because he promised to tame the chaos she feared. It became critical that she convince herself that "he, he alone was sensible and sane and if she abandoned him out of some adolescent fantasy she would be abandoning truth and progress; she would be regressing to the place of wildness . . . to the place of betrayal and danger."

Clare has always feared uncontrolled emotion and behavior. She began her relationship with David, she now admits to herself and her siblings, because she was in flight from a real love: an Italian woman, Julia. Julia was wild, unpredictable; "when we make love," Julia had promised her, "the volcano will wake up, and throw off that mingy little city, hurl it through the air as a firework display just for you and me." And Clare had run in fear, "fled the dangerous joy," run right back to England, and into David's sane and sensible arms.

Clare must dig back still deeper, though, to find the root cause of her fear–for the question by now has become not so much what she has forgotten but rather why she has done so. She discovers the answer while lying on the Scottish hillside watching a meteor shower with her brothers and sisters, in a scene that seamlessly interweaves present and past, Scotland and Zimbabwe, and memories still more distant:

> Her parents, her real parents, before James and Hester, before this was her family, her real parents had been powerful magicians. . . . they made fireworks. . . . Her parents' best display was their last, on a crisp November evening.
>
> She had knelt on the broad window seat quivering with anticipation.
>
> Her mother had advanced into the middle of the lawn and lit the fuse.
>
> Then she had joined her husband against the laboratory wall. When the pause ended all heaven broke loose; the windows shattered, cold glass diamonds joining the hot fire ones. In a flash of sulphur lightning, she saw them embrace, and explode.
>
> Clare watched her parents explode in a cloud of stars.

Clare has always known that James and Hester are really her aunt and uncle, her brother and sisters really cousins–it is not this memory that shocks her. Rather, it is the newly recovered memory of how her parents died–that they had been laughing as it happened. The chaos she has always feared was the explosive power that took her parents from her–and it was something they cherished.

James and Hester, Clare's new parents, have always tried to guard her, to teach all their children that they will be protected if they put their trust in God and in the safety of his love. But it is Clare's very desire for safety, ironically, that has put her at risk–that has led her to the point where she can wish her lover dead and not know whether if, by wishing, she has killed him. An alternate creed is instead espoused by Clare's youngest sister, Ceci, a nun, who complains that "People are always talking about God being safe. I don't get it. In the final count, it seems to me, God isn't safe, God is the only danger big enough." Ceci remarks that "God doesn't say, be safe, be cosy" but instead commands

> Bend and break the will, discipline and scourge the flesh, face blindly the unknown, the enormous, the terrifying. Love your life, and you'll lose it.
>
> Risk it and–half blind, mangled, limbless, maimed–maybe, just, you'll totter into heaven; the place of both annihilation and total knowledge.
>
> The risk is absolute, you'll get nothing else out of it, not pleasure . . . not comfort, and certainly not safety. Just beauty.

This beauty, the beauty of risk–and annihilation–took Clare's parents from her. But as she has discovered–perhaps too late–it was also her inheritance: the knowledge that "risk must be desired, hunted, feared, embraced. . . . that beauty and danger walk hand in hand and cannot be separated."

In the final analysis, Clare still does not know whether or not she killed David; she will have to live

Dust jacket for Maitland's 1996 volume of collected stories, which depict the lives of past and present women in the context of classical mythology, folktales, and Bible stories (Richland County Public Library)

with that lack of knowledge about who she is, perhaps forever. She has learned, however, what it will take to move on in her life, to slowly rebuild her ability to live, and to love. The novel closes with a dream: Clare envisions herself as a tightrope walker, balanced precariously over a void:

> That was the challenge, the moment of hope, to dance as near the edge of destruction as was possible, to be willing to fall and still not fall. And the audience cheered, because it was beautiful . . . and she had made it beautiful.

Home Truths earned Maitland a place on the shortlist for the McVitie's Prize for the Scottish Writer of the Year.

Between 1993 and 1996 Maitland published three more volumes of short stories: *Women Fly When Men Aren't Watching* (1993), *Angel and Me: Short Stories for Holy Week* (1995), and *Angel Maker: The Short Stories of Sara Maitland* (1996). The thirty stories–many previously published–in *Angel Maker* are trademark Maitland: drawing on classical mythology, classic European folktales, biblical tradition, and her own expansive imagination, these tales explore women's lives past and present in witty, startling, and evocative ways. Several of the stories give a new spin on familiar themes, presenting stock characters from fiction and fable in a new light: in "The Wicked Stepmother's Lament," a story included in *More Tales I Tell My Mother,* the title character attempts to explain and justify her legendary cruelty; "Triptych," previously collected in *A Book of Spells,* presents the story of Abraham, Sarah, and Hagar from all three points of view; the narrator of "An Un-Romance," a self-acknowledged "Ice Queen," asks that "next time you hear a piteous tale of unrequited love, and its heroic courage, just spare a thought for the real victims of romance: the unrequiting lovers." Some stories center on explicitly feminist issues and events: originally collected in *Telling Tales: Short Stories* (1983), "An Edwardian Tableau" features a young woman whose decision whether or not to marry hinges on her suitor's reaction to her participation in a suffragette action; another story from *Telling Tales,* "The Tale of the Beautiful Princess Kalito," is a fairy-tale rendering of a young girl's footbinding. Throughout the collection, women such as Cassandra and Artemis, sirens and seal-women, mix with the contemporary and the mundane. Short and pithy–few more than ten pages long–the tales open unexpected windows into corners of the world, and corners of the human psyche, that are mysterious and familiar at the same time.

Angel and Me occupies a position slightly off to the side of Maitland's other short-story collections, and its contents are not replicated in *Angel Maker.* Originally commissioned by the BBC for daily radio broadcast during the Holy Week before Easter, the book consists of four sequences, "Mother of the promise," "Women of the passion," "Sisters of the Spirit," and "Angel and me," each of which offers a loose reinterpretation of the events of Holy Week, as expressed through stories of women from the Old and New Testaments, European history, and–finally–Maitland herself, in conversation with her guardian angel. This project, Maitland writes in the introduction, "solved a real problem for me: how I could bring together two parts of myself which feel integrated inside me but don't seem to sit comfortably together in public. The part of me that is feminist novelist and the part of me that is a Christian and would-be theologian." An example of what she terms "artful theology," *Angel and Me* participates in what Maitland sees as a long–although recently neglected–tradition of narrative Christianity.

In her novel *Brittle Joys* (1999) Maitland returns once more to the idea of angels. The protagonist of the novel, Ellie McCauley, is a renowned artisanal glassblower; her pieces are highly sought after and are included in the permanent collection of the Victoria and Albert Museum. In her mid forties, Ellie has recently begun receiving visits from what she must assume is her guardian angel–although "no guardian angel chosen by Ellie for Ellie would have remotely resembled Angel," an intrusive and bossy, adenoidal-voiced presence that manifests itself "somewhere in the region of her *corpus callosum.*"

Throughout the novel, Angel's visits occur with some regularity, interspersed with the ordinary events of Ellie's life: work in the glass studio; outings with her closest friends, Judith and Hugo, as well as with the assortment of young gay men she cultivates; the comfortable rhythms of her now sexless twenty-five-year-old marriage. At times these visitations take the form of conversations; at other times Ellie is dropped without warning into visions from throughout history, all having to do with glass. While Ellie wonders if she is perhaps going insane, Angel insists that she has only just become aware of its presence because of menopause: "lots of physical changes take place in women at the climacterium, gaining consciousness of your angel may very well be one of them."

The physical changes Ellie is undergoing, however, pale in comparison with the emotional shifts and stresses of this period of her life. A self-proclaimed "fag hag" living in the middle of the AIDS crisis, Ellie is perpetually faced with the illnesses and deaths of friends. Her mother, a dour and hypercritical woman from whom she fled in her teens, would perhaps like to see her–or so her equally dour and critical brother claims. Meanwhile, her daughter, Stephanie, has fled from her in turn, "denounced her as an interfering, dangerous bitch"–furious with Ellie for trying secretly to have her removed from a primatological field expedition because of her epilepsy. And Stephanie is not the only one in flight: unexpectedly, her husband, Henry, asks for a fifty-fifth birthday present–a divorce. In an uncharacteristic moment of viciousness he tells her he is leaving her for a "grown-up" with whom he can live a normal life: "she loves me and she's capable of doing so. I am belly sick and bored with your immaturity, your inability to relate to normal human beings and your bizarre perverse neurosis and your strings of little queens who are dying of nasty illnesses."

Mary, her current apprentice, is infiltrating her life in ways that Ellie finds threatening: taking the absent Stephanie's place in Ellie's heart; planning to have the child that Ellie cannot with Hugo; testing her wings with ambitious solo work that will take Ellie's studio in a new direction. "Mary is a thief," Ellie thinks: she has stolen Ellie's love and Ellie's craft–and she may also be actually stealing Ellie's favorite creations from the studio shelves.

The thief, though, turns out to have been Angel. Always connected with glass, delighted by its fragility and toughness, Angel has come to love glass too much–to desire it. And, as Angel tells Ellie of its kind, "if we desire we develop a sickness: we call it Angeloid

Paperback cover for the U.S. edition of Maitland's 1995 collection, which reinterprets the events of Holy Week through the stories of biblical women, European history, and an imagined dialogue between the author and her guardian angel (Richland County Public Library)

Incarnational Delusional Sickness." Ellie must let Angel go away for testing; she must also accompany Hugo to finally be tested for HIV, before he donates his semen to Mary. Ellie's glass treasures are returned to her; she agrees to the divorce; she writes Stephanie to apologize. "Nothing would get easier. Lots of things would get harder." Her angel is gone. But Angel's parting gift is a moment of inspiration, annunciation, that leads her into perfect creation: a "glowing blue, light-refracting, light-distorting bubble, free of the rod, free and filled with inspiration"–as free and filled as Ellie herself has learned to be.

In 2000 Maitland moved to live on top of a moor–in part, she told Feingold, to explore ideas about solitude and silence. She spoke of her plans to draw a book out of this experience, "a big cultural history of silence." She also reported that she was working on a new themed collection of stories, this one about the women missing from fairy tales, the menopausal women: "first you're a young heroine," she explained, "and then you're a young mother and then you're an old crone, but most of us actually have a bit of space in between for which we have no models–so I'm finding them, or inventing them." The collection of women she has come up with is, as one might expect, eclectic: Helen of Troy, Guinevere, Eve, the Delphic Sybil, Deborah, the Virgin Mary, Jocasta, Maid Marian. Some stories will be about historical women; some, about invented modern ones. Many of these women, she realizes, people are used to thinking of as young–but, she points out, "Helen of Troy was 50 when she ran away with Paris; people made references to this, but it's somehow just disappeared from our consciousness." She will do her best to reimplant it there.

Sara Maitland has produced a varied, and remarkable, body of writing in a career that began in the 1970s. Critics have praised her range, with an unsigned review of *Angel Maker* in *Kirkus Reviews* (15 June 1996) calling her "among the best of her generation." Sally Cunneen, in her review of the same collection in *Cross Currents* (Winter 1997–1998), cited her "astonishing freedom of style and voice," while Laurie Muchnick, in a piece in *The Village Voice Literary Supplement* (March 1994), noted the consistency of her vision: "a heightened, changeable reality in which religion, mythology, feminism, and chaos theory are stirred together in a witches' brew of weirdness and possibility." Many marvel at the seemingly heterogeneous collection of creeds that define her life and work–feminism, socialism, Catholicism–observing, as did Daria Donnelly in her review of *Ancestral Truths* for *Commonweal* (19 August 1994), that her "joy in both synthesis and contradiction" brings her writing much of its power. As Cunneen noted, Maitland herself says, in defining her theology, "incompatible discourses may sometimes be needed to provide a full description of human or divine reality."

Ultimately, what unifies Maitland's work is her fundamental commitment to narrative and to the power of stories to change lives. In her philosophy, stories are where everything began: as she points out in her March 1997 Anne Spencer Memorial Sermon, "Telling Tales: Theology and the Art of Fiction," according to the Judeo-Christian tradition "it is not just that our God creates in some general sense, but that our God creates by speaking, by words. We are socially constructed within this very particular mythology." The universe, then, is God's story:

> you could call the whole creation God's work of fiction. And it is worth noticing that contemporary, post Newtonian (indeed now post-Einsteinian) physics and cosmology are giving us a sense of what an unboundedaried, open-ended evolving universe we have: that is a universe that feels increasingly like a fiction, or epic, rather than like a painting or building.

Likewise, theology is at its heart simply "telling stories about the divine." And fiction? In the end it is perhaps as difficult to draw lines between Maitland's theology and her fiction as it is to separate her realism from her fabulism. Religion, politics, and story all derive their meaning from their potential for transformation. Drawing tight the link between the magic in her fiction and the magic of storytelling itself, Maitland is quoted by Muchnick as saying: "what I'm really interested in is what I think fiction can do, which is to make magical changes happen in people's lives. . . . All fiction, however social realist . . . is in fact part fantasy."

Interview:

Jon Elsen, "'Infidelity is very boring,'" *New York Times Book Review,* 13 March 1994, p. 12.

References:

Caroline Guerin, "Iris Murdoch–A Revisionist Theology?: A Comparative Study of Iris Murdoch's Nuns and Soldiers and Sara Maitland's Virgin Territory," *Literature and Theology: An International Journal of Theory, Criticism and Culture,* 6, no. 2 (1992): 153–170;

Andrea Gutenberg, "Thresholds and Boundaries: Limit Plots in Eva Figes, Penelope Lively and Sara Maitland," in *Engendering Realism and Postmodernism: Contemporary Women Writers in Britain,* edited by Beate Neumeier (Amsterdam & New York: Rodopi, 2001), pp. 191–205;

Susan J. Leonardi, "The Long-Distance Runner (The Loneliness, Loveliness, Nunliness of)," *Tulsa Studies in Women's Literature,* 13, no. 1 (1994): 57–85;

Laurie Muchnick, "Bewitched: Sara Maitland Stirs It Up," *Village Voice Literary Supplement,* 123 (March 1994): 28–29;

Sara Maitland, novelist, fabulist, feminist <http://trace.ntu.ac.uk/voices/maitland.htm> [13 September 2002].

Hilary Mantel

(6 July 1952 -   )

Michael R. Molino
Southern Illinois University

BOOKS: *Every Day Is Mother's Day* (London: Chatto & Windus, 1985; New York: Holt, 2000);

Vacant Possession (London: Chatto & Windus, 1986; New York: Holt, 2000);

Eight Months on Ghazzah Street (London: Viking, 1988; New York: Holt, 1997);

Fludd (London & New York: Viking Penguin, 1989; New York: Holt, 2000);

A Place of Greater Safety (London & New York: Viking, 1992; New York: Atheneum, 1993);

A Change of Climate (London & New York: Viking, 1994; New York: Atheneum, 1994);

An Experiment in Love (London: Viking, 1995; New York: Holt, 1996);

The Giant, O'Brien (London: Fourth Estate, 1998; New York: Holt, 1998).

OTHER: "Alas for the Egg," in *Best Short Stories 1987,* edited by Giles Gordon and David Hughes (London: Heinemann, 1987), pp. 180–198;

"If the Glance of a Woman Can Sour Cream," in *My Lord's: A Celebration of the World's Greatest Cricket Grounds,* edited by Tim Heald (London: Willow, 1990), pp. 77–80;

"King Billy Is a Gentleman," in *New Writing,* edited by Malcolm Bradbury and Judy Cooke (London: Minerva, 1992), pp. 40–49;

"Harley Street," in *The Time Out Book of London Short Stories,* edited by Maria Lexton (London & New York: Penguin, 1993), pp. 145–155;

"Growing a Tale," in *The Agony and the Ego: The Art and Strategy of Fiction Writing Explored,* edited by Clare Boylan (London & New York: Penguin, 1993), pp. 35–46;

"The Nature of the Trade," in *New Writing 3: An Anthology,* edited by Andrew Motion and Candice Rodd (London: Minerva, 1994), pp. 48–72;

"Lippy Kid," in *The Daily Telegraph Book of Contemporary Short Stories,* edited by John Coldstream (London: Headline Review, 1995), pp. 213–219;

Hilary Mantel (photograph © Jerry Bauer; from the dust jacket for the U.S. edition of A Place of Greater Safety, *1993)*

"Ties That Bind," in *New Writing 5,* edited by Peter Porter and Christopher Hope (London: Vintage, 1996), pp. 487–493.

SELECTED PERIODICAL PUBLICATIONS–UNCOLLECTED:

FICTION

"Poor Children," as Hilary McEwan, *Punch,* 276 (21 February 1979): 314–316;

"A Dying Breed," *London Magazine,* 26, nos. 1–2 (1986): 21–28;

"Something for Sweet," *Literary Review* (Edinburgh), 102 (December 1986): 57–59;

"Dog Days," *Encounter,* 68 (1987): 15–21;

"Nadine at Forty," *Granta,* 56 (1996): 121–127;

"Terminus," *London Review of Books,* 19 (22 May 1997): 20;

"Destroyed," *Granta,* 63 (1998): 41–55.

NONFICTION

"Last Morning in Al Hamra," *Spectator* (24 January 1987): 23–26;

"Learning to Talk," *London Magazine,* 27, nos. 1–2 (1987): 102–110;

"Third Floor Rising," *Times* (London) *Magazine* (23 December 2000): 16–20, 22.

In "Growing a Tale," her 1993 essay about the process of writing fiction, Hilary Mantel confesses that "I have sat, at the moment of purest heartbreak, in mental agony, and put my thoughts on paper, and then I have taken those thoughts and allocated them to one of my characters, largely for comic effect." Those final four words startlingly shift the reader's perspective, as if the author intended to lure the reader in only to spring a trap at the end. Such traps–if indeed they deserve such a negative designation–recur throughout Mantel's novels, resulting in moments when the reader discovers humor amid horror, pleasure amid pain, the ridiculous amid the somber, and the profane amid the sacred. Mantel's novels typically blend black comedy, political intrigue, and social criticism in a manner that reveals the way the past plays upon the present and impacts people's lives in ways even the individuals involved find difficult to comprehend.

Mantel has much in common with two of her British contemporaries, Graham Greene and Muriel Spark. Like Greene, Mantel writes the darkest of black comedies, evokes a sense of impending misfortune, sets her novels against political or cultural backdrops to intensify the sense of apprehension, and occasionally suggests the need and means of redemption for whatever is hidden in the past. Underlying much of Mantel's fiction, despite the relish with which she satirizes most things, is a humanitarian desire to heal whatever is injured, lacking, or well hidden in her characters. Like Spark, Mantel's prose style is crisp and ironic, filled with vivid images and description. She has a tendency to create what the British refer to as "spiky" characters, and her heroines often possess caustic or relentless personalities. Again like Spark, Mantel has a ear for sardonic dialogue that she places within narratives that oscillate forward and backward in time. And like Spark's, her stories are both fables of human intrigue and malevolence and satires of social institutions and the complacency with which people accept those institutions.

Many of the traits Mantel has in common with Greene and Spark she also shares with the Irish novelists Brian Moore and Edna O'Brien. The identification with both British and Irish writers is not an idle feature. Mantel is the oldest of three children born to Irish Catholic émigrés, Margaret Foster and Henry Thompson, who moved to the English Midlands. Hilary Mantel was born on 6 July 1952 in Hadfield, Derbyshire–a town she portrays to comic and grotesque effects as Featherhoughton in her novel *Fludd* (1989). In Hadfield, Mantel attended St. Charles Borromeo Catholic school, which she has described as a "holding pen for future sub-literates." Mother Malachy, the headmistress at the school, was the model for Mother Purpit in *Fludd.* During her early childhood Mantel and her family lived in her maternal grandparents' house, which was also populated with her grandmother's Irish brothers and sisters.

Two influential events occurred when Mantel was young. The first event resulted in a kind of change in culture climate. On the evening before her eleventh birthday Mantel and her family moved eight miles from Hadfield to Romiley in the neighboring county of Cheshire. The geographical distance between the two towns may be short, but the cultural distance was great. In her essay "Learning to Talk" (1987), Mantel describes the difference: "In Cheshire people didn't live in rows of stone terraces, but behind pebbledash or mock-Tudor facades. They cultivated lawns and flowering trees, and kept bird-tables. They had family cars, known as 'little runabouts.' At dinner time they had their lunch, and at tea-time they had their dinner. They cleaned themselves up in things called bathrums." While living in Romiley, Mantel attended Harrytown High School, a convent school similar to the one portrayed in her novel *An Experiment in Love* (1995).

As is often the case in her fiction, Mantel presents comically the family shift in social status in her short story "Destroyed" (1998), in which the family dog, Mike, keeps "betraying mongrel origins," which, of course, the family members share. The narrator explains how Mike's bad manners concerned her mother most: "When my mother saw the neighbors leaning over the larchlap, imparting gardening tips, she thought they were talking about Mike." The mother's concern over neighborhood gossip hints at the second significant event in Mantel's early childhood. Around the time Mantel's family moved to Romiley, an old flame, Jack Mantel, reentered her mother's life. The two never married, but Jack Mantel moved into the house shortly after Mantel's father moved out. Consequently, the family became the object of odium and scandal in the small town. Both of these events echo in the characters and themes of Mantel's novels. Many of her characters, for instance, are haunted by, but nonetheless struggle to overcome, the stigma of class distinctions. Many of her characters are outsiders who know

Paperback cover for the U.S. edition of Mantel's 1985 novel, about a psychic woman's attempts to care for her autistic daughter in their apparently haunted house (Richland County Public Library)

they are marked by their northern accent or common education. Likewise, many of her novels satirize individual or social moral hypocrisy. What characters hide often hurts them far worse while hidden than it does once revealed. Rarely is childhood portrayed as a happy time in a person's life.

Frequently ill as a child, Mantel often had time to read on her own. In an interview for the *Sunday Star Times* (12 March 2000), Mantel told Iain Sharp about her early reading habits and education: "I grew up in a very unliterary milieu. I was the first one in my family to have a university education or even a proper secondary education. I read voraciously as a child–but uncritically. I never understood that certain books were supposed to be too hard for me." Many of her beliefs and actions made Mantel a suspicious character by middle-class standards. By age sixteen Mantel had abandoned her religion and joined the Young Communist League. Despite her working-class origins, in 1970 Mantel gained entrance to the London School of Economics, where she, like Carmel in *An Experiment in Love,* intended to study law. After several years Mantel had to acknowledge the fact that she would never be able to afford the costs of a postgraduate degree in legal studies, so she moved to Sheffield University, where her husband, Gerald McEwan, was studying geology. The two had married in 1972. Mantel graduated from Sheffield with a B.Jur. degree in 1973.

After graduation Mantel worked briefly as a social worker in a geriatric hospital and then for three years as a shop assistant in Manchester. The shop work was not demanding, which gave Mantel time to think about the French Revolution, a topic that obsessed her. Although she was not an aspiring novelist at this point, she was already contemplating the story that became *A Place of Greater Safety* (1992). This time in Mantel's life is captured in the short story "The Nature of the Trade" (1994), in which a writer, presumably in her forties, looks back to her twenties and recalls not only the lives of her friends but also the stages by which she learned to trust her imagination. Mantel began writing *A Place of Greater Safety* in 1974.

In 1977 McEwan accepted a job with the Geological Survey in Botswana, so the two moved to a small town called Lobatse near the South African border. With much time on her hands Mantel began writing. Her first published piece was a short story for *Punch,* which Mantel claims was written in three hours on St. Patrick's Day in 1978. The story, "Poor Children" (1979), the root of the novel *An Experiment in Love,* introduces the character of Carmel and other girls attending a convent school. "Poor Children" explores the different trajectories three girls take in life as they come of age. The story also presents the hostilities, rebukes, and unaccountable qualities that occur in human relationships, even friendships. While in Africa, Mantel wrote two drafts of *A Place of Greater Safety* from notes she had brought with her. While on leave in England in 1980 she dropped the 1,080-page manuscript off with a publisher who had expressed interest in the novel. At the same time, a long-term illness required Mantel to stay in hospital and undergo surgery. Mantel emerged from the hospital only to discover her manuscript rejected by the publisher and forty pages of it missing. In spite of her initial failure Mantel began to work on another novel, a black comedy that satirized the English social-services system. She shuttled back and forth between Africa and Britain for several years, writing and working at various jobs. In 1983 McEwan completed his contract in Botswana and took a position in Saudi Arabia with the Ministry of Petroleum and Mineral Resources. Mantel and her husband moved to Jeddah, where she completed work on her first novel and began her second.

Every Day Is Mother's Day, published in 1985 by Chatto and Windus, reveals the utter failure of governmental social services to address the problems that plague people's lives–dismal marriages, child abuse, psychological isolation, lingering despair, and cavalier indifference. Like many of Mantel's novels, the opening pages of *Every Day Is Mother's Day* keep the reader off balance by eschewing traditional explication and character introduction in favor of immersing the reader in the language, lives, and idiosyncrasies of several characters. Time and place shifts early on add to this sense of disorientation. Without transition or forewarning, the reader encounters memos between social workers, letters written to Evelyn Axon from various social workers, and even excerpts from the Axon case file. This onslaught of professional jargon is interspersed with Evelyn's peculiar memories and experiences as a professional psychic who cares for her mentally retarded adult daughter, Muriel. As characters and events come into focus, the reader gains not just an appreciation of the various self-inflicted problems that disrupt the characters' lives, but a clearer perception of what the characters themselves fail to see. Even the reader, however, is kept in the dark about several factors, affording Mantel the opportunity to resolve the story with a surprising twist.

The novel follows the lives of neighbors who have lived next door to each other for years without ever making real contact each other–even though their lives nonetheless intersect in odd, eerie, and eventually violent ways. Most of the events in the Axon household are presented from the perspective of Evelyn, who struggles to cope with both Muriel and the spirits haunting her house. A professional spiritualist familiar with the ways of the spectral world, Evelyn assumes that hostile spirits are wreaking havoc on her home and making unreasonable demands that restrict her access to portions of the house. When Isabel Fields, one in a long line of social workers to handle the Axon file, tries to assist the Axons, she encounters resistance and hostility from Evelyn, who seemingly controls all her daughter's actions. Isabel recommends that Muriel spend time out of the house interacting with others; thus, the novel seems to present a conflict between the rational goals and practices of social service versus the delusions of an old woman. Things are rarely as they seem in Mantel's fiction, however.

When Mantel shifts the perspective from Evelyn's view of events to her daughter's, she employs Bruno Bettleheim's research into autism to reveal the workings of Muriel's mind. When the novel shifts briefly to Muriel's psychological world, the story of the Axon household changes dramatically. Muriel's sense of the world is based on peculiar perceptions and assumptions about cause and effect, language, and human emotions. Muriel lacks a view of the world with herself and her actions in it as well as any sense of empathy for or connection with others. As the novel progresses, the reader must reassess the Axon household and decide if the problems that plague it spring from material or spectral forces. Moreover, Muriel's movements outside her home, the consequence of Fields's intercession, prove something less than benign. While Muriel's sense of isolation and her lack of imagination apparently spring from her psychological impairment, the other characters in the novel likewise exist in a world sealed off from others, oblivious to the consequences of their actions or the lives of those around them. The other characters, though, who do not suffer from Muriel's mental disability, imprison themselves through their attitudes and actions.

Just as Evelyn struggles to care for Muriel, her neighbor, Florence Sidney, struggles to care for her aged mother, who lives safely ensconced in a world where she is a member of the royal family. Florence demands and receives help from her brother, Colin, who visits the house to make repairs and assist as he can. Colin Sidney–bored with his roles as teacher, parent, and husband–begins an affair with Isabel Fields, unaware that she is the social worker for the Axons. The reader is hard-pressed to blame Colin for his marital transgression. The Sidney household is a place where human rather than spiritual forces wreak havoc on the lives of its members.

When Isabel presses Colin to leave his wife, Sylvia, Colin impregnates Sylvia and then chooses responsibility over happiness. Whether Colin impregnated Sylvia by design or chance is not clear. Whether Isabel indeed represented the happiness Colin hoped to achieve is equally unclear. The end of the novel brings a resolution to several story lines but not certainty to the characters. All seems good on the surface. Colin buys the Axon house cheaply when Evelyn is killed and Muriel institutionalized. This moment of well-being represents only a hiatus in the intersections, however.

John Mellors in *London Magazine* (March 1985) affirmed that "Hilary Mantel has written an accomplished novel of striking originality, as funny as it is frightening, about the different kinds of hell men make for themselves on earth." When the novel was published in the United States, it received equally favorable reviews. Writing for *The New York Times Book Review* (30 April 2000), Kathryn Harrison describes Mantel thus: a "gifted writer whose descriptions convey the infrared precision of a powerful night scope, she provides an amusement that is similarly guilty, even aerial. In a cosmos that spawns a Muriel Axon, there may be no God, but there is the compensation of a godlike

Paperback cover for the U.S. edition of Mantel's 1989 novel, in which a young curate may be the reincarnation of seventeenth-century alchemist Robert Fludd (Richland County Public Library)

presence: that of the author, who draws her readers into complicity, making them privy to secrets withheld from the suffering." Besides a smattering of positive reviews, *Every Day Is Mother's Day* made Mantel £2,000 and a £4,000 advance for a second novel.

In a 1989 interview for *Contemporary Authors,* Mantel explains the impetus for her second novel, *Vacant Possession* (1986), a sequel to *Every Day Is Mother's Day:*

> *Vacant Possession* is a much more exuberant book with, however, a higher mortality rate among the characters. The starting point was the policy decision to close long-term hospitals for the mentally ill and mentally retarded, and release their former inmates into "the community"–a community which on the whole did not want them and had done nothing to prepare for them. This policy frees Muriel Axon to take revenge on the people whom she believes injured her. Though it is hard to imagine how events in *Vacant Possession* could take place in real life, I hope that in the book they have a threatening logic of their own.

The novel does have a threatening logic to it, and the source of that logic is Muriel, who has been released after ten years of institutional care. Muriel has learned an important skill during the past ten years: she knows how to become other people, to assume an identity but remain unnoticed. Thus, when Muriel has the opportunity to enter the lives of the Sidneys and others she seeks revenge upon, she does so in plain sight as Lizzie Blank or Poor Mrs. Wilmot.

In the preceding ten years the other characters from *Every Day Is Mother's Day* have moved on. Isabel, locked now in a failing marriage, decides to write a novel based on the Axon case, a decision that recalls events from the earlier novel when Colin's boss finds the Axon file that Isabel misplaced and decides to do the same. Sylvia Sidney is now a fit and fashionable woman, mobile rather than trapped in the house, socially and politically active and apparently engaged in an affair of her own with the vicar. The Sidneys' eldest daughter, Suzanne, now eighteen, follows in her father's perfidious footsteps. She is having an affair with a married man, James Ryan, who just happens to be married to Isabel Fields. Colin is moving up in his career, now that his boss has drunk himself into retirement. At one point Colin contemplates his world and, surprisingly for a Mantel character, has an epiphany of sorts that identifies the logic at work in the novel: "Everything he had done and thought had been contained within the streets, the gardens, the motorway loops of this sad English town. But why did he need a wider sphere of action? The town was in itself a universe, a universe in a closed box. There was no escape, no point of arrival, and no point of departure. Every action, however banal, opened into a shrapnel blast of possibilities; each possibility tail-ended or nose-dived into every other, so that there was no thought, no wish, and no perception that did not in the end come home to its begetter." *Vacant Possession* charts the course of those shrapnel pieces as they fly through the air and rip through the lives of the Sidney family, Isabel Fields, and various others.

The events from *Every Day Is Mother's Day* are told often from Muriel's perspective, revealing the extent to which Muriel hated her mother and planned her revenge. Muriel's thinking is still as odd and eerie as it was in the earlier novel, but her intentions are much more focused and the path to her goals clearer. Throughout the novel Mantel avoids a moralistic tone, opting instead for a dispassionate presentation of horrifying events. Thus, the logic of the story to which Mantel refers in her *Contemporary Authors* interview represents both Muriel's laser-like focus on her task and the obliviousness of the others to the malignant force in their midst. Muriel as Lizzie becomes the Sidneys' maid in the house that was once hers and her mother's. Quickly, the Sidneys become dependent on Lizzie to do almost everything for them. When things go wrong, rather than blaming rambunctious spooks the way Evelyn Axon did, the Sidneys blame each other, but never Lizzie. As a result Lizzie is able to infiltrate the Sidney household and wreak as much havoc as she did in her mother's home. Muriel is able to repeat this infiltration in the lives of Mrs. Sidney, Colin and Florence's mother, as well as Isabel's father, who turns out to be the father of Muriel's child.

Muriel is the agent of much of the action in the novel. Colin at one point wishes for what comes naturally to Muriel: "I could do with being two people really, he thought; people who could live quite alternative lives, and meet up from time to time to compare notes. I am incapable of a decision, and always have been; I wait for circumstances to make my decision for me, and just as I pray for resolution, so I dread it. Act, and you might as well be dead. Action is the great abortionist. It wipes out freedom. It terminates desire." In this way, Muriel is Colin's foil. While Colin lets much of life occur to him, Muriel takes the initiative to obtain her desire. Colin wishes he could be more than one person, but Muriel becomes more than one person. Colin believes that action terminates desire; Muriel's desire fuels her actions. As the novel concludes, Colin stands hopelessly in his new empty home, while Muriel carries out the resolution of her plans.

In his review of *Vacant Possession* for *The New Statesman* (30 May 1986) Bill Greenwell compares Mantel favorably to two of her contemporaries: "I mentioned [Sue] Townsend and [Tom] Sharpe. Hilary Mantel is a sort of antidote to both. Where Sue Townsend is barmily soothing about the social services, Mantel is busily putting her subtle boot in. But Sharpe? Mantel reminds me why I have packed in Sharpe, who always managed half a bundle of laughs before abandoning his novels to vitriol and anarchy. Mantel maintains a very firm hold on her material, sustaining a tale of such irony as might dazzle the most accomplished farceur." In her review for the *Wall Street Journal* (31 March 2000) Merle Rubin places Mantel's novels like *Vacant Possession* into a larger context of postwar British fiction: "Ms. Mantel's wry humor and finely honed prose style are reminiscent of early Muriel Spark. The dysfunctional world she depicts would not have shocked readers accustomed to novels like Martin Amis's 'Dead Babies' (1975). Indeed, so much postwar British fiction mines this vein of black humor that it has become something of a national mannerism."

Around the time *Vacant Possession* was published, Mantel and McEwan moved back to England for good. By this time in her personal life, Mantel was concerned about the dangers of being permanent expatriates. In a 7 March 1995 interview with Hunter Davies for *The Independent* (London) Mantel explains that "Nine years as an expat was enough. We'd loved Botswana, but life in Jeddah was not very pleasant for a woman. I feared if we stayed any longer, we would develop the mind-set of the expat–complaining about welfare state scroungers and singing 'God Save the Queen' at every opportunity. It's like rabies. You must move before the signs appear, because when they do, you're lost."

Back in England, Mantel had a stroke of good fortune. She entered and won a contest for travel writing, and that award led to other writing opportunities. Mantel won the Shiva Naipaul Prize for "Last Morning in Al Hamra," an essay whose sensibility informs *Eight Months on Ghazzah Street* (1988), her third novel. From a pool of 206 entries the judges recognized Mantel because of "her ability to convey not only the discovery of culture new to her but also the distaste which the discovery aroused." *The Spectator* subsequently offered Mantel the position of movie reviewer, replacing Peter Ackroyd, who had moved on. Over the next four years Mantel wrote movie and book reviews while continuing work on her fiction.

By this time in her career Mantel had developed a regimented process of preparation and writing, which she explains in the essay "Growing a Tale": "the planning stage of a book takes me a long time. I go through a phase where I know what is to happen, and to whom–and at this stage I can write a synopsis if it is needed–but I don't quite know what the book is *about.* I have not teased out all its themes. I tease them out through the act of writing itself. I am very seldom conscious of the metaphors I may embed in a book, of recurring images, of the links that (for a reader) hold a book together and give it integrity and a characteristic tone." Mantel also contends that her strength as a writer lies in the link between ideas and action: "What talent I have is for seeing the connection between things, and in finding a dramatic form for abstract ideas. It seems to me that my books are ideas-driven–they are dramatic expression of what interests me or preoccupies me or obsesses me at the time."

What obsesses Frances Shore in *Eight Months on Ghazzah Street* involves real cultural conflicts that distinguish a British from an Arab view of the world as well as imagined or assumed intrigues at work in the apartment building where Frances and her husband, Andrew, live. The cultural conflict of the novel stems from a country eager to employ foreigners to build and rebuild their country while nonetheless resenting their presence at every moment. The expatriates living in Saudi Arabia only compound this cultural conflict while making it a continual topic of contemptuous conversation. Many of the expatriates work in the Kingdom because of the money to be made, making them a kind of industrial or technical mercenary for hire. Frances sees both sides of this equation clearly and refuses to keep her views to herself: "I'm not one of those people who think that when you go to a foreign country you must leave your judgment at home." She and Andrew choose to live in town rather than in the compound housing most of the expatriates. Although Mantel lived for four years in Saudi Arabia, *Eight Months on Ghazzah Street,* like her other novels, is not a fictionalized account of personal events but a story of conflicting cultural beliefs propelled by suspenseful ambiguity.

Structured in chapters identifying the months in the lunar Hijra calendar, the novel fluctuates between the action of the various characters and Frances's diary entries. Frances quickly discovers how intolerant the Saudis are of Western ways in general and Western women's rights in particular. Once in the Kingdom, Frances, a cartographer by training, finds independent movement dangerous, humiliating, and disorienting. As a result she finds herself trapped in her apartment for extended periods of time while Andrew works long hours on the building he is designing. Since she cannot enter the street where the men move freely, Frances moves within her building, making friends with two of the women–Yasmin, a Pakistani, and Samira, a Saudi. Frances's exchanges with these two women reveal the utter incompatibility of the cultures that define them. Central to this incompatibility is Frances's observation that, unlike Western cultures, Islam does not distinguish between public order and private morality, which opens the door then to public actions vigorously or forcefully imposed upon private choices.

Into the mix Mantel adds several mysteries. The first involves a secret contained in a supposedly vacant apartment in the building, in which Frances is sure someone is being hidden or held. The other mystery, which is never really resolved, involves the unexpected death of a British air-conditioning consultant, Adam Fairfax, who arrives in the Kingdom for just a short visit. The two mysteries may be connected, but Frances cannot be sure. Despite her best efforts to discover some kind of truth regarding these mysteries, she discovers only more mysteries or a willingness on the part of both Saudis and British to leave them unexplained. Frances and Andrew eventually move onto the company compound because they realize that they can no longer live on Ghazzah Street. In the end the reader watches Frances either progress toward a state of accommodation with an alien culture or regress from the world to a state of isolation where she spends her days idly moving about her new apartment:

> I pick up the chair, bounce it gently on the concrete to shake out the dust. I turn with it, and catch my reflection in the glass doors. My face is black, deeply shadowed, with empty eyes, and a pale ragged aureole encircles my head. I have become the negative of myself. I go back into the house and put down the chair. I look out through the glass, on to the landscape, the distant prospect of traveling cars. Window one, the freeway; window two, the freeway. I turn away, cross the room to find a different view. Window three, the freeway; window four, the freeway.

Anita Brookner's review of *Eight Months on Ghazzah Street* for *The Spectator* (14 May 1988) presents the novel as "a detective story that fails to tie up the loose ends." Brookner believes that some readers will find this trait unrewarding but argues that the strength of the novel is that "Everything is withheld. This tightness of control is perhaps the novel's eeriest feature." In her review in *The New York Times Book Review* (20 July 1997), Francine Prose links the mysteries in the novel with its cultural context: "the violence that shatters the final chapters . . . is presented as an almost unavoidable consequence of the tension rife in contemporary Arab culture. What makes this trickier is that the crimes and disasters are so plausibly rendered that we never feel we're reading dire jingoist or racist fantasies. . . . Some readers may find themselves re-examining their own ideas about the artist's right or obligation to render politically uncomfortable truths."

Mantel's next novel, *Fludd,* portrays how upsetting religious change and liberation can be. *Fludd* may not begin on the proverbial dark and stormy night, but almost everything changes at the Church of St. Thomas Aquinas in the small northern town of Featherhoughton when a young curate, presumably sent by the bishop to modernize the church, arrives on such a night. Once the curate takes his place in the rectory, small, though not necessarily holy, miracles occur on a regular basis. Father Angwin's whiskey bottle, like the biblical loaves and fishes, is never depleted; the wart on Miss Dempsey's face disappears, only to reappear later on the face of Mother Perpetua; Sister Philomena, in a rare case among Mantel's women, escapes the confines of the convent and finds a chance at happiness. Startling confessions accompany these small miracles. Father Angwin admits that he has lost his faith, even his belief in God's existence. Mother Perpetua, in a moment of secular glee, revels in the clothes shed by the other sisters upon arrival at the convent. The curate, who may be an incarnation of seventeenth-century alchemist Robert Fludd, does not transform base metals into gold but exposes what is psychologically or emotionally hidden and reveals opportunities when none seemed possible before.

In contrast to Mantel's other novels, where a cool uncertainty prevails at the end, in *Fludd* the guilty are punished and the just offered mercy, but this mercy comes only after change. The process of change occurs in dramatic ways to base metals, but that same change seems to occur in subtle ways through fiction and the ideas it explores:

> But everything that is going to be purified must first be corrupted; that is a principle of science and art. Everything that is to be put together must first be taken apart, everything that is to be made whole must first be broken into its constituent parts, its heat, its coldness, its dryness, its moisture. Base matter imprisons spirit, the gross fetters the subtle; every passion must be anatomized, every whim submit to mortar and pestle, every desire be ground and ground until its essence appears. After separation, drying out, moistening, dissolving, coagulating, fermenting, comes purification, recombination: the creation of substances that the world has until now never beheld.

Peter Parker in his review of *Fludd* in *The Listener* (7 September 1989) identifies the novel as "a courageous departure for Mantel, whose previous novels have been noted for their high comedy. . . . In the past, Hilary Mantel has been compared to Muriel Spark; here she tackles Sparkish concerns and arrives at something altogether her own." *Fludd* was the last of Mantel's novels to be released in the United States, but it received equally positive reviews as it did in England when first published. According to Patricia T. O'Conner in *The New York Times Book Review* (2 July 2000), "Mantel manages to make us laugh even as our hair stands on end. . . . The writing is characteristically Mantel: mordant, pitiless, razor sharp."

What is clear throughout Mantel's fiction is her interest in characters who struggle with some kind of internal conflict–an excess of will, faith, conscience, or an absence thereof. In *The Age* (6 March 2000) Mantel explained to Stephanie Bunbury her preoccupation with conflicted and damaged people: "There's not much mileage for a fiction writer in calm people or happy people. You want to write about people who are prepared to put a bomb under things. Literally, in the case of the [French] Revolution, but also simply people who are inconvenient, who keep asking questions when they are told not to ask questions, people who run against the grain." Muriel Axon from the first two novels and Frances Shore from *Eight Months on Ghazzah Street* represent fictional characters who in different ways inconveniently impact the world around them. The mysterious assistant in *Fludd,* whether a reincarnation of the real Robert Fludd or just another person to pass through Featherhoughton, certainly runs against the grain of local habit. In her fifth novel, *A Place of Greater Safety,* Mantel chose historical figures and an actual revolution to find people willing "to put a bomb under things."

Dust jacket for the U.S. edition of Mantel's 1992 historical novel, which portrays the events leading up to and during the French Revolution from the perspectives of some of its principal instigators (Richland County Public Library)

A Place of Greater Safety, which Mantel began in 1974 and reworked over the years, takes place in the eighteenth century, during the years of and prior to the French Revolution. The topic of this novel in its largest sense is the event that changed not just France but all of Europe as well. In this novel, her most ambitious, Mantel takes full advantage of the strengths and liberties afforded the fiction writer but unavailable to the historian. Mantel tells the stories of L. S. C. Desmoulins, known as Camille; Georges Jacques Danton; and Maximilien de Robespierre as well as the people they love and encounter in life. The perspective is more close detail than sweeping vistas, though Mantel does not ignore the political story that informs the national narrative in favor of the personal story. Mantel also imaginatively fills in the story of the childhoods of these characters, providing detail and scope that reveal changes in characters over time. As a result the intellectual and emotional turmoil that brought about the French Revolution and the violence and change that followed in its wake are portrayed in detail. Mantel's efforts were recognized, and *A Place of Greater Safety* won the *Sunday Express* book prize, which includes a £20,000 award.

In her review of a collection of essays on Robespierre (*London Review of Books,* 30 March 2000) Mantel discusses the difficulty of writing about such a man. In the process she reveals something of the design behind her novel:

> To write about Robespierre you have to find the courage to allow yourself to be mistaken. Otherwise every sentence will be freighted with conditionals and qualifiers, and every quotation prefaced by "alleged to have said." You will contradict yourself, because he contradicts himself. If you want to know why he excites such extremes of adoration and loathing, you have to study not just the biographies but the life stories of the people who write them. . . . It's not only novelists who perpetuate fiction, and it seems that whatever you say about him, you say about yourself. . . . Intending only to look at Robespierre, we see ourselves with our own startled eyes, starved or gross, inflated or diminished.

The political concerns of the day were not history, of course, at the time; they were topics of discussion by those interested in issues or simply those interested in being fashionable about issues. For some people, issues that will later be identified as central to the day blend indistinguishably with the mundane. Mantel begins one section of the novel with the large picture of 1790 France but quickly allows Lucile's thoughts to telescope the narrative into the thoughts of others, including the trivialities by which her mother assesses current events:

> That year the Assembly made bishops and priests into public officials, salaried by the state and subject to election, and in time also required of them an oath of loyalty to the new constitution. To some it seemed a mistake to force priests to a stark choice; to refuse was to be counted disloyal, and dangerous. Everybody agreed (at her mother's little afternoon salons) that religious conflict was the most dangerous force that could be unleashed in a nation. From time to time her mother would sigh over the new developments. "Life would be so prosaic," she complained. "The constitution, and the high-mindedness, and the Quaker hats."

As the section reaches its conclusion, Lucile's question slowly emerges, revealing a more probing and serious mind than her mother's. Lucile, however, is not just talking politics of the day, for she knows the character of the person she asks the question will bear up the answer she receives. The revolution had factions because its leaders had differing points of view and emphasized different things: "So has this revolution a philosophy, Lucile wanted to know, has it a future? She dared not ask Robespierre, or he would lecture her for the afternoon on the General Will; or Camille, for fear of a thoughtful and coherent two hours on the development of the Roman republic. So she asked Danton. 'Oh, I think it has a philosophy,' he said seriously. 'Grab what you can, and get out while the going's good.'"

Although he found some passages "forced," Oliver Bernier praised Mantel's novel in *The New York Times Book Review* (9 May 1993): "As a work of fiction, 'A Place of Greater Safety' is unquestionably a success. Ms. Mantel understands how people feel, how they react, how they think. She has the kind of long view that enables her convincingly to take up a character in childhood and bring him or her to dramatic adulthood. Just as important, she knows how to make us sympathize. To meet Danton as the unruliest of boys, then as a happily married young lawyer, helps us to comprehend his emotions as he progresses to the revolutionary leadership he eventually assumes." Bernier's point is echoed by Annette Kobak in her *TLS: The Times Literary Supplement* review (23 May 1997) of Marge Piercy's French Revolution novel *City of Darkness, City of Light.* Kobak contends that Piercy fails to reveal the changes in characters such as Danton. Kobak compares Piercy's novel unfavorably to Mantel's: "Piercy doesn't register any of these moments, although she deals with the events. Hilary Mantel . . . notes them all and, of course, much else besides."

For her next novel Mantel leaves eighteenth-century France for twentieth-century Africa. *A Change of Climate* (1994) explores the seemingly singular trajectory a person's life takes–questioning whether or not a person chooses which paths to follow or which option to take and whether a person over time evolves or stagnates as a result of those choices. To address such questions, of course, demands that the individual read the past rather than ignore it, and that is where the conflict of Mantel's sixth novel begins. *A Change of Climate* fluctuates between distinct points in the life of Ralph Eldred, a middle-aged man who has dedicated his life to the charitable service of others. Ralph and his wife, Anna, are professional Christians who articulate their goodwill through good deeds. Ralph divides the world into "sad cases" and "good souls," of which he and Anna would qualify as the latter. The novel begins as the trajectory of one character's life concludes. Ralph and Anna attend the funeral of Felix Palmer, a family friend. After the funeral Ralph learns of an affair between Felix and his sister, Emma. Ralph is stunned by his utter ignorance of events that were known by virtually everyone else, including Felix's wife, Ginny. Ralph's realization that an entirely different version of history coexisted with his own sense of the past triggers a series of events and recollections that force him to reexamine his own present and past.

In the days following Felix's funeral Ralph recalls his childhood years in a home dominated by an overbearing and overpious father. Wealthy enough to ensure, and thus manipulate, his children's financial stability, Matthew Eldred forces young Ralph to choose the path in life Matthew wishes him to take. A cunning manipulator, Matthew sends his wife to do his dirty work, a threat that if Ralph does not enter the family business and forget his desire to study geology, then Matthew will see to it that the doors to Emma's future slam shut. Ralph, betrayed by both his parents, acquiesces and thereby opens the door through which Emma can pursue her career in medicine: "Payment was due, he reckoned, a tribute from the past to the future." His path of choice blocked to him, Ralph follows the one opened for him, which involves taking a wife and beginning his missionary service in Africa.

Like so many of Mantel's novels, *A Change of Climate* blends personal tragedy and political intrigue, the small story writ against the large. In her review of the novel in the *Los Angeles Times* (14 September 1997) Charlotte Innes praises the "chilling moments in this darkly humorous book (perhaps Hilary Mantel's best), encapsulating the push and pull between emotion and repression, self-sacrifice, pragmatism and confusion, goodness and evil–in fact, all the complicated 'business of being human'–that animates everything Mantel writes." The story of the Eldred missionary work plays out against the apartheid system of South Africa, though the story is not simply a portrait of unjust whites imposing their will on unfortunate blacks. Neither evil nor goodwill knows culture or skin color. Moments before an event that haunts Ralph and Anna for years, Ralph contemplates the trajectory that a person's life takes and his own contentment with the imposed trajectory his own life has taken:

> If in the course of his life he had done one thing differently, one tiny thing, perhaps he would not be where he is now; his frail wife in his arms, his twins on the knee of their dark nanny, his convalescent dog at his feet, ribs heaving with delight at mere survival. Everything in the universe declines to chaos and waste; he knew this, he is not so poor a scientist. But he believes that his choices have been the right ones, that this is where he wishes to be; believes it simply, as he believed in Bible stories when he was a child. If his choices have led to this, have brought him to this moment, they have an intrinsic rightness; as for those other worlds, the alternative universe, he will not inquire. And surely, in the end, he says, my will is free?

Paperback cover for the U.S. edition of Mantel's 1994 novel, in which a Christian missionary is compelled to face uncomfortable truths about a family friend after the man's death, as well as about his own past and present (Richland County Public Library)

Ralph and Anna hold a secret for much of their adult lives, and that secret slowly changes them from good souls to sad cases. At the conclusion of the novel an opportunity arises, in the form of a child emerging from the mud, for the two to find redemption and work together as they did so many years before.

Mantel reveals in her *Contemporary Authors* interview that *An Experiment in Love* "is a joke-variant of Muriel Spark's novel *The Girls of Slender Means.* It explores the question of how a girl invents herself into a woman, and considers what role models she will embrace as she moves into adulthood. . . . As in *A Place of Greater Safety* I wanted to hover at the point of interconnection between the personal and the political,

Dust jacket for the U.S. edition of Mantel's 1995 novel, about the educational experiences of three girlfriends from varying social classes (Richland County Public Library)

but this book puts a feminist spin on the question." Told by the adult Carmel McBain, who lives safely ensconced in her middle-class existence, the novel recounts the lives of Carmel and her friends–Julianne "Julia" Lipcott and Karina, whose last name Carmel assures the reader is unpronounceable–from their early childhood in Lancashire to their early adult years at the University of London. Wrapped in this bildungsroman is a whodunit that is, like most challenging questions in Mantel's fiction, identified but never answered. Childhood is presented not as innocent but as merely parochial, and forgetfulness and malice rather than empathy and affection typically recur between friends. Financial or professional success is presented as far more attainable than authentic friendship. Moreover, the common traits of geography, class, and community play far greater roles in the lives of Carmel and Karina than other factors in the maturation process. Carmel and Karina are not friends really, although they grow up and spend most of their formative years together. In fact, the novel suggests that friendships are not easily attained and rarely lifelong, even though relationships may prove life-changing.

When Carmel arrives first to check into the college residence hall, she chooses to share a room with Julia rather than Karina. At first, it seems that Carmel makes this choice for Julia's sake, but it becomes clear that Carmel and Karina share a past but little else. Both were born into poor, working-class families in which their mothers envision better lives for their daughters than was offered to them. Carmel's mother, for instance, is domineering and relentless in her daughter's pursuit of success. Mrs. McBain eagerly pressures Carmel to gain entrée into a world she does not really understand. When Carmel has the chance to win a scholarship to the prestigious Holy Redeemer convent school, Mrs. McBain makes the long journey from the family home to the school, losing her way in the process. The fact that Carmel and Karina, who also wins a scholarship, must leave for school early in the morning and take several buses to reach school is less a factor than the success that education will bring.

The education Carmel receives falls into two basic categories, the pedagogy and the ideology informing that pedagogy. In the first category, Carmel includes a laundry list of facts and ideas that mark her education, along with a few things she also learned along the way:

> Year I, I learnt:
> a. The ground plan of a medieval monastery;
> b. That it is vulgar to use a ballpoint pen instead of a fountain-pen;
> c. That parallel lines meet in infinity.
> Year II, I learnt:
> a. The product of Ecuador;
> b. The mountain sheep are sweeter, / But the valley sheep are fatter;
> c. To prefer the active to the passive voice.
> Year III, I learnt:
> a. The anatomy of a rabbit;
> b. That beauty is truth, truth beauty;
> c. How to apply liquid eyeliner.
> Year IV, I learnt:
> a. The ablative absolute;
> b. The composition of blood;
> c. Something of the nature of the task before me.

Later on, when Carmel successfully moves through that system, she looks back and observes that the model for her education was based on the model commonly applied to young men by a system eager to replicate similar, if not identical, versions of earlier models: "and this is what we were. . . . not so much little nuns, but little chappies, little chappies with breasts. . . . Our school kept from us, for as long as they could, the disastrous, disruptive, upsetting knowledge of our own female natures."

An Experiment in Love garnered rave reviews and won the distinguished Hawthornden Prize. Brookner in *The Spectator* (4 March 1995) praised Mantel's novel: "*An Experiment in Love* differs from any other novel I can think of written to this particular formula, which has become a commonplace: although we are to assume a rite of passage this is never enacted. . . . A clear-eyed examination of female alliances may well be needed in these misleading times. *An Experiment in Love* may well be such an examination, cool, unsentimental, and unassumingly authoritative." Margaret Atwood's assessment of the novel in *The New York Times Book Review* (2 June 1996) presents both the most recurring positive sentiments of Mantel's fiction as well as the most common critique: "Moral confusion reigns, and moral questions also: What makes bad people? Even more mysteriously, what makes good people good? . . . If there's any complaint, it's that we want to know more: like Carmel herself, the book could have been fatter. . . . But perhaps that's the point: it's what you'll never know that haunts you; and with all its brilliance, its sharpness and its clear-eyed wit, *An Experiment in Love* is a haunting book."

Loosely based on real characters from the eighteenth century, Mantel's eighth novel, *The Giant, O'Brien* (1998) chronicles the lives of and eventual encounter between the Scottish anatomist and scientist John Hunter and Charles O'Brien, the "Surprising Irish Giant, the Tallest Man in the World." Hunter represents the newly emergent methodology of scientific inquiry–whose spirit the real Fludd, reincarnated in Mantel's earlier novel, so earnestly resisted. In contrast, the giant–emerging from the misty world of turf fires, hedge schools, wandering poets, and fairies–represents the rapidly fading oral tradition of Ireland, a country that has fallen prey to the imperial designs of England. Hunter is that aspect of human nature that strives to classify, control, name, and possess everything. O'Brien, who freely combines fact and fancy, is that aspect prone to telling stories to explain the world, and O'Brien's stories range from those handed down within the Irish literary tradition to variations on tales of Hans Christian Andersen and the brothers Grimm.

Mantel discussed her motivation for writing the novel in a 27 November 1998 interview on Canadian radio. In the interview she explains that she was reading a book in which the story of O'Brien was sketched in a brief footnote. The footnote merely relayed basic facts about the giant–his 7'10" frame, his pituitary condition, and his final resting place. Mantel recognized the possibility for a novel and began research. To her surprise Mantel discovered that "What is known about Hunter fills volumes. What is known about the giant, you can write on the back of a postcard." The real giant was probably mentally retarded, and most certainly not the loquacious storyteller who appears in her novel. Just as she took certain liberties in *A Place of Greater Safety* to tell the story of the childhoods of Danton and Robespierre, however, Mantel creates a thoroughly fictional story whose central characters are historical figures. In the case of her French Revolution novel Mantel explores through fiction what is unknown through history, the early years of her characters. In *The Giant, O'Brien* Mantel gives voice to a character who was probably mute or inarticulate in order to tell the story of two countries and two colliding traditions.

The novel charts the journey of O'Brien and his followers (Jankin, Claffey, Pybus, and Joe Vance) from Ireland to England. The group leaves Ireland, where

Dust jacket for the U.S. edition of Mantel's 1998 historical novel, which tells the intertwined stories of Scottish anatomist John Hunter and the freakishly large Irishman Charles O'Brien in eighteenth-century England (Richland County Public Library)

starvation, if not total destruction, is imminent, to make their way to a London eager for the latest freak show. The year is 1782, when the giant, under the stage name of Charles Byrne, goes on exhibit in London. The novel follows the rising and falling success of the giant as a curiosity and the gradual corruption of his fellow travelers. A year later the giant is dead and his body secured by Hunter for his collection of bones. The journey of Hunter, which the novel also charts, begins in 1748 when the twenty-year-old travels from Scotland to England to become a scientist, surgeon, collector, and distinguished member of the Royal College of Surgeons, in whose museum the bones of the real giant remain on display today.

The difference between the two men is presented not only in the broad viewpoints or traditions the two represent, but also by their dialogue with others and their sensibilities toward the world around them. Just as O'Brien has his band of followers, Hunter has his, a troop of grave robbers he employs to obtain the corpses he needs for his anatomy experiments. When he explains the procedures the men should follow to obtain the corpses, Hunter portrays human emotion and action in a causal and condescending, Hobbesian manner: "Leave the grave as you found it. No slovenly workmanship, for that conduces to suspicion, and suspicion conduces to lying in wait, and lying in wait conduces to apprehension, and apprehension conduces to a mob, and a mob conduces to a smashed pate and a broken leg, and a noose if you are unlucky." In contrast, when he and the others encounter various freaks on the streets of London, O'Brien reveals a wonderment at the mysteries of God's creation reminiscent of Gerard Manley Hopkins: "They are wonders, they are prodigies, the Giant tells them; they are nature's curlicues and flourishes, extravagances of flesh . . . the fruit of God's absentmindedness." Jankin, typically the most foolish of the group, responds, "'Charles O'Brien, I never thought it–but there's lower than Irish.'"

Mantel also introduces her usual comic perspective even amid dire surroundings when the band of Irishmen arrive in London and encounter a multistory building for the first time. Joe Vance, the erstwhile agent who has arranged the trip, eager to demonstrate his worldly wisdom, explains why men, and not women, occupy the upper floors of buildings: "No. The women cannot fly. They remain on what is called the lower storey, or ground floor, where men are able to join them as they please, or, when they sicken of their nagging chatter and wish to smoke a pipe of tobacco, they unfold the wings they keep under their greatcoats, and flutter up to what they call the upper storeys." The end result, then, is a marvelous tale that both charms and horrifies the reader. Just as she did in *A Place of Greater Safety,* Mantel skillfully re-creates the world in which her characters live. Eighteenth-century London is presented as a teeming, violent, stinking place where kindness easily gives way to greed, and a human storyteller gives way to a trophy skeleton in a museum.

John Bayley, in his review for the *New York Review of Books* (8 October 1998), places Mantel in rare company indeed: "*The Giant, O'Brien* offers a different and more bizarre glimpse of unquiet history. More like Swift than Scott, its dazzling technique has Swift's way of taking the extraordinary for granted, while demurely drawing our attention to some silly spectacle that attracted the crowds. . . . Her method has relations with that of Ackroyd in *Hawksmoor, Chatteron,* or *Milton in America,* where the past has been transformed into a scholarly fantasy of equal originality. But Mantel's vision is the more oblique and economical, the precision of her language–a language appropriate to an Irish giant and his myrmidons–as sharp-pointed as poetical, leaving the reader to rejoice in a continual dance of subtle inference."

At this stage in her career Hilary Mantel has written eight remarkably different novels. Regarding the difference among her novels, Mantel told Ruth Nichol in the *Evening Standard* (14 March 2000), "I can't help it. I don't think I could produce last time's book even if I wanted to because I'm a different person each time; it's a different person writing." Among her future plans Mantel is writing a novel, tentatively titled "Beyond Black," a modern-day black comedy about a professional psychic, set in Surrey in the Thames Valley, where Mantel currently resides. She is also working individually on a BBC production of *The Giant, O'Brien* and collaboratively with several production companies on motion-picture versions of her novels. Mantel admits to having three new novels in hand; a memoir of her time in Africa, tentatively titled "The Complete Stranger"; and several nonfiction pieces. Whichever of these project appears in print first, it will certainly differ from its predecessors and pave the way in turn for future variations.

Interviews:

"Hilary Mantel," in *Contemporary Authors,* 125 (Detroit: Gale, 1989), pp. 310–311;

Kate Kellaway, "Two Doors: Which One Will You Open?" *Guardian,* 13 March 1994;

May Derwent, "In the Grip of a Passion for Words," *Times* (London), 23 February 1995;

Hunter Davies, "A Fantasist Hidden in Suburbia," *Independent,* 7 March 1995, p. 21;

Sue Fox, "How We Met: Hilary Mantel and Lesley Glaister," *Independent,* 10 March 1995, p. 56;

Nicci Gerrard, "Orderly Conduct," *Observer,* 26 May 1996, p. 9;

Fiona Malcolm, "Hometown," *Times* (London) *Magazine,* 29 March 1997, p. 50;

"Arts Today," CBC Radio One, 27 November 1998;

Stephanie Bunbury, "The Mantel of Malcontent," *Age* (6 March 2000);

Iain Sharp, "Mantel Pieces," *Sunday Star Times,* 12 March 2000, p. F2.

Reference:

A. S. Byatt, *On Histories and Stories: Selected Essays* (Cambridge, Mass.: Harvard University Press), pp. 54–58, 74–75.

Allan Massie

(16 October 1938 -)

Sarah Elizabeth Clere
University of North Carolina at Chapel Hill

BOOKS: *Change and Decay in All Around I See* (London: Bodley Head, 1978);

Muriel Spark (Edinburgh: Ramsay Head Press, 1979);

The Last Peacock (London: Bodley Head, 1980);

Ill Met By Gaslight: Five Edinburgh Murders (Edinburgh: Paul Harris, 1980);

The Death of Men (London: Bodley Head, 1981; Boston: Houghton Mifflin, 1982);

The Caesars (London: Secker & Warburg, 1983; New York: F. Watts, 1984);

One Night in Winter (London: Bodley Head, 1984);

A Portrait of Scottish Rugby (Edinburgh: Polygon, 1984);

Colette (Harmondsworth, U.K.: Penguin, 1986; New York: Penguin, 1986);

Augustus: The Memoirs of the Emperor (London: Bodley Head, 1986); republished as *Let the Emperor Speak: A Novel of Caesar Augustus* (Garden City, N.Y.: Doubleday, 1987); republished as *Augustus: A Novel* (Sevenoaks: Sceptre, 1987); republished as *Augustus* (New York: Carroll & Graf, 1995);

101 Great Scots (Edinburgh: Chambers, 1987);

Byron's Travels (London: Sidgwick & Jackson, 1988);

How Should Health Services Be Financed? A Patient's View, Hume Paper, no. 9 (Aberdeen: Aberdeen University Press, 1988);

The Novelist's View of the Market Economy, Hume Occasional Papers, no. 7 (Edinburgh: David Hume Institute, 1988);

Glasgow: Portraits of a City (London: Barrie & Jenkins, 1989);

A Question of Loyalties (London: Hutchinson, 1989);

The Novel Today: A Critical Guide to the British Novel 1970–1989 (London & New York: Longman/British Council, 1990);

The Hanging Tree: A Romance of the Fifteenth Century (London: Heinemann, 1990);

Tiberius: The Memoirs of the Emperor (London: Hodder & Stoughton, 1991; New York: Carroll & Graf, 1993);

Scotland and Free Enterprise, by Massie, Ewan Marwick, and Douglas Mason (London: Aims of Industry, 1991);

The Sins of the Father (London: Hutchinson, 1991; New York: Carroll & Graf, 1992);

Caesar (London: Hodder & Stoughton, 1993; New York: Carroll & Graf, 1994);

These Enchanted Woods: A Comedy of Morals (London: Hutchinson, 1993; New York: Random House, 1994);

The Ragged Lion (London: Hutchinson, 1994);

Edinburgh (London: Sinclair-Stevenson, 1994);

The History of Selkirk Merchant Company 1694–1994 (Selkirk: Selkirk Merchant Co., 1994);

King David (London: Sceptre, 1995);

Shadows of Empire (London: Sinclair-Stevenson, 1997; New York: Random House, 1997);

Antony (London: Sceptre, 1997);

Nero's Heirs (London: Sceptre, 1999);

The Evening of the World: A Romance of the Dark Ages (London: Weidenfeld & Nicolson, 2001).

PLAY PRODUCTIONS: *The Minstrel and the Shirra,* Selkirk, Bowhill Little Theatre, 1989;

First-Class Passengers, Pitlochry Festival Theatre, 1995.

OTHER: *Edinburgh and the Borders, in Verse,* edited, with an introduction, by Massie (London: Secker & Warburg, 1983);

"Calvinism and Catholicism in Muriel Spark," in *Muriel Spark: An Odd Capacity for Vision,* edited by Alan Bold (London: Vision / Totowa, N.J.: Barnes & Noble, 1984), pp. 94–107;

"Scott and the European Novel," in *Sir Walter Scott: The Long-Forgotten Melody,* edited by Bold (London: Vision / Totowa, N.J.: Barnes & Noble, 1984), pp. 91–106;

Alfred Eisenstaedt, *Eisenstaedt: Aberdeen: Portrait of a City,* text by Massie (Edinburgh: Mainstream/Mobil North Sea, 1984);

P.E.N. New Fiction II, edited by Massie (London: Quartet, 1987);

Walter Scott, *The Bride of Lammermoor,* introduction by Massie, Everyman's Library (London: J. M. Dent / Rutland, Vt.: Charles E. Tuttle, 1993);

Robert Graves, *I, Claudius: From the Autobiography of Tiberius Claudius, Emperor of the Romans, born 10 BC, Murdered and Deified AD 54,* introduction by Massie, illustrated by Neil Packer (London: Folio Society, 1994);

John O'Hara, *Appointment in Samarra,* introduction by Massie, Penguin Twentieth-Century Classics (London: Penguin, 1997);

Richard White, ed., *King Arthur in Legend and History,* foreword by Massie (London: J. M. Dent, 1997; New York: Routledge, 1998);

Eric Linklater, *The Dark of Summer,* introduction by Massie (Edinburgh: Canongate, 1999).

SELECTED PERIODICAL PUBLICATIONS–UNCOLLECTED: "Ten Years of Fiction," *Daily Telegraph* (London), 1 September 1992, p. 30;

"Death on the Shelf," *Daily Telegraph* (London), 16 October 1993, p. 1;

"The Problem Faced by Fashion's Victims," *Daily Telegraph* (London), 22 November 1997, p. 6.

Allan Massie's many and diverse writings have made him one of Scotland's leading men of letters. Massie's most notable characteristic is the diversity of his fiction. Although mainly known for historical novels about the Roman Empire, he has also written espionage novels, novels set in the Middle Ages, and contemporary novels of manners, in addition to many works of nonfiction. In all his fiction Massie is concerned with the instability of society, and this sense of flux and mutability provides the basis for most of his work. Massie's novels are chiefly plot driven; he has a vigorous narrative technique and is primarily interested in action. His historical fiction does not have the wealth of quotidian details that some period novelists employ to add density and verisimilitude to their work. All of his novels benefit from his vigorous storytelling and vivid characterization. His nonfiction includes biographies of Muriel Spark, Colette, and George Gordon, Lord Byron; books about Edinburgh and other Scottish cities; and works of literary criticism.

Allan Johnstone Massie was born in Singapore on 16 October 1938 to Alexander Johnstone Massie and Evelyn Jane Wilson (Forbes) Massie. His father, a rubber planter in Malaya, was taken prisoner when the Japanese army captured Singapore in early 1942 and was held in an internment camp for the majority of World War II. Before the Japanese invasion Evelyn Massie returned to Aberdeenshire with Allan and his brother and sister. Massie began his formal education at Drumtochty Castle, a Scottish preparatory school. He continued his schooling at Glenalmond and then at Trinity College, University of Cambridge, where he read history. After completing his degree in 1960, he returned to Drumtochty Castle in the position of master. At Drumtochty he first met Alison Agnes Graham Langlands. After the school went bankrupt in 1971, Massie began teaching English in Rome. In 1973 he married Alison, and in 1975 the couple returned to Scotland, settling in Edinburgh. They have three children: two sons and one daughter. In 1975 he began reviewing fiction for *The Scotsman,* a task that he continues to perform. He became a television critic for *The Sunday Standard* in 1981 and a columnist for *The Herald* (Glasgow) and *The Sunday Times Scotland* in 1985 and 1987 respectively. Since 1991 he has written a column for *The Daily Telegraph* (London), and he has been a columnist for *The Scotsman* since 1992 and *The Daily Mail* (London) since 1994. He has managed to balance a busy career as a journalist with continued productivity as a novelist. In 1982 he was made a Fellow of the Royal Society of Literature.

Massie's novels of ancient Rome are his strongest and have the widest readership and perhaps the highest critical esteem. Joseph Farrell, for instance, writing in *The Scotsman* (20 November 1999), noted that "Anyone who wishes to examine the intriguing relationship between fiction and history, or to consider the element of creativity in historiography and the measure of observation in fiction, will find ample material in the work of Allan Massie." Massie himself has explained the appeal of historical fiction, writing in the 16 October 1993 issue of *The Daily Telegraph* (London): "Many mainstream novelists have turned to the historical novel in recent years, and most of them will tell you that these books are far more popular than their novels set in our own time. The historical novel is an elastic form, which can be used for various purposes, but its first purpose is to escape from the present. That is what readers look for."

Massie writes primarily about the latter days of the Roman Empire, with a particular emphasis on the precariousness of the government. Taking Roman emperors as his subjects, he provides a credible picture of the political climate of the Roman Empire. In his Roman novels Massie owes a particular debt to Robert Graves and his historical novels *I, Claudius* (1934) and *Claudius the God and His Wife Messalina* (1934). Massie's accessible, somewhat racy narratives are a direct inheritance from Graves. In a 27 September 1986 review of *Augustus: The Memoirs of the Emperor* (1986) in *The Financial Times* (London) Martin Seymour-Smith noted that "the excellent Allan Massie" was attempting to follow in

Graves's footsteps, indicated that the attempt had not been wholly successful, but concluded: "However, historical fiction is difficult to write–perhaps nothing is quite as difficult–and certainly all devotees of it will appreciate Massie's effort." A literary antecedent of both men is Titus Livius, known as Livy, an historian of the Augustan period, who, in the writing of his histories, was concerned not so much with detail and strict historical accuracy as with conveying the ideas and mood of the period and its central figures. Massie, like Livy, takes liberties with documented history in order to give a lively and compelling account of historical events.

Although his historical fiction has received the most exposure, Massie's first four novels are not directly concerned with the Roman Empire. The first of these books is *Change and Decay in All Around I See* (1978). The title of the novel elucidates the themes of flux and deterioration common to Massie's work. *Change and Decay in All Around I See* is a postmodern send-up of contemporary English society. The protagonist of the novel, Atwater, inherits a small legacy from his grandmother. As he attempts to collect his money, he encounters Jeremy, perhaps the most inefficient solicitor in England, and Jeremy's discontented girlfriend, Clare. Through Jeremy and Clare he enters a world populated with a whole cast of zany characters including an Anglo-Catholic Tory M.P. who lusts after her young female secretary, the secretary's mother–a suicidal sculptor obsessed with Great Danes–and a Jamaican gambler named Aloysius.

Atwater, who has always made it his policy not to become involved, becomes heavily involved with these people, eventually marrying Polly, the young secretary. Meanwhile, Clare, who has left an obviously gay Jeremy, falls in love with Polly's father, known simply as the Colonel. The novel resolves itself into a marriage plot and ends in a manner weirdly reminiscent of Jane Austen's *Pride and Prejudice* (1813).

Change and Decay in All Around I See is much different from most of Massie's later work; it is a decidedly literary novel, a so-called novelist's novel. Yet, certain themes and conventions are already established. Massie is concerned with a society on the brink of some uncertain change. In the novel he depicts an uneasily pluralistic London society, in which racism, homophobia, and anti-Semitism run rampant. Such things are dealt with humorously; yet, as with all effective satire, their dark ramifications are chillingly obvious.

Massie's novels are all full of allusions, and *Change and Decay in All Around I See* is no exception. It opens with the line "'My first disobedience,' sighed Atwater–'but it was no good–was the fruit,'" an ironic allusion to the opening lines of book 1 of John Milton's *Paradise Lost* (1667): "Of Mans First Disobedience, and the Fruit / Of that Forbidden Tree, whose mortal tast / Brought Death into the World, and all our woe." Later in the book there is an allusion to A. E. Houseman's 1896 poetry collection, *A Shropshire Lad,* when Jeremy, bemoaning his homosexuality and the effect on the family firm should the Shropshire clients find out, is told by Clare: "'Perhaps you haven't found the right boy yet. You never know, a Shropshire lad maybe.'"

The Last Peacock (1980), Massie's second novel, is much more a conventional novel of manners. The book was well received, winning the Frederick Niven Award. William Boyd, writing in *TLS: The Times Literary Supplement,* commented, "Amongst other things, *The Last Peacock* offers us an acute and fascinating portrayal of the Scottish landed gentry"; he called the work "an accomplished novel" and Massie "a fine and talented writer." The Meldrum family, remnants of the landed gentry, gathers at the deathbed of their elderly matriarch, Grace, whose passing indicates the vanishing of an old way of life. The title of the novel refers to the literal death of a peacock, the last on the estate. Colin Meldrum takes the peacock to a taxidermist to be stuffed. It is tempting to view this act as a symbolic gesture indicating that the Meldrums will retain some form of their old life. However, Massie is careful to subvert the symbolism of the peacock. He writes of the stuffed bird, "The job had been well done. The bird had retained its panoply of finery, yet didn't at all suggest it was anything more, in any way, than a stuffed peacock in a case." After Grace's funeral the family again scatters, and Colin is left alone with the peacock.

The Last Peacock has little in the way of plot; the turbulence of a change in authority gives the novel its force. The issues of imperialism and homophobia that are satirically referred to in *Change and Decay in All Around I See* are here given a thoughtful treatment. Yet, despite its depiction of social unrest, the novel holds little promise of social and political improvement. One imperfect political and social structure will replace another, and the lives of ordinary people will not be much affected.

In *The Last Peacock* and in several nonfiction works–for instance, his *Muriel Spark* (1979), a biography of the Edinburgh-born writer; *Ill Met By Gaslight: Five Edinburgh Murders* (1980), a "true-crime" recounting of famous homicides in the capital city of Scotland; *101 Great Scots* (1987), a collection of brief biographies; and *Glasgow: Portraits of a City* (1989), which uses contemporary accounts to trace the history of the largest city in Scotland–Massie demonstrates his essential Scottishness. In the 24 August 1997 installment of his weekly column in *The Sunday Times* (London) on the reviewing climate, Harvey Porlock (pseudonym of Terence Blacker) quoted Ross Leckie as declaring that "Almost alone,

Allan Massie has for 20 years kept Scottish letters alive," and though this statement may exaggerate the loneliness of his dedication, it is a dedication nonetheless.

In his third novel, *The Death of Men* (1981), Massie gives an even more direct picture of political instability. *The Death of Men,* which won a Scottish Arts Council Award, is a novel of political intrigue set in 1978 Rome. Loosely based on the abduction and murder of Italian politician Aldo Moro, the novel is narrated primarily from the perspective of Raimundo Dusa, whose brother Corrado, a politician with liberal leanings, is kidnaped by fascists and murdered. Members of the Dusa family, who, as Massie takes pains to point out in his introduction, bear no resemblance to the Moros, are all affected by Corrado's kidnaping. Most shocking is Bernardo, who helped engineer his father's capture. The idea of political loyalties superceding family allegiance is a theme that Massie returns to frequently in his work. The title comes from a line by Oliver Wendell Holmes, that "every society rests upon the death of men."

Massie's years in Rome are evident in his detailed and believable portrayals of the daily life of the city. The thoughtfully explored familial arrangements and strongly defined setting of *The Death of Men* link it to Massie's previous two novels; however, in this novel interpersonal relationships are superseded by a definite and dramatic plot. *The Death of Men* has thoughtful and discursive elements; yet, it is primarily a thriller–this book is Massie's first really fast-paced novel and prefigures the course he follows in the majority of his later work.

In *One Night in Winter* (1984) Massie revisits provincial Scotland and its disintegrating social order. The protagonist of the novel is Dallas Graham, a middle-aged husband, father, and failed antique store owner living in England. Dissatisfied with his current life, he decides to write a memoir, through it revisiting his Scottish youth. The landscape of Graham's young adulthood is peopled with types almost as bizarre as those found in *Change and Decay in All Around I See.* Chief among these characters is Fraser Donnelly, a prosperous local contractor, would-be politician, and uncontrolled alcoholic, at war against what he thinks of as bourgeois moral conventions. In his battles against local mores Fraser, as he is referred to throughout the novel, crosses boundaries, not of societal propriety but of decency and humanity. His manipulation and coercion render the area's narrow moral code enlightened and kind by comparison. His passive wife, Lorna, watches Fraser destroy her own life and the lives of others until, one night in winter, she finds his brutality more than she can bear and shoots him.

Graham, as witness to these events, recalls them years later. His family was the local gentry, and he is referred to as "the young laird," affectionately or derisively, depending on the speaker. He is intelligent, witty, and humane–the exact opposite of Fraser. Yet, Fraser, though uncouth and brutal, has a force and charisma that Graham lacks. Graham also lacks all conviction, while Fraser is full of passionate intensity. The vitality of the lower classes supersedes birth.

Dust jacket for the U.S. edition of Massie's 1986 novel Augustus, *the first in his series of fictionalized accounts of the lives of Roman emperors (Richland County Public Library)*

Richard Cobb calls *One Night in Winter* the best novel about drink he has ever read, and indeed, the book can be seen as the story of one man's slide into alcoholism. However, the book has distinct elements of the thriller and has much more of the fast-paced tone of *The Death of Men* than the meditative melancholy of *The Last Peacock.*

Massie followed another biography, *Colette* (published in May 1986), with his first historical novel and the first in a quartet of novels about Roman emperors, *Augustus: The Memoirs of the Emperor,* published in September 1986 and first published in the United States the following year as *Let the Emperor Speak.* The novel traces

Dust jacket for the U.S. edition of Massie's 1991 novel, about a romance between the daughter of a Jewish Holocaust survivor and the son of a former Nazi (Richland County Public Library)

young Octavian's rise to power after the death of Caesar, who has named him his heir. Massie, with characteristic vividness, gives interesting portraits of Augustus's contemporaries. Octavian's first meeting with Livia is delineated, and the reader gets a glimpse into the beginning of perhaps the most infamous marital alliance of ancient Rome. Mark Antony, a fellow triumvir, and Octavian's loyal supporter and general, Marcus Vipsanius Agrippa, get similar treatments, as does the courtier Maecenas. The only infelicitous characterization is that of the poet Virgil. Massie deserves congratulations for resisting the temptation to portray the poet as a mere pamphleteer, eager to curry favor with the emperor. However, he presents a portrait every bit as simplistic in another direction. Massie's Virgil is a simple, apolitical dreamer who is possessed of "a quiet northern voice that never sounded without offering a rustic comfort." Virgil's portrait of pastoral life, the *Bucolics* (also known as the *Eclogues,* 42/41–39/38 B.C.), and his didactic work on farming, the *Georgics* (36–29? B.C.), are anything but simple and comforting. Massie's diminishment of Virgil erodes the verisimilitude of the novel.

A Question of Loyalties (1989) also deals with the clash of family and ideology. The novel, as is *One Night in Winter,* is narrated in the third person by a cynical middle-aged man looking backward. Massie uses this device often; it allows both immediacy and rhetorical distance. The narrator and protagonist, Etienne de Balafre, must delve into the past of his father, Lucien de Balafre, in order to gather material for a biographer. In the process Etienne must confront his father's activities as a collaborator in Vichy France.

The narration shifts between accounts of Lucien's life delivered by way of journal entries that Etienne unearths and the story of Etienne's own young adulthood. Etienne is in South Africa with his mother and her new husband at the time of Lucien's death and has barely known his father. Nevertheless, the course of his own life is profoundly affected by his father's actions. In an incident of coincidence so extreme as to seem clichéd, Etienne falls in love with a young woman whose mother, a French Jew, died in the Nazi concentration camp of Bergen-Belsen. The girl's father was instrumental in Lucien's arrest for collaboration by the French authorities and, like that of Romeo and Juliet, the lovers' relationship is doomed from its beginning.

Massie in all his work is as concerned with his ignoble characters as his good figures. His books do not contain purely evil Iagos, and readers may, uncomfortably, find themselves sympathizing with the cruel and corrupt. The question of loyalties referred to in the title is Etienne's loyalty to his father versus his loyalty to a democratic France and humanistic values in general. If Lucien, the collaborationist, represents extreme nationalistic zeal, then Etienne's daughter Sarah, a vehemently liberal, yet unsympathetic, human-rights advocate, is the other end of the spectrum. In *A Question of Loyalties,* as he does in *The Death of Men,* Massie portrays political and social extremism as debilitating. In his 25 August 1989 review in *The Independent* (London) Auberon Waugh called it "a brilliant novel, taking in the whole agony of Europe leading up to its present happy state." It received *The Scotsman* /Saltire Scottish Book of the Year Award.

Massie's next novel, *The Hanging Tree: A Romance of the Fifteenth Century* (1990), marked his first foray into the setting of the Middle Ages. It had been written five years earlier, at a time when, Victoria Glendinning reports in her review of the book in the 22 November 1990 issue of *The Times* (London), Massie felt that his fiction was "too cerebral and reflective." *The Hanging Tree* is set in fifteenth-century Scotland and begins with the hanging of the patriarch of the Laidlaw clan, a family of uncouth and unprincipled vagabonds. Laidlaw's four sons exact their revenge in a medieval version of frontier justice. After the death of their father the novel follows the fortunes of the young brothers, particularly Maurie, a hunchbacked miscreant with a persuasive tongue. Maurie infiltrates English society, and the novel is filled with both English and Scottish political intrigue.

Readers may find the novel hard going as it contains difficult-to-decipher Scots dialect as well as many English archaisms. In her review Glendinning pointed out that "Scottish people have always contrived to decode the assorted dialects of English people, and the least Allan Massie's non-Scots readers can do is to return the compliment." Harry Ritchie comments, "To his compatriots Massie seems much more Anglo than Scottish, and, in a literary culture characterized by the dominance of the working class and the vernacular, his writing stands out like a Union Jack at Hampden Park." *The Hanging Tree* comes across as clichéd and hackneyed as Massie unsuccessfully tries to meld a chanson de geste with a history text.

Following his interesting and authoritative *The Novel Today: A Critical Guide to the British Novel 1970–1989* (1990), Massie returns to ancient Rome with *Tiberius: The Memoirs of the Emperor* (1991). As does *Augustus, Tiberius* has a frame narrative; the book is ostensibly the emperor's unearthed autobiography. Massie's Tiberius is a surprisingly sympathetic character. The notoriously severe and taciturn general is a loving husband (who nevertheless divorces his beloved wife, Vipsania Agrippina, mother of his son Drusus, at a word from Augustus), a devoted father, and a compassionate conqueror. In this novel as in others, Massie does a masterful job exploring the characters' relationships with each other. In *Tiberius* the rivalry between Drusus and Sejanus for the emperor's affection is compelling and plausible. When Tiberius discovers that Sejanus is responsible for his son's death, the reader is as shocked and saddened as the emperor. Reviewer Miranda Miller praised *Tiberius* in *The Guardian* (27 December 1990), writing that "Roman history provides all the political and sexual excesses of a bonkbuster plot [that is, a popular novel with much sex]. When it is well written and vividly characterised, as it is here, it is fascinating stuff: I look forward to traveling backwards in time to *Augustus,* the first in the trilogy."

The Sins of the Father, Massie's next novel, also appeared in 1991. The novel begins in Argentina and describes the romance of Becky Czinner and Franz Schmidt–only Franz's last name is not really Schmidt but Kestner, and his father, Rudi Schmidt, is actually Rudi Kestner, a former Nazi who was responsible for sending Becky's Jewish father to a concentration camp. Becky's father, now blind, recognizes the elder Kestner's voice and reports him. The former Nazi's trial is to take place in Israel. Franz and Becky also go to Israel, he to support his father, she to support her fiancé. The stress Czinner's revelation and the subsequent trial put on the couple's relationship is extreme; however, they stay together, and at first it appears that they can transcend their parents' animosity. The relationship between Czinner and Rudi Kestner is one of the most interesting aspects of the novel. Czinner is an eminent German economist who contributed to the Third Reich's economic policy, never believing he would become a target of Nazi persecution. Because of Czinner's cooperation with the Nazi regime, the relationship of the two men is thus more complex than that of victim and victimizer and is explored more fully when the setting of the novel shifts to Israel, where Kestner's trial is held.

The Sins of the Father is gripping and readable, yet the whole premise seems somewhat improbable. Massie used the plot device of a Jewish girl whose parent had been in a concentration camp falling in love with the son of a Nazi previously in *A Question of Loyalties,* and it is not any more believable a second time around. Lachlan Mackinnon, however, praised the novel in a 28 September 1991 review in *The Independent* (London): "The philosopher Kierkegaard once said that he wished he were a novelist, as the novelist showed philosophy in action. Allan Massie bears him out, treating evanescent joys and enduring terrible questions with a patient art that begins to feel like life."

With *The Sins of the Father,* Massie became embroiled in one of the more vivid controversies of the almost-always controversial Booker Prize for Fiction. His book was among the long list of nominated titles. When the shortlist–that is, the list of the six finalists–was announced, Massie was not included. The stir arose from the noisy resignation from the judging panel of Nicholas Mosley, third Baron Ravensdale; a distinguished novelist, Mosley is the eldest son of Oswald Mosley, the British fascist leader. He resigned because the other judges on the panel had–unfairly, he believed–rejected all six of his nominations, which included Massie's book. Massie himself had helped to judge the Booker Prize in 1987. Perhaps his experience in 1991, as well as his wide knowledge of the publishing, reviewing, and prize-giving worlds of British letters, has colored some of his views on that world. In the 1 September 1992 issue of *The Daily Telegraph* (London) he wrote a column in which, while referring to the 1991 controversy over his book, he comments on the "gulf . . . between the books the public buys and reads and those the critics praise"; suggesting that there is a bias against strong stories in the reception of the "literary novel"; and concludes wistfully that "in some moods, at least, one feels the game is up: the novel, that beautiful and flexible art-form, is on the way out." Massie is considered something of a conservative in his political stance; he also espouses traditional values in his criticism and has deplored the tendency of the press to celebrate young writers, sheerly out of hunger for novelty, while older, established writers, as Massie observes in the 22 November 1997 issue of *The Daily Telegraph* (London), "constantly write good readable, intelligent novels and find themselves neglected by their publishers (as the authors think), and passed over by reviewers in search of the new."

Caesar, published in 1993, is the third of Massie's fictionalized accounts of Roman emperors' lives. The novel is narrated from the perspective of the emperor's friend and comrade in arms, Decimus Junius Brutus, called Mouse by Julius Caesar. Mouse admires the emperor and is loyal to him; yet, he feels even more loyalty to the empire. In his mind, Caesar's assassination was essential to the survival of Roman freedom. Through Mouse's narration the reader sees how Caesar actually begins to believe his own propaganda. By the time of Caesar's assassination on 15 March 44 B.C. by a group of conspirators led by Mouse's cousin Marcus Junius Brutus, it seems Caesar really does believe himself to be a deity. Critical reaction to the novel was mixed, as usually seems to be the case with Massie's books. In his 5 May 1993 review in *The Herald* (Glasgow) Archie Hind commented that "The events of the Ides of March in 44 B.C. have incited the imagination of many writers–historians and dramatists–and Massie has legitimately responded to them. But while readable and lively enough this book is also curiously slight and peremptory." Alan Taylor, writing in *Scotland on Sunday* (9 May 1993), was much more positive, both about *Caesar,* of which he said, "Massie writes with his customary clarity," and about Massie's project of which it is a part: "Individually the novels demonstrate just how much could happen on the way to the Forum; together they are building towards a kind of epic grandeur, a splendid fictional corrective to the renowned fallibility of historians."

In the same year that *Caesar* was published Massie published another book about Scotland, giving rise to David Robson's somewhat perplexed attempt, in the 1 August 1993 issue of *The Sunday Telegraph* (London), to characterize his output:

> Allan Massie's fictional career is beginning to resemble a golfer zig-zagging down the fairway, going from the right-hand rough to the left-hand bunker; he doesn't drop many strokes to par, but his way of playing the course is eccentric. He has divided his energies equally between ancient Rome and his native Scotland, and, although he has served both venues well, there is an inconsistency in his output which makes me wonder if he wouldn't do better as an out-and-out specialist.

In his eleventh novel, *These Enchanted Woods: A Comedy of Morals* (1993), Massie returns to the Scotland of *The Last Peacock* to revisit the Meldrum family. The focus this time is on Colin's sister Fiona, a minor character in the earlier novel, in which she makes a brief appearance as a vain perfectionist who has married for money and position. Now the money is gone and the social position jeopardized, as Gavin, her alcoholic husband, injures a child in a drunk-driving accident. The Fiona of *These Enchanted Woods* is almost a prototype of the unfulfilled and discontented woman. An affair offers a partial solution to Fiona's problems; yet, the end of the novel finds her too tied to her old life to relinquish it.

Massie returned to an even earlier Scotland with the publication of *The Ragged Lion* in 1994. *The Ragged Lion,* which purports to be Sir Walter Scott's memoir, is another example of that blend of biography and fiction of which Massie is so fond. In his introduction to the novel Massie calls Scott "not only the greatest Scottish writer . . . he was also, if not the greatest Scotsman, which is perhaps a meaningless term, the most thoroughly Scottish of our great men." *The Ragged Lion* is narrated by Scott from the perspective of his debt-ridden old age and shows his prodigious energy and the vast amount of writing he completed to pay off those debts. Although the introduction is a witty piece of badinage tracing the fictional history of the purported memoir, the novel itself is a serious treatment of an author whom Massie obviously believes to be truly heroic. Historian Glendinning assessed the novel shrewdly in her 18 June 1994 review in *The Daily Telegraph* (London), in part by noting similarities between author and subject; aside from an interest in a hitherto unexpected dark side to Scott, Glendinning remarked that "The other aspect that interests Massie, himself the author of historical novels, living in Scott's own Border country, is the quality of Scott's Scottishness. Romantically patriotic, Scott nevertheless believed in the union with England." She noted Scott's belief that when writing he was possessed, and summarized that "Massie, writing as Scott, must have experienced something of the same weird phenomenon. It is impossible to disentangle quite who is possessed by whom. *The Ragged Lion* is a cunning piece of work, as well as an act of homage."

Reminders of Scott haunt Edinburgh, the cultural capital of Scotland and the subject of Massie's nonfiction book *Edinburgh* (1994). In his 18 September 1994 review in *The Sunday Telegraph* (London) Martin Gayford called Massie's book "an elegant historical portrait of the place."

King David (1995) is narrated by the title character from the vantage point of his old age. The novel has, in addition to the donnée of a fictional autobiography, the somewhat racy tone that characterizes Massie's historical fiction, opening with the king in bed with a young slave girl–young slave girls and boys seem to be a staple of Massie's historical fiction. Indeed, the novel deals more with David's human relationships, such as his friendship with Jonathan, son and heir of King Saul (whose death, along with his father's, in battle against the Philistines cleared the way for David to become king), than it does with his relationship to God. Massie falls squarely into the camp of those who think David and Jonathan had an amorous relationship, further contemporizing his treatment of the biblical figure. Massie's David is ultimately betrayed in his human alliances–his eventual successor, the calculating Solomon (traditionally seen as the wisest and greatest king of Israel), eagerly awaiting his father's death, is depicted by Massie as unfavorably as is his half brother, Absalom, who attempted to overthrow their father and is referred to in 2 Sam. 3–19 as being physically attractive but unmatched in his insolence and treachery. The novel does not explore the perhaps larger and more complex issue of betrayal by God. One reviewer, Michael Arditti, praised it in *The Independent* (London) of 12 August 1995 as "a fascinating story excitingly told" while expressing disappointment at its failure to go beyond that familiar story. In a 23 July 1995 review in *The Observer* (London) Matthew Reisz compared King David to Alan Clark, a contemporary Tory politician known for epigrammatic cruelty and unreconstructed sexism, and summed the book up in a somewhat grudging way: "Along with this unexpected love triangle [David, Jonathan, and Jonathan's sister Michal], Massie creates some splendid dramatic setpieces from biblical hints, as when David uses music to cure Saul's depression. While rather lacking in deeper resonances, this is skillful, straightforward storytelling which offers a powerful variation on a familiar theme."

In *Shadows of Empire* (1997), Massie revisits the setting of World War II–era Europe, previously explored in *A Question of Loyalties* and *The Sins of the Father*. Alec Alan, the narrator of the novel, has an impressive Scottish pedigree, including a father who is a minister in the Church of Scotland. As a journalist living in Berlin in the 1930s, Alan witnesses firsthand the descent of Europe into the madness of war. His three brothers pursue different careers, and by giving thumbnail sketches of their lives, Alan narrates both the decline of British imperialism and the torturous relationship Scotland has with England. Perhaps the most interesting of these brothers is George, who, like Massie's father, becomes a planter in Malaya and is subsequently detained in a Japanese prison camp. The strongest section of the novel is its depiction of the decadence of pre–World War II Berlin with its cabarets and cafés, a description that owes much to Christopher Isherwood's portrait of prewar Germany in his so-called Berlin stories, the novels *Mr. Norris Changes Trains* (1935) and *Goodbye to Berlin* (1939). In the first part of the novel Massie is so evocative that the reader might be tempted to find the fate of Europe more interesting than that of Scotland. In her 10 August 1997 review in *The Sunday Telegraph* (London) Caroline Moore recognized the theme of the novel as the "demoralization of the British Establishment," pointed out that all the Alans are failures, and commented that the end of the novel becomes "suddenly moving. Massie has always excelled at depicting the sadness of old age: here, his vision of emotional bleakness becomes almost elegiac." A more telling reaction camc from Isabel Colegate, also an author of historical novels tracing the twentieth century in Britain. In her 9 August 1997 review in *The Daily Telegraph* (London) she remarked, "Novels which look

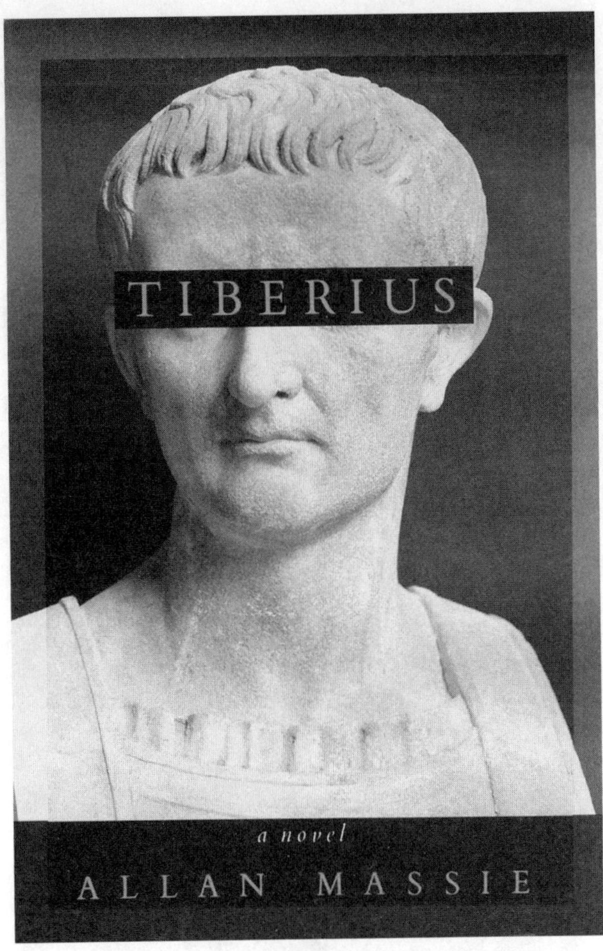

Dust jacket for the U.S. edition of Massie's 1991 novel, a fictionalized autobiography of the third Roman emperor (Richland County Public Library)

Dust jacket for the U.S. edition of Massie's 1993 novel, an account of Julius Caesar's life from the perspective of a friend torn by his loyalty to Caesar and his loyalty to the Roman Empire (Richland County Public Library)

thoughtfully at the Europe in which we live and the reasons why it might have become what it is are a rarity to be welcomed. The scope of this one is ambitious, and the big themes seem sometimes to outweigh the small people; but it is an admirable novel, serious in intent and consistently interesting to read."

With *Antony* (1997) Massie completes his quartet of novels on the lives of Roman emperors. The elderly Mark Antony dictates his memoir to a clerk, Critias, who feels free to interrupt the emperor's narration with his own descriptions of events and eventually takes over the memoir himself. In Massie's previous historical novels Antonius is portrayed as an uncontrolled buffoon with a penchant for alcohol and attractive boys. In this novel Antonius does not drink any less; however, his debauchery is treated more sympathetically, and his primary flaw is his generous nature. Antony's relationships with Octavian and Cleopatra are delineated here; his betrayal at the hands of the former is particularly heart-wrenching. The only unsuccessful element in the novel is the usage of modern slang expressions, in which Massie indulges in nearly all his historical fiction: the frequent use of "bugger" strikes a jarring note. Hugo Barnacle's 16 November 1997 review in *The Sunday Times* (London) may have been responding to such anachronisms when he suggested that "Massie has not altogether solved the historical novelist's perpetual problem of finding a secure and flexible idiom." But he found the book "modern and impressive" and declared that "The ending is quite remarkably sad, considering we know it well already. Massie appears to achieve this by avoiding full-blown sentimentality and instead using understatement and irony."

Nero's Heirs, published in 1999, is, as the title indicates, another Roman historical novel. It depicts the events of A.D. 69, the infamous "year of the four emperors." Because Nero had no official heir, the empire was thrown into tumult as Servius Sulpicius Galba, Marcus Salvius Otho, Aulus Vitellius, and Titus Flavius Sabinus Vespasianus seized power in turn. As do many of Massie's novels, *Nero's Heirs* has a frame narrative. The story is told from the perspective of Scaurus, a boyhood friend of Domitian, Vespasian's son. Scaurus appears to be a fictional creation, as, other than the Marcus Aemilius Scaurus who was consul in 115 and 107 B.C. and his son and namesake, who was quaestor to Pompey (74–64 B.C.), no one else by that name appears in the historical record. Massie's Scaurus is enlisted by the historian Cornelius Tacitus to give an account of this tumultuous period of Roman history. *Nero's Heirs* is rife with colorful characters and bloodshed–what reviewer Adam Lively called "no-nonsense, in-your-face action" in the 2 January 2000 issue of *The Sunday Times* (London)–but at times there is simply too much going on. A dramatization of this most disorganized of periods cannot help but be disorganized itself. Lively found it "an entertaining, gripping read, but in the end it is the potboiler that wins the day, leaving behind those shadows and shadings that had suggested a deeper, richer novel."

The Evening of the World: A Romance of the Dark Ages (2001), Massie's seventeenth novel, is set during the early Middle Ages. It is the first volume of a projected trilogy about the Dark Ages, which presumably will resemble the series of novels about Roman emperors. Framed as a recovered medieval manuscript, *The Evening of the World* is a parody of a romantic quest. The hero of the novel, Marcus, must navigate a veritable morass of literary archetypes. In the course of his travels he meets a Wandering Jew, a princess in distress, and even the Green Knight, whose depiction as a British rustic is one of the cleverer elements of the novel. Other plot devices, such as a tribe of lascivious women whose extremely obese leader forces Marcus and his friend Lycus to become her sexual slaves, are somewhat less compelling. In this novel, as in some others, Massie's depiction of sex, particularly same-sex relationships, may be problematic to some readers. Massie almost always either links homosexuality with pedophilia, treating it in a sniggering manner, or shows it as emblematic of submission and degradation.

Massie blends classical myth, Arthurian legend, and Christian doctrine, and the result is somewhat convoluted. The narrative gets bogged down in digressions and allusions; as Peter Parker commented in his 22 July 2001 review in *The Sunday Times* (London), "The story itself is hugely diverting, but Massie adds layer upon layer to what he calls this 'strange farrago.'" Reviewing the book for *The Scotsman* (30 June 2001), Paul Johnston read the complications as part of a somewhat postmodern approach to the historical novel, which, he said, "in recent years has taken on board the prevailing ideas of literary criticism, primarily the unreliability of text, author and narrator, to attain complexity far beyond the ken of the genre's inventor, Sir Walter Scott." In this development, Johnston believed, "Another success is the deliberate use of anachronism, both with historical events and literary allusions. There are references to TS Eliot and Tennyson and Sir Gavin has 'a cunning plan': in the post-modern historical novel even Blackadder has a place." And demonstrating the variability of responses to the excess of *The Evening of the World,* Parker acclaimed it as "a book that can be recommended to anyone who thinks that the historical novel is moribund."

Writing in his 24 August 1997 "Harvey Porlock" column in *The Sunday Times* (London), Blacker noted of Massie and another Scottish novelist, Iain Banks: "You produce a novel a year. You get the favourable reviews, the respectful profiles. Your books sell well, but not indecently. You become part of the literary scene. And yet still you find yourself mysteriously barred from that most exclusive of establishments, the top novelists' club. . . ." Blacker went on to remark that when such a novelist produces a new book, "it is not so much what is said in reviews that matters as who says it (critics making their names rather than the established big guns) and in what tones." Reviews of Massie's work often seem to have a perfunctory quality and are often marked by faint praise, seemingly bestowed grudgingly. This apparent critical disdain may arise from his role in the literary scene–frequent critic, author of a book of criticism of the contemporary novel–from his ambiguous quality of Scottishness in an age of literary nationalism, from his defense of the traditional, plot-driven novel, or from his dedication to historical fiction.

Allan Massie is a man of letters in a sense that few writers attempt today. Although he may surprise his readers with a pamphlet on health care or a history of rugby, he is foremost a novelist. At least two of his forthcoming books will probably be novels set in the Dark Ages–and he will likely continue his "zig-zagging" path, taking in the modern world as well as the ancient in his ambitious attempt to maintain the Scott tradition of thoughtful historical fiction.

References:

Douglas Dunn, "Divergent Scottishness: William Boyd, Allan Massie, Ronald Frame," in *The Scottish Novel Since the Seventies: New Visions, Old Dreams,* edited by Gavin Wallace and Randall Stevenson (Edinburgh: Edinburgh University Press, 1993), pp. 149–169;

Colin Riordan, "The Sins of the Children: Peter Schneider, Allan Massie and the Legacy of Auschwitz," *Journal of European Studies,* 27 (June 1997): 161–180.

John Mortimer

(21 April 1923 -   )

Anne Daniel
Princeton University

See also the Mortimer entries in *DLB 13: British Dramatists Since World War II* and *DLB 245: British and Irish Dramatists Since World War II, Third Series.*

BOOKS: *Charade* (London: Bodley Head, 1947; New York: Viking, 1986);

Rumming Park: A Comedy (London: Bodley Head, 1948);

Answer Yes or No (London: Bodley Head, 1950); republished as *The Silver Hook* (New York: Morrow, 1950; London: Transworld, 1952);

Like Men Betrayed (London: Collins, 1953; Philadelphia: Lippincott, 1954);

The Narrowing Stream (London: Collins, 1954; New York: Viking, 1989);

Three Winters (London: Collins, 1956);

With Love and Lizards, by Mortimer and Penelope Mortimer (London: Joseph, 1957);

Three Plays: The Dock Brief; What Shall We Tell Caroline?; I Spy (London: Elek, 1958; New York: Grove, 1962);

The Dock Brief: A Play (London & New York: S. French, 1959);

What Shall We Tell Caroline? (London: S. French, 1959);

I Spy: A Play in One Act (London & New York: S. French, 1960);

Sketches from One to Another, by Mortimer, N. F. Simpson, and Harold Pinter (London & New York: S. French, 1960)–includes *Triangle, Cleaning Up Justice, Collector's Piece,* and *Conference,* by Mortimer;

The Wrong Side of the Park: A Play in Three Acts (London: Heinemann, 1960):

Lunch Hour, and Other Plays (London: Methuen, 1960)–comprises *Lunch Hour, Collect Your Hand Baggage, David and Broccoli,* and *Call Me a Liar;*

Collect Your Hand Baggage: A Play in One Act (London: S. French, 1960);

Two Stars for Comfort (London: Methuen, 1962);

The Judge (London: Methuen, 1967);

Come As You Are: Four Plays (London: Methuen, 1971; London & New York: S. French, 1971)–comprises *Mill Hill, Bermondsey, Gloucester Road,* and *Marble Arch;*

John Mortimer (photograph by Rosemary Herbert; from the dust jacket for the U.S. edition of Titmuss Regained, *1990)*

A Voyage Round My Father (London: Methuen, 1971; London & New York: S. French, 1971);

Collaborators (London: Eyre Methuen, 1973; London & New York: S. French, 1974);

Knightsbridge (London: S. French, 1973);

Will Shakespeare (London: Hodder & Stoughton, 1977); republished as *Will Shakespeare: The Untold Story* (New York: Delacorte, 1977);

The Bells of Hell: A Divine Comedy (London & New York: S. French, 1978);

Rumpole of the Bailey (Harmondsworth & New York: Penguin, 1978);

The Fear of Heaven: A Play (London & New York: S. French, 1978);

The Trials of Rumpole (Harmondsworth & New York: Penguin, 1979);

Rumpole's Return (Harmondsworth & New York: Penguin, 1980);
Regina v. Rumpole: Rumpole for the Defence, and, Rumpole's Return (London: Allen Lane, 1981);
Rumpole for the Defence (Harmondsworth & New York: Penguin, 1982);
Clinging to the Wreckage: A Part of Life (London: Weidenfeld & Nicolson, 1982; New Haven, Conn.: Ticknor & Fields, 1982);
The Liberty of the Citizen, by Mortimer, Franklin Thomas, and John Hunt, Baron Hunt of Tanworth, Granada Guildhall Lectures, 1982 (London & New York: Granada, 1983);
Rumpole and the Golden Thread (Harmondsworth & New York: Penguin, 1983);
In Character (London: Allen Lane, 1983);
Edwin and Other Plays (Harmondsworth: Penguin, 1984)–comprises *Edwin, Bermondsey, Marble Arch, The Fear of Heaven,* and *The Prince of Darkness;*
Edwin: A Play (London: S. French, 1984);
Paradise Postponed (London: Viking, 1985; New York: Viking, 1986);
Character Parts (London: Viking, 1986; New York: Penguin, 1987);
Rumpole's Last Case (Harmondsworth: Penguin, 1987; New York: Penguin, 1988);
Summer's Lease (London: Penguin, 1988; New York: Penguin, 1989);
Rumpole and the Age of Miracles (London & New York: Penguin, 1988);
Titmuss Regained (London & New York: Viking, 1990);
Rumpole à la carte (London: Penguin, 1990; New York: Penguin, 1993);
Rumpole on Trial (London & New York: Viking, 1992);
Dunster (London: Viking, 1992; New York: Viking, 1993);
Under the Hammer (London: Penguin, 1994);
Murderers and Other Friends: Another Part of Life (London & New York: Viking, 1994);
Rumpole and the Angel of Death (London: Viking, 1995; New York: Penguin, 1997);
Rumpole and the Younger Generation (London: Penguin, 1995);
Felix in the Underworld (London & New York: Viking, 1997);
The Sound of Trumpets (London & New York: Viking, 1998);
The Summer of a Dormouse (London: Viking, 2000; New York: Viking, 2001);
Rumpole Rests His Case (London: Viking, 2001; New York: Viking, 2002);
Hock and Soda Water (London: Oberon, 2001);
Naked Justice (London: Oberon, 2002);
Rumpole and the Primrose Path (London: Viking, 2002).

Edition and Collections: *Five Plays* (London: Methuen, 1970)–comprises *The Dock Brief, What Shall We Tell Caroline? I Spy, Lunch Hour,* and *Collect Your Hand Baggage;*
Rumpole (London: Allen Lane, 1980)–comprises *Rumpole of the Bailey* and *The Trials of Rumpole;*
A Voyage Round My Father; The Dock Brief; What Shall We Tell Caroline? (Harmondsworth & New York: Penguin, 1982);
The First Rumpole Omnibus (Harmondsworth & New York: Penguin, 1983)–comprises *Rumpole of the Bailey, The Trials of Rumpole,* and *Rumpole's Return;*
The Second Rumpole Omnibus (London: Viking, 1987; New York: Penguin, 1988)–comprises *Rumpole for the Defence, Rumpole and the Golden Thread,* and *Rumpole's Last Case;*
Like Men Betrayed (New York: Viking, 1988);
The Rapstone Chronicles (London: Viking, 1991; New York: Penguin, 1993)–comprises *Paradise Postponed* and *Titmuss Regained;*
The Best of Rumpole, selected, with an introduction, by Mortimer (London & New York: Viking, 1993);
Rumpole, selected, with an introduction, by Mortimer, illustrated by Paul Cox (London: Folio Society, 1994);
The Third Rumpole Omnibus (London and New York: Viking, 1997)–comprises *Rumpole and the Age of Miracles, Rumpole à la carte,* and *Rumpole and the Angel of Death;*
Collected Plays (London: Oberon, 2001–).

PLAY PRODUCTIONS: *The Dock Brief* and *What Shall We Tell Caroline?* Hammersmith, Lyric Theatre, 9 April 1958; London, Garrick Theatre, 20 May 1958;
I Spy, Salisbury, Salisbury Playhouse, 16 March 1959;
Triangle, Cleaning Up Justice, Collector's Piece, and *Conference,* in *One to Another,* by Mortimer, Harold Pinter, and N. F. Simpson, Hammersmith, Lyric Theatre, July 1959;
The Wrong Side of the Park, London, Cambridge Theatre, 3 February 1960;
Lunch Hour, Salisbury, Salisbury Playhouse, 20 June 1960; London, Criterion Theatre, 13 February 1961;
Collect Your Hand Baggage, London, London Academy of Music and Dramatic Art, December 1961;
One over the Eight, includes sketches by Mortimer, music by Lionel Bart, London, 1961;
Two Stars for Comfort, London, Garrick Theatre, 2 April 1962;
Changing Gear, includes sketches by Mortimer, music by Bart, 1965;

A Flea in Her Ear, translated from Georges Feydeau's *La Puce à l'oreille,* London, National Theatre at the Old Vic, 8 February 1966;

The Judge, Hamburg, Deutsches Schauspielhaus, 29 January 1967; London, Cambridge Theatre, 1 March 1967;

Cat among the Pigeons, translated from Feydeau's *Un Fil à la patte,* London, Prince of Wales Theatre, 15 April 1969;

Come As You Are, London, New Theatre, 27 January 1970–comprises *Mill Hill, Bermondsey, Gloucester Road,* and *Marble Arch;*

A Voyage Round My Father, London, Greenwich Theatre, 25 November 1970; London, Haymarket Theatre, 4 August 1971; Oxford, The Playhouse, 2 May 1995;

The Captain of Köpenick, translated from Carl Zuckmayer's *Der Hauptmann von Köpenick,* London, National Theatre at the Old Vic, 9 March 1971;

I, Claudius, adapted from Robert Graves's *I, Claudius* and *Claudius the God and His Wife Messalina,* London, Queen's Theatre, 11 July 1972;

Collaborators, London, Duchess Theatre, 18 April 1973;

Heaven and Hell, London, Greenwich Theatre, 28 May 1976–comprises *The Fear of Heaven* and *The Prince of Darkness;*

The Lady from Maxim's, translated from Feydeau's *La Dame de chez Maxim,* London, National Theatre, 18 October 1977;

When That I Was, Ottowa, Arts Centre, 1982;

A Little Hotel on the Side, translated from Feydeau and Maurice Desvallières's *L'Hôtel du Libre-Echange,* London, National Theatre, 9 August 1984;

Die Fledermaus, translated from Carl Haffner and Richard Genée's libretto, London, Royal Opera House, 9 January 1989;

A Christmas Carol, adapted from Charles Dickens's novel, London, Royal Shakespeare Company at the Barbican Theatre, 28 November 1994;

Naked Justice, Leeds, West Yorkshire Playhouse, 26 January 2001;

Hock and Soda Water, Chichester, Minerva Theatre, 28 November 2001;

Full House and *The Hairless Diva,* translated from Eugène Ionesco's *La Cantatrice chauve,* Watford, Palace Theatre, 17 April 2002.

PRODUCED SCRIPTS: *Like Men Betrayed,* radio, BBC, 1955;

No Hero, radio, BBC, 1955;

The Dock Brief, radio, BBC Third Programme, 12 May 1957;

The Dock Brief, television, BBC, 16 September 1957;

I Spy, radio, BBC Third Programme, 19 November 1957;

I Spy, television, BBC, 28 January 1958;

Call Me a Liar, television, BBC, 22 April 1958;

Three Winters, radio, BBC, 1958;

Ferry to Hong Kong, motion picture, screenplay by Lewis Gilbert and Vernon Harris, additional dialogue by Mortimer, Rank, 1959;

David and Broccoli, television, BBC, 26 January 1960;

Lunch Hour, radio, BBC Third Programme, 25 June 1960;

The Innocents, motion picture, adapted by Truman Capote and William Archibald from Henry James's novel *The Turn of the Screw,* additional scenes and dialogue by Mortimer, 20th Century-Fox/Achilles, 1961;

Guns of Darkness, motion picture, adapted from Francis Clifford's novel *Act of Mercy,* Associated British/Cavalcade Pictures/Concorde, 1962;

I Thank a Fool, motion picture, adapted by Mortimer and Karl Tunberg from Audrey Erskine-Lindop's novel, Eaton/M-G-M, 1962;

Lunch Hour, motion picture, adapted by Mortimer from his play, London Films, 1962;

Collect Your Hand Baggage, television, Anglia Television, 29 August 1963;

The Running Man, motion picture, adapted from Shelley Smith's novel *The Ballad of the Running Man,* Peet Productions, 1963;

A Voyage Round My Father, radio, BBC Third Programme, 1963;

Personality Split, radio, BBC, 1964;

Education of an Englishman, radio, BBC, 1964;

Bunny Lake Is Missing, motion picture, adapted by Mortimer and Penelope Mortimer from Evelyn Piper's novel of that title, Columbia/Wheel, 1965;

A Rare Device, radio, BBC, 1965;

The Head Waiter, television, *Wednesday Play,* BBC1, 9 November 1966;

A Choice of Kings, television, Associated Rediffusion, 1966;

The Exploding Azalea, television, Thames Television, 1966;

Hughie, television, by Mortimer and Brian Cooke, *Comedy Playhouse,* BBC1, 19 May 1967;

The Other Side, television, BBC, 1967;

Infidelity Took Place, television, BBC1, 8 May 1968;

A Flea in Her Ear, motion picture, adapted from Georges Feydeau's *La Puce à l'oreille,* 20th Century-Fox, 1968;

A Voyage Round My Father, television, *Plays of Today,* BBC2, 16 October 1969;

John and Mary, motion picture, adapted from Mervyn Jones's novel of that title, Debrod/20th Century-Fox, 1969;
Married Alive, television, CBS, 23 January 1970; ITV, 6 June 1970;
Mill Hill, television, *Thirty-Minute Theatre,* BBC2, 22 May 1972;
Lunch Hour, television, *Thirty-Minute Theatre,* BBC2, 29 May 1972;
Swiss Cottage, television, *Thirty-Minute Theatre,* BBC2, 5 June 1972;
Alcock and Gander, television, Thames Television, 5 June - 10 July 1972;
Knightsbridge, television, *Thirty-Minute Theatre,* BBC2, 12 June 1972;
Bermondsey, television, *Thirty-Minute Theatre,* BBC2, 19 June 1972;
Rumpole of the Bailey, television, *Play for Today,* BBC, 3 December 1975;
Mr Luby's Fear of Heaven, radio, BBC, 1976;
Two Stars for Comfort, television, ITV, 6 June 1977;
Rumpole of the Bailey, television, Thames Television, 3 April - 15 May 1978;
Will Shakespeare, television, Anglia Television, 1978;
The Trials of Rumpole, television, Thames Television, 29 May - 3 July 1979;
Rumpole's Return, television, Thames Television, 30 December 1980;
Unity, television, adapted from David Pryce-Jones's book *Unity Mitford,* BBC2, 20 March 1981;
Brideshead Revisited, television, adapted by Mortimer and Charles Sturridge from Evelyn Waugh's novel of that title, Granada Television, 12 October - 22 December 1981;
Edwin, radio, 1982;
A Voyage Round My Father, television, Thames Television, 1982;
Rumpole and the Golden Thread, television, Thames Television, 11 October - 15 November 1983;
The Ebony Tower, television, adapted from John Fowles's short story of that title, Granada Television, 1984;
Edwin, television, 1984;
Paradise Postponed, television, Thames Television, 15 September - 24 November 1986;
Maschenka, motion picture, adapted from Vladimir Nabokov's novel *Mashen'ka,* Channel 4 Television Corporation / Clasart Film / France 3 / Jörn Donner Productions / Zweites Deutsches Fernsehen, 1986;
Rumpole's Last Case, television, Thames Television, 19 January - 23 February 1987;
Rumpole and the Age of Miracles, television, Thames Television, 23 November - 28 December 1988;
Summer's Lease, television, adapted by Mortimer from his novel of that title, Thames Television, 1989;
The Waiting Room, television, 1989;
Titmuss Regained, television, Thames Television, September 1991;
Rumpole à la Carte, television, Thames Television, 28 October - 2 December 1991;
Rumpole on Trial, television, Thames Television, 29 October - 3 December 1992;
Under the Hammer, television, Meridian / ITV, 1994;
Cider with Rosie, television, adapted from Laurie Lee's autobiography, Carlton Television, 1998;
Tea with Mussolini, motion picture, adapted by Mortimer and Franco Zeffirelli from Zeffirelli's autobiography, Cattleya / Cineritmo, 1999;
Don Quixote, television, adapted from Miguel de Cervantes y Saavedra's novel of that title, Turner Network Television, 9 April 2000;
In Love and War, television, adapted from Eric Newby's book *Love and War in the Apennines,* CBS Television, 18 November 2001;
Ceremonial in Three Flats, radio, *Afternoon Play,* BBC Radio 4, 4 June 2002.

OTHER: Harry Hodge and James H. Hodge, eds., *Famous Trials,* selected, with an introduction, by Mortimer (Harmondsworth: Penguin, 1984);
Georges Feydeau, *Three Boulevard Farces,* translated, with introductions, by Mortimer (Harmondsworth & New York: Penguin, 1985);
Carl Haffner and Richard Genée, *Die Fledermaus; or, The Bat's Revenge,* translated by Mortimer (London: Viking, 1989);
Edward Marjoribanks, *Famous Trials of Marshall Hall,* introduction by Mortimer (London: Penguin, 1989);
Great Law & Order Stories, edited, with an introduction, by Mortimer (London: Bellew, 1990; New York: Norton, 1992); republished as *The Penguin Book of Great Law & Order Stories* (London: Penguin, 1991);
The Oxford Book of Villains, edited by Mortimer (Oxford & New York: Oxford University Press, 1992).

SELECTED PERIODICAL PUBLICATION–UNCOLLECTED: "Courting Disaster on the Small Screen," *Daily Telegraph* (London), 27 April 1996, p. 3.

An extremely prolific and versatile writer–accomplished playwright, scriptwriter, and memoirist as well as fiction writer–John Mortimer is also well known as a barrister. Combining his interests in writing and the law, he created the character Rumpole of the Bailey–

Mortimer as a law student at Brasenose College, Oxford, early 1940s (from Clinging to the Wreckage: A Part of Life, *1982)*

featured initially in a television series, then in a series of books–for whom he is likely to be best remembered. But he is also the author of several novels that are not about Rumpole.

John Clifford Mortimer was born on 21 April 1923, the only child of a former art teacher, Kathleen May Smith Mortimer, and a successful divorce lawyer, Clifford Mortimer. His father, who went blind when John Mortimer was a boy but continued to practice law, was the chief inspiration for his son–both in Mortimer's life, as he went into his father's profession, and in Mortimer's imagination, as he used his father as the model for his best-known fictional character, Horace Rumpole. In some of his fiction, his play *A Voyage Round My Father* (published 1971), and all his memoirs, Mortimer writes out of his great admiration for his father.

John Mortimer's first love was acting out plays, particularly those of William Shakespeare, for his parents. His father took him to Stratford when John was a boy, and Clifford Mortimer had *Hamlet* and other Shakespeare plays from memory; Mortimer learned this love, and many others, from his father. As he was an only child, John had to play all the roles in the plays as he put them on at home. This early experience with acting served him well in the courtroom, as a playwright, and onstage in later life, when he gave readings from his work and participated in productions at literary festivals.

From 1937 to 1940 Mortimer attended Harrow School (also the alma mater of his beloved George Gordon, Lord Byron). While there he became a communist. In an interview published in *The Jerusalem Post* (24 March 1995), Pearl Sheffy Gefen quoted Mortimer as remarking, "I was the only communist cell at Harrow, and because it was the time of the Hitler-Stalin pact, I was told to slow down production on the factory floor. So I told everyone to translate Virgil slowly." Communism proved flawed, so Mortimer took up anarchy. "But it's quite difficult to be an anarchist, because they don't have rules or anything like that. So I became a socialist." Mortimer has, more or less, maintained this political allegiance all his life. His detractors routinely refer to him as a "champagne socialist," presumably because he comes from the southern upper classes rather than the northern working classes, and he is known to live well (thus, the implication is, his socialism is hypocritical); his frequently expressed response is "champagne for everyone!" A supporter of the more left-leaning Old Labour party, he has not much faith in the New Labour that arose in the 1980s and 1990s; nevertheless, he was knighted in 1998 by Tony Blair's Labour government.

At Brasenose College, University of Oxford, from 1940 to 1942 Mortimer read law and performed with the Oxford University Dramatic Society. He went from Oxford to a brief wartime service as a writer for the Crown Film Unit, the British wartime propaganda movie company. After the war he went into his father's chambers as an apprentice lawyer, joining the bar in 1948. However, his interest in the movies and, later, television remained. Years later, after the Rumpole series on television made him a rich man, Mortimer founded his own independent motion-picture production company, New Penny Productions, with Jacqueline Davis, producer of the Rumpole shows.

As did his father, Mortimer began his professional career as a divorce lawyer, and in a report in *The New York Times* (19 April 1999) Mel Gussow quoted him as telling a New York audience that "I was raised, housed, and educated entirely on the proceeds of adultery." He turned to writing to make a little extra money, at first, to support his wife, Penelope Fletcher Dimont, whom he married in 1949, her four children from her first marriage, and their two together, Sally and Jeremy. He also wrote romances for "ladies' magazines," among other assignments. Mortimer soon switched his practice to criminal law, becoming a Queen's Counsel (senior barrister, or trial lawyer) in 1966 and defending many criminals of varying degrees of innocence.

Mortimer's first wife published novels and memoirs during and after their marriage under the name

Penelope Mortimer. During the 1960s and 1970s she serialized their "perfect" family life for *The New Yorker,* and then, in the 1990s, wrote viciously of their marriage in her second volume of autobiography, *About Time Too: 1940–1978* (1993). Five years older than Mortimer, she had four daughters when they met during his undergraduate years at Oxford, and they divorced in 1972 after twenty-three years of marriage. In a 20 October 2001 interview for *The Times* (London) Mortimer spoke sadly to Ginny Dougary of the "really nasty book about us, a long time after we parted"–but in his own memoir, he told Dougary, he tried only to "remember the good things about her." As to her charges of adultery, in which she also evidently engaged, Angela Levin reports his reply, in a 26 July 1997 interview for the *Courier-Mail,* that "I do like women and at one point was a bit of a ladies' man, although not more than the average bank manager from Waltham Cross." In 1972 he married again, to Penelope Gollop, with whom he had two more children, Emily and Rosie.

Although his own writing career turned successful by the late 1950s, with a BBC radio play, *The Dock Brief* (published 1959), that won the Italia Prize in 1957, Mortimer's law career remained even more successful. Freedom of speech was an important issue to him, even in the midst of a primarily family-law practice, and Mortimer soon got out of divorce law and into trial law, defending those charged with misdemeanor and criminal offenses. In the 1960 *Lady Chatterley's Lover* obscenity case, Mortimer served as a junior counsel on behalf of Penguin Books, which had published an unexpurgated version of D. H. Lawrence's 1928 novel. On behalf of freedom of speech, always one of his favorite causes, Mortimer represented Richard Neville, Felix Dennis, and Jim Anderson of the "underground" magazine *Oz* when they were charged in June 1971 for conspiracy to "corrupt the morals of young children and other young persons" for publishing a drawing of the popular children's cartoon character Rupert Bear engaged in sex; the punk-rock band the Sex Pistols on obscenity charges for the title of their album *Never Mind the Bollocks Here's the Sex Pistols* (1977); and the right-wing British National Party. He defended these clients because, as he was quoted as saying in a 13 May 2001 report in *The Observer* (London) about some controversial cases in which Cherie Booth (wife of Prime Minister Blair and a lawyer) was involved, "nasty horrible people need representing just like anyone else." Dressed, as he described himself to Dougary in their 2001 interview, in "velveteen trousers with bell bottoms and a sort of Nehru jacket and bangles and beads and things hanging around my neck," he enjoyed swinging London but still regrets, as he told Dougary, "missed opportunities." When Alix Madrigal, in an interview for the *San Francisco Chronicle* (7 April 1996), asked Mortimer what it was like to defend murderers, he replied

> I liked doing murders because I found murderers rather nice clients as opposed to people in divorce cases. My sort of murderers usually killed the one person in life that was really bugging them, so they were peaceful and grateful for any little thing you could do for them. And they didn't ring you up at 3 in the morning, like people in divorce cases did, saying, "You'll never guess what he's done now."

However, after his *Rumpole* stories became immensely successful, Mortimer found it more difficult to practice law, as he related in an anecdote to Gefen: after one client was convicted of murder, he reproached Mortimer with the words "Rumpole would have got me off." In 1977 Mortimer lost an important libel case when his client, Denis Lemon, the editor of *Gay News,* was convicted of the ancient common-law offense, nearly forgotten in English law, of blasphemous libel, for publishing a poem by James Kirkup, "The Love That Dares to Speak Its Name," that graphically depicts a Roman centurion's sexual love for Jesus Christ. Lemon drew a suspended sentence but narrowly avoided going to prison. Two years later, Margaret Thatcher became prime minister in, to Mortimer's dismay, a newly conservative England. He soon gave up his practice to write full-time.

Although he is retired from practicing law full-time, Mortimer is still a most active observer of English law, particularly where freedom of speech and expression are concerned. When the English legal system did away with an accused's right to silence (not unlike the American equivalent of pleading the Fifth Amendment to avoid self-incrimination), Mortimer was horrified. As he put it in a 1994 interview with Heather Mallick of the *Toronto Sun,* "even Americans, who execute people, have the right to silence."

Mortimer spoke out in a 27 April 1996 editorial in *The Daily Telegraph* (London) against permitting cameras in courtrooms. "The fatal effect of television on trials," wrote Mortimer, "was finally demonstrated in the OJ Simpson performance, in which everyone acted for the benefit of the cameras and justice became a somewhat decadent form of mass entertainment." He admitted that courtroom dramas such as the television version of *Rumpole,* and movies made from novels by Scott Turow and John Grisham, are immensely popular–but argued that real trials are damaged by becoming dramas. For judges and lawyers to seek, and play for, the cameras is, Mortimer believes, fatal to both justice and entertainment: "Nothing could have a worse

Mortimer (standing at center) and his family in 1958: stepdaughters Madelon (standing at left) and Deborah (reclining in foreground); stepdaughter Caroline, wife Penelope, son Jeremy, daughter Sally, and stepdaughter Julia (seated) (photograph by Michael McKeown, Daily Express*)*

effect, both on the standards of entertainment and on the administration of justice." While reading crime fiction is pleasant–"There is nothing so enjoyable as sitting comfortably by the fire and reading about the terrible things that are happening to other people"–watching "real prisoners become part of the entertainment industry" is "close to the trials put on by dictators in the sports arena." The other, deepest difference between fact and fiction in the law is, as he remarked to Madrigal, "If you do a case badly, someone goes to prison for 14 years. If you write a bad book, nobody goes to prison, which is a great relief."

In June of 2001 Mortimer went to court for the first time in fifteen years to help defend Richard Meade, a vocal and well-known supporter of foxhunting in England. His own socialist convictions might have made his defense of foxhunting seem paradoxical. But his participation demonstrated his lifelong commitment to liberal tolerance. While he made it clear that he did not support hunting–he himself does not hunt, and never has–he spoke against the intolerance of others' freedoms he saw in the proposed ban on hunting. In a 9 May 2000 article in *The Daily Telegraph* (London), Charles Clover quoted him as saying, "The idea that things we dislike should be made a criminal offense is repulsive to many people. . . . what is not permissible is for one sector of the community buttressed by a statistical majority to criminalise an honest, honourable and decent section of the community who regard hunting as a perfectly legitimate way of life."

In spring 2002 Mortimer again emerged from retirement as a lawyer, again in defense of individual freedoms, this time to involve himself for the defense against the proposed criminal prosecution, for blasphemy, of television presenter Joan Bakewell. Bakewell had recited on television some lines from Kirkup's poem "The Love That Dares to Speak Its Name," the same poem that had landed *Gay News* editor Lemon in trouble some twenty-five years earlier. Mortimer stepped in to defend Bakewell, as he had earlier defended the gay journal that had published the poem, saying, "it's idiotic that the police should spend time on this."

Mortimer has written nearly fifty novels, plays, and other books, and, although he is fully aware that he will be best remembered as the creator of Rumpole, his career as an author is much longer and more varied than the many years of Rumpole stories and scripts would suggest. His fiction writing falls into three main phases. In the first, he wrote six novels between 1947 and 1956. He was already practicing law and wrote his early novels, he told Jean W. Ross in a brief 1987 interview for *Contemporary Authors,* out of "desperation, because I had all those children to support." After 1956, when *Three Winters* was published, there was a thirty-year interval during which he wrote no more mainstream fiction. During that time, of course, he turned to writing for the theater, producing nearly a play a year; he continued at the bar; and he wrote many scripts for radio, television, and motion pictures.

Then, in 1985, with *Paradise Postponed,* he resumed the writing of full-length novels (the Rumpole books are collections of stories). Typically, he wrote *Paradise Postponed* both as a novel and as a script for television. When asked by Ross how hard it was to write successfully in so many different media, he replied, "I've never thought that they were that different. I know people think they're all terribly different, but most of the successful things I've done have appeared in several forms. *Voyage Round My Father* was a radio play, a stage play, and then a television film. *Paradise Postponed* is a television series and a novel." Mortimer has been both impressively inventive and cannily economical in the use of his material.

Written when Mortimer was twenty-four, *Charade* (1947) is itself something of a combination, including elements of the bildungsroman (as its young narrator decides what to do with his life, involving a renunciation of art in favor of "life"), a mystery story involving the solution of a murder, and a satire on moviemaking. The narrator is a callow youth who is serving as an assistant director on a wartime film; at the seaside location he encounters a collection of strongly caricatured figures from the world of cinema, from the pretentious director down to drunken crew members.

Rumming Park (1948) is another of the early social-realistic, or "social-realist-comic," novels that Mortimer has expressed some disquiet about, suggesting that they (perhaps along with his earlier plays) were written in haste to support his family. In a 1986 interview with Francis X. Clines for *The New York Times* he commented on these apprentice years. "It took him a while to sort out his own voice," Clines noted, "and it did not happen until he tried writing a radio play, which is still a fine art form in England." That play was *The Dock Brief,* "about a criminal defendant who comes to pity his bungling but well-meaning counsel, an economical, two-actor play still produced on stages around England." Clines quoted Mortimer:

> "Suddenly, I found a voice for writing," he recalls, his relief still clear. "It probably came out of hearing the elaborate dialogue of the courts. Whatever it was, it was my own, and although I've missed it frequently and can't achieve it always, I know it when it's there."

Neither *Rumming Park* nor *Three Winters* has been published in the United States or reprinted in the United Kingdom, even when in the aftermath of his Rumpole celebrity many of his earlier books were brought out.

Answer Yes or No (1950; republished as *The Silver Hook,* 1950), like *Charade,* involves its protagonist in an adulterous relationship with another man's wife. Here the main character, Ransom, is a practicing barrister whose entanglement with Caroline Letts earns him the enmity of her husband; it also reminds him of analogies between his own behavior and aspects of the divorce case in which he is appearing. The reviewer for *The Times Literary Supplement* (23 June 1950) commented that "the skill with which his [Ransom's] nature–humane but sturdy, conscientious but not diffident–is conveyed through action, in a double sense of that word, is admirable. Mr. Mortimer has a mature conception of characters and relationships in public life, but an immature conception of private emotions and conflicts."

Like Men Betrayed (1953) also centers on a lawyer, though this one, Christopher Kennet, is a solicitor rather than a barrister. His life is disrupted when his son Kit embezzles money from one of Kennet's clients and goes on the run into the criminal underworld; Kennet follows, leaving what has been his safe zone and facing threats and other changes, including, once again, adulterous love. Reviewers of this novel disagreed widely. Reviewing the 1988 edition for the *Los Angeles Times* (29 March 1989) when it was republished in the United States on Rumpole's coattails, Clancy Sigal said, "It's a bad novel, overwritten, mechanically fatalistic, its prose at once stilted and exhausted," while Jonathan Yardley praised it in *The Washington Post* (15 February 1989), though he was apparently unaware that it had been published in the United States in 1954: "Mortimer does a great deal more within the relatively brief space he has allotted himself. His portrait of the Hume-Monument family is a devastating spoof of provincial English gentility, and he has assembled a delightful array of politicians, crooks and other scoundrels. . . . Its American debut is no less auspicious for being so long delayed."

*Mortimer and daughter Emily at home in Turville Heath, Buckinghamshire, 1982 (*Daily Express*)*

The Narrowing Stream (1954) was also published in 1989 in the United States once Mortimer had become famous for Rumpole. It is a sort of detective story, the kind in which an unwitting and unwilling amateur is dragged into investigation. Its main character is the thirty-eight-year-old Julia Swinton, who lives with her husband and children alongside a river. The mysterious death of an actress living in a houseboat further down the river, followed by the actress's brother's visit to Julia, bringing with him a cigarette case belonging to Julia's husband that he found in his sister's home, springs the plot into action. Reviewer Ann Arensberg praised Mortimer's plot in *The New York Times* (15 October 1989): "Every part of its construction dovetails neatly: motive with action; subplot with plot; symbol with psychology. The hand of the master, the intelligence that moves and interprets the events, is felt very strongly; but it is a deft hand, and it never robs the characters of their spontaneity or obstructs the rising tide of suspense." She concluded that "'The Narrowing Stream' is a mature and original accomplishment, as fascinating and ominous as the river that runs through its pages."

After publishing six novels in his first nine years as a professional (though not full-time) writer, Mortimer turned decisively to other genres. The first of these, and the first in which he really made his mark, was drama, writing for the West End stage, though with his usual versatile (or economical) facility in making his works serve more than one purpose, his works for the stage are also usually works intended for broadcast on radio or, latterly, on television.

His first success as a playwright came with the play *The Dock Brief,* which was broadcast on radio in May 1957 and on television in September 1957 before being produced at the Lyric Theatre, Hammersmith, 9 April 1958. In his entry on Mortimer for *Contemporary Dramatists* (1988), Henry Raynor sums up the reasons for its success: it "proved to be witty, imaginative, unusual, and cleverly worked out." The stage version has frequently been revived; the play was also adapted by Pierre Jouve as a 1962 motion picture, starring Peter Sellers as the bumbling solicitor and Richard Attenborough as the hapless defendant, released in the United States as *Trial and Error.* Mortimer was a contemporary of such "angry" playwrights as John Osborne and

Arnold Wesker, though his social and cultural allegiances were always different, and he is discussed in John Russell Taylor's book on the period, *The Angry Theatre: New British Drama* (1962). Taylor comments that "the differences between his works and those of the other new dramatists" consist mostly in that he "applies his exploratory techniques to the middle classes in decline rather than the working classes ascendent." Taylor traces that fact to Mortimer's unusually privileged middle-class background, unusual among the playwrights of the late 1950s and early 1960s. Though to call someone an author of "well made plays" usually counts as damning with faint praise, it is true of Mortimer. He often works in the comic, and, though this range includes some bedroom farces–for instance, *Lunch Hour* (1960)–Taylor quotes Mortimer as declaring that

> Comedy is, to my mind, the only thing worth writing in this despairing age, providing the comedy is on the side of the lonely, the neglected and the unsuccessful, and plays its part in the war against established rules and against the imposing of an arbitrary code of behaviour upon individual and unpredictable human beings.

As a playwright, Mortimer is best known for the play *A Voyage Around My Father* (retitled *A Voyage Round My Father* in later stage and published versions). Clifford Mortimer's favorite actor, Laurence Olivier, played him in the second, 1982 filmed version. Mortimer has written a screenplay with Franco Zeffirelli (*Tea with Mussolini,* 1999) and has adapted many novels for television, including a 2000 version of Miguel de Cervantes y Saavedra's *Don Quixote* (1605, 1615) with John Lithgow in the title role, and the popular 1981 version of Evelyn Waugh's *Brideshead Revisited* (1945), starring Jeremy Irons, Claire Bloom, Olivier, and Anthony Andrews.

During the thirty years of his greatest dramatic activity Mortimer wrote scripts for television and movies and wrote plays (frequently for radio, then the stage) of all types and lengths. He is something of a specialist in one-act plays; if there is a subject that recurs in his works, beyond a kind of comedy of human loneliness and inadequacy, it may be the law, as several of his plays (including his most famous, *The Dock Brief* and *A Voyage Round My Father*) concern the justice system. In December 1975 he began what became his most famous and successful branch of writing, the production of television shows and stories about Horace Rumpole. In that month *Rumpole of the Bailey* was broadcast by the BBC on the *Play for Today* television series; three years later the first Rumpole series, also called *Rumpole of the Bailey,* went out on Thames Television (a part of the commercial ITV network), followed by broadcast in the United States.

Mortimer published his first Rumpole stories in 1978 under the title *Rumpole of the Bailey*. The setting, the criminal courts of London, chiefly the Old Bailey, and cast of characters were positively Dickensian. There were Liz Probert and Judge Bullington, the delightfully despicable head of chambers, Soapy Sam Ballard, south London scourge Peanuts Molloy, and the wonderful old lawyer doing his best to defend his difficult and wacky clients among them–Horace Rumpole, whose crankiness, political incorrectness, and social liberalism are his leading characteristics. Rumpole's priorities, John J. O'Connor noted in a review of the broadcast of the sixth Rumpole series in *The New York Times* (29 May 1993), are "Steak and kidney pudding, the jury system, presumption of innocence and Wordsworth." Horace, inspired by Mortimer's father–Juliet Herd, in *The Weekend Australian* (3 January 1998), quoted Mortimer as remarking, "I find it difficult to distinguish between them"–plodded home every night to the inimitable and unrelenting Hilda, best known to the thousands of Rumpole fans as "She Who Must Be Obeyed." Rumpole's nickname for his wife comes from H. Rider Haggard's fin de siècle sensation *She* (1886), but Hilda, unlike her namesake, can be unexpectedly sweet at the end of her husband's long days in court when he makes his exhausted way back to their depressing flat in Froxbury Mansions.

Rumpole's irascibility, political incorrectness, bucking of authority, and successful independence made the aging barrister, and the supporting characters in the stories surrounding him, immensely popular in England, Australia, and, to a degree, in the United States, running for many seasons on the PBS series *Mystery*. Actor Leo McKern played Rumpole in the first play and all of the series. The role of his wife, Hilda, was originated by Joyce Heron; Peggy Thorpe-Bates played Hilda in the 1978, 1979, and 1983 series and the 1980 television special, *Rumpole's Return,* and Marion Mathie adopted the role in the next five series, which originally aired from 1987 to 1992.

Some of Mortimer's more unorthodox clients made it into the *Rumpole* stories with little fictionalizing required. In the title story of the 1995 collection, *Rumpole and the Angel of Death,* Rumpole is called to defend a practitioner of euthanasia whose "clients" are not always at death's door. It is based on an actual case of Mortimer's, in which he successfully defended, he told Madrigal in their 1996 interview, "Mr. Lyons, an awful man with a bobble hat and plastic bags. He'd give you whiskey and aspirins and put a plastic bag over your head, [and] he'd say things like, 'Hurry up and die because I've got two more to do this afternoon.'"

Leo McKern (as barrister Horace Rumpole) and Dave King in a 1987 episode of Rumpole's Last Case, *one of the several Rumpole series Mortimer wrote for Thames Television (Everett Collection)*

The immense success of the Rumpole television series enabled Mortimer to retire from actively practicing law and devote himself to writing full-time. Consistently compared to P. G. Wodehouse for his chronicling of middle-class English life and recreational pursuits, Mortimer is rather more like Shakespeare or Charles Dickens, in his eye for what happens in the streets and courts of London, and for describing those who perpetrate, prosecute, and defend outrages. As he told Gefen in their 1995 *Jerusalem Post* interview, Rumpole gives him a chance to speak out in a way that people are more apt to listen to: "I've always tried to be on the side of the underdog and the oppressed, and against pomposity and the abuse of power. But you can only encourage these attitudes if you do it in a funny way so people enjoy it. If I say these things myself, they sound trendy and left wing and abrasive. If Rumpole says them, they sound rather cuddly and grumpy and attractive."

In 1998 BBC Radio 4 decided not to run a series of Rumpole stories because–in a real case of paradox–Mortimer included a feminist character who was too outspoken and forceful about her views. In a 13 January 1998 report for *The Independent* (London), Paul McCann quoted a BBC spokeswoman as declaring, "The BBC feels that the feminist politics of the last Rumpole offering were dated and old-fashioned."

Marcel Berlins, in a 22 October 1995 article for *The Sunday Times* (London), wrote that "more people know about the English legal system through watching and reading John Mortimer's *Rumpole* than from any other source. Because English trials are not televised, and only a minority has attended a real trial, the English courtroom has been accessible partly through newspaper reports, but mainly through fiction; and, of all fictional courtroom tales, the *Rumpole* books and television series have been easily the most popular."

In 2001 Mortimer published the twelfth volume of his Rumpole stories. Titled *Rumpole Rests His Case,* this book looks to be the last hurrah of Horace Rumpole. These seven stories, populated by the usual cast of characters, are as progressive and timely as their predecessors; Rumpole defends an Afghan seeking asylum in England, and one case involves a stalker who works through e-mail. The usual cast of characters have become–except for Rumpole–frightfully contemporary and politically correct: Soapy Sam eats muesli, and

Hilda Rumpole wants to engage in interior decoration, both of which are things to horrify Rumpole into retirement or worse. Mortimer is as subtle as ever in his contemporary details: poor Rumpole can no longer smoke his cigars in court or even in his office; he is consigned to puff away outdoors in the usually inclement London weather. *Rumpole Rests His Case* ends with Rumpole in an ambulance on his way to the hospital, after being stricken while on his feet in the courtroom. Paul Magrath, in his 18 December 2001 review in *The Times* (London), spoke for many fans of "the Old Bailey hack" when he wrote, "there is something to be cherished in Rumpole, the loss of which would diminish us all." Whether Mortimer will permit his alter ego to return to the bar, as he himself has so often done, is uncertain. Mortimer admitted, in his 2001 interview with Dougary, "Basically, I need Rumpole to say what I think about the world."

The death on 23 July 2002 of McKern, the actor who came to embody the character on television, makes future television series problematic; as Clive Anderson wrote in his 28 July 2002 column for *The Independent* (London), "I suppose Rumpole, like James Bond, could be played by a succession of actors, but the fictional English barrister and the real-life Australian actor have become so closely associated that another portrayal of Rumpole seems scarcely imaginable." He noted, however, that "Rumpole can live on in written form," and he reported on a recent conversation with Mortimer in which the author "assured us he had just written another batch of Rumpoles."

In his 1996 interview with Madrigal for the *San Francisco Chronicle,* Mortimer likened his career track to a traditional pattern: "I was like a woman who wanted to be a film star and did a bit of waitressing; law was my day job. But I got too good at it and stuck there too long." Although popular, the Rumpole stories had, for the most part, little political content–that may be why they were so popular. Mortimer might have been spurred into writing novels again by his distaste for the direction Britain was going after the election of Thatcher as prime minister in 1979; he deplored her government, he told Catherine Bennett in a 24 April 1988 interview for *The Times* (London), as "bringing out the worst elements in society, the most greedy, and the most money-oriented feelings of people, and the least compassionate, and therefore the least English." In 1985 he returned to mainstream and full-length fiction, for the first time since 1957, with his novel *Paradise Postponed.* This book was the first of three featuring unattractive protagonist Leslie Titmuss–Mortimer told Alan Franks in a 12 September 1986 interview in *The Times* (London) that "Leslie represents all that I hate"–a trilogy now called "The Rapstone Chronicles," set in the halls of power of London but also, more importantly, in the quirky and inimitable little village of Rapstone Fanner. These novels–*Paradise Postponed, Titmuss Regained* (1990), and *The Sound of Trumpets* (1998)–were written specifically with television adaptation in mind. Many of the filmed English versions of Mortimer's books, including the Leslie Titmuss saga, have come to the United States and Canada by way of the PBS series *Masterpiece Theatre.*

Paradise Postponed, as the title suggests, is something of a condition-of-England novel. The young man Leslie Titmuss is a working-class lad determined to make good; he tries to "improve" his telltale working-class accent by mimicking the announcers on the BBC cricket broadcasts. But his rise is disturbing, in part because of its methods (reminiscent of Dickens's Uriah Heep) and because of its aims, to squirm into the Tory ascendancy. The novel, not surprisingly, contains, along with some effective satire, a powerful mystery. The Rev. Simeon Simcox, a rural Anglican of impeccable left-wing credentials, has died and, greatly to everyone's surprise, has left a £2 million legacy to Titmuss, whom he knew as a boy. Simcox's two grown sons react differently: Henry, a novelist whose own leftist principles seem to be suffering some erosion, wants to overturn the will by showing that his father was mentally disturbed; Fred, a doctor, decides to pursue the truth of why his father acted as he did. The title of the novel raises the question of why Paradise (the earthly Paradise, which Simeon Simcox seemed determined to build in England's green and pleasant land) is always postponed. Reviewing the novel in the 22 September 1985 issue of *The Times* (London), Julian Symons noted the acuteness with which the book raises this question; he went on to comment that it "operates, as Eliot said a play might, on two levels: that of the faintly Rumpoleish Simcox secret, and another concerned with an England that has changed, not for the better." In her *Christian Science Monitor* (11 April 1986) review, Pamela Marsh concluded that "It would be a mistake to suppose that Mortimer has nothing but bitter comedy, mystery, and echoes of other men to offer us. His own voice can be heard soberly warning, through his characters' machinations, that most men's ideas of paradise are doomed to be indefinitely postponed or dissolved into ashes."

Mortimer postponed the second volume of his "Rapstone Chronicles" for *Summer's Lease* (1988), a novel set in Tuscany among wealthy British folk who summer there in what Mortimer named (it has since entered the language) "Chiantishire." *Summer's Lease,* according to interviewer Bennett, "fits comfortably into the tradition of 'comic-serious eccentric English writing,' as Mortimer calls it; complete with farcical couples, absurd names, and a comment on the human condition." In addition there are murder and mystery. But the main aim seems to be a satire on a certain sector of British society: middle class, educated, cultured, probably of liberal to socialist attitudes, like Mortimer himself: in fact, the champagne socialist class to which his critics assign him. That he may be attempting something symbolic or allegorical along the lines of *Paradise Postponed* is one inference from the name of the central villa in the novel: "La Felicita" (happiness). The main strengths of this work, however, are in the knowing satire on well-drawn types and the kind of world they create for themselves in an Italy they only partially understand.

Published in 1990, *Titmuss Regained* returns to the successful Conservative politician, this time involved in a question of development. He is now the Minister for Housing, Ecological Affairs and Planning; he has acquired a new, upper-class wife (to replace the one he lost in *Paradise Postponed*) and a stately home, Rapstone Manor, in which to house her. His determination to keep a proposed "new town" out of his neighborhood has a dual significance. In one sense it is a satire on what the British call *Nimbyism* (from the acronym *NIMBY*: "Not in My Back Yard"), a term popularized in Britain by Nicholas Ridley, Thatcher's environment secretary, to denigrate those who opposed rural development–among whose ranks were numbered some of Mrs. Thatcher's cabinet, including Ridley, who was later revealed to have secretly opposed the building of new housing visible from his country home. In another it reveals Leslie's indifference to less-favored Britons, of the sort he used to be, now that he has "made it." Of course, the conflicts in Leslie are like the conflicts in his ministry–building housing is almost always bad for ecological affairs. Mortimer himself is antidevelopment, so that the theme of the novel is slightly confused by the repellent Titmuss (who allegedly represents everything his author hates) opposing the expansion of urban ugliness to the country. In her 24 March 1990 review for *The Independent* (London) Zoe Heller pounced on this apparent confusion: "Throughout this novel, Mortimer drags a lot of comic mileage not just out of Titmuss but also out of Titmuss's upper-middle-class detractors. He sends up, for example, the guests at an Oxford lunch party, who snicker when Titmuss exposes his ignorance of opera. Given his own amusement at Titmuss's petit-bourgeois ways, and the pages of ribald fun he has with working-class solecisms, many will conclude that Mortimer is trying, rather recklessly, to have his cake and eat it."

That Mortimer may be acknowledging his own complicity in the matters he depicts is suggested by his inclusion in his next novel, *Dunster* (1992), of a character who denounces a left-wing professor as a champagne socialist; the professor's reply–that "his brand of socialism meant that champagne would be freely available to all but until that bright day dawned, at least it would be available to socialist cabinet ministers"–is more or less Mortimer's own response: "champagne for all" (by and by). Mortimer, in other words, sees both sides of things. As David Robson, reviewing *Dunster* in the 28 March 1992 issue of *The Daily Telegraph* (London), wrote, "the instinctive distrust of the Establishment, which runs like a golden thread through John Mortimer's writings, is generally balanced by a scepticism about the motives and methods of those who would replace the Establishment with something better. In *Dunster,* this tension between the forces of reaction and subversion finds its clearest and most forceful expression yet." There are two lifelong friends at the heart of this book–the dull narrator, Progmire (a name as suggestive as Titmuss), and his more dashing and irresponsible friend Dunster, who has spent a lifetime causing trouble, not least to Progmire. His leveling charges of war crimes at Progmire's boss leads to a libel trial that looms large in the novel.

Other reviewers differed sharply; thus, in an 18 April 1992 review for *The Independent* (London) Amanda Craig declared that it was a "skimpy mixture of comedy, detective story and court-room drama . . . *Dunster* seems to have been written on autopilot." For her part, Isabel Quigly described the novel in the 28 March 1992 issue of *The Financial Times* (London) as "masterly" and thought that, compared with *Summer's Lease,* "it goes much deeper, and more darkly, though the surface has a similar exactness and exuberance and a similar deadpan wit."

Under the Hammer (1994), set in a London auction house, is a satire on the art business, a world of dubious authentifications and outright fakery. Though published as a novel, the book is a sort of novelization of Mortimer's television series of the same title, which aired in 1993.

Felix in the Underworld (1997) is a warning about the ease with which joblessness and homelessness can happen in today's world to those who have no reason to expect them. Felix Morsom, a once-famous novelist, meets a woman at a mysterious book signing and is suddenly being hounded, to his horror and disbelief, by an organization called the Parental Rights and Obligations Department (PROD) for child support this woman, Miriam Bowker, now demands. She says they had a child ten years earlier; Felix has never, as best he can remember, met her before. When he is also suspected of murder, and finds his snobby, self-involved lawyer, Septimus Roache, to be of no help to him at all, poor Felix joins the large homeless population of London both for refuge and out of necessity. Mortimer mercilessly lashes the failings of the British Child Support Agency and various organizations instituted to help the homeless in this scary, and somehow all-too-possible, novel. For his research for *Felix in the Underworld,* Mortimer ventured into "Cardboard City," accompanied by the chaplain from the Savoy Chapel or the policemen stationed at Charing Cross. Most of the homeless he talked to were men, whom he described to Valerie Grove in a 1991 interview as "confused middle-aged men who just can't cope after their families fall apart."

Mortimer's 1998 novel, *The Sound of Trumpets,* is the conclusion to the Rapstone Chronicles and a searing satire of Blair's "Cool Brittannia." In it, Labour candidate Terry Flitton, bored by his beautiful and stupid young wife, has an affair with fifty-year-old Agnes Simcox, the ultimate heroine of the novel. Gussow quoted Mortimer as saying, "I'm so fed up with stories of middle-aged men leaving their middle-aged wives for beautiful young girls. I wanted to write a story with a man leaving a beautiful young girl for a wonderful, hard-drinking, hard-smoking middle-aged woman." Leslie Titmuss is now Lord Titmuss, ennobled by Mrs. Thatcher on her way out. Terry Flitton is something of a marker for New Labour, on which Mortimer comments acerbically. Like most of his novels, this one relies on sexual intrigue and murder mystery; at the heart of it, however, is the relationship between Titmuss and Flitton, who form an unlikely and unequal (and unwise) partnership based on their apparent similarity; the result is the rise and fall of Terry Flitton alongside the rise and continued rise of Leslie Titmuss. In his 5 March 1999 *Los Angeles Times* review Michael Frank summed up the novel (and in a way the trilogy):

> Along the way . . . Flitton's personal world is reduced to shambles, and "the dark presence that seemed to have taken control of his life" is not so easily cast off. After satirizing the suburbanization of the English countryside, the sexual peccadilloes of politicians, the prying perseverance of the press and his countrymen's comic disputes over fox hunting, Mortimer closes "The Sound of Trumpets" with a set piece that shows Titmuss's devilry undiminished and, if anything, rather sharpened by his retirement to the apparent sidelines. Terry Flitton may flit on out of the center of Rapstone, but Leslie Titmuss will surely remain on hand for a good while yet.

Alongside his work as a playwright, scriptwriter, and novelist, Mortimer has become a distinguished memoirist. His autobiographies run to three volumes. *Clinging to the Wreckage* (1982) is the story of his youth and young manhood, ending in the 1970s, and the sec-

Dust jacket for the U.S. edition of Mortimer's 1990 novel, the sequel to Paradise Postponed *(Richland County Public Library)*

ond volume, *Murderers and Other Friends* (1994), tells of his middle life and career as a writer. It is more about the "other friends" like David Niven, Tony Richardson, and Robert Graves than about the murderers Mortimer has defended, but is, appropriately, a chronicling of the last years of his legal practice and his joyful departure from family and criminal law for a life entirely in letters. The third volume is *The Summer of a Dormouse* (2000), a rather elegiac work, whose title is taken from Mortimer's favorite line from Byron, an entry in his journal for 7 December 1813: "When one subtracts from life infancy (which is vegetation), sleep, eating and swilling, buttoning and unbuttoning–how much remains of downright existence? The summer of a dormouse." The story of one year in Mortimer's late life–"a year of growing old disgracefully," he says–*The Summer of a Dormouse* deals much with mortality. In it Mortimer talks of the glaucoma that has cost him the sight in one eye, the asthma that plagues him, and the thousand other ills that aging brings, with his usual ironic humor. Of his fading eyesight, Levin quoted him

Dust jacket for the U.S. edition of Mortimer's 1992 novel, about a libel trial that affects a lifelong friendship (Richland County Public Library)

as saying, "It means I can no longer judge distances, which makes stairs difficult to deal with, and I pour wine onto the table." Yet, in the words of Michael Langan, in his review for the *Buffalo News* (29 July 2001), to see "this urbane and witty fellow standing on line in the short queue for eternity with the nominal belief that God may be only a 'Great Perhaps'" calls "for more stoicism than I can muster."

Aside from his memoir writing, it is as a playwright and actor that Mortimer is still most active. In 2001, two new Mortimer plays opened in England. *Naked Justice,* a courtroom drama rather along the lines of a Rumpole story, is a story of three aging judges and their relationship to their profession and each other, while *Hock and Soda Water* added yet another chapter to Mortimer's self-inspired dramas. The central figure in this play is a Mortimeresque seventy-year-old named (with Mortimer's constant eye to the timely even in his preference for the past) Harry Pottinger, looking back at his younger self. Most unlike the eponymous protagonist of Byron's long satiric poem *Don Juan* (1819–1824), from which the title comes, Mortimer's Pottinger falls again and again into a nice middle-class complacency and predictability despite–or, perhaps, because of–his young dreams of excitement and grandeur. Charles Spencer, reviewing the play in the 29 November 2001 issue of *The Daily Telegraph* (London), summed it up as a long and loving look at "an England now disappearing from view: a world of church fetes, halves of mild at the local pub, and transports of sexual delight in the back of a Ford Popular." Yet, Spencer also noted, "our hero's determination to seek new horizons in old age makes you want to cheer." This encomium is something all who enjoy the act of reading can apply to Mortimer, as he, despite his age, shows no sign of diminishment in his enthusiasm for writing or for life. On 17 April 2002, a double bill of new Mortimer plays premiered at the Watford Palace. An original play by Mortimer, *Full House* is a drawing-room farce that hinges on mistaken identity, involving a writer named Sam who is invited to a meeting with a producer to whom he hopes to sell his new story. In her 18 April 2002 review for *The Evening Standard* (London), Rachel Haliburton criticized the production as a "flailing farce" and remarked the "result is old-guard rather than avant-garde." Benedict Nightingale, in a 20 April 2002 review for *The Times* (London), remarked that "the denouement is visible early on" but "This doesn't matter, or wouldn't matter if Kate Sinclair's cast had brought more pep and energy to confusions that spiral, Feydeau-style, towards but not quite into chaos." Both critics spoke more favorably of the second play, *The Hairless Diva,* an adaptation of Eugène Ionesco's *La Cantatrice chauve* (1950; usually translated as *The Bald Soprano*), Haliburton remarking that "Mortimer has proved a revivifying force for Ionesco" and Nightingale approving the "skill and panache" with which the cast delivered Mortimer's "freeish translation."

Mortimer remains a social critic. As Glenys Kinnock (wife of former Labour Party leader Neil Kinnock) said in a 17 January 1999 article for *The Independent* (London), "He loves debunking. He loves it if you attack pretentiousness or poseurs–there's a lot of that in his writing. I think he quite likes no-nonsense people." And his politics are far more left-wing than those associated with "New Labour"–the triumphant Blair administration and its supporters. Mortimer is most outspoken about current world affairs; though haunted by the destruction of the World Trade Center towers, an act that recalled the Blitz of London to him, Mortimer insisted to interviewer Dougary that neither the United States nor Britain can "achieve anything by bombing a lot of people in tents."

He never shrinks from making his opinions plain. Horrified by the state of prisons, Mortimer was quoted by Ian Burrell in the 30 April 2001 issue of *The Independent* (London) as criticizing Blair's home secretary, Jack Straw, and prison system administrator Paul Boateng for the "hopeless, terrible condition" of existing prisons and the non-solution of building more prisons without focusing instead on stopping crime in prisons, which are rife with drug sales and rape. He has also spoken out on behalf of asylum seekers, often "lawyers and teachers," who come to England only to be treated badly and sent away–and wrote one of his last Rumpole stories about this subject.

The father of four children, stepfather of many more, and grandfather to a legion of children today, Mortimer has said repeatedly, in his memoirs and through his fictional characters, how much he loves parenting–and how much comic material for his writing he finds therein. The children of his first marriage, Sally and Jeremy, are now a special education teacher and an executive with the radio drama division of the BBC, respectively. Emily and Rosie, his two daughters from his second marriage, are now an actress and a model, respectively.

John Mortimer lives in the Chilterns, on the border of Oxfordshire and Buckinghamshire, with his wife, Penny, in the house his father built when John was a boy. He still begins writing before sunup in the morning and, as did Anthony Trollope, goes on until lunchtime. Afternoons are for rest, recreation, conversations with family and friends, and listening to opera. He told Nigel Reynolds of *The Daily Telegraph* (London) in a 6 March 1999 interview, "I think when you get old, there is nothing else to do except work." He also uses work to stave off his increasing host of ills, reflecting, as he told Levin in 1997, that bad health is "brought on by boredom" and that "keeping ill health at bay is one reason why I work so hard." But the fears and hazards of being "A Writer" continue; in the 15 April 1995 issue of *The Daily Telegraph* (London) Mortimer admitted that, "like all writers, I'm extremely unsure of myself. I never think I'm going to be able to do it again and, when I've done it, I'm not sure if it's any good. I see disaster round every corner." Yardley marveled in a review of *Murderers and Other Friends: Another Part of Life* in the *Chicago Sun-Times* (23 March 1995), "Mortimer is rich and famous, thanks largely to his 'Rumpole of the Bailey' tv series, but he regards his good fortune with gratitude and surprise. Both emotions, in this age of celebrity, are as welcome as they are uncommon."

Interviews:

Alan Franks, "A Flower of the Left, Hiding in the Snobbery," *Times* (London), 12 September 1986;

Francis X. Clines, "Of 'Paradise' and John Mortimer," *New York Times,* 19 October 1986, II: 31;

Rosemary Herbert, "Murder by Decree: An Interview with John Mortimer," *Armchair Detective: A Quarterly Journal Devoted to the Appreciation of Mystery, Detective, and Suspense Fiction,* 20 (Fall 1987): 340–349;

Jean W. Ross, "*CA* Interview," in *Contemporary Authors, New Revision Series, Volume 21* (Detroit: Gale, 1987), pp. 316–320;

Catherine Bennett, "Our good-humoured commentator on the human condition," *Times* (London), 24 April 1988;

Valerie Grove, "A Voyage Round Cardboard City," *Times* (London), 24 June 1991;

Pearl Sheffy Gefen, "Rumpole Made Him," *Jerusalem Post,* 24 March 1995, p. 23;

Scott Rosenberg, "Champagne for Everyone!" *Salon.com* (15 February 1996) <http://www.salon.com/11/features/mortimer1.html>;

Alix Madrigal, "Checking in with Rumpole," *San Francisco Chronicle,* 7 April 1996, p. 4;

Angela Levin, "Courting Disaster," *Courier-Mail* (Queensland), 26 July 1997, p. 7;

Juliet Herd, "Muse That Must Be Obeyed," *Weekend Australian,* 3 January 1998, p. R07;

Nigel Reynolds, "Mortimer is on a Roll," *Daily Telegraph* (London), 6 March 1998, p. 20;

Ginny Dougary, "How Do You Plead, Mrs. Mortimer?" *Times* (London), 20 October 2001;

Jonathan Heawood, "This Much I Know: Sir John Mortimer," *Observer* (London), 26 May 2002, Magazine section, p. 8.

References:

John Russell Taylor, "In the Air," in *The Angry Theatre: New British Drama* (New York: Hill & Wang, 1962), pp. 214–226;

Sharon Villines, "John Mortimer," in *Mystery and Suspense Writers: The Literature of Crime, Detection, and Espionage,* edited by Robin W. Winks and Maureen Corrigan, volume 2 (New York: Scribners, 1998), pp. 689–698.

Papers:

Collections of John Mortimer's typescripts, drafts, corrected proofs, and other papers are held by the Department of Special Collections, Mugar Memorial Library, Boston University; and the Harry Ransom Humanities Research Center, University of Texas at Austin.

Geoff Nicholson

(4 March 1953 -)

Jayne Thexton
Stafford College

BOOKS: *Street Sleeper* (London: Quartet, 1987);
The Knot Garden (London: Hodder & Stoughton, 1989);
What We Did on Our Holidays (London: Hodder & Stoughton, 1990);
Big Noises: Rock Guitar in the 1990s (London: Quartet, 1991);
Hunters and Gatherers (London: Hodder & Stoughton, 1991; Woodstock, N.Y.: Overlook, 1994);
The Food Chain (London: Hodder & Stoughton, 1992; Woodstock, N.Y.: Overlook, 1993);
Day Trips to the Desert: A Sort of Travel Book (London: Hodder & Stoughton, 1992);
The Errol Flynn Novel (London: Hodder & Stoughton, 1993);
Still Life with Volkswagens (London: Quartet, 1994; Woodstock, N.Y.: Overlook, 1995);
Everything and More (London: Gollancz, 1994; New York: St. Martin's Press, 1995);
Footsucker (London: Gollancz, 1995; Woodstock, N.Y.: Overlook, 1996);
Bleeding London (London: Gollancz, 1997; Woodstock, N.Y.: Overlook, 1997);
Flesh Guitar (London: Gollancz, 1998; Woodstock, N.Y.: Overlook, 1999);
Female Ruins (London: Gollancz, 1999; Woodstock, N.Y.: Overlook, 2000);
Bedlam Burning (London: Gollancz, 2000; Woodstock, N.Y.: Overlook, 2002).

SELECTED PERIODICAL PUBLICATION–UNCOLLECTED: "The Strung Out Look: Phallic yet curvaceous, electric guitars will always look cool–to men," *Independent* (London), 8 July 2000, p. 18.

Geoff Nicholson (photograph by Colin Ramsay; from the dust jacket for the U.S. edition of The Food Chain, *1993)*

Geoff Nicholson is a highly prolific writer, having produced some thirteen works of fiction and two of nonfiction over a period of fourteen years. This consistently regular output has kept him in the literary public eye, and his quirky and daring subject matter has earned him a particular niche in current literature. He has striven with a great deal of success to resist a formulaic approach to narratives, and there is a remarkable variety and imaginative zeal to his novels. Nicholson's reputation is primarily linked to his wickedly risqué and satirical black humor; many of his works are seriously silly, taking the form of farces with dark undertones.

It took Nicholson some years to identify his métier. Born in Sheffield, England, on 4 March 1953, Geoffrey Joseph Nicholson is the only child of blue-collar parents; his father, Geoff, was a joiner and his mother, Violet, a bookkeeper, "good working class people," he said in an unpublished interview, "who believed in education even if they hadn't had much themselves." Writing from an early age, Nicholson decided quickly that he wanted to be a writer but admits, "I didn't know what kind of writer I was, not even what I wanted to be." This uncertainty continued until he was in his mid thirties, when he wrote his first novel. A difficult time at grammar school (where his achievements were few except in English) was followed by more-assured years at Gonville and Caius College, Cambridge, from which he received a B.A. degree in 1975 and an M.A. in 1978. Nicholson read English and was much involved with student theater, to the point at which he decided that playwriting was the way forward. Having developed an interest in the works of such writers as Harold Pinter, William S. Burroughs, and Jack Kerouac, Nicholson moved on to receive an M.A. in drama, which he completed in 1978 at the University of Essex. At this point he had aspirations to become what he calls an "avant-garde playwright/director." Titles produced at Essex for performance at the Edinburgh Festival and on the London Fringe include *Oscar* (1975), *Don't Blame It on the Moonlight* (1978), and *Angst for the Memory* (1987). None were published, and Nicholson himself is reluctant to recall these early efforts, describing them as "pretty awful."

Having moved into the London area, he supported himself in the early to mid 1980s with brief jobs such as gardening, bookselling, bar work, and selling furniture in Harrods department store. He married Tessa Robinson in January 1984, and, according to the autobiographical passages in *Still Life with Volkswagens* (1994), learned to drive, acquiring a Volkswagen Beetle. Nicholson and his wife became friendly with fellow Beetle enthusiasts and integrated with the Volkswagen clubbers' social scene. These last details would seem fairly insignificant ones in the biography of another author, but in the case of Nicholson these events provided him with inspiration for his first novel. Having put aside playwriting for the foreseeable future, Nicholson wrote *Street Sleeper* (1987). It was his turning point. He comments: "Once I started writing novels, I realized that was what I did best."

Nicholson's signature theme is obsession. Whether it is an obsession with Errol Flynn, feet, collections, London, sex, or Volkswagens, Nicholson is fascinated with the anatomy of desire. He writes about the ways in which people manage their obsessions and addresses the question of whether an obsessive personality denotes deviancy and madness. Frequently, the novels seem to draw the opposite conclusion, that obsessiveness is a symptom of humanity and a manifestation of the need to exert a controlling influence on the shapeless unpredictability of modern life. Collectors anchor their private universes through responsibility for something unique. In this way Nicholson's characters seek to transcend mundane mortality. Despite their ambitions, though, many of his creations follow similar blueprints. The principal males are frequently adrift in the world, dislocated and embarking on life-changing journeys, whereas female characters are often highly sexed yet emotionally unattainable and enigmatic. Nicholson's progress has been that of a journeyman, noticeably honing his craft and developing his skills as a writer over the years. Themes may be repeated and characteristics remain like signposts to previous efforts, but the overall style and scope matures and enlarges in his later publications. The 1997 nomination of *Bleeding London* (1997) for a Whitbread Award signaled an arrival of sorts and a recognition.

Nicholson exploited his passion for the Volkswagen Beetle to shape his first novel as an homage to the car and was rewarded with a nomination for the *Yorkshire Post* First Work Award. A light and witty satire of the "road novel" genre, *Street Sleeper* is an antidote to the serious introspection of novels such as Kerouac's *On The Road* (1957). The plot follows the attempts by a librarian and self-styled "Zen Road Warrior" to find himself. This effort involves quitting his job and fiancée, changing his name from Barry to Ishmael, and taking to the road in "Enlightenment," his new Beetle. Along the way he falls in love and becomes the improbable spiritual leader to a motley assortment of lost souls. Ishmael is a hugely pretentious homespun philosopher, trying to "find himself" while seeking adventure but hoping desperately for sexual gratification along the way. When his comic search for self appears to be over and he actually becomes the road warrior of his own fantasies, events threaten to engulf him.

The paradox of the novel, which is repeated later in *Still Life with Volkswagens,* is that the Beetle is wielded by the characters as a weapon for tolerance and "new age" causes against far-right racial and social bigotry, whereas the vehicle itself, readers are told, is a product of Nazi values, Adolf Hitler's own "Strength through Joy" car. Interspersed with the main plot are fictionalized historical passages charting the history of the Beetle, from its conception by Hitler before World War II through its postwar development and ensuing worldwide success. They re-create the story of how the Volkswagen made the jump from a symbol of Nazi philosophy to the international "people's car." This process is no more bizarre than the events in Ishmael's tale; as the events in the story grow ever more wild and surreal, however, the "factual" passages keep the novel as a whole grounded in something that resembles reality.

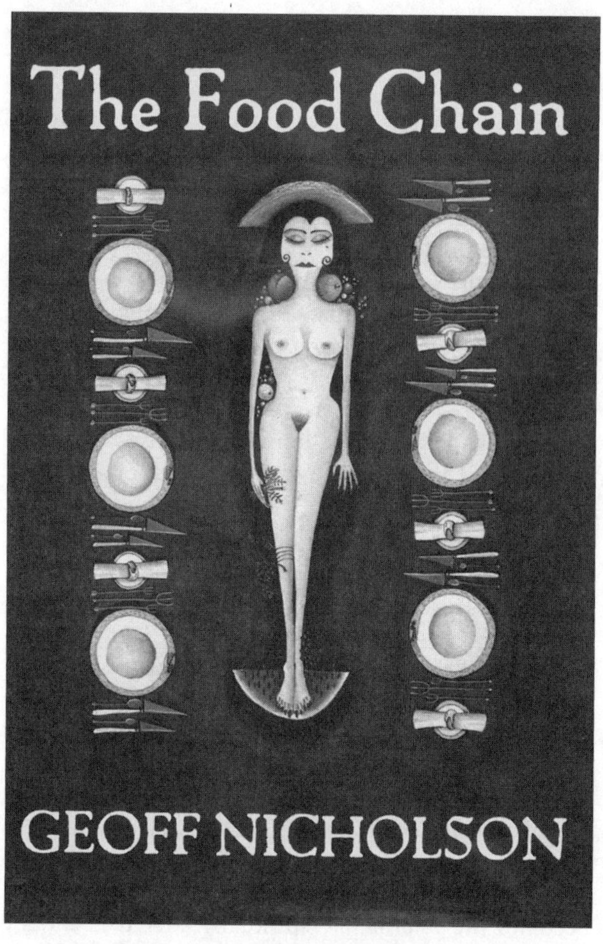

Dust jacket for the U.S. edition of Nicholson's 1992 novel, in which a young restaurateur is initiated into a mysterious society devoted to gluttony (Richland County Public Library)

Nicholson's follow-up was a murder-mystery satire, the somewhat tangled *The Knot Garden* (1989), later changed to *A Knot Garden.* Involving many first-person narrators, it tells of a widow's efforts to uncover the truth behind her husband's death: was it suicide or murder? Every character has a monologue, and all are held together by the central mystery. Twists and turns abound, and there are clues, hints, and false trails, but none of these prepare the reader for the revelations of the final chapter. The narrative is not so much a knot garden as a maze. The central character is undeniably the dead man–no other protagonist dominates the action to the same extent. His intimate life is recalled by so many observers and acquaintances that he is the most recognizable character in the novel, as a minor television celebrity and writer, herb garden specialist, prankster, and sexual adventurer. His complex life is recalled in detail and gradually reassembled by those investigating his demise, but the solutions make no sense at all–bizarre clues point to illogical conclusions, and the confusion fuels his widow's mental breakdown.

A Knot Garden reads like a risqué Agatha Christie novel as Nicholson pokes fun at that most popular of literary genres, the whodunit. None of his sleuths possesses the clairvoyance of Christie's Miss Marple, however, which is required to solve the crime. They are a tribute to his burgeoning development as a writer, for he has managed to give voice to at least sixteen original characters, each bearing the mark of individualism and authenticity. A rash of conspiracies and clues are uncovered, but these confuse rather than clarify. Nothing is explained or revealed until the final chapter, when the majority of the characters are summoned to a hotel by a mysterious invitation. Naturally, a figure emerges from the shadows of the plot to explain all, and a frustrating conclusion is drawn that no reader could possibly have reached unaided. Nicholson takes a risk by imitating the type of thriller writer who denies the reader a chance at solving the mystery. Crucial evidence is withheld and the reader is misled in order to produce a total surprise at the climax. Nicholson thus leaves himself open to the same criticisms as the thriller writers he is satirizing.

With *What We Did on Our Holidays* (1990) Nicholson made the leap from unlikely comedy to black satire and farce. Reminiscent of some of playwright Alan Ayckbourn's wilder dramas, *What We Did on Our Holidays* deposits a freakish family in a surreal holiday park, populated by homicidal Spaniards, carnivorous fish, a hysterical police inspector, and sexually rapacious dwarves on unicycles. Nicholson revels in the progressive humiliation and persecution of his strait-laced diarist and narrator, Eric, whose wife, son, and daughter grudgingly accompany him to the Tralee Carapark and Holiday Centre in the coastal town of Skegness. This peculiarly English variety of holiday has traditionally been reserved for the unadventurous tripper, but Eric finds to his horror that his focus of cherished nostalgia has been invaded by the forces of modern philistinism. Even the apparently kindly and civilized characters he meets at the park prove to be bizarre extremists, such as the "old gent" who asserts that the "younger generation" should be "flogged and made to perform disgusting sex acts, and have electrodes attached to their genitals and have their feet eaten by red ants." Eric is alone among savages, as his son goes back to nature, his daughter becomes a religious zealot, and his wife an insatiable sexual addict. Eventually cracking, he exacts steely-eyed, sadistic revenge on the world at large.

Nicholson uses the innocuous location to amplify the sense of horror, particularly in the bloodbath that follows Eric's personal epiphany. The violence dispensed is quite appalling, yet could almost pass without comment in a conventional horror/thriller. He attacks routine acceptance of gratuitously violent "entertainment" by lifting the genre out of the context that comforts the audience or reader. Thus, this parody appears in stark relief against an unlikely background. As in movies, the arbitrary violence has no negative consequences–there is no grief or repentance for the many dead, and Eric has no regrets whatsoever about his crimes. *What We Did on Our Holidays* is a comedy of the absurd, yet the humor is uneasy. Nicholson's skill is in compelling the reader to confront his or her attitude to violence as entertainment, sweetening the unpalatable with injections of comedy.

His next novel, *Hunters and Gatherers* (1991), can in many ways be seen as a quintessential Nicholson work. Generally well received, it forms a characteristic whole from the themes and devices seen elsewhere in isolation. John Skow in *Time* (23 January 1995) wrote, "Nicholson's tale is not so much a novel as it is a collection of loosely related fiction riffs, but it does not suffer at all from its lack of connective tissue." Characters and events hang together largely because of huge and unbelievable coincidences that intertwine and overlap throughout the story. Here it seems Nicholson is satirizing the process of novel writing itself. Plot devices are knowingly obvious and outrageously contrived as Nicholson pokes fun at the tricks of his own trade. The central character, Steve Geddes, is a writer and former barman, recently divorced and intrigued by people's individual obsessions. Nicholson has commented, "It seems I generally write about characters who are obsessed one way or another. . . . I write about the relationship between people and objects." Geddes pursues information for a book on collectors, but as he researches he becomes afflicted with writer's block and distracted by a growing obsession with a little-known and reclusive author named Thornton McCain. The works of McCain make up the thread that holds all the characters' independent tales together.

As Geddes goes from collector to hobbyist, expecting to find them amusing and pathetic, Nicholson creates a series of strong and weird characters. There is the nymphet, who collects sexual conquests and will have sex with anyone at all providing it offers a unique experience. There is the teenage girl who records sound in all imaginable forms, including different types of silence. There is the beer-can collector who may or may not have held and lost the finest collection in the world. Gradually Geddes's stock of research forms into his own collection, which he tries in vain to shape into coherent prose. The touchstone idea present throughout Nicholson's work emerges fully in this novel. Writing in *Booklist* (1 December 1994), reviewer Donna Seaman identified it, commenting on "people's attempts to bring meaning and order into their lives through acquisition." Geddes realizes that collecting "is an act of appropriation. . . . You decide what matters and what's valuable. You make a neat world." Obsession and accumulation are all about control, Nicholson observes, about having power over one's life and influencing one's environment. People's collections mimic perfect imaginary worlds.

In the same year he published *Hunters and Gatherers,* Nicholson also published his first nonfiction book. *Big Noises: Rock Guitar in the 1990s* (1991) has a cultish appeal, mainly to fans of rock music. Nicholson offers critiques of famous (and not so famous) electric guitarists, introduced with a humorous scene in which he (as author) is examined by a psychiatrist and espouses his idea of great music and guitar heroes. He explains why he has chosen the thirty-seven individuals whose short but impassioned biographical sketches make up the book. Nicholson summarizes the respective styles and talents of his chosen heroes and closes the book with "One Hundred More Mighty Guitar Moments," a tongue-in-cheek "listening list." It is difficult to imagine the book exciting a reader who is not already interested in rock music, but from the immediate inclusion of technical details, Nicholson is presumably preaching to a converted readership. His own affection for his subject dominates the book, just as in *Street Sleeper.* Clearly, by now Nicholson was prepared to take risks with his career–having found his feet in the world of novel writing, he quickly branched off to try something different.

In Nicholson's fifth novel, the darkly complex comedy *The Food Chain* (1992), black humor holds sway. The critical reception to the book was largely favorable: the reviewer for *Publishers Weekly* (6 September 1998), writing on the audio version of the novel, maintained that it "sets him firmly in the contemporary British mode of savvy, morbid humour pioneered by compatriots like Martin Amis and Pete Davies." *The Food Chain* has certain elements of the Nicholson formula–the male central character, struggling to solve a mystery while "finding himself" in the process, and the sexually uninhibited supporting female are both present. Here the focus is firmly on appetite–for food, sex, and death. Nicholson's hero is an arrogant and largely unpleasant young restaurateur, Virgil Marcel. Invited to join an exclusive and ancient English society called the Everlasting Club, he is initiated into a world of wanton and sickening gluttony, reminiscent of James Joyce's "Lestrygonians" sequence in *Ulysses* (1922). As Marisa Januzzi pointed out in the *Review of Contemporary Fiction* (Fall 1993),

Dust jacket for the U.S. edition of Nicholson's 1991 novel, in which a writer develops an obsession with a reclusive fellow author (Richland County Public Library)

"though we can elevate cooking and even hunger to the status of art, the act of eating . . . can be enough to ruin a civilised appetite." The members gorge on overly rich, mismatched food and drink, but Nicholson gives an indication from the first that there is more to this feasting than meets the eye. The darker purpose, hints the club name and history (excerpts of which appear regularly interspersed with the main text), is of vampirish significance. Not until the final chapter of the book does Nicholson reveal whether the club members are cannibals.

Virgil's refusal to join the club results in his kidnapping, whereupon he is taken on a gastronomic and sexual tour of Britain by Rose, who is being paid by the Everlasting Club to "fatten him up." Nicholson makes Rose into a mine of information on the regional delicacies and folklore of British food. She forces Virgil to consume everything he enjoys to excess, until he loathes all things carnal and culinary. This loathing becomes his redemption–stripped of desire for sensual pleasures, Virgil develops into an unselfish and sympathetic character. The Christian ideals of sin and redemption are inverted by his transformation–it is gluttony, not fasting, that saves Virgil, overindulgence rather than self-denial. His tortuous trip around the food of Britain becomes a pilgrimage of sorts, and by the close of the novel he is a charitable, likeable character dedicated to overseas "food aid."

The more disturbing aspects in the novel are the "Scenes from the History of the Everlasting Club." A few of these sections are merely humorous. Others, though, involving the savagely sexual and cannibalistic murders of young boys in Germany between the wars, the poisonous excesses of the Marquis de Sade, and the infamous consumption of dead teammates by a Uruguayan rugby team stranded after a plane crash, to name a few, make grim and at times stomach-turning reading. Again and again Nicholson confronts the reader with a grisly Eucharist, all suggesting that what perpetuates the Everlasting Club is the continuity that comes from consuming its own members. This grimy detail of the novel makes it uncomfortable and often shocking to read. If anything, it prompts a reassessment of what readers find humorous, which may or may not be what Nicholson is encouraging. Here is death, here are "unnatural acts," and the reader is able to read on with amusement and revulsion in similar measures.

While writing *The Food Chain,* Nicholson was gathering material for another book, his second book of nonfiction. *Day Trips to the Desert: A Sort of Travel Book* (1992) is a confessional of sorts, a highly intimate and personal snapshot of Nicholson's life around this time. Although he had intended the book to be a desert travelogue, a "wry, oblique, possibly comic account of travelling through the desert southwest with a certain timidity and a rented car," the reality of life interrupted this ideal, and in the event the book became "about" a great many other things. Nicholson had recently separated from his wife and returned to London after a spell in his native Yorkshire when he began researching the book, but his father suddenly died from cancer, and this unexpected event inevitably colors most of his desert experiences, from the Australian outback to Death Valley. While it was obviously important to him at the time to write about such private events in an exposed and honest way, Nicholson has come to regret the baring of his soul in *Day Trips to the Desert,* remarking, "I wouldn't write that book if I had my time again." The book is raw with guilt and regret, as he confesses intimate details about his divorce, his family, and his barely suppressed desire to escape the pressures of his father's illness. "We all do things we regret," comments

Nicholson, "unfortunately when you're a writer you do them on paper." *Day Trips to the Desert* borders on the uncomfortable–the reader knows Nicholson a little too well by the end–but it is well written, atmospheric, and affecting. It was clearly an emotionally draining effort and part of his grieving process, which perhaps goes some way toward explaining the limitations of the next book he published.

Although published the year after, the knowingly titled *The Errol Flynn Novel* (1993) was also in production while the events chronicled in *Day Trips to the Desert* were taking place. Throughout 1991, while the end of his marriage and death of his father infused the research for his book on deserts, Nicholson was also writing *The Errol Flynn Novel.* He comments, "Having a non-fiction and a fiction project on the go at the same time seems to work quite well–each is a respite from the other." While *The Errol Flynn Novel* is at least brightly entertaining in parts, it remains unsatisfying, a big idea that never fulfills its promise. The skeletal plot and characters in the novel never flesh out convincingly, and it seems a step backward from the solid and self-assured *Hunters and Gatherers* and *The Food Chain.* Nicholson remarks that it was "pretty much ignored" by most critics.

The narrator, Jake, guides the reader through this uncertain tale, recounting how as a young English actor he played the lead in an Errol Flynn movie biography, directed by an American hustler, Dan Ryan. Nicholson has clearly researched the movie star in great detail, since a succession of diverting biographical details are duly trotted out by Jake as he researches his role. Erratic production on the movie, however, suddenly halts, and a dubious plot device takes the story to Las Vegas. Characters and events seem senseless, and it is difficult to deduce what Nicholson wants his readers to conclude from them. Ryan's wife, Tina, and his leading lady, Sacha, are both sexually exploited by him, though they seem passive and willing accomplices. Both offer sexual favors to Jake to help Ryan's causes; indeed, Sacha's complicity seems all the more bizarre as she claims to have been raped by Ryan. Ryan himself, emulating Errol Flynn, ruthlessly uses and abuses people in general, and Jake rails indignantly yet feebly against his injustices. The anticlimactic ending caps off the sense of dissatisfaction.

With *Still Life with Volkswagens* Nicholson returned to confessional mode and seemed to hit his stride again with a much more full and complex novel. It is ostensibly a sequel to *Street Sleeper* but, distractingly, also has snatches of autobiographical material, in which Nicholson describes his relationship with the Volkswagen Beetle and its role in his friendships, his marriage, and its ending. The tone is personal but anecdotal, and the passages are as much about the car as they are about his former wife and friends. Also included are more quasi-factual moments from the history of the Beetle–including its use by Elvis Presley, Charles Manson, and Ted Bundy. Even in the main plot many different characters and story lines jostle for attention, making it anything but a still life. A tremendous effort is discernible as Nicholson strives to keep all the threads moving independently of one another, finally binding them together at the climax of the novel. Various characters from *Street Sleeper* reappear, and new ones include a troop of neo-Nazis bent on reclaiming the Volkswagen as a symbol of fascist terror. Their leader is in pursuit of a famous piece of Beetle memorabilia made for Hitler himself–a Holy Grail of fascism.

Some critics seemed to regard it as a romp with little substance, as the reviewer in *Publishers Weekly* (21 August 1995) put it: "Nicholson's satiric talent has enough horsepower to make thrilling a meandering ride to nowhere in particular." Full of incident, *Still Life with Volkswagens* is another look at the love/hate relationship between people and objects of desire. The ruthless collector will kill, kidnap, and torture in order to possess an automaton made for Hitler. On the other hand, a hatred of objects and a desire to destroy them is embodied in Ishmael's great love, Marilyn Lederer's father and Fat Les, the former Beetle fan who now bombs the cars. Extreme emotions climax in a violent clash at an enthusiasts' rally, demonstrating the terrible dangers of obsession. What is interesting is that Nicholson can celebrate the quirks of cult culture–the love of objects, the desire to collect–while simultaneously warning against attaching too much importance to objects of desire or, indeed, anything. Extremes are almost always dangerous–extreme love and hate become virtually inseparable.

Everything and More (1994) is a satirical slice of department-store life, no doubt inspired by Nicholson's spell working at Harrods as a furniture salesman in the days before he became a novelist. Haden Brothers is a grandiose concern by even the standards of Harrods, improbably housed in a 1930s re-creation of Pieter Bruegel's painting of the Tower of Babel and claiming to sell "everything and more." Critical praise abounds for the novel. Mary Carroll in *Booklist* (1 June 1995) wrote, "Nicholson's clockwork emporium provides a vivid setting for this very British yet universal comedy of modern manners and morals." Truly, the Haden Brothers building is layered with all imaginable goods and secrets. Arnold Haden, the owner (invoking the lifestyle of reclusive millionaire Howard Hughes), lives in a sterile apartment on the top floor, insulated from reality. Below in the basement lurks a

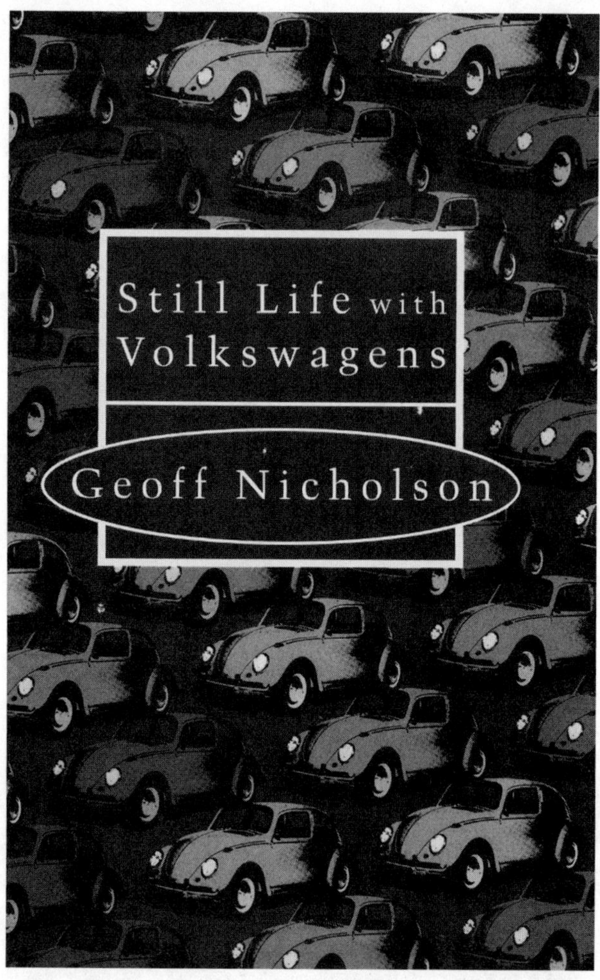

Dust jacket for the U.S. edition of Nicholson's 1994 novel in which the competing obsessions of Volkswagen enthusiasts lead to violent clashes (Richland County Public Library)

similar apartment, secret home of the shop's architect, who (in a neat allusion to Gaston Leroux's *The Phantom of the Opera,* 1910) has been hiding out in a network of secret passages, a world within a world, where he can observe life without involvement. Nicholson opens the novel with the climactic events of the story and then proceeds to tell, using flashback and character monologues, what brought the protagonists to this situation. Suspense is maintained until the final chapters, mysteries are gradually unfolded, and the many pieces fall into place to provide a satisfying and complete conclusion. The many characters achieve what they aim to achieve, though not in a manner anticipated or welcomed.

Everything and More treats the themes of obsession and collecting that govern most of Nicholson's novels in a refreshing manner. Arnold Haden is the only character who could be termed obsessed; haunted by his past, he has shrunk into his penthouse hermitage, alone with his fantasies. In this way he controls his world absolutely. Nicholson's comment about his work charting the relationship between people and objects is often true, and *Everything and More* is no exception. The difference here is that Haden does not collect objects; in his quest for "anonymity and featurelessness," he has removed "anything he might attach himself to." Instead of the dangers of fixative collecting, readers are shown the dehumanizing effect of eschewing all objects. Haden's rehabilitation into the living world is signified by the redecoration of his blank white apartment, when colors and objets d'art are permitted to intrude at last.

Nicholson's next novel was the risqué *Footsucker* (1995), which details the private life of a committed foot and shoe fetishist. Nothing so half-baked as a "partialist," he is at pains to point out, the narrator is a fully fledged fetishist, for whom the female foot is the beginning and end of erotic desire. Much of the criticism for *Footsucker,* though undoubtedly favorable, was colored by reviewers' determination to have their own jokes with the subject matter. For instance, Susan Jeffreys puns in the *New Statesman and Society* (8 December 1995): "You do find yourself seeing the beauty of a good foot and have some idea what these chaps get so worked up about–a sort of Footsucker Proxy." The hero and narrator of this novel remains, unusually for Nicholson, anonymous, but he is anything but an enigma. His anonymity seems consistent with his professed desire to keep his fetishism a secret from even his closest friends. At variance with this concealment are his elaborations on the most lurid details of his personal life, including his tastes, fantasies, and relationship with Catherine, possessor of the feet of his dreams.

Nicholson explores fetish psychology convincingly, as his hero introduces his world with unashamed and articulate candor. He visualizes his perfect foot in painstaking detail, along with the kinds of shoes he adores and abhors, listing shoe designers and styles with the ease of the fanatic. Nicholson is well versed in shoes and psychology, as his hero mulls over the professional opinions of various psychologists (from Sigmund Freud to the pioneer theorist of fetishism, Richard von Kraft-Ebbing) on what engenders the fetishist personality. Most of these positions are dismissed–the hero hates to be labeled or defined and, it appears, likes to distinguish himself from other fetishists. His desires are reasonable, whereas others' are "unhealthy." Unsurprisingly for a Nicholson hero, the fetishist has a collection, an "archive" of which he is the "curator," an attempt at validation that is both touching and disturbing. As in other Nicholson stories, the enthusiast has a minutely researched, indexed

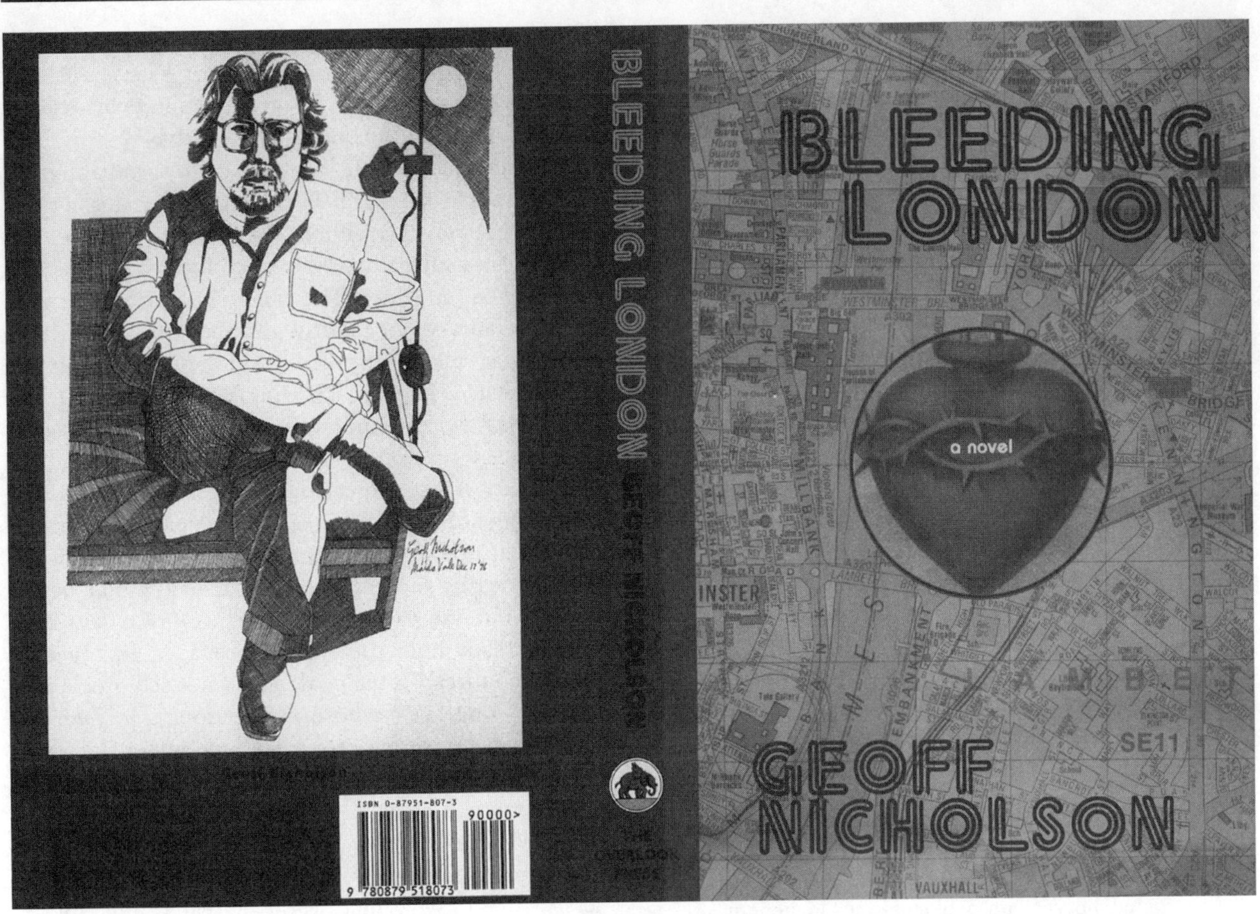

Dust jacket for the U.S. edition of Nicholson's 1997 novel, in which the three main characters are obsessed with the geographical layout of London (Richland County Public Library)

shrine at which to worship, in this case a multimedia library of shoes. This collection symbolizes the secret personality of the character–the more extreme aspects of his nature being folded up and locked away from his closest friends.

Nicholson is neither condemnatory nor congratulatory of his hero's habits, but he does show the disastrous effect of allowing his private obsession out of the hidden recesses of the archive. As the narrator guides the reader around his secret shrine to shoes and feet, he speaks of "the urge to share it with someone." Catherine is the only character to know the full implications of his obsession, and this invasion of his private consciousness, however much he welcomes it, is its undoing. As he becomes more daring and unguarded, the couple's activities lead to murder. The hero's anonymity and dignity are stripped away and the secret obsession routed, but, having endured psychological and physical trials, the character achieves a fresh start. The plotline involving the murder is introduced late in the novel and seems incongruous, featuring as it does an implausible policeman (highly reminiscent of *What We Did on Our Holidays*) who tortures and terrorizes the hero. Although the plot device is worked in to become the motivation behind the hero's development, its juxtaposition is at odds with the convincing realism of previous chapters.

Nicholson followed *Footsucker* with his most accomplished and intensely detailed novel to date, *Bleeding London.* In spite of mixed reviews, it was shortlisted for the 1997 Whitbread Novel of the Year Award. It focuses heavily on obsession and coincidence; the events and characters twine tightly around each other to form a complete and complex whole. London itself is the prime mover, providing location, motivation, and impetus, moving the story line like an omnipotent presence. There are three major characters, around whom the many other secondary characters revolve. The one with whom the reader becomes most familiar is Mick Wilton, the peculiarly moralizing "hired gun" from Nicholson's native Sheffield in the North of England. Mick travels to London to revenge himself on six alleged rapists of his girlfriend, setting about the task with method and imaginative flair. He meets Judy Tanaka, a memorable addition to Nicholson's stock of sex-addict females, who is ambitious to experience congress in every postal district of London. To this end she marks off her every sexual experience against a map of the city. One who coincides with many of these trysts is Stuart London, the third major character in the novel. Stuart has an obsession in common with Judy–a fascination with the city of London. Having founded a thriving tour-guide company, he finds his interest in the business is overwhelmed by his love of London itself. He decides to walk every street in the city, marking them on an A-Z map and recording his experiences in a secret diary, before committing suicide.

Marilyn Lederer, introduced in *Street Sleeper* and *Still Life with Volkswagens,* appears briefly as the presenter of a late-night radio phone-in program. Nicholson has included her as an anchor to his previous works, a signpost to his first novel to chart how far he has matured as a writer. *Bleeding London* is indeed a far cry from the adventures of Ishmael and his friends–it is deeply immersed in place and character, displaying a great deal of complexity, with authority about London, demonstrated impressively in Stuart's diary entries:

> In Bentinck Street, Mayfair, I saw a tall imposing bay-fronted house with a blue plaque in honour of Edward Gibbon, author of *Decline and Fall of the Roman Empire*. . . . I read the plaque more closely and Gibbon didn't actually live in *this* house but in a house "on this site." I felt a little cheated, and then I realised that was how it was always likely to be. When we say Edward Gibbon lived here, or this was where Elizabeth Browning met Byron, or this was where Christopher Marlowe was killed, or this is where Samuel Johnson walked, what do we mean by "here"? The here has gone just as surely as the now.

Stuart and Mick are convincing, as are most of the characters, with the exception of Judy, whose notion that she is somehow "becoming" London (by the end of the novel she has acquired a tattooed map of the River Thames on her body) is not really explained, nor is her fixation with geographical sex. Tim Haigh of *The Independent on Sunday* (18 May 1997) wrote: "Although she has many attractive quirks, Judy is never a really convincing character. Her sexuality is a plot device." Many of the female characters in Nicholson's novels seem mainly to be creatures of ardent and fixative sexual appetite, comparable with sirens or succubi. The principal females in *What We Did on Our Holidays, Hunters and Gatherers, The Food Chain, The Errol Flynn Novel,* and *Bedlam Burning* (2000) exhibit this quality. While some of his novels feature fully realized female characters who can equal the males in sensitivity and depth (such as Jenny Slade or Vita Carlisle), it is difficult to know what Nicholson expects his readers to conclude from the ones such as Judy.

Flesh Guitar (1998) harks back to the avant-garde playwriting with which Nicholson began his writing career. The novel is without plot, or at best has a loose one, set in a surreal world evoked by disjointed fables and broken time lines. The central character is a figure of male fantasy, a beautiful girl and the greatest electric guitar player in the world, whose instrument bleeds when played. The book opens with Jenny Slade's last performance and proceeds to recall a selection of scenes from her life history. It is soon clear that the reader is not expected to take these scenes seriously–Nicholson contrives to have his character present at notorious moments in rock history, including the deaths and epiphanies of several guitar heroes throughout the twentieth century. Only a few common threads hold the story, such as it is, together. One such thread is the evidence of her self-proclaimed "number-one fan," whose publication, *The Journal of Sladean Studies,* provides several sections of the narrative. This fanzine compounds the fantasy atmosphere of the novel as a whole–for instance, the weird and cleverly funny "Moby Dick" entry, in which a musician known as Johnny Ahab or "the Captain" relentlessly pursues what he calls the "Great White Noise."

Nicholson describes the novel as having received "some poisonous reviews." It is obviously a personal novel, written, as was his earlier homage to the electric guitar, *Big Noises,* with real passion for the music and its players. Nicholson's interest in the subject matter could be said to have drowned out the narrative. As Pam Barrett puts it in *The Sunday Times* (21 March 1999), "Sounds great, but what does it mean? . . . The effect is like standing too close to a speaker, the cacophonous prose hitting you in a squall of white noise." Andrew Smith, however, also writing in *The Sunday Times* (6 December 1998), assessed *Flesh Guitar* as a "rock novel," finding the work "imaginative," "very funny," and "priceless."

Following *Flesh Guitar* is *Female Ruins* (1999), another novel to feature a female central character. Kelly Howell is not one of Nicholson's familiar sexual obsessives but a likably flawed creation, a believable heroine ill at ease with herself and her past. The novel is interspersed with essays written by her now-deceased father, a well-known academic architect and revered theorist; he is the past that she simultaneously wants to forget but longs to recall. Kelly is disconnected in her own life; she feels a failure in the sense that she has not pursued a creative career comparable with her father's. A taxi driver in rural Suffolk, she lives alone and seems to have no real friends. Nicholson offers snapshots of a blank, unfulfilled life, stifled by loneliness. As she acknowledges, "There was a need in her that she feared the mere presence of another person could never wholly satisfy. It wasn't about sex or love, it was about vacuity, hollowness."

An odd, similarly flawed character appears, demanding a guided tour around East Anglia, which leads to a whistle-stop trip around architectural and historical points of interest, places Nicholson obviously knows well. Kelly guides Dexter around ruins, ancient churches, and seaside towns, and they collect souvenirs, convenient miniatures of buildings, safe versions of a real world to add to Dexter's father's model town. Eventually, Kelly discovers that he owns the only building her father ever completed, and Dexter takes her to see it in California. She expects some kind of epiphany, and there is indeed one, but Nicholson makes sure that it disappoints and leaves a void at the close of the novel. The knowledge that her father thought himself as much of a failure as she considers herself liberates Kelly to pursue her life exactly the way she wants to. She seems to decide to carry on just as she always has, and the reader is left with a sense of waste and irresolution. As Dominic Bradbury confirmed in the 13 February 1999 edition of *The Times* (London), "he has created a disappointment because, like Kelly, Nicholson's reader is desperate for a deeper truth, some sense of purpose to emerge from her father's life. Kelly's final acceptance of his fallibility may be fearsomely realistic, but it is also shot through with sadness and–ultimately–futility."

With *Bedlam Burning* Nicholson returns to a scene briefly visited in *Still Life with Volkswagens.* Charles Lederer's experiences in the asylum, related in the earlier work, give intriguing glimpses of a colorful collection of mental patients. Five years on, perhaps seeing the potential for further development, Nicholson took these small elements and wove a complete novel around them. He creates a patient, Charles Manning, whose blazer-clad gentility strongly resembles Lederer's character, perhaps by way of an homage to the original inspiration. The story is narrated by the central character, Mike Smith, who progresses from a handsome youth (and seller of collectible books valued by the condition of their covers) to a man who ultimately comes to rely not on his appearance but on his voice, as a radio presenter. He tells how the small deception of allowing his picture to be used on the jacket of Gregory Collin's newly published novel leads to him impersonating the author at a book reading and landing the post of "writer-in-residence" at the Kincaid Clinic, an asylum dedicated to experimental treatments.

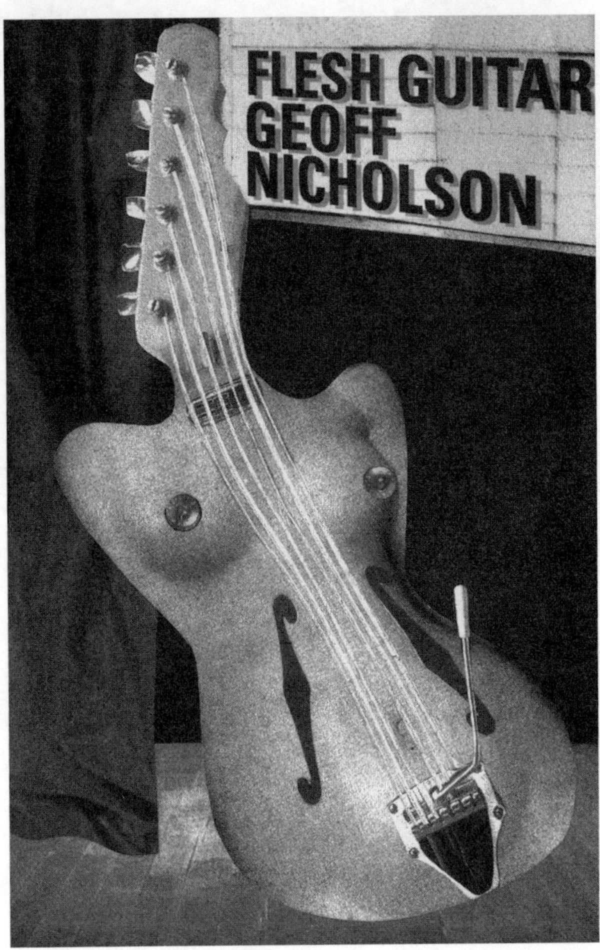

Dust jacket for the U.S. edition of Nicholson's 1998 novel, about a female rock musician whose guitar bleeds when she plays it (Richland County Public Library)

The theory at the heart of this clinic gives the novel its focus and thematic pulse. It postulates that the root of madness is visual stimulation and that only by depriving the insane of any graven images can they be cured. The clinic is as blank and featureless as Arnold Haden's apartment in *Everything and More;* even the food tins in the kitchen have been stripped of their "inflammatory" labels. The written word is deemed an integral part of the cure, thus the need for a writer-in-residence. The paradox is that Smith owes his position at the clinic not to the written word, but to an image; his photo on the jacket of a book. Since most of the staff at the Kincaid Clinic seem at least as mad as the patients, there is plenty of fodder for what D. J. Taylor in *The Independent* (23 September 2000) called "predictable jokes about insanity."

When the patients hint they are just affecting madness so that they can stay on indefinitely and avoid the everyday terrors of the outside world, the reader is left to guess who is sane and who is not. Dr.

Alicia Crowe is a case for debate. She contrives to have wild sex with Smith under cover of darkness, shouting obscenities as encouragement, while shunning him by day. The visual is rejected in favor of the verbal, and the removal of images and objects is shown to have a dehumanizing effect. Black bags are pulled over the patient's heads to "calm" them, but this technique has the dual effect of allowing others to see them as objects. Gill Hornby wrote for the 23 September 2000 edition of *The Times* (London), "there is a darker side at work here. . . . Nicholson has his eye on bullies and repressives everywhere." Smith is dehumanized in his sexual liaisons with Crowe, and at the end of the novel a bag over his head allows others sufficient power to ensure he will never be seen in the same way again. He is disfigured by the author on whose book his picture appears. Just as Smith appropriated Collins's writing, so Collins takes Smith's face. He destroys what is, to the literary world, his own image and so symbolically frees himself.

Geoff Nicholson has only been writing since 1987, and yet his output is impressive both in quantity and quality. He has a workman-like attitude toward his craft, determinedly writing every day and usually developing more than one project simultaneously. Always a keen traveler with a particular affection for the United States, he divides his time between Maida Vale in London and Brooklyn in New York. A significant portion of his work comprises articles and essays for journals and newspapers on both sides of the Atlantic, notably for *The Independent* (London). As varied as his fiction, these articles cover a range of topics from literary review to rock music, gardening, and architecture. Nicholson, it seems, does not intend to stagnate. As he comments, "I have been known to say that I write about people who are obsessed–with women's feet or Volkswagens or whatever–and I certainly understand obsession–but my own obsession is with writing." Roughly half of his novels have been optioned by motion-picture production companies, and he has converted a few into movie scripts, though no movies have appeared as yet. It remains to be seen whether Nicholson will pass from critical notoriety to popular success, as contemporaries such as Iain Banks have done. Given his age and rate of productivity, there is a strong probability that his best work is yet to come.

References:

Dalya Alberge, "McEwan in Final Round for Whitbread Award," *Times* (London), 11 November 1997, p. 14;

Harvey Porlock, "Byline," *Sunday Times* (London), 7 January 1996, p. 2.

Robert Nye

(15 March 1939 -)

Rob Spence
Edge Hill College of Higher Education, Ormskirk, England

See also the Nye entry in *DLB 14: British Novelists Since 1960.*

BOOKS: *Juvenilia 1* (Lowestoft: Scorpion Press, 1961);
Juvenilia 2 (Lowestoft: Scorpion Press, 1963);
Taliesin (London: Faber & Faber, 1966; New York: Hill & Wang, 1967);
March Has Horse's Ears (London: Faber & Faber, 1966; New York: Hill & Wang, 1967);
Doubtfire (London: Calder & Boyars, 1967; New York: Hill & Wang, 1968);
Bee Hunter: Adventures of Beowulf (London: Faber & Faber, 1968; New York: Hill & Wang, 1968); republished as *Beowulf, the Bee Hunter* (London: Faber & Faber, 1972);
Darker Ends (London: Calder & Boyars, 1969; New York: Hill & Wang, 1969);
Tales I Told My Mother (London: Calder & Boyars, 1969; New York: Hill & Wang, 1969);
Wishing Gold (London: Macmillan, 1970; New York: Hill & Wang, 1971);
Sawney Bean, by Nye and William Watson (London: Calder & Boyars, 1970);
Poor Pumpkin (London: Macmillan, 1971; New York: Hill & Wang, 1972); republished as *The Mathematical Princess and Other Stories* (New York: Hill & Wang, 1972);
Agnus Dei (Rushden: Sceptre Press, 1973);
The Seven Deadly Sins: A Mask, words by Nye, music by James Douglas (Rushden: Omphalos Press, 1974);
Two Prayers (Richmond: Keepsake Press, 1974);
Five Dreams (Rushden: Sceptre Press, 1974);
Cricket: Three Tales (Indianapolis: Bobbs-Merrill, 1974); republished as *Once Upon Three Times* (London: Benn, 1978);
Three Plays (London: Calder & Boyars, 1976)–includes *Fugue* [screenplay], *Sisters,* and *Penthesilea,* adapted by Nye from Heinrich Von Kleist's play;
Falstaff (London: Hamilton, 1976; Boston: Little, Brown, 1976);

Robert Nye (photograph by Fay Godwin; from the dust jacket for the U.S. edition of Merlin, *1979)*

Divisions on a Ground (Manchester: Carcanet New Press, 1976);
Out of the World and Back Again (London: Collins, 1977); republished as *Out of This World and Back Again: Three Stories* (Indianapolis: Bobbs-Merrill, 1978);
Merlin (London: Hamilton, 1978; New York: Putnam, 1979);
The Bird of the Golden Land (London: Hamilton, 1980);
Faust (London: Hamilton, 1980; New York: Putnam, 1981);

Harry Pay the Pirate (London: Hamilton, 1981);
The Voyage of the Destiny (London: Hamilton, 1982; New York: Putnam, 1982);
The Facts of Life and Other Fictions (London: Hamilton, 1983);
A Collection of Poems, 1955–1988 (London: Hamilton, 1989);
The Memoirs of Lord Byron: A Novel (London: Hamilton, 1989);
The Life and Death of My Lord Gilles de Rais (London: Hamilton, 1990);
Mrs. Shakespeare: The Complete Works (London: Sinclair-Stevenson, 1993; New York: Arcade, 2000);
Collected Poems (London: Sinclair-Stevenson, 1995);
Lord Fox and Other Spine-Chilling Tales (London: Orion, 1997);
The Late Mr. Shakespeare (London: Chatto & Windus, 1998; New York: Arcade, 1999).

PLAY PRODUCTIONS: *Sawney Bean,* by Nye and William Watson, Edinburgh, 1969;
Sisters, Edinburgh, 1973;
The Seven Deadly Sins: A Mask, words by Nye and music by James Douglas, Stirling, 1973;
Mr. Poe, Edinburgh, 1974.

PRODUCED SCRIPTS: *Sisters,* radio, BBC, 1969;
A Bloody Stupit Hole, radio, BBC, 1970;
Reynolds, Reynolds, radio, BBC, 1971;
Penthesilea, radio, BBC, 1971;
The Devil's Jig, radio, script by Nye, music by Humphrey Searle, BBC, 1980;
Mrs. Shakespeare, radio, BBC, 1998.

OTHER: *A Choice of Sir Walter Raleigh's Verse,* edited by Nye (London: Faber & Faber, 1972);
William Barnes: A Selection of His Poems, edited, with an introduction, by Nye (Oxford: Carcanet, 1972); republished as *Selected Poems* (Manchester & New York: Carcanet, 1988);
A Choice of Swinburne's Verse, edited by Nye (London: Faber & Faber, 1973);
"Visakha," in *Scottish Short Stories,* edited by the Scottish Arts Council (London: Collins, 1973);
"The Lesson," in *Scottish Short Stories, 1974* (London: Collins, 1974);
"The Whole Story," in *Factions,* edited by Giles Gordon and Alex Hamilton (London: Joseph, 1974);
"Remember Young Cecil?" in *Scottish Short Stories, 1975* (London: Collins, 1975);
The Faber Book of Sonnets, edited by Nye (London: Faber & Faber, 1976); republished as *A Book of Sonnets* (New York: Oxford University Press, 1976);
The English Sermon 1750–1850, edited by Nye (Manchester: Carcanet, 1976);
"The Facts of Life," in *Arts Council Stories* (London: Hutchinson, 1978);
"The Second Best Bed," in *Shakespeare Stories,* edited by Gordon (London: Hamilton, 1982);
First Awakenings: The Early Poems of Laura Riding, edited, with an introduction, by Nye, Elizabeth Friedmann, and Alan J. Clark (Manchester: Carcanet, 1992; New York: Persea, 1992);
A Selection of the Poems of Laura Riding (Manchester: Carcanet, 1994; New York: Persea, 1996).

The career of Robert Nye might usefully be compared to that of Anthony Burgess. Like Burgess, Nye is a prolific writer with an extensive bibliography and a reputation as a critic. Again, like Burgess, he is primarily known as a novelist but has written with distinction in other modes too, although he would claim that his true vocation is poetry and that the writing of novels merely supports his principal calling. His work as a poet and author of children's fiction has won acclaim, and his collection of short stories *Tales I Told My Mother* (1969) won the James Kennaway Memorial Award. Less-well-known achievements include editing various volumes of poetry by poets as diverse as William Barnes and Sir Walter Ralegh and editing a volume in a series on the English sermon. He has also written several plays for radio. His reputation rests, however, mainly on his novels. These novels, again recalling some of Burgess's work, deal with archetypal and mythical themes and are often intensely intertextual, utilizing both real and fictional characters.

Born in London on 15 March 1939 to Oswald and Frances Weller Nye, Robert Nye attended Southend High School and began to write at an early age. He published some poems in the prestigious *London Magazine* at the age of sixteen. After leaving school, he spent the second half of the 1950s in a succession of mostly menial jobs before becoming a full-time writer in 1961. In 1959 he married Judith Pratt, and the couple had three sons before divorcing in 1967. He became a respected critic during the 1960s, writing for various journals and becoming poetry editor of the *Scotsman.* He later became poetry critic for *The Times* (London) and reviewed fiction for *The Guardian.* After a time in the early 1960s when he lived in North Wales, a region whose mythology provided material for some of the children's books he wrote at the time, Nye lived with his second wife–Aileen Campbell, whom he married in 1968–in Edinburgh, where he was writer in residence at the University of Edinburgh in the academic year 1976–1977. The couple has one daughter. Since then he has made his home in the west of Ireland, where he continues to live. Thus, like Burgess, he has lived much of his life outside his native country.

Following the publication of two volumes of poetry in the early 1960s, his novel-writing career began in 1967 with the publication of *Doubtfire*. This boldly experimental work is not typical of Nye's mature style but still includes elements recognizable in his later writing. The novel, which may be partly autobiographical, set as it is in a seaside town not unlike the one in which Nye grew up, chronicles the thoughts and feelings of William Retz, an adolescent boy enduring a crisis of identity. This bald summary does not convey anything of the extraordinary flavor of this dark composition, in which various narratives compete for the reader's attention. Some passages are written in relatively straightforward third-person narrative and deal with the encounters Retz has with a series of other characters, who are transformed through Retz's consciousness into stylized symbols. The woman (Joan Dark, or Jeanne d'Arc), the enemy (Ben Flamel), the psychiatrist (Dr Sphinx), the father (Og), and the mother (Lil) all feature obsessively in Retz's self-enclosed world. Their appearances are rendered in a bewildering variety of styles, ranging from Beckett-like dialogue, to Joycean stream of consciousness, to pastiche modernist free verse, to collages of tourist material and monologue. Literary and historical references abound in a swiftly changing sequence of scenes, juxtaposed with little or no connecting narrative. The effect is almost cinematic rather than novelistic. In one of the stream-of-consciousness sections, for example, Retz's mind jumps from the realization that the date is the vernal equinox to a meditation on crucifixion:

> The disciples drinking the blood of the slaughtered (poleaxed) bull. The Virgin whore. St John, the viper's son. Good thief. Bad thief. Hamnet, prince of darkness. Lance. Chalice. Sheath. Sang Royal. Real. Quarrel. Vinegar. Adam. Maikpeblis. Did the angel write you a letter? *Je, Jehanne*. Tattooed with ivyleaf. Emptyflesh. The halcyon. His allseeing incredulous butterface. His ornate gingerbread-Gothic heart. Her mother must've eaten a poemgranate seed. You mean a pomegranate? Thicking them with honey. Bubbles. And castrated himself, my dear, to tinkling tangling tingling murmuring music, flutes and drums and symbols. When circumstance permitted. *Remember?*

The richly suggestive and playful language here is typical of many passages in the novel. This allusive, and occasionally elusive, style is both the major strength and weakness of the work. P. H. Porosky, writing in the *Northwest Review* (Summer 1968), suggests that the reader must penetrate the forest of allusions to arrive at the core of the novel: "The reality of Nye's intricately clever nowhere somewhere else is not real because he teaches us that no reality is real. Madness, grotesque bizarreness replace so-called lucidity because, as Nye's characters learn, lucidity is really a fiction, a process of imagination, the mirror image, or finally, as in the case of William Retz, the poem."

Dust jacket for the U.S. edition of Nye's 1976 novel, a fictionalized memoir in which a character created by William Shakespeare recounts his bawdy adventures (Richland County Public Library)

In retrospect, perhaps, this first novel, or anti-novel, can be seen as an attempt by Nye to define his fictional world. Many of the themes and characters that are prominent in later novels are announced in *Doubtfire.* Joan of Arc and Gilles de Retz, or Rais, most obviously feature in *The Life and Death of My Lord Gilles de Rais* (1990), but are also present in *Falstaff* (1976). Merlin, who surfaces occasionally in *Doubtfire* as part of a cluster of intertextual references to T. S. Eliot's *The Waste Land* (1922) and Arthurian literature, is the eponymous subject of Nye's novel of 1978. Christopher Marlowe, a major source for *Faust* (1980), also features at one point. This novel certainly announced Nye as a major and unusual new talent.

Nye's novel-writing career did not resume until the publication of *Falstaff* in 1976. Between *Doubtfire* and *Falstaff,* Nye published three children's books: his retelling of the Beowulf story, *Bee Hunter* (1968); *Wishing Gold* (1970), a fairy tale set in a mythical Ireland; and *Poor Pumpkin* (1971), a collection of stories culled from a variety of folk traditions. In addition, he also published *Tales I Told My Mother,* several plays, and some poetry.

Falstaff was much praised on its publication, and Nye quickly followed this success with two more novels in similar vein, *Merlin* and *Faust.* All three novels take fictional characters and construct an elaborate biography for them. The novels are shot through with bawdy, even lewd, humor but still address large existential issues.

The full title of *Falstaff* gives some indication of the excesses to follow. The title page reads *Falstaff: Being the "Acta Domini Johannis Fastolfe"; or, "Life and Valiant Deeds of Sir John Faustoff"; or, "The Hundred Days War," As Told by Sir John Fastolf, K. G., to His Secretaries William Worcester, Stephen Scrope, Fr. Brackley, Christopher Hanson, Luke Nanton, John Bussard, and Peter Bassett–Now First Transcribed, Arranged, and Edited in Modern Spelling by Robert Nye.* The most common adjective used of the novel at its publication was "Rabelaisian," and with some justice. The narrative celebrates the life of William Shakespeare's character, dwelling chiefly upon his conquests, both martial and amatory, and "correcting" the version revealed in Shakespeare's plays. The central conceit is that Falstaff, at the end of a long and vigorous life, is dictating his memoirs to a series of scribes. As with *Doubtfire,* there is little sense of a plot or character development in the conventional sense. Instead, Nye presents the reader with an avalanche of pungent reminiscences in one hundred short chapters, by turns scatological, bawdy, or sacrilegious, but most of all humorous.

The novel begins, like Laurence Sterne's *Tristram Shandy* (1760–1767), with the begetting of the chief character and shares some other characteristics with Sterne's novel as well, most noticeably the use of digressions and extratextual features. Where Sterne has a chapter on noses, for example, Nye includes one on "The Art of Farting," complete with graphic representations of the particular emissions of some of the characters.

This indicates the playful excess of the narrative, which mirrors the personality of the main character. After dealing with his conception, on the Cerne Abbas giant (a 180–foot figure with an erect phallus carved into a chalk down in Dorset), the novel treats Falstaff's life chronologically. Falstaff manages to explain away his apparent death in Shakespeare's *Henry IV,* part 2 (circa 1597), on the grounds that it was faked to avoid pursuing creditors. This conceit allows Nye to present Falstaff's life, as he tells it to his succession of amanuenses, as a riot of adventure and excess, peopled with characters whose names are drawn almost exclusively from Shakespeare's plays. Sir John is seen as a monk, a nun, a lady-in-waiting, a friend of princes and kings, a soldier, but mostly as a sexually voracious lecher, able to use his "mainspring" (one of twenty-six aliases for his phallus in the chapter "About Sir John Fastolf's Prick") to good effect with an endless succession of compliant women. Of course, Falstaff is, like Shakespeare's character, a liar of epic capacity, and it is no surprise when, following the scribe Scrope's itemized list of charges for his services in "this book of lies," in the penultimate chapter, "Sir John Fastolf's Confession to Friar Brackley," he finally admits the magnitude of his deceit: "Father, I am a vain man, and conceited, and all through these memoirs I have sought, however curiously, the admiration of secretaries and whoever should one day cast his eye upon them. These tricks were mostly through fictitious immodesties. I always cared to picture myself as a great man. I was only ever a fat man, father."

Falstaff was awarded both the Hawthornden Prize and *The Guardian* Fiction Prize in 1976. Critics were especially impressed by the vitality of Nye's language and the liveliness of the execution. A noticeably laudatory assessment was by Anthony Burgess, whose *Nothing Like the Sun* (1964) had covered similar ground more than a decade before. In his *Ninety-Nine Novels: The Best in English Since 1939* (1984), he included *Falstaff,* writing that Nye "combines, very successfully, the forward drive of modern fiction with the divagations of a more monkish tradition."

The second in Nye's series of biographies of fictional characters, *Merlin,* appeared in 1978. The familiar Arthurian tale is given an initial twist by Nye's conception of the hero as the offspring of Satan and a virgin, making him a kind of Antichrist. Again, Nye employs a first-person narrative to tell his tale, which is recognizably that of the familiar legend. Typically, though, Nye embellishes the ancient material with a blend of bawdy humor and recherché learning, the effect of which is to transpose the mood of the ancient tale into a more comic vein while still addressing some of the larger issues suggested by the material. In particular, Nye uses Merlin, a man "locked in the present tense," as a means to discourse on matters of good versus evil and free will versus predestination. The somewhat chilling conclusion is that the world is a book and the devil its author.

As is the case with *Falstaff,* the reader may enjoy Nye's rewriting of familiar material, but what characterizes this book most obviously is the use of humor.

Again, like *Falstaff,* the language and subject matter often verges on the obscene. In *Merlin* Nye again uses a suggestive mixture of the sacred and the profane, juxtaposing sexual innuendo and erudition, pitting low comedy against elaborate artifice. That these comments might equally have been made of *Falstaff* and, to a lesser extent, *Doubtfire* might suggest that Nye was writing in an almost programmatic way at this stage in his career. A more sympathetic viewpoint would be that Nye, after a long apprenticeship, had found his novelist's voice. Certainly, the emphasis on the sexual that disturbed some reviewers of *Falstaff* is present in *Merlin,* but it is a sexuality that by turns appalls and delights. Nye does not use his characters' sexual nature to titillate; rather, he uses it as an element in his re-creation of a thoroughly realized medieval world.

The next novel in Nye's sequence of fictional recreations, *Faust,* was published in 1980. Again, it is a first-person account, though in this case the narrator is not Faust but his "familiar servant and disciple," Kit Wagner. The novel is arranged in three parts: the first, "The Tower," is set in Faust's castle in the Staufen, near Freiburg; the second, "The Road to Rome," is an account of the journey Faust, Wagner, and their entourage make to seek the Pope's blessing and, therefore, regain Faust's soul; and the third part, "Holy Week," concerns the events that befall the group in Rome. This tripartite plot is more tightly structured than Nye's other fictions and is further constrained by a time scheme that limits the action to the forty days of Lent between Ash Wednesday and Good Friday in 1540. Rather than the short chapters favored by Nye in his other novels, this book comprises altogether 178 sections, many of them consisting of just a few lines.

Wagner's narrative begins with an account of an act of necrophilia by Faust, who, in contrast to the versions of Marlowe and Johann Wolfgang von Goethe, is characterized throughout as a foul-smelling, foul-mouthed drunkard. The inhabitants of the castle also include Faust's consort, Helen of Troy; seven girls, each representing one of the languages spoken by Wagner, whose function, it seems, is to offer sexual gratification to them at every opportunity; and a sinister capuchin monkey, Akercocke. The central portion of the novel, concerning the journey to Rome, is an extended tale of debauchery and violence, narrated in laconic style.

The voice of Wagner marks this novel off from Nye's other ventures into this territory. Wagner, who has a minor role in Marlowe's play, takes center stage here. In some respects he is as much the central character as is Faust. Having supplied this character with a first name borrowed from Marlowe, Nye gives Wagner a demotic, aggressively modern voice rather than equip

Dust jacket for the U.S. edition of Nye's 1978 novel, a reworking of Arthurian tales narrated by the legendary wizard (Richland County Public Library)

him with a register replete with medieval locutions, as he did with Falstaff. The title page, like that of *Falstaff* an extravagant, mock-learned description of the contents, suggests that the narrative is "now for the first time Englished from the Low German" by Nye. Certainly, the English of Wagner/Nye is racy, slangy, idiomatic, occasionally obscene, and determinedly twentieth-century throughout. So, a knight in armor is referred to as "a chainmail freak"; Faust is a "screwball" and a "fuck-up"; Helen of Troy is "a sweetie"; the disappearance of Justine, one of Wagner's girls, is greeted with a shrugged "easy come, easy go."

Although there is more emphasis on plot than is the case with Nye's earlier novels, there is still room for a series of strictly irrelevant episodes and jokes. When Wagner finds himself toward the end of the novel in the catacombs of Rome with a snoring Faust, he fills his time by killing flies (one of which, in a Shandean joke, manifests itself on the printed page) and writing jests about Martin Luther.

More seriously, the novel explores the nature of reality and illusion, using the Faust materials in a way similar to the approach Nye uses in *Merlin* as a springboard for the discussion of issues such as determinism and free will. There is also, as is the case in all of Nye's work, an emphasis on the constructed nature of the text. The fictional Wagner reminds readers that he is sticking to the facts, as the truth about Faust is stranger than fiction and is anyway "beyond my imaginative range."

As it must, *Faust* concludes with the damnation of the hero. Typically, though, Nye completes his version with a plot twist that, although not entirely unexpected given the several hints earlier in the novel, provides a new perspective on the familiar story.

Nye's next novel, *The Voyage of the Destiny* (1982), is another first-person narration by a well-known figure. In this case, the figure is an historical, rather than a fictional one: Sir Walter Ralegh. The novel purports to be the journal kept by Ralegh as he sails home from his abortive final South American exploration, searching for gold along the Orinoco, concluding shortly before his execution for treason in 1618. As with *Faust,* the imposition of a rigid time frame produces a certain tightness in the text, as the journal records Ralegh's thoughts over an eight-month period. The overall effect, however, is more akin to the impression produced in *Falstaff,* as Ralegh includes, for the benefit of his son, to whom the journal is addressed, various documents relating to his life: for example, he presents the warrant for his arrest; a document including an insincere apology to the king for the failure of his expedition; and a letter to the Privy Council written by the chaplain of the *Destiny*. The novel is more of an autobiography than a journal, as Ralegh reflects on his life and his mortality, with the final entry being dated 28 October 1618, the day before his execution.

The connotations of the ship's name are not lost on Ralegh or the reader. At one point, in the self-reflexive mode so characteristic of Nye's protagonists, he reflects on the nature of his work in writing the journal:

> This book, I see now, is the log of three voyages.
>
> The first: The Voyage of the Destiny. Set in the present time. . . .
>
> The second: The voyage of my history. The tale of my life and fortunes. . . .
>
> The third voyage is the most difficult to define. . . . The Voyage of the Destiny. That's my third voyage. The true task.

Ralegh, then, is aware of his status both as an historical figure, evidenced in the legal documents and letters that frame his journal, and also as a fictive construct, the subject of the novel that the reader holds. This postmodern blurring of fiction and reality, together with a pervasive playful intertextuality, is typical of Nye's mature style.

The Voyage of the Destiny was followed by a collection of short stories, *The Facts of Life and Other Fictions* (1983), a title that encapsulates Nye's ambivalent attitude to the status of story. This volume once again demonstrates Nye's ability to mix biography and fiction to illuminating effect. Figures such as James Joyce and Anne Hathaway make appearances in a lively and inventive series of tales.

The Memoirs of Lord Byron (1989) continues the trend in Nye's fiction begun in *The Voyage of the Destiny*. Once again, instead of treating fictional characters as historical figures, as he had done in the three-novel sequence beginning with *Falstaff, The Memoirs of Lord Byron* re-creates the Romantic poet as a fictional character. The conceit on which the novel is based concerns the real memoirs of the poet, supposedly destroyed by a committee of family and friends after his death, on the grounds that they were "fit only for a brothel." Nye takes his cue from this opinion, recorded by Byron's executor, Sir John Cam Hobhouse.

In what was by now a familiar style, Nye's first-person narrative begins with the nine-year-old Byron's earliest sexual experiences, at the hands, literally, of his Scottish Calvinist governess. The narrator establishes his current circumstances early on: "I begin these *Memoirs* half-way through my thirtieth year to hell, here at my best stopping-place so far, the Palazzo Mocenigo, in Venice, on Friday the thirteenth of July, 1818, recovering from a dose of the clap and having nothing worse to do."

The novel then proceeds chronologically through Byron's life, though the narrative is framed by interpolations from the thirty-year-old poet in his Venetian convalescence, detailing his affair with the Venetian baker's wife, Margarita. It concludes with two postscripts concerning the deaths of Byron's daughter, Allegra, and of Percy Bysshe Shelley, finishing with a premonition of his own death, which is then duly recorded in an additional third-person passage, headed "Epilogue."

The narrative takes on an episodic, picaresque quality, as the central figure proceeds from school to fame as the author of *Childe Harold's Pilgrimage* (1812–1818), to notoriety as the lover of Lady Caroline Lamb and ostracism after committing incest with his half sister, Augusta. The short chapters are headed in a manner reminiscent of Daniel Defoe or Henry Fielding: "I Inherit a Great Number of Tree Stumps" is one, and "I Proceed on My First Pilgrimage, and Swim the Hellespont, and Save a Girl in a Sack" is another. The narrative is characterized by bawdy humor, with Byron never failing to provide the often racy details of his hectic love life. The chapter headed "(XXX)", in which Byron confesses to incest with his half sister, is the only chapter in the novel in which the ironically colloquial, self-mocking tone, reminiscent of *Don Juan* (1819–1824), is replaced by a poignantly tender voice, wistfully evoking a doomed relationship that resulted in Byron's permanent exile from his homeland.

The Byron who emerges from Nye's novel is a surprisingly sympathetic hero, deeply flawed but nonetheless attractive. Certainly, he is "mad, bad and dangerous to know," as Lady Caroline called him, but also brilliantly witty, generous, extravagant, impulsive, and distinctly vulnerable. Nye's publisher claims on the dust jacket that the book was "scrupulously researched over many years," and that claim is borne out in the mass of incidental detail with which the novel is furnished. It is a completely believable self-portrait of a hugely interesting figure, as well as an accomplished historical novel.

For his next novel Nye returned to a familiar motif first encountered in *Doubtfire:* the story of Joan of Arc and her captain, Gilles de Retz, Marshal of France. Toward the end of *Falstaff,* the knight presents his thoughts on "Joan of Arc. Joan la Pucelle. Joan the Maid. Joan the Puzzell" and her companion "Gilles de Retz. Gilles de Laval. Marshal of France. Bluebeard." Falstaff has, he says, been "a witness to the edges" of their story, claiming to have seen Joan's execution. The chapter leads Falstaff to reflect on the "images of contradiction" symbolized by the relationship between the two and on the confluence of good and evil.

In *The Life and Death of My Lord Gilles de Rais* Nye gives full rein to the story of this Bluebeard figure. As in *Faust,* the perspective is provided by an apparently lowly witness of the events, this time a priest, Dom Eustache Blanchet, who spends the three years prior to de Rais's execution as his servant. The priest is, the reader learns, writing this account in 1457 at the Great Hospital in Milan, where he is being treated for leprosy. He finishes his work on Holy Innocents' Day, a feast of terrible significance in his story.

The novel is organized in three parts of ten chapters each. The first relates Blanchet's history from Christmas Eve 1437, when he is dismissed by his patron, the Bishop of Saint Malo, and resolves to enter the service of de Rais, to the moment two years later when he celebrates Holy Innocents' Day at Tiffauges, the seat of the marshal. The second section concerns the events leading to the arrest of de Rais in the autumn of 1440. The final section is an account of his trial and execution in October 1440.

As in his previous novel, Nye is scrupulous to include dates and real events to lend authenticity to his work, and as in *Faust,* the witness is driven by a desire

Dust jacket for the U.S. edition of Nye's 1982 novel, written in the form of a journal by Sir Walter Ralegh (Richland County Public Library)

to present facts. At the beginning of the third section, for example, Blanchet announces:

> My function for the trial of Gilles de Rais is editorial. I intend to give you all the facts, and to reproduce the necessary documents for your inspection. The story is dire and no story, and I would rather have left it untold, in the darkness to the left and the right of my hand, beyond the margins of saying: but I have no choice.

Like many of Nye's narrators, Blanchet is a compulsive storyteller, though not an unreliable one: the narrative is a serious document, related by one who feels the need for an accurate record. At one point, relating certain alchemical experiments, Blanchet writes: "The reader who considers all this black drivel has my sympathy. I do not approve or condone it, and my function in repeating it here is purely historical." This tone of dogged sobriety lends Nye's narrative its authority. The events treated in this novel are horrific, and Blanchet's self-deprecating and measured prose style points them up more effectively than a more self-consciously dramatic rendition might have done.

Nye is at pains in a note appended to the novel to emphasize the historical accuracy of the work, citing a list of archival and other sources. This insistence on historical verisimilitude, perhaps, combined with an equally heavy emphasis on the primacy of story, characterizes his working methods.

For his next novel Nye returned to Elizabethan England and Shakespeare for his source material. *Mrs. Shakespeare: The Complete Works* (1993) purports to be the writings of Anne Hathaway, compiled in a vellum volume given to her by her daughter, Susanna, in 1622. The novel is, in some ways, a return to the style of *Falstaff.* In a series of short chapters, printed in italics to suggest handwriting, Shakespeare's wife reflects on her life with her husband and casts light upon issues that have exercised Shakespeare's biographers. For example, she gives an account of the famous "second-best" bed and why it was bequeathed to her, and also identifies the dark lady of the sonnets as herself. She professes not to have read her husband's works, preferring her Bible instead, but Nye insinuates some of Shakespeare's best-known phrases into her account, suggesting she might have been the source of such lines as "I know a hawk from a handsaw" from *Hamlet* (circa 1600–1601).

The novel is lighthearted in tone, with much of the humor deriving from the ironic juxtaposition of Shakespeare's genius and Anne's determinedly down-to-earth sensibilities. The whole is a gallimaufry of pleasant delights, replete with recipes, anecdotes, and reports of historical events. The Anne who emerges from this account is more than a Warwickshire housewife: she is a lively, intelligent woman with a sharp preference for plain speaking at all times. She entreats her husband at one point to abandon his poetic language and "tell us in plain words." Nye has Anne completing her story in 1623, the year of the First Folio of Shakespeare's collected plays: her "complete works" are thus ranged against his.

Nye returned to this material shortly afterward with the publication of *The Late Mr. Shakespeare* (1998), another novel in which a minor player–literally, in this case–observes a major historical figure. The narrator here is Pickleherring, an eighty-one-year-old former boy actor, looking back on his career from a Restoration London recently free of the plague and about to be engulfed by the Great Fire. Nye's choice of narrator echoes that of Burgess in *A Dead Man in Deptford* (1993), in which another fictional boy actor presents an account of his life with Marlowe.

Like *Falstaff,* the novel is arranged in a hundred short chapters with often whimsical titles: "In which Anne Hathaway" and "About silk stockings" are two examples, but this book is a much more substantial offering than *Mrs. Shakespeare.* Anecdotes about the life of Shakespeare are interspersed with digressions on Pickleherring's room and the whore he can observe plying her trade through a peephole in the room below. Having baldly stated "All the facts about Mr Shakespeare" on one page, Pickleherring, like others of Nye's narrators, emphasizes the fictional nature of his enterprise:

> These twelve facts are all there is to be known for sure about William Shakespeare from the public records.
>
> But a man's life does not just consist of facts.
>
> Least of all, the life of our Shakespeare.

Nye takes these bare facts and weaves them dextrously into an energetic narrative that includes not only the various legends that have attached themselves to Shakespeare's biography (for example, the youthful stealing of deer) but also some bizarre new inventions (competing suggestions that Shakespeare's mother might have been Elizabeth I or that his father might have been the vicar of Stratford, for instance). One noticeable feature of Pickleherring's narrative is the anachronistic inclusion of various well-known remarks about Shakespeare, either in their correct form or, more commonly, somewhat adapted. The reader is implicitly invited to identify the sources from a list appended as a postscript: some sixty-six names are listed, from Shakespearean scholars such as Samuel Schoenbaum and John Dover Wilson, to contemporaries of Shakespeare such as Marlowe and Ralegh. Also included are a range of writers who have, at some point, commented on Shakespeare–including Jorge Luis Borges, John Keats, Ralph Waldo Emerson, and Thomas Hardy. In a typical in-joke, one name on the list is Robert Nye, and one of Pickleherring's chapters, "Some tales that Shakespeare told his mother," echoes the title of Nye's early collection of short stories.

Pickleherring has a theory for every detail of Shakespeare's career and presents alternative versions for several episodes. For example, the "lost years" are, he suggests, either spent at sea (his preference), as a tutor (as Burgess suggested in *Nothing Like the Sun*), as an apprentice to a lawyer, or as a soldier. In each case textual references are ingeniously adduced to support the competing theories. In the case of the sea theory, Shakespeare's knowledge of seafaring practice in many plays is mentioned, but the detail that convinces Pickleherring, and perhaps the reader, is Jaques's use of the obscure term "remainder biscuit" in *As You Like It* (circa 1599–1600).

At times, the novel reads like a speculative investigation into the biographical evidence provided by the works of the type written by A. L. Rowse, for instance. Nowhere is this quality more apparent than when Pickleherring presents the case of four women who might have been the Dark Lady of the sonnets. The conclusion, that the lady was a prostitute, Lucy Negro, is enlivened by an account of her working practices.

Nye's ludic narrative includes several other postmodern elements. As does Julian Barnes in *Flaubert's Parrot* (1984), Pickleherring offers readers a mock examination paper on his subject. He also presents a "missing" sonnet by Shakespeare, beginning "Shall I compare thee . . . " but continuing with lines culled from various other sonnets, and reproduces the "Shakespeare" section from the play *Sir Thomas More.* At one point Pickleherring muses, "Sometimes I think that Mr Shakespeare lived a life of allegory, and his work was a commentary upon it." Nye's novel uses the work to illuminate the man and in so doing attempts, as Pickleherring puts it, "to come at the truth by telling lies."

The Late Mr. Shakespeare was particularly well received by the critics. Jonathan Bate, in *TLS: The Times Literary Supplement* (5 January 1998), called it a "rich plum-pie" of a novel and praised its inventiveness and wit. The whole, he wrote, is "a glorious confabulation." Once again, Nye has produced a fiction presented as factual, which is nevertheless conscious of its own fictional status. Pickleherring sets out the parameters of his work in an early chapter headed "About this book." In another echo of *Tristram Shandy,* he writes: "This book must not be thought of as a fable or an old wives' tale. Nor is it so much of a cock and bull story as you might care to think. Being jocose, it could even be said to be not incompatible with a taste or a hunger for truth. . . . This is the story of William Shakespeare. It is a pack of lies, and my heart's blood."

Robert Nye's achievement in more than thirty years of prose fiction writing has been to produce a diverse body of work that displays his own wide learning and his passionate concern with the art of storytelling. His work, rooted in English myth, legend, and literature, explores the boundaries between art and life, between fact and fiction, between illusion and reality. His strength is the vitality of his language, richly suggestive and filled with jokes, puns, allusions, quotations, and learned disquisition. Nye has said of his own work: "I do not write short stories as much as tall stories, fibs, lies, whoppers." This applies as much to the novels as to the short stories, and might equally be applied to many of Nye's eccentric gallery of narrators. Nye has tested the boundaries of fiction and continues to do so, offering his readers new challenges with every volume.

Dust jacket for the U.S. edition of Nye's 1998 historical novel, narrated by an elderly man remembering his days as a boy actor in London during William Shakespeare's time (Richland County Public Library)

References:

Anthony Burgess, *Ninety-Nine Novels: The Best in English Since 1939: A Personal Choice* (New York: Summit, 1984);

Andrew Hassam, "Literary Exploration: The Fictive Sea Journals of William Golding, Robert Nye, B. S. Johnson, and Malcolm Lowry," *Ariel: A Review of International Literature,* 19 (July 1988): 29–46;

P. H. Porosky, "The Moth Becomes the Flame," *Northwest Review,* 10 (Summer 1968): 100–104.

Papers:

Collections of Robert Nye's manuscripts and correspondence are held at the University of Texas at Austin; at Colgate University, Hamilton, New York; at Edinburgh University; and at the National Library of Scotland, Edinburgh.

Simon Raven

(28 December 1927 – 12 May 2001)

Nicolas Tredell
University of Sussex

BOOKS: *The Feathers of Death* (London: Blond, 1959; New York: Simon & Schuster, 1960);

Brother Cain (London: Blond, 1959; New York: Simon & Schuster, 1960);

Doctors Wear Scarlet (London: Blond, 1960; New York: Simon & Schuster, 1961);

The English Gentleman: An Essay in Attitudes (London: Blond, 1961); republished as *The Decline of the Gentleman* (New York: Simon & Schuster, 1961);

Close of Play (London: Blond, 1962);

Boys Will Be Boys (London: Blond, 1963);

The Rich Pay Late (London: Blond, 1964; New York: Putnam, 1965);

Friends in Low Places (London: Blond, 1965; New York: Putnam, 1966);

Royal Foundation and Other Plays (London: Blond, 1966)–comprises *Royal Foundation, The Move Up Country, The Doomsday School, The Scapegoat, Panther Larkin, The High King's Tomb, The Gaming Book, Sir Jocelyn,* and *The Minister Would Like a Word;*

The Sabre Squadron (London: Blond, 1966; New York: Harper & Row, 1967);

Fielding Gray (London: Blond, 1967; New York: Beaufort Books, 1985);

The Judas Boy (London: Blond, 1968);

Places Where They Sing (London: Blond, 1970);

Sound the Retreat (London: Blond, 1971; New York: Beaufort Books, 1986);

Come Like Shadows (London: Blond & Briggs, 1972);

Bring Forth the Body (London: Blond & Briggs, 1974);

The Fortunes of Fingel (London: Blond & Briggs, 1976);

The Survivors (London: Blond & Briggs, 1976);

An Inch of Fortune (London: Blond & Briggs, 1980);

The Roses of Picardie: A Romance (London: Blond & Briggs, 1980);

Shadows on the Grass (London: Blond & Briggs, 1982);

September Castle: A Tale of Love (London: Blond & Briggs, 1983);

Morning Star (London: Blond & Briggs, 1984);

The Face of the Waters (London: Blond, 1985);

Before the Cock Crow (London: Muller, Blond & White, 1986);

Simon Raven (photograph by Jerry Bauer; from the dust jacket for the U.S. edition of The Sabre Squadron, *1966)*

The Old School: A Study in the Oddities of the English Public School System (London: Hamilton, 1986);

The Old Gang: A Sporting and Military Memoir (London: Hamilton, 1988);

New Seed for Old (London: Muller, 1988);

Bird of Ill-Omen (London: Hamilton, 1989);

Blood of My Bone (London: Muller, 1989);

In the Image of God (London: Muller, 1990);

"Is There Anybody There?" Said the Traveller: Memories of a Private Nuisance (London: Muller, 1990);

The Troubadour (London: Hutchinson, 1992);

The Islands of Sorrow (London: Winged Lion, 1994).

PRODUCED SCRIPTS: *Triad,* radio, loosely based on Thucydides' *History of the Peloponnesian War,* BBC, 1965–1968;

Point Counter Point, television, based on the novel by Aldous Huxley, BBC2, 1968;

The Way We Live Now, television, based on the novel by Anthony Trollope, BBC, 1969;

Unman, Wittering and Zigo, motion picture, based on the play by Giles Cooper, Paramount, 1971;

The Pallisers, television, based on the novels by Trollope, BBC, 1974;

An Unofficial Rose, television, based on the novel by Iris Murdoch, BBC, 28 December 1974;

Edward and Mrs Simpson, television, based on the biography *Edward VIII* by Frances Donaldson, Thames Television, 1978;

Love in a Cold Climate, television, based on the novels by Nancy Mitford, Thames Television, 1980;

The Blackheath Poisonings, television, based on a novel by Julian Symons, Thames Television, 1993.

OTHER: *The Best of Gerald Kersh,* edited by Raven (London: Heinemann, 1960).

Simon Raven was a highly productive writer who made a significant and distinctive contribution to postwar English fiction, especially in the ten novels of his "Alms for Oblivion" sequence, published between 1964 and 1976. The world that Raven explores in his work is the intricate, influential world of the British upper middle classes in the convulsive period from 1945 to the 1970s: his main characters emerge from and move between the key institutions of that world–the public school, Cambridge, the army, the Houses of Parliament, the intellectual journal, the publishing house that aims to combine culture with commerce. His characters also rub shoulders with and sometimes enter into other, less public zones, however: of prostitution of a kind that caters to idiosyncratic sexual tastes; of homosexuality in a society in which, until 1967, same-sex relationships between those defined as consenting adults were illegal; of Cold War espionage; of popular journalism. Raven portrays a stratum of society that is deeply threatened both by its own desires and follies and by social and political change: his novels aim to dramatize key aspects of the history of postwar England such as the loss of empire, the fiasco of Suez, the recognition of military and economic subordination to the United States, the election of Labour governments in 1945, 1964, and 1966, the growth of student protest in the later 1960s, and the increasing importance of the media, especially television.

To an extent Raven's work might be seen as elegiac, the portrayal of what he himself called an ancien régime, and one that might seem destined for oblivion. Raven's fiction could also appear to demonstrate, however, the resilience and adaptability of that ancien régime, its capacity to make concessions in order to retain its influence and power. His fiction is marked by a tension between nostalgia and energy, between lamenting a world that seems to be dying and registering its ability to renew itself. Raven's portrayal of this world is extremely skillful; his best work combines lucid, witty narrative prose, strong dialogue, and complex, compelling plots.

Simon Arthur Noel Raven was born 28 December 1927, the son of Arthur Godart Raven and Esther Kate Raven (née Christmas). His father lived on the proceeds of his share of the hosiery business that his grandfather, William Raven, had built up. Simon Raven's early years were spent mainly in Virginia Water, Surrey; at the age of eight, in May 1936, his parents sent him as a boarder to Cordwalles School in Camberley, where, by his own account, the games master seduced him. In 1941 he won a scholarship to Charterhouse, a leading English public school. He proved a good classical scholar, and the reading of ancient Greek and Latin texts continued to be important throughout his life and contributed to the economy of his prose style and to the robustness of his worldview. In his own eyes, however, his greatest achievement was to win a place in a First XI cricket team that included Peter May, later captain of the England cricket squad, and James Prior, who became a minister in Margaret Thatcher's government and finally a peer. Raven's career at Charterhouse came to a scandalous end, however, when he was expelled in 1945 for homosexuality, an event that receives fictional treatment in the fourth novel of the "Alms for Oblivion" sequence, *Fielding Gray* (1967). He was already acquiring an identity that remained with him throughout his life, as an "inside outsider," with friends and contacts in the most influential echelons of British society but with a reputation for transgression that often threatened to put him beyond the pale.

Raven did his national service in the Parachute Regiment, when he was posted as an officer cadet to Bangalore in India and commissioned. His experience of India in the last days of the British Raj fed into the seventh volume of the "Alms for Oblivion" sequence, *Sound the Retreat* (1971). He returned to England in 1948 and went up to King's College, Cambridge, to read the classics. As he had done at Charterhouse, he did well academically and on the sports field, taking a first in Part 1 of the Classical Tripos and winning two English essay prizes, and playing cricket and squash for his college and royal tennis for the university. He also, however, drank, gambled, got into debt, and engaged in both homosexual and heterosexual adventures. He hoped to become a fellow of King's, but failed to obtain a First in his finals, gaining only a 2:1 (Upper Second) degree; King's nonetheless awarded him a studentship

Dust jacket for Raven's 1962 novel, in which a young man drops out of Cambridge and becomes a pimp and a murderer (Bruccoli Clark Layman Archives)

that provided financial support for him to research the influence of the classics on Victorian public schools.

Raven then learned that Susan Mandeville Kilner, a student at Newnham College, Cambridge, with whom he had been having an affair, was pregnant. He married her in 1951, and their child, Adam, was born in March 1952. He disliked married life, however, and distanced himself from its claims; he was divorced in 1957. He became notorious for his response to a telegram that said "Wife and baby starving. Send money soonest." Raven replied: "Sorry no money. Suggest eat baby." Raven's treatment of Susan and his son confirmed his reputation as a cad.

He also failed to do any research work; he had, however, been laying the foundations of a literary career by reviewing novels for *The Listener* and working on a novel of his own, called "A Passage to Biarritz." The manuscript has many of the ingredients of Raven's later novels; it is the story of Esme Sangrail Sa Foy, who is taken on as a holiday tutor to a rich woman's son and becomes a blackmailer and a swindler. "A Passage to Biarritz" drew significantly on some of Raven's own recent experiences, and it was not published because of fears that it would provoke actions for libel. It eventually came out, under the title *An Inch of Fortune,* in 1980.

The rejection of "A Passage to Biarritz" made Raven decide to turn away from literature for a time; he enlisted again in the army, and from 1953 to 1956 he served in the KSLI–the King's Own Shropshire Light Infantry–in Germany and Kenya before being posted back to Shrewsbury in England. As an officer he was expected to represent the regiment at local horse-race meetings but went well beyond the call of duty in incurring debts that he could not meet–conduct unbecoming an officer and a gentleman that would have resulted in a court-martial and probable dismissal if an official complaint had been made. His commandant engineered his discreet resignation, and he left the army to become a full-time writer. While he continued to drink, gamble, and behave promiscuously as long as his health and finances held out, he also proved a disciplined writer, settling down to work assiduously at 9:30 each morning whatever the dissipations of the night before and producing an enormous body of high-quality material: novels, memoirs, nonfiction books, articles, reviews, radio plays, and television plays and adaptations.

Raven's first novel, *The Feathers of Death* (1959), was commissioned by the publisher Anthony Blond on the basis of a synopsis Raven submitted to him. Blond continued to publish his work for many years and provided an important element of stability in his life, paying him a regular stipend and insisting that he live more than fifty miles from London to avoid the temptations of the capital; Raven did most of his work in Deal, on the Kent coast. Raven completed *The Feathers of Death* in ten weeks, sending it in sections to Blond, who was soon convinced of its quality. *The Feathers of Death* focuses on the love affair between two soldiers, Lieutenant Alistair Lynch and Drummer Malcolm Harley. The story is told by Andrew Lamont, an intelligence officer in a mounted infantry regiment that has been posted to the British colony of Pepromene. After a skirmish in the foothills with African guerrillas, Harley is found dead, killed not by the enemy but by Lynch, who claims that he shot him for disobeying orders. Simes, Harley's friend, claims that Lynch murdered Harley because Harley had publicly rejected him. Lamont knows, from talking privately to Lynch, that the issue of Lynch's guilt is ambiguous, but Lynch is acquitted at his court- martial. Simes then, however, administers his own rough justice by killing Lynch with a bayonet thrust in the back.

The Feathers of Death received good, though qualified, reviews. John Coleman in *The Spectator* (30 January 1959) found that Raven "handles the development of his complex plot with considerable mastery" and "has a cool, balanced style, as precise and unlyrical" as that of Evelyn Waugh. The comparison between Raven and Waugh was a recurrent one in Raven's career, though more often to Raven's disadvantage than not. Coleman also felt, however, that Lynch was too lightweight as a central figure–once again, a charge that continued to be brought against Raven's central characters, right up to the figure of Raisley Conyngham in his final series of novels. In *The New Statesman* (31 January 1959), however, James Kennaway praised Raven for "the clarity of his characterisation, the simplicity of his prose, and the design of his plot" but detected, "Superimposed upon much closely-observed detail," "a sort of grand neo-classical dream in which men are brave, arrogant, rich, 'civilized' . . . and ambidextrous"–by which Kennaway meant "bisexual." Kennaway perceptively observes, in Raven's first novel, a tension between realism and romanticism that persists throughout his work. There is one aspect of *The Feathers of Death,* however, in which romanticism and realism fruitfully converge to provide a powerful analysis and indictment of homophobia. Here, for example, is the narrator's description of one of the officers at the court-martial, Brigadier Milner:

> Bullying, insistent, flat-voiced, common, he did not even have the advantage of being an ex-ranker, with all the understanding such experience normally confers. He had proceeded in 1939 . . . straight from his employment in a midland factory to a commission in the R.A.O.C. [Royal Army Ordnance Corps], had hung on and prospered after the war, and had now come to represent all the worst features of the post-war Army, in which such as he, with their grubby technical know-how, had of necessity to be retained. Everything about Alistair, his voice, appearance, uniform and mental attitude, was calculated to annoy Milner; and the mention of homosexuality could not fail to be an additional irritant. He had all the makings, to judge from his presence, of a man pathologically inimical to homosexuals and their behaviour; and even if this were not the case, a man of Milner's background and attainments could only view Alistair's affair with Harley at best as the irresponsible and malignant pastime of a degenerate wordling.

Milner's attitude contrasts with those of Major-General Osborne and Colonel Grail: "I could not imagine that either of them would be unduly dismayed by the idea of a homosexual liaison–they were surely above middle- class prejudices of that kind." In a way that is characteristic of Raven, reactionary snobbery is combined with an affirmation of sexual liberty.

The treatment of homosexuality in *The Feathers of Death* was remarkably frank for its time, and the controversial nature of Raven's first novel combined with favorable review responses to promote its rise toward the best-seller lists and to result in the sale of paperback, movie, and American rights. Raven was launched as a novelist with a distinctive identity. His next novel, *Brother Cain* (1959), features a protagonist, Jacinth Crewe, whose caddish career bears some resemblance to Raven's; Crewe is expelled from school for homosexuality, is sent down from Cambridge, and resigns from the army because he cannot pay his debts. Needing £5,000 urgently, he joins a terrorist organization secretly financed by the British government that uses dirty tricks–including murder by the transmission of venereal disease–to combat Communism in the Mediterranean. *Brother Cain* was less well received than *The Feathers of Death:* the anonymous review in the 23 October 1959 edition of *The Times Literary Supplement* (*TLS*) charged that Raven "calls Kraft-Ebbing and Havelock Ellis to add the spice of perversity to the insipidities of Edwardian romance," especially as represented by "the dream-world of John Buchan." This sort of comparison with popular authors was a frequent refrain in reviews of Raven's work; Coleman in *The Spectator* (23 October 1959) detected in "the chilly, jolly tone" of *Brother Cain* faint echoes of Ian Fleming, author of the James Bond novels, as well as of Daisy Ashford, famous for a novel she wrote at the age of nine, *The Young Visiters* (1919). A more positive response to *Brother Cain* came, however, from Paul West in *The New Statesman,* who concluded that "Raven's fable has a clear point, is pungently written and starts disquieting trains of thought."

Raven's third novel, *Doctors Wear Scarlet* (1960), focuses on a young Cambridge archaeologist, Richard Fountain, whose scholarly and sporting prowess seems to promise much but whose sadomasochistic tendencies emerge strongly when, staying in Greece, he becomes involved with a female vampire. At a time when English fiction was still strongly dominated by the idea of realism, the introduction of the vampire seemed to relegate the novel to a lower literary status and provoked comparisons with popular writers: Buchan again; Bram Stoker, the author of *Dracula* (1897); Dennis Wheatley, one of whose specialities was the satanic thriller; and the crime writers Dornford Yates, Edgar Wallace, and Sapper (H. C. McNeile). The sense of the way in which *Doctors Wear Scarlet* mixed genres and hovered between literary respectability and subcultural sensationalism is summed up in the description in the anonymous review in *TLS* (2 December 1960), which called the novel "a gruesome mixture of *Brideshead Revisited,* Buchan and Bram Stoker."

Dust jacket for Raven's 1964 novel, the first in his ten-volume "Alms for Oblivion" series, which chronicles the corruption of the British upper middle class (Bruccoli Clark Layman Archives)

In 1961 Raven published his first nonfiction book, *The English Gentleman: An Essay in Attitudes*–an entertaining history of "that honourable figure of a vanished age" that is also a kind of autobiography that provides glimpses into Raven's own experiences of Charterhouse, Cambridge, and the army that complement his fiction. Raven began writing for radio and television in 1961, and nine of his radio and television plays were published in 1966 in a volume called *Royal Foundation and Other Plays.* While developing his career as a radio and television writer, Raven continued to produce reviews and articles for *The Listener, The Observer* (London), *Punch,* and *The Spectator.* He was most at home in *The Spectator,* in which he published some of his best journalism and showed his capacity both to please and outrage the largely conservative readership of that journal.

His main energies went into his fiction, however, and his fourth novel, *Close of Play,* appeared in 1962. Like *Doctors Wear Scarlet,* this novel features another promising young man who goes to the bad. Hugo Warren, in his final term at Cambridge, throws away all his opportunities, betrays his friends, and becomes a pimp and finally a murderer who dumps his mistress's body in the desert, only to find that her contraceptive device prevents the evidence of his crime from being totally consumed by vultures. The comparison between Raven and Waugh was once more invoked, this time by Laurence Lerner in *The Listener* (15 November 1962), who judged that, despite the resemblances, the novel lacked "the sharp reality that gives an edge to Waugh's comedy" and was finally more of a thriller than a satire. The mixing of genres was once again observed by the anonymous reviewer in *TLS* (16 November 1962), who judged that, while "always pungent," its combination of "sex, melodrama, demimonde debauches and self-conscious amorality, with simple English goodness symbolized by glorious *Boy's Own* afternoons on the cricket field, does not really come off." Maurice Richardson in *The New Statesman* (16 November 1962) also found *Close of Play* "weirdly uneven" but nonetheless called it "a most diverting moral tract."

It was becoming clear that Raven's literary reputation was an insecure one. To stake his claim on posterity, he proposed to Blond that he embark on a sequence of novels that would focus on English upper-middle-class life since the end of World War II and, in particular, on the role his own generation had played and was playing in that life. In a passage quoted in Michael Barber's biography *The Captain: The Life and Times of Simon Raven* (1996), Raven says that his intention was "to write ten independent stories with common characters and a common theme. In short, a roman-fleuve." The common theme was concisely summarized in Raven's contribution to *Contemporary Novelists* (1986): "the vanity of human wishes." That theme is echoed by the title of the sequence, which comes from Ulysses' speech in act 3, scene 3 of William Shakespeare's play *Troilus and Cressida* (circa 1601–1602)–"Time hath, my lord, / A wallet at his back, wherein he puts / Alms for oblivion." Raven claimed, however, that the more immediate source of the title was Herman Wouk's blockbuster novel *Youngblood Hawke* (1962), whose eponymous writer-hero has written a novel called *Alms for Oblivion.*

Blond commissioned the whole series. It was a time at which the novel sequences of Anthony Powell, "A Dance to the Music of Time" (twelve novels between 1951 and 1975), and of C. P. Snow, "Strangers and Brothers" (eleven novels between 1940 and 1970), were still in progress and receiving considerable attention. Raven planned to start the sequence with a story set in 1945, but Blond wanted a more contemporary tale to begin with, so the first novel of "Alms for Oblivion" to appear, *The Rich Pay Late* (1964), is set in the buildup to a watershed moment in postwar British history: the attempt in 1956 of British, French, and Israeli forces to regain control of the Suez Canal after it had been nationalized by President Gamal Abdel Nasser of Egypt. The novel introduces significant characters who recur in later novels of this sequence and, in many cases, in Raven's later sequence, "The First Born of Egypt." The most memorable of these is Somerset Lloyd-James, the editor of an influential commercial and political journal called *Strix,* a complex young man who combines an unprepossessing physical appearance, considerable personal presence, a capacity for ruthless manipulation, a devout Roman Catholicism, and a taste for being spanked. Other key characters include Peter Morrison, a large, slow, honorable, slightly pompous member of Parliament who leads a group of reforming Conservatives, and Tom Llewellyn, a Welshman of left-wing leanings who has risen from a humble background and is on the verge of becoming a successful writer of books on politics and economics, but who still has a tendency to outrageous behavior.

The plot centers on the attempt by a thrusting young partner in a printing firm, Jude Holbrook, to buy *Strix* from its owner, Lord Philby, despite clauses in the constitution of the magazine that prohibit such a sale; Holbrook attempts to coerce Morrison, who is on the board of *Strix,* to fall in with his plans by threatening to rake up an alleged scandal in which, as a teenager, Morrison made a young working-class woman pregnant. Although the allegation is questionable, Morrison nonetheless uses it as a pretext to resign his parliamentary seat because he feels that if he remains an MP, he will have to criticize the behavior of the government in the impending Suez crisis.

The Rich Pay Late plunges the reader into a world of intrigue, chicanery, hypocrisy, and imminent scandal, in which even apparently honorable behavior starts to look dubious. Although the novel is set in 1956 and vividly evokes aspects of Britain immediately prior to the Suez crisis, its vision of English upper-middle-class life seemed especially resonant in the year of its publication, 1964, which was still experiencing the fallout from the Profumo scandal of the previous year that had revealed an intricate network of links between high life and low life, government, espionage, and sexual transgression.

The main plot of the novel is accompanied by a range of subplots; for example, a piece of cruel black comedy in which Holbrook's secretary, Miss Beatty, finally gets her senile mother into an old people's home and hopes to make up for lost time by inviting a man back to her flat–only to be murdered by her first visitor. (Ashley Dexterside, who works for Holbrook's firm, recalls the mother's response to the news of her daughter's death: "You know what the idiot mum did when we told her? She sat there and screamed with laughter.") Throughout *The Rich Pay Late,* Raven employs a highly skilled narrative technique, combining dialogue, authorial comment, and free indirect style in which the thoughts of characters are rendered in the third person and the past tense but employ the words and phrases that those characters might actually be expected to use. He cuts effectively from scene to scene to create suspense and give a sense of the way in which events take place simultaneously and the way in which they converge to create climaxes. *The Rich Pay Late* also provides an example of one of Raven's specialities–a social or public event at which things go wrong. In this novel it is a party with echoes of those in F. Scott Fitzgerald's novel *The Great Gatsby* (1925) and Federico Fellini's motion picture *La Dolce Vita* (1960), where the host has some money stolen and Llewellyn makes a scene and insults Morrison and his wife. Despite its technical accomplishments, *The Rich Pay Late* was criticized by reviewers for its thin characterization, its weak dialogue, and its heartlessness. In *The New Statesman* (2 October 1964), the critic Christopher Ricks, contemplating the future of the series, observed: "one can't help wondering whether the author has enough malice, squalor and perversion in reserve."

Friends in Low Places (1965), set in 1959, employs the same narrative and stylistic techniques as *The Rich Pay Late* and is equally vivid, comic, and compelling. The main plot in this novel focuses on the quest for a letter that implicates government ministers in chicanery over Suez; Lloyd-James, continuing to show the capacity for ruthless self-interest that he revealed in *The Rich Pay Late,* wants to use the letter to secure his nomination as a Conservative candidate against Morrison, who is seeking to return to Parliament; Holbrook, who has now become an out-and-out criminal, is also keen to secure the letter. The novel combines the threat of scandal that was also an important aspect of *The Rich Pay Late* with a thriller element, particularly evident in a powerful scene in which Holbrook tortures Lloyd-James in order to force him to disclose the whereabouts of the letter–a scene that also sets up an analogy between Holbrook's self-serving physical sadism and Lloyd-James's manipulation of others through intrigue to get what he wants. Holbrook is finally outwitted by Fielding Gray, a figure crucial to the "Alms for Oblivion" sequence as a whole: Gray first appears in this novel as a former soldier, disfigured by a bomb in Cyprus, who wants to become a writer but still shows himself capable of being a man of action.

Friends in Low Places is also notable for its comedy–for example, in its portrayal of Lord Canteloupe, who, having turned his stately home into a profitable public attraction, is appointed Parliamentary Secretary for the Development of British Recreational Resources and decides to open a series of holiday camps that will combine leisure activity with moral uplift. Raven's capacity for the highly amusing orchestration of dialogue is shown in the discussion between Canteloupe and Lloyd-James of their plans for the first camp:

> "This one that'll be ready in June . . . where is it?"
> "Somerset. No, not you–the Quantocks."
> "Splendid. We'll give it some sensible west country name . . . 'Drake,' perhaps–"
> "–Wasn't he a Devon man?–"
> "–No need to be pedantic. A bracing west country name, a royal opening on television, and presto, in moves the first lot of campers–"
> "–Wearing lederhosen–"
> "–Singing Jerusalem–"
> "–Men and women hand in hand, but peeling off emphatically to separate quarters–"
> "–Except for the family parties with bright-eyed children to prove it–"
> "–Service of dedication–"
> "–Taken by Donald Soper–"
> "–Accompanied by a skiffle group–"
> "–And I've got just the name. Westward Ho!"

High comedy, with darker undertones, also characterizes the big social event that features in this novel and that suffers a more spectacular disruption than the party in *The Rich Pay Late.* The anonymous reviewer in *TLS* (14 October 1965) called the novel "mostly political comedy with deftly mentioned elements of the thriller, echoes of the early Waugh and, incongruously or otherwise, of Trollope." The comparison to Anthony Trollope anticipates Raven's later adaptation of Trollope's Palliser novels for television.

The third novel in the "Alms for Oblivion" sequence, *The Sabre Squadron* (1966), adopts a different technique. Instead of the often rapid crosscutting between different scenes and the viewpoints, thoughts, and feelings of different characters, the narrative, though told in the third person, focuses on one character, Daniel Mond. The novel travels back in time to 1952. Daniel Mond, a brilliant, half-Jewish Cambridge mathematician, goes to Göttingen in Germany on a postgraduate research fellowship to study the hitherto undeciphered mathematical notation of the Dortmund papers, left behind by a physicist who died in 1938. He is befriended by Earle Restarick, an American who later turns out to be an intelligence agent and who is interested in the possible military applications of Dortmund's work. Restarick's plan to extract information from Mond is thwarted, however, because soldiers of a British squadron who are in Germany on exercises to deal with the aftermath of a possible nuclear attack take Mond under their wing. One of the soldiers is Fielding Gray, prior to his disfigurement by the Cyprus bomb. When Mond succeeds in deciphering Dortmund's notation, he feels that he has discovered a secret that poses an even more profound threat than atomic fission, a threat to the structure of the universe itself; but it is clear that the Americans are determined to force him to yield up his secret. The soldiers of the British squadron try to help him to escape, but things go wrong, and he eventually ends up in Restarick's hands. When he is told that he must reveal Dortmund's secret or the soldiers who helped him will be denounced and disgraced, he decides to kill himself. The novel ends at this point. While *The Sabre Squadron* certainly engages with crucial issues, it is a rather uneasy mixture of a Cold War thriller, a metaphysical speculation, and a romance of male bonding. Review responses were lukewarm, although the novelist William Cooper, in *The Listener* (20 December 1966), applauded Raven as "a fine narrator," and John Daniel, in *The Spectator* (14 October 1966), called him "a moralist."

Fielding Gray, the fourth novel in the "Alms for Oblivion" sequence, is the one that Raven had originally intended to write first. The novel takes the form of a journal in which Gray recalls the latter part of his life at school; Gray's journal starts in the school chapel in 1945, with a memorial service to commemorate the dead and contemplate the future. While reading the "Alms for Oblivion" sequence in the chronological order of the events it describes may make for greater clarity, it does remove one of the fascinating aspects of reading the sequence in the order in which its novels first appeared–encountering characters such as Lloyd-James and Morrison, whom the reader has already got to know in later life, at earlier stages of their existence. The focus of this novel is on Gray himself and on the series of traumas that he suffers: learning about these traumas, the reader feels that the physical disfigurement that Gray is later to suffer is a kind of culmination and correlative of his emotional and intellectual disfigurement. The first trauma is his love for, and brief sexual encounter with, a younger pupil, Christopher, who subsequently kills himself because he believes, not without reason, that Gray has rejected him. This loss is compounded by Gray's expulsion from school and then by the determination, first of his father, and then, after his father's death, of his mother, to thwart his attempts to go to university. *Fielding Gray* is an absorbing, deeply felt novel in which a young man is painfully marked, early in life, by the consequences of transgression and by the frustrations of his ambitions; and, like Dorian Gray, whose surname he shares, the marks will eventually show on his face. William Buchan, in *The Spectator* (22 September 1967), commended Raven's "skill and power as a moralist," though he overidentifies with those characters in the novel, such as Morrison, who roundly condemn Gray's behavior toward Christopher. *Fielding Gray* shows not only Gray's culpability but also what Desmond Mac Namara, in his review of the novel in *The New Statesman* (15 September 1967), calls the "virtuous hypocrisy" of Gray's self-appointed judges. The anonymous review in *TLS* (14 September 1967) makes the interesting claim that *Fielding Gray* has the "occasional flavour of a right-wing E. M. Forster," a remark that could be developed and applied more widely to Raven's fiction.

The fifth novel of the "Alms for Oblivion" sequence, *The Judas Boy,* was published in 1968. Like *The Sabre Squadron, The Judas Boy* is a rather uneasy amalgam of a Cold War thriller and a homoerotic romance that tends toward sentimentality, even though it has some powerful moments. Gray, now a recognized and moderately successful novelist, is asked by Llewellyn, who has briefly become a British Broadcasting Corporation (BBC) producer, to investigate the possibility that, in the Cyprus conflict, General Grivas, the leader of the Greek Cypriot underground group EOKA, was encouraged by the Americans to employ terrorist methods. In an incident that might have come straight out of the James Bond novels, an attempt is made to kill Gray as he is on his way to Athens to try to contact Grivas, by separating the railway coach he is in from the train that is pulling it and letting it run off the edge of a cliff. Gray survives, however, and reaches Greece, where a powerful means of distraction is arranged; a young Greek boy, Nicos, appears, as if by magic, who seems like a reincarnation of Christopher, the dead love of his school days. Meanwhile, Tom is sacked from the BBC because of irregularities over his National Insurance payments, so Gray's project no longer enjoys any backing; but he has become obsessed with Nicos and is devastated when he learns that Nicos was a plant, deliberately intended to distract his attention, who apparently never cared for him at all.

Dust jacket for the U.S. edition of Raven's 1966 novel, the third in his "Alms for Oblivion" series, in which a Cambridge mathematician in Germany is caught between the competing interests of the American and British militaries (Richland County Public Library)

Returning again and again to Mycenae, the scene of the revelation of Nicos's perfidy, and obsessively reenacting their separation, Gray is eventually rescued by Harriet Ongley, a wealthy American who becomes his partner for several years. Although some of the scenes both in London and Greece are powerful, the novel does not quite hang together, and it hovers between sensationalism and seriousness. As the novelist and critic Auberon Waugh observed sardonically in *The Spectator* (27 September 1968), "it never quite makes up its mind whether it is a Bond-style thriller or whether it is yet another important modern novel." The anonymous review in *TLS* (3 October 1968) found it "more Eric Ambler than Ian Fleming" and felt that the "Alms for Oblivion" series was becoming "increasingly odd."

Raven had greater success in 1968 with a television adaptation of a novel that employed a technique of rapid crosscutting between scenes and characters similar to that which he himself had employed in the first two novels of the "Alms for Oblivion" series; the novel was Aldous Huxley's *Point Counter Point* (1928), and Raven's version, broadcast on BBC2, received a good critical reception. Raven followed up its success in 1969 with a television adaptation of Trollope's massive novel *The Way We Live Now* (1874–1875).

Places Where They Sing (1970), the sixth novel of the "Alms for Oblivion" sequence, returns to England and to the student revolts of the later 1960s. The setting is Lancaster College, Cambridge, where Llewellyn is now a research fellow. The plot of the novel focuses on the debate within the college over the most appropriate way in which to use a surplus of £250,000 that has been acquired through the sale of land. Radical students and their supporters seize on the issue to provoke disruption: the novel culminates in another superbly sustained scene of a public event that is disrupted–in this case, a madrigal concert in the college chapel that is interrupted when a brass band and a procession of student rebels invade the sacred premises and come close to destroying the precious east window. While Raven is effective and entertaining in his rendering of this disruption and in his evocation of the internal debates in the college committee, his portrayal of the radical students and their allies is less successful, falling into vagueness and caricature, in a way rather similar to that of Snow in his attempts to deal with student revolt in *The Sleep of Reason* (1968). *Places Where They Sing* is also an oddly insular novel. Whereas earlier novels in the sequence had shown an awareness of the global dimensions of national and local political struggles, this one, apart from a few joking references to Fidel Castro and Che Guevara, ignores them, most notably making no mention of the Vietnam War. *Places Where They Sing* received poor reviews: the reviewer in *TLS* (26 February 1970) said that "The pattern is well-wrought but only as a collage of odd juxtapositions which jar and startle."

Raven is on firmer ground with the seventh novel of the "Alms for Oblivion" sequence, *Sound the Retreat,* which is set mainly in India in 1945, where Morrison, then a second lieutenant, is involved in the suppression of a campaign of civil disobedience mounted by his former commanding officer, Gilzail Khan–a campaign that is aimed at preventing rather than hastening British withdrawal, which Khan believes will lead to internecine conflict between Hindu and Muslim. The British authorities, however, find Khan an irritant–they want to quit India as soon as is decently possible–and a chain of events is set in motion that leads to Khan's death and earns Morrison, along with two of his brother officers, a viceregal commendation that seems to mark him for future success. The reader who comes to *Sound the Retreat* after the previous volumes of "Alms for Oblivion" is already aware that Morrison's career will be a complex and checkered one, however. Reviewers praised the readability of the novel but found it pessimistic and deeply dispiriting.

Come Like Shadows (1972) returns readers, in the eighth novel of the "Alms for Oblivion" sequence, to Gray and draws to some extent on the experience Raven himself had gained of the motion-picture industry when he had been asked to improve the script of the James Bond movie *On Her Majesty's Secret Service* (1969). Gray's project, however, seems at first to have high-cultural credentials; Llewellyn has asked him to undertake, for a tempting fee, a movie adaptation of *The Odyssey.* Fielding accepts the task and is gratified at its financial rewards; but he also has a strong sense of responsibility to Homer, his favorite poet since the age of fifteen: "as Fielding considered the task before him, he recognized a duty as well as a mere means to money. He must keep faith with Homer and show his gratitude even while supplying his greed."

The task is complicated by a range of economic and political pressures, however–for example, the plan of a young actress involved in the movie, Sasha Grimes, to provide Odysseus with a social conscience so that he repents his killing of the Cyclops, who is really no more than an innocent shepherd; suffers acute guilt at his exploitation of Circe and Calypso; and gives away his land, money, and power to found a commune when he returns to Ithaca. Gray becomes sexually involved with Sasha and also gains control of the finances of the movie in a way that enables him to hold the film company to ransom. The company contrives to have him arrested by the Greek colonels as a dangerous subversive, and with the help of the American secret agent Earle Restarick, an attempt is made to turn him into a heroin addict so that he will confess to plotting against the regime. Rescue comes just in time, and he returns to England to find, to his relief, that

Harriet has left; he settles down to work on a book on Joseph Conrad.

Like some of the earlier novels in the sequence, such as *The Judas Boy, Come Like Shadows* is uneven. When Raven focuses on Gray, he sometimes loses his detachment, allowing Gray to become an outlet for a streak of sentimentality or a mouthpiece for unexamined prejudices and irritations; the latter aspect is to the fore in *Come Like Shadows*. The theme of the collision between the writer and the movie industry is a familiar one–it occurs in Christopher Isherwood's *Prater Violet* (1945), for example–and Raven handles it quite effectively but without any great originality. The most interesting aspects of the novel are its explorations of the processes of adaptation, but these are weakened by the heavy-handed satire on progressive attitudes, in which *The Spectator* columnist all too often takes over from the novelist. The largely negative review responses sometimes broadened into reflections into the "Alms for Oblivion" series as a whole, now that it was nearing completion. The reviewer for *TLS* (27 October 1972) summed up the series as "capable yarns which are often funny and clever, which sometimes read like parodies of low pornography and occasionally achieve an uncomfortable memorability." In *The New Statesman* (27 October 1972), Peter Buckman reflected that, "Considering the immense talent and craft of his earlier novels, the series might be seen as an albatross which he and some of his critics could be glad to see slip beneath the waves."

The ninth novel of the "Alms for Oblivion" sequence, *Bring Forth the Body* (1974), is a much more successful work than *Come Like Shadows*. It opens with a startling and unexpected event: the discovery of Lloyd-James dead in his bath, with his wrists slashed. The suicide at first seems inexplicable: Lloyd-James is a Roman Catholic and, by now, a wealthy man and a highly successful politician. The novel becomes a kind of detective story in which Captain Detterling, a figure who has featured in several of the previous novels, explores Lloyd-James's earlier life and tries to discover the reasons for his self-slaughter. *Bring Forth the Body* works well because of the focus provided by the mystery of Lloyd-James's motives and because it is more concerned to search the past than to try to engage with the present–a present from which, on the evidence of *Places Where They Sing* and *Come Like Shadows,* Raven had become increasingly alienated. It began to seem that he was now at his best reviving the past for the present. His appeal was not only to an older generation of readers, however. *Bring Forth the Body* received particular praise from a younger critic who has himself become a distinguished novelist, Peter Ackroyd. In *The Spectator* (2 November 1974) Ackroyd called the novel "a British

Dust jacket for the U.S. edition of Raven's 1967 novel, the fourth in his "Alms for Oblivion" series, in which the title character remembers his school days and a homosexual affair that came to a tragic end (Richland County Public Library)

fiction of the most traditional and entertaining kind, and all the more solid for being self-consciously so." This commendation might be part of a recipe for Ackroyd's own later fiction and implicitly raises the more general question of Raven's influence on later generations of British novelists. Raven's capacity to revive the past for the present was apparent in 1974, not only in *Bring Forth the Body* but also in the twenty-six episodes of his adaptation for BBC television of Trollope's six Palliser novels (1864–1880), a series that was successful although it received some criticism for taking too many licenses with Trollope's original. Raven himself inserted an amusing self-congratulatory reference to the series in his later novel *The Troubadour* (1992), where one of the characters asks: "What was it that Trollope said of the old Duke of Omnium–the one played by Ronald Culver in that admirable dramatisation by Simon Raven?"

In 1974 Raven's adaptation of Iris Murdoch's novel *An Unofficial Rose* (1962) was broadcast on BBC

TV, and in 1976 the tenth and final volume of the "Alms for Oblivion" sequence, *The Survivors,* was published. The novel is set in Venice and makes full use of the associations of decay and corruption which that city has acquired in literature. The survivors who gather there in 1973 include Gray, Llewellyn, Captain Detterling, and Mond, who survived the suicide attempt at the end of *The Sabre Squadron* but who is now gravely ill. Detterling finds that he has inherited Lord Canteloupe's marquessate in lieu of any other heir, while Gray, intrigued by an unexplained young man in a late-eighteenth-century family portrait, carries out an investigation that reveals the true Canteloupe descendant. Mond dies, and Morrison, now minister of commerce, arrives in Venice determined to put the needs of commerce above those of conservation. The novel ends with a roll call of familiar characters that modulates into a powerful image of corruption as a dark stain spreads across the lagoon.

The completion of the tenth and last "Alms for Oblivion" novel prompted reviewers to offer their verdict on the sequence as a whole. These assessments ranged from the hostile to the highly positive. The case against Raven was forcefully made in *The New Statesman* (11 June 1976) by the critic and novelist Julian Symons, who judged the series readable but "artistically negligible," a mere "collection of strip cartoons." Raven's talents lay in the fields of melodrama and "wild, lubricious comedy" but were not suited to sustain a grand overall theme. At the other end of the critical spectrum, T. G. Rosenthal, in the 21 June 1976 edition of *The Times* (London), found in "Alms for Oblivion" "the splendid architectonic skill of a flawlessly executed grand design."

With "Alms for Oblivion" finished, Raven turned to other writing. His connection with BBC TV lapsed, but he made further significant adaptations for Thames TV. *Edward and Mrs Simpson* (1978), a serial based on Frances Donaldson's biography of Edward VIII, was well received, and in 1980 his eight-part dramatization of Nancy Mitford's novels *The Pursuit of Love* (1945) and *Love in a Cold Climate* (1949) proved highly entertaining. Also in 1980, his first novel since the completion of the "Alms for Oblivion" sequence was published. *The Roses of Picardie: A Romance* gave full vent to Raven's Gothic and Romantic impulses while reintroducing two minor characters from "Alms for Oblivion," Jacquiz Helmut and Balbo Blakeney, each of whom embarks independently on a quest for the roses of the title, which are in fact twelve enormously valuable rubies strung on a necklace. The novel divided critics. In *The Listener* (14 February 1980) John Naughton judged that the "whole outrageous mixture, nonsense on stilts from beginning to end, is marvellously entertaining, civilized, erudite and decadent," but Francis King in *The Spectator* (19 January 1980) felt that this "farrago of crime, intrigue, sex, the occult and science fiction" was too far removed from reality.

In 1982 Raven began another venture with his memoir *Shadows on the Grass,* which was followed by further memoirs: *The Old School: A Study in the Oddities of the English Public School System* (1986), *The Old Gang: A Sporting and Military Memoir* (1988), *Bird of Ill-Omen* (1989), and *"Is There Anybody There?" Said the Traveller: Memories of a Private Nuisance* (1990). These memoirs were unconventional in that they employed dialogue in the manner of a novel and seemed, not least to some of those people mentioned in them, to be more fictional than factual. In a review of *"Is There Anybody There?" Said the Traveller* in *The Spectator* (26 January 1991), Raven's long-time publisher, Blond, observed that the book was seared by the "savage searchlight of the novelist's imagination" and proceeded to sue Raven for libel–one of a flurry of writs that caused the withdrawal of the book. Raven was on safer ground with fiction. The novel that followed *The Roses of Picardie, September Castle: A Tale of Love* (1983), is, like its predecessor, in a Gothic and Romantic mode and focuses again on a competitive quest, this time for the truth about, and treasure of, the Lady Xanthippe, a thirteenth-century Greek princess once held hostage in the Castle of Arques. Philip Howard, in the 3 March 1983 edition of *The Times* (London), called the novel "ghoulish, indecent, stylish, funny, clever," and Valentine Cunningham in *TLS* (26 June 1983) felt that, while *The Roses of Picardie* had been a "long drawn-out dud," *September Castle* was a "short," "sparky," and "cumulatively powerful fiction."

Raven was not willing to rest content with one-off successes, however: the lure of the novel sequence was drawing him again. His next novel, *Morning Star* (1984), was presented as the inaugural volume of a second series, "The First Born of Egypt," which might be seen as a partial continuation of "Alms for Oblivion" because it featured characters from the previous series and their children as they moved into adolescence and toward adulthood. The children were to be the focus of the series: its overall theme was announced as "the purposes, beliefs and ways of life of the growing young as observed, deplored or encouraged by their elders." The older characters included Gray, Morrison, the Marquess Canteloupe (formerly Captain Detterling), Gregory Stern, Tom (now Sir Thomas) Llewellyn, and Maisie Malcolm, the compliant prostitute who had serviced most of the leading men of "Alms for Oblivion" at one time or another. The "growing young" included Jeremy Morrison, Maisie's daughter (known discreetly as her "niece") Tessa Malcolm, Rosie Stern, and, most prominently, the half-Jewish Marius Stern, who in

Morning Star follows in the footsteps of earlier Raven protagonists by behaving in a way that puts him in danger of being expelled from school and whose life becomes more complex when his parents are kidnapped in the Middle East by Arab militants. The novel received some harsh reviews. Frances Hill, in *The Spectator* (30 June 1984), judged that Raven had "abandoned any attempt to make characters, plotting and dialogue the slightest bit credible" and felt that his "energy, imagination and technique have all failed him." In the 21 June 1984 edition of *The Times* (London), Nicholas Shakespeare was equally unsparing, calling *Morning Star* "diabolically uninteresting–puerile in content" and "shambolic in structure."

Raven persisted with the new series, however, and a second novel, *The Face of the Waters,* appeared in 1985. A complex plot mixed elements from *Fielding Gray* and *The Survivors*–the impact of sexuality on an adolescent and the intertwining of art history and the family history of the Canteloupes–with an anti-Zionist conspiracy that entraps Stern and leads to a literally excruciating climax. This aspect of the novel showed a sharp engagement with the contemporary world and took on a topic that was an especially sensitive one for Raven, who had sometimes been suspected of anti-Semitism. In other respects, however, *The Face of the Waters* reiterates old themes. Hugh Barnes observed in *The Times* (London) for 25 July 1985 that Raven's "frame of reference recalls not only a period but a vanished way of life," while Toby Fitton in *TLS* (13 September 1985) judged that Raven's new crop of younger characters were "relatively colourless."

The third novel in the series, *Before the Cock Crow* (1986), takes up Gray's discovery of the true heir to the Canteloupe fortune in the last book of the "Alms for Oblivion" sequence, *The Survivors.* When the Marquess Canteloupe himself finds out that a poverty-stricken Italian may have a claim on his fortune, measures are set in hand to try to deal with the threat that involves Greco Barraclough, an anthropology don, and his page, Nicos, in a strange journey. Meanwhile, Stern and Tessa Malcolm fall under the spell of Milo Hedley and, more significantly, of his classics teacher, Raisley Conyngham, a figure who is the evil genius of the rest of the "First Born of Egypt" series. A third strand in the complex plot of the novel concerns the scion of the Morrison family, Jeremy, who leaves Cambridge to get back to his roots in the land owned by his family but also finds the object of Milo's machinations. The characters finally converge on a racecourse that provides Raven with an opportunity for another of the dramatic, surprising public set pieces at which he is so adept.

Before the Cock Crow was better received than its two predecessors in the "First Born of Egypt" series, with Christopher Hawtree, in *TLS* (5 September 1986), feeling that it showed "a return to focus." Praise was not unqualified, however. Harriet Waugh, in *The Spectator* (9 August 1986), found the latest work of this "elegant, amusing and disgusting writer" entertaining but empty, while Howard, in *The Times* (London) for 24 July 1986, called it "Gothic, camp, and snobbish," characterizing it as a mixture of the fiction of the camp fantasy of Ronald Firbank and of the thriller writers Dornford Yates and, because of its racecourse climax, Dick Francis. An interesting feature of reviews of Raven's later novels is that the comparisons with Powell that were made when the "Alms for Oblivion" series was in progress give way to comparisons to Firbank and to more popular writers, such as Yates, who had been invoked in reviews of his earliest novels.

The fourth novel in the "First Born of Egypt" series, *New Seed for Old* (1988), concerns the removal of Canteloupe's retarded son (fathered by Fielding Gray) and the attempt to replace him with another, more satisfactory child, of whom fifteen-year-old Marius Stern is to be the father. While the theme of surrogate parenthood was a topical one, the novel otherwise tended to replay Raven's familiar motifs. As Christopher Hawtree observed in *TLS* (4 March 1988), it was "the mixture as before," "as though one had been watching ghosts (the young among them), figures from another age." Hawtree conceded that *New Seed for Old* was entertaining, however, and Brian Morton emphasized this aspect of the novel in the *Times Educational Supplement* (4 March 1988), calling it "a hilarious and remarkable read." As Howard had done with *Before the Cock Crow,* Morton found in *New Seed for Old* traces of Firbank, combined this time with elements that called to mind the satirical novelist Tom Sharpe. Morton did also discern, however, a residual touch of Powell.

The sense, however, that Raven was reshuffling a well-worn repertoire of themes persisted in responses to his next novel, the fifth in the "First Born of Egypt" sequence, *Blood of My Bone* (1989). This novel focuses on the spiritual and ethical fate of Marius in the aftermath of the demise of Llewellyn, the provost of Lancaster College, who on his deathbed warns Marius that he must "turn his back" on both Raisley Conyngham and Milo Hedley, who are "striving to enslave and corrupt" him. Toby Fitton, in *TLS* (10 March 1989), echoed exactly Hawtree's comment on *New Seed for Old* when he called *Blood of My Bone* "very much the mixture as before," a novel in which "Most of Raven's themes crop up again" and "Retrospection is rampant." The anonymous reviewer of *Blood of My Bone* in *Private Eye* expressed some exasperation with Raven's project: "The First Born of Egypt is merely Alms for Oblivion part two, with the dying old characters replaced by

Dust jacket for the U.S. edition of Raven's 1971 novel, the seventh in his "Alms for Oblivion" series, set during the last days of British colonial rule of India (Richland County Public Library)

their worse offspring, in an internal propagation system." The review claimed that, as Raven grows older, his fictional world, "ever more remote from reality, has become ever more perverse and his novels, instead of coming forward in time, have slipped back into never-never land."

The struggle for Marius's soul in *Blood of My Bone* continues in the next novel of the sequence, *In the Image of God* (1990), but once more there is a sense of recycling previously used material; Jasper Rees, in *The Times* (London) for 15 February 1990, found "the same old team of vastly unlikeable (and entirely unbelievable) mind-gamesters conniving, bitching and sinning in standard vein." By this stage of Raven's career it seemed that familiarity was starting to breed contempt among some readers and reviewers. His work could still receive enthusiastic endorsement, however–for example, in Paul Golding's response to the final novel of the "First Born of Egypt" series, *The Troubadour,* in which Raisley Conyngham finally gets his comeuppance. In *The Times* (London) for 20 February 1992, Golding set the new novel in the context of both the "First Born of Egypt" and the "Alms for Oblivion" series, pointing out that, taken together, they constitute the longest roman-fleuve in contemporary literature. He also argued, however, that the test of any novel sequence was that each novel that it comprises should be a successful work in its own right, and he felt that *The Troubadour* triumphantly passed this test: it "can, and amply does, hold its own." By contrast, in *TLS* (28 February 1992), Fitton, who had written negative reviews of some of the previous "First Born of Egypt" novels, found the concluding one no more successful. In particular, he observed that Raisley Conyngham, a key figure for much of the series, had "failed to develop adequately as an evil character." Fitton was clearly relieved to reach the end of what he called "this creaking and jaded sequence."

Raven's last published work of fiction was a novella, *The Islands of Sorrow* (1994). Like the last book of the "Alms for Oblivion" sequence, *The Survivors,* it is set largely in Venice, but it shows more of the Gothic strain that comes through in his novels after "Alms for Oblivion," opening with a striking account of a dream–"Last night I dreamt I had two pricks"–and ending with spontaneous decomposition: "the thing that had been Formosa was quivering and sinking. Her face was liquefying jelly, dripping, then descending with a kind of suck, on to the table cloth." It is a well-turned but lightweight tale that received little attention. By now Raven was unwell, and in December of the following year he entered Sutton's Hospital in Charterhouse Square in the City of London, an institution that shared its foundation with Raven's old school. This male enclave, secluded but central, was a welcome haven in his final years. On 12 May 2001, at the age of seventy-three, he died after a stroke.

Raven's death prompted a range of assessments of his literary standing. There seems little doubt that his greatest achievement is the "Alms for Oblivion" sequence and that this series will survive as a highly entertaining, if idiosyncratic, chronicle of British upper-middle-class life from 1945 to 1973. It lacks the subtlety of Powell's "Music of Time" and the earnestness of Snow's "Strangers and Brothers," but it has a distinctive vision to offer–the vision of the "inside outsider," of the lover of institutions who could never wholly fit into them, of the reactionary who was never respectable. The "First Born of Egypt" sequence is less successful because of its repetitive quality and because it seems to be out of touch with the younger generation on which it claims to focus; but it provides many pleasures for the reader and gives greater license to a Romantic, Gothic vein in Raven that sometimes fitted uneasily into the ostensibly realist framework of "Alms for Oblivion" but that is more in accord with the expansive scope of more recent British fiction.

If Raven's earlier novels sometimes seem to strain against the restrictions of realism in a way that may now look commendable, they are also notable for the way in which they challenge constraints on writing about sexuality, especially male homosexuality. In this field Raven is a pioneer, and he later took full advantage of the freedoms that did not prevail when he began his career as a novelist. His frankness about male homosexuality is matched by a frankness about female sexuality that complicates any simple account of him as a misogynist. It is undoubtedly true that he has little time for women in their domestic and maternal roles, but he does provide vigorous portrayals of sexually active women, most notably Angela Tuck in "Alms for Oblivion," the one female character in the list of the dramatis personae of the series whose name, like those of the leading male characters, is endowed with importance by being printed in capital letters. In view of this aspect of his work, it is not altogether surprising that a 19 February 1988 interview in *The Times* (London) quotes this crusty reactionary as saying: "I think I'm in favour of these new feminists. Of course they can be tiresome and terribly silly, but they do seem to be getting off their backside and doing something, which is more than my generation's lot ever did."

For Simon Raven, sexuality is a rich source not only of low comedy but also of potential tragedy, as in the death of Christopher in *Fielding Gray;* and tragedy leads, in his work, to serious considerations of necessity and morality. In Raven's writing, sentimentality, melodrama, and laughter can vitiate seriousness; but seriousness is never wholly absent. His vision, at its highest, is a classical one, informed by his lifelong reading of the ancient Greek and Roman authors; it is a vision of a world ruled by necessity, to which human beings must submit, though not without getting the most out of life first. As Raven himself says, as quoted in a *Guardian* obituary (16 May 2001) by his biographer Michael Barber: "we aren't here for long, and when we do go, that's that. Finish. So for God's sake enjoy yourself now–and sod anyone who tries to stop you."

Interview:

Chris Peachment, "Simon Raven," *Times* (London), 19 February 1988, p. 18.

Biography:

Michael Barber, *The Captain: The Life and Times of Simon Raven* (London: Duckworth, 1996).

References:

Kerry McSweeney, "The Novels of Simon Raven," *Queen's Quarterly* (Spring 1971);

"Simon Raven," in D. L. Kirkpatrick, ed., *Contemporary Novelists* (London & Chicago: St. James, 1986).

Vikram Seth

(20 June 1952 –   )

Cynthia Ho
University of North Carolina at Asheville

See also the Seth entry in *DLB 120: American Poets Since World War II, Third Series.*

BOOKS: *Mappings* (Saratoga, Cal.: Vikram Seth, 1980; Calcutta: Writers Workshop, 1981; New Delhi & London: Viking, 1994);

From Heaven Lake: Travels Through Sinkiang and Tibet (London: Chatto & Windus, 1983; New York: Vintage, 1987);

The Humble Administrator's Garden (Manchester: Carcanet, 1985; New Delhi: Viking, 1994);

The Golden Gate: A Novel in Verse (New York: Random House, 1986; London & Boston: Faber & Faber, 1986);

All You Who Sleep Tonight (New York: Knopf, 1990; London: Faber & Faber, 1990);

Beastly Tales from Here and There, illustrated by Ravi Shankar (New Delhi & New York: Viking, 1992; London: Phoenix House, 1993);

A Suitable Boy: A Novel (1 volume, New Delhi: Viking, 1993; London: Phoenix House, 1993; New York: HarperCollins, 1993; 3 volumes, London: Phoenix House, 1995; 2 volumes, 1995);

Arion & the Dolphin: A Libretto (London: Phoenix House, 1994; New Delhi & New York: Penguin, 1994);

Arion and The Dolphin, illustrated by Jane Ray (London: Orion, 1994; New York: Dutton, 1995);

Riot at Misri Mandi: From "A Suitable Boy" (London: Phoenix House, 1996);

An Equal Music (New Delhi: Viking, 1999; New York: Broadway Books, 1999; London: Phoenix House, 1999).

Collection: *The Poems, 1981–1994* (New Delhi & New York: Penguin, 1995).

PLAY PRODUCTIONS: *Arion and the Dolphin,* libretto by Seth, music by Alec Roth, Plymouth, Royal Navy Dockyard, H.M.S. Drake Drill Shed, 14 June 1994;

Chinese Gardens, words by Seth, music by Roth, Chester, Town Hall, 13 July 1998;

Vikram Seth (photograph © 1992 by Aradhana Seth; from the cover of the U.S. paperback edition of A Suitable Boy, *1994)*

Earth and Sky, words by Seth, music by Roth, London, Royal Albert Hall, 18 July 2000.

TRANSLATION: *Three Chinese Poets: Translations of Poems by Wang Wei, Li Bai and Du Fu* (London & Boston: Faber & Faber, 1992; New York: HarperCollins, 1992).

The tradition of the great writers of preindependence India, such as Raja Rao, R. K. Narayan, and Mulk Raj Anand, has given way to Indian writers of the global village led by two important and fundamentally different authors, Salman Rushdie and Vikram

Seth. These two writers brought Indian literature in English to the attention of a wider Western reading public, first with Rushdie's *Midnight's Children* (1981) and then with Seth's *The Golden Gate* (1986). Rushdie's wildly imaginative experimentation with postmodernism contrasts with Seth's conservative approach to poetry and prose, but both writers established the economic viability of Indian writing and paved the way for the wave of South Asian writers in the market today that includes Bharati Mukherjee, Arundhati Roy, Rohinton Mistry, and Romesh Gunesekera. Seth has promoted himself as a traditionalist uninterested in literary theory and the tastes of what he has called, in a 1999 interview with Katherine Knorr, "the mad critics" and deconstructionists of the universities. Nevertheless, he is one of the most popular and best regarded of the current generation of Indian authors who write in English. He refuses to categorize himself, even though he jokingly writes in the introduction to his *The Poems, 1981–1994* (1995) that *Time* magazine "dubbed him a member of the Empire-Writes-Back Generation."

Seth was born 20 June 1952, in Calcutta, India, an important cultural center that was also the home of the poet Rabindranath Tagore (1861–1941) and movie director Satyajit Ray (1921–1992). He comes from a family of high achievers. His mother, Laila Seth, took her London bar exams just three months after the birth of Seth's younger brother, receiving top scores, and she went on to become the first woman chief justice of India. His father, Premnath Seth, is a self-made successful businessman who, Jeremy Gavron noted in a 27 March 1999 interview-profile of Vikram Seth, rose "to a position of such respect in the Indian shoe business that he is known in Delhi as Mr. Shoe." Although Vikram Seth once complained that his father was too distant with the children when they were young, the two have since grown close. In "Departure Lounge," a poem in his collection *Mappings* (1980), he signals their new understanding: "If I could / Have had a better father years ago / I could not now, I know." Seth is the oldest of three children–his brother conducts Buddhist meditational tours, and his younger sister serves as an Austrian diplomat.

Seth was educated in India, Great Britain, the United States, and China. After prep school he attended Doon, the so-called Eton of India. He excelled academically at the school, though he was unhappy there; according to Gavron, when Seth gave the Founder's Day speech at Doon in 1992, he shocked the audience by remarking, "I had a terrible feeling of loneliness and isolation during my six years here. . . . Sometimes at lights out I wished I would never wake up. I was teased and bullied by my classmates and my seniors because of my interest in studies and reading, because of my lack of interest in games, because of my unwillingness to join gangs and groups." From India he went to Corpus Christi College, University of Oxford, where he earned a B.A. in 1975. He chose to study "pure maths, applied maths, physics" because, he told Chelvanayakam Kanaganayankam in an interview published in 1995, "I really liked reading, but it seemed pointless to study literature as a subject." He then attended Stanford University, intending to earn a doctorate in economics. Although he did receive an M.A. in 1979, he became more interested in learning Chinese and writing poetry in English. Seth told Kanaganayankam that he "never had any passion for economics, not what I felt for writing poetry," but nevertheless regrets not finishing his Ph.D. As a consequence of his interest in poetry while at Stanford, he received a Wallace Stegner Fellowship in Creative Writing from 1977 to 1978. Returning to his economic studies, he worked from 1982 to 1983 at Nanjing University in China on a research project about the Chinese birth control program.

Although Seth has attributed some of his poetic technique to Indian tradition, such as the rhyme of Hindi poetry, he gives most credit to the American poet Timothy Steele and the British poet Donald Davie, both of whom he encountered at Stanford when he was becoming interested in poetry. "I wanted to have some contact with the writing programme," Seth told Gavron, "So I went to this office and asked if there was anyone who could help with poetry. There were two poets there," he recalled, "and the one nearest the door was Timothy Steele, who writes with rhyme and metre. If the other fellow had been closer, I'd probably have turned out a poet of free verse." Steele's *Missing Measures: Modern Poetry and the Revolt Against Meter* (1990) and Dana Gioia's *Can Poetry Matter? Essays on Poetry and American Culture* (1992)–which chronicles public estrangement from much modern American poetry–are two works from the Stanford school that reflect the aesthetics Seth adopted. Gavron noted that Seth acknowledges both Steele and Davie as giving him the models and guidance in formal rhyme and meter that characterize his approach to poetry, which could be called "Conservative New Formalism."

Seth's first collection of poems, *Mappings,* was self-published in 1980. The poems are personal, anecdotal, and somewhat autobiographical about life in India, China, and the United States. In his foreword Seth relates that because he "stood outside the orbit of the latest critical theories, and did not realize that writing in rhyme and metre would make me a sort of literary untouchable," the book was rejected by every publisher to whom he sent it. He tried to sell the books himself to San Francisco bookstores and finally gave

Dust jacket for the U.S. edition of Seth's 1986 novel-in-verse, which chronicles the relationships of a group of yuppies in the San Francisco Bay area (Richland County Public Library)

many away to family and friends. Seth complained to Knorr in their 1999 interview that "poetry lists are the preserve of people who don't expect to sell" and that poetry editors "publish their friends and their fellow poets in their particular school of writing." Seth sent a typescript of *Mappings* to Philip Larkin, who replied with helpful comments, including "words of encouragement," Seth told Gavron, that "kept me going for five years." Anthony Thwaite's edition of *Selected Letters of Philip Larkin, 1940–1985* (1992), however, includes a letter to Robert Conquest in which Larkin calls Seth's poetry a "load of crap," saying it "comes of his being an oriental." *Mappings* was republished in 1981 by an Indian company, The Writer's Workshop.

With considerable self-confidence Seth pushed ahead with the publication and promotion of his second book of poetry, *The Humble Administrator's Garden* (1985). His effort was rewarded with the 1985 Commonwealth Poetry Prize for Asia. With what Devesh Patel has called "a mixture of muted and terse tones" Seth employs the natural settings of the three locales important to him. Each of the three sections–"Wutong" (China), "Neem" (India), and "Live Oak" (California)–uses images of trees and leaves to unify the volume. Utilizing such forms as sonnet, quatrain, epigrammatic couplet, and on occasion, tightly controlled free verse, he celebrates the trivia of life. The authorial voice that appears in Seth's subsequent works makes a strong debut here: conversational, approachable, clever, and sometimes flippant. And the ideas he introduces here appear throughout his career as well–traditional, even tried and true themes, presented in a way that some readers find filled with unexpected originality.

Each of the emblematic trees reflects the cultural identity of a country; Wutong, for example, is an Asian gum tree that is a favorite motif in classical Chinese poetry. It is also notable for a useful product, a sticky gum. All of the trees in fact have some function in addition to their symbolic value. The first poem in "Wutong," "A Little Night Music," begins with all the themes that will continue to appear in Seth's poetry: music, nighttime, memory, and hope for a meaningful human connection. The title sonnet introduces the "humble administrator" in his garden acquired by "dubious means." The poem "Research in Jiangsu Province" opens with the image of Seth's tape recorder: "From off this plastic strip the noise / of buzzing stops. A human voice / asks its set questions, pauses, then / Waits for responses to begin." He goes on to record a catalogue of Chinese village life from his research interviews. Tiny details make the scene come alive. The "Neem" section, named for the tree whose bitter bark is used as a tonic, ranges over an expanse of Indian experience and anticipates topics that appear later in his novel *A Suitable Boy* (1993). "The Comfortable Classes at Work and Play" delivers snatches of an upper Indian family life that seem to reflect bits of his own family: "The mother takes a volume in half-calf / From off the wall, and wrestles with a judgment / Of Justice Krishna Iyer of the Supreme Court." To reiterate that India is the land of memories, this section ends with a dramatic monologue titled "From the Babur-Nama, Memoirs of Babur, First Moghul Emperor of India." The third part is "Live Oak," named for the evergreen oak cultivated for its shade and noted for extremely durable wood. This American section focuses on California, Seth's home at the time he was writing the collection. In these poems the United States, despite all its comforts and pleasures, is lonely and dangerous. All of the themes introduced earlier return–music, nighttime, love–but this time with a sense of loss. The final poem, "Unclaimed," comments upon a passing sexual encounter, "To make love with a stranger is the best / There is no riddle and there is no test." The last section was generally seen as the weakest of the three, but *The Humble Administrator's Garden* was critically well received.

While studying at Nanjing University in conjunction with his work at Stanford, Seth took an organized student trip. He chafed under the constraints of the programmed tour and desired to explore for himself. When the students were asked to perform for their guests, Seth sang an Indian movie theme song, "The Wanderer," that was wildly popular in China, so popular that it impressed his hosts and allowed him to make the contacts necessary to obtain a rare pass to Lhasa, the Tibetan capital. In the summer of 1981 he hitchhiked the land route home to Delhi by way of Tibet and Nepal. Back in Delhi, his father suggested his journeys might make a book, and the resulting travelogue, *From Heaven Lake: Travels Through Sinkiang and Tibet* (1983) is stimulating travel literature at its best. Subsequently winning the Thomas Cook Travel Book Award, Seth says, gave him the confidence to start thinking of himself as a writer. On his trip he travels from the oases of northwest China to the Himalayas and crosses four Chinese provinces: Xinjian, Gansu in the northwestern desert, then the basin and plateau of Qinghai, and finally Tibet. Wearing the blue trousers, jacket, and visored cap of the Chinese peasant, he battles Communist bureaucracy, climatic extremes, and the discomfort of riding long distances in bad weather over inferior roads in antiquated trucks. The liveliness of Seth's engagement with the experience and his linguistic ability to deal with people from various ethnic groups make it an engaging and stimulating account.

Seth's move from writing poetry to writing fiction came about in an unusual way. While he was filing data on Chinese villages into a computer as part of his economics research project, Seth could not stand the tedium and went to the Stanford Bookstore where he picked some poetry books at random off the shelves. Providentially, one book he chose was *Eugene Onegin,* Charles Johnston's 1977 translation of Aleksandr Sergeevich Pushkin's novel in verse, *Evgenii Onegin* (1825–1833). He told Akash Kapur in an interview for *The Atlantic Unbound* (23 June 1999) that "I was so astonished by it, and so affected by it, that I decided that rather than continue working on my dissertation I would take time off to write a novel using the same stanza form, but set in California. I didn't realize then that I would never finish my dissertation; I thought it was a temporary time out."

In 1986 Seth published his first novel, *The Golden Gate.* This Byronesque story is a sonnet sequence of 590 rhyming tetrameter poems telling the romantic tale of young professionals in San Francisco. All of the apparatuses of the novel, the acknowledgments, dedication, and author page, are also in the same sonnet form. Since his name is pronounced something like "sate," he has made even the title page rhyme: "The Golden Gate / by Vikram Seth." Seth's intention was to use formal poetry to portray modern morals. Two significant influences played a considerable part in this idea. First is Steele's poetry, here again a model for Seth's formalism, but now also for his content. He told Knorr in their 1999 interview that after he saw Steele's works, "I realized that one could write about one's own times with a modern sensibility and yet use these forms which have existed in the language for hundreds of years, full of the resonance that they had and the clarity that they almost forced upon one." This realization is in line with the New Formalism, which called for a return to older forms, though in a colloquial rather than self-consciously "literary" manner, and an engagement with popular culture.

The second, and major, influence is Pushkin's masterpiece, *Evgenii Onegin.* Seth read the work through two steps of translation. Pushkin's verse novel was first translated in unrhymed iambics by Vladimir Nabokov, with commentary, in a version published in four volumes in 1964. Then, this rendering offered Johnston the basis for his own version, which uses Pushkin's meter and rhyme scheme. Seth's chance reading of Johnston's version ignited his own sonnet project; having enjoyed Johnston's translation, "like champagne / Its effervescence stirs my brain," Seth adopted the complex and flexible iambic tetrameter structure that marks Pushkin's composition. This choice is an interesting one, considering, as Seth admits in *The Golden Gate,* that the "once noble" meter "capers before the proud pentameter, Tyrant of English." The Johnston/Seth sonnet stanza follows Pushkin's in using three possible ways of building quatrains with two rhymes, and it matches Pushkin's masculine and feminine rhymes. In addition to the form, Pushkin's poem also provides the model for the playful tone and the theme of personal quest. Seth told Kapur in their 1999 interview that "Pushkin is very close to my heart because I like his mixture of levity and deep seriousness. He refused to be pompous, and to become a venerable man of letters." *Evgenii Onegin* begins with the hero complaining to himself about his situation, just as *The Golden Gate* opens with the hero, hit in the head with a red Frisbee, asking the meaning of life: "He thought, 'If I died, who'd be sad? / Who'd weep? Who'd gloat? Who would be glad?'" Rhymes made of bumper sticker sayings and billboard slogans are part of the lighthearted appeal of the work.

The hero of Seth's saga is John, a Silicon Valley executive, who represents the 1980s Yuppie: "Well-paid, congenial employment; / A house; a modicum of wealth; / Some sunlight; coffee and the papers; / Artichoke hearts adorned with capers; / A Burberry trench

Cover for the U.S. paperback edition of Seth's 1993 novel, which centers on four large families in India during the political turmoil of the early 1950s (Richland County Public Library)

coat; a Peugeot." In his search for love, John asks his friend Janet Hayakawa, a sculptor and drummer in a band called Liquid Sheep, to help him put a personal ad in the *Bay Guardian.* Responses to his want ad provide the rest of the plot and the characters of the novel: Liz Dorati, the love interest, is a lawyer who eloquently protests against Lungless Labs and nuclear bombs and has an "anti-nuclear cat," Charlemagne; Phil, a divorced father unsure of his sexuality; Ed, member of a Sonoma wine family and owner of an iguana named Arnold Schwarzenegger; and Ed's sister Elizabeth, another attorney. As characters combine and recombine relationships, the constant theme is the need to find a loving relationship. Although the fairly simple plot is a romp through light subjects and mock-heroic catalogues, the underlying theme nevertheless satirizes urban cultural pretensions and blind materialism. The book shows the considerable sympathy for California life that Seth himself developed after moving to Stanford. He told Knorr in their 1999 interview, "'I thought, oh my God, thick-headed beach boys and no intellectual conversation. But then I met people who were both very intelligent and interested in things of the mind, and who would think nothing about teaching you to swim butterfly. For me it was like a revelation in a wonderful way. That's why 'The Golden Gate,' in a way, for all its tragedy, it's a happy book."

The narrator of the poem, who is Seth, is one of its most important characters. As such, Seth plays with many levels of self-reflexive comment and self-representation. At the beginning of chapter 5 the narrator describes his encounter with an editor at a publishing party "Hosted by (long live!) Thomas Cook / Where my Tibetan travel book / Was honored." The editor, interested in Seth's next work along the same lines as *From Heaven Lake,* inquires into his plans, to which Seth replies that he is working on a novel in verse: "'How marvelously quaint,' he said, / And subsequently cut me dead." As Seth was writing *The Golden Gate,* friends as well as editors scoffed; the novel reports his friends asking, "Drivelling in rhyme's all very well / The question is does spittle sell?" Nabokov had particularly derided feminine endings in his discussion of Pushkin, so Seth anticipates criticism of his poetic form: "How do I justify this stanza? / These feminine rhymes? My wrinkled muse? / This whole passe extravaganza? / How can I (careless of time) use / The dusty bread molds of Onegin / In the brave bakery of Reagan?" In defense of his own style Seth takes a jab at critics who deride the traditional in favor of the avant-garde when Janet receives a bad critical review of her art. In addition to his authorial comments, Seth also places a character, Kim Tarvesh, much like himself, within the work: "While bowed down with the gray futility / Of his pedant thesis, Kim Tarvesh / Ogles convexities of flesh / and maximizes his utility / By drowning in his chilled Chablis / His economics Ph.D." Despite some critics who felt the book was an uncomfortable mix of fiction and poetry, the reception of *The Golden Gate* was generally favorable.

After the publication of *The Golden Gate,* Seth returned to his family home in India to write and research his first prose novel. His problems in finding a publisher for his verse novel made him realize that he needed a literary agent. Seth interviewed several agents before selecting the London-based Giles Gordon, a legendarily tough negotiator, who agreed to represent Seth though he had no completed manuscript. Work on the novel went slowly, and Seth took breaks to work on other projects. His *All You Who Sleep Tonight* (1990) is a slim but nicely produced volume that marks his return to shorter verse. It includes representatives of the main forms that interest him, from translations to epigrams. Many of Seth's previous concerns–remembering, detachment, observation, and exile–coalesce in this volume. *All You Who Sleep Tonight* has five parts: "Romantic Residues," a first-person narrator addressing past loves; "In Other Voices," a collection of dramatic monologues; "In Other Places Around the World," comprising poems mostly about China, with the fiftieth anniversary of the Golden Gate Bridge added in; "Quatrains," a miscellany of things from "Telephone" to "Door"; and finally "Meditations of the Heart," a collection about those who "Sleep alone" for noble or less compelling reasons.

The opening piece, "Round and Round," is an eighteen-line poem in three stanzas about the poet's memories when he sees a red bag at the airport baggage claim. This "excess baggage" sets the tone for this section about ended relationships. The strongest section is "In Other Voices," with passages directly inspired by the works of Mizra Ghali (a Farsi and Urdu poet of the nineteenth century); by *Kommandant in Auschwitz: Autobiographische Aufzeichnungen* (1958; translated as *Commandant of Auschwitz: The Autobiography of Rudolf Hoess,* 1959), the prison memoirs of the Nazi war criminal Rudolf Hess; and by *Hiroshima Diary: The Journal of a Japanese Physician August 6 – September 30, 1945* (1955) by Michihiko Hachiya. Drawn from Hachiya's work, "A Doctor's Journal Entry for August 6, 1945," with its journalistic monologue, relays eyewitness shock at the atomic bomb: "Arms stretched straight out, shoulder to dangling hand; / It took some time for me to understand / The friction on their burns caused so much pain / They feared to chafe flesh against flesh again." Overall critical opinion of the collection was not favorable. Although Thomas Disch of *The Washington Post* (25 April 1991) praised it as "a work [that gives] pleasure to the ideal Common Reader," many reviewers found it too lacking in imagination and depth. The critical split that developed here continues to appear in subsequent appraisals of Seth's work. While one group of readers finds Seth's work moving and even profound in its traditional expression of common experience, others believe Seth to be talented, a learned rhymer, but missing in the essential spark of invention.

In his introduction to his next published work, *Beastly Tales from Here and There* (1992), Seth explains that he wrote a collection of beast fables because distractingly hot weather drove him to write about mangoes and a river. This verse collection is a combination of the ancient Sanskrit framed didactic tales, the tradition of Reynard the Fox, and the fables of Jean de La Fontaine. While many of the stories are familiar, they have a lighthearted and modern twist. In the "Hare and the Tortoise" story, for example, Teddy Tortoise wins the race, but the delicate hare gets all the prizes and accolades for her beauty (including book and movie rights). Of the ten whimsical tales told in lighthearted couplets, two each come from India, China, Greece, and the Ukraine. The final two are Seth's own creation, which he says came to him directly from "the Land of Gup." Ravi Shankar, a famous Indian cartoonist, illustrated the volume.

Seth's intense interest in learning Chinese led him to his next published project, *Three Chinese Poets: Translations of Poems by Wang Wei, Li Bai and Du Fu* (1992). In this work he translates three important poets of the Tang dynasty. He offers an excellent introduction to the works of the three, their commonalities and differences. About this project, which is much different from his earlier work, Seth told interviewer Kapur: "I was just suddenly compelled to do it for one or two months late in 1989, and I can't explain why. It isn't something I see myself as being: a translator." As a way of justifying his work to the reader he comments in the foreword to the book that "Works in translation from languages I do not understand have had as deep an influence on my own writing as works I can read in the original." His role models in translation are Robert Fitzgerald's *The Iliad* (1963), Richard Wilbur's *Tartuffe* (1954), and, of course, Johnston's *Eugene Onegin.* The introspective Wang Wei writes about the comforts of nature in "Deer Park": "Empty hills, no man in sight– / Just echoes of the voice of men. / In the deep wood reflected light / Shines on the bluegreen moss again." The poems of Li Bai (or Li Po), on the other hand, are energetic and full of delight in the world, as in "Drinking Alone with the Moon": "A pot of wine among the flowers. / I drink alone, no friend with me. / I raise my cup to invite the moon. / He and my shadow and I make three." Du Fu (or Tu Fu) writes poems sadly reflective of the difficult political times in which he lived, as in his "An Autumn Meditation": "Failure and grief is all these hundred years have brought . . . My ancient land and times of peace come to my thoughts."

A Suitable Boy, published in 1993, continues Seth's tradition of writing each new book unlike all of his books that have come before. Each of his works evokes a narrowly specific world, and the focus of this text is modern India. According to his 1993 interview with Michele Field, Seth felt that because *A Suitable Boy* was "a distinctly Indian novel," it should be first published in India. He remarked, "I was in Calcutta, and I knew I wanted the novel to be typeset once–once only. I couldn't bear to proofread a book of this length for three different English-language publishers: I would have hated it by the end. I decided to do it in India to show that we could." He worked closely with David Davidar, editor of Penguin of India, which published the novel under the Viking imprint in February of 1993; the British edition was brought out by Orion under the Phoenix imprint in March, and the U.S. edition appeared under the HarperCollins imprint in May.

A Suitable Boy is so large that commentators developed different measurements to register amazement at its size: it is the longest single-volume novel ever published in English, with 1,349 pages, comprising six million words, two feet high in typescript, and weighing four pounds in the paperback edition. Thus, the opening epigram from Voltaire, "The secret of being a bore is to say everything," seems self-referential. Interestingly, the length of the novel became a marketing tool to promote it; prepublication publicity pointed out that because it was too excellent to be edited to a smaller size, special glue had to be developed to hold the paperback binding together. According to Field, Seth and his literary agent, Gordon, also set a new record in the advance they received from Orion: £250,000, at that time the largest advance ever paid for a first novel in Britain. The novel sold more than one million copies worldwide and won The Connect Award in 1993.

After *The Golden Gate* had been published, Seth had planned "to write a series of five short novels" about India. But as he explained to Amit Roy in a 29 August 1992 interview for *The Telegraph* (Calcutta), "Instead, I wrote one rather long novel which deals with a period I did not, at first, think was very interesting–the early 1950's." He thought that after dealing swiftly with this period, he would "go forward to the Sino-Indian war, the Emergency and all that kind of stuff. Instead, I got stuck in that period." In a sense, Seth's novel is Jane Austen's *Pride and Prejudice* (1813) enlarged. Austen's novel opens with the famous line, "It is a truth universally acknowledged, that a single man in possession of a good fortune must be in want of a wife," and as Seth's novel opens, Mrs. Mehra is searching for a husband for her youngest daughter. The search soon involves four large families whose destinies are played out against the political upheavals of India in the 1950s. The central issue that the novel addresses, the problems of marriage for the Indian middle class, with its quagmire of caste, religion, and tradition, has never been so fully addressed in English. The characters in the novel reflect the Hindu and Muslim cultural mix that produced tensions following the independence of India and led to the partition of the subcontinent into India, mostly Hindu, and Pakistan, mostly Muslim. The same kind of historically based violence portrayed in the novel broke out about the time the novel appeared. While some critics praised him for being prescient, Seth told Knorr in their 1999 interview that "I had no idea that what I was writing about–the attacks of temples and mosques–actually would take place two months before the book–while the book was actually being typeset." He did, however, have an important moral intent for the novel, as he told Jill Rachlin in an interview for *People Weekly* (24 May 1993), "I don't normally consider myself a political person, but I feel deeply about this. India is a secular country and no place for religions to aggrandize themselves and do their countrymen down. It's tragic. I hope the book will be a force of tolerance."

The modern, urban setting for the novel is Calcutta, which has a progressive English-educated middle class, the heritage of its lengthy Raj. Religious conflict occurs between Hindus and Muslims in the city of Brahmpur, an invented city on the Ganges in the invented state of Purva Pradesh, where the story is also set. In the 1950s the freedom fighters had become the new government, and a number of important changes took place. Gandhi was assassinated in 1948, and his deputy Vallabhbhai Jhaverbhai Patel died in 1950, making Jawaharlal Nehru the absolute head of both party and nation. The historical Nehru is joined in the novel by three fictional politicians, S. S. Sharma, Mahesh Kapoor, and L. N. Agarwal. Thus, the political setting in which India searches for a suitable place in the family of nations is interwoven with the search of Mrs. Mehra for a suitable boy for her daughter. Despite the multiple interlacings of the plot, the story unfolds as a traditional linear narrative. Seth believes modern writing has been contorted by academic critics and diverted from its course by an obsession with stylish experimentation. He told Gavron in their 1999 interview, "I don't read a lot of modern fiction, but it seems to me that too much of it is thesis fodder." Seth maintains that he writes to disprove the assumption that "subjects such as love, ambition and family are worthy only of the airport novel."

In *A Suitable Boy,* Seth examines the interconnectedness of four families–the Mehras, the Chatterjis, the Kapoors, and the Khans. The widowed Mrs. Rupa Mehra and Lata, her marriageable but rebellious youngest daughter, are the two characters who initiate the action and connect the multitudinous strands of the plot. Rupa Mehra's mission throughout the novel is to insure the smooth running of her family, and an imperative element of that mission is to find a suitable (defined as Khatri Hindu) husband for Lata. Lata, a student of English literature at the University of Brahmpur, experiments with making her own love matches, first with the charming Kabir Durrani. He is unsuitable most obviously because he is Muslim but also because of the powerful passionate response he evokes in Lata. Kabir is replaced by the contrasting Amit Chatterji, easygoing and familiar. Amit, despite being a witty, cosmopolitan, and sophisticated writer, is rejected because Lata feels he is too preoccupied with his writing to make a good husband. After Lata unsuccessfully tries to find love for herself, her mother makes an unromantic match for her with Haresh, an uncouth but intelligent, self-made rising businessman. Haresh is a sensible, rational choice with the added advantage that "he isn't the kind of man to ask" for a dowry. Incidents of Haresh's life, such as trying to force his way into the management of a Czech shoe company, are from the life of Seth's father. Seth's admiration for his father's craft shows when he praises the link between business and art: "No poet ever worked harder or more inspiredly to craft a poem than Haresh worked for the next three days on his pair of shoes." While Lata's choice might be a disappointment to some readers, Seth seems to be pointing to sensible and practical choices in the private domain to contrast with the chaotic and fanatical choices being made in the public sphere. Tradition has its place when combined with common sense. Although Shyam Agarwalla quotes Seth as insisting, "I use very little symbol, metaphor, allegory in my books," many critics have seen Haresh as a symbol of the new modernizing India that will replace Muslim, British, and Hindu factionalism.

The entire Mehra clan represents the hardworking Indian middle class. Vivid renderings of individual personalities make up the family unit. Mrs. Rupa Mehra, the heroine's sentimental mother, is based in part on Seth's grandmother (also named Rupa Mehra) whom Seth called "the muse of the project. Mrs. Mehra's son Arun is married into the Chatterji family, which brings their large and idiosyncratic group into the novel. Two judges head the family of five children. All have money and time to pursue their own passions: Amit is a poet, Meenakshi (the wife of Arun Mehra) is the adulterous social climber, Dipankar is the lazy middle brother seeking the meaning of life, Kakoli is an exaggerated example of the flighty teenage girl, and Tapan is a schoolboy. Also in the mix is Cuddles, the dog, who mirrors many of the Chatterjis' snobbish ways. They are the main source of the Raj values that hover in the background of the novel, and they express their identification with the English through such things as their obsession for good spoken English and their high regard for a light complexion. At their least admirable moments they are engaged in a self-absorbed materialism disconnected from Indian reality. The ambiguous presentation of the Chatterjis is perhaps surprising since they are in many ways Seth's family. Seth claims that he began rhyming (in English) at the age of three, which vividly recalls the boisterous Chatterji family, who incessantly rhyme and even improvise doggerel couplets at the breakfast table. Amit Chatterji, one of Lata's suitors, is clearly modeled on Seth himself. One of Amit's sisters observes he is not husband material: "Jane Austen is the only woman in his life." Amit sits around all day staring out of the window while his family carefully nurtures his talents, in the same way

Dust jacket for the U.S. edition of the 1994 children's book that Seth adapted from his libretto for an opera based on Greek mythology (Richland County Public Library)

Seth's parents are said to have tiptoed around and provided all his needs while he stayed with them in India to complete the novel. Like Seth, Amit is writing an historical novel about India that is more than one thousand pages long, but he humorously derides the project: long books "make me pant with the effort of holding them up for a few minutes . . . I still bear the scars of *Middlemarch*."

The Kapoor clan is headed by Mahesh Kapoor, revenue minister in the ministry of Purva Pradesh. His wife, Mrs. Kapoor, is deeply religious, superstitious, and conservative. His daughter, Veena, is a close friend of Lata, and his elder son Pran is an asthmatic lecturer in English at Brahmpur University. This family is the most political of the clans, for Mahesh Kapoor is a veteran freedom fighter, a confidant of Nehru, and a radical socialist. He is determined to abolish the feudal system of Zamindari (the method of landholding that kept the majority of Indians hopelessly tied to a subsistence life) in Purva Pradesh. This plotline recalls another hot topic of the early 1950s, the condition of the scheduled castes (formerly called "untouchables") and the call of Gandhi to abolish untouchability. Lata (as a student) and Pran (as an instructor) in the English department at Brahmpur University provide Seth with several occasions to satirize the academic establishment.

In a display of the pettiness of academic politics, a reactionary professor tries to block Pran Kapoor from putting James Joyce on the university syllabus. Pran negotiates for a readership in the university in what becomes a struggle between the adherents of Joyce and those of T. S. Eliot. Eliot here becomes a symbol of the unthinking stodginess of Indian education and Indian society. Pran laments the uncritical adulation of Eliot in India: "he gave a great deal of respect to India. We are delighted when anyone pays us any attention and so we give adoration where we receive interest." When Lata attends a meeting of the Brahmpur Literary Society, the title of the lecture for next week is announced: "Professor Mishra on 'Eliot: Whither?'"

In contrast to these three Hindu families are the Khans, led by the aristocratic Muslim Nawab Sahib of Baitar. Through this family, readers see a different view of India, equally as complex as the Hindu side. The Nawab Sahib is the greatest opponent of his friend Mahesh Kapoor concerning the Zamindari Abolition Bill because, as a large landlord, he stands to lose his way of life. His two sons, Imtiaz Khan and Firoz Khan, pursue the richness of Moghul literary and musical culture and pursue a courtesan who illustrates artistic dependence on feudalism. The two main women of the family illustrate the different roles available to Muslim women. His daughter, Zainab, manages her family from purdah, while in interesting contrast his sister-in-law, the Begum Abid Kahan, is an aggressive and public political firebrand.

Rushdie's *Midnight's Children* successfully exploited the English actually spoken in India, providing a model for younger Indian writers. In *A Suitable Boy,* Seth capitalizes on the great variety and different environments of Indian English in a much wider ranging way than Rushdie. Because Seth's characters are from highly anglicized society, he is able to depict a range of dialects of Indian English–Hinglish, Bengalish, Tanlish, Urglish, and Pucka Sahibish. Much of this depiction is quite subtle and gives Western readers information about Indian customs and manners. The Kapoors and Mehras speak Hinglish and display certain cultural norms of North India; for example, these women do not call their husbands by name. The Chatterjis use Banglish, and it is in this dialect that Kakoli and Meenakshi endlessly rhyme and mime: "Famous poet, so they say / 'Besh' decent in every way" ("Besh" is Bengali for "all right"). Muslim Moghul expansion into India gave birth to Urdu, which uses Persian, Arabic, and Turkish words. In *A Suitable Boy,* the Nawab and his family speak Urdu and provide a vivid description of the various Muslim customs, social and religious festivals. Despite this playful use of the language, the novel remains clear to Western readers, even though some culturally specific elements, such as death rituals and marriage decisions, can still be misunderstood.

Through all of its characters, the novel plays out the importance of personal hopes in a time of national distress. Although Seth shows an India losing its idealism through corruption and disharmony, he establishes the importance of the ties of family, caste, and religion which offer a continuity with the past. The novel was well received by critics around the world. To the chagrin of many, *A Suitable Boy* not only failed to win the Booker Prize for 1993, it failed to make even the shortlist of six finalists.

Music has been a constant backdrop to Seth's literary and poetic achievements, and he was commissioned by the Baylis Programme at the English National Opera to write a libretto based on the Greek legend of Arion, a young musician at the court of Periander, ruler of Corinth in ancient Greece. Arion is sent by Periander to compete in a musical contest on the island of Sicily; when the victorious Arion sails for home, the sailors steal his prize money and throw him overboard. He is saved by a dolphin, who befriends him. The resulting opera, *Arion and the Dolphin* (with music by Alec Roth), was performed for the first time in June 1994. The libretto was published by Phoenix House to coincide with the premiere of the opera, and Orion Children's Books subsequently published a picture book based on the opera in which Seth's words are illustrated by Jane Ray. This unusual children's book combines verse and prose to tell the fairly sophisticated story of Arion, who is imprisoned by Periander when he returns home without the money, and the dolphin, who is captured to be used as a performer and dies in captivity. Seth dedicates the book to "the wild dolphin 'Fungie,'" with whom he swam in the Dingle Bay of Ireland. Seth also collaborated with Roth on *Chinese Gardens,* a song cycle for voice and guitar that premiered at the Chester Summer Music Festival in 1998, and *Earth and Sky,* a children's choral piece that was commissioned by the British Broadcasting Corporation for the BBC Proms 2000, where it was performed by the Finchley Children's Music Group, conducted by Nicholas Wilks.

In his novel *An Equal Music* (1999) Seth once again takes on a completely new subject, this time the European world of classical musicians. Seth himself insists that this setting was not an intentional departure from previous topics. He told Jay Currie and Michèle Denis in a 1999 interview that "I don't try to do something new each time, it's just that I don't flee from it if it happens to be new." All his books are "different, one-offs," he has said, though this book came as a special surprise to many of his readers. The title is taken from a line in John Donne's "The House of

Dust jacket for the U.S. edition of Seth's 1999 novel, about a failed romance between two classical musicians (Richland County Public Library)

God" in his *XXVI. Sermons* (1660): "No noise, nor silence, but one equal music, no fears nor hopes, but one equal possession."

The ill-fated lovers of this romantic novel are violinist Michael Holme and pianist Julia McNicholl. Ten years before the story begins, their romance dissolved when their school days ended. The daughter of an Oxford professor, Julia had introduced him to art and literature, and they found that they could make beautiful music together. When Michael has a breakdown, he leaves Vienna with not much explanation to Julia. But when playing the music of Ludwig van Beethoven in London reawakens Michael's longing for Julia, he providentially glimpses her on a bus. His subsequent search for her and the consequences of their reunion are the stuff of the story. Michael has all the elements of the self-made artist: his working-class family in the north of England do not appreciate his classical music, his fine education, or his career. His love of music was fostered fortuitously when he was nine years old by a kind neighbor who took him to hear George Frideric Handel's *Messiah* (1741). Later, Michael recalls, "More than anything else, I wanted to be a part of that noise." Borrowed instruments, a scholarship to the Royal Northern College of Music in Manchester, membership in a master class at the Musikhochschule in Vienna, and many benefactors make his dream of becoming a professional violinist come true. Michael's character also allows for subdued political commentary about urban decline and cultural priorities. Julia is a much less complex or vexed character. She is simply the perfect love object for the hero, and her three impediments (her marriage, her son, and her deafness) make her all the more compelling. When she breaks off the affair, Michael reacts by breaking all links with human passion and with music. In the end he reconciles with the other members of his quartet, and they all reunite like a happy family. The plot thus loosely mimics the myth of Orpheus and Eurydice. Although Orpheus successfully rescues his love with his music, he still loses her in the end.

In his author's note Seth begins by saying "Music to me is dearer even than speech," and *An Equal Music* is above all a novel in which music matters. Although Seth had some early training in Indian classical music and only studied Western music, specifically piano and cello, later–he told Knorr "it's pointless coming to it at the age I came to it"–it is Western classical music that matters in this book. The length of Franz Schubert's "Trout Quintet" (1819), the discovery of a Beethoven opus, and ownership of a certain violin are all as important in the plot as the characters themselves. To accompany the novel, Seth produced a double compact-disc set that offers performances conducted by Sir Neville Marriner of music featured in the story, most particularly Beethoven's String Quintet in C minor and "Trout Quintet," which was released on the Uni/Decca label as *Vikram Seth: An Equal Music* (2000). The most highly praised element of the novel is the way it accurately represents the social and musical dynamics that govern string quartets. In Michael's Maggiore Quartet, the human aspects of music-making, with its contentious rivalry of egos, do not destroy the musical harmony. In addition to his own expertise with music, Seth also acknowledges the research he did both with the deaf and ear specialists to understand "the intersection of the world of wordlessness with those of heard, of half heard and of imagined sound."

Once again, the plot is straightforward. Seth has defended the seeming simplicity of his work: "I don't try to make things deliberately referential or obfuscating so the general reader can't read it," he told Knorr in their 1999 interview. The style of *An Equal Music,* however, is decidedly that of *A Suitable Boy.* There is a distinct musicality in the writing, a crossover into poetry at some points: "Panes of ice, frosted and clear: the wind pushed them onto the southern shore. They slide upon each other, give gently and creak clean. Seven layers thick, half-beached, they lie as clear as glass and creak and shift as the water moves with the wind." Sometimes the playfulness of the wordplay of *The Golden Gate* appears: "It's the weirdest thing, a quartet," one member remarks. "I don't know what to compare it to. A marriage? a firm? a platoon under fire? A self-regarding, self-destructive priesthood?" The most startling difference from *A Suitable Boy,* aside from its more manageable 380 pages, is the change from Seth's usual wry and ironic third-person narrative to a first-person narrator. He explained this change to interviewers Currie and Denis, saying "The only way I could write about music in the first place was to talk from inside his [John's] thoughts, otherwise it would just sound like program notes or something."

As in his other works, Seth sets up a self-referential critical scene. A pretentious music critic rejects Schubert's "Trout Quintet" for an avant-garde piece for baritone and vacuum cleaner, a sly jab at those who favor postmodern fiction over more traditional narrative. Seth's artistic goals seem to mirror those of the Maggiore Quartet, who spurn modern music in favor of the "classic" repertoire, against the grain of fashion-obsessed music critics. At one point Michael tells Julia, "I don't know how I've lived without you all these years," only to realize, "how feeble and trite my words sound to me, as if they have been plucked out of some housewife fantasy." Michael here echoes the conundrum felt by readers of the novel: is it profound in its remarkable psychological portraiture and representations of "real life" or does it descend into an overly sentimental romance cliché?

This novel, written after Seth had taken up residence in London, is the most Western of Seth's works, with the exception of *The Golden Gate.* Whether it is to escape being pigeonholed as an "Indian author," or, as Meenakshi Ganguly suggested in *Time International* (24 May 1999), to colonize "the fictional space of the West," or simply to present his authentic global self, Seth has decidedly looked for his materials from the West. The literary theorist Aijaz Ahmad has suggested that much Indian writing in English could have as easily been written in any of the other Indian languages. But this suggestion is certainly not true of Seth's works. Rather than aligning himself with a particular cultural tradition, he seems much more interested in following in the footsteps of his literary inspiration, Pushkin, who, as Seth remarked to Kapur in their 1999 interview, "wrote in all sorts of different forms. He didn't succumb to the temptation to repeat himself simply to please a public or a publisher."

In 1995 Vikram Seth published *The Poems, 1981–1994,* a collection of all his poetic writings and his libretto for *Arion and the Dolphin.* In the introduction he looks back over his career and reaffirms that although he desires to escape categorization, he considers himself primarily a poet. Where his career will take him in the future is unsure: "The wish to write about anything is such a rare and mysterious feeling," he says, "that it is pointless to preempt or constrain it by notions of subject or geography or genre."

Interviews:

Amit Roy, interview, *Telegraph* (Calcutta), 29 August 1992;

Michele Field, "Vikram Seth," *Publishers Weekly,* 240 (10 May 1993): 46–47;

Jill Rachlin, "Talking with . . .Vikram Seth: Creating an Indian 'Romeo and Juliet,'" *People Weekly,* 39 (24 May 1993): 65;

Eleanor Wachtel, "Eleanor Wachtel with Vikram Seth," *Malahat Review,* 107 (Summer 1994): 85–102;

Sudeep Sen, "A Poet at Heart," *Wasafiri: Journal of Caribbean, African, Asian and Associated Literatures and Film,* 21 (Spring 1995): 22–25;

Chelvanayakam Kanaganayankam, "Vikram Seth," *Configurations of Exile: South Asian Writers and Their World* (Toronto: TSAR, 1995);

Jeremy Gavron, "A suitable joy," *Guardian Unlimited* (27 March 1999) <http://www.guardian.co.uk/Archive/Article/0,4273,3845046,00.html>;

Katherine Knorr, "Vikram Seth Plays to His 'Truest Judges,'" *International Herald Tribune* (23 April 1999) <http://www.iht.com/IHT/KK/00/kk042399.html>;

Akash Kapur, "The Seth Variations," *Atlantic Unbound* (23 June 1999) <http://www.theatlantic.com/unbound/ interviews/ba990623.htm>;

Jay Currie and Michèle Denis, "Hearing a Different Music," *January* (June 1999) <http://www.januarymagazine.com/profiles/vseth.html>.

References:

Shyam S. Agarwalla, *Vikram Seth's "A Suitable Boy": Search for an Indian Identity* (New Delhi: Prestige Books, 1995);

Angela Atkins, *Vikram Seth's "A Suitable Boy": A Reader's Guide* (New York: Continuum, 2002);

Emilienne Baneth-Nouailhetas, "Forms of Creation in *A Suitable Boy,*" *Commonwealth Essays and Studies,* 22 (Spring 2000): 69–83;

John Bemrose, "Full-Lotus Fiction," *Maclean's,* 106, no. 22 (1993): 46–48;

Jay Curlin, "'The World Goes On': Narrative Structure and the Sonnet in Vikram Seth's *The Golden Gate,*" *Publications of the Arkansas Philological Association,* 22 (Fall 1996): 13–26;

Thomas Disch, "Onegin's Children: Poems in the Form of a Novel," *Parnassus: Poetry in Review,* 17/18 (1993): 166–186;

Santosh Gupta, "*The Golden Gate:* The First Indian Novel in Verse," in *The New Indian Novel in English: A Study of the 1980s,* edited by Viney Kirpal (New Delhi: Allied Publishers, 1990), pp. 91–100;

John Hollander, "Yuppie Time in Rhyme," *New Republic,* 194 (21 April 1986): 39–47;

Makarand R. Paranjape, "*The Golden Gate* and the Quest for Self-Realization," *ACLALS Bulletin,* 8, no. 1 (1989): 58–73;

John Oliver Perry, "*All You Who Sleep Tonight,*" *World Literature Today* (Summer 1991): 549–550.

William Sutcliffe

(9 March 1971 –)

Merritt Moseley
University of North Carolina at Asheville

BOOKS: *New Boy* (London & New York: Penguin, 1996);

Are You Experienced? (London: Hamilton, 1997; New York: Penguin, 1999);

The Love Hexagon (London: Hamilton, 2000; New York: Penguin, 2000).

SELECTED PERIODICAL PUBLICATIONS–UNCOLLECTED: "It's cool not to travel with 'Heat and Dust.' Off to India? William Sutcliffe offers some fashion tips on paperbacks for backpackers," *Daily Telegraph,* 9 August 1997, p. 7;

"No sex please, we're dancing," *Daily Telegraph,* 27 October 1997, p. 14;

"Travel: Why I loathe that backpacker baloney," *Sunday Telegraph,* 28 June 1998, p. 19.

William Sutcliffe is one of the most accomplished of the younger British novelists, the author of three books that mine familiar territory for many men of his age (including himself–there is a strong autobiographical component to them): school, adolescent travel, angst, uncertainties about love and sex, uncertainties in general. He commented in a 2000 interview on the website of the publisher Penguin: "Evelyn Waugh rendered any distinction between popular and literary fiction irrelevant because his novels are undoubtedly brilliant in every sense. That's what I aspire to. I want to write books that can communicate to people with all kinds of interests." Waugh is an ambitious model, but there are obvious connections. Like Waugh, Sutcliffe is primarily a comic writer, using comedy for the purposes of satire. He deflates many forms of human pretension. His first novel is about a school in which neither the masters nor the students are quite so completely grotesque as those in Waugh's *Decline and Fall* (1929); but the resemblance is there.

William Sutcliffe was born in London on 9 March 1971 and raised in Harrow, a northwest London suburb. He was educated for seven years at the Haberdashers' Aske's School for Boys in Elstree, Hertfordshire, and then at Cambridge University. There he was a member of Cambridge Footlights, a well-known performance troupe that mounts several shows a year. They are often written by the cast. After graduation Sutcliffe worked as a television researcher for several independent production companies based variously in West London, Soho, and Cardiff. Two of the characters in his third novel, *The Love Hexagon* (2000), are television researchers, and the explanation of their careers may reflect the author's own experience: "Elemental Productions, like the whole industry, was entirely dependent on the free labour supplied by arts graduates in their early twenties suffering from the temporary delusion that having an interesting job was more important than earning enough money to pay rent." He also worked as a tour guide, taking American teenagers around continental Europe. Since he began to publish novels–all of which have sold well–Sutcliffe no longer works in television. In a recent interview he said that he lives in London and writes, and that is all.

His first novel, *New Boy,* appeared in 1996. It is the account of life in a boys' school, much (even controversially) like his own Haberdashers' Aske's School, particularly focused on the relationship between the narrator, Mark, and new boy Barry. The moving force in the novel is the powerful attraction between Mark and Barry, whom he soon identifies as "sex on legs." Though he looks at Barry in the dressing room, Mark regularly insists that he is no "bender–I didn't get an erection or anything when I was looking at Barry. I just . . . I just felt a certain manly admiration for his beauty. I think maybe I was jealous of his power to attract women. The reason why I couldn't stop thinking about him or staring at him was that I wanted to look like him so that I could have sex with lots of women. That's what it was."

After some delicate courtship by Mark, he and Barry become friends. Barry even begins to serve as Mark's surrogate in the world of sex. Though Mark is obsessed with sexuality and talks about it incessantly, even poring over celebrity biographies to glean anecdotes and facts with which to amuse his friends, he is not only a virgin but also deeply convinced that he will remain so; he is insistent on his own ugliness. This conviction combines with the inaccessibility of females (they go to a different school, even though adjacent) to keep him chaste. Barry is a different matter, however, and Mark is able to arrange, effortlessly, for Barry to sleep with "the best-looking girl in North West London." From there Barry, abetted by Mark, actually moves on to Mrs. Mumford, a married French teacher, launches a passionate affair with her that loses her her job, and moves in with her.

Through a series of further moves, involving both Mark's brother and Barry's sister, the love relationships become more complicated, at the end of which Barry is having an affair with Mark's gay brother. Mark's sputtering outrage at this development is not entirely convincing, and the reader is inclined to agree with Barry's sister, who tells Mark that he lusts after Barry and is "just too repressed to admit it."

The texture of homosexual relations between boys and between boys and masters in the novel assured two results. One of these was considerable attention to Sutcliffe's old school, where, according to David Rowan in *The Guardian* (21 August 1996), "the novel became the intense focus of telephone calls across north-west London." Sutcliffe acknowledged carefully, "It is a fiction, but a very accurate satire of a certain place at a certain time. There are definitely certain uncomfortable truths it brings to light." Rowan, referring to Sutcliffe, sees the book as a "way of highlighting the repressed homosexuality in a school such as his." The other result is the acceptance, or celebration, of the novel as gay fiction, with inclusion on gay websites and sales through gay book clubs.

Sutcliffe's reference to satire, and his ambition to be like Waugh, suggest a quality to this novel that transcends its love plot or the highlighting of homosexuality, repressed or otherwise. It is an accomplished and funny satire on adolescence and social striving. Narrator Mark is knowing about his school, which has somehow come to be populated mostly by Asian and Jewish boys. The Jewish/Christian contrast (though waived, mostly, for Gentile Barry) is the source of much of the humor. The opening paragraph strikes the brash tone:

> Along with the rest of the staff, the chaplain at my school failed to notice that the place had long since been taken over by Jews and Asians. He was the kind of chirpy Englishman who Christians think of as "a character" but we Jews prefer to call "a wanker."

Later Mark, talking with the Gentile Piers, a posh misfit in the school, "began to form hideous and exaggerated images of what must indeed be an awful, chilling crea-

Paperback cover for Sutcliffe's 1996 novel, about an adolescent schoolboy's awakening sexuality (Collection of Merritt Moseley)

ture–the non-Jewish mother." Sutcliffe is Jewish, though not religious.

More humor circulates around adolescent sex. When Mark discovers that his nickname among the girls is Bruno, he understands that this refers in the cruel shorthand of adolescents (via Frank Bruno, British heavyweight boxer) to an unfortunate incident at a party when, trying to pet with a girl, he accidentally punched her instead, in the crotch. Explaining a rash of graffiti at the school, consisting of drawing penises on every available surface, he urbanely comments,

> Anyone at all sceptical about the ability of men to work in harmony and sympathy should look on this as an irrefutable example of modern man at his very best. Maybe the first generation of New Men is only just arriving–we, the children of the seventies, the first generation to be raised by feminist mothers–we are arriving at last to overturn decades of slander against the male gene. Wait for us! We're completely different from everything you've ever seen before.

His rather cruel indifference to older people, including his parents as well as the staff at the school, comes out in his harshness to Mrs. Mumford (though jealousy of her affair with Barry may also be involved), as when he sees her dressing to look younger but describes her garment as "a cross between a poncho, a pair of dungarees, and a carpet."

This sardonic kind of observational humor reappears in *Are You Experienced?* (1997), a novel about young people "doing" India in their "gap years"–that is, between school and university. Like *New Boy,* it has a generous basis in Sutcliffe's own life: "I myself was a culprit of every one of the classic backpacker sins (yes, including the clothes) as a middle-class 19-year-old on a Year Off in India," he writes in "Why I loathe that backpacker baloney" (*Sunday Telegraph,* 28 June 1998). "Although I am pleased that I did the trip, I feel deeply sorry for the people who had to put up with me, not to mention nauseous with embarrassment." Sutcliffe is particularly adept at making comedy out of embarrassment, as he showed in his debut, and the road to India affords more, or at least more different, venues for young people to embarrass themselves with humorous results. His protagonist, Dave, continually finds himself in predicaments, some resulting from his own dislocation (or from his discovery that India is not what he had expected), some from his innocence or clumsiness, some from his mixture of motives–for instance, realizing that he is miserable in India but unable to admit it because of what others will think.

In addition, Sutcliffe is acute on the traditional objects of satirical comedy, pretentiousness and affectation, and the incongruities between reality and pretense. He knows that the motives people have for their pilgrimage are often mixed or inadmissible; so Dave pretends to be seeking spiritual enlightenment, while in reality he has sex in mind. His friend James "launched into some enormous long-winded theory about imperialist cultural assumptions and putting yourself into a situation where you're challenged to think about things that are taken for granted in the West, but I could tell that what he actually meant was 'The dope really *is* cheap.'" In Pushkar, Dave and Liz, his traveling companion, meet two English girls who have just spent three months at a leper colony, provoking Liz's envy:

> "How did you get a place there? I mean I've heard it's quite competitive."
>
> "I was lucky. One of mother's friends runs a leprosy organization in London, and I was put to the head of the queue. I could put in a good word for you if you like."

Sutcliffe penetrates the pretensions of his English travelers in various ways–by having them expose themselves, as in this conversation; by permitting Dave to score sarcastic points against them; and finally by inserting a real blast from an English journalist, who tells Dave that he is going to put him into an article–"something about how it's not hippies on a spiritual mission who come here any more, just morons on a poverty-tourism adventure holiday. The real point would have to be about how going to India isn't an act of rebellion these days, it's actually a form of conformity for ambitious middle-class kids who want to be able to put something on their CV that shows a bit of initiative."

Reviewer Laurence O'Toole, in *The Independent* (London) for 23 August 1997, called this book "a comic novel of oneupmanship and bickering between young people desperate to be liked by each other. It is therefore both very modern and timeless." The reviewer for *The New Statesman* called it "extremely and incisively funny . . . just as [Oscar] Wilde held a mirror up to the Victorians, Sutcliffe satirises British youth. . . . Guaranteed to make you run screaming from the Lonely Planet."

Christopher Hart, who called it "spot-on satire and very funny" in the *Daily Telegraph* (13 September 1997), nevertheless expressed the wish that "for his third novel one hopes that Sutcliffe will try for something more ambitious, less autobiographical." *The Love Hexagon* is more ambitious. Whether it is less autobiographical is unclear; two of its six main characters are television researchers, doing the job Sutcliffe held at the time his first novel was published–and there is some funny material about their jobs. For instance, one of them is proposing to develop a series on celebrities and their bathrooms, approval for which would guarantee her earning some money, and she receives it during the course of the book by pretending a star is interested in presenting the show. The trick is in substituting a much less prestigious presenter without losing the commission.

The Love Hexagon differs from Sutcliffe's first two books in its distributed focus. As the title suggests, there are six main characters, and the book traces the permutations in their love and/or sex relationships with one another. They are Guy and Lisa, who have been living together for five years, apparently in a stable and "good relationship"; Josh, Lisa's coworker (they are the television researchers, though "whenever there was nothing in production . . . the job title changed to development researcher and the salary went down"); Keri, Lisa's best friend, an unattached single woman of great beauty and sexiness; Graham, Guy's best male friend, a luckless single

Paperback cover of the first edition of Sutcliffe's 1997 novel, about the adventures of pretentious young Britons backpacking in India (Bruccoli Clark Layman Archives)

man who, as the novel opens, has just been dumped by his girlfriend, using the pager she insisted he buy; and Helen, Guy's best female friend, also unlucky in love. During the course of the book, all the alliances change. The catalyst seems to be the desire of the paired, Guy and Lisa–who think they are happily in love but really have an increasingly shallow relationship masking genuine dislike–to attract others into their condition. Guy sets up Helen and Graham; Lisa sets Keri up with Josh. Guy and Lisa part, and Lisa is first Josh's lodger, then his lover; Guy follows a one-night stand with Keri (after a humiliating fight with Lisa at their anniversary party) with the pursuit and eventual discovery of Helen; both Helen and Keri have had unsuccessful dates with Josh; and Keri, the cool, beautiful, apparently unapproachable woman, ends up with the hapless Graham.

It is not so much that each of the characters gets from point A to point B that matters in this novel as the sparkling observation, of behavior and psychology, and the wittiness of the dialogue along the way that make *The Love Hexagon* a successful novel. The threat to Guy and Lisa is evident in chapter 1, as they get ready to go out together: "Although Lisa talked more, laughed more, drank more, fell over more, and generally lived more than Guy, she rarely went anywhere without him. . . . They bundle out of the house together and rush off to the party of a friend of a friend of Lisa's, with Guy already wondering what time they will be able to leave and hoping there are some decent magazines in the toilet." Later, when Josh, who is vaguely upper-class but unsuccessful with women, is on his date with Helen, "he brushes off Helen's refusal to ask him any questions, and embarks on a lengthy monologue about his relationship with Lisa, and his job. Perhaps not exactly *his* job, but a job resembling it, with more authority, more excitement, higher wages, and less photocopying." Lisa, who sets out to arrange a breakup

Paperback cover for Sutcliffe's 2000 novel, about the shifting sexual pairings of a group of young Londoners (Bruccoli Clark Layman Archives)

with Guy, "loved feeling wronged. Aside from anything else, it allowed her to get angry–and anger was Lisa's hobby. She had mastered the phrasing, instrumentation, dynamic control, pacing, breathing technique and tonal colouring required to generate symphonic masterpieces of rage." The humor coexists with serious psychological observation. Talking with Josh, she regrets an insult and recognizes that "Every time she discusses her friend, she always finds herself riding piggyback on the sexual superiority exuded by Keri to end up in easy man-squashing games."

There is some evidence that *The Love Hexagon* means to expose the nullity of the twenty-something generation; for instance, when Graham tells Guy (admittedly in the throes of a transitory passion for a forty-year-old woman), "I mean–people our age are . . . are just . . . there's nothing to us." Sutcliffe declares in "No sex please, we're dancing" (*Daily Telegraph,* 27 October 1997) that "My generation–the twentysomethings of this decade–is afraid of sex." His characters do not seem to be *afraid* of sex, though they are uncomfortable in pursuing it, unsure of how to read the signals, and (in some cases) no good at it. Several critics read the novel as a critique of Sutcliffe's generation. Carrie O'Grady, in *The Guardian* (22 January 2000), wrote that "the loveless, opportunistic world of modern relationship-hunting is expertly picked apart" and called it a "chilly exposé of the modern mindset." Charlotte Mendelson described it in *The Independent* (London) for 2 January 2000 as "a genuinely funny running commentary on the failures, falsehoods, and constant self-assessments which are the twentysomething's natural state."

Perhaps this exposé-of-a-generation theme is overplayed. There are, after all, only six characters; they are all twenty-somethings, it is true, but the novel hardly invites readers to generalize their mischances and miscommunications into an indictment of their whole cohort. Moreover, all the characters in the novel do in fact like sex and are successful in achieving it, despite the varying degrees of satisfaction they may derive from it or bestow by it. The difference between a love hexagon and a love triangle is that the latter cannot be reduced to two couples. The love hexagon can always produce, as this one does, three pairs, suggesting that the possibilities of pairing up properly–or at least *more* properly–do exist.

Two reviewers of *The Love Hexagon* named deeper qualities that characterize all three of William Sutcliffe's novels and raise them above the reports from the territory of youth they are sometimes mistakenly taken to be. Emma Hagestadt, in *The Independent* (London) for 8 January 2000, identified Sutcliffe's "sparkling repartee and narrative sophistication," and William Leith, in the *Daily Telegraph* (15 January 2000), after identifying Sutcliffe as "a master of the trivial domestic snit," goes on to conclude that "the author is telling us, convincingly, how easily and often our veneer of social decorum is destroyed by the sexual urge." This is the traditional work of the satirist: to show the distance between what people would be and what they are, between the head and the heart, between the arrangements of society and sexuality. Sutcliffe, in his first three novels, earns his aspiration to elide the distinction between popular and literary fiction, like Waugh.

Interview:

Interview with Sutcliffe, *Penguin UK* <http://www.penguin.co.uk/static/packages/uk/articles/sutcliffe.html>.

Colm Tóibín

(1955 -)

Tim Middleton
Bath Spa University College

BOOKS: *Martyrs and Metaphors,* Letters from the New Island, volume 1, no. 2 (Dublin: Raven Arts Press, 1987);

Walking Along the Border, photographs by Tony O'Shea (London: Queen Anne Press, 1987); republished as *Bad Blood: A Walk Along the Irish Border* (London: Vintage, 1994);

Dubliners, photographs by O'Shea (London: Macdonald, 1990);

Homage to Barcelona (London: Simon & Schuster, 1990; revised, 1991; republished, with new introduction by Tóibín, New York: Penguin, 1992; revised edition, London: Picador, 2002);

The South (London: Serpent's Tail, 1990; New York: Viking, 1991);

The Trial of the Generals: Selected Journalism, 1980–1990 (Dublin: Raven Arts Press, 1990);

The Heather Blazing (London: Pan, 1992; New York: Viking, 1993);

The Sign of the Cross: Travels in Catholic Europe (London: Cape, 1994; New York: Pantheon, 1994);

The Story of the Night (London: Picador, 1996; New York: Holt, 1997);

Finbar's Hotel, by Tóibín and others, edited by Dermot Bolger (London: Picador / Dublin: New Island Books, 1997; San Diego: Harcourt Brace, 1999);

The Blackwater Lightship (London: Picador, 1999; New York: Scribner, 2000);

The Irish Famine (London: Profile/London Review of Books, 1999); enlarged, with documentary materials, as *The Irish Famine: A Documentary,* edited by Tóibín and Diarmid Ferriter (London: Profile/London Review of Books, 2001; New York: Thomas Dunne/St. Martin's Press, 2002);

The Modern Library: The Two Hundred Best Novels in English Since 1950, by Tóibín and Carmen Callil (London: Picador, 1999; revised and enlarged, 2000);

Love in a Dark Time: Gay Lives from Wilde to Almodóvar (London: Picador, 2002); republished as *Love in a Dark Time: And Other Explorations of Gay Lives and Literature* (New York: Scribner, 2002);

Colm Tóibín (photograph by Perry Ogden; from the dust jacket for the U.S. edition of The Blackwater Lightship, *2000)*

Lady Gregory's Toothbrush (Dublin: Lilliput Press, 2002; Madison: University of Wisconsin Press, 2002).

OTHER: *Seeing Is Believing: Moving Statues in Ireland,* edited by Tóibín (Mountrath, Ireland: Pilgrim Press, 1985; Bucks: Colin Smythe, 1985);

Soho Square 6: New Writing from Ireland, edited by Tóibín (London: Bloomsbury, 1993); republished as *New Writing from Ireland: A Soho Square Anthology* (Win-chester, Mass.: Faber & Faber, 1994); republished as *New Irish Writing* (London: Bloomsbury, 1997);

The Guinness Book of Ireland, edited by Tóibín and Bernard Loughlin (London: Gulane, 1995);

Francis Stuart, *Black List, Section H,* foreword by Tóibín (Dublin: Lilliput Press, 1995; London: Penguin, 1996);

The Kilfenora Teaboy: A Study of Paul Durcan, edited by Tóibín (Dublin: New Island Books, 1996);

Micheál Tóibín, *Enniscorthy: History & Heritage,* introduction by Tóibín (Dublin: New Island Books, 1998);

The Penguin Book of Irish Fiction, edited, with an introduction, by Tóibín (New York & London: Viking, 1999; London: Penguin, 2001);

The Irish Times Book of Favourite Irish Poems, introduction by Tóibín (Dublin: Irish Times Books, 2000);

James Baldwin, *Another Country,* introduction by Tóibín (London: Penguin, 2001);

Andrew Hinds, *The Starving and October Song: Two Contemporary Irish Plays,* foreword by Tóibín (Dublin: Caryfort Press, 2001);

L. P. Hartley, *The Go-Between,* foreword by Tóibín, New York Review Books Classics (New York: New York Review Books, 2002).

Colm Tóibín is one of the leading contemporary Irish authors. His output is varied, including novels, works of prose nonfiction, travelogues, and works of literary criticism. Tóibín's distinctive traits as a novelist include a spare style and compressed but powerful prose that owes as much to the American writer Raymond Carver as it does to any modern Irish writer. In his works Tóibín has tackled the problems that the modern Irish have had in dealing with the legacy of the troubled past of their country, examined the effects that repressive and illiberal states have on individuals, and addressed questions of sexuality and the impact of AIDS. Academic study of Tóibín's work is limited, but his novels are widely reviewed in newspapers as well as weekly and monthly periodicals. Tóibín's work has been written in a culture undergoing tremendous change and in which the certainties of the past are subject to revision. As critic Richard Kearney suggests in his *Transitions: Narratives in Modern Irish Culture* (1988), "A central problem facing contemporary Irish culture is how to mediate between the images of past and future; how to avoid the petrification of tradition and the alienation of modernity." Tóibín's work may readily be located as part of what Terence Brown, in his *Ireland: A Social and Cultural History,* called that "vital energy of contemporary Irish art in its engagement . . . with crises of identity, violence and historical consciousness."

Colm Tóibín was born in Enniscorthy, County Wexford, Ireland, in 1955. His father, Micheál Tóibín, a schoolteacher and local historian, died when Tóibín was twelve. Tóibín's family had long-standing connections to the area and to the tradition of resistance against British rule. His grandfather Patrick Tobin and his granduncle Michael Tobin were members of the Irish Republican Brotherhood. Patrick Tobin was jailed in 1915 for tearing down British army recruiting posters; he took part in the Enniscorthy uprising in support of the 1916 Easter Uprising in Dublin and was imprisoned once more by the British authorities. Colm Tóibin's older sister, Bairbre Tóibín, a history teacher in Colaiste Bhride, has written a novel based on their grandfather's experiences, *The Rising* (2001). Colm Tóibín was educated at St. Peter's College, Wexford, and studied English and history at University College, Dublin. He went to Spain in 1975, where he taught English in Barcelona, before returning to Ireland in 1979. He began his writing career as features editor of *In Dublin* from 1981 to 1982, was an editor of the current-affairs magazine *Magill* from 1983 to 1985, and has worked as a journalist for the *Sunday Independent* (Dublin) since 1985. He has been a regular contributor to *Esquire, London Review of Books, New Statesman, TLS: The Times Literary Supplement,* and *The Irish Review.* Tóibín lives and works in Dublin.

Tóibín's first novel, *The South* (1990), is a haunting work that tells the story of Katherine Proctor, the only child of a broken Anglo-Irish home, who flees her marriage with Tom and abandons their young son, Richard, for Spain, where she meets and falls in love with Miguel, a political artist. The reasons for Katherine's departure are complex and only partly stem from her husband's insistence on prosecuting a legal claim against a local Catholic family. Spanning two decades from the 1950s to 1970s, with recollected sequences from the 1920s and 1930s, the novel weaves Katherine's childhood memories of being burned out of her family home during the Irish Civil War (1922–1923) with Miguel's troubled recollections of his violent acts during the Spanish Civil War (1936–1939). Miguel and Katherine leave Barcelona for a house in the Catalonian Pyrenees mountain village of Pallosa, where he had been during the civil war, and his anarchist past returns to haunt him. While in the mountains Katherine develops her talent as a painter, and the couple continues to see much of their mutual friend, the Catholic Irishman Michael Graves, who comes from the same region of Ireland as does Katherine. She and Miguel have a daughter, Isona, but soon Katherine is finding the relationship fraught, and it is clear that, like her own mother, she lacks strong maternal feelings–"she had not wanted a child; she was not prepared to go through such fear and agony."

Miguel's memories, coupled with the brutal treatment by the police of his old comrade Carlos Puig, become too much for him, and in a bleak sequence he takes his own life and that of their daughter by driving off a mountain road. It is part of the oblique narrative style of the novel that the deaths are followed by a jump in time and a shift to the first person–the reader sees from Katherine's perspective, but this shift comes some time after the initial horror has passed and she has begun to build up a new life for herself as a painter in Barcelona. The reader knows that there is pain because she says so–"I cannot think about what happened. It is something I stop myself doing at all hours of the day and night"–but the reader is never presented with the details.

When Katherine returns to Ireland, she continues to develop her career as a painter. After a holiday with her mother she decides to contact her son, who has married a Catholic and converted to Catholicism, and she arranges to go and visit him and his family in the old family home. Katherine settles in with the family, and the novel ends with her in a platonic relationship with Michael Graves and achieving success as an artist.

In summary the novel may sound rather flat, and although, the suicide apart, it lacks major incidents, it tells a powerful story of self-discovery, carefully narrated to allow the reader to see glimpses of Katherine's mind while eschewing intrusive interventions. Set in and around the Wexford country of Tóibín's birth and drawing upon his knowledge of Barcelona and Catalonia, *The South* carefully establishes the complex intersection of place and identity. Placing human relationships at the center of its account of the troubled histories of two nations, this book is a simple yet stunning first novel. An unsigned review in *Publishers Weekly* (5 July 1991) praised it as "an exceedingly well crafted novel about divided countries and divided people, about how the past commands the present" and noted Tóibín's "extraordinary skill for rendering time and place." In the *Chicago Tribune Books* (20 October 1991) Judith Dunford called it "a book of sustained lyrical beauty and power," while in her review for *The Washington Post Book World* (22 September 1991) Barbara Probst Solomon described it as "a tour de force" in "making a woman artist's sensibility the focus" of its narration. He won the *Irish Times*–Aer Lingus International Fiction Prize and was short-listed for the Whitbread First Novel Prize for *The South* in 1991.

Dust jacket for the U.S. edition of Tóibín's first novel, in which a married Irish woman becomes romantically involved with a painter haunted by his memories of the Spanish civil war (Richland County Public Library)

Tóibín's second novel, *The Heather Blazing* (1992), focuses upon the emotional awakening of Eamon Redmond, an aging High Court judge whose indifference to those around him stems from a difficult childhood. The novel is set in Tóibín's birthplace, the Wexford town of Enniscorthy. The narrative moves between past and present and, like *The South,* explores Irish history through the lives of the central characters. Redmond's father, a local historian and schoolteacher, brings him up single-handedly following the early death of his mother; the boy's childhood during World War II, when Ireland was neutral, plays off Redmond's emotional isolation against the political isolation of the nation. In his introduction to *The Penguin Book of Irish Fiction* (1999) Tóibín argues that "Fathers in Irish writing are absent, or angry, or mad, or strangely silent," and Redmond falls into the last category. Redmond's austere public persona is revealed to be an armor that he uses both to keep in his childhood pain and to keep out emotional engagement with those around him; he is dominated by his past because he finds it "more real and vivid and focused than anything that had happened since."

In charting Redmond's rise to public office Tóibín also charts the emergence of a new Ireland–an Ireland with which the law that Redmond represents is increasingly unable to engage–"it was the world in which these things happened which made him uneasy, a world in which opposite values lived so close to each other." In two key cases that the reader sees him judge–one concerning the state's duty of care toward a disabled child, the other regarding the rights of a pregnant teenager–Redmond finds in favor of institutions, not individuals. In a subtle critique of the Catholic foundations of the Irish state, Redmond is shown coming to the slow realization of the implications of his growing uneasiness with the legal decisions he makes:

> What was a family? The Constitution did not define a family, and at the time it was written in 1937 the term was perfectly understood: a man, his wife, and their children. But the Constitution was written in the present tense. . . . It was his job to define and redefine these terms now. . . . He was not certain about right and wrong, and he realized that this was something he would have to keep hidden from the court.

Redmond's emotional detachment also features in his private life, affecting his marriage with Carmel and his parenting of their daughter, Niamh, and son, Donal. Faced by his wife's serious illness and his unmarried daughter's pregnancy, he is unable to provide love and affection, and it takes the death of his wife to bring him closer to his children. Changes in his inner life become apparent, and, during the course of a long walk alone on the beach near their holiday home, the reader sees a rare emotional response–"his eyes filled up with tears"–and his character begins to become more sympathetic to the reader. This scene comes immediately after one of the time shifts of the novel to Redmond's childhood, in this case to the death of his father–the only other occasion when "His eyes filled up with tears." The novel closes with Redmond finding a new emotional equilibrium, enjoying his relationship with his daughter and grandson and apparently perceptive to the emotional needs of others in a way not seen before:

> Eamon held his grandson under the arms and lifted him high so the sun was on his back, and then lowered him into the water until his legs were wet, holding him firmly all the time. He ducked him down in to the water and out again, but it was too much for him. He was frightened. Eamon began to carry him slowly towards the shore.

This scene echoes an earlier beach scene with Redmond and his father and brings the novel to a close with a suggestion that he has come to terms with his past as well as his present.

An unsigned review in *Publishers Weekly* (23 November 1992) commented that "Tóibín's acclaimed prose style–measured and restrained as a Victorian memoir yet poetic in precision–makes a character of the brooding, enigmatic Irish weather and gives voice to the darker side of the Irish character" and noted Joycean echoes in the "epiphany of sons" that concludes the novel. *The Heather Blazing* won the Encore Award for best second novel published in Britain in 1993 and the E. M. Forster Prize from the American Academy of Arts and Letters in 1995.

Tóibín's third novel, *The Story of the Night* (1996), marked a departure in terms of setting, the bulk of the action taking place in Argentina in the 1970s and 1980s–a period that included military rule, the war with Britain over the Falkland Islands, and the postwar attempt to redevelop the nation. Tóibín has visited Argentina several times; as a journalist he covered the downfall of the military dictatorship in 1985–some of his reportage is collected in *The Trial of the Generals: Selected Journalism, 1980–1990* (1990). In terms of theme and style the novel remains on familiar ground, but Tóibín makes a marked shift in narrative style by choosing to tell the story in the first person.

Richard Garay is born to an English mother and Argentinean father. Following the death of his father, his mother retreats into a narrow circle of English associates, increasingly bitter at her straitened circumstances. At the start of the novel Richard ekes out a living as a teacher of English; later, through the family of one his pupils, he meets and comes to work for Donald and Susan Ford, U.S. economic advisers backed by the Central Intelligence Agency, for whom his inside but distanced knowledge of the Argentine political scene proves useful. An outsider because of his partly English heritage, Richard is also an outsider in the macho culture of Argentina because of his homosexuality, and together nationality and sexuality conspire to make him "see the world as separate from myself."

Much of the novel revolves around Richard's views on and experience of Argentinean politics in the aftermath of the Falklands war. At times this political dimension sits uneasily with the more private story of Richard's romantic and sexual life, and the novel is rather uneven–long sequences about political machinations and equally long sequences of sexual adventures that never quite jell into anything coherent or cohesive. The novel is retrospective first-person narration, but Tóibín does little to exploit the gap between the older, experienced narrator and the younger, experiencing self. At times the reader is brought up against the unreliability of Richard's narration, but whether this unreliability stems from his mixed nationality or his sexuality, or both, remains unclear. What is clear, however, is that Richard is set up as an outsider whose prejudices are slowly eroded by the weight of personal experience. On balance, the gay bildungsroman aspect of the novel is stronger than the political plotline–scenes of tentative sexual awakening and promiscuous gay sex are drawn with Tóibín's usual spare but deft touch.

After the death of his mother Richard is free to develop his gay life, but the key event is his meeting with the Fords, who arrange for him to take a job as a translator for economists from the International Monetary Fund. Richard takes to this new world with naive enthusiasm: "I enjoyed standing in front of them, wearing the same clothes as they wore, mimicking their masculinity, and seeming to be in control." As he gains power and business contacts, he is also developing a relationship with Pablo Canetto, the brother of his one-time pupil. Richard rents a large house, and he and Pablo plan their life together. These scenes are carefully drawn, and the first-person narrative allows Tóibín to build up a sense of Richard's optimism and newfound harmony only to shatter it with the arrival of Pablo's friends Jack and Mart. Mart is dying of AIDS, and the latter part of the novel plays off the emergence of a reformed and seemingly less corrupt Argentina with Richard and Pablo's eventual infection with AIDS. The novel ends with Pablo and Richard living from day to day, uncertain of how much future they might have.

The novel is about the self-delusions of Richard Garay, cut off not only from the politics of the country he inhabits but also, toward the end of the novel, seemingly reluctant to face up to the reality of his infection with AIDS. As was the case with Tóibín's earlier protagonists, Garay is emotionally distant for much of the novel, and here the first-person narration makes less visible the kind of growing self-awareness that was a feature of the closure of the earlier texts. In a 14 April 1997 review for *The Spectator* (London) James Simmons noted the "meandering plot" but found much to praise in the tact with which Garay's ingrained self-denial is portrayed. Mary Ellen Quinn, reviewing the novel for *Booklist* (15 May 1997), noted that "questions of identity haunt this novel" and suggested that Tóibín's "careful prose works well with Richard's dispassionate way of conveying his life story." An unsigned review in *Publishers Weekly* (14 April 1997) called the novel "a rewarding narrative that blends themes of personal intensity and historical import" and remarked that "The book succeeds seamlessly on two levels. Through Richard's work, we get a fascinating view of Argentina in transition. . . . Through Richard's own coming of age story, we also bear witness, in Tóibín's evocative cadences, to a more international yet deeply personal crisis: the devastation of AIDS."

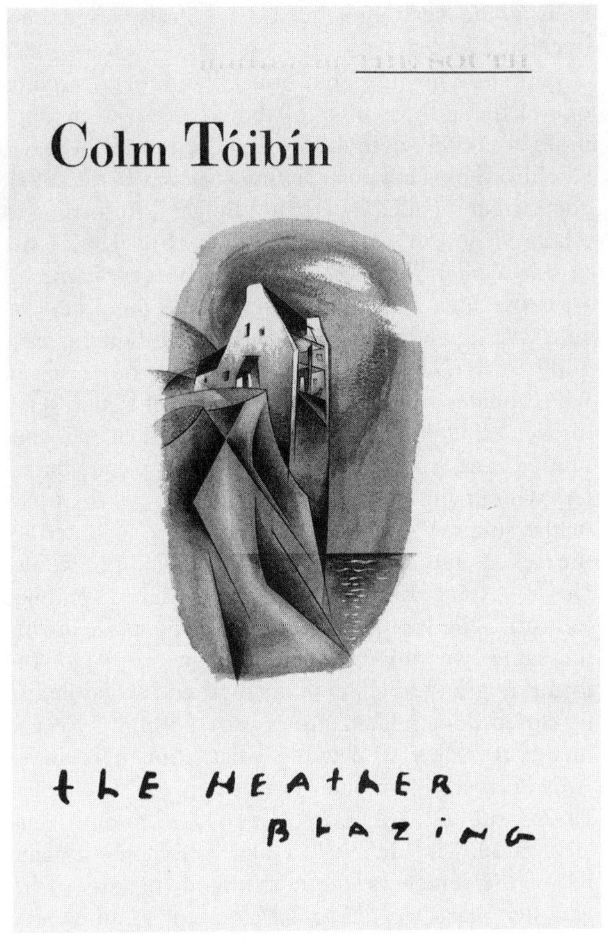

Dust jacket for the U.S. edition of Tóibín's 1992 novel, in which an emotionally detached High Court judge is brought closer to his children by the death of his wife (Richland County Public Library)

In a long review for the *New Statesman* (20 September 1996) Victoria Radin suggested that *The Story of the Night* was Tóibín's most explicit insight into the figure of "the outsider." Radin praised the strongly drawn Mrs. Garay, seeing her as "an antidote to Richard's and perhaps his author's parsimonious making do." However, the dominant note of Radin's review is one of critique of Tóibín's uneven plotting and handling of theme in the novel. Radin is especially critical of the closure of the novel, suggesting that Tóibín does not bring together the development of Garay's "self concealment and emotional dandyism" with the "gay romance" of the concluding chapters: "Quite soon, with the arrival of a very camp couple from San Francisco, we are brutally in AIDS country. The novel, as all of Tóibín's work, tries to insert a grace note at the very end, but here it feels desperately banal and forced."

Before his next solo novel, Tóibín appeared as one of the authors of a collaborative novel–perhaps more accurately described as a collection of short stories linked by a common setting–*Finbar's Hotel* (1997), "devised and edited by Dermot Bolger." According to Alain de Botton's account in the 27 July 1997 issue of *The Sunday Telegraph* (London), Bolger "came up with the idea, in part to escape the loneliness of solo-writing and spend time with the authors he most admired. He sent a 20-page letter to the other six, in which he described an (imaginary) hotel in the Quay district of Dublin, assigning each of them a room number and asking them to dream up some characters who might have checked into the hotel on a particular summer's night." The chapters contributed by the seven authors (Bolger himself, Tóibín, Roddy Doyle, Anne Enright, Hugo Hamilton, Jennifer Johnston, and Joseph O'Connor) all take place during the same twenty-four-hour period in the life of the formerly grand hotel, now decrepit and scheduled to be closed down. The authors were faithful, it seems, in not revealing who wrote what, though reviewer Anne Haverty, for one, declared in the 4 October 1997 issue of *The Daily Telegraph* (London) that "Room 107" is "definitely Colm Tóibín–the elegant fall of the sentences, the odd unknowingness of his gangster character." *Finbar's Hotel* occupies an anomalous place in Tóibín's body of work, as it is not quite a co-authored novel, but his contribution is more than just a short story. In 1998 Tóibín wrote the foreword to a selection of his father's essays on local history, *Enniscorthy: History & Heritage.*

In his fourth solo novel, *The Blackwater Lightship* (1999), Tóibín returns to an Irish setting–the Wexford locations of his earlier work are once again to the fore–but continues to address the subject of AIDS. Once again Tóibín shows mastery of the convoluted and surprising ways in which childhood shapes and informs adult attitudes. Parental emotional detachment is again a subject for insightful inquiry, and the theme of self-delusion is also present in the inability of Helen, the central character, to see that her career-mindedness and marital tensions make her far more like her mother, Lily, than she cares to recognize.

The novel commences in the home of Helen and Hugh, both teachers, who are enjoying an end-of-term party at their home. Surrounded as they are by friends, colleagues, and neighbors, their suburban life is superficially tranquil and rewarding, but the reader soon sees deep-seated tensions within Helen, whose marriage merely patches over "the raw areas in her which were unsettled and untrusting." Soon the causes of this lack of contentment resurface as she learns that her brother, Declan, is dying from AIDS-related illnesses and her rather unhappy family are asked to gather around Declan at his grandmother's home in Cush, County Wexford, to nurse him during a last weekend at home in the final stages of his illness.

The three women in the family–Dora Devereux, her daughter, Lily, and her granddaughter, Helen–grapple with the legacy of years of bitterness and mistrust while trying to nurse the ailing Declan and cope with the presence of his gay close friends Paul and Larry. While there are moments of humor and shared understanding, the dominant note is one of pain and misunderstanding for much of the novel. Tóibín handles the material adroitly, giving the reader Declan and Helen's childhood and the death of their father with his customary tact and subtlety. Readers are shown causes of present problems but also the ways in which memory can occlude and obscure the truth. Tóibín's wonderful economy of writing is still evident in his reluctance to give the reader full access to characters' inner feelings, but by playing off the memories of three generations of women he gives the reader a rich insight into family history, studded with telling moments.

Against this backdrop of mutual recrimination the reader witnesses Declan's decline and the tentative and uncertain moves toward reconciliation between the women. The key themes, as was also the case in *The South* and *The Heather Blazing,* are the compromises and concessions involved in belonging to a family and in calling somewhere "home":

> She realised that for the first time in years–ten years, maybe–she was back as a member of this family she had so determinedly tried to leave. For the first time in years they would all be under the same roof, as though nothing had happened. She was back home, where she had hoped she would never be again, and she felt, despite herself, almost relieved.

Portrayed largely from Helen's perspective, the novel underscores Tóibín's ability to draw complex female characters. Declan's illness, although portrayed in unflinching detail, is really little more than a catalyst for Helen's reconciliation with her family. The exploration in the novel of the redemptive power of death in a modern setting might be seen as of especial significance in a Catholic nation.

Unlike Tóibín's earlier novels, *The Blackwater Lightship* is less engaged with the political history of Ireland. Aspects of social change are touched upon incidentally in detailing Lily's childhood or the lives of Declan's gay friends Paul and Larry, but the main focus is the mistrust between Helen and her mother and grandmother. Gradually, Lily reveals a more compassionate side and Helen finds "the new softness in her mother . . . impossible to resist"; however, there is no easy reconciliation. The family's fumbling attempts at change are set against the natural process of erosion that is eating away the coastline close to the family home in Cush. As in *The Heather Blazing,* Tóibín uses the liminal space of the beach as a setting for the beginning of Helen and Lily's reconciliation, and the novel ends with the muted triumph of Lily spending the night at Helen's home after returning the now severely ill Declan to the hospital in Dublin.

This quiet novel achieves its effects gradually and with subtlety. It was short-listed for the Booker Prize for Fiction in 1999 and the International IMPAC Dublin Literary Award in 2001. In *Lambda Book Report* (October 2000) Elizabeth Flynn suggested that the novel "captures adult human life in all its complexity" and praised the work's deft narrative structure. The reviewer for *Publishers Weekly* (12 June 2000) remarked that this book was not a "'dying of AIDS' story" but rather a "delicately powerful story of a family's failure to face difficult feelings and their stubborn refusal to admit need." In the *New Statesman* (11 October 1999) Martyn Bedford noted that "Tóibín understands this human tension between selfishness and altruism when a loved one is dying" and praised the "visceral and unsparing" depiction in the novel of Declan's illness, remarking that his "graphic deterioration in the final stages of his illness and its impact on those around him ought to move any reader." Reviewing the U.S. edition in *The Gay & Lesbian Review Worldwide* (July 2001) Felice Picano noted that the novel approached the subject of AIDS obliquely, suggesting that the "core fable is that of a broken family being reunited with their gay son" and concluding that while the novel is "Unremarkable, simple, almost prosaic," it nonetheless delivers a "powerful kick."

In 1999 the massive anthology *The Penguin Book of Irish Fiction,* edited by Tóibín, was published, as was *The Modern Library: The Two Hundred Best Novels in English Since 1950,* an annotated listing by Tóibín and collaborator Carmen Callil of what they perceived to be the most significant English-language novels of the second half of the twentieth century. That same year Tóibín also published *The Irish Famine,* a monograph on the mid-nineteenth-century famine that devastated Ireland. Tóibín's historiography was republished as the introduction to the follow-up volume, *The Irish Famine: A Documentary* (2001), which includes a wide range of contemporary documents, such as

Dust jacket for the U.S. edition of Tóibín's 1999 novel, in which a woman tries to reconcile with her family while caring for her brother, who is dying from AIDS (Richland County Public Library)

letters, newspaper articles, and relief commission reports, compiled by Tóibín and his collaborator, historian Diarmid Ferriter. In his review of the 2001 volume for *The Spectator* (London) Kevin Myers called Tóibín's introduction "a very model of wisdom, of profound moral engagement and of scholarship" and concluded that "This small but brilliant book reaches right into the heart of the most tragic period in Irish history. I recommend it unreservedly."

In 2000 Tóibín was one of the judges for the International IMPAC Dublin Literary Award. In 2000 and 2001 Tóibín held a fellowship at the New York Public Library (NYPL) Center for Scholars and Writers. During his research on *The Irish Famine* he had become interested in Sir William Gregory, a seemingly generous landlord who nevertheless was responsible for legislation that forced applicants for public assistance to give up all land holdings, thus causing the ruin of many Irish families during the famine. Tóibín's research at the NYPL focused on

Gregory's wife, Lady Isabella Augusta Persse Gregory, who was a patron to William Butler Yeats and other writers and arguably the driving force behind the early-twentieth-century Irish literary renaissance. Although he was said to be working on a novel based on Lady Gregory, the first result of Tóibín's research is a short biographical sketch, *Lady Gregory's Toothbrush* (2002). The novelist William Trevor, in a 20 April 2002 review in *The Spectator* (London), remarked that "Biographical portraits are too often nowadays smudged in a surfeit of words: using so few that they amount almost to a paucity, this one is a brilliant illumination."

In 2002 Tóibín also published *Love in a Dark Time: Gay Lives from Wilde to Almodóvar,* a series of essays on gay artists and writers that mostly originated in pieces written for the *London Review of Books.* In a 10 March 2002 review for *The Sunday Telegraph* (London) Mark Sanderson noted that the theme of the book "is not coming out–declaring one's sexuality to the world–but coming to terms with one's self" and remarked that "Tóibín may once have been 'uneasy' about his sexuality but these fascinating essays suggest his critical faculties have always been assured."

Colm Tóibín has established himself as a major and distinctive voice in contemporary Irish fiction. While his work makes much of the complex associations between people and place, he eschews easy stereotypes of Irishness in favor of the often contradictory impulses that pull on contemporary lives. In his introduction to *The Penguin Book of Irish Fiction,* Tóibín argues that Irish writers "inherit a tradition in which it is readily accepted that the novel cannot compete with the world"–it is perhaps because of this anxiety about the relationship between world and writing that so much Irish writing is, Tóibín suggests, concerned with "dislocation and displacement and where it does focus upon the social it is by dramatizing the small details, the moments of pure truth" that "tell you very little about 'Irish society' and a great deal about the human heart." Tóibín's work may readily be fitted into this category of contemporary Irish writing.

Interview:

Lynne Tillman, "Colm Tóibín," *BOMB,* 38 (Winter 1992): 22–23.

References:

Colm Tóibín Website, 14 January 2002 <http://colmtoibin.com>;

Tom Herron, "ContamiNation: Patrick McCabe and Colm Tóibín's Pathographies of the Republic," in *Contemporary Irish Fiction: Themes, Tropes, Theories,* edited by Liam Harte and Michael Parker (Houndmills, U.K.: Macmillan / New York: St. Martin's Press, 2000), pp. 168–191;

Kim Wallace, "Dissent and Dislocation in Colm Tóibín's *The Story of the Night,*" *BELLS: Barcelona English Language and Literature Studies,* 11 (2000): 257–273.

Sue Townsend

(2 April 1946 –)

Peter D. Kittle
California State University, Chico

BOOKS: *The Secret Diary of Adrian Mole Aged 13 3/4* (London: Methuen, 1982; New York: Avon, 1984);

Bazaar and Rummage, Groping for Words, Womberang: Three Plays (London & New York: Methuen, 1984);

The Great Celestial Cow (London & New York: Methuen, 1984);

The Growing Pains of Adrian Mole (London: Methuen, 1984; New York: Grove, 1986);

The Secret Diary of Adrian Mole Aged 13 3/4: The Play, with songs by Ken Howard and Alan Blaikley (London: Methuen, 1985);

The Secret Diary of Adrian Mole Song Book, music and lyrics by Howard and Blaikley (London: Methuen, 1985);

Rebuilding Coventry: A Tale of Two Cities (London: Methuen, 1988; New York: Grove Weidenfeld, 1990);

Mr. Bevan's Dream (London: Chatto & Windus, 1989; New York: Trafalgar Square, 1990);

The True Confessions of Adrian Albert Mole, Margaret Hilda Roberts, and Susan Lilian Townsend (London: Methuen, 1989);

Ten Tiny Fingers, Nine Tiny Toes (London: Methuen Drama, 1990);

Adrian Mole: From Minor to Major: Ten Years of the Adrian Mole Diaries (London: Methuen, 1991)–comprises *The Secret Diary of Adrian Mole Aged 13 3/4, The Growing Pains of Adrian Mole, The True Confessions of Adrian Mole, Margaret Hilda Roberts, and Susan Lilian Townsend,* and "Adrian Mole and the Small Amphibians";

The Queen and I (London: Methuen, 1992; New York: Soho, 1993);

Adrian Mole: The Wilderness Years (London: Methuen, 1993);

The Queen and I: A Play with Songs, with songs by Ian Dury and Mickey Gallagher (London: Methuen, 1994);

Plays: 1 (London: Methuen Drama, 1996);

Ghost Children (London: Methuen, 1997; New York: Soho, 1998);

Adrian Mole: The Cappuccino Years (London: Joseph, 1999; New York: Soho, 2000);

The Public Confessions of a Middle-Aged Woman Aged 55 3/4 (London: Joseph, 2001);

Number Ten (London: Joseph, 2002).

Editions: *The Adrian Mole Diaries* (London: Methuen, 1985; New York: Grove, 1986)–comprises *The Secret Diary of Adrian Mole Aged 13 3/4* and *The Growing Pains of Adrian Mole;*

Adrian Mole: The Lost Years (New York: Soho, 1994)–comprises *The True Confessions of Adrian Albert Mole, Margaret Hilda Roberts, and Susan Lilian Townsend* and *Adrian Mole: The Wilderness Years.*

PLAY PRODUCTIONS: *Womberang,* London, Soho Poly Theatre Club, 20 October 1979;

The Ghost of Daniel Lambert, Leicester, Phoenix Theatre Company, 1981;

Dayroom, London, Croydon Warehouse Theatre, 1981;

Bazaar and Rummage, London, Royal Court Theatre Upstairs, 10 May 1982;

Captain Christmas and the Evil Adults, Leicester, Phoenix Theatre Company, 1982;

Groping for Words, London, Croydon Warehouse Theatre, 10 March 1983; revised as *Are You Sitting Comfortably,* Watford, Palace Theatre, 1986;

The Great Celestial Cow, London, Royal Court Theatre, 30 March 1984;

The Secret Diary of Adrian Mole Aged 13 3/4, Leicester, Phoenix Theatre Company, 6 September 1984; London, Wyndham's Theatre, 12 December 1984;

Ten Tiny Fingers, Nine Tiny Toes, Manchester, Library Theatre, November 1989;

The Queen and I, Leicester, Haymarket Theatre, 29 March 1994.

PRODUCED SCRIPTS: *The Secret Diary of Adrian Mole Aged 13 3/4,* television, by Townsend and Trevor Waite, 1985;

Sue Townsend (photograph © Jane Bown; from the dust jacket for the U.S. edition of Adrian Mole: The Cappuccino Years, *2000)*

The Growing Pains of Adrian Mole, television, Thames Television, 1987;

The Refuge, television, by Townsend and Carole Hayman, BBC4, 1987;

Adrian Mole: The Cappuccino Years, television, BBC, 2 February 2001.

In the realm of publishing, novelist Sue Townsend dominated England in the 1980s. Creator of Adrian Mole, a character described by *Spectator* reviewer Claudia FitzHerbert in 1992 as "a twerpish teenage boy from Leicester with a heart of gold and an unparalleled gift for bathos," Townsend was the best-selling English author of the decade.

An established playwright in her native Leicester, Townsend emerged from local writer to national (and later worldwide) publishing phenomenon in the 1980s. Her new role as a national best-selling author began with her publication of *The Secret Diary of Adrian Mole Aged 13 3/4* in 1982, which was followed by *The Growing Pains of Adrian Mole* in 1984, *The True Confessions of Adrian Albert Mole, Margaret Hilda Roberts, and Susan Lilian Townsend* in 1989, *Adrian Mole: From Minor to Major* in 1991, *Adrian Mole: The Wilderness Years* in 1993, and *Adrian Mole: The Cappuccino Years* in 1999. Each of these, which taken together form a satiric bildungsroman, were best-sellers, with the first novel spending more than a year in the number-one spot. Townsend's other work includes the novels *Rebuilding Coventry: A Tale of Two Cities* (1988), *The Queen and I* (1992), and *Ghost Children* (1997), in addition to plays produced in Leicester, Manchester, and London, among other areas of the United Kingdom. The chord that resonates most clearly throughout Townsend's work is the intersection of politics and family–particularly working- and middle-class families.

Townsend writes of such family situations with an authenticity grounded in experience. The eldest of three daughters, Susan Lilian Johnstone was born to John and Grace Johnstone on 2 April 1946 (her nebbish creation, Adrian, shares her birthday). She commented in the 28 November 1984 edition of *The Times* (London) that her parents, both of whom worked as bus conductors, were "clever enough to have been anything under different circumstances." Although unable to provide material wealth to Townsend's childhood–the family lived on an estate of prefabricated houses in Leicester known as "the rabbit hutches"–the Johnstones amply fed her intellect, especially in their own devotion to reading. Townsend has repeatedly commented that her family's regular use of public libraries led to her self-proclaimed addiction to print. She was particularly enamored of Richmal Crompton's *Just William* books, which featured adventures in the great outdoors not unlike those Townsend herself experienced in the peaceful wooded countryside surrounding her childhood home. Not all was idyllic, however; in an 11 October 1999 *Daily Telegraph* (London) article, Elizabeth Grice notes that as a child, Townsend had witnessed a murder while sitting in a tree with two other children but had told no one for fear that adults would not believe her.

This distrust of adults did little to help Townsend in the formality of school settings; she finally left school permanently a week before her fifteenth birthday. With no official qualifications, she worked at a series of unskilled jobs in dress shops, shoe factories, garages, and in encyclopedia sales before meeting and marrying Keith Townsend, a sheet-metal worker, when she was eighteen years old. When her husband left her for a younger woman in 1971, Townsend was left to raise their three young children alone. She soon found herself in need of public assistance and was forced by economic necessity to move into government-subsidized council housing, where she more than once was reduced to searching for loose change down the back of her sofa to pay for food.

All the while Townsend was writing, although she hid that fact "for twenty years–a period which encompassed my first marriage and the birth of three of my four children," as she writes in the introduction to *Plays: 1* (1996). The closest she came to going public with her writing was in the mid 1970s, when she was working with children, first at a local evening youth club and later at an after-school "adventure playground" program. Townsend wrote scripts for pantomimes–a traditional British dramatic form, usually performed around Christmas, which takes as its plot folk stories or other familiar tales–which were performed by the children for their parents. Twenty years later Townsend reflected that her experience directing the children's plays "was the best introduction to professional theatre I could have had."

At this time she met Colin Broadway, who became father to Townsend's fourth child in 1977. (The couple married later, in 1985.) At Broadway's urging, Townsend joined fellow local playwrights in the Phoenix Writers Group in 1978. Her play *Womberang* was soon written, workshopped, and eventually produced in London in 1979, winning Townsend a £2,000 Thames Television Playwrights Bursary that year and effectively launching her professional writing career. *Womberang* was followed by commissioned plays and, eventually, books. The character of Adrian Mole–initially named Nigel Mole, but changed because of the similarity to another fictional British schoolboy, Geoffrey Willans's Nigel Molesworth–originated in Townsend's years of secret writing and was revived as an audition piece for an actor. Eventually, the brief piece was expanded and submitted to Radio 4 of the British Broadcasting Company (BBC), where its broadcast as a half-hour comedy garnered Townsend a commission for a book about Adrian.

The 1982 publication of *The Secret Diary of Adrian Mole Aged 13 3/4* changed Townsend's life dramatically. Within three years she had two books on the best-seller list (*The Growing Pains of Adrian Mole* followed in 1984), a successful West End play, a television series, a range of official Adrian Mole writing products, and even a computer game to her credit. When Townsend adapted her novel for the stage, the initial nine-week run of the play in Leicester sold out completely within two days, causing, as Sally Brompton reported in the 28 November 1984 edition of *The Times* (London), "terrible scenes outside the theatre with people trying to fight their way in. In London, Wyndham's Theatre took £12,000 in advance bookings in the first 48 hours." The novels are popular with readers ranging from schoolchildren to adults. By 1986 they had been translated into sixteen languages (as of 2000, that number had increased to twenty-eight languages) and were "widely used as classroom texts" in Britain and elsewhere, according to a 4 October 1985 article in *TES: The Times Educational Supplement.*

Townsend has traced the genesis of Adrian Mole to overheard conversations at the youth club she worked in during the 1970s–conversations that, as she said in an undated interview with Mick Cowar, revealed the myriad aspects of pubescent life usually invisible to adults. *The Secret Diary of Adrian Mole Aged 13 3/4* gives voice to that combination of angst and uncertainty, naiveté and egocentrism, that defines adolescence; the commercial success of the novel–it spent more than a year at the number-one spot–would indicate that it was a voice many were anxious to hear. The novel is written, as its title implies, entirely in diary form, giving the narrative a necessarily episodic and staccato feel, as well as severely limiting the perspective afforded to the reader.

Adrian Mole, a thirteen-year-old boy living in Leicester, has high aspirations: he believes himself to be an intellectual, continually writes poetry that he

Dust jacket for the U.S. edition of Townsend's 1992 novel, in which the British monarchy is abolished and the royal family has to adapt to life in a public-housing project (Richland County Public Library)

hopes will one day be broadcast by the BBC, and envisions a life of riches resulting from his literary endeavors. The story begins with Adrian's composing his New Year's resolutions for 1981 and carries on through April 1982. During that period Adrian agonizes over his complexion, worries about his peer relationships at Neil Armstrong Comprehensive School, criticizes his parents' seemingly lax morals, and pines for a treacle-haired classmate named Pandora Braithewaite. He deals with a school bully named Barry Kent, takes care of a communist old-age pensioner named Bert Baxter, and watches the marriage of his working-class parents, Pauline and George, apparently dissolve, only to be repaired after a few months of separation. At the same time, Adrian notes the historical happenings on the periphery of the scene: the closure of factories and rise of unemployment under Margaret Thatcher; the marriage of Prince Charles to Diana Spencer; and the outbreak of war with Argentina over the Falkland Islands.

Townsend's filtering of these diverse threads of the narrative through Adrian's subjectivity gives *The Secret Diary of Adrian Mole Aged 13 3/4* its appeal. As Lynn Barber said in the 10 October 1999 issue of *The Observer Magazine* (London) the juxtaposing of "idealism versus trivia, high-mindedness versus low worries about acne" helps delineate not just Adrian's values but the important issues of his time. Early in the book Adrian's parents, arguing over the fact that Pauline is obviously (to everyone except Adrian) having an affair with their neighbor, neglect to prepare the evening meal, forcing Adrian to fend for himself at a local Chinese take-out. Later, his father tries to talk with Adrian about the troubles he and Pauline are facing: "he said my mother and him are 'going through a bad patch.' He asked me if I had anything to say. I said he owed me thirty-two pence for the Chinese chips and soy sauce. He gave me a pound. So I made a profit of sixty-eight pence." Adrian's prioritizing of a few pence over the welfare of his family appears to be the "willful naivete" that Casey Greenfield in *Newsday* (27 August 2000) called "Adrian's trademark."

At the same time, Townsend allows a bit of sharp political acumen to surface on occasion, as when Adrian speculates about the reasons for the nutritionally deficient lunches at his school: "Perhaps Mrs Thatcher wants us to be too weak to demonstrate in years to come." Thatcher is the target of various barbs in Adrian's diary, perhaps most notably when he considers voting for her during a mock school election: "Sometimes I think Mrs Thatcher is a nice kind sort of woman. Then the next day I see her on television and she frightens me rigid. She has got eyes like a psychotic killer, but a voice like a gentle person. It is a bit confusing." Townsend deftly raises the political and economic uncertainty of the times by making them manifest in her protagonist. As she said in the 30 June 1985 edition of *The Sunday Times* (London), she sees the Adrian Mole books not just as simple comedy but also as "an attack on the British class system."

The comedy in *The Secret Diary of Adrian Mole Aged 13 3/4* is not simply peripheral, however. For sheer comic effect, Townsend has Adrian compulsively measure and record the length of his "thing" and likewise throws in the odd malapropism, as Adrian's response shows when Pandora's father gives him Robert Tressell's *The Ragged Trousered Philanthropists* (1914) to read: "I haven't looked through it yet but I'm quite interested in stamp collecting so I will read it tonight." Townsend has said that her use of comic effects is deliberate and is intended to make her audience read more carefully. In an interview with Ellen Kanner of *Bookpage* (December 1994) Townsend noted that "if I tell people something serious, they don't listen. If they laugh, they listen. They listen acutely. You can get in whatever you want to say in comedy." Her comedy is employed not simply to entertain but to help her get her serious political ideas across–political ideas that Barber characterized as far to the left of the Labour Party.

These political ideas maintain their presence in *The Growing Pains of Adrian Mole.* Before the book even opens, Adrian's hand-scribbled "basic table of interpersonal relationships" places Thatcher in the list of "Enemies of Family," along with his school principal, bully Barry Kent, and his father's boss. The tone, tenor, and style of the book is consistent with the first volume and continues to follow the same story lines: Adrian's growing relationship with Pandora runs into problems because of Pandora's squarely middle-class status, while family matters become far more complicated when both Pauline and Doreen Slater, a woman with whom George had an affair in *The Secret Diary of Adrian Mole Aged 13 3/4,* turn up pregnant.

These problems, of a more complex and mature nature, show development in Adrian's character, yet the comic voice maintains: "I have just realized that I have never seen a dead body or a real female nipple. This is what comes of living in a cul-de-sac." After the birth of his new sister, Rosie, and half brother, Brett, Adrian captures the contradictions and complications of life in contemporary England: "My father was ironing baby clothes when I got home from school. He said, 'If you laugh, I'll kill you.' My mother was feeding the baby, with her feet on the dog's back. It was a charming domestic picture, only spoiled when my father put the ironing board away and went home to his other family." These types of observations, positing the unpleasant truth of broken families within a comic frame, exemplify what Nicolas Shrimpton, in his *Sunday Times* (London) review (5 August 1984) of *The Growing Pains of Adrian Mole,* called "the natural strength of books like these."

As was the case with *The Secret Diary of Adrian Mole Aged 13 3/4, The Growing Pains of Adrian Mole* was a best-seller; combined sales of the English-language editions of the two books had topped five million copies by mid 1986. The Mole phenomenon seemed to be a publishing juggernaut when Townsend vowed, shortly after finishing *The Growing Pains of Adrian Mole,* to refrain from writing more about Mole until 1992 (although the third book actually appeared in 1989), despite tremendous pressure from both her publisher and the public. In an interview with Sally Brompton in 1986, Townsend said of a third Mole book that "There's something almost distasteful about it because I *know* it would sell and I would feel I was cashing in on it." Earlier that same year, Townsend, then approaching her fortieth birthday, suffered a massive heart attack, owing to a combination of factors: her recently diagnosed insulin-dependent diabetes, a lifestyle that included both cigarettes and alcohol, and an overload of work-related stress resulting from the success of the Mole books.

While the public was clearly enamored of Mole, the critics were often less kind. Reviews of the Mole books have often emphasized that they are popular rather than literary works (for instance, they have been featured infrequently in the more highbrow *TLS: The Times Literary Supplement*). In a 9 September 1984 review in *The Sunday Times* (London) of the play adaptation of *The Secret Diary of Adrian Mole Aged 13 3/4,* John Peter was quick to let the reader know that he is "one of the few people in the western hemisphere" who found Adrian Mole "totally unfunny," although he conceded that the rest of the audience "didn't find it unfunny at all." In his review of *The Growing Pains of Adrian Mole* Shrimpton described Townsend's creation as "the curse of Mole." Roy Hattersley, while calling Adrian Mole "an invention of genius" in *The Sunday Times* (London) for 13 September 1992, hastened to add that he has "never been a devotee of Townsend's agonised adolescent." Drawing on the popularity of Mole, a compilation edition of the two Mole novels, *The Adrian Mole Diaries,* was published in 1985.

Townsend's next book, *Rebuilding Coventry,* struck those familiar with the Mole books as something of a radical departure, but it is actually quite similar in theme to plays such as *Womberang* and *Bazaar and Rummage* (1982). The protagonist of the novel, a woman named Coventry Dakin, is the married mother of two teenage children, living with a tortoise-fancying husband, Derek, in the Midlands of England. The plot is predicated on an unexpected action taken by Coventry: the killing of her neighbor Gerald Fox, a man who had previously spread rumors of an affair between himself and Coventry and who was, when Coventry took action, in the process of throttling his own wife in front of their children. Witnessing Gerald's actions, Coventry runs across the road to the Fox household, picks up a stray Action Man doll, and brings it down on the base of Gerald's skull, instantly killing the man.

From then on, the story follows the aftermath, alternating between first-person chapters detailing Coventry's flight to and respite in the anonymity of London and third-person chapters covering the effects Coventry's actions have on the family she leaves behind. Her family discovers aspects of Coventry's character that had been kept hidden from them, particularly the fact that she had an alter ego, Lauren McSkye, a free spirit who kept a secret diary,

Dust jacket for the 1994 collection comprising The True Confessions of Adrian Albert Mole, Margaret Hilda Roberts, and Susan Lilian Townsend *(1989) and* Adrian Mole: The Wilderness Years *(1993), two books featuring Townsend's most popular character (Richland County Public Library)*

took art classes, and referred to Coventry's husband and children as "the drearies." Coventry, meanwhile, becomes one of the teeming homeless of London but is lucky enough to find a "posh" friend, Dodo, an upper-class vagrant whose brother is a former cabinet minister. Through a series of improbable machinations Coventry and Dodo flee the country, but not before Coventry has the opportunity to explain herself to her children.

While *Rebuilding Coventry* did not approach the success of the Mole books, it received predominantly positive reviews. Kate Cruise O'Brien, in a *Sunday Times* (London) review (4 September 1988), called the book a "feminist fairy tale fantasy" written with "great charm and conviction," although the narrative seemed "oddly uneven" to her. *TES* reviewer Frances Spaulding (4 November 1988) praised both Townsend's "superb ventriloquizing talent" as well as her "hard look at loveless aspects of contemporary Britain." Shena Mackay, writing in *TLS* (16 September 1988), noted that "one of Sue Townsend's recurrent themes" is that "the mass of women lead lives of quiet desperation," a theme rendered in the "uneasy synthesis of fantasy and reality" in the book. In *Rebuilding Coventry* Townsend succeeds in showing that the Mole books are not her only means of presenting the condition of England, even if the pacing and characterization of the novel are somewhat inconsistent.

"Inconsistent" might also be used to describe Townsend's next book, *The True Confessions of Adrian Albert Mole, Margaret Hilda Roberts, and Susan Lilian Townsend.* A compilation of Mole pieces that had mostly been printed elsewhere is linked here with Townsend's travelogue on a trip to Majorca and a series of fictional childhood diary entries by a pubescent Margaret Thatcher (née Roberts). The confessions of Mole take Adrian from age eighteen through his early twenties and are only partially in diary form: radio monologues, a series of letters between Adrian and prison inmate Barry Kent, a painfully overwrought period of infatuation for Sarah Ferguson, and a trip to Moscow are matched with diaries of Adrian's leaving Leicester for Oxford and his subsequent work tracking newt populations at the Department of the Environment.

The Adrian Mole of this book seems, more than in the previous book, to be suffering from growing pains. The willful naiveté of the young adolescent sits less comfortably on the shoulders of a twenty-something and pushes the limits of the reader's suspension of disbelief. Adrian's love poetry at age thirteen ("Pandora! / I adore ya. / I implore ye / Don't ignore me.") may be remarkably bad, but it certainly fits his age; more than five years later, however, a poem Adrian sends to Sarah Ferguson on the eve of her wedding to Prince Andrew shows that neither his maturity nor his poetry seem to have grown: "Sarah Ferguson, oh Sarah Ferguson, / Your name is on my lips constantly. / Don't marry Andy, his legs are bandy. / Come to Leicester, come to Leicester, marry me!" DJ Taylor commented in his 15 October 1989 review in *The Sunday Times* (London) that "Whereas the early Mole has some sort of remote anchorage in reality, his present incarnation, chuntering on about 'Mole on lifestyle' and thinking that Sarah Ferguson will marry him, is a ludicrous fantasy figure." The satire of a young Thatcher's diary is likewise heavy-handed, with the future prime minister dressing up in a crown and faux-ermine robes, practicing until she has "almost perfected the regal wave." While much of the charm of the earlier books was derived from the humanity beneath the satire, Townsend's reliance in *The True Confessions of Adrian Albert Mole, Margaret Hilda Roberts, and Susan Lilian Townsend* upon caricature rather than character led reviewers–for example, Martin Spence in *The Times* (London) for 31 August 1989–to label it "childish, embarrassing, and a mistake."

Between the publication of *The True Confessions of Adrian Albert Mole, Margaret Hilda Roberts, and Susan Lilian Townsend* and Townsend's next book, the political climate in England took a dramatic turn. After leading the country for more than a decade, Thatcher was turned out of office, replaced by John Major, another Conservative Party leader, in November 1990. The new prime minister's name (and rather moleish persona) played a punning role in the title of *Adrian Mole: From Minor to Major* (1991), an anthology of the first three Mole books with the addition of the brief "Adrian Mole and the Small Amphibians." This latter section takes Adrian from July 1989, when he is twenty-two years old, through New Year's Day 1991 and recaptures the humane tone in its briefer and less comprehensive entries. He continues to suffer from growing pains, but less awkwardly; the responsibilities of adulthood weigh heavily on Adrian, who compulsively makes lists of his worries (which include the pregnancy of a former girlfriend) and continues to have difficulty prioritizing his life. A spoiled lettuce, for instance, reduces him to the same state of tearfulness as does a dressing down from his tyrannical boss, complete with the threat of being sacked, at the Department of the Environment. Townsend here also returns to Adrian's failing literary aspirations (neither his epic poem, "The Restless Tadpole," nor his vowel-free novel, "Lo! the Flat Hills of My Homeland," have found publishers). Taken together, these elements point to a return to verisimilitude that is more in line with the initial Mole offerings.

A close semblance to reality likewise imbues *The Queen and I,* a satire focusing on the British royal family. As with her prior regular targeting of Thatcher, Townsend's choice of satiric object here is rooted in her political beliefs. Townsend's socialist tenets include supporting the transformation of England into a republic by abolishing the monarchy. The conceit of *The Queen and I* is that the election results on 9 April 1992 bring to power neither Conservative nor Labour administrations, but Jack Barker of the People's Republican Party. The first order of business Barker faces is the expulsion of the royal family from their respective estates, relocating them to a poverty-ridden public-housing project in Leicester.

The several plots of the novel focus mostly upon the adjustments the royal family must make to survive in their new milieu. The Queen Mother, suffering from Alzheimer's disease, dies peacefully within weeks of the relocation, all the while believing she remains the object of national adoration. Princess Margaret and Prince Philip prepare to make the worst of their situations, maintaining haughtily arrogant attitudes and acting, for the most part, like spoiled children. Siblings Princess Anne and Prince Charles both relish their release from the strictures of royal life, while Princess Diana pursues interests in fashion and parenting. The children quickly learn to discard their upper-class accents and fall into the colloquial speech patterns of the families in the neighborhood because, as young Prince Harry says, "If I speak proper I get my cowin' face smashed in." The Queen, somewhat baffled at first by day-to-day life without servants, adapts quickly in order to brave the kinds of problems common to most residents of her street, Hellebore (known to locals as "Hell") Close: running short of money, having delinquent children, trying to receive timely medical attention.

The narrative is wittily written and its premise radical, especially to the British public; only the ending of the book, which reveals that it was all just the Queen's nightmare, smacks of a tired cliché. The strength of the novel is the careful juxtaposing of two varieties of traditional British families: royal and working class. The Queen's experiences with her neighbors, and their experiences with her, serve to bridge what Townsend sees as an artificial and ideological gap separating them. Both the royals and their working-class neighbors are painted simply, as families with the same characteristics and problems as any other family. Coming from a strict antiroyalist such as Townsend, the depiction is, as Claudia FitzHerbert said in a review in *The Spectator* (26 September 1992), "an extraordinarily loving look at our beleaguered monarch."

Townsend's next book, *Adrian Mole: The Wilderness Years* (the 1994 U.S. edition, *Adrian Mole: The Lost Years,* combines *The True Confessions of Adrian Albert Mole, Margaret Hilda Roberts, and Susan Lilian Townsend* and *Adrian Mole: The Wilderness Years*), covers the years 1991 to 1992 and follows Adrian up through his twenty-fifth birthday. In it, Adrian loses his job at the Department of the Environment, gains and then loses a girlfriend, is repeatedly called a young John Major, falls in love with his therapist, moves to London, and continues, fruitlessly, to pursue his literary career. In an effective display of self-deprecation, Townsend gives Adrian's hoped-for publishing success to his nemesis, Barry Kent, who writes a wildly successful novel called *Dork's Diary.* Kent's novel focuses on Aiden Vole, who "is obsessed with matters anal. He is jingoistic, deeply conservative and a failure with

Dust jacket for the U.S. edition of Townsend's 1997 novel, in which a man and woman reunite years after an abortion ended their romantic relationship (Richland County Public Library)

women. 'Aiden Vole' is an outrageous caricature of me, without a doubt."

While Adrian's anger is no surprise, the fact that he recognizes himself in Kent's book shows that Townsend is, if only incrementally, continuing to mature the character. This process is probably most evident in the ending of the novel, which is more hopeful than that of any prior Mole book. Adrian meets and begins to romance JoJo, a Nigerian artist, just prior to his leaving for a two-week writing institute on a Greek island. When the writing institute instructor, novelist Angela Hacker, pronounces one of his ideas "brilliant," and he then returns to England to find JoJo waiting at the airport, Adrian's days as a born loser seem to be over. The criticisms of Townsend's earlier work as uneven do not hold true here; the depiction of Mole is accomplished, polished, and professional. With *Adrian Mole: The Wilderness Years,* both Adrian and Townsend have matured.

That maturity is reflected in the serious nature of Townsend's 1997 novel *Ghost Children.* The book follows two couples, neither particularly sympathetic, as their lives intersect over the ephemera of ghost children. Christopher Moore and Angela Carr, lovers seventeen years prior to the time line of the novel, reunite after Christopher, out for an early morning walk, makes a grisly discovery: a bag of late-term fetuses from an abortion clinic, carelessly discarded in a park field. The small, lifeless bodies remind Christopher of Angela's late-term abortion many years earlier, and, determined to confront her about the issue that broke up their relationship, he finds her an unhappy, overweight travel agent stuck in a materially successful but loveless marriage. They meet several times in a dumpy, dirty tearoom frequented by Tamara and Crackle Natas and their small daughter, Storme. Crackle is a crack-addicted satan-worshiper, and Tamara is developmentally delayed and illiterate, while Storme suffers from both neglect and abuse. The novel weaves together two trajectories which, as Tamsin Dean wrote in the 4 October 1997 *Daily Telegraph* (London), are equally bleak: "the horrors of abortion are not made to seem more dreadful than the alternative of letting babies come into the world to be tortured and neglected by inadequate parents."

Ghost Children "got mixed reviews in England (and raves in America)," according to Barber, who also reports that the story line of the novel is rooted in Townsend's personal experience. Between the birth of her fourth child in 1977 and the beginning of the meteoric rise of her career, Townsend had what she calls two "careless" pregnancies that ended in abortions. "Children are in your head all the time, like splinters. I had four children. I just felt I didn't have room inside my head for any more," she said in an 11 October 1999 *Daily Telegraph* interview. Only after *Ghost Children* was written did Townsend speak of the abortions to her husband and children; the revisiting of such vivid, visceral memories in the book made its composition a "painful" process: "I was scared a lot of the time, because I exposed myself an awful lot." The intimacy of Townsend's knowledge of the subject helped her find "a degree of humanity" in all of the characters in the book, as Jonathan Yardley wrote in the *Washington Post* (29 April 1998): "It is, in the end, her deep feeling for all her characters that is this novel's greatest strength." Despite such praise, Townsend acknowledges that "The book didn't sell. They didn't reprint. People were waiting for the next Mole."

That next Mole came two years later, in the fall of 1999, with the publication of *Adrian Mole: The Cappuccino Years.* Beginning just days before Tony Blair's landslide Labour victory in 1997, the novel finds

Adrian in possession of some of the fame he has always sought, although not in literature; rather, he is a celebrity chef at the trendy Soho restaurant Hoi Polloi, where he prepares such traditional English set-menu meals as scrag-end of lamb with marrowfat peas and a Kit Kat bar. This success lands Adrian a job as a television chef on *Offally Good!,* where he is an unwitting, pedantic stooge upstaged by his copresenter. On the family front, Adrian is the single father of three-year-old William, a mixed-race child from Adrian's unsuccessful marriage to Nigerian artist JoJo (Townsend herself has mixed-race grandchildren); Adrian's mother marries Pandora's father, leading his father to move in with Pandora's mother; and Adrian finds himself, midway through the book, suddenly given custody of Glenn Bott, a son he had fathered twelve years earlier during the time frame of *The True Confessions of Adrian Albert Mole, Margaret Hilda Roberts, and Susan Lilian Townsend* (although paternity had never before been proved).

In *Adrian Mole: The Cappuccino Years* Townsend gives Blair's government no more support than she gave to Thatcher's or Major's in earlier Mole books. Pandora is a newly elected Labour member of Parliament, one of "Blair's Babes" who pays lip service to her supposedly socialist principles while wearing Chanel suits and carrying Prada handbags. Townsend told Elizabeth Grice in the 11 October 1999 *Daily Telegraph* (London) that the title beverage in *Adrian Mole: The Cappuccino Years* is "the perfect metaphor for New Labour: three-quarters froth and very, very little coffee presented in a very nice cup." Adrian, mirroring Townsend's own beliefs, feels shortchanged by a lack of any substantive change under Blair. Although Adrian is less savvy than Townsend, he is nonetheless, as Lynne Raughley wrote in the *Chicago Tribune* (3 September 2000), "the perfect lens through which to take a satirical look at contemporary Britain."

Reviewers seem to agree with Raughley's assessment that Sue Townsend's satiric depictions of England show a remarkable clarity of vision. At the same time, however, her vision is literally failing. In early 1999, as she was finishing *Adrian Mole: The Cappuccino Years,* her diabetes again delivered a blow against Townsend's health: diabetic retinitis has left her partially sighted. The biggest impact of this development has been on Townsend's ability to read, which can only be accomplished by using a large, bulky magnifier. Looking optimistically at the situation, Townsend told Barber, again in her interview for *The Observer Magazine,* that less reading led to more thinking, which was "a revelation. I don't think I've had an original thought in years–maybe as Mole, but not as Sue Townsend. It's wonderful really." By

Dust jacket for the U.S. edition of Townsend's 1999 novel, in which her popular protagonist becomes a well-known chef and television personality (Richland County Public Library)

March 2001 not even the magnifier was of any help; Townsend had been diagnosed and registered as totally blind. Her general perspective, however, retains its wry observational power, and she considers her blindness "a challenge," as she said to Nicci Gerrard in a 25 March 2001 interview for *The Observer* (London): "I was in a kind of rut, you know, and this is a change. All my life I have loved big changes. I mean, I wouldn't go as far as dashing out my eyes for change–but now they've been dashed out anyway, well, I'm off the treadmill."

Facing her new challenge head-on, Townsend has continued to read and write, albeit with the help of assistants and her family. *Public Confessions of a Middle-Aged Woman Aged 55 3/4* was published in December of 2001. The book collects columns Townsend wrote over the previous decade for *Sainsbury's,* a popular

British cooking and lifestyle magazine. That many of the columns center on family issues is no surprise given the magazine's focus, but, as with her fiction, Townsend manages to meld the political and domestic. A column focusing on the acquisition of a new Aga cooktop/oven, for instance, comically raises the class issues inherent in such conspicuous consumption. At a meeting to introduce new Aga owners to their appliances' features, Townsend notes that "it was an exceptionally well-dressed audience, we would not have been out of place in the Royal Opera House." A new novel, *Number Ten* (October 2002), likewise hones in on British social values through comedy. The plot follows Labour Prime Minister Edward Clare as he travels incognito around England in an attempt to discover what the British public really wants from its leadership. Prepublication press releases from publisher Michael Joseph call the novel "the most perceptive and hilarious examination of British life since *The Queen and I*." The comparison to the previous novel is apt, it would seem, with the target this time not the Royal Family but the First Family. Whether this book achieves the level of success Townsend found in *The Queen and I* is yet to be seen, but its likelihood of eclipsing the success of the Adrian Mole series is doubtful. As *Rumpole of the Bailey* creator John Mortimer noted in the *Observer Review* (17 October 1999), Adrian Mole "is one of literature's most endearing figures," and Townsend's future writing will tell whether he is one of the most enduring ones as well.

Interviews:

Sally Brompton, "Secret Agony of Adrian's 'Mum,' Aged 40," *Times* (London), 13 October 1986, p. 13;

Ellen Kanner, "The Nerd Extraordinaire Is Back," *Bookpage,* December 1994, p. 9;

Lynn Barber, "Mole Vision," *Observer Magazine* (London), 10 October 1999, pp. 25–28;

Elizabeth Grice, "Sue at 53 1/2–The Turbulent Years," *Daily Telegraph* (London), 11 October 1999, p. 13;

Nicci Gerrard, "How the World Went Dark for Sue Townsend," *Observer* (25 March 2001).

References:

Sally Brompton, "Secret Diary of Sue Townsend," *Times* (London), 28 November 1984, p. 10;

Val Hennessy, "Secret Fears of the Real Adrian Mole," *Sunday Times* (London), 30 June 1985, p. 36;

David Lister, "Dead Awful–A Mole's Eye View of the Staffroom," *TES: The Times Educational Supplement,* 4 October 1985, p. 3.

Rose Tremain

(2 August 1943 –)

Merritt Moseley
University of North Carolina at Asheville

See also the Tremain entry in *DLB 14: British Novelists Since 1960.*

Rose Tremain (photograph by John Rawson; from the dust jacket for the U.S. edition of Music & Silence, *2000)*

BOOKS: *The Fight for Freedom for Women* (New York: Ballantine, 1973);
Stalin (New York: Ballantine, 1975);
Sadler's Birthday (London: Macdonald & Jane's, 1976; New York: St. Martin's Press, 1976);
Letter to Sister Benedicta (London: Macdonald & Jane's, 1978; New York: St. Martin's Press, 1979);
The Cupboard (London: Macdonald, 1981; New York: St. Martin's Press, 1982);
The Colonel's Daughter and Other Stories (New York: Summit, 1984; London: Hamilton, 1984);
Journey to the Volcano, illustrated by Alan Marks (London: Hamilton, 1985);
The Swimming Pool Season (London: Hamilton, 1985; New York: Summit, 1985);
The Garden of the Villa Mollini and Other Stories (London: Hamilton, 1987);
Restoration (London: Hamilton, 1989); republished as *Restoration: A Novel of Seventeenth-Century England* (New York: Viking, 1990);
Sacred Country (London: Sinclair-Stevenson, 1992; New York: Atheneum / Toronto: Maxwell Macmillan Canada / New York: Maxwell Macmillan International, 1993);
Evangelista's Fan & Other Stories (London: Sinclair-Stevenson, 1994; Bath, U.K.: Chivers / Thorndike, Me.: Thorndike Press, 1995);
The Way I Found Her (London: Sinclair-Stevenson, 1997; New York: Farrar, Straus & Giroux, 1998);
Music & Silence (London: Chatto & Windus, 1999; New York: Farrar, Straus & Giroux, 2000).

Collection: *Collected Short Stories* (London: Sinclair-Stevenson, 1996)–comprises *The Colonel's Daughter and Other Stories, The Garden of the Villa Mollini and Other Stories,* and *Evangelista's Fan & Other Stories.*

PRODUCED SCRIPTS: *The Wisest Fool,* radio, BBC Radio 4, April 1976;
Dark Green, radio, BBC Radio 4, June 1977;
Blossom, radio, BBC Radio 4, November 1977;
Don't Be Cruel, radio, BBC Radio 4, October 1978;
Leavings, radio, BBC Radio, November 1978;
Down the Hill, radio, BBC Radio 4, November 1979;
Halleluiah, Mary Plum, television, BBC 2, 1979;
Half Time, radio, BBC Radio 4, May 1980;
Findings on a Late Afternoon, television, BBC 1, 1981;
A Room for the Winter, television, BBC 1, 1981;
Temporary Shelter, radio, BBC Radio 4, 5 March 1984;
The Kite Flyer, radio, BBC Radio 4, 1989;
Music and Silence, radio, BBC Radio, 1992;

Who Was Emily Davison? radio, BBC World Service, 1996;

The End of Love, radio, BBC World Service, 23 October 1999;

One Night in Winter, BBC World Service, 2000.

OTHER: *Temporary Shelter,* in *Best Radio Plays of 1984: The Giles Cooper Award Winners* (London: Methuen/ BBC Publications, 1985), pp. 175–218.

Rose Tremain is one of the most important and most celebrated of her generation of British novelists. In 1983 her name appeared in the famous list of the twenty "Best Young British Novelists" published in *Granta* magazine, alongside those of Martin Amis, Pat Barker, Julian Barnes, Salman Rushdie, Ian McEwan, and other promising contemporaries (Tremain, born in 1943, just made it under the cutoff of forty); since then her novels and short-story collections have amply proved her claim to inclusion. Her two most acclaimed books–*Restoration* (1989) and *Music & Silence* (1999)–are historical fictions, set in the seventeenth century, and this fact has led some observers to think of her as an historical novelist. She resists this characterization, telling Helen de Bertodano in a 23 January 2000 interview in *The Sunday Telegraph* (London): "A historical novel implies that everything you're going to read is safely in the past so you don't need to think or care about it. But the emotional and intellectual truth of those characters is timeless. It's annoying because it implies a kind of shallow emptiness, and I don't really think my books have that." As this comment suggests, she is equally accomplished with the twentieth century and the challenges of contemporary life, and she is successful in her novels, whatever the distance from the present day, in creating timeless emotional and intellectual truth. She is, as interviewer Sylvia Brownrigg declared in *Long Island Newsday* (12 July 1998), "one of the most exciting, inventive and humane of contemporary British novelists."

Rose Thomson was born 2 August 1943 to Keith Nicholas Home Thomson and Viola Mabel (Dudley) Thomson. Born in London, she grew up there and attended Francis Holland School, then the Sorbonne in Paris, where she received a diploma in literature in 1963. She then read English at the University of East Anglia (UEA) and received a B.A. with Honours there in 1967. After two years of teaching French and history in a primary school, she spent another year as an editor at British Printing Corporation Publications in London. From 1971 on she was a writer, and for the most part a full-time writer, though she was a part-time lecturer on the teaching staff at the Creative Writing course of the University of East Anglia from 1988 to 1995. This association (which began when, as an undergraduate, she met novelist Angus Wilson, who was teaching at UEA), has presumably been advantageous to her; it has also involved her in some of the resentment, or perhaps envy, critics and others express about what Louis Doughty, in an article in *The Guardian* (9 November 1992), called "the UEA mafia–you know, that gang of poisonous academics with a stranglehold on English letters."

In 1971 she married Jon Tremain; during this seven-year marriage she had a daughter, Eleanor Rachel. In 1982 she married Jonathan Dudley. After that marriage ended, she met the biographer Richard Holmes, in 1992, and they now live together in a Regency house near Norwich.

Rose Tremain's career as a published writer began in 1973 with *The Fight for Freedom for Women,* an illustrated history book for nonspecialist readers, published in New York, which was followed two years later by *Stalin,* an illustrated biography. Her first novel, *Sadler's Birthday,* appeared in 1976; her first collection of stories, *The Colonel's Daughter and Other Stories,* in 1984; in that year she won the Dylan Thomas Short Story Prize. She has written many radio and television plays; in 1984 she received a Giles Cooper Award for Best Radio Play for *Temporary Shelter.*

In 1983, the same year she was named by *Granta* as one of the twenty best young British novelists, Tremain became a fellow of the Royal Society of Literature. Her 1989 historical novel, *Restoration,* was on the shortlist for the Booker Prize for fiction and was named the *Sunday Express* Book of the Year. In 1993 her novel *Sacred Country* won the James Tait Black Memorial Prize and in 1994 the Prix Femina Etranger in France, and *Music & Silence* was named the Whitbread Novel of the year in 1999.

Her beginnings as a book author were more modest. *The Fight for Freedom for Women* is standard popular history, including photographs. It begins with John Stuart Mill in 1867, continues through the suffragist period, the Pankhursts, and women's enfranchisement, and includes some reflections on the recent past (for example, Germaine Greer). The part that seems most to appeal to the author is the story of the famous young woman who died by throwing herself under the hooves of the king's horse in a race,

> a young suffragette called Emily Wilding Davison, arrested in Parliament Street while trying to stuff a burning, petrol soaked rag into a pillar box. . . . Emily Davison's ever-present desire to do impulsive and sensational things was changed by her prison experiences into something like an obsession. . . . Like many others, Emily Davison was uncommitted to anything but the cause. But a degree of mental unbalance had created in

> her the belief that she must offer the movement her greatest gift–life itself.

This interest bore fruit in Tremain's later fictions, *The Cupboard* (1981) and, less directly, the title story of *The Colonel's Daughter and Other Stories* and the 1996 radio play *Who Was Emily Davison?*. In 1975 she published *Stalin,* another short, illustrated popular history from Ballantine Books in New York, part of "Ballantine's Illustrated History of the Violent Century" series, as was her first book.

In the following year her first novel appeared, *Sadler's Birthday.* In her interview with Brownrigg, Tremain explained that in her books she looks for a character who is "slightly marginalized, who is on the edge of the main event." The title character, Jack Sadler, is just such a marginal man. He is an aging former servant who, after years of faithful service as butler to Colonel and Mrs. Bassett, inherited their home when they both died, almost simultaneously, on Coronation Day. Now he lives in the big house alone, except for a dog, and is visited by a woman named Mrs. Moore, who helps out. During the day of the book it becomes clear that she is no longer willing to come in because of Sadler's increasing oddity and dreaminess.

He was born in 1900 and came to the Bassetts' in 1939, just before the war. The day on which the novel takes place may or may not be his birthday–he has become shaky on time. Not a great deal happens, though the vicar comes to tell him that Mrs. Moore is quitting, and at the end of the day he revisits his old room where, while a servant, he had a passionate relationship with a boy named Tom, an evacuee during the war. He does find an old birthday card from his mother under the bed.

This sequence is part of the evocative reminiscence that occupies most of the book. Sadler's mother, Annie, was a talented pianist, daughter of a piano tuner, but was seduced and abandoned with her child and had to go into service. She loved her son Jack and raised him in homes where she was a servant; in one of them she was threatened with dismissal because, at his request, she played the piano.

Sadler's Birthday has a powerful feeling of nostalgia and loss. In his most important reflection Sadler thinks

> Because what's there in the past to give you any clue? What's to show for all that time? An awareness of your mediocrity, a growing despondency. That was all. Nothing else of any note, was there? After seventy-six years–from soft-skinned child grubbing on a green square to a blotchy old man who limped, and whose mouth, for some humiliating reason, made too much saliva–was that all he could think of to say? He searched, of course. The search had become frenzied. Now hardly an hour went by without him finding some buried splinter of his existence and picking at it. But, probe as he did, he could find nothing much of any significance: just the odd day–odd *hour,* really, because that was the burning time of the fuses occasionally lit with happiness–yes, the odd hour of wonder. . . . There were, he decided, about seven or eight of these in all that time.

Dust jacket for the U.S. edition of Tremain's 1989 historical novel set during the reign of Charles II (Richland County Public Library)

Two years later Tremain published her second novel, *Letter to Sister Benedicta* (1978), another story of contemporary sadness set against an historically resonant background. A fiftyish Londoner named Ruby Constad writes a letter, which she does not intend to mail, to her old teacher in India, Sister Benedicta, about her current problems. Most notably, her husband, Leon, has had a stroke and is in a nursing home. Ruby visits him on most days, though he is largely unresponsive. During the course of the novel he gets better, begins walking therapy, then dies from another stroke. Ruby's children, Noel and Alexandra, are estranged from their parents; as Ruby's story continues, it becomes clear that the trouble started the previous

Christmas when, instead of coming to visit their parents, the two stayed together in a Norfolk cottage, and, in the absence of Alexandra's lesbian lover, Sue, they begin an incestuous affair. Ruby is unable to inform them of their father's death.

Questionable causation is one of the themes of the book. Ruby worries about her own responsibility for her children's troubles; she worries about her relationship with her husband, Leon–she thinks she loves him but is not sure, and she doubts that he loves her but blames herself to some extent because she is extremely fat. There is a masochistic and self-lacerating quality to her thoughts throughout.

Her colonial background is important to the story. She grew up in India before the Partition, the daughter of an unhappily married British officer, and attended parochial school, where she came to admire Sister Benedicta. During the course of the novel, partly in an effort to understand the way her life is going and, perhaps, to help pass the time while she waits for a change in her husband's condition, she gets a library book about contemporary India, learning about its poverty and inequality, and at the end of the book she sets off to India. This choice seems to be partly a result of a loss of faith–though she visits the Brompton Oratory frequently, lights candles, and so on, her Roman Catholicism is attenuated–and she has also been impressed by the rootlessness of her son and one of his American friends, and her departure for India is her way of loosening ties.

Letter to Sister Benedicta is interesting for its treatment of religion, family, and a depressed marriage. A friend named Gerald Tibbs, heartbroken because his wife has left him, shares Ruby's bed briefly and (at least on her part) joylessly; and her dying husband, who was frequently unfaithful to Ruby, remains the object of her baffled and intermittent love, though she never remembers anything lovable about him.

Published in 1981, *The Cupboard* lacks the same sure touch. This book is another moderately historical novel, featuring another child of the century. Unlike Jack Sadler, this one is not obscure; instead, Erica March has been a celebrity much of her life, a famous author, a suffragist, a friend of Virginia Woolf, Bertrand Russell, Emily Davison, and Pablo Picasso. The situation of the novel is that an American journalist, Ralph Pears, has come on assignment for a magazine called *Bulletin Worldwide* to write Erica's story. He is fascinated by her; his editor is not. His insistence on continuing to write her story, to the point of being fired, helps to assign importance to Erica's life.

She grew up on a farm in Suffolk; after her mother's weird death (stamped to death by a bull she was sexually arousing so he would mate with the cows) she goes to stay in London with her father's flamboyantly gay brother, Chadwick, and is introduced into metropolitan life. She spends time in prison for blowing up mailboxes in the cause of women's suffrage. Her first novel, begun during World War I, is a sort of antiwar allegory and a success; when she goes to Paris to oversee its translation, she begins a long, passionate affair with a French artist, Gerard Guerard (abandoning her English lover, Sam Green). Guerard dies (perhaps predictably) in the Spanish Civil War. After returning to England, she lives with another man. She writes three novels. On the death of her father she inherits the family farm but gives it away; she has also inherited Chadwick's money but let it slip away. The one thing she has kept is the cupboard of the title, left to her by her mother, and she insists on dying in it and being buried in it. It seems to symbolize the restraints on women in the twentieth century.

This now-neglected woman, who has done almost everything in the world of twentieth-century art and thought, imposes on Ralph because of the power of her novels: he says of one of them, "*The Hospital Ship* held an extraordinary compulsion. It was one of the few books–of the many he owned–that he would read again and again throughout his life." His own life is sketched in; he is the child of neglectful rich parents and has spent time in Tennessee. (Like East Anglia, Tennessee is a region to which Tremain returns in her fiction.) This part of the story is impaired by an inadequate attempt at rendering American speech: Ralph's grandmother says, "I never saw in any-*wun* have what you' Ma do have, Ralphie, and that is leprosy of the soul. Now you must mind it ain't catchin!" and a black maid comments on this grandmother, "she was one stubborn old lady, your Gran . . . there ain't no more like her left. She all was the last one, man!"

Erica March is contrasted with Ralph Pears in obvious ways. The most important way, apparently, and the one that constitutes her hold over him, is the one he diagnoses:

> It is only since she has begun to talk about passion . . . that I've begun to see something of what separates me from her, my time from her time. I knew, after the first few days' talking, that there was some fundamental thing, informing what I must call Erica's life but which also goes outward from her and *informs* the times she lived in. I believe this thing is passion, or desire, or call it what you will, a craving of the spirit that's lacking not just in me but whose lack *characterizes this era.*

The creation of Erica as emblem of the passionate life and of a passionate world now gone never seems to catch fire in this book, however.

In 1984 Tremain's first collection of short stories, *The Colonel's Daughter and Other Stories,* appeared.

Like those in her two later collections, *The Garden of the Villa Mollini and Other Stories* (1987) and *Evangelista's Fan & Other Stories* (1994)–these three volumes were republished together as *Collected Short Stories* (1996)–these stories are the work of an extremely accomplished writer, whose mastery of the short-story form would justify her high standing as a fiction writer irrespective of her novels. *The Colonel's Daughter and Other Stories* demonstrates an impressive breadth of reference, of tone, and of type of story, while maintaining a high standard of excellence.

The title story is about a troubled young woman, devoted to "revolution," who robs her parents, brings about the deaths of two men, and inadvertently involves an American writer, who notes (in his planning to write the story himself): "'Exile (Voluntary. American),' he begins, 'Finds himself at centre of case which will shock this nation (in ways particular to this nation and its class system) more than far more terrible things i.e. deaths in Lebanon.'"

"Wedding Night," set in Paris, is convincingly narrated by a man; Tremain has always had an assured way with speaking through the other gender. "Autumn in Florida" is a comic/shocking account of the visit, by a British couple, to some friends who now live in a secure development in Florida, which becomes increasingly creepy. "My Love Affair with James I" is about an actor working on a movie that is set during the Stuart era, and perhaps anticipates *Restoration.* In "The Stately Roller Coaster," a bluff and coarse old man delivers a monologue to a young female reporter, saying things such as "Nice breasts. But too tall. How tall are you? Five ten? If more women had good breasts, they wouldn't need brassieres."

The best story in the collection is "Current Account," a brittle story about the princesse de Villemorin, a divorced fortune hunter (no longer entitled to the title), and her gigolo. He ends up sleeping with her daughter, Lorna, in a scene in which the Princesse is "the invisible onlooker": "As they enfold each other, there she is tangled in their moist hair, there she is in their breaths. And afterwards–the glorious knowledge that together they had conquered her, where each had failed to conquer alone. As they walk back, they hear it, the click-clack of Penelope's high heels, the clink and tinkle of Mother's bracelets. Perfect, thinks Guy. Perfect, thinks Lorna."

In *The New York Times* (27 May 1984) reviewer Caryn James praised these stories for the author's "precise, mature artistic voice" and wrote that

> Her storytelling devices range from conventional third-person narration to monologues delivered as interviews to a news reporter and a social worker. But always there is a sense of impending psychic violence; this tension, which at any moment might shatter an ordinary conversation about crossword puzzles, turning it into a lament about an empty marriage, gives the stories their originality and power.

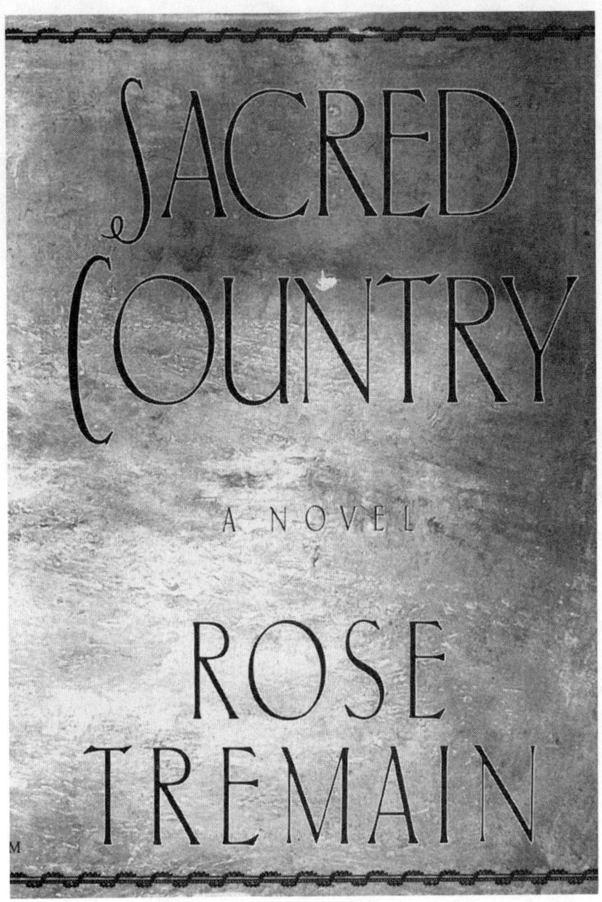

Dust jacket for the U.S. edition of Tremain's 1992 novel, in which a transsexual from rural England ends up in Nashville, Tennessee (Richland County Public Library)

The book won the Dylan Thomas Award (£1,000), established to encourage poetry and short-story writing.

In the next two years Tremain published a new novel, a novel for young people, and another collection of short stories. *The Swimming Pool Season* (1985) continues the use of Continental locations, and to some extent the dislocation of English people into them, seen in some of the stories of *The Colonel's Daughter and Other Stories.* The main characters, Larry and Miriam Kendal, are in France as the novel begins. Larry has failed in business, and they have retreated to what had been their second home. Overly impressed by the hot English summer of 1976, he began Aquazure, a company installing outdoor swimming pools, but it has now gone broke, leaving him humiliated and at loose ends. The "season" of the title refers both to 1976 and to the present day, as Larry is now at work trying to install a pool at their French home and get his business started up again. The spring of the action comes when Leni, Miriam's mother, summons her back to Oxford because she is ill. From that point the novel runs on parallel tracks.

In Oxford, Miriam falls under the spell, to some extent, of her malicious and fascinating mother, a snobbish don's widow who disapproves of Larry and clearly intends to spoil their marriage. Leni betrayed her own husband with frequent infidelities and sometimes wonders if she shortened his life, but easily justifies herself: "So many men wanted a share of what they said she was–beautiful. No age has ever side-stepped the physical beauty of woman. It was always hard currency. And if you're rich with it, as she was rich, how can you bear to hide it and not spend it?" One of Leni's friends declares his love for Miriam. When Leni dies Miriam realizes that she does want Larry and calls him to Oxford. He, meanwhile, has been working on his pool, making friends with his neighbors–aside from one wealthy and malevolent woman who is determined to block his pool–and becoming more acclimated to life in his French village, including a one-night affair with a Polish villager.

More than in previous books Tremain seems to be investigating what love is. Early on,

> Miriam sleeps. Larry can feel, a few inches from the sighs that keep heaving and falling, heaving and falling inside his ribcage, the lovely warmth that is his sleeping wife. . . . He doesn't know whether he should call this feeling of being warmed "love." Love has always seemed such a sumptuous word to Larry Kendal that he has kept it apart from his private vocabulary, like a medal kept hidden in a leather box and never pinned on.

After Leni's death, her gay lodger, referring to her and her dead husband, initiates the following exchange with Miriam,

> "A marvellous 'pair.' How I envy the ones who get this right, this pairing."
>
> "It always has its problems."
>
> "Yes. Yet it's what we all ache for. Like lemmings, you might say. Lemmings who learned how to swim!"

And in the successful reconciliation, Larry and Miriam discuss the happy result of their summer-long separation:

> ". . . you wouldn't have started the pool if I hadn't gone."
>
> "Maybe. But you didn't stay away for me, Miriam. You stayed away for you."
>
> "Yes. Mainly."
>
> "And you had a lover, did you? One of Leni's courtiers?"
>
> "No. There was an offer. I declined."
>
> "Why?"
>
> "I don't know. Isn't that odd? He was so kind to me. Bought me expensive suppers. But I didn't want him."
>
> Larry lowers his head and kisses Miriam's face. He wants, after this odd confession of hers, to tell her about Nadia, but the smell of his wife's body is too heady and he can't find the words.

In her review in *The New York Times* (1 September 1985) Sheila Gordon found the ending a bit too pat but called the author "a talented writer extravagant, almost, with her gift." Richard Eder commented in his *Los Angeles Times* review (30 June 1985) that "The drama in this mysterious and ultimately tender comedy is achieved not by the characters' development but by their acting and living out the consequences of their own and each other's actions. And the combination of these actions goes beyond the actions themselves to suggest an unspoken but affecting sense of life's orders and patterns."

In *Journey to the Volcano* (1985), a novel for young people, another married couple separates for a summer. The focus is a boy named George Lewis. His father is English, his mother (Anna) Sicilian. His mother more or less abducts George and takes him back to Sicily; she has decided that her elderly mother, Violetta, is about to die and wants George to meet her. George likes it there but misses his father, Robert; he does not particularly like the poverty; he enjoys his cousin Guido but does not want to become like him; and he is worried about a local man who has returned from the United States who is clearly a Mafioso and is known to have killed another man. The father misses his son and wife but eventually reaches some clarity when he realizes that he has ignored his own father and goes down and stays with him. Eventually, Etna erupts, killing Violetta; Robert flies out to Sicily, and there is a reconciliation.

George treats his father with amused condescension, but he loves him. There is an echo of E. M. Forster's novel *A Room with a View* (1908) in contrast between unstated English routine and Italian passion that is sketched out in a conversation between George and his father:

> "I always did my best for Anna," Robert said.
>
> "Did your best? Well, maybe. But was your 'best' any good? Was it worth doing? That's the question to ask."
>
> "I worked. I supported her, I was a good husband . . ."
>
> "Were you any fun, though, Bertie?"

In *The Garden of the Villa Mollini and Other Stories* Tremain covers some of this same ground. The title story is a masterful study of power and ruthlessness. An Italian tenor, Antonio Mollini, buys a villa in 1877 and renames it for himself. He dominates the nearby peasants because he is famous, and they think they are lucky to have him. He betrays his wife with a soprano whom he brings back to the villa; later he betrays her with another singer. He is domineering to the villagers, damming up their stream and taking their common land for his use. He reminds the reader of other overbearing figures in Tremain's fiction, including the intolerant woman who used her moneyed influence to have Larry Kendal's pool filled in.

"La Plume de mon Ami" is a retrospective account of a youthful love affair between a student and a schoolmaster, viewed from their adult meeting in a London park. In "Strawberry Jam," a misunderstanding of Austrian refugees leads the narrator to suspect the sad Zimmerlis of murder. The most interesting story may be "The Kite Flyer," which revisits Tremain's territories of East Anglia and feminist history. Here Olivia, the middle-aged wife of a troubled vicar, becomes more independent as he starts to lose his faith (eventually going off to a retreat house). She becomes interested in Anna of Didsmill, who fought, disguised as a man, for the Parliamentary forces against the king; was captured, tried for treason, and hanged. Olivia begins writing about her, gives talks, and ends up joining the women of Greenham Common (a radical women's protest of U.S. nuclear forces) and starting a campaign against more missiles on a local U.S. base.

In 1989 came the publication of the book with which Tremain "hit the big time," *Restoration.* It was her first "historical" novel, at least her first set more than a century in the past (*The Cupboard* and *Sadler's Birthday* had shown a keen and subtle use of twentieth-century history), and her first long novel.

The rich, yeasty, detailed picaresque plot centers on a man named Robert Merivel. He is the son of a glovemaker and a student of anatomy. Because his father makes gloves for the king, he ends up in a fortunate position where, by healing one of Charles II's dogs, he gets himself a place at court. Charles seems to like him, treating him as a sort of fool, a designation that Merivel encourages. Soon the king makes him a member of the Order of the Garter (thus, Sir Robert), gives him an estate in East Anglia, and marries him to one of his own mistresses, Celia Clemence. It is a marriage of convenience–the king's convenience, since Celia's marriage to Merivel is designed only to avert suspicion of the king and Merivel is denied any of the privileges of marriage, including consummation or even the companionship of his wife. Merivel goes off to his estate and spends money, enjoying himself, though a bit worried that Charles shows no further interest in him. Then Celia arrives; she has overstepped her bounds and has been banished. She usually treats Merivel with scorn but is occasionally kind to him, though she says that he was chosen as her husband because he is so contemptible and that Charles never had any liking for him. Merivel makes the mistake of falling in love with his wife, makes a sort of play for her, and is rebuffed. Elias Finn, a portrait painter who has been teaching Merivel to paint and is now doing Celia's portrait for the king, reports his crime. He is summoned to London and his estate is taken away from him. All this drama, however, is the lesser part of his activity.

He goes to the Fens, to be with his Cambridge friend Pearce, now living in a communal refuge where he helps to care for the mentally ill. Pearce is a Quaker who has turned up from time to time usually to tell Merivel that he is living wrong. Having sinned against the purity of the commune by impregnating a deranged woman, Merivel is expelled, and the couple goes to London and lives with her mother. Merivel becomes a successful physician; the portrait painter turns up in London, having been ruined by the king. Turbulent events, including births and deaths, culminate in 1666 in the Great Fire of London, which breaks out while Merivel is once again being received at court. Both his parents had died in a house fire; now, he rescues a deaf woman from a burning house. Finally, the king restores his favor to him and lets him go back to his old estate (though it is now the king's estate), where he will be given the best room.

Merivel is a fascinating character in his own right: ambitious, sexually voracious, not entirely honest, not entirely lucid, overly fascinated by the king, whom he loves despite his capricious behavior. *Restoration* is hardly dazzled by royalty. Charles, though powerful, is amoral and cruel; his mistress, Celia, matches him in this respect; and the secret of success at court is not what one would expect: "A year passed most profitably and pleasurably. My nature, I quickly understood, was in every particular well suited to life at Court. My fondness for gossip and laughter, my brimming appetites, my tendency to sartorial chaos and my trick of farting at will made me one of the most popular men at Whitehall."

Early in the book Merivel provides a reflection that resonates over this long plot: "What she [his mother] couldn't see, and what I had not the heart to point out, was that we no longer live in an honourable age. What has dawned instead is the Age of Possibility. And it is only the elderly (as my mother was) and the truculently myopic (as my friend, Pearce, is) who

Dust jacket for the U.S. edition of Tremain's 1997 novel, about a thirteen-year-old English boy in Paris who rescues his much older love interest from kidnappers (Richland County Public Library)

haven't noticed this and are not preparing to take full advantage of it."

In *The New York Times Book Review* (15 April 1990) Florence King praised *Restoration:* "Readers of this splendid story . . . will find that the title has yet a third meaning"–beyond the "restoration of the hero's spiritual sanity" and the Restoration of Charles II–"Rose Tremain, its author, has restored the historical novel to its rightful place of honor after nearly two decades of degeneration into the sweet-savage imbecility of so-called historical romance." Reviews of the novel were generally favorable. In a 30 September 1989 review in *The Independent* (London) Kate Saunders called it "a most beautiful and original novel." Critical reaction became complicated, nevertheless, in discussions of the status and claims of the historical novel. The tendency of readers to label historical fiction with words like "rollicking" was one that even Isabel Quigly, who admired it, could not avoid, titling her 30 September 1989 review in *The Financial Times* (London) "Historical Romps." When *Restoration* was named to the six-book shortlist of finalists for the Booker Prize (eventually won by Kazuo Ishiguro, fellow UEA alumnus, for his study of an aged servant not unlike Jack Sadler, *The Remains of the Day*), generic considerations again raised eyebrows. In the 24 September 1989 issue of *The Times* (London) John Walsh commented, "Tremain has written a novel in which the historical details provide a fascinating backdrop and rarely threaten to swamp the delicate process of guiding its hero to his own psychological restoration. Nonetheless, a costume drama which should count itself extremely fortunate to be shortlisted." The 1995 motion-picture adaptation, with a screenplay by Rupert Walters and starring Robert Downey Jr. as Merivel, met with some critical success.

In a 25 September 1989 interview with Harry Eyres for *The Times* (London) Tremain expressed some exasperation: "I hate the label historical novel, which is bound to be applied to this book. To me historical novel denotes something shallow which is only concerned with itself." She went on to comment on the parallels between the late 1980s and the Restoration period, but she explained, "Of course one wants to write seriously about the present. The problem is that the present has become really so very painful that I find I can't get any authorial distance from it, and secondly, everything is moving so fast that if you locate something in September 1989, by the time the book's published it's gone."

Nevertheless, in her next novel she did turn to the present day and some of its problems. *Sacred Country* (1992), like *The Swimming Pool Season* and *Restoration,* has a multivalent title. Rather surprisingly, one of the meanings has to do with country music. Set in two of the author's recurrent locales, East Anglia and Tennessee, this novel aroused considerable comment by its placement, at the center, of a transsexual. On 15 February 1952, during the two-minute silence for the death of King George V, Mary Ward realizes something is wrong: "And then, hearing the familiar screech of her guinea fowl coming from near the farmhouse, she thought, I have some news for you, Marguerite. I have a secret to tell you, dear, and this is it. I am not Mary. That is a mistake. I am not a girl. I'm a boy. This was how and when it began, the long journey of Mary Ward." Mary is the child of a dysfunctional farm family: her father, Sonny, is an abusive man depressed since part of his ear was shot off on the Rhine during World War II; her mother, Estelle, is unbalanced and in and out of asylums; and her brother, Timmy, is a disappointment to his parents, later becoming a vicar.

Mary thinks of herself as Martin; as an adult she becomes a cross-dresser, has an affair with a lesbian, and takes some steps (limited surgery, hormone therapy) toward becoming a man. Somewhat surprisingly, Mary receives considerable sympathy; her grandfather encourages her and calls her Martin; her teacher sympathizes and gives her a home when her father rejects her. She soon goes to London and participates in the life of the "Swinging Sixties," living in Chelsea and working on a radical magazine. There she meets (again) the other main character of the novel, a man named Walter Loomis. Walter's family owns the butcher shop in Mary's village, Swaithey; he, however, turns to music and, under the tuition of his uncle Pete, tries to learn country singing. In London, where he is working as a busker, he tells Mary of his plans to go to Nashville, because

> "People are kinder there."
> "Why?"
> "Why are they kinder? Because they're country people."
> "Swaithey people are 'country people.'"
> "It's not the same. Swaithey people think they know things. They think they've got everything mapped out. Country Music isn't about knowing things, it's about knowing nothing and discovering everything for the first time and then writing about it."

She and Walter end up in Nashville, where he works toward a country music career, and she lives in a barn on a judge's farm, taking care of fowls (as she had been doing, as a little girl, when she received her notice of gender reassignment).

Sacred Country is narrated in a variety of voices, as befits its somewhat loose, multiply focused structure: there are first-person portions from Mary's point of view, her mother's, and other people's, as well as omniscient third-person narration. The dramatis personae include several eccentrics: Uncle Pete, with his wandering eye, who lives in an abandoned trolley bus; Mary's mother, Estelle, who becomes more and more zombified by watching television and is hopelessly in love with Bobby Moore, the captain of the victorious 1966 English World Cup soccer team; and a cricket-bat maker named Edward Harker, who marries one of Mary's friends and has an illusion that sharply looks forward to *Music & Silence:* "Though he seldom talked about God or the universe, he held an unshakeable belief in the transmigration of souls. He was fairly certain that, three centuries ago, he had been a lutenist at the court of the Danish king, Christian IV."

Natasha Walter, in a long and perceptive 12 September 1992 review of *Sacred Country* in *The Independent* (London), commented on the pervasive misery of the characters but said that "Two things keep the sad parade of *Sacred Country* on the road. First, the odd quickness and sparkle of Tremain's writing . . . precise, lucid observations and sparks of funniness lead to the second great strength of *Sacred Country:* its unusually sweet and hopeful sense of ethics." In the 10 September 1992 issue of *The Times* (London) Caroline Moore called it a "remarkable novel, which manages to combine bleakness and richness in its vision." There were dissenters from the generally positive reaction (which led to expectations, later disappointed, of a Booker Prize short-listing): in a 20 September 1992 "review of reviews" in *The Sunday Telegraph* (London) William Startle wrote that "Michael Dibdin in *The Independent on Sunday* put his finger on the problem with *Sacred Country* when he said it was 'easier to admire than like.'" When the book was published in France in 1994, it received wide critical acclaim and won the Prix Feminina Etranger.

Evangelista's Fan & Other Stories, Tremain's third collection, appeared in 1994. The stories are, as one would expect, original, different, and highly accomplished. The title story is a bit incoherent–the tale of a Piedmontcsc clock maker, who goes to London and becomes a barometer maker, and his inconclusive love. "Trade Wind Over Nashville" is again somewhat betrayed by shaky Tennessee dialect, but it is an interesting story of "trailer-trash" types involving the Grand Ole Opry and the boon to a roofer from a big storm that tears the tops off buildings. More impressive are "The Candle Maker," about a Corsican woman and her bitterness over past betrayal, "Two of Them," in which a boy is seduced by twin neighbor girls in the summer when his father has gone insane, and particularly "The Unoccupied Room," in which Marianne, having been struck on the head at a conference, remembers a murder that took place in an unoccupied room next to her childhood bedroom.

The Way I Found Her (1997) carries over into the novel, for the first time, some of the sensational events that Tremain has always put into her short fiction. It modulates from a somewhat conventional coming-of-age novel into a thriller complete with espionage, kidnapping, and violent death. Set in and around Paris, the novel recounts the story of Lewis Little, the narrator. With his mother, he leaves his father in Devon to spend the summer in Paris. His mother is the English translator for Valentina Gavril, a French author of medieval romances, and they move into Valentina's large Paris flat. Lewis is left to his own devices. His mother is working, or so it seems; soon it becomes clear that she is having an affair, though one is never entirely sure with whom. Lewis spends his time walking Valentina's dog, wandering around Paris, and getting to know an existentialist laborer who is at work on the roof outside his window. Lewis becomes more and more self-reliant, necessarily. His translation of Alain-Fournier's *Le Grand Meaulnes* (1913; translated as *The*

Dust jacket for the U.S. edition of Tremain's 1999 historical novel, about an English lutenist who performs with the royal musicians at the Danish court of King Christian IV (Richland County Public Library)

Wanderer, 1928) is a key part of his development, as is his growing love for Valentina, a passionate forty-year-old of Russian background; and he has charmingly revealed relations with Babba, the African maid; Didier, the roofer (who may be his mother's lover); Valentina's mother; and another Russian émigré named Grigory Panin. Lewis comes to realize that Valentina, under pressure from her publisher and fearing writer's block, is actually plagiarizing her work in progress from Panin. He spends some time worrying about his father, an unimpressive schoolteacher, back in Devon constructing a "hut" for his wife to write in and obviously unhappy about her indifference to him.

The plot accelerates when Valentina disappears. Lewis, who at first seems the only one who cares, thinks she has been hauled back to Russia as a punishment for plagiarism. Later a note artfully playing on his knowledge of *Le Grand Meaulnes* leads him into trouble, and he is kidnapped and reunited with Valentina in a house outside of Paris, where they communicate through the wall. Eventually, he leads her in an escape attempt. The novel ends with the Little family reunited, uneasily, back in England, though Lewis is doing badly and now occupies the hut his father was building.

The novel succeeds well in two somewhat daunting challenges: making Paris a real and vital place, and convincingly impersonating a thirteen-year-old boy. Tremain did considerable research to reacquaint herself with Paris, though stopping short of climbing onto roofs. As for Lewis, interviewer Victoria Glendinning commented in the 3 May 1997 issue of *The Daily Telegraph* (London) that he "is startlingly knowing, and sexually aware (and sexually active) to a degree that may shock some readers." In her interview with Glendinning, Tremain insisted that "the young do have quite extreme sexual fantasies," and further explains the virtues of her narrative choice: "I feel comfortable inside a first-person narrative. It makes it impossible to condescend to your character, you have to inhabit him." Lewis "had to be clever, and he had to love following trails. So he's good at chess and maths, the antithesis of me." One reviewer, Greg Morago in *The Hartford Courant* (2 August 1998), fulminated over this novel: "One longs to give Lewis a healthy kick in the pants and say, 'Go out and play like normal kids.' Lewis, obviously, is no normal boy. And 'The Way I Found Her' is no normal Tremain book. It is neither entrancing nor convincing. It is, plainly, ridiculous. A crime by Tremain, a punishment for readers." In her 26 April 1997 review for *The Independent* (London) Ruth Brandon celebrated "the recent return of plot to the British literary novel." She worried a bit over Lewis Little's precocity but concluded, "the reader becomes immersed in the inexorable adolescent logic of his world. He is a formidable creation." In her review for *The Guardian* (29 May 1997) Brownrigg identified the chief marvel of this novel when she credited its enchantment to "how deep we get into Lewis's consciousness."

In her next novel, *Music & Silence* (published in 1999), Tremain turned to the consciousness of another character remote from her own personality, Peter Claire, who seemingly is the "lutenist at the court of the Danish king, Christian IV" of whom Edward Harker dreamed in *Sacred Country.* As the novel begins, Claire has come to Denmark to perform with the royal musicians. Through him the reader is introduced to the most fascinating character, King Christian, a would-be savior of his people, a military hero, and an unfortunate husband and monarch. The king's consort is in love with a German count and makes the king ridiculous by her infidelity; she also has a lady-in-waiting with whom Peter Claire eventually falls in love.

The plot here is multifarious, with the court moving from one castle to another and to a far-off tundra where coal mining is supposed to save the economy; the consort banished, along with her ladies, to rural retirement; and the narrative filling in interesting detail about Christian's childhood, about the wars of religion, about early astronomer Tycho Brahe, and about Peter Claire's family back in East Anglia, where his father is a pastor and his sister is engaged to a landowner. This novel could have been a trying farrago, but Tremain does a beautiful job of holding it together, certainly not in a limpid single line, but in a meaningful harmony of different voices. The way the king's ensemble works (made up of natives of many lands, they perform in a cold dark cellar so their music can be wafted up to his presence through unseen passages, his own invention) is vivid, and one believes in Peter Claire's musicianship.

In *The New Yorker* (5 June 2000) Joan Acocella commented on the strengths of this novel:

> *Music & Silence* is very contemporary in its preoccupation with history and in its "appropriations." Shakespeare is invoked repeatedly. The name of Claire, the "angel," comes from Hardy. The Brothers Grimm are there, and not just in the wicked stepmother; the language sounds like a fairy tale grown up. Above all, we feel the impress of the seventeenth-century world, a world that its creatures thought they understood yet looked on with awe, born of the rise of commerce and the explorations of the New World. . . . But the novel wears its learning lightly. Indeed, it seems less a novel than a fable.

She emphasizes the importance of music in the novel, not just as subject matter:

> The structure is musical, too. In its jumping from subplot to subplot, and in the doubling of characters and events, the novel imitates harmony, counterpoint. It has fine, brassy climaxes and, in the end, a gentle diminuendo.

It is hard to imagine anyone thinking of *Music & Silence* as a "costume drama," though of course the characters wear period "costume." It is a brilliant book, with a brilliance that melds intelligence and emotion, history and mystery, male and female, Denmark and Norfolk. Reviewers hailed it: in a 28 August 1999 review in *The Daily Telegraph* (London) Patrick Gale called it "a narrative as funny as it is compelling"; in *The Guardian* (4 September 1999) Steven Poole described it as "a wonderful, joyously noisy book"; in the *Milwaukee Journal Sentinel* (16 April 2000) Robert Allen Papinchak extolled it as "a glorious saga with grand themes, larger-than-life characters and a sweeping narrative"; and in the 16 September 1999 issue of *The Irish Times* (Dublin) Katie Donovan praised the novel for its combination of "bawdy wickedness and haunting images of hope and despair." It was considered a surprising omission from the shortlist for the Booker Prize, but the judging panel for the Whitbread Awards chose it as the 1999 Novel of the Year.

Tremain has explained that the germ of her novel was the discovery, on a trip to the castle at Rosenberg, of the cellar in which Charles's musicians were kept, out of sight, to provide music when needed. Peter Claire, a member of that hidden band, is thus one of those characters she has always looked for, a character "slightly marginalized, who is on the edge of the main event." The marginal character (like Merivel in *Restoration*) provides a sufficiently interesting focus in his own right while permitting a refracted view of what ordinarily would be "the main event"–the doings of kings and queens.

In the aftermath of *Music & Silence* the author was once again at some pains to clarify her genre. She told Donovan in their 1999 interview for *The Irish Times* (Dublin), "I have written a total of eight books, so it's maddening to be limited by that definition. My American publishers can't grasp the idea that I don't always write historical novels." She went on to declare that "I want my writing to take me to places I wouldn't dare to go, somewhere out of my day-to-day existence." Readers can be grateful to Rose Tremain for the way her novels take them, as well, to such places as the mind of a young transsexual, a burning London with a heroic quack, and the roof of a kidnapper's house where an imaginative English teenager and his middle-aged Russian novelist lover leap for safety. As Brownrigg remarked in the 1998 interview, Rose Tremain "uses a magical and distinctive prose to make the exotic seem familiar, and the familiar strangely charmed."

Interviews:

Harry Eyres, "For Kings and Currency," *Times* (London), 25 September 1989;

Victoria Glendinning, "The Arts: The Craft of Dreaming," *Daily Telegraph* (London), 3 May 1997, p. 5;

Sylvia Brownrigg, "Talking with Rose Tremain: Making It All Up," *Long Island Newsday,* 12 July 1998, p. B11;

Clare Colvin, "The Books Interview: Chance of a Lifetime," *Independent* (London), 4 September 1999, Features section, p. 9;

Katie Donovan, "Bridging Reason and Instinct," *Irish Times* (Dublin), 16 September 1999, Arts section, p. 12;

Helen de Bertodano, "Features: An Inherited Restlessness," *Sunday Telegraph* (London), 23 January 2000, p. 3.

Reference:

Susanne Fendler and Ruth Wittlinger, "Rose Tremain's *Restoration* and Thatcherism," *Culture & Communication,* 3 (Winter 2000): 29–50.

Irvine Welsh

(1958 -)

James F. Ketcham
Creighton University

BOOKS: *Past Tense: Four Stories from a Novel* (South Queensferry, Edinburgh: Clocktower Press, 1992); revised and enlarged as *Trainspotting* (London: Secker & Warburg, 1993; New York: Norton, 1996);

The Acid House (London: Cape, 1994; New York: Norton, 1995);

Marabou Stork Nightmares: A Novel (London: Cape, 1995; New York: Norton, 1996);

Ecstasy: Three Tales of Chemical Romance (London: Cape, 1996; New York & London: Norton, 1996);

Trainspotting & Headstate, by Welsh and Harry Gibson (London: Minerva, 1996);

You'll Have Had Your Hole (London: Methuen, 1998);

Filth: A Novel (London: Cape, 1998; New York & London: Norton, 1998);

The Acid House: A Screen Play (London: Methuen, 1999);

Glue (London: Cape, 2001; New York: Norton, 2001);

Porno (London: Cape, 2002; New York: Norton, 2002).

Collection: *The Irvine Welsh Omnibus* (London: Cape/ Secker & Warburg, 1997)–comprises *Trainspotting, The Acid House,* and *Marabou Stork Nightmares.*

PLAY PRODUCTIONS: *Headstate,* by Welsh in collaboration with Boilerhouse Theatre Company, Glasgow, Tramway, 18 October 1994;

You'll Have Had Your Hole, Leeds, West Yorkshire Playhouse, 25 February 1998; London, LA2, 9 February 1999;

Blackpool, by Welsh and Harry Gibson, music by Vic Godard, Edinburgh, Queen Mary's University College, Gateway Theatre, 19 February 2002.

PRODUCED SCRIPTS: *The Acid House,* motion picture, adapted by Welsh from his book of that title, Channel Four Films, 1999;

Dockers, television, by Welsh, Jimmy McGovern, and others, Channel 4, 11 July 1999.

OTHER: Nick Waplington, *Weddings, Parties, Anything,* essay by Welsh (New York: Aperture, 1996);

Irvine Welsh (photograph by Robert Clifford; from the dust jacket for the U.S. edition of Marabou Stork Nightmares,*1996)*

4 Play: Based on the Novels and Novellas of Irvine Welsh, introduction by Welsh (London: Vintage, 2001)–comprises *Trainspotting,* adapted by Harry Gibson; *Marabou Stork Nightmares,* adapted by Gibson; *Ecstasy,* adapted by Keith Wyatt; and *Filth,* adapted by Gibson.

To open his book *Ecstasy: Three Tales of Chemical Romance* (1996), Irvine Welsh used an epigraph taken from *I Need More: The Stooges and Other Stories* (1982), the autobiography of the so-called Godfather of Punk, Iggy Pop: "They say that death kills you, but death doesn't kill you. Boredom and indifference kill you." This statement seems to encapsulate the theme of not only Welsh's fiction but also his life. Welsh and his characters fight against the boredom and indifference created by their living conditions in Scotland. They use drugs, women, and violence to bash their ways through life, trying to find a way out. Welsh's first novel, *Trainspotting,* crashed onto the British scene in 1993, kicking up controversy in its wake. The book was critically acclaimed for portraying Scottish youths in a gritty and often violently realistic way, yet scathingly condemned by more conservative critics who accused Welsh of glorifying drug use and violence. The book was tremendously popular; however, first-time book buyers formed the bulk of the readership. Because of his overwhelming popularity among the people about whom he is writing, Welsh feels free from the pressure of critical reactions, and he is able to create extraordinary glimpses into his culture.

Welsh was born in Edinburgh, Scotland, in 1958. He is not overly forthcoming about his life up to the publication of *Trainspotting,* but some details have emerged. As Anna Burnside noted in a 17 February 2002 profile-interview, however, such details "are blurred between facts, misinformation and Welsh's own fiction and he likes to keep it that way." In several interviews he has said that his father was a dock worker and his mother a waitress, that he grew up in Leith, living in surroundings characterized by poverty, and that his family moved to a new housing scheme (housing project) in Muirhouse when he was young. Welsh uses this term "scheme" often in his writing, sometimes describing the place, but mostly describing the people. They are "schemies," branded and shaped by the neighborhood where they grew up. At a younger age he never considered the possibility of being a writer, saying in a 1998 interview with Simon Reynolds for *The Village Voice,* "Back then, the idea of someone being a writer, you'd think of graffiti spray painted on the walls." Instead, Welsh was beginning his experiences with drugs, relating to Mary Riddell in an interview for the *New Statesman* (1996) that he "bought Airfax kits, threw away the plane and inhaled the glue." He was also arrested around this same time for playing soccer in the projects. A passage from *Marabou Stork Nightmares* (1995) reflects this experience: "We were kicking a ball around in a patch of grass outside the block of flats we lived in. There were no NO BALL GAMES signs up, but we should have known, even at that age, that as the scheme was a concentration camp for the poor; this like everything else, was prohibited." This idea of the scheme being a place to escape from is prevalent in all of Welsh's fiction; however, he demonstrates that it is not easy to break free, as his characters are snared by the complications of poverty: drug addiction, sex, violence, and many other criminal and destructive activities.

Welsh makes no secret of his drug use. During the early 1980s he often changed jobs, and, according to Riddell, "After leaving school underqualified and almost innumerate, he drifted between Scotland and London–working as a TV repairman, sleeping rough, playing the guitar and, in an Orwellian interlude, washing dishes in a restaurant." As he said in the Reynolds interview, he worked "crap jobs and the dole" using "drugs, specifically heroin and speed." However, as Riddell observed in the *New Statesman* interview, "Welsh also hedged his bets. He gradually acquired a portfolio of useful qualifications–from a City and Guilds certificate in electrical engineering to an MBA from Heriot-Watt." However, there was another tremendous influence on Welsh, and that was the developing rave scene, bringing together acid house music and ecstasy.

Welsh claims that his distinctive linguistic style, which mixes the dialect of Edinburgh with terms and phrases from the rave community, has its genesis there. He remarked in a 1999 interview with Carlo McCormick, "When I started writing, I was getting into house music and raving, and it was tied to this, where the text was the effects over the beats and the language was an approximation of those rhythms." He added to this observation in a 2001 interview with Christopher Kemp of the online magazine *Salon,* saying, "I wanted to get the rhythms in it and beats into it, and Standard English isn't a very rhythmic language . . . The kind of language that I use, a lot of words are Gypsy words and it's a Celtic oral storytelling tradition. It's very informative, it's got that aspect to it that drives it on for me." Welsh fuses the rhythm of the rave scene with the desperation of the schemes to graphically portray the conditions.

Welsh's first novel, *Trainspotting,* follows a group of Edinburgh youths who are all battling in different ways to escape Scotland in general and the schemes in particular. An earlier version was published by Duncan McLean of the Clocktower Press in pamphlet form as *Past Tense: Four Stories from a Novel* (1992); the London publishers Secker and Warburg, Ltd. published the final version the following year. The novel was critically acclaimed and thrust Welsh into the public consciousness. Some praised him for his graphic representation of the complications and degradation of drugs, while others accused him of glorifying drug use. He claimed in the McCormick interview that drug use "has to be brought up . . . You can't celebrate or condemn them. Drugs are just so close to being a general metaphor for life; it seems to be such an intrinsic part of it. When people are talking about life in its excess, all its pleasures and disappointments, it's almost as if drugs sharpen our awareness of

Paperback cover for the U.S. edition of Welsh's 1993 novel, about a group of young Edinburgh heroin addicts (Richland County Public Library)

what life's about–the good times, morality and our great fear of the Grim Reaper."

The point of view in *Trainspotting* is mostly first person, jumping from character to character; however, the last section is written in the third person. The story follows the lives of many characters, each illustrating how easy it is to fall into the traps of poverty and desperation. Mark Renton, who narrates the most chapters, is a heroin addict who eventually double-crosses his friends at the end of the novel. Sick Boy is a malicious part-time addict who uses sex to gain control of his world, and Franco Begbie violently lashes out at everyone around him, friend and foe alike. Spud also is an addict but lacks Renton's ability to protect himself. Tommy eschews heroin at first, but after shooting up with Renton, he quickly gets hooked, eventually dying of AIDS from infected needles. While all of these characters, except Begbie, are heavy drug users, drugs are only a symptom of the larger problem: the poverty and stagnation in the schemes. Renton demonstrates how he feels about Scotland when he denounces, in a typically profane passage,

> Fucking failures in a country ay failures. It's nae good blamin it on the English fir colonizing us. Ah don't hate the English. They're just wankers. We are colonised by wankers. We can't even pick a decent vibrant, healthy culture to be colonized by. No. We're ruled by effete arseholes. What does that make us? The lowest of the . . . low, the scum of the earth. The most wretched, servile, miserable pathetic trash that was ever shat intae creation. Ah don't hate the English . . . Ah hate the Scots.

This hate manifests itself in Renton's and Spud's disregard of their health as they destroy themselves with heroin, Sick Boy's misogynistic and cruel behavior, and Begbie's uncontrolled violence. When deciding how to deal with the pressures of life, Renton reveals his beliefs, saying, "Choose mortgage payments; choose washing machines; choose cars; choose sitting oan a couch watching mind numbing and spirit crushing game shows . . . Choose rotting away . . . Choose life. Well, ah choose not tae choose life." However, Renton eventually takes action, although to escape he must steal the money he and his friends have made from a drug deal. Assuring that his ties to Edinburgh are cut off is the only way for him to break free. The novel ends with the lines:

> Ripping off your mates was the highest offense in the book . . . Renton had used Begbie, used him to burn his boats completely and utterly. It was Begbie who ensured he could never return. He had done what he wanted to do. He could now never go back to Leith, to Edinburgh, even to Scotland, ever again. There, he could not be anything other than he was. Now, free from them all, for good, he could be what he wanted to be. He'd stand or fall alone.

Welsh's next book, *The Acid House* (1994), is a group of short stories and a novella, all still grounded in Welsh's experiences in Scotland. However, the tales range from the grittily realistic to the magically fantastic. The book includes a surreal tale called "The Granton Star Cause" about a man who loses everything in one day, only to be turned into a fly by God. He is eventually squashed by his mother after witnessing his parents engaged in kinky, perverted sexual acts. In another story a newly born baby and a man heavily into an acid trip exchange bodies during a lightning storm. And the novella that ends the collection, titled "A Smart Cunt," not only feels like *Trainspotting* but also repeats characters from that novel; for instance, Spud puts in an appearance. Welsh explained the fantastical elements of the book in the interview with McCormick, saying, "people are used to thinking in different, much less linear ways . . . the gaps between realism, surrealism, magic realism and pure fantasy are gone now . . . It is as if Standard English is on the way out. People absorb and process information in a much broader way." Some of the stories stray from Scotland, but even in those, a character from Edinburgh is sure to appear. When asked by Kemp in the *Salon* interview if he worried whether his characters were universal, Welsh replied, "I think they're universal. With *Trainspotting* everybody went on about it being a drug thing, but it was all about the characters. I go to Tokyo or Moscow or New York and everybody says, 'Oh we know a Begbie, we know a Sick Boy,' and I think if you get good characters they have universal application." These stories present a range of styles that paves the way for the textual distortions Welsh uses in his next novel.

Welsh uses Standard English in *Marabou Stork Nightmares,* but it is only one of three layers woven into this deep introspection into one character's mind. Roy Strang, injured in some type of accident, is confined to a hospital bed in Edinburgh. The reader does not know why Roy is there, only that his mind twists and turns trying to face the reality of what he has done and searching for some forgiveness. Gradually, it becomes apparent that Roy has been involved in a brutal gang rape and that he has tried to kill himself by putting a plastic bag over his head. Welsh uses rising and falling text patterns to show the transitions between the three stories taking place:

> No way.
>
> Deeper
>
> deeper. In fact I'm further up
> get because I can hear Patricia
> can't Devine telling me that
> This is disturbing because I I have a visitor. I'm
> so
> conscious, I'm almost
> awake. I fear waking up.
> I fear it more than ever.

Roy tries to sink deeper into his fantasy, but, as the text suggests, he is drawn back up to the surface. The reader must follow the flow of the text instead of reading traditionally from left to right. Welsh remarked in a 1996 interview with Jenifer Berman for *Bomb* magazine, "There's so many different levels of things going on, and you can create the feel for the kind of dislocation and fragmentation in people's lives by using these techniques . . . The text moves all over the place, in and out of different realities, like Roy does in order to suspend a lot of the truth. The text is a dislocater, so he can escape the real world of the rape and his confusion. Like the storks are dopplegangers for his fears." Welsh uses the textual patterns to portray the flow of Roy's thoughts, outlining the battle being fought in his head.

The people who visit Roy in the hospital–his parents, brothers, doctors, nurses, and the rape victim, Kirsty–keep trying to pull Roy to the surface; however, Roy only desires to sink into his surreal fantasy of a trip to Africa to hunt the scavenger/predator Marabou Stork. He believes killing the stork will somehow relieve him of his crushing guilt: "I want to keep hunting the Stork. The Stork's the personification of all this badness. If I kill the Stork I'll kill the badness in me." When he cannot sink all the way into his fantasy, he narrates his life, starting with his childhood and leading up to the suicide attempt that leaves him in a coma. As the novel climaxes, the levels start to mix, ending with him finally admitting the two important truths of the novel. First, he reveals that he was much more involved in the rape than he has admitted to the reader; instead of his being an unwilling participant, his victim indicates, Roy prolonged the attack, viciously abusing her. The second is that Roy's abuse at the hands of his uncle was far more intrusive than he has acknowledged. The revelation of these two facts illustrates that Roy's compulsion to find the stork is not the simple search for forgiveness that Roy suggests, but more of a search for the truth that he has not even admitted to himself. Roy's overwhelming depression eventually drives him to make the suicide attempt that puts him in the coma, but before his depression weighs him down he tries to escape by moving to Manchester, England. When he makes the move, Roy is suffering from depression that has settled on him since he and his friends were found not guilty of the rape charges. Anti-rape posters plastered all over Edinburgh haunt him. In Manchester, however, he tries ecstasy for the first time, and it has a tremendous effect on his life.

Throughout the novel, drugs are surprisingly missing from Roy's life compared to their importance for previous Welsh characters. In Welsh's world, however, drugs are only a method of escape, and Roy instead turns to fighting. Roy joins "the casuals," groups of soccer hooligans who attend the matches with the sole purpose of "swedging" (fighting) with the casuals from other cities. For Roy the involvement in this primal violence puts him on a destructive path that eventually ends with the rape. His violence escalates from fighting at soccer matches to torturing his family's dog and eventually blowing off its head with fireworks. Eventually, his violence culminates in the brutal gang rape of a girl by whom he felt slighted. When he tries to escape his violent past in Manchester, he takes ecstasy for the first time. When Roy feels love for the first time in his life while taking ecstasy, there is a sense that not only is his opinion of drugs changing, but so is Welsh's. Roy says, "You can either use drugs as a validation of the joy of life or you can use them as an escape

Dust jacket for the U.S. edition of Welsh's 1995 novel, about a comatose soccer hooligan who alternately hallucinates about being in Africa and relives his brutal life (Richland County Public Library)

from its horrors." Roy's use of ecstasy makes him realize that these violent compulsions are reactions to a lack of love. He admits that his hatred of the dog is a result of his perception that his family loves that dog more than him. When the dog maimed him when he was a child, his memory is of his father begging Roy not to tell the authorities so they will not take the dog away.

Welsh provides an explanation for Roy's behavior but not a justification. The guilt eventually drives Roy to try to commit suicide. Ironically, it is his victim who ends his life. Roy recognizes the role he played in turning his victim into a murderer. He remarks, "I understand her. I understand her hurt, her pain, how it all just has to come out. It just goes round and round, the hurt. It takes an exceptionally strong person to just say: no more. It takes a weak one to just keep it all to themselves, let it tear them apart without hurting anyone else. I'm not an exceptionally strong person. Nor is Kirsty. We're both just ordinary and this is shite. We both understand everything." Roy understands her rage because it is his rage. The fact that Roy hides his role in the rape from the reader is equal to his unwillingness to face the truth about the rape he suffered at the hands of his uncle. Roy has this rage going "round and round," and once he sees the depths that he has sunk to through his experiences with ecstasy, suicide is his only avenue of escape. Reviewers were generally positive in their reactions to the novel.

Trainspotting was adapted by John Hodge into a motion picture, first released in March 1996. The movie was hugely successful, grossing more than £12 million in the United Kingdom and $16.5 million in the United States, and made a star of Ewan McGregor, who played Renton. The success of the motion-picture version of his book also helped propel Welsh to greater literary notoriety, particularly in the United States, where the book was published by W. W. Norton in June 1996, just before the 21 July 1996 U.S. premiere of the movie.

In his next book, *Ecstasy,* Welsh continues to explore the world of raves and the use of MDMA (ecstasy). Three novellas make up the book, and each includes the usual complement of drugs, sex, and violence found in Welsh's works. However, *Ecstasy* is different in the way that it deals with these topics. There seems to be a shift in Welsh's view of drugs near the end of *Marabou Stork Nightmares,* when he suggests that some drugs can be used to emphasize the joy in life instead of just masking the pain. The three stories in this volume all use the drug ecstasy to kick off the characters' transformations. In the first story, "Lorraine Goes to Livingston: A Rave and Regency Romance," a romance writer, Rebecca Navarro, suffers a minor stroke, and during her hospital stay she meets Lorraine, the nurse assigned to care for her. Rebecca is overweight and lives mainly for her writing and secretly gorging on bon-bons. After her stroke, as she is working to recover, she finds out about her husband's disturbing perverted behavior. Her experiments with ecstasy do help her to open up and feel loved, but the story is driven by her need to punish her husband, which she does with Lorraine's help. The story ends with her sitting in the "chill out" room at a rave, "the drug . . . taking her to new heights with the music."

The second story, "Fortune's Always Hiding: A Corporate Drug Romance," is set up like a mystery, revolving around thalidomide, a scandalously dangerous drug formerly prescribed for morning sickness that caused many babies to be born with birth defects. Eventually, Samantha and others like her seek revenge against the makers and marketers of the drug. Underlying this quest is the main character's relationship with Samantha, as he falls in love with her despite her deformity and obsession for revenge. Both stories have surreal elements and Scottish ties but feel lighter than Welsh's previous work. The last story, "The Undefeated," seems to inhabit the same world as *Trainspotting,* with heroin being replaced by ecstasy. The point of view jumps from character to character, as Lloyd and Heather break away from their worlds eventually to find each other.

Ecstasy was not applauded by critics as his first three novels were, and even Welsh admits *Ecstasy* was flawed because so many ordinary people came up to him and told him how bad they thought it was. Welsh is often scornful of what he sees as the literary elite, and instead values the opinion of ordinary people; however, those he considers ordinary are not the middle classes. In the Berman interview Welsh said that Scotland is "seen as a very middle class place. And that was never my experience growing up in a housing scheme outside the city. The problem with that touristy kind of culture is that it tends to marginalize the people who live there and the issues and the problems they face." The characters trapped in the scheme repeatedly fall into the available traps of alcohol, drugs, sex, and violence because, Welsh said in the same interview, "There are two kinds of working class philosophies, a radical revolutionary one that sees the middle and upper classes as the enemies; and another more individualistic desire to escape from the working class and assimilate into the upper classes. That antagonism is always going on in a working class head."

Filth takes this conflict and studies it from the opposite side. The word *filth* is Scottish slang for the police but also accurately describes the main character, Bruce Robertson, a corrupt policeman. The cover of the book shows a pig in a policeman's helmet (which caused much controversy in itself); however, the pig is not necessarily a slur on the police in general but rather an apt metaphor for Robertson in particular: he lies, steals, and abuses the guilty and innocent alike. As is *Marabou Stork Nightmares, Filth* is set in the mind of one character, but there is the sense that while Welsh might feel sympathy toward Roy Strang, he feels nothing but loathing for Robertson. In the Reynolds interview Welsh remarked, "You hate his racism, his sexism, even his musical taste, everything about him. But when you dive into that kind of cesspool, it's quite creepy, because you do get into it. You have to, to make it believable."

Drugs also play a role in *Filth,* although again Welsh switches the primary drug, this time to cocaine. Robertson is not a man who would embrace the loving feelings inspired by ecstasy; cocaine, however, matches his personality. Welsh told Reynolds, "Cocaine is the ultimate consumer capitalist drug . . . And Robertson's got that ideology of pure consumption. You can see that in the worm as well." The worm to which he is referring is a tapeworm growing in Robertson's intestines. The presence of the worm adds a surreal element breaking up and sometimes imposing on Robertson's narration. Welsh shapes the text, as in *Marabou Stork Nightmares;* except in *Filth* the presence of the worm is shown through squiggly worm-like borders that cut right through the text. The tapeworm at first appears consumed by hunger but soon becomes concerned for its survival and tries to provide some guidance to Robertson. Its help fails, however, and it is pushed from Robertson's body as he kills himself in the final scene. Again, a Welsh character turns to suicide as the only way out of the black hole he has dug for himself.

Welsh's 2001 book, *Glue,* combines many of the elements found in his earlier novels, but his treatment of Scotland has changed somewhat. The book is similar to *Trainspotting* in that it is also set in Edinburgh and the characters speak the same rich language. Welsh remarked in the Kemp interview, "the similarity really is the fact that it's very much character-based rather than plot based. I didn't really have a plot for this, I just thought, well, I did want to get back to the feel of *Trainspotting,* the idea you've got these characters that are, sort of, sparking off each other and they take the story from there." However, while *Glue* might feel like *Trainspotting,* many things have changed in Edinburgh. The title is a reference to the relationship between the four main characters: Carl, Terry, Billy, and Gally. As in *Trainspotting,* the point of view is first person, jumping from character to character until the end of the book, when it switches to third person. Unlike in *Trainspotting,* however, the relationships of the main characters do not end in betrayal at

Paperback cover for the U.S. edition of Welsh's 2001 novel, which depicts the close friendship of a group of boys in an Edinburgh housing project (Richland County Public Library)

the conclusion. In fact, the bond between these friends is what gives them some hope.

Glue starts in the early 1970s and runs into the year 2002, providing a long-range view of the characters. Using this large time frame allows Welsh not only to detail the influences that lead to the complications in their lives but also to show the few things that offer some hope. The four main characters echo those from *Trainspotting.* Terry, like Sick Boy, uses sex to drown out the nastiness in his life. Gally is lost and searching like Spud. The characters face many of the same demons produced by the scheme, but in *Glue* partially manage to subdue them. Carl, for example, is shown to have a stable family structure. In fact, his father presents him with a set of rules that helps to guide his conduct:

NEVER HIT A WOMAN
ALWAYS BACK UP YOUR MATES
NEVER SCAB
NEVER CROSS A PICKET LINE
NEVER GRASS FRIEND OR FOE
TELL THEM NOWT (THEM BEING POLI, DOLE, SOCIAL, JOURNALISTS, COUNCIL CENSUS, ETC.)
NEVER LET A WEEK GO BY WITHOUT INVESTING IN NEW VINAL
GIVE WHEN YOU CAN, TAKE ONLY WHEN YOU HAVE TO
IF YOU FEEL HIGH OR LOW, MIND THAT NOTHING GOOD OR BAD LASTS FOR EVER AND TODAY'S THE START OF THE REST OF YOUR LIFE
GIVE LOVE FREELY, BUT BE TIGHTER WITH TRUST

This list marks a sharp difference between the characters of *Glue* and those of *Trainspotting.* In *Glue,* characters such as Carl and Billy have a solid parental structure and consequently have an easier time surviving. So while Carl may experiment with drugs, his love of music, which is inspired by his father, offers some hope of escape. This idea of love being a way to escape their condition is important. In a 1998 interview in *Time* magazine with Joel Stein, Welsh remarked, "That's one of the points of the book: when there is an absence of love, the void is filled by bitterness, manipulation, anger and resentment and unrest." Some critics were bothered by this transformation. Steven Poole ended his *New Statesman* (7 May 2001) review by saying that "inside every posturing hard man lurks a maudlin sentimentalist." Linda Gardiner claims in a 2001 *Nation* review, "in Edinburgh the basics never change." As with all his books, however, Welsh does not really care about literary critics. More than half of his readership for *Trainspotting* and subsequent books consists of those people whom he considers ordinary. Welsh commented in the Berman interview, "I've been fortunate enough to discover my readership in my lifetime–and what that's done is completely negate any part of these liberal critics who only like things that affirm their own values, but won't challenge them."

Welsh has experimented in other genres. Although he did not write the screenplay for *Trainspotting,* he did adapt *The Acid House* into a movie. At first intended for broadcast as a miniseries by Channel 4 Television, the movie was instead given a theatrical release in 1999, apparently after the television executives realized the language and content made the project unsuitable for broadcast. Many of his novels, including *Trainspotting, Marabou Stork Nightmares,* and *Filth,* were adapted by Harry Gibson for the stage. Welsh first tried his hand at playwriting with *Headstate* (produced 1994; published 1996), a collaborative work undertaken with the Boiler House Theatre Company of Edinburgh. His next play, *You'll Have Had Your Hole* (published 1998), premiered in Leeds in 1998 and opened in a London rock club the following year. Neither work was considered a success by critics. He also collaborated with Gibson on *Blackpool,* a musical staged by final-year drama students at Queen Mary's University College in Edinburgh in February 2002, for which Vic Godard, former frontman for the punk band The Subway Sect, contributed original music. Music continues to be a passion for Welsh, and he helped put together an album produced by Creation Records.

In August 2002 Welsh published *Porno,* the long-awaited sequel to *Trainspotting.* The novel reunites the main characters from his first novel, now dispersed: as the story opens, Sick Boy is in London, working in a strip club and trying to become a pimp; Begbie is finishing out a sentence in a Scottish jail and plotting revenge against whoever it is that keeps sending him parcels of gay pornography; Renton is hiding out in Amsterdam, where he absconded with the loot he took in the first novel; and Spud is still in Leith, now with a girlfriend and baby, trying to keep himself off drugs and write a history of his hometown. Now an Armani-clad con man and a heavy cocaine user, Sick Boy returns to Leith and takes over his aunt's run-down pub, planning to use the upstairs room to film pornographic movies. Various new characters appear as well, notably, Nikki Fuller-Smith, a beautiful English film studies student who works in a massage parlor and is soon cast as the star of Sick Boy's porn video "Seven Rides for Seven Brothers."

As John Walsh noted in his 12 August 2002 interview with Welsh for *The Independent* (London), the characters "are like the components of a time bomb waiting to go off": what, for example, will happen when the psychopathic Begbie discovers that Sick Boy was the sender of the "poof's porn"? Renton becomes Sick Boy's partner in distributing pornography, but, as John Burnside remarked in his 17 August 2002 review in *The Times* (London), both are conscious "throughout their dealings that Sick Boy must exact his pound of flesh for Renton's former betrayal." Burnside argued that "The suspense, however, lies in the potential reunion between Renton and Begbie, *Porno*'s most surprising and oddly touching love hate relationship–and it has to be said that, when the two meet, the power of the writing and Welsh's subtle handling of that love-hate will astonish even his most dedicated fans." Burnside called Welsh's characterization of Nikki "striking," though Ali Smith, in an otherwise favorable review for *The Guardian* (24 August 2002), called her a "two-dimensional creation" and "an upmarket Welshian exercise in stereotyping, desperate for sexual satisfaction and fame as a means of control."

When Walsh asked Welsh why he had written a sequel to *Trainspotting,* he said, "I always liked them [the characters], and I always wanted to go back and see what happened to them. But it took me a while to really want to do it, because you've got to make it feel like it's still them, but 10 years further on. It's got to stand up to the test of the original, you know?" After remarking "almost gloomily" that a movie version was nearly inevitable, Welsh said, "You know what I'm really afraid of? . . . Sick Boy becoming a franchise. I worry that I may be turning him into a schemie, coke-fuelled Harry Potter."

Irvine Welsh is one of the most important representatives of the so-called Scottish literary renaissance. Although he lives mainly in London and Amsterdam, he still retains a flat in Edinburgh. He has come a long way from the Muirhouse scheme, but assuredly Welsh and his characters will always be a part of Scotland, searching for ways to escape.

Interviews:

Jenifer Berman, "Irvine Welsh," *Bomb,* 56 (1996): 56–61;

Mary Riddell, "Irvine Welsh: The Voice of a Chemical Generation," *New Statesman,* 128 (1996): 22–23;

Simon Reynolds, "Filthy Mind: Irvine Welsh Dishes the Dirt on Literary Hypocrisy, Drug Culture, and His Nasty New Novel," *Village Voice,* 43 (1998): 70–76;

Joel Stein, "Irvine Welsh," *Time,* 152 (28 September 1998): 13;

Carlo McCormick, "The House that Welsh Built: How Irvine Welsh made *Trainspotting* look like kid's stuff," *Paper,* August 1999 <http://staging.papermag.com/magazine/mag_99/mag_aug99/welsh/welsh0899.html>;

Christopher Kemp, "Irvine Welsh," *Salon* (9 July 2001) <http://www.salon.com/people/conv/2001/07/09/welsh/index/html>;

Anna Burnside, "Rock and a Hard Place," *Sunday Times* (London), 17 February 2002, Features section;

John Walsh, "Irvine Welsh: Upwardly Mobile," *Independent* (London), Features section, 12 August 2002, pp. 4–5.

References:

Martin Bruggemeier and Horst W. Drescher, "A Subculture and Its Characterization in Irvine Welsh's *Trainspotting,*" *Anglistik & Englischunterricht,* 63 (Winter 2000): 135–150;

Alan Freeman, "Ghosts in Sunny Leith: Irvine Welsh's *Trainspotting,*" in *Studies in Scottish Fiction: 1945 to the Present,* edited by Susanne Hagemann (Frankfurt-am-Main & New York: Peter Lang, 1996), pp. 251–262;

Patricia Horton, "*Trainspotting:* A Topography of the Masculine Abject," *English: The Journal of the English Association,* 50 (Autumn 2001): 219–234;

Ellen-Raisa Jackson and Willy Maley, "Birds of a Feather? A Postcolonial Reading of Irvine Welsh's *Marabou Stork Nightmares,*" *Revista Canaria de Estudios Ingleses,* 41 (November 2000): 187–196;

Robert A. Morace, *Irvine Welsh's "Trainspotting": A Reader's Guide* (New York: Continuum, 2001).

Books for Further Reading

This is a selective list of studies concerning contemporary British fiction and aspects of the modern novel in English. Additional information may be obtained from the annual *Modern Language Association International Bibliography* and the reference series *Contemporary Literary Criticism* and *Contemporary Authors*. Bibliographies of criticism on twentieth-century British novelists include Irving Adelman and Rita Dworkin, *The Contemporary Novel: A Checklist of Critical Literature on the English Language Novel Since 1945,* second edition (Lanham, Md.: Scarecrow Press, 1996); Helen H. Palmer and Anne Jane Dyson, comp., *English Novel Explication: Criticisms to 1972* (London: Bingley, 1973; Hamden, Conn.: Shoe String Press, 1976) and its supplements; A. F. Cassis, *The Twentieth-Century English Novel: An Annotated Bibliography of General Criticism* (New York: Garland, 1977); Paul Schlueter and June Schlueter, *The English Novel: Twentieth Century Criticism: Volume II, Twentieth Century Novelists* (Chicago & London: Swallow Press, 1982); The British Council, *The Novel in Britain and Ireland Since 1970: A Select Bibliography* (London: British Council, 1994); and Peter Parker, ed., Frank Kermode, consultant ed., *The Reader's Companion to the Twentieth Century Novel* (London: Fourth Estate / Oxford: Helicon, 1994).

Acheson, James, ed. *The British and Irish Novel since 1960.* Basingstoke: Macmillan, 1991; New York: St. Martin's Press, 1991.

Allen, Walter Ernst. *The Modern Novel in Britain and the United States.* New York: Dutton, 1964.

Astbury, Raymond, ed. *The Writer in the Market Place: Papers Delivered at a Symposium Held at the Liverpool School of Librarianship, April 1968.* London: Bingley, 1969.

Bergonzi, Bernard. *The Situation of the Novel.* London: Macmillan, 1970; Pittsburgh: University of Pittsburgh Press, 1971.

Bergonzi, ed. *The Twentieth Century.* Volume 7 of *History of Literature in the English Language.* London: Sphere, 1970; London: Barrie & Jenkins, 1970.

Blair, John G. *The Confidence Man in Modern Fiction: A Rogue's Gallery with Six Portraits.* New York: Barnes & Noble, 1979.

Booker, M. Keith. *The Modern British Novel of The Left: A Research Guide.* Westport, Conn. & London: Greenwood Press, 1998.

Booker and Dubravka Juraga. *The Caribbean Novel in English: An Introduction.* Oxford: James Currey, 2000; Portsmouth, N.H.: Heinemann, 2001.

Bradbury, Malcolm. *Dangerous Pilgrimages: Transatlantic Mythologies and the Novel.* London: Secker & Warburg, 1995; New York: Viking, 1996.

Bradbury. *The Modern British Novel.* London: Secker & Warburg, 1993; London & New York: Penguin, 1994.

Bradbury. *No, Not Bloomsbury.* London: Deutsch, 1987; New York: Columbia University Press, 1988.

Bradbury, ed. *The Novel Today: Contemporary Writers on Modern Fiction.* Manchester: Manchester University Press / Totowa, N.J.: Rowman & Littlefield, 1977.

Bradbury, ed. *Possibilities: Essays on the State of the Novel.* London & New York: Oxford University Press, 1973.

Bradbury and Judy Cooke, eds. *New Writing.* London: Minerva in Association with The British Council, 1992.

Bradbury and David Palmer, eds. *The Contemporary English Novel.* London: Arnold, 1979; New York: Holmes & Meier, 1980.

Burgess, Anthony. *Ninety-nine Novels: The Best in English Since 1939: A Personal Choice.* London: Allison & Busby, 1984; New York: Summit Books, 1984.

Burgess. *The Novel Now: A Student's Guide to Contemporary Fiction.* London: Faber & Faber, 1967; New York: Norton, 1967.

Burns, Alan and Charles Sugnet, eds. *The Imagination on Trial: British and American Writers Discuss Their Working Methods.* London & New York: Allison & Busby, 1981.

Cope, Jackson I. and Geoffrey Green, eds. *Novel vs. Fiction: The Contemporary Reformation.* Norman, Okla.: Pilgrim Books, 1981.

Crosland, Margaret. *Beyond the Lighthouse: English Women Novelists in the Twentieth Century.* London: Constable, 1981; New York: Taplinger, 1981.

Dervin, Daniel. *Matricentric Narratives: Recent British Women's Fiction in a Postmodern Mode.* Lewiston, N.Y.: Edwin Mellen Press, 1997.

Federman, Raymond, ed. *Surfiction: Fiction Now–and Tomorrow,* enlarged edition. Chicago: Swallow Press, 1981.

Firchow, Peter. *The Writer's Place: Interviews on the Literary Situation in Contemporary Britain.* Minneapolis: University of Minnesota Press, 1974.

Fletcher, John. *Novel and Reader.* London & Boston: Boyars, 1980.

Gindin, James Jack. *Postwar British Fiction: New Accents and Attitudes.* Berkeley & Los Angeles: University of California Press, 1962.

Glicksberg, Charles I. *The Sexual Revolution in Modern English Literature.* The Hague: Martinus Nijhoff, 1973.

Gray, Nigel. *The Silent Majority: A Study of the Working Class in Post-War British Fiction.* London: Vision, 1973; New York: Barnes & Noble, 1973.

Gunn, James E. *Alternate Worlds: The Illustrated History of Science Fiction.* Englewood Cliffs, N.J.: Prentice-Hall, 1975.

Hall, James. *The Lunatic Giant in the Drawing Room: The British and American Novel Since 1930.* Bloomington: Indiana University Press, 1968.

Hazell, Stephen, ed. *The English Novel: Developments in Criticism Since Henry James.* London: Macmillan, 1978.

Head, Dominic. *An Introduction to Modern British Fiction, 1950–2000.* Cambridge & New York: Cambridge University Press, 2002.

Hennessy, Val. *A Little Light Friction.* London: Harrap, 1989.

Holmes, Frederick Michael. *The Historical Imagination: Postmodernism and the Treatment of the Past in Contemporary British Fiction.* Victoria, B.C.: English Literary Studies, University of Victoria, 1997.

Jameson, Storm. *Parthian Words.* London: Collins/Harvill, 1970.

Kaplan, Sydney Janet. *Feminine Consciousness in the Modern British Novel.* Urbana: University of Illinois Press, 1975.

Klaus, H. Gustav, ed. *The Socialist Novel in Britain: Towards a Recovery of a Tradition.* Brighton: Harvester, 1982; New York: St. Martin's Press, 1982.

Lee, Alison. *Realism and Power: Postmodern British Fiction.* London & New York: Routledge, 1990.

Lewald, H. Ernest, ed. *The Cry of Home: Cultural Nationalism and the Modern Writer.* Knoxville: University of Tennessee Press, 1972.

Lodge, David. *After Bakhtin: Essays on Fiction and Criticism.* London & New York: Routledge, 1990.

Lodge. *The Art of Fiction: Illustrated From Classic and Modern Texts.* London: Secker & Warburg, 1992.

Lodge. *The Language of Fiction: Essays in Criticism and Verbal Analysis of the English Novel.* London: Routledge & Kegan Paul / New York: Columbia University Press, 1966.

Lodge. *The Modes of Modern Writing: Metaphor, Metonymy, and the Typology of Modern Literature.* London: Edward Arnold, 1977.

Lodge. *The Novelist at the Crossroads and Other Essays on Fiction and Criticism.* London: Routledge & Kegan Paul, 1971; Ithaca, N.Y.: Cornell University Press, 1971.

Lodge. *The Practice of Writing: Essays, Lectures, Reviews and a Diary.* London: Secker & Warburg, 1996.

Lodge. *Working With Structuralism: Essays and Reviews on Nineteenth- and Twentieth-Century Literature.* London & New York: Routledge,1986.

Madden, David. *A Primer of the Novel: For Readers and Writers.* Metuchen, N.J. & London: Scarecrow Press, 1980.

Massie, Allan. *The Novel Today: A Critical Guide to the British Novel 1970–1989.* London & New York: Longman in Association with The British Council, 1990.

McEwan, Neil. *The Survival of the Novel: British Fiction in the Later Twentieth Century.* London: Macmillan, 1981; Totowa, N.J.: Barnes & Noble, 1981.

Miles, Rosalind. *The Fiction of Sex: Themes and Functions of Sex Difference in the Modern Novel.* London: Vision, 1974; New York: Barnes & Noble, 1974.

Morris, Robert K. *Old Lines, New Forces: Essays on the Contemporary English Novel, 1960–1970.* Rutherford, N.J.: Fairleigh Dickinson University Press / London: Associated University Presses, 1976.

O'Connor, William Van. *The New University Wits and the End of Modernism.* Carbondale: Southern Illinois University Press, 1963.

Peters, Joan Douglas. *Feminist Metafiction and the Evolution of the British Novel.* Gainesville: University Press of Florida, 2002.

Ross, Stephen David. *Literature and Philosophy: An Analysis of the Philosophical Novel.* New York: Appleton-Century-Crofts, 1969.

Shapiro, Charles, ed. *Contemporary British Novelists.* Carbondale: Southern Illinois University Press, 1965.

Smith, David J. *Socialist Propaganda in the Twentieth-Century British Novel.* London: Macmillan, 1978; Totowa, N.J.: Rowman & Littlefield, 1979.

Spilka, Mark, ed. *Towards a Poetics of Fiction.* Bloomington & London: Indiana University Press, 1977.

Staley, Thomas F., ed. *Twentieth-Century Women Novelists.* London: Macmillan, 1982.

Stetz, Margaret D. *British Women's Comic Fiction, 1890–1990: Not Drowning, But Laughing.* Aldershot, U.K. & Burlington, Vt.: Ashgate, 2001.

Stevenson, Randall. *The British Novel Since the Thirties: An Introduction.* Athens: University of Georgia Press, 1986.

Sutherland, John. *Fiction and the Fiction Industry.* London: Athlone, 1978.

Swinden, Patrick. *The English Novel of History and Society, 1940–1980: Richard Hughes, Henry Green, Anthony Powell, Angus Wilson, Kingsley Amis, V. S. Naipaul.* London: Macmillan, 1984; New York: St. Martin's Press, 1984.

Swinden. *Unofficial Selves: Character in the Novel from Dickens to the Present Day.* London & Basingstoke: Macmillan, 1973; New York: Barnes & Noble, 1973.

Taylor, D. J. *A Vain Conceit: British Fiction in the 1980s.* London: Bloomsbury, 1989.

Todd, Richard. *Consuming Fictions: The Booker Prize and Fiction in Britain Today.* London: Bloomsbury, 1996.

Werlock, Abby H. P., ed. *British Women Writing Fiction.* Tuscaloosa: University of Alabama Press, 2000.

West, Paul. *The Modern Novel.* London: Hutchinson, 1963.

Wicker, Brian. *The Story-Shaped World: Fiction and Metaphysics: Some Variations on a Theme.* London: Athlone, 1975.

Wilson, Colin. *The Craft of the Novel.* London: Gollancz, 1975.

Ziegler, Heide and Christopher Bigsby, eds. *The Radical Imagination and the Liberal Tradition: Interviews with English and American Novelists.* London: Junction Books, 1982.

Contributors

Ingibjörg Ágústsdóttir . . . . *University of Iceland*
Nicholas Birns . . . . *New School University*
Andrew Biswell . . . . *King's College, Aberdeen University*
Sarah Elizabeth Clere . . . . *University of North Carolina at Chapel Hill*
Anne Daniel . . . . *Princeton University*
Ruth P. Feingold . . . . *St. Mary's College of Maryland*
Gillian Fenwick . . . . *University of Toronto*
Dan Friedman . . . . *Yale University*
Ann Hancock . . . . *University of the West of England, Bristol*
Graeme Harper . . . . *University of Wales, Bangor*
Michael J. Hayes . . . . *University of Central Lancashire*
Cynthia Ho . . . . *University of North Carolina at Asheville*
Cecile M. Jagodzinski . . . . *Illinois State University*
James F. Ketcham . . . . *Creighton University*
Peter D. Kittle . . . . *California State University, Chico*
Tim Middleton . . . . *Bath Spa University College*
Michael R. Molino . . . . *Southern Illinois University*
Merritt Moseley . . . . *University of North Carolina at Asheville*
S. J. Newman . . . .
Michael C. Prusse . . . . *Zürcher Hochschule Winterthur & Universität Zürich*
Lorena Russell . . . . *University of North Carolina at Chapel Hill*
Rob Spence . . . . *Edge Hill College of Higher Education, Ormskirk, England*
Jayne Thexton . . . . *Stafford College*
Nicolas Tredell . . . . *University of Sussex*
Juliette Wells . . . . *Yale University*

Cumulative Index

Dictionary of Literary Biography, Volumes 1-271
Dictionary of Literary Biography Yearbook, 1980-2001
Dictionary of Literary Biography Documentary Series, Volumes 1-19
Concise Dictionary of American Literary Biography, Volumes 1-7
Concise Dictionary of British Literary Biography, Volumes 1-8
Concise Dictionary of World Literary Biography, Volumes 1-4

Cumulative Index

DLB before number: *Dictionary of Literary Biography,* Volumes 1-271
Y before number: *Dictionary of Literary Biography Yearbook,* 1980-2001
DS before number: *Dictionary of Literary Biography Documentary Series,* Volumes 1-19
CDALB before number: *Concise Dictionary of American Literary Biography,* Volumes 1-7
CDBLB before number: *Concise Dictionary of British Literary Biography,* Volumes 1-8
CDWLB before number: *Concise Dictionary of World Literary Biography,* Volumes 1-4

A

B

C

D

E

F

G

H

I

J

K

L

M

N

O

Q

R

S

T

U

V

W

X

Y

Z

ISBN 0-7876-6015-9

9 780787 660154